HISTORICAL DICTIONARIES OF AFRICA
Edited by Jon Woronoff

1. *Cameroon,* by Victor T. Le Vine and Roger P. Nye. 1974. *Out of print. See No. 48.*
2. *The Congo,* 2nd ed., by Virginia Thompson and Richard Adloff. 1984. *Out of print. See No. 69.*
3. *Swaziland,* by John J. Grotpeter. 1975.
4. *The Gambia,* 2nd ed., by Harry A. Gailey. 1987. *Out of print. See No. 79.*
5. *Botswana,* by Richard P. Stevens. 1975. *Out of print. See No. 70.*
6. *Somalia,* by Margaret F. Castagno. 1975. *Out of print. See No. 87.*
7. *Benin (Dahomey),* 2nd ed., by Samuel Decalo. 1987. *Out of print. See No. 61.*
8. *Burundi,* by Warren Weinstein. 1976. *Out of print. See No. 73.*
9. *Togo,* 3rd ed., by Samuel Decalo. 1996.
10. *Lesotho,* by Gordon Haliburton. 1977. *Out of print. See No. 90.*
11. *Mali,* 3rd ed., by Pascal James Imperato. 1996.
12. *Sierra Leone,* by Cyril Patrick Foray. 1977.
13. *Chad,* 3rd ed., by Samuel Decalo. 1997.
14. *Upper Volta,* by Daniel Miles McFarland. 1978.
15. *Tanzania,* by Laura S. Kurtz. 1978.
16. *Guinea,* 3rd ed., by Thomas O'Toole with Ibrahima Bah-Lalya. 1995. *Out of print. See No. 94.*
17. *Sudan,* by John Voll. 1978. *Out of print. See No. 53.*
18. *Rhodesia/Zimbabwe,* by R. Kent Rasmussen. 1979. *Out of print. See No. 46.*
19. *Zambia,* 2nd ed., by John J. Grotpeter, Brian V. Siegel, and James R. Pletcher. 1998.
20. *Niger,* 3rd ed., by Samuel Decalo. 1997.
21. *Equatorial Guinea,* 3rd ed., by Max Liniger-Goumaz. 2000.
22. *Guinea-Bissau,* 3rd ed., by Richard Lobban and Peter Mendy. 1997.
23. *Senegal,* by Lucie G. Colvin. 1981. *Out of print. See No. 65.*
24. *Morocco,* by William Spencer. 1980. *Out of print. See No. 71.*
25. *Malawi,* by Cynthia A. Crosby. 1980. *Out of print. See No. 84.*
26. *Angola,* by Phyllis Martin. 1980. *Out of print. See No. 92.*

Historical Dictionary of Libya

Fourth Edition

Ronald Bruce St John

Historical Dictionaries of Africa, No. 100

The Scarecrow Press, Inc.
Lanham, Maryland • Toronto • Oxford
2006

SCARECROW PRESS, INC.

Published in the United States of America
by Scarecrow Press, Inc.
A wholly owned subsidiary of
The Rowman & Littlefield Publishing Group, Inc.
4501 Forbes Boulevard, Suite 200, Lanham, Maryland 20706
www.scarecrowpress.com

PO Box 317
Oxford
OX2 9RU, UK

British Library Cataloguing in Publication Information Available

Library of Congress Cataloging-in-Publication Data

St John, Ronald Bruce
  Historical dictionary of Libya / Ronald Bruce St John. — 4th ed.
    p. cm. — (Historical dictionaries of Africa)
  Includes bibliographical references.
  ISBN-13: 978-0-8108-5303-4 (hardcover : alk. paper)
  ISBN-10: 0-8108-5303-5 (hardcover : alk. paper)
  1. Libya—History—Dictionaries. I. Title. II. Series.

DT223.3.S7 2006
961.2003—dc22

                                        2006002525

∞™ The paper used in this publication meets the minimum requirements of
American National Standard for Information Sciences—Permanence of
Paper for Printed Library Materials, ANSI/NISO Z39.48-1992.
Manufactured in the United States of America.

To Frances Bailey St John
Mother, Teacher, Friend

Contents

Editor's Foreword

Few national leaders have stirred up as much controversy over the past decades as Muammar al-Qaddafi, who has ruled Libya since 1969 and will be around somewhat longer. While much has been written about the Qaddafi regime, often to take sides and praise or condemn, not enough effort has been made to understand where he comes from and how the country is ruled. Indeed, not much is said about Libya as a state in its own right, a relatively recent one but with roots reaching far back into the past. Some of these gaps are filled by *Historical Dictionary of Libya*, which provides considerable information both about the Libyan leader and about Libya—about its long and frequently painful history, about the economy, about the society and culture of its people, and, last but not least, about the "revolutionary" government.

This is particularly important now that, after so many years, Qaddafi and Libya are returning to the fold and participating more positively in the activities of the region and the world. There is also considerable change afoot in the economic and social sectors, although there is thus far no progress to report in the political arena. Still, given its geographic location, its abundant oil resources, and the nature of its leader, it is helpful to have a dictionary with hundreds of entries—including a fair number of new ones in this updated edition—on important persons, places, events, institutions, and so on. The introduction, which has been expanded, now has sections on its political, economic, and social development. Further background is provided by appendixes and a glossary. Meanwhile, the bibliography, more ample than ever, points to further reading.

This fourth edition of *Historical Dictionary of Libya* was written by Ronald Bruce St John, who also wrote the second and third editions and knows the country well. He has been observing Libyan affairs closely for more than three decades and has visited the country frequently.

During this time, Dr. St John has written more than a hundred articles on the Qaddafi regime as well as two books, *Qaddafi's World Design: Libyan Foreign Policy, 1969–1987* and *Libya and the United States: Two Centuries of Strife*. He is thus one of the best Libya-watchers around, with the perspective to integrate the present into the past to keep us abreast of major events.

Jon Woronoff
Series Editor

Preface

This dictionary is the product of almost three decades of observation, investigation, and reflection that began in the fall of 1977 when I first visited the Great Socialist People's Libyan Arab Jamahiriya, more commonly known as Libya. In the intervening period, I have visited that North African country countless times and traveled over much of its territory. In preparing this dictionary, I have drawn freely from a number of earlier publications in book, journal, and newspaper form, although many conclusions have been substantially modified both by hindsight and by changed circumstances. Nevertheless, I would like to acknowledge those editors who have allowed earlier approximations of parts of the present material to appear under their auspices in the books and articles listed under my name in the bibliography.

This edition of *Historical Dictionary of Libya* has been substantially revised and updated with special attention paid to developments since the publication of the last edition in 1998. New information has been included on the economy, society, and culture of Libya. Some of the more important new entries cover the following topics: the African Union, foreign policy, Russia, Saif al-Islam al-Qaddafi, and terrorism. In addition, all existing entries have been revised and updated to reflect important changes and new developments. For example, the entries on Muammar al-Qaddafi, the opposition, the United Nations, and the United States have been thoroughly revised if not largely rewritten.

The bibliography has been updated and expanded considerably to incorporate the wealth of new material published in recent years. Some of the appendixes have been retained and updated to provide the reader with easy access to general background information on Libya as well as more detailed information on subjects such as the Karamanli dynasty, Turkish governors, the first Revolutionary Command Council, and the Libyan government today. Finally, a series of maps has been included to facilitate understanding of the territorial disputes in which Libya was involved over the last century.

Acknowledgments

This book is dedicated to my mother, for all she has done, in so many ways. I would also like to thank my wife, Carol, and my two sons, Alexander and Nathan, for the encouragement, support, and counsel they have given me in the completion of this dictionary as well as many related manuscripts. A study of this scope requires an enormous amount of time and energy, much of which would otherwise have been devoted to them.

Reader's Note

Conventional spellings and forms have been used where they exist; where they do not, foreign words and names have been rendered into English according to accepted scholarly methods. In the case of Libya, this is not an easy task, as the Latin spelling of Libyan personal and place names has never been standardized. In many cases, the spelling of Arabic names and places was fixed in the Latin alphabet by early explorers, adventurers, diplomats, or colonial officials who were not necessarily linguists. As a result, Latin spellings in use are often a mixture of English, French, and Italian adaptations, colloquial variations, and spellings based on the written Arabic. For example, one source has estimated that there are almost 650 possible Latin-alphabet permutations of the name of the individual identified in this dictionary as Muammar al-Qaddafi.

Definite articles that form part of a name are not taken into account in the alphabetical ordering. Thus, al-Qaddafi is listed under "Q" rather than under "a." At the same time, the Arabic definite article, variously "al" or "el," has been hyphenated although actual practice varies considerably. Titles, such as "Sayyid" and "Sheik," are not considered part of a person's name but are generally included in the dictionary listing. Hence, Sayyid Muhammad bin Ali al-Sanusi is entered under "S" as "Sanusi, Sayyid Muhammad bin Ali al-." In all cases, Arabic names and words are written without diacritical marks in an effort to make the information and analysis contained in this dictionary accessible and understandable to the widest possible audience. Names and terms are generally listed as they typically appear in the English-, French-, or Italian-language literature on Libya. Where more than one variation of a name is frequent, the most common variations are included. Although this approach may offend some Arabists and linguists, it has been adopted here because it will make this dictionary more intelligible to a wider audience.

In many cases, alternative titles, headings, or spellings have been listed and cross-referenced to the title under which the entry appears. For example, "Popular Committee" is listed with a *See* to refer to "People's Committee"; "Oil" is listed with instructions to refer to "Petroleum"; and "Corsairs" is listed with instructions to see "Barbary States." In all entries, extensive cross-references have been included to facilitate the location of information. Cross-references found within the text of the entry are printed in boldface type; additional related topics appear at the end of the entry under *See also*.

Acronyms and Abbreviations

ABEDA	Arab Bank for Economic Development in Africa
ADB	African Development Bank
AFESD	Arab Fund for Economic and Social Development
AIDS	Acquired Immunodeficiency Syndrome
AL	Arab League
AMF	Arab Monetary Fund
AMU	Arab Maghrib Union (also Union du Maghreb Arabe or UMA)
ASU	Arab Socialist Union
AU	African Union
AWACS	Airborne Warning and Control System
BPC	Basic People's Congress
CAEU	Council of Arab Economic Unity
CCC	Customs Cooperation Council
COMESA	Common Market for Eastern and Southern Africa
COMESSA	Community of Sahel-Saharan States
DN	Dinar
EC	European Community
ECA	Economic Commission for Africa
ELF	Eritrean Liberation Front
EPSA	Exploration and Production-Sharing Agreement
EU	European Union
FAO	Food and Agriculture Organization
FAR	Federation of Arab Republics
FRG	Federal Republic of Germany
Frolinat	Front de Libération Nationale du Chad (Front for the National Liberation of Chad)
G-77	Group of 77
GMR	Great Manmade River

GPC	General People's Congress
HIV	Human Immunodeficiency Virus
HRH	His Royal Highness
IAEA	International Atomic Energy Agency
IBRD	International Bank for Reconstruction and Development
ICAO	International Civil Aviation Organization
ICJ	International Court of Justice
IDA	International Development Association
IDB	Islamic Development Bank
IFAD	International Fund for Agricultural Development
IFC	International Finance Corporation
IFRCS	International Federation of Red Cross and Red Crescent Societies
ILO	International Labor Organization
ILSA	Iran-Libya Sanctions Act
IMF	International Monetary Fund
IMG	Islamic Militant Group
IMO	International Maritime Organization
Intelsat	International Telecommunications Satellite Organization
Interpol	International Criminal Police Organization
IOC	International Olympic Committee
IRA	Irish Republican Army
ITU	International Telecommunications Union
LD	Libyan Dollars
LIPETCO	Libyan General Petroleum Company
LNG	liquefied natural gas
MILF	Moro Islamic Liberation Front
MNLF	Moro National Liberation Front
NAM	Nonaligned Movement
NATO	North Atlantic Treaty Organization
NFSL	National Front for the Salvation of Libya
NOC	National Oil Company
NPOI	National Public Organization for Industrialization
OAPEC	Organization of Arab Petroleum Exporting Countries
OAU	Organization of African Unity
OIC	Organization of the Islamic Conference

OIIC	Oil Investments International Corporation
OPEC	Organization of Petroleum Exporting Countries
PC	People's Committee
PLO	Palestine Liberation Organization
Polisario	Frente Popular para la Liberación de Saguia el-Hamra y Rio de Oro (Popular Front for the Liberation of Saguia el-Hamra and Rio de Oro)
RC	Revolutionary Committee
RCC	Revolutionary Command Council
UMA	*See* AMU
UN	United Nations
UNCTAD	United Nations Conference on Trade and Development
UNDP	United Nations Development Program
UNESCO	United Nations Educational, Scientific, and Cultural Organization
UNIDO	United Nations Industrial Development Organization
UNITAR	United Nations Institute for Training and Research
UNSCR	United Nations Security Council Resolution
UPU	Universal Postal Union
WFTU	World Federation of Trade Unions
WHO	World Health Organization
WIPO	World Intellectual Property Organization
WLGP	Western Libya Gas Project
WMO	World Meteorological Organization
WTO	World Trade Organization

MAPS

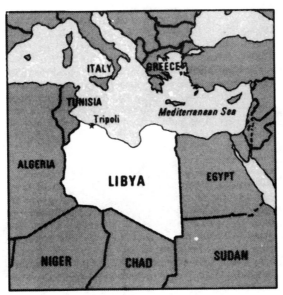

Map 1.   Libya in the Region

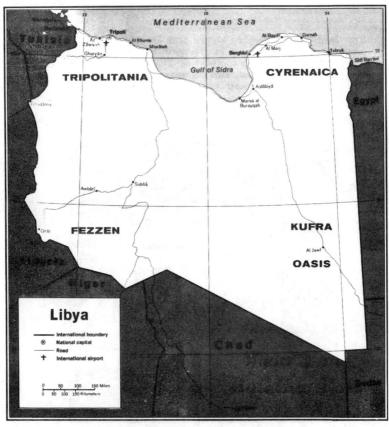

Map 2. Great Socialist People's Libyan Arab Jamahiriya

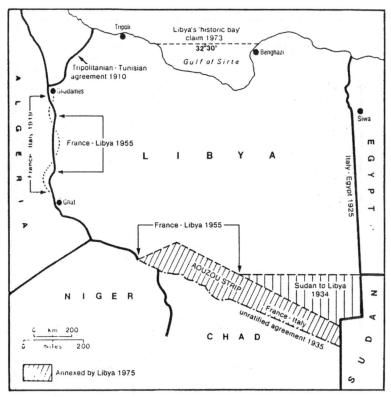

Map 3.   Libyan Boundary Disputes and Settlements

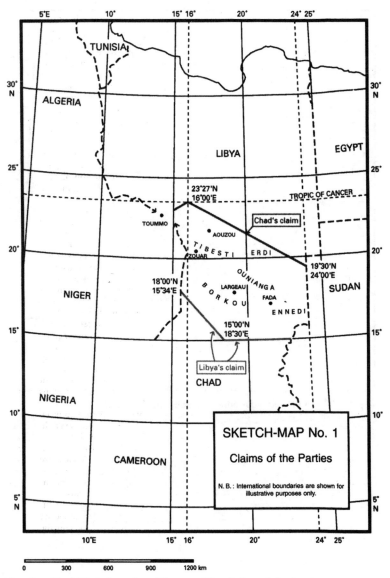

Map 4.   Chad-Libya Boundary Disputes. The Claims of the Parties

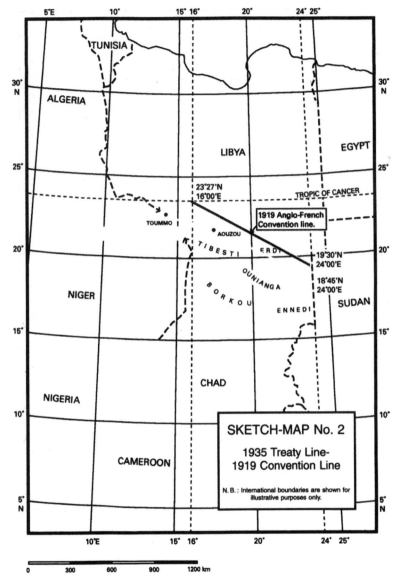

Map 5.   Chad-Libya Boundary Disputes. 1935 Treaty Line and 1919 Convention Line

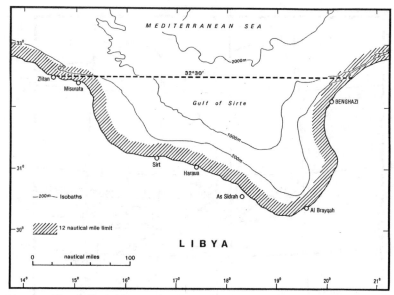

Map 6.   The Gulf of Sidra Closing Line

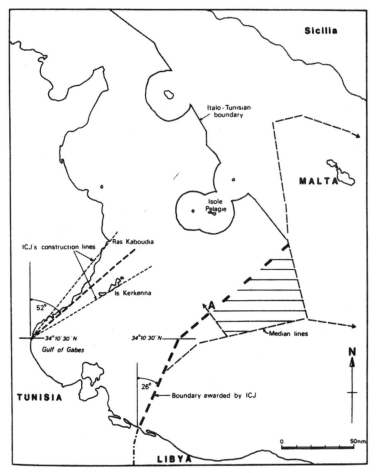

Map 7.   The Libya-Tunisia Maritime Boundary Line Recommended by the
International Court of Justice

Chronology

1551 Beginning of Ottoman rule.

1711 Initiation of the Karamanli dynasty.

1832 Abdication of Yusuf Karamanli. Civil war breaks out.

1835 Ottoman reoccupation. End of Karamanli dynasty.

1842 Sanusi Order establishes first *zawiya* in Cyrenaica.

1856 Sanusi Order moves to Giarabub and is recognized by the sultan.

1860 Mahmud Nadim Pasha governor until 1866.

1866 Ali Ridha governor until 1870 and again in 1872–1874.

1881 Ahmad Rasim Pasha governor until 1896.

1896 Namiq Pasha governor until 1898.

1902 Sanusi Order suffers first military defeat at the hands of the French. Contacts opened with the Italians.

1904 Marshal Rajib Pasha governor until 1908.

1911 Italians invade Libya.

1912 Congress of Aziziya.

1915 Battle of Qasr Bu Hadi. Idris becomes leader of the Sanusi Order.

1917 Italian-Sanusi Agreement of Akramah.

1918 Tripoli Republic.

1919 Agreement of Qalat al-Zaytuna between the Italian government and the Tripoli Republic. Italians promulgate the *Legge Fondamentale*.

1920 **25 October:** Accord of Al-Rajma between the Italian government and Sayyid Muhammad Idris concluded.

1921 **11 November:** Italian-Sanusi Accord of By Maryam.

1922 Idris accepts the amirate of Libya.

1923 Italian government abrogates all Libyan agreements and begins the *Riconquista.*

1929 Italians unite Tripolitania, Cyrenaica, and the Fezzan into one colony known as Libya.

1932 Battle of Hawaria.

1937 First state-sponsored Italian settlers arrive in Libya.

1942 British government pledges Libya will not be returned to Italian control.

1943 British and French military forces defeat Italian armies in Libya and establish military administrations to govern their respective territories.

1949 Big Four Powers turn over disposition of Libyan territories to the United Nations.

1951 Libya is proclaimed an independent kingdom.

1952 First general elections held.

1953 Libya joins Arab League. Anglo-Libyan Agreement signed.

1954 American-Libyan Agreement signed. Succession limited by royal decree to the Idris branch of the Sanusi family.

1955 Franco-Libyan Agreement signed. Libya joins the UN.

1959 Major petroleum deposits confirmed at Zelten in Cyrenaica.

1961 First major oil exports.

1962 Libya joins the Organization of Petroleum Exporting Countries (OPEC).

1969 **1 September:** Libyan Free Unionist Officers movement overthrows monarchy. **13 September:** Muammar al-Qaddafi nominated president of the Libyan Arab Republic. **29 October:** Libya demands withdrawal of British troops and liquidation of military bases. **30 October:** Libya demands liquidation of Wheelus Air Force Base. **14 November:** First foreign banks and hospitals in Libya are nationalized. **11 December:** Constitutional Proclamation promulgated. **27 December:** Tripoli Charter unites Egypt, Libya, and the Sudan.

1970 **28 March:** Last British forces evacuated. **5 May:** First colloquium of Libyan revolutionaries and intellectuals debates the revolutionary course of the nation. **16 June:** Last American forces evacuate Wheelus Air Force Base. **21 June:** Italian properties confiscated and Italian workers expelled. **5 July:** Revolutionary Command Council (RCC) issues first major law relating to the nationalization of the oil industry. **29 November:** Tripoli Cathedral converted into the Gamal Abdul Nasser Mosque. **10 December:** RCC establishes a Jihad Fund to promote struggle against Israel.

1971 **15 January:** Libyan Producer Agreements announced. **17 April:** Federation of Arab Republics unites Egypt, Libya, and Syria. **12 June:** Arab Socialist Union created. **15 October:** Libyan insurance companies nationalized. **7 December:** British Petroleum Company nationalized.

1972 **18 February:** RCC formally abrogates nine treaties concluded by the former Kingdom of Libya with the United States. **4 March:** First Libyan-Soviet cooperation announced. **7 April:** Arab Socialist Union holds its first congress in Tripoli. **2 August:** Benghazi Declaration by Egypt and Libya announces union plans. **28 October:** Committee created to "Islamize" the Libyan legal system.

1973 **15 April:** Qaddafi issues Third Universal Theory marking the commencement of the Popular Revolution. **2 June:** Popular Committees take over Libyan radio and television stations. **8 June:** Libya accuses the United States of infringing on its 100-mile restricted airspace off the Mediterranean coast. **11 June:** Bunker Hunt Oil nationalized. **18 July:** Green March to the Egyptian frontier in support of Libyan union with Egypt. **11 August:** Libya nationalizes 51 percent of Occidental Petroleum followed shortly by the nationalization of 51 percent of all foreign oil companies. **6 October:** Third Arab-Israeli War begins. **26 October:** Libya embargoes oil exports to the United States because of U.S. support for Israel.

1974 **12 January:** Creation of the Arab Islamic Republic by Libya and Tunisia. President of Tunisia soon repudiates the agreement. **11 February:** Libya nationalizes three U.S. oil companies: Texaco, Libyan American Oil Company, and California Asiatic. **May:** Abdel Salaam Jalloud makes official visit to Soviet Union and concludes first major Soviet-Libyan arms agreement. **6 September:** Popular revolution revitalized.

1975 **3 January:** Libya lifts oil embargo against the United States. **12 May:** Soviet prime minister Alexei Kosygin visits Libya. **13 August:** First major coup attempt against Qaddafi. **26 August:** Revolutionary courts created. **September:** Chad confirms Libyan annexation of the Aouzou Strip. **12 September:** Imposition of first U.S. economic sanctions against Libya. **November:** First Basic People's Congresses created.

1976 **5–18 January:** First session of the General People's Congress. **25 May:** Qaddafi announces creation of special committees to intensify the revolution. **17 September:** Publication of part 1 of *The Green Book* entitled "The Solution of the Problem of Democracy: The Authority of the People." **13–24 November:** Second session of the General People's Congress.

1977 **2 March:** Declaration of the Establishment of the People's Authority. Revolutionary Command Council is disbanded. **5 April:** Twenty-two military officers implicated in an abortive August 1975 coup attempt are publicly executed. **21–24 July:** Egypt-Libya border war. **November:** Third session of the General People's Congress. Publication of part 2 of *The Green Book*, "The Solution of the Economic Problem: Socialism." **6 November:** First revolutionary committee established in Tripoli. **1–5 December:** Creation of the Steadfastness and Confrontation Front between Libya, Algeria, Syria, and the Palestine Liberation Front.

1978 **2 March:** General People's Committee replaces cabinet. **6 May:** New real estate regulations virtually eliminate ownership of rental properties. **1 September:** Qaddafi exhorts workers to assume management of their places of employment; banking and petroleum sectors are excluded from such measures. Qaddafi calls for the establishment of revolutionary committees outside Libya. **19 December:** Qaddafi resigns as secretary general of the General People's Congress to dedicate more time to the revolution.

1979 **January:** Libyan intervention in Uganda. **1 June:** Publication of part 3 of *The Green Book*, entitled "The Social Basis of the Third Universal Theory." **1 September:** People's Bureaus begin to replace Libyan embassies throughout the world. The initial takeovers are staged in Rome, Paris, London, Bonn, Madrid, and Valletta. **2 December:** Mobs attack U.S. embassy in Tripoli, setting it on fire.

1980 **30 January:** Tunisia expels the Libyan ambassador and withdraws the head of the Tunisian diplomatic mission in Tripoli in reaction to an apparent Libyan-sponsored commando attack on the Tunisian town of Gafsa. Libyan citizens, protesting French support of Tunisia in the ensuing diplomatic confrontation, attack and burn the French embassy in Tripoli. **7 February:** The U.S. embassy in Tripoli effectively closes. Six embassy staff are recalled, leaving only an administrative officer to look after U.S. property and the needs of some 2,500 Americans working in Libya. A Department of State spokesman says the move is being taken to prevent an attack on the embassy after the United States speeds up military aid to Tunisia. **4 May:** Four Libyan diplomats are ordered to leave the United States for allegedly intimidating Libyan expatriates. Several Libyan dissidents living in Europe are assassinated in the course of the year. **14 July:** Billy Carter, brother of U.S. President Jimmy Carter, registers as a foreign agent of Libya to avoid a federal grand jury investigation. **6–20 August:** Military unit near Tobruk revolts. Libyan officials deny reports of insurgency. **1 September:** Qaddafi proposes a merger with Syria and threatens to resign and join the fedayeen in Palestine if his proposal is rejected. The Syrian government immediately accepts the proposal, and the two governments declare their intention to work toward a unified government. **3 October:** Military confrontation off the Libyan coast as U.S. fighter jets challenge Libyan fighters threatening a reconnaissance plane. **Fall:** Libyan regular army units deployed in Chad. France warns Libya against further military intervention in the civil war in Chad, indicating it is ready to support African moves to maintain Chad's unity and independence. A growing number of African states also voice concern over Libyan intervention, especially after Libyan forces occupy N'Djamena, the capital of Chad, in mid-December.

1981 **3 January:** Libya unfolds its 1981–1985 development plan, which calls for expenditures of LD18.5 billion ($62.5 billion), more than double the amount allocated for the previous five-year plan (1975–1980). **20 March:** The secretary-general of the general secretariat of the General People's Congress announces that the private sector is to be entirely abolished by the end of the year. All foreign trade has already been nationalized and large supermarkets have been set up to replace privately run shops. **6 May:** The U.S. government orders Libya to close its diplomatic mission in Washington and to remove the mission staff from the country. In support of the closure, a State Department statement cites a wide range of Libyan provocations, including support for global terrorism. **19 August:** U.S. aircraft shoot down two Libyan aircraft over the disputed Gulf of Sidra. Qaddafi later threatens to attack U.S. nuclear depots and cause an international catastrophe if U.S. forces again attack Libyan aircraft in the Gulf of Sidra.

1982   12 March: U.S. government bans all exports to Libya, with the exception of food and medicine. **13 December:** Qaddafi announces all Libyan military personnel will be demobilized and replaced by a People's Army.

1983   June: Libya again invades Chad.

1984   4 March: Revival of assassination campaign against Libyan dissidents living abroad. **18 April:** London police besiege Libyan embassy. A policewoman is killed and 11 others are injured when shots are fired from inside the embassy. Great Britain breaks diplomatic relations with Libya and closes the Libyan embassy. **13 August:** Treaty of Oujda signed by Libya and Morocco declares a union between the two states. Through the treaty, Morocco obtains an end to Libyan aid to the Polisario and Libya an end to Moroccan support for French forces in Chad. **18 September:** France and Libya announce a mutual phased withdrawal of their troops from Chad. While France and Libya later announce the completion of the mutual withdrawal of troops from Chad, evidence soon surfaces to suggest Libyan troops remain in northern Chad. **30 November:** Malta and Libya sign a five-year treaty for security and military cooperation, calling for Libya to defend Malta if the Mediterranean island nation requests assistance.

1985   July–September: Libyan government expels several thousand guest workers.

1986   8 January: U.S. government increases economic sanctions on Libya in the wake of late-1985 terrorist attacks on Rome and Vienna airports and later attacks targets around Tripoli and Benghazi. **29 August:** Morocco unilaterally withdraws from its union with Libya.

1987   1 January: Qaddafi declares al-Jufra the new capital of Libya. **6 August:** Libyan forces advance on Chad. **19 August:** Qaddafi inaugurates the Brega concrete pipe factory, a center for the production of pipes for the Great Manmade River project. **5 September:** Chad invades Libya for the first time, occupying the Matan al-Sarra air base 60 miles north of the frontier. **11 September:** Libya and Chad agree to a cease-fire in response to an Organization of African Unity (OAU) appeal. **17 September:** Qaddafi declares an end to the war with Chad after claiming victories at Matan al-Sarra and in the Aouzou Strip. **24 September:** Libya and Chad submit their border dispute to the OAU for mediation. **22 November:** Qaddafi criticizes Revolutionary Committees for too much enthusiasm. **28 December:** Libya and Tunisia restore diplomatic ties broken in September 1985 after the expulsion by Libya of some 35,000 Tunisian laborers.

1988   28 January: Qaddafi denounces the Muslim Brotherhood, calling it the worst of God's enemies and accusing it of destroying the Arab nation. **31 March:** The Tobruk oil refinery at al-Batan opens with a capacity of 220,000 barrels a day. **31 August:** Libya announces plans to abolish both the regular army and the police and to replace them with an "armed people," whose service would be voluntary. **3 October:** Chad and Libya announce plans to restore diplomatic ties. **25 October:** U.S. Central Intelligence Agency accuses Libya of building a chemical weapons plant. **3 November:** Qaddafi outlines plans to restructure the armed forces into three separate branches: regular army units called "Jamahiriya Guards," conscripts with a compulsory service of two years, and part-time recruits. **21 December:** Pan Am flight 103 explodes over Lockerbie, Scotland.

1989   4 January: United States downs two more Libyan aircraft over the Mediterranean Sea. **19 January:** U.S. president Ronald Reagan announces plans for the modification of trade regulations to allow U S. companies to resume operations in Libya. **20 January:** Libya cancels a World Cup soccer match, conceding victory to Algeria because the two teams "are in fact one team." **17 February:** Algeria, Libya, Mauritania,

Morocco, and Tunisia create the Arab Maghrib Union. **8 March:** Qaddafi complains that movements such as the Muslim Brotherhood are trying to obtain power through the use of religion. **11 June:** Announcement of the creation of the Qaddafi International Prize for Human Rights, with jailed black South African activist Nelson Mandela as the first winner. **1 September:** Twentieth anniversary of the Libyan revolution. Libya agrees to submit Aouzou dispute to the International Court of Justice. **19 September:** UTA flight 772 explodes over Niger. **16 October:** Qaddafi visits Egypt for the first time in 16 years. **25 October:** Qaddafi admits that Libya has supported groups accused of terrorism but claims such aid was halted when it became apparent that these groups were doing more harm than good. **28 October:** Libya warns Italy it will press for reparations unless Rome pays for the thousands of Libyans killed, injured, or deported during the 1911–1943 period of colonial rule.

1990 March: U.S. government calls for pressure on Libya to end chemical arms production. A fire at the controversial chemical plant at Rabta, 45 miles southwest of Tripoli, kills two people. **5 March:** Libya and Sudan agree to sign integration pacts paving the way for possible union in four years. **22 March:** Czechoslovakian government reveals that the country's former Communist government sold Libya 1,000 tons of Semtex, an odorless explosive often used by terrorists. **26 March:** Chad accuses Libyan-backed rebels of attacking two government garrisons on its eastern border with Sudan. **April:** France credits Qaddafi with assisting in the release of three European hostages. **1 April:** Ethiopia expels two Libyan diplomats after a minor explosion at an Addis Ababa hotel. **3 April:** Qaddafi states that Jewish emigrants should go to the Baltic republics, Alaska, or Alsace-Lorraine but not to Israel. **11 June:** China denies it is helping Libya or any other country to develop chemical weapons. **16 June:** Libya denies it was behind a riot of Shiite Muslims in southern Thailand. **31 August:** Aouzou Strip dispute submitted to the International Court of Justice. **11 October:** Nine European and North African states, including Libya, forge a regional structure to promote political stability and economic development in the Mediterranean region.

1991 11 March: Washington admits a two-year-old secret program to destabilize the Libyan government with Libyan commandos trained by the U.S. has ended in failure. **30 March:** Qaddafi, in pursuit of the elusive goal of Arab unity, uses a bulldozer to knock down a border gate between Libya and Egypt. **28 August:** Qaddafi hosts a celebration marking the opening of the Great Manmade River, a pipeline for transporting water from wells in eastern and central Libya to the coast. **October:** Western sources renew claims that Libya was behind the 1988 bombing of Pan Am flight 103 over Scotland. **November:** United States claims to have fresh evidence that Libya is again producing poison gas at Rabta, as well as building a factory nearby for the manufacture of chemical weapons.

1992   21 January: UN Security Council approves Resolution 731, which requires Libya to cooperate with the investigation Great Britain, France, and the United States are conducting into the destruction of Pan Am flight 103 over Lockerbie and UTA flight 772 over Niger. United States charges Libya is expanding its chemical weapons program and dispersing chemical stockpiles to avoid detection. **3 February:** The International Atomic Energy Agency (IAEA) announces that Libya has informed its director general that all Libyan nuclear facilities are open for IAEA inspection. **15 April:** Japan, Italy, Belgium, Denmark, and Sweden ask Libyan diplomats to leave their countries and flights are canceled to Libya as UN sanctions take effect. **9 June:** Libya relays information to the British government concerning past contacts with the Irish Republican Army. **14 June:** *Al-Jamahiriya*, official organ of the revolutionary committees in Libya, continues a week-long series of articles attacking Qaddafi policies. **14 August:** UN Security Council retains sanctions imposed on Libya for failing to hand over two suspects in the 1988–1989 bombings of the Pan Am and UTA aircraft. **4 September:** New legislation takes effect in Libya permitting individuals or companies to engage in industry, agriculture, health care, and trade. **26 October:** Libya demands compensation from Italy for the 32-year Italian occupation of Libya, as well as information on the whereabouts of more than 5,000 Libyans allegedly deported to Italy during the occupation to work as forced labor. **31 December:** U.S. officials announce they have frozen $260 million in Libyan cash assets to further punish Libya for alleged support of international terrorism, bringing the total assets frozen to $950 million.

1993   20 February: Libya denies U.S. allegations it is constructing a chemical weapons plant near Tripoli and invites any neutral international group to inspect the site. **23 February:** Reports indicate that Libya plans to move foreign embassies, together with its foreign and oil ministries, to Ras Lanuf, a semidesert region southeast of Tripoli. **2 July:** U.S. Department of State, complying with the international embargo against Libya, refuses entry to a delegation of 79 Libyan athletes seeking to participate in the World University Games in Buffalo, New York. **October:** Army rebellion by units stationed near Misurata is put down by units loyal to Qaddafi. **22 October:** United States warns Thailand that Thai contractors are the main companies involved in the construction of chemical weapons plants in Libya. When Thailand opens an investigation into the U.S. allegations, Qaddafi on 9 November orders the expulsion of thousands of Thai workers in retaliation. **11 November:** UN agrees to tighten its embargo against Libya, freezing Libyan assets overseas, banning some sales of oil equipment, and strengthening flight bans into Libya.

1994   3 February: International Court of Justice awards the Aouzou Strip to Chad, voiding Libya's claim to the disputed territory. **September:** Libya pledges to stop discriminating against Thai workers. **1 September:** Libya celebrates 25th anniversary of the revolution. **18 November:** Libya sets a multiple exchange rate for the dinar one week after a devaluation.

1995   1 March: Libya announces the release of more than 300 prisoners and the destruction of the last prison in the country. **23 March:** U.S. Federal Bureau of Investigation announces a $4 million reward for the arrest of the two Libyans wanted in connection with the bombing of Pan Am flight 103. **31 March:** UN Security Council extends the sanctions imposed earlier on Libya because of the country's failure to surrender the two Libyans suspects in the Lockerbie bombing. **5 April:** Qaddafi threatens to defy the UN ban on flights to Libya and to quit the United Nations. **19 April:** UN Security Council eases its travel ban on Libyan flights to allow Libyan pilgrims to make the hajj to Mecca. **6 June:** Libya awards a $5.7 billion contract for the third stage of the Great Manmade River project to South Korea's Dong Ah Construction. **14 August:** Libya bans all diplomatic travel outside Tripoli without a special pass. **1–8 September:** Islamists clash with government forces in Benghazi. Up to 70 people are reported killed and the government later arrests 3,500 Islamists. **17 October:** Libya announces it will no longer seek a seat on the UN Security Council, citing hostile U.S. domination of the world organization. **27 November:** Opposition leader Ali Muhammad Abu Zayd is stabbed to death in London. **30 November:** Italian police seize 10 tons of weapons and related military hardware en route to Libya from Canadian, British, and U.S. manufacturers. **11 December:** British government expels a Libyan diplomat based in the Saudi Arabian embassy in London on charges of spying.

1996   24–26 January: Louis Farrakhan, leader of the Nation of Islam movement in the United States, meets with Qaddafi in Tripoli to discuss organizing and mobilizing American Muslims to influence elections in the United States. **9 February:** Opposition sources report a Libyan court has issued death sentences to 12 officers involved in an October 1993 uprising against the Qaddafi government. **24 February:** U.S. intelligence sources identify a factory in Tarhuna, scheduled for completion in 1997, as the world's largest chemical weapons plant. **15 April:** Qaddafi demands the United States hand over the planners and pilots involved in the 1986 attack on Libyan cities for trial in Libyan courts. **29 April:** Relatives of Lockerbie bombing victims file a $10 billion lawsuit against Libya in U.S. courts. **May:** Moro National Liberation Front leader Nur Misuari visits Tripoli to seek Libyan support before agreeing to head the Southern Philippines Council on Peace and Development proposed by the Philippine government. **27 May:** Opposition forces report armed clashes with security forces in Benghazi after a security officer is killed on 24 May. **22 June:** Qaddafi flies to an Arab summit in Cairo, ignoring a UN ban on flights from Libya. **9 July:** Up to 50 people reportedly die at a soccer match in Tripoli during an altercation between the bodyguards of one of Qaddafi's sons and unknown hecklers. **5 August:** U.S. president Bill Clinton signs a controversial new law imposing sanctions on foreign individuals or companies that invest $40 million or more in gas or oil projects in Libya or Iran. **27 August:** U.S. government rejects an application from Farrakhan to receive a $1 billion gift from Libya; Farrakhan later accepts the Qaddafi International Prize for Human Rights but declines the $250,000 stipend that accompanies the award. **5–7 October:** Prime Minister Necmettin Erbakan of Turkey visits Libya to promote plans to forge an alliance of Muslim states. He also emphasizes the need for stronger trade cooperation and reiterates Turkey's rejection of the UN sanctions imposed on Libya. Qaddafi responds by assailing Turkish ties with the Israel, NATO, and the United States.

1997   1 January: Libyan state television reports a court has sentenced six senior military officers and two civilians to death for spying. **11 March:** The Vatican establishes full diplomatic relations with Libya. **10 June:** The Armed Forces Revolutionary Council in Sierra Leone denies it sent a delegation to Libya to seek military support from Qaddafi. **21 September:** Arab League approves a resolution that defies UN sanctions by permitting planes carrying the political leadership of Libya or Libyan delegations participating in regional and international meetings to land on the territory of Arab countries and to permit other flights for religious and humanitarian purposes. **29 October:** South African president Nelson Mandela bestows his country's highest award, the Order of Good Hope, on Qaddafi in recognition for Libya's support in the struggle against apartheid. **30 October:** Two German businessmen are jailed for illegally supplying Libya with electronic components for use in making chemical weapons. **19 November:** A trial opens in Berlin in which the prosecution seeks to prove that the Libyan People's Bureau was directly responsible for the 1986 bombing of the La Belle discothèque.

1998   27 February: Rejecting arguments by Britain and the United States, the International Court of Justice rules it has the authority to decide whether Libya must surrender two of its citizens for trial on charges of blowing up Pan Am flight 103. **20 March:** During a UN Security Council debate, Libya presses its case for an end to UN sanctions imposed in the wake of the 1988 Lockerbie bombing. **28 March:** President Mandela of South Africa, the first recipient of the Qaddafi International Prize for Human Rights back in 1989, defends his right to maintain friendly relations with Libya. **29 March:** A Libyan Arab Airways plane carrying Muslims on the annual pilgrimage lands in Saudi Arabia in defiance of UN sanctions. **19 May:** Germany and Libya sign an economic cooperation agreement in the fields of industry, finance, and tourism. **26 August:** Libya provisionally accepts the joint British-U.S. proposal to try two Libyan suspects under Scottish law in The Hague for the Lockerbie bombing. **28 August:** UN Security Council votes unanimously to suspend sanctions against Libya once it has remanded the Lockerbie bombing suspects. **August–September:** Official delegations from neighboring African states visit Libya in violation of the UN flight ban.

1999   9 February: United Nations approves Libyan flights for travel to Saudi Arabia for the hajj. **February–March:** Prolonged negotiations result in Libyan leader Qaddafi agreeing to remand the two Lockerbie suspects by 6 April for trial by Scottish judges in the Netherlands. **10 March:** A French antiterrorism court sentences six Libyans to life imprisonment in absentia for the 1989 downing of UTA flight 772 over Niger. **5 April:** Libya hands over the two Lockerbie suspects, Abdel Basset Ali al-Megrahi and Al-Amin Khalifa Fhimah, for trial by a Scottish court in the Netherlands. In response, the United Nations immediately suspends its sanctions against Libya. **7 July:** Libya accepts responsibility for the 1984 shooting of a policewoman outside the Libyan embassy in London, agrees to cooperate with a British police investigation, and offers compensation to the family of the victim. **20 August:** Qaddafi calls on African nations to create a United States of Africa. **7 September:** Qaddafi celebrates his 30th year in power with a military parade in Tripoli. **1 December:** Italian prime minister Massimo D'Alema flies to Tripoli for a two-day official visit, the first Western head of government to visit Libya in eight years.

2000   January: The British government confirms newspaper reports that a crate of Scud missile parts destined for Libya had been discovered in late November 1999 on a British Airways flight. **February:** For the first time in a decade, Libya contributes officers to a UN peacekeeping mission. **March:** Qaddafi abolishes most central government executive functions, devolving responsibility to the 26 municipal councils making up the General People's Congress. **22 August:** Libya agrees to pay $1 million for each of 12 foreign hostages held by Muslim rebels in the southern Philippines. **September–October:** Diplomatic sources report widespread racial violence in Libya, where mobs have been attacking black African migrant workers.

2001   31 January: After a 12-year investigation and an 84-day trial, costing an estimated $106 million, three Scottish judges sitting in a special court in the Netherlands find guilty only one of the two defendants in the Lockerbie trial. **June:** Germany asks Libya for compensation for the victims of the La Belle discothèque bombing. **September:** Libya pledges a total of $2 billion in development assistance to several Caribbean islands, raising concern in the U.S. government about increased Libyan influence in its backyard. **October:** Libya selected for a new seat on the UN Social and Economic Council. **November:** U.S. State Department extends for another year restrictions on the use of

U.S. passports for travel to Libya. **20 December:** Qaddafi notifies officials in the Netherlands that Libya is prepared to sign the international treaty banning chemical weapons.

2002   January: U.S. president George W. Bush extends the U.S. sanctions first imposed on Libya in January 1986 for another year. Libya launches an Internet website that offers a $1 million reward for information on individuals, mostly regime opponents affiliated with Islamic movements, wanted by Libyan officials. **March:** Libya rejects a U.S. report that charges it has a poor human rights record. An appellate court ruling upholds the January 2001 guilty verdict in the Lockerbie trial, bringing some closure to the case. **June:** Australia announces it is moving to reestablish diplomatic relations with Libya because it believes the Libyan government is no longer actively involved in promoting terrorism. Talks continue between American, British, and Libyan officials regarding a proposed $2.7 billion compensation package for the families of the victims of the Pan Am flight 103 bombing. A U.S. federal appeals court rules the United States has the right to sue Libya for terrorist attacks on American soil. **July:** The African Union, a regional group modeled after the European Union, replaces the 39-year-old Organization of African Unity. **September:** The British prime minister asks Qaddafi to stop supporting the Robert Mugabe regime in Zimbabwe and to dispose of weapons of mass destruction. **October:** Franco-Libyan group meets in Paris for the first time in 20 years, three days after the French foreign minister completes a trip to Libya.

2003   January: Qaddafi indicates Libya is exchanging intelligence on the al-Qaeda terrorist network with the United States. Libya is elected chairman of the UN Commission on Human Rights. **March:** Secret talks open in London between American, British, and Libyan officials aimed at dismantling Libya's unconventional weapons program. **August:** Britain, Libya, and the United States reach agreement that Libya will accept responsibility for the 1988 bombing of Pan Am flight 103; Libya transfers $2.7 billion to the Bank for International Settlements in Switzerland to compensate the families of the victims of the Lockerbie bombing. Qaddafi also announces a final compensation deal with the relatives of the victims killed in the 1989 bombing of UTA flight 772 over Niger. **12 September:** UN Security Council permanently lifts its 11-year-old sanctions regime on Libya. **19 December:** Libyan foreign minister announces his country has decided of its own free will to be completely free of internationally banned weapons.

2004   23 April: President Bush removes most of the remaining sanctions on doing business in Libya, authorizing establishment of a diplomatic mission in Tripoli. **27 April:** Libyan leader Qaddafi begins a visit to Europe with an announcement in Brussels that he will again support "Freedom Fighters" if the West refuses his offer of peace. **5 May:** A Libyan court sentences five Bulgarian nurses and a Palestinian doctor to death by firing squad. The six defendants were convicted of deliberately infecting more than 400 children in a Benghazi children's hospital with HIV in an effort to find a cure for AIDS. **29 June:** Libya and the United States restore diplomatic relations after a 24-year gap. **31 July:** A plea bargain in a U.S. court details plans of an alleged Libyan plot to assassinate Saudi Arabian crown prince Abdullah. **20 September:** President Bush revokes trade embargo on Libya, but Libya remains on U.S. list of state sponsors of terrorism. **11 October:** European Union foreign ministers agree to lift arms embargo on Libya. **November:** Libya sends four peacekeepers to the Philippines to oversee implementation of the cease-fire negotiated between the Philippine government and the Moro Islamic Liberation Front. **1 November:** Prime Minister Shukri Ghanem announces Libya intends to abolish some $5 billion worth of subsidies on electricity, fuel, and basic food items in a move to liberalize the economy. **December:** Libyan Central Bank withdraws $1 billion in assets frozen in U.S. banks since 1986.

2005   3 February: U.S. corporation Boeing announces sale of up to six 737-800s to Buraq Airlines, a privately owned Libyan company. The sale to Buraq, Libya's first private airline, is valued at $367 million. **9 February:** U.S. assistant secretary of state William Burns meets with Libyan leader Qaddafi in talks intended to improve U.S.-Libyan relations. **1 March:** Qaddafi argues pending UN reforms should abolish the Security Council. **15 March:** General People's Congress approves a measure allowing foreign banks to open branches in Libya and to contribute as shareholders in local banks. **20 May:** U.S. officials discuss plans to restore military cooperation with Libya, including arms exports and training of Libyan military and security forces. **9 June:** Nine Libyan policemen and a physician are cleared of charges they tortured five Bulgarian nurses to force them to confess to infecting Libyan children with

HIV. **25–26 June:** Libyan opponents to the Qaddafi regime, gathering in London to discuss plans to remove him from power, reject foreign military support. **23 July:** An Austrian bank, BAWAG P.S.K., is the first Western bank to open a branch in Tripoli. **28 September:** President Bush waives some defense export restrictions to allow U.S. companies to participate in the destruction of Libya's chemical weapons stockpile, as well as to refurbish eight transport planes purchased by Libya in the 1970s but held in storage in the United States since that time.

2006   May: United States restores full diplomatic relations, removing Libya from the U.S. State Department list of State Sponsors of Terrorism and omitting it from the annual certification of countries not fully cooperating with American antiterrorism efforts.

Introduction

Of all the states of the Middle East and North Africa, Libya is the country about which the least is known. It is only in recent times that scholars and the general public alike have begun to appreciate the complexity of Libya's turbulent history under Ottoman and Italian rule, as well as the extensive, prolonged violence that accompanied the passage after 1911 from one form of colonial bondage to another. The transition to independence in 1951 was scarcely more propitious, as the United Kingdom of Libya under the rule of King Idris I was considered by many to be a caricature of the neocolonial state. A deeper understanding of this turbulent background to contemporary times places the Qaddafi era in a larger context and helps clarify policies and programs that otherwise might seem inexplicable.

LAND AND PEOPLE

The Great Socialist People's Libyan Arab Jamahiriya, still generally known as Libya, is bounded on the north by the Mediterranean Sea, on the east by Egypt, on the west by Tunisia and Algeria, and on the south by Niger, Chad, and the Sudan. With an area of 1,759,540 square kilometers (approximately 680,000 square miles), it ranks fourth in geographical size among the countries of Africa and 15th among the countries of the world. While Libya is two and a half times the size of the state of Texas, less than 2 percent of the country receives enough rainfall for settled agriculture, with the heaviest precipitation occurring in the Jabal al-Akhdar region of Cyrenaica. There are no permanent rivers or streams in Libya, and no true mountains with the exception of the Tibesti range, which rises to a height of almost 2,300 meters (7,500 feet), near the Chadian border.

Both an African and an Arab country, Libya's strategic location on the northern rim of Africa has been of considerable importance to its historical and modern development. Early African trade routes, several of which passed through Libya, ran from Central Africa through the Sahel to the North African coast. These trade links, coupled with Libya's location well into the Sahara Desert, explain the long-term Libyan interest in the affairs of Central and Eastern Africa. In terms of the Arab world, a tongue of the Libyan Desert reaching almost to the Mediterranean Sea has traditionally split Libya into two parts, with the eastern half looking toward the Mashriq while the western part focused on the Maghrib. In the last century, the Libyan-based Sanusi Order reinforced this tendency to look to both the Arab and African worlds by establishing religious lodges south to Chad and west to Senegal. After World War II, the major powers of the world recognized Libya's strategic importance as a link to the Arab states of North Africa and the Middle East, as well as a springboard to African states.

While the desert predominates in Libya, the country is characterized by surprising variety. Less than 20 percent of its territory is covered by sand dunes, notably the Awbari and Murzuk Sand Seas in the Fezzan, and the Kalanshiyu and Rabyanah Sand Seas in Cyrenaica, with much of the remainder covered by rocky or gravel plains. With the Mediterranean Sea and the Sahara Desert as the dominant influences, some five separate climatic zones have been identified in Libya. These range from the coastal lowlands, where the climate tends to be Mediterranean with hot summers and mild winters, to the desert interior, which experiences very hot summers and extreme temperature ranges. Rates of rainfall are relatively high in the high plateaus of Cyrenaica and Tripolitania, and snow is not unknown. The prevailing coastal winds are from the northeast, with occasional north winds. In the summer, hot winds known in Libya as the *ghibli* occasionally blow northward from the desert; this weather condition raises the ambient temperature well above normal and fills the air with sand and dust. In the south, the prevailing winds shift from the northeast to the southwest. The winds blowing off the Sahara Desert are hot in the summer and cold in the winter.

With the exception of a few oases, the most productive agricultural areas are the coastal strip and the highland steppes just south of it. In most areas, antiquated farming methods and erosion due to overgrazing have taken a toll on land that was generally marginal in productivity at the outset. An accelerated use of subsoil water deposits along the coast has also led to growing problems with soil salinity. The main crops in Libya are barley, olives, citrus fruits, vegetables, wheat, and dates. The traditional crop is barley, and a considerable amount of cropland is devoted to its cultivation. The main citrus crops are tangerines and lemons. Almonds and dates are other significant tree crops. In the past, wild esparto grass was gathered for use in papermaking. Herds of sheep and cattle are on the increase, as are poultry stocks, while the number of goats and camels is decreasing. Everywhere, the government has encouraged the use of modern range management practices to eliminate overgrazing and maximize the use of available pasture land.

A high birthrate, encouraged and supported by the government, has raised Libya's population from around 1,000,000 at the time of independence in 1951 to an estimated 5,631,585 in 2005. More than two-thirds of this population lives in the cities along the Mediterranean coast, with around half of this number in Tripoli itself. The composition of the Libyan population is overwhelmingly young, with more than a third of all Libyans alive today under 14 years of age and well over half born after the Libyan Free Unionist Officers movement seized power in 1969.

The ethnic composition of the Libyan population remains diverse but has changed considerably in recent years. The 30,000 or so Italians who were living in Libya after World War II were mostly expelled by the revolutionary government in 1970. Similarly, a Jewish population that numbered around 35,000 in 1948 had shrunk to no more than 100 residents by 1973. The remainder of the Libyan population is largely a mixture of Arab and Berber stock. Tripolitania has three Arab tribes that trace their origins back to the Bani Hilal, and five tribes that go back to the Bani Sulaim. Cyrenaica is occupied mainly by the Bani Sulaim, which are divided into two main branches, the Jibarna and the Harabi. Berbers were once dominant throughout North Africa, but in Libya today, they are a marginal, conservative people who tend to reside in remote mountain areas or desert localities. Other ethnic groups include a few thousand Tuareg living in southwest Libya, black Libyans who are mostly descendants of sub-Saharan Africans, Tebu who live in the southern desert, and Duwud living near the salt flats of the western Fezzan.

With the Arab conquest, Islam penetrated North Africa in general and Libya in particular. Over the next 12 centuries, the North African shore, especially Libya, assumed a distinct Arab-Islamic character. In the early

19th century, Sayyid Muhammad bin Ali al-Sanusi established the Sanusi Order in Cyrenaica between Benghazi and Derna. An orthodox order of Sufis, the Sanusi were a revivalist, as opposed to a reformist, movement dedicated to spreading religious enlightenment into areas where Islam was at best only lightly observed. They concentrated their efforts away from the main population centers of the Mediterranean Sea and North Africa and among the more inaccessible peoples of the Sahara and the Sudan. The brothers of the order carried their message to large parts of Islamic and pagan Africa, eventually establishing almost 150 lodges in the region. In most areas, the Sanusi Order brought law and order, curbed raiding, encouraged peaceful trade, and promoted agricultural development in a remarkable civilizing mission amid highly unpromising surroundings. Centered in Cyrenaica, Sanusism later spread to the Fezzan but never achieved the widespread following in Tripolitania that it enjoyed in southern and eastern Libya.

When Italy invaded Libya in 1911, most Libyans viewed its colonial policies as a direct attack against Islam and responded by declaring jihad. In this sense, the sustained resistance to Italian occupation was motivated far more by religious zeal than by European-style nationalism. Forty years later, Islam as epitomized by the Sanusi movement gave both continuity and legitimacy to the independent kingdom established in 1951. Thereafter, the role of religion as a legitimizing force in Libya declined for a variety of reasons, including increased education and growing urbanization. Nevertheless, Islam has continued to exert a major influence on Libyan history and society.

The vast majority of Libyans belong to the Sunni branch of Islam and adhere to the Malikite school of Islamic law. One of four orthodox Sunni sects, the Malikite rite holds that the Koran and the hadith are the principal sources of truth. In line with their orthodox Islamic beliefs, Libyan Muslims also practice the Five Pillars of Islam, which are the profession of faith, alms giving, prayer five times daily, fasting during the holy month of Ramadan, and pilgrimage to Mecca.

HISTORY

Early History

Given Libya's location at a strategic crossroads of Europe, Africa, and the Middle East, it should come as little surprise that its history has been one of successive invasions. Before the 12th century B.C., Phoenician traders were active throughout the Mediterranean, and the depots they established along the African coast were links in a maritime chain that stretched from modern-day Lebanon to Spain. At about the same time, trade routes were opened that carried slaves and merchandise from Central Africa through Libya to the Mediterranean Sea until the early years of the present century. By the fifth century B.C., the city-state of Carthage controlled much of the region, which included permanent settlements along the Libyan coast at Oea (Tripoli), Labdah (later Leptis Magna), and Sabratah in an area known collectively as Tripolis ("Three Cities"). Carthage continued to dominate Tripolis until it was defeated by Rome in the Punic Wars (264–241 and 218–201 B.C.). With the final destruction of Carthage in 146 B.C., Tripoli became a Roman colony; however, Cyrenaica was colonized by the Greek states from the seventh century B.C. until the sixth century A.D. Fezzan, the third major region of modern Libya, was loosely controlled by the Garamantes after 1000 B.C. They established a powerful kingdom in the desert astride the trade route from the western Sudan to the Mediterranean Sea. Cyrenaica was later subjugated by the Persians and then annexed by Rome in 74 B.C.

While Libya has experienced many invaders, it was the Arabs who had the greatest impact as they grafted both their culture and their religion onto indigenous Berber peoples. In A.D. 642, Arab Muslims swept across Cyrenaica and continued westward until they seized Germa, the capital of the Garamantes, in 663. The Arab Fatimid dynasty was established in Egypt in 910 and later extended its control to Tripolitania. A century later, the Fatimids responded to growing Berber opposition to their rule by inviting two bedouin tribes from the Arabian Peninsula, the Beni Hilal and the Beni Sulaim, to come to North Africa and quell the revolt. While each wave of Arab invaders stamped its character on the Libyan people, it was this last group that ensured the Arab character of the region.

Although Tripolitania later returned to Berber rule for a short period of time, it was the Ottomans who eventually controlled Libya for most of the next 400 years. After the Turks conquered Egypt in 1510, Cyrenaica passed under Ottoman control, as did Tripolitania 41 years later after the Turks drove out the Knights of St. John of Malta. While contemporary Libya remained a part of the Ottoman Empire from 1551 to 1911, Turkish control over its North African domain was generally lax. Consequently, the three regencies in the Ottoman Maghrib, Tripoli,

Algiers, and Tunis, experienced recurrent periods of revolt followed by the reassertion of Ottoman control. In 1711, an army officer in Tripoli established the Karamanli dynasty, a manifestation of local autonomy, which governed Libya until 1835 when the Ottomans restored direct control. With the Ottoman empire already in serious decline, Turkish rule in Libya became increasingly remote with control over the region reaching a low ebb by the beginning of the 20th century.

The Colonial Era

Italy was one of the last European powers to engage in imperial expansion. Because the Italian city-states were not united until 1870, the Italian government was not in a position to exploit early colonial opportunities in Africa. At the beginning of the 20th century, Libya was one of the few remaining African territories not occupied by Europeans, and its proximity to Italy—at its closest point only 550 kilometers (350 miles) from Italy's boot—made it an irresistible target for Italian colonial policy. On 29 September 1911, Rome declared war on the Ottoman Empire, and four days later, Italian forces occupied Tripoli. Although the Turks abandoned Libya to Italian administration 12 months after that, Libyan forces continued to oppose Italian rule in a struggle that took on aspects of a holy war.

The Italians had occupied most of Tripolitania by 1913, but military progress elsewhere in the country was slow. An invasion of the Fezzan achieved some early success; nevertheless, by early 1914 bedouin resistance had largely driven the invaders out. In Cyrenaica, the Sanusi Order effectively rallied and led resistance against the Italians for much of the next two decades. As a result, the Italians in early August 1915 controlled little more than the Libyan coastal cities of Tripoli, Benghazi, Derna, and Tobruk.

Events during and after World War I strengthened Italian determination to dominate Libya. As part of the inducement to Italy to enter the war on the side of the Allies, the April 1915 Pact of London promised the Italian government all of the rights that Turkey had enjoyed in Libya. In 1917, the Italians concluded a peace agreement with the Sanusi Order in Cyrenaica, and in 1918 Rome agreed to a measure of self-government in Tripolitania. The Misurata-based Tripoli Republic was established in 1918, and two years later, Italy recognized the head of the Sanusi Order as the hereditary amir of Cyrenaica, thus recognizing his authority over much of the interior. This series of political achievements encouraged the political factions in Libya to increase their cooperation, and in 1922 the Cyrenaicans accepted a Tripolitanian offer to recognize the head of the Sanusi Order as the amir of all Libya.

While political developments in Libya appeared to favor the Libyans, decisive events were taking place in Rome. With the Fascist rise to power in October 1922, the Italian government of Benito Mussolini embarked upon a more rigid colonial policy, including the pacification of Libya. In 1923, Italy's armed forces began a brutal reconquest of Libya that enjoyed early success due to an overwhelming superiority in men and equipment. Tripolitania was quickly subdued, and the Fezzan was finally pacified at the end of the decade. In Cyrenaica, Sanusi tribesmen employed guerrilla warfare to prolong the struggle, but resistance finally ended in September 1931 with the capture of Sidi Umar al-Mukhtar, the most effective Cyrenaican resistance leader. On 24 January 1932, Italian authorities declared an official end to the war begun in 1911.

After 1934, the Libyan territories were administered by a governor-general who in 1937 was designated first consul. He was supported by a general consultative council and a council of government made up exclusively of Italians. In 1937, Mussolini proclaimed himself the Protector of Islam, and in early 1939, the colony of Libya was incorporated into metropolitan Italy and from then on considered an integral part of the Italian state. Throughout the 1930s, Italy devoted a considerable amount of time and money to the colonization and development of Libya. Approximately 110,000 Italians emigrated to Libya, and public services and works were expanded and improved. Unfortunately, most of these improvements were for the benefit of the Italian settlers and a few Libyan collaborators, with the average Libyan citizen reaping very few advantages from colonial rule.

Where World War I had smoothed the way for the Italian occupation of Libya, World War II led to its end. During the war, Great Britain occupied Tripolitania and Cyrenaica, while France gained control of the Fezzan. This division of Libya between two new colonial masters augured ill for the future, but eventually led to a declaration of independence. At the July 1945 Potsdam Conference, the Soviet Union proposed that a trusteeship be established over Tripolitania, and in April

1946 Great Britain suggested immediate independence for all of Libya. With the Big Four Powers (France, Great Britain, the Soviet Union, and the United States) unable to agree on a future course, the 1947 Treaty of Peace with Italy left open the question of the final disposition of Italy's former colonies. Even though a Big Four commission of investigation dispatched to Libya in 1948 reported the country was not ready for independence, the Big Four Powers eventually referred the question to the UN General Assembly. Under a November 1949 General Assembly resolution, the United Kingdom of Libya, the first North African state to achieve statehood and the first state to emerge under the auspices of the United Nations, was proclaimed on 24 December 1951 under the rule of Muhammad Idris al-Mahdi al-Sanusi.

Independence and Monarchy

Libya under King Idris I could best be characterized as a conservative, traditional Arab state. The 1951 constitution established a hereditary monarchy with a federal state divided into the provinces of Tripolitania, Cyrenaica, and Fezzan. This arrangement was the subject of much criticism and was eventually replaced in 1963 with a unitary system. A constitutional amendment joined the three provinces together in a united kingdom with a parliamentary legislature.

In the interim, forces and movements inside and outside Libya pressured the monarchy to accelerate economic, social, and political change. The discovery of major deposits of petroleum and natural gas in 1959 later precipitated dramatic changes in the Libyan economy, accelerating the transformation of the nation's socioeconomic fabric. As this process continued, the gulf between the traditional ruling elite and emerging new social groups widened.

At the same time, the Libyan government and people were enmeshed in the growing politicization of the Arab world. Colonial struggles in neighboring states, the Palestine imbroglio, and the growth of Nasserist and Baathist pan-Arabism did not augur well for a conservative monarchy that had expended its anticolonialist credits. Dependent in the early years on the income from U.S. and British military bases, the Idris regime pursued a policy of cooperation with the West that it was unable to reverse once rapidly growing oil revenues broadened its political options. On 1 September 1969, in what became known as the One September Revolution, the Libyan monarchy was overthrown by the Revolutionary Command Council (RCC), led by Colonel Muammar al-Qaddafi.

The Qaddafi Era

Soon after seizing power, Qaddafi and the RCC set about redirecting the domestic and foreign policies of the old regime. They opened negotiations with Great Britain and the United States aimed at an early termination of agreements providing for military bases in Libya. Italian-owned assets were confiscated, and the Italians living in Libya were expelled. The RCC also pursued other domestic policies that emphasized its opposition to colonialism and imperialism. Outside Libya, the RCC consistently advocated war—broadly defined to include economic and political as well as military actions—as the only solution to the Arab-Israeli dispute. The revised Libyan stance on Palestine also influenced its policy toward an overall Middle East settlement in addition to many other areas of foreign policy, especially its posture toward terrorism.

On 11 December 1969, the RCC repealed the 1951 constitution, issuing a constitutional proclamation that described itself as the highest authority in Libya. The RCC assumed both executive and legislative functions, together with the power to take whatever measures it deemed necessary to protect the regime and revolution. In the area of foreign affairs, for example, the proclamation gave the RCC the power to declare war, conclude and ratify treaties, and control the armed forces. Described as a temporary document that would remain in place only until the so-called nationalist democratic revolution was completed, the 1969 constitutional proclamation was never replaced.

In theory, Libya's policy of nonalignment should have translated into a refusal to join any alliance of non-Arab powers, especially either of the two superpower blocs that developed after World War II. Consistent with this approach, early pronouncements by the RCC rejected both communism and capitalism as unsuitable for Libya. Communism was described as a rejected, atheistic system alien to Islam in general and Arab socialism in particular. Nevertheless, the Soviet Union was much more assertive than the United States in seeking to improve and expand its relations with Libya. A military arms agreement between Libya and the Soviet Union was first concluded in 1970; and by the end of the decade, Soviet arms deliveries were estimated to exceed $12 billion. Libyan leader Qaddafi threatened repeatedly to join the Warsaw Pact, but never made good on his threat.

In the course of the revolution, Qaddafi gave the tenets of his strain of Arab nationalism a theoretical underpinning in what came to be known as the Third Universal Theory. In so doing, he sought to develop an alternative to capitalism and communism, both of which he found unsuitable to the Libyan milieu. In the Third Universal Theory, Qaddafi condemned both economic models as monopolistic, the former a state monopoly of ownership and the latter a monopoly of ownership by capitalists and companies.

Qaddafi based the Third Universal Theory on nationalism and religion, two forces he described as the paramount drives moving history and humankind. Nationalism was considered to be the natural result of the world's racial and cultural diversity and thus a necessary and a productive force. Arab nationalism was considered to have especially deep and glorious roots in the ancient past. Because the Arab nation was the product of an age-old civilization based on the heavenly and universal message of Islam, Qaddafi argued that it had the right as well as the duty to be the bearer of the Third Universal Theory to the world.

Qaddafi never produced a coherent, comprehensive discussion of religion, but his thoughts in various seminars and statements focused on the centrality of Islam to religion and the Koran to Islam. Considering Islam to be God's final utterance to humanity, he argued that there was nothing in life for which the principles were not found in Islam. For Qaddafi, the essence of religion was the unity of God; consequently, he made no distinction between what he called the followers of Muhammad, Jesus, and Moses. Since there was only one religion and that religion was Islam, he considered all monotheists to be Muslims. Qaddafi firmly believed that Islam was not addressed only to the followers of the Prophet Muhammad but that Islam meant a belief in God as embodied in all religions. He referred to his contention that anyone who believed in God and his apostles was a Muslim as the "divine concept of Islam."

Qaddafi based his call for Islamic revival on the Koran, arguing that Muslims had moved away from God and the Koran and must return. In the process, he sought to correct contemporary Islamic practices that he considered contrary to the faith. He rejected formal interpretation of the

Koran as blasphemy and sin, contending that the Koran was written in Arabic so that every Arab could read it and apply it without the help of others. Similarly, he criticized the hadith on the grounds that the Koran was the only real source of God's word. He was also very critical of the various schools of Islamic jurisprudence on the grounds they were largely the product of a struggle for political power and thus unconnected to either Islam or the Koran. In the process, the Islamic character of Qaddafi's brand of Arab nationalism and the supposed universal elements of the Third Universal Theory became increasingly paradoxical. In response, Qaddafi continued to emphasize the centrality of Islam to Arab nationalism while deemphasizing Islam's role in the Third Universal Theory.

POLITICAL DEVELOPMENT

Since it gained independence in December 1951, Libya has been ruled by only two governments, the monarchy of King Idris I and the revolutionary government dominated by Qaddafi that gained power in 1969. In April 1973, Qaddafi proclaimed a popular revolution, calling for the election of People's Committees at the zone, municipal, and governorate levels. The RCC continued into 1977 as the supreme instrument of government, but its powers were then assumed by a new, national level representative body known as the General People's Congress (GPC). Thereafter, the Libyan political system evolved into a unitary state governed by this unique combination of committees and congresses. The GPC meets annually, and the general secretary of the GPC serves as the chief executive's staff and advisory body. The GPC includes a General People's Committee, which serves as the cabinet. Qaddafi resigned his post as general secretary of the GPC in 1979, assuming the title Leader of the Revolution.

In theory, the committee and congress system created by Qaddafi in the 1970s rules Libya today. In his self-appointed role of Leader of the Revolution, Qaddafi claims to be outside the decision-making process, serving without official position as counselor and guide to the Libyan people. In practice, Qaddafi and a small circle of men, with the assistance of the armed forces, security services, and revolutionary committees, control and direct all facets of the Libyan government. They approve delegates to the GPC and designate members of the General People's Committee. In addition, all important domestic and foreign policy initiatives are approved by the Leader of the Revolution.

ECONOMIC DEVELOPMENT

Well into the 20th century, more than 80 percent of the population of Libya was engaged in agriculture and animal husbandry. The Mediterranean littoral, constituting only some 3 percent of Libya's total area, has long been its most heavily populated space as well as the one most suitable for agriculture. Another 6 percent of the country is semi-desert and has historically been dedicated to grazing. Unfortunately, poor soil, insufficient rainfall, and limited usable ground water restricted most agriculture to dry farming. For this reason, Libya at independence was known as the Desert Kingdom.

In the early 1950s, the World Bank considered Libya to be one of the least developed countries in the world. Its capacity to generate foreign exchange earnings was so limited that a significant contribution came from the export of esparto grass and the scrap metal collected from disabled World War II armored vehicles. Libya's fortunes improved later in the decade after the successful negotiation of long-term military base agreements with Great Britain and the United States led to annual cash payments, food shipments, and ongoing developmental assistance.

The discovery in 1959 of sizable petroleum and natural gas deposits drastically modified the Libyan economy. By 1966, Libya was exporting 1.5 million barrels of oil daily. Thereafter, oil and gas exports generally accounted for upward of 99 percent of export earnings. In less than a decade, Libya went from one of the poorest countries in the world to one with a gross domestic product far exceeding its North African neighbors.

The revolutionary government after 1969 trumpeted socialism as the solution to Libya's economic problems. Libyan socialism was doctrinal rather than pragmatic. It was also highly nationalistic, in an area of the world where socialism and nationalism have often been found together. Early statements underscored the indigenous nature of Libyan socialism, describing it as an integral part of Libyan political culture as well as a necessary corrective action. Early economic policies emphasized social welfare programs, which enjoyed widespread popular support. The regime's support for increased housing and improved health care was especially strong, while its enthusiasm for education was comparatively weaker and somewhat selective.

The Libyan approach to socialism clarified in 1978 with the publication of part 2 of *The Green Book*, entitled "The Solution of the Economic Problem: Socialism." Humanity's basic needs were defined as a house, income, and a vehicle. Renting out houses and hiring out vehicles were described as forms of domination over the needs of others. Ownership of land was prohibited because land was the property of society and not the individual. The accumulation of savings beyond a level necessary to satisfy individual needs was considered exploitative, on the assumption that all societies suffer from a scarcity of economic goods and thus to accumulate wealth beyond one's immediate needs was to do so at the expense of others.

Qaddafi developed a theory of natural socialism based on equality among the three economic factors of production—raw materials, an instrument of production, and a producer. In his mind, each of these factors was equally important in the process of production and thus each was entitled to an equal share in what was produced. According to Qaddafi, the problem with earlier approaches to socialism was that they focused on ownership, wages, or only one of the factors of production; as a result, they did not address the real economic problem, which was production itself. For Qaddafi, the salient characteristic of contemporary economic structures was the wage system, because it deprived the worker of a share in production. Advocating abolition of both profit motive and wage system, he argued this would lead to the disappearance of money. Depicting salaried employees as wage slaves, Qaddafi urged them to rise up and become partners in production.

After 1975, the socialist theories outlined in *The Green Book* were gradually translated into laws that extended and tightened controls over private enterprise. This process accelerated after March 1978, when the general secretariat of the General People's Congress issued Resolution Four, establishing new guidelines for home ownership. All Libyans were given the right to own their own home, but with few exceptions, no one could own more than one. In September 1978, after Qaddafi urged greater self-management of public and private enterprise, workers rushed to take over some 200 companies. In May 1980, all currency in denominations larger than one Libyan dinar was declared void, and citizens were given one week to exchange the money in their possession. In early 1981, the general secretariat announced the state takeover of all import, export, and distribution functions by year-end. A series of state-run central and satellite supermarkets was constructed to replace the private sector.

A socialist revolution thus occurred in Libya after 1969, in that the management of the economy was increasingly socialist in intent and effect. This process continued well into the 1980s when the revolutionary government signaled an interest in returning to a more open, free-enterprise system in a package of measures, often described as "green *perestroika*." In a March 1987 speech before the General People's Congress, Qaddafi announced the first of a series of economic and political reforms that would eventually modify many of the socialist policies followed earlier by his regime. This speech was followed by additional public pronouncements on 23 May and 1 September in which Qaddafi called for a new role for the private sector as well as increased political liberalization.

In the wake of Qaddafi's 1 September 1987 speech, the secretary of industry announced a new timetable for the privatization of economic enterprises. In less than a year, approximately 140 companies were turned over to self-management committees; in theory, such companies would no longer receive subsidies from the government. At the 1 September 1988 anniversary celebration, Qaddafi announced the state import and export monopoly had been abolished. At the same time, many of the injunctions against retail trade were lifted, and markets in the cities began to reopen.

A variety of economic and political factors combined to reverse the socialist policies the Qaddafi regime had pursued for almost two decades. The state supermarket system, established in 1981, faltered under the weight of corruption and a disorganized distribution system. The illegal, albeit unofficially tolerated, black market provided little relief to the average Libyan citizen. The expulsion of large numbers of expatriate workers after 1985 brought much of the service and agricultural sectors to a standstill. The impact of these issues was then compounded by the diplomatic isolation Libya experienced in the second half of the 1980s. Libyans were unable to travel abroad freely, and the country was belabored with a conflict in Chad that consumed more and more resources, increasing popular discontent. Aware of the politically explosive impact of the economic crisis, Qaddafi responded with a number of corrective measures that eventually changed the face of Libyan socialism.

The liberalization measures implemented in Libya at the end of the 1980s were notable for their widespread popularity. Qaddafi's approval ratings soared for a time as he seized the initiative in imposing necessary reforms. Nevertheless, this early program of economic and political liberalization must be counted a resounding failure. Lacking a clear political strategy conducive to private investment, the economic results of the reforms were mostly limited to the reappearance of simple arts and crafts traders, primarily gold merchants. The program did not attract much desired overseas investment, in large part because modest attempts to create an internal market and accompanying institutions were not accompanied by the necessary reversal of the political experiments in place since 1969. As a result, Libya remained a rentier state trapped in a paradoxical position in which its use of oil revenues blocked the development of the political institutions necessary for the economy to expand and diversify beyond dependence on hydrocarbons.

With the lifting of economic sanctions in 2003, Libya took fresh steps to liberalize its still largely socialist economy. Early policy changes included application for World Trade Organization (WTO) membership, the reduction of economic subsidies, and the announcement of plans for privatization. While the government later indicated some 360 public-sector entities were slated for divestment, including large companies like the Arab Cement Company and the National Company for Feed and Mills, it remained unclear how quickly Libya would be able to implement its privatization plans. Steps taken in 2004–2005 laid the groundwork for a transition to a more market-based economy, but the experience of other socialist states suggested the liberalization process could be long and difficult.

SOCIAL DEVELOPMENT

Arabic-speaking Muslims of mixed Arab and Berber ancestry constitute the bulk of the Libyan population, and Arabic influence permeates the culture. Successive waves of Arabs arrived in the 7th, 9th, and 11th centuries, imposing Islam and the Arabic language, along with political domination. The cultural impact of the Ottoman period and the Italian occupation, while significant, was not as strong as that of the Arab invasion.

Urban migration began under the Italians, resulting in an infusion of progressively larger numbers of workers and laying the basis for the modern working class. This process accelerated in the 1960s and after as the development of hydrocarbon deposits generated stronger economic activity in urban areas. The cities became attractive centers of attention, drawing people from traditional village and tribal systems and in the process dissolving the bonds that held those systems together. As urban migration accelerated, the resulting housing shortage destroyed the social solidarity formerly present in the old ethnic quarters of Libyan cities. Urban migration also weakened extended family, clan, and tribal ties, the basic social units of traditional rural society. In this sense, the cities have become the crucibles of social change in modern Libya.

In the countryside, traditional Arab life, including customary dress, predominated at the time of independence. However, urban migration and the new wealth from petroleum made inroads into traditional modes of dress. In the cities, already somewhat Westernized at the time of independence, younger men and women generally adopted Western clothing, with older people continuing to dress traditionally. In the countryside, traditional dress remained more common.

The distinction between individual tribes has long been as significant in Libya as any distinction between Arab and non-Arab. Tracing their descent to common ancestors, tribal groups in Libya form kinship and quasi-political units, binding them by loyalties that override all others. The revolutionary government took measures to discourage the nomadic way of life basic to tribal existence, but the tribe for many Libyans has remained the primary economic and social framework. Political loyalty often derives from tribal loyalty, as opposed to commitment to a set of ideas or principles. Limited opportunities available to participate in occupational or interest groups in revolutionary Libya added to the importance of tribal affiliation.

Initially, the revolutionary government opposed tribalism; however, Qaddafi later constructed a power base largely dependent on tribal support. Striving to achieve a representative balance among the tribes, the

Libyan leader has frequently shifted the mix of tribal representation within the government to prevent any one faction from becoming too powerful. Qaddafi's own tribe, the Qadadfa, is well represented within the upper ranks of the government, armed forces, and security services; nevertheless, the alleged involvement of tribal members in a failed 1996 coup d'état suggests even its allegiance is not guaranteed.

The revolutionary government's treatment of women and youth accelerated social change in Libya. The population in 1969 was among the youngest in the world; therefore, the Qaddafi regime understandably devoted considerable effort to mobilizing Libyan youth in support of the revolution. A survey of Libyan students published in 2001 indicated these efforts met with some success. The survey suggested the regime was particularly successful in the area of gender issues and in instilling revolutionary values in the younger generation. It was less successful in creating politically participant citizens and largely failed to develop acceptable alternative kinship ties. For most of the students surveyed, tribes remained a source of identity and economic welfare.

From the outset of the One September Revolution, Qaddafi urged females to take a more active role in society, devoting the longest section of part 3 of *The Green Book* to the rights and duties of women. They were encouraged to participate in the committee and congress system, and one of the regime's more impressive accomplishments has been the advancement in the quantity of education available to them. In the 1970s, women were absent from the workplace and mostly isolated at home, but by 2005, women were seen everywhere from university hallways to office buildings. The status of women in Libya may not yet be completely equal to men; however, they have made notable social progress over the last three decades.

THE DICTIONARY

– A –

ABBASID DYNASTY (750–1258). Founded by Abbas, a descendant of the Prophet Muhammad's uncle, the Abbasid dynasty was a successor to the **Umayyad dynasty**. The Abbasid coalition, which consisted of Shiite, mawali (non-Arab Muslims), and other dissidents, moved the capital from Damascus to Baghdad. Recognizing the difficulty of governing their vast domains from Baghdad, the Abbasids made little effort to deter regional governors and military officers from asserting their autonomy as long as they recognized the spiritual leadership of the caliph and paid an annual tribute. The fragmentation of the Abbasid empire eventually weakened the power of the caliphs, diluting their political authority and finally leaving them with only attenuated spiritual powers.

ABD AL-MUMIN (ABD AL-MUMIN IBN ALI) (?–1163). First and greatest caliph of the **Almohad dynasty**. Born in southern **Morocco** to the son of a potter of the Kumiya tribe of Zenata **Berbers**, Abd al-Mumin distinguished himself in **Islamic** studies, which led him to Tlemcen and later to Bejaia, both in modern Algeria. Eventually, he met **Ibn Tumart**, the founder of the Almohad dynasty, who was impressed with Abd al-Mumin and chose him to be his khalifa or deputy. Following the death of Ibn Tumart, Abd al-Mumin became the caliph and organized an army, which operated first in the Atlas Mountains and later in the Rif. Eventually, he confronted the **Almoravids** near Tlemcen in 1145, defeated them, and pushed their forces into the coastal plain near Oran. Abd al-Mumin captured Fez and then Marrakesh in 1147, which signaled the end of the power of the Almoravid dynasty.

1

ADEM BASE, AL-. World War II British air base near Tobruk. Under the terms of the **Anglo-Libyan Agreement**, dated 29 July 1953, the **Idris** government granted **Great Britain** continued use of the Al-Adem base. Evacuation of Al-Adem and other foreign-controlled military facilities in Libya was a first priority of the revolutionary government that seized power in Libya on 1 September 1969. When the British evacuated the base on 28 March 1970, the revolutionary government made the day an official public holiday, **Evacuation Day**.

AFRICA. Libya has enjoyed a prolonged political, **economic**, and **religious** relationship with sub-Saharan Africa. Precolonial trade routes ran from central Africa through the Sahel to the North African coast. These trade links, coupled with Libya's location well into the **Sahara Desert**, largely explain early Libyan interest in the politics of central and eastern Africa. Commercial intercourse was reinforced by religious ties as **Islam** became a major social and political force in the region. Centuries ago, Muslim missionaries in the form of **Sufi** holy men and Muslim traders brought Islam to central and west central Africa. More recently, the Libyan-based **Sanusi Order** buttressed this development by establishing religious lodges south to **Chad** and west to Senegal. The French government correctly viewed the spread of the Sanusi Order as a threat to its influence in central Africa, and after 1902 it waged war on the order, progressively destroying its Saharan centers.

With independence in 1951, the African policy of the Libyan monarchy focused on Chad. Diplomatic relations with the remainder of the states in sub-Saharan Africa were of little consequence and were generally conducted within the framework of the **Organization of African Unity** (OAU). The **Revolutionary Command Council** (RCC) changed this approach as it broadened Libyan diplomatic objectives in the area and developed a variety of institutions to support its goals. In 1970, the **Association for the Propagation of Islam** was established to train Muslim missionaries sympathetic to **Muammar al-Qaddafi**'s reformist approach to Islam. About the same time, a **Jihad Fund** was set up to strengthen the Libyan **armed forces** and to support the **Arab** nation in its struggle against so-called Zionist forces and imperialist perils. Finally, toward the end of the 1970s, an

Islamic Legion, largely consisting of African recruits, was organized to support Libyan **foreign policy** in sub-Saharan Africa.

While the RCC never formally adopted **Egyptian** president Gamal Abdul Nasser's "three circles" strategy, which focused on the Arab, African, and Islamic worlds, Africa in effect became the third circle of Libyan foreign policy. Especially in the early 1970s, sub-Saharan Africa was the scene of intense Libyan diplomatic activity aimed at supplanting **Israeli** influence in the region. At the same time, the Libyan government moved to reduce all Western power and influence on the continent by eliminating Western military bases and undermining moderate African governments opposed to Libyan policies.

In terms of strategy, the RCC generally established diplomatic relations with African states, offered one or more forms of aid, and then urged the recipients to break diplomatic and commercial relations with Israel. Libya also provided financial and other support to African liberation movements and regularly denounced the white minority regimes in southern Africa. For example, Libya began providing military assistance to liberation movements in Angola, Guinea-Bissau, and Mozambique in the early 1970s, and it closed Libyan airspace to South African overflights in 1973.

Often, Libyan foreign policy in Africa assumed an Islamic hue, in that preference was given to governments and groups that expressed their opposition to the status quo in religious terms. On the other hand, it is important to keep the Islamic element of Qaddafi's African policies in perspective. Islam was only one of several elements—others included Arab **nationalism**, **positive neutrality**, and Arab **unity**—that both motivated and constrained Libya's foreign relations. The Islamic dimension of Qaddafi's policies was never dominant to the extent that Libya automatically took the Muslim side in any dispute, and Libya never equated the Islamic revival with anti-communism. For example, the Libyan government supported the Marxist regime in **Ethiopia** against the predominantly Muslim Eritrean independence movement and also supported the **Soviet** intervention in Afghanistan.

By 1980, Libyan diplomacy in Africa, as well as elsewhere, was coming under extreme pressure, in large part due to growing French and American opposition. The ongoing involvement of

Libya in Chadian affairs alarmed policy makers within and outside Africa in part because they feared success would encourage intervention elsewhere. By the end of the year, nine African states, including Gabon, Gambia, Ghana, and Senegal, had expelled Libyan diplomats, closed Libyan embassies, or broken diplomatic relations with Libya. In addition, strong tensions or a serious deterioration in diplomatic relations had occurred in at least six other African states, including Uganda and Upper Volta.

In the second half of the 1980s, the Libyan diplomatic agenda continued to assign Africa a high priority, but there was little new in the policies pursued by Qaddafi. While Israel remained a central concern, the **United States** became actively involved in helping Israel to restore diplomatic links with African states. In mid-1986, Cameroon became the fourth African country—following the Ivory Coast, Liberia, and Zaire—to resume diplomatic relations with Israel; other African states followed suit later in the decade.

In the final analysis, a variety of regional, extraregional, and domestic concerns combined to frustrate Libyan foreign policy in Africa after 1969. However, the core of the problem remained the inability of the Qaddafi regime to impart a minimum of credibility to its political and ideological aims in Africa. Throughout the continent, Libya's African interests came to be seen by Africans as secondary to, if not incompatible with, Qaddafi's global policy objectives. Consequently, where the Arab world saw Qaddafi's ideology as inflexible, if not anachronistic, the African world viewed it as simply irrelevant.

Following the suspension of UN sanctions in early 1999, Qaddafi undertook a number of new initiatives in Africa, most notably calling for the creation of a United States of Africa. In conjunction with these regional initiatives, he launched a series of diplomatic efforts to resolve disputes in the Congo, the Horn of Africa, Sierra Leone, and the **Sudan**. He brokered a cease-fire agreement between Congolese president Laurent Kabila and Ugandan president Yoweri Museveni in April 1999 and dispatched Libyan troops to Uganda as part of an African peacekeeping force in May. Libya later hosted a five-nation summit on the Congo in October 1999. In the Horn of Africa, where Eritrea and Ethiopia in July 1999 accepted a Libyan plan to end their border conflict, a final solution proved as elusive as in the Congo.

Qaddafi also dispatched an envoy to the Sierra Leone peace talks in Togo and met with government and opposition leaders in the Sudan in an effort to end the civil war there. While this wave of diplomatic initiatives yielded few practical results, Qaddafi clearly hoped to leverage the sympathy received from African governments during the UN sanctions years to play a wider role in regional issues.

The Libyan government also expanded bilateral ties with a number of African states. Qaddafi flew to South Africa in June 1999 on a three-day tour to mark Nelson Mandela's retirement and the inauguration of his successor, Thabo Mbeki. The last official guest of the Mandela administration, Qaddafi was described by his host as one of the revolutionary icons of our time. The Libyan government also extended bilateral financial aid to several African states, including Ethiopia, the Ivory Coast, Malawi, Mali, Senegal, Tanzania, Uganda, and Zimbabwe. Libya also announced joint venture investment projects in Chad, Ethiopia, Mali, and Tanzania. Ironically, some observers saw the agreement with Chad, which established a joint company to promote **petroleum** extraction, as a throwback to Libya's former policy of seeking control over African resources. Qaddafi's courtship of Africa suffered a setback in late September 2000 when several days of riots, first in Zawiya and later in other Libyan cities, left scores of expatriate African workers dead or injured. While the government described the riots as isolated instances in which no Libyan nationals were involved, independent observers confirmed the participation of Libyans as well as nationals from other African states in disturbances that left to up to 650 dead and greatly complicated Qaddafi's pan-African diplomacy.

Libya focused after 2001 on the African continent to the virtual exclusion of the Middle East. At the opening of the OAU summit in Lusaka in July 2001, for example, Qaddafi concentrated on African issues, ignoring the Palestinian cause in general and the intifada in particular. Earlier, the **Tripoli** People's Court had sentenced to death seven people for their part in September 2000 riots that officials said were part of a plot to derail Qaddafi's drive for African unity. The riots were an embarrassment to the Qaddafi regime, whose unionist pledges encouraged poor people from neighboring states to come to oil-rich Libya in search of work. Elsewhere, Qaddafi occasionally referenced the Palestinian issue, but his comments were often a curious blend of ideology and indifference as he distanced himself from an issue that had dominated Libyan foreign policy three decades earlier. *See also* AFRICAN UNION.

AFRICAN UNION (AU). The African Union, a regional organization modeled after the **European Union** and intended to rejuvenate an impoverished continent, replaced the 35-year-old **Organization of African Unity** in July 2002. Libyan leader **Muammar al-Qaddafi** was a longtime supporter of enhanced African **unity**, calling for the creation of a United States of **Africa** as early as 1999. Accorded a prominent speaking role at the opening ceremonies of the AU, Qaddafi rejected all conditions on foreign aid, openly contradicting the call of the AU chairman, South African president Thabo Mbeki, for Western states to steer aid and investment to African nations demonstrating good governance. Qaddafi later bowed to Mbeki's promotion of the New Partnership for Africa's Development (NEPAD), a program promoting democracy and good government in Africa in return for greater aid and investment from the developed world.

Uneasy with Qaddafi's push to base the AU's parliament, development bank, and standing army in Libya, Mbeki later discounted Qaddafi's idea of a standing, continental army. Instead, the AU supported the concept of a standby force consisting of multidisciplinary civilian and military contingents based in countries of origin but ready for deployment as needed. The AU later deployed an observer mission to the troubled Darfur region of **Sudan** in mid-2004.

The pan-African parliament, the AU's most ambitious institution, met for the first time in mid-September 2004 in its permanent seat in South Africa. In July 2005, Qaddafi hosted an AU summit meeting at a purpose-built administrative center in Sirte. Celebrating the third anniversary of the union's formation, the Libyan leader called for the creation of a single African passport to facilitate freer movement on the continent. *See also* FOREIGN POLICY.

AGIP. A wholly owned subsidiary of **Italy**'s **ENI**, Agip has long been an important oil producer in Libya and is currently the largest foreign oil producer operating in the country. It first became involved in Libya in the late 1930s when the Italian government of Benito Mussolini asked it to undertake a survey of **petroleum** reserves. Following World War II, an Agip affiliate was awarded an oil concession in Libya that proved unsuccessful; however, when Agip took over the acreage, it eventually yielded three producing fields in the 1990s. In 1977, Agip also discovered the offshore Bouri field, from which it began production in the late 1980s. In 2005, Agip enjoyed established equity production of around 80,000 barrels a day from the Bu' Attifel field in the **Sirte Basin** and the Bouri field in the NC-41 Block. With the takeover in December 2004 of the exploration company Lasmo, Agip gained a majority interest in the 600-million-barrel Elephant field in the **Murzuk Basin**, which could eventually add 150,000 barrels a day to current production.

AGRICULTURE. The main crops in Libya are barley, olives, citrus fruits, vegetables, wheat, and dates. Barley is the traditional crop, and the largest amount of cropland is devoted to its cultivation. It is grown throughout the country, but the highest barley yields are generally produced on farms in the **Tripoli** area. Wheat production is scattered along the coastal region, and output varies considerably from year to year. Millet is the chief grain grown in southern oases.

The main citrus crops are tangerines and lemons. Other important fruits include apples, figs, and olives. Almonds and dates are other significant tree crops. Most farms have an orchard of some description. Vegetable cultivation is largely restricted to irrigated areas because of the limited rainfall. Tobacco cultivation has been encouraged by the government to help meet the growing demand for tobacco products. Esparto grass, which grew wild, was gathered in the past for use in papermaking.

In the late 1950s, agricultural production in Libya stagnated or declined as farmers moved off the land to seek employment in urban areas or the nascent **petroleum** industry. Agricultural output in the early 1960s was also adversely affected by a government program that offered long-term loans to Libyan nationals to buy land from **Italian** settlers. The program increased land prices and took land out of production, since many urban dwellers purchased farms primarily for use as rural retreats. As farm labor became increasingly scarce, farm wages improved, though not fast enough to stem the flow of workers from rural areas.

In the early 1960s, the Libyan government increased its emphasis on agricultural development, and output improved as investment increased. Incentives were given to absentee landlords to put their farms into production, and foreign workers were introduced into the agricultural sector to replace the Libyans migrating to the towns. Nevertheless, the agricultural sector of the **economy**, including **fishing** and forestry, remained of marginal importance in the late 1960s and early 1970s. At that time, this sector contributed less than 3 percent of gross domestic product and provided jobs for less than 30 percent of the nation's employed. Moreover, Libyan agriculture had the lowest yields per unit area of cereals in North **Africa** and produced less than 40 percent of the nation's food requirements.

Given the prevailing state of Libyan agriculture, it should come as no surprise that the revolutionary government put considerable emphasis on this economic sector. Over much of the last three decades, government programs to increase both crop and **livestock** production have included massive allocations of funds to a variety of state agencies, corporations, and development projects. The goals of government programs in agriculture have included the preservation and expansion of existing **water resources**; the distribution of loans, grants, and technical assistance to herdsmen and farmers; and the allocation of confiscated or other government-controlled land to nomads and farm laborers. Several of the government's agricultural projects have proved to be relatively successful in terms of the quantity of goods produced, but the unit cost of production has frequently been much higher than world market prices.

Self-sufficiency in key agricultural commodities remains an articulated but highly elusive goal in Libya. Despite the capital inflows and the promises of Libyan leader **Muammar al-Qaddafi**—who declared 1990 the year of agriculture in Libya—the agricultural sector has failed to live up to its potential. Cereal output has increased and self-sufficiency has been achieved in white meat and vegetable production, but the food import bill has steadily risen. In an attempt to reverse this trend, the Libyan government continues to address the two major obstacles to the success of its agricultural **development plans**: the shortage of water and the shortage of labor.

The provision of water from the **Great Manmade River** (GMR) project is central to future agricultural growth. Inadequate rainfall, coupled with the increasing salinity of the aquifers located on the coastal agricultural belt, make the GMR the only obvious solution both to inadequate and unreliable water supplies and the lack of arable land. The original master plan for the GMR envisaged using water brought from the southern part of Libya to set up 37,000 model farms on the Mediterranean coast that would cultivate an extra 180,000 hectares (450,000 acres) of grain and feed crops in the summer. The wisdom of apportioning such huge amounts of water to agriculture was repeatedly questioned, but that has not prevented the government from pressing ahead.

Labor shortages are the second major problem that Libyan agriculture must address. As in many oil-rich Arab states, the rural population of Libya has steadily drifted toward the urban areas over the last three-plus decades in search of salaried jobs in the public sector. In the early 1960s, around half of Libya's working population was engaged in agriculture; the comparable figure today is less than 15 percent. In part for this reason, the average annual growth rate of agricultural and food production, both in total terms and per capita, was zero or negative in the second and third decades of the revolution. *See also* BUDGETS.

AHMAD, MUSA. One of only two senior military officers (the other being **Adam Said Hawwaz**) not purged at the outset of the **One September Revolution** in 1969. Ahmad was initially appointed minister of interior in the eight-member **Council of Ministers**, but he was arrested in December 1969 in connection with an abortive plot to overthrow the revolutionary government. Both Ahmad and Hawwaz were sentenced to long prison terms, which were later increased.

AIRPORTS. At last count, Libya had a total of 146 domestic and international airports. The main airports at **Tripoli**, **Benghazi**, and **Sebha** offer international service. Domestic service is available from all of these, plus smaller airports at Beida, **Ghadames**, Ghat, Houn, Al-Kutrah, **Misurata**, Tobruk, and others. In addition, there are numerous smaller airstrips, without ground services, in the **petroleum**-producing areas that are used mainly by oil company aircraft.

Jamahiriya Libyan Arab Airways, formerly Libyan Arab Airlines, is the national carrier. It was reorganized in 1973 when it was transformed into a public sector company. The airline experienced rapid growth in the 1970s, providing domestic service, as well as a variety of international routes before the **United Nations** implemented its embargo on Libya. *See also* TRANSPORTATION.

AJAL, WADI. Drainage system located in the **Fezzan** on the southern boundary of the Awbari Sand Sea. The Wadi Ajal contains several oases that extend northeastward from Ubari (Awbari) to Al-Abyad. It may be extended northeastward to include **Sebha** (Sabhah) and the oases of Timmenhent (Taminhant), Az-Zighan, and Umm al-Abid. Historically, a large percentage of the population living in the Fezzan has been concentrated in several chains of oases along the northern and southern edges of the sand dune areas.

AJDABIYAH (AGEDABIA). Often associated with the coastal **road** running east to **Benghazi**, Ajdabiyah actually stands 18 kilometers (11 miles) from the Mediterranean Sea. The city is well connected to the interior of Libya through routes running in a southerly direction to Awjilah (Augila) and then on to the oasis at Al-Kufrah. In all periods of history, the importance of Ajdabiyah has derived largely from the fact that wells were located here. As early as Roman times, and very likely before, invading armies sought water at the wells of Ajdabiyah as they established stations along the coast of Libya.

AL-. *See* entry at root word (e.g., QADDAFI for AL-QADDAFI).

ALMOHAD DYNASTY (AL-MUWAHHIDUN) (1147–1269). **Berber** tribal dynasty that dominated the Maghrib and Muslim Spain for much of the 12th and 13th centuries. **Ibn Tumart** (1080–1130), the founder of the Almohad dynasty, preached a doctrine of moral regeneration through reaffirmation of a vigorous, strict, and orthodox **Islam**. He imposed upon the Almohads a hierarchical, theocratic, and centralized government that respected but transcended the existing **tribal** structure.

Originating in **Morocco**, the movement swept eastward across the Maghrib, supplanting the Normans from their strongholds in Ifriquiya and **Tripolitania**. The Almohads conquered the **Almoravid** capital of Marrakesh in 1147 and reasserted Islamic rule in a number of Spanish cities that had turned against the Almoravids, notably Seville and Cordoba, in 1149. At its height, the Almohad Empire embraced all of North Africa from **Tripoli** in Libya to Tinmallal in Morocco and from Islamic Spain to the western Sahel. While the Almohads failed to promote the doctrines of Ibn Tumart consistently, they left behind a splendid architectural legacy, including the Kutubiya Mosque in Marrakesh and other structures still visible in towns such as Rabat and Sousse.

Despite the military prowess of the Almohads, the Andalusian states of Spain and the city-states of **Italy** launched an uncoordinated but successful counterattack in the following two centuries. Through a combination of economic and military means, their combined efforts led to the eventual expulsion of Islam from Spain (completed in 1492), the creation of small Christian political and trading enclaves in North Africa, and the division of the Almohad state among three competing dynasties: the Marinids (1244–1420), who ruled principally in Morocco; the Zayinids (1236–1318), in Algeria; and the Hafsids (1228–1574), in **Tunisia** and Tripolitania. *See also* ABD AL-MUMIN.

ALMORAVID DYNASTY (AL-MURABITUN) (1073–1147). The state apparatus of the Almoravids, whose capital was Marrakesh, rested on a reformist version of Maliki Sunnism and a military and administrative elite recruited among the Sanhaja **Berbers** of the middle Atlas and western **Sahara Desert**. Maliki Islam allowed the Almoravids to portray their defense of **Islam** as one that combined a strict and rigorous implementation of Islamic law with a zealous propagation of the faith. The challenge and reward of both included the control of lucrative trans-Saharan trade routes to West Africa and **jihad** or holy war against the Christian states of Andalusia. At its height, the Almoravid state stretched from southern Morocco east to Algiers and north into Spain. *See also* ALMOHAD DYNASTY.

AMERICAN-LIBYAN AGREEMENT. The 1953 **Anglo-Libyan Agreement** was followed 13 months later by a treaty with the **United States**. Dated 9 September 1954, the "Agreement between the Government of the United States and the Government of the United Kingdom of Libya" permitted the U.S. government to maintain military facilities in Libya until 24 December 1970. In return, Washington pledged to provide Libya with financial aid and economic cooperation. Shortly after the agreement came into effect, the U.S. government elevated its legation in Libya to the status of an embassy.

Whereas the monarchy in Libya had viewed the Anglo-Libyan Agreement as primarily a deterrent to outside aggression, it viewed the American-Libyan Agreement principally as a source of economic assistance and only secondarily as a defensive alliance. The U.S. government, on the other hand, considered Libya a strategically important base for the air defense of North Africa and the Mediterranean against **Soviet** encroachment. In addition, military facilities in Libya provided Washington with a valuable transit stop for forces moving to and from the Far East as well as an important training base for NATO forces in a region that had witnessed major battles during World War II.

Under the terms of the American-Libyan Agreement, the U.S. government retained **Wheelus Air Base** and could construct communications facilities outside the areas in which it operated military equipment. In return, Washington agreed to provide substantial economic assistance to Libya, and early levels of aid were later increased in 1956 and 1959. During fiscal year 1955–1956, for example, U.S. aid to Libya totaled $9 million in development aid and 25,000 tons of wheat in famine relief. In the following year, U.S. aid increased to $11 million together with an additional 5,000 tons of wheat and enough military aid to expand the Libyan army to 1,000 troops. *See also* FOREIGN POLICY.

ANGLO-LIBYAN AGREEMENT. Dated 29 July 1953, the "Treaty of Friendship and Alliance between Her Majesty in Respect of the United Kingdom of **Great Britain** and Northern Ireland and His Majesty the King of the **United Kingdom of Libya**" granted the British government the right to maintain military facilities in Libya for two decades in return for financial assistance over the duration of the agreement. Libya received a pledge of financial assistance over a 20-year period as well as £5 million for economic development and £2.75 million in budgetary aid in the first five years. At the end of each subsequent five-year period, the signatories agreed to reassess the total amount of Libya's aid needs together with the fields in which it should be spent.

In return, Great Britain received military facilities and a military base in Libya. The facilities consisted of airstrips at the **airport** in **Tripoli** and at **Al-Adem** near Tobruk in **Cyrenaica**. Both locations were highly desirable as they were situated on the strategic air corridors to far-flung British interests in **Africa**, the Indian Ocean, and the Far East. Moreover, the facilities provided British forces with excellent opportunities, virtually year-round, to train in **desert** conditions.

In addition to the provision of financial aid, the Anglo-Libyan Agreement was important to the United Kingdom of Libya because the movement of British air and land forces in Libya, together with the supply of equipment and arms to the Libyan **armed forces**, helped ensure the protection of Libyan territory from outside aggression. At the time, it was thought by the monarchy that the agreement, combined with a similar agreement forthcoming with the **United States**, the **American-Libyan Agreement**, would allow Libya to pursue domestic and **foreign policies** largely unfettered by outside powers, especially the **Egyptian** government. In this assumption, the **Idris** regime was later proved to be mistaken.

The Anglo-Libyan Agreement created a storm of controversy in the **Arab** world. The Egyptian government labeled it an act of treason, while the **Arab League**, threatening to obstruct the treaty, offered Libya an annual grant equivalent to £4 million to reject or amend it. In Tripoli and elsewhere in Libya, police forces had to suppress demonstrations opposed to the agreement.

In the end, the United Kingdom of Libya rejected the offer of the Arab League and ratified the agreement with Great Britain. In so doing, it recognized that the defense aspects of the treaty, as opposed to its **economic** components, were the central elements. At this early stage in the independence era, independence and the protection of national borders were the core foreign policy objectives of the Libyan government. Membership in the Arab League, which supported Libya's status as an independent Arab state, combined with the Anglo-Libyan Agreement, which provided protection from military aggression, seemed to the monarchy the best approach to achieve these objectives.

AOUZOU STRIP. *See* CHAD; FRONTIERS.

APOLLONIA. The ancient **Greek** city of Apollonia was built to provide a port for **Cyrene**. After Cyrene, it is probably the most enjoyable archeological site in **Cyrenaica**. Situated on the coast with the sea in front and hills behind, the site features several important monuments, including a theater carved into the rock and a complex of baths.

ARAB ISLAMIC REPUBLIC. *See* LIBYA-TUNISIA UNION.

ARAB LEAGUE. The League of **Arab** States was founded on 22 March 1945, a few weeks before the **United Nations** Conference on International Organization in San Francisco. With greater Arab **unity** long a goal in the Middle East, the Arab League gave some institutional form to the sense of **nationalism** and unity among its members. On 28 March 1953, Libya became the eighth member of the Arab League.

Libya's decision to join the Arab League so soon after winning independence and before it concluded treaties with the major Western states was a product of political pressure from the other Arab states, especially the government of Gamal Abdul Nasser in Cairo. **Egypt** hoped to use the Arab League to bring influence to bear on the foreign and domestic policies of the monarchy in Libya.

The **Muammar al-Qaddafi** regime continued to participate in Arab League affairs; however, Libyan **foreign policy** in the modern era has had little impact on the Arab League or its policies. Conversely, the Arab League has exerted very little influence on Libyan foreign policy over the last three decades. In an effort to isolate the Egyptian government, Qaddafi has called periodically for the transfer of the Arab League's headquarters to **Tunisia** or Kuwait.

ARAB MAGHRIB UNION (AMU). In February 1989, Libya joined Algeria, Mauritania, **Morocco**, and **Tunisia** in a regional organization intended to increase **economic** cooperation and efficiency. Directly inspired by the European Community, the Arab Maghrib Union was considered essential for presenting a common economic front in the face of a single European market after 1992. Upcoming changes in what would soon become the **European Union** posed a direct threat to the export markets of the Maghrib, especially in such areas as **agricultural** products, textiles, and light **industrial** products. In addition, labor migration from the Maghrib to Europe had slowed, and European **tourism** in North **Africa** was also declining.

In conjunction with the promotion of economic development and integration, the function of the AMU was to provide a forum for regular discussions among North African leaders to prevent the bilateral frictions that had marred regional cooperation in the past. The administrative framework created by the union treaty included a Council of Heads of State, a rotating chairmanship, committees to oversee the integration process, a consultative Maghrib Chamber, and a Maghrib Court. The pact also included a mutual defense clause, indicating that no state was to tolerate on its soil the presence of any organization prejudicial to the security of a fellow member state. At the same time, state sovereignty was to remain intact, as there was no question of political **unity**.

Libya's enthusiasm for Maghribi integration in general and the AMU in particular was often questioned by member states. At times, **Muammar al-Qaddafi** appeared to be deliberately controversial— such as when he proposed that **Chad**, Niger, Mali, and **Sudan** should be allowed to join the union or when he argued that the organization's resources should be mobilized to continue the struggle against **Israel** for Palestine. The January 1990 summit meeting of the AMU highlighted some of its problems. The opening session was postponed twice and Qaddafi's participation was never certain. Once the meeting was convened, a proposal to create a Maghribi identity card created much discussion, with some member states expressing concern that such a card could fall into the hands of subversive groups. The following year, discussion centered on the location of a permanent seat for the AMU, with most member states feeling that their own country offered the optimum site.

The members of the AMU reached a number of economic and political accords; nevertheless, the governments of Algeria, Mauritania, Morocco, and Tunisia found it increasingly difficult to maintain close links with Libya. The **frontiers** between Libya, Tunisia, and Algeria, for example, were closed on more than one occasion in the mid-1990s as Libya's neighbors expressed their unhappiness with Qaddafi's support for radical **Islamic** factions within their societies. The members of the AMU also expressed concern at Libya's occasional attempts to include **Egypt** in North African affairs. Finally, the mandatory sanctions imposed on Libya by the **United Nations** after 15 April 1992 added to Libya's regional and international isolation, thwarting any serious attempts at economic or political integration.

When the UN sanctions were suspended in April 1999, Qaddafi moved immediately to revitalize the Arab Maghrib Union. In May 1999, representatives of the five member states attended the first session of the AMU follow-up committee held in more than three years. At the meeting, the delegates agreed to convene before the end of 1999 the first summit in five years. Libya also expressed interest in increasing the scope of the AMU, possibly integrating the Community of Sahel and Saharan States, a creation of Qaddafi's that included Burkina Faso, Chad, Mali, Niger, and Sudan. In November 1999, the Moroccan prime minister visited **Tripoli**, concluding several economic and social accords, including restoration of direct flights between the two states.

Libya and Tunisia in June 2000 announced the creation of a free trade zone, together with a resumption of air travel. At the same time, Qaddafi and Tunisian president Zine El Abidine Ben Ali called for the North African summit, postponed from November 1999, to take place as early as possible. Algerian Airways in August 2000 became the third AMU member-state airline to resume flights to Tripoli. In October 2000, the **General People's Congress** agreed to nominate 30 members to an expanded Maghrib assembly and approved the final draft of a pledge supporting a move toward **Arab-African union**. Dialogue aimed at reactivating the AMU continued throughout 2000, but a variety of factors—including the conflict in the Western Sahara, the **Lockerbie incident**, and the domestic political situation in Algeria—combined to block meaningful progress.

As Libya continued its efforts to revitalize the moribund AMU, it was generally supported by the heads of state of the other member nations; it was not political will but contentious political issues that blocked forward motion. However, with the Lockerbie issue on the road to resolution, the persistent violence in Algeria coming under control, and a resolution of the Western Sahara question in the offering, the stage finally seemed set in early 2001 for a concerted effort to revitalize the AMU. Instead, member states focused on internal issues, marginalizing collective interest in resuscitating the AMU.

Morocco's King Mohammed in January 2001 made his first visit to Libya since his enthronement in July 1999; talks during his 24-hour visit focused on improved bilateral relations and increased **trade**. In May 2001, Libyan foreign minister Mohammed Abderrahman Chalgam again turned to the Western Sahara question, labeling the Algeria-Morocco dispute over the issue of the Polisario the main obstacle to joint Maghrib action. At the same time, he called for his Arab Maghrib neighbors to abolish borders, barriers, and the use of passports. AMU foreign ministers met in Algiers in January 2002 but were unable to agree on a venue for the AMU summit that had been pending since 1999. The summit was again postponed in May 2005 when Morocco rejected Algerian attempts to include the Western Sahara issue on the agenda. Informed observers agreed that sustained progress was unlikely until Algeria and Morocco resolved the Saharan dispute. *See also* ARAB ISLAMIC REPUBLIC; ARAB SOCIALIST UNION; FOREIGN POLICY.

ARAB SOCIALIST UNION (ASU). On 11 June 1971, **Muammar al-Qaddafi** announced the formation of the Arab Socialist Union, an official mass mobilization organization patterned after its **Egyptian** namesake. The **Revolutionary Command Council** (RCC) intended the ASU to become the primary link between the government and the people, filling the void left by the abolition of the **tribal** system. Envisioned as an organization stretching from the local to the national level, the ASU offered the masses an opportunity to participate in the establishment and execution of local policies. At the same time, it promised a pervasive network of organizations throughout Libyan society capable both of monitoring citizens at all levels and of becoming a source of support for revolutionary policies whenever such support was required. The ASU was thus conceived of as an organization that mirrored government policy and interests while remaining sensitive to public demands and aspirations.

The ASU was organized at the national, **governorate**, and basic or local levels. Both the governorate and basic units consisted of a congress representing the general membership and a smaller committee for leadership. Membership was based on both place of residence and occupation or workplace. Application for membership could be made either where the individual lived or at his or her workplace; however, the individual could not join the ASU at both locations. The basic committee consisted of 10 people elected by and from the basic congress to serve as its executive body. The governorate congress consisted of two or more representatives elected from each basic unit, with the final number selected dependent on the size of the basic unit's membership. The governorate committee consisted of 20 people elected by and from the members of the governorate congress. Since colleges and universities were considered equivalent to a single governorate, basic units were also created among staff and faculty. Committees at both the basic and the governorate levels elected secretariats and appointed subcommittees to investigate issues and suggest policies.

Membership in the ASU was open to any Libyan citizen of the working people who was at least 18 years of age, in good legal standing, of sound mental health, not a member of the royal family, not associated with the previous monarchical government, and not specifically barred by the RCC. Working people were defined as farmers, intellectuals, soldiers, workers, and owners of nonexploitative capital. The ASU charter specified that 50 percent of all members must be workers and farmers.

The ASU structure at the national level was the National General Congress, a forerunner of the **General People's Congress**. The National General Congress was made up of 10, 14, or 20 representatives from each governorate, depending on the membership of that body. It also included members of the RCC, the **Council of Ministers**, and delegates from certain functional organizations such as the **armed forces**, police and **youth** organizations, professional associations, and **trade unions**. Scheduled to meet every two years, the term of National General Congress members was six years. The ASU was firmly controlled by the RCC, with Qaddafi serving as president and the other members of the RCC designated the Supreme Leading Authority of the Arab Socialist Union.

To a large extent, the ASU was stillborn. The rigid control insisted on by the RCC stifled local initiative and suffocated local leadership. Moreover, the organization was never able to resolve its fundamental contradiction of seeking simultaneously to reflect government interests and articulate local demands. In particular, the members of the ASU failed to understand the traditionalism of the people of Libya and the central role of traditional leaders in the development of public perceptions. Finally, the ASU was undercut by existing government ministries and organizations, which viewed it as a competitor for authority. Since the ASU system largely paralleled governmental machinery already established by the RCC, there was frequent conflict between party organizers and government functionaries, with the latter generally supported by the traditional leaders within and outside their ranks. For all of these reasons, the ASU was gradually replaced after 1976 by a new political system based on direct popular authority. *See also* DECLARATION OF THE ESTABLISHMENT OF THE PEOPLE'S AUTHORITY; FOREIGN POLICY; UNITY.

ARAB-AFRICAN UNION. On 13 December 1984, the governments of Libya and **Morocco** concluded a union agreement, known as the Treaty of Oujda, which called for the creation of a federation in which both signatories retained their sovereignty. Known officially as the Arab-African Union, the new organization provided for considerably less than Qaddafi's oft-stated goal of full and integral Arab **unity**. The treaty established a joint presidency, which alone had decision-making powers; a rotating permanent secretariat; a joint legislature; a court of justice; and advisory councils at various levels. It also called for common approaches in **foreign policy** as well as closer cooperation in **economic**, social, and political matters, but it allowed either state to enter into pacts with third nations without the prior agreement of the other. One article stipulated that an act of aggression against one party would be regarded as an act of aggression against the other, making it in effect a mutual defense pact. The official objective of the union was greater Maghrib and **Arab** unity, and it provided for third parties to adhere as long as both signatories approved. Referenda in Morocco and Libya on 31 August 1984 and 1 September 1984, respectively, approved the Treaty of Oujda by massive majorities.

Both Libya and Morocco gained from the 1984 treaty. It reduced the diplomatic isolation Libya experienced as the result of earlier policy initiatives, and it struck a blow for the sacred cause of Arab unity. It also reduced the isolation the Moroccan government suffered as a result of the war in the Western Sahara and the Algeria-**Tunisia**-Mauritania entente of 1983. Morocco later suggested another benefit of the accord was that it implied Libyan recognition of Morocco's claim to the Western Sahara, which, even if true, probably overestimated the political value of such recognition. Other mutual benefits stemming from the treaty included formal Libyan agreement to end support for the Polisario Front in return for Moroccan agreement not to interfere in **Chad**. Since Morocco considered the Western Sahara issue an internal affair, it probably also viewed the treaty article that prevented the signatories from interfering in each other's internal affairs as a form of insurance policy. The Moroccan government also received promises of Libyan financial support, together with assurances that Libya would no longer aid opponents of the monarchy. Finally, the accord helped demonstrate Moroccan independence from the **United States** and thus buttressed King Hassan's domestic political position.

While the treaty provided considerable benefits to both signatories, the long-term prospects for the Arab-African Union were never good. The political outlooks of Morocco and Libya were diametrically opposed, the former being essentially a status quo power interested in little or no change and the latter remaining a regional center for dynamic revolutionary change. This basic incompatibility was increasingly obvious over the next two years as newly created commissions struggled to translate treaty clauses into functioning administrative bodies. With the accord in jeopardy for some time, King Hassan eventually declared it null and void on 29 August 1986. As a pretext, he cited a joint Libyan-Syrian communiqué, issued earlier in the week, that described his recent meeting with **Israeli** prime minister Shimon Peres as an act of treason. *See also* AFRICA; ORGANIZATION OF AFRICAN UNITY.

ARABS. In the 7th, 9th, and 11th centuries, successive waves of Arabs arrived in North **Africa**, including Libya, to impose political domination together with **Islam** and the Arabic language. The spread of Islam was generally complete by 1300. The replacement of **Berber** dialects with the Arabic language proceeded much more slowly; even today, a few Libyan communities contain native Berber-speakers.

In the beginning, many Berbers fled into the **desert** to escape the Arab invaders; consequently, Islam initially was largely an urban **religion**. Only in the 11th century did **tribes** of the Beni Hilal and Beni

Sulaim invade first **Cyrenaica** and later **Tripolitania** and impose their Islamic faith and nomadic way of life. A new influx of Arabic-speaking peoples entered the region in the 15th and early 16th centuries in response to the collapse of the last Muslim strongholds in Spain to Christian forces. Many Spanish **Jews** as well as Muslims—faced with a choice of baptism, death, or exile—migrated from Iberia to North Africa, where they settled mostly in coastal cities.

Authorities suggest that the total number of Arabs to arrive in North Africa during the first two migrations probably did not exceed 700,000 and that the total Arab population of the area was no more than 10 percent of the whole as late as the 12th century. While Arab blood was later reinforced from Spain, the Berbers continued to outnumber the Arabs throughout North Africa for a prolonged period. On the other hand, waves of Arabs reached Libya earlier than elsewhere in the region because Libya was situated closest to the Middle East. As a result, the Arabization of the Berbers undoubtedly advanced faster in Libya than elsewhere in the Maghrib.

At the time of independence, traditional Arab life, including customary dress, was still common in the Libyan countryside. Over the last half-century, this situation has slowly changed as oil wealth, urban migration, and social change eroded traditional ways. In urban areas today, younger men and **women** frequently wear Western dress, although older women can still be seen in traditional costume. In the countryside, men often wear loose cotton shirts and trousers covered by a wool *barracan* which resembles a Roman toga. Women wear a loose-fitting garment known by the same name.

ARMED FORCES. The September 1969 coup d'état—the **One September Revolution**—was totally military in conception, planning, and execution. It was accomplished without the participation, or even knowledge, of organized civilian groups. In the early years of the revolution, the **Revolutionary Command Council** (RCC) insisted on maintaining its military direction. Under attack from all facets of the former elite structure, the RCC worked to create a reliable coercive arm capable of sustaining the revolution.

By the end of 1970, the military establishment had tripled in size, largely due to the merger of regional and specialized security forces. It continued to grow in quantity and improve in quality throughout the ensuing decade. In May 1978, the government issued a conscription law making military service compulsory, and in January 1979 it announced that both men and **women** would be conscripted. Expenditures for equipment also increased dramatically, and the Libyan armed forces entered the 1980s with the highest ratio of military equipment to manpower in the Third World. While the war with **Chad** later exposed the real limits of Libya's ability to employ modern armaments effectively, the revolutionary government continued to maintain a substantial inventory of military equipment. For the most part, the pursuit of a constant arms purchase policy continued until **petroleum** revenues declined in the mid-1980s.

Although there were occasional coup attempts, the military rewarded **Muammar al-Qaddafi**'s paternalism with a general absence of major upheavals or open dissension in the early years of the regime. At the same time, military opposition grew as Qaddafi increasingly advocated a **people's militia** to offset the power of the professional military organization. His insistence on compulsory military service for females, a measure opposed by the 1984 **General People's Congress**, was especially unpopular both within the military and among the general populace. Military involvement in antiregime activities increased in the second half of the 1980s and continued at a high level as the Qaddafi regime approached its fourth decade in power.

Often expressing distaste for traditional armies, Qaddafi repeatedly talked of replacing them with people's militias. As a result, a variety of paramilitary organizations have been established over the years parallel to the regular army. These included the Popular Resistance Forces; the Deterrent Battalion, which was responsible for security within the armed forces; the People's Defense Committee; the **Jamahiriya** Guard; and the **Islamic Legion**. The latter organization consisted of an estimated 8,000 recruits from **Egypt**, **Sudan**, and the Sahel states. In addition, all sectors of Libyan society were encouraged to undergo military training.

In the final analysis, Qaddafi's relationship with the Libyan armed forces mirrors the more contradictory elements of his complex ideology and values system. On the one hand, a powerful Libyan military establishment remains essential to his dreams of power and **Arab** leadership. With a small population base, Qaddafi's visions of regional prestige and influence rest largely on his ability to militarize Libyan society. On the other hand, the Libyan armed forces remain the most obvious threat to Qaddafi's security. Most observers would agree that any significant challenge to the revolution will almost certainly originate within the armed forces because the military at present is the only group in Libya with the requisite power and organization. Elements of the armed forces have initiated most of the coup attempts against Qaddafi, and the military will likely be in the forefront of any future coup attempts. In a word, Qaddafi desperately needs the Libyan armed forces, but he also needs a military he can control.

Reliable, up-to-date information on the size and composition of Libya's armed forces is difficult to obtain. The defense budget in 2003 was estimated to be $1.2 billion, with active-duty Libyan armed forces personnel totaling 76,000, including some 38,000 conscripts. An additional 40,000 troops were held in reserve in the People's Militia. *See also* CYRENAICAN DEFENSE FORCES.

ASABAA, BATTLE OF. When the **Italians** invaded Libya, **Suleiman Baruni**, a former deputy for **Tripolitania** in the 1908 Turkish parliament, tried to rally the **Berbers** of **Jabal Nafusah** to fight for their independence. His efforts failed when the Italians, advancing from **Tripoli**, defeated his followers between Garian and Yefren in March 1913.

ASSOCIATION FOR NATIONAL REFORM. *See* TRIPOLI REPUBLIC.

ASSOCIATION FOR THE PROPAGATION OF ISLAM. An organization founded by the revolutionary government in 1970 to train Muslim missionaries. By the end of the decade, the association had reportedly deployed a force of several hundred missionaries, most of whom were non-Libyans. *See also* ISLAM.

AZIZIYA, CONGRESS OF. Following the conclusion of the 1912 peace treaty between **Italy** and the **Ottoman Empire**, a number of provincial notables and administrators met to determine their stance on the empire's grant of autonomy to Libya and Italy's declared annexation of the province. In an acrimonious meeting, two opposing positions emerged, with one side favoring negotiations with Italy while the other pressed for a continuation of armed resistance. **Farhat al-Zawi** was the principal proponent of the first position, and **Suleiman Baruni** advocated the second. Baruni felt the autonomy accorded the province by the Ottomans afforded a better chance of realizing his objective of an autonomous Ibadi province. In turn, Zawi, who was familiar with the **French** protectorate in **Tunisia**, hoped to gain for Libya the apparent advantages of European tutelage through cooperation. The Congress of Aziziya ended without agreement, but when Zawi later approached the Italian governor to sound out Italian intentions, the latter mistook the overture for a reflection of general opinion. *See also* YOUNG TURK REVOLUTION.

– B –

BAB AL-AZIZIYA BARRACKS. Fortified area of **Tripoli** that serves as a residence for Libyan leader **Muammar al-Qaddafi**. The Bab al-Aziziya Barracks was heavily damaged during the U.S. air raid on Tripoli in 1986. After the attack, it was converted into a museum to highlight American aggression.

BADOGLIO, PIETRO (1871–1956). The commander of the **Italian** pacification campaign under Governor-General **Giuseppi Volpi**, Marshal Badoglio was named governor of both **Tripolitania** and **Cyrenaica** in January 1929. He quickly issued a proclamation offering peace, clemency, and generosity to all Libyans prepared to submit to Italian rule; at the same time, he promised to wage war with all modern systems and means if his offer of peace was rejected. The Badoglio proclamation met with little response from the Libyan people, setting the stage for the final brutal campaign of the **Italian** occupation. Badoglio became head of the Italian government after Benito Mussolini was overthrown in July 1943.

BADRI, ABDEL QADIR (ABDUL GADER AL-BADRI; ABDUL QADER AL-BADRI). Appointed prime minister in June 1967 to restore order in Libya in the wake of the June 1967 Arab-**Israeli** War,

Badri had risen to political prominence through his position as a **tribal** leader in western **Cyrenaica**. After serving in parliament, he was first minister of **industry** and later minister of **housing** and state. Retaining virtually all the ministers from the previous cabinet, he pledged to liquidate the foreign bases in Libya and to maintain a ban on **petroleum** exports to **Great Britain** and the **United States**. His draconian measures stirred political recriminations leading to his early resignation in October 1967. *See also* UNITED KINGDOM OF LIBYA.

BADRI, ABDULLAH SALEM AL- (1940–). Chairman of the **National Oil Company** (NOC). Badri has some 25 years of experience in the **petroleum** sector, having served previously as chairman of the local firm Oasis Oil, first secretary of oil, and secretary of energy until that post was abolished in 2000. After serving briefly as NOC chairman, he was promoted to deputy secretary (deputy prime minister) for services in the General People's Committee, later adding assistant secretary-general to the secretary (prime minister) of the General People's Committee to his title. As part of the 2003 government reorganization, Badri returned to NOC as chairman. *See also* GENERAL PEOPLE'S CONGRESS.

BAKKUSH, ABDEL HAMID (ABDUL HAMID AL-BAKKUSH) (1932–). Prime minister from October 1967 to September 1968. Son of a lower-middle-class family, Bakkush received a **law** degree from Cairo University in 1957. In **Egypt**, he became involved in liberal Arab **nationalist** politics. Returning to Libya, he first served as a judge and later established a successful law practice, specializing in the large foreign companies. Regarded as a progressive, Bakkush attempted to modernize the small and ineffective Libyan **armed forces** and reform the grossly inefficient Libyan bureaucracy. Both the nature and the speed of his reforms were opposed by conservative elements, and he was eventually forced to resign. Bakkush later opposed the revolutionary government as head of the Libyan Liberation Organization. *See also* OPPOSITION; UNITED KINGDOM OF LIBYA.

BALBO, ITALO (1896–1940). The colonization of Libya is closely linked to the name of Italo Balbo, **Italian** governor from 1934 until his death in a mysterious plane crash. Owing much to the work of his predecessors, Balbo was fortunate to become governor at an opportune moment for the colony's development in that he assumed office after the destruction of the **Sanusi** resistance. For the first time in more than two decades of occupation, the Italians could concentrate on the **economic** development of Libya. At the same time, an interrelated cluster of economic and social issues in Italy favored the colonization of Libya in the early 1930s. A negative balance of trade, combined with a strong lira, aggravated Rome's chronic unemployment problem. During the winters of 1931–1935, for example, up to 15 percent of the agricultural workers were unemployed—a rate only relatively higher than industrial workers.

Balbo was also fortunate that the Mussolini regime at that time was less interested in the costs of colonization than in the prestige the projects might reflect. A modern, highly colonized Libya promised a strong card in Mussolini's bid for Mediterranean hegemony and an **African** empire. On a less belligerent note, the Libyan example, with its emphasis on large-scale public works and resettlement projects, appeared to offer new answers to a world troubled by depression and unemployment. Finally, the colonization of Libya struck a respondent chord in the hearts of patriotic Italians, many of whom dreamed of creating population outlets under the Italian flag in Africa.

In a real sense, Balbo oversaw the creation of the state later known as Libya. At the time, the territory consisted of two colonies, together with the vast expanse of the **Fezzan** in the **Saharan** interior. Under Balbo, the Italian state, originally founded in 1861, now extended across the Mediterranean Sea to incorporate the two coastal provinces of **Cyrenaica** and **Tripolitania** into metropolitan Italy proper, with the Fezzan accorded the status of a colonial province. For the first time, the entire colony was defined and delineated, in European legalistic terms, as Italian Libya.

If one moment epitomized the Balbo era, it was the *ventimila*, in which 20,000 colonists were transported to Libya in a single mass convoy in October 1938. While Balbo also led a second emigration of about 10,000 persons in 1939, the *ventimila* was his most spectacular and last great public triumph. The parade and carnival aspects of mass emigration later came under increasing criticism in Italy. In Libya and the Arab world as a whole, mass emigration was also poorly received, provoking violent demonstrations in Baghdad and elsewhere.

Balbo's blueprint for Libya's future prosperity faded with the outbreak of World War II. As the North African campaign seesawed across Cyrenaica, many Italian colonists were eventually evacuated. With the end of the war, and the end of Italian subsidies for colonization, the remaining settlement schemes in Tripolitania also faltered. *See also* LEGGE FONDAMENTALE.

BANI HILAL. *See* TRIBES.

BANI SULAIM. *See* TRIBES.

BANKING. Banking policy in contemporary Libya falls into two distinct phases. Soon after the **Libyan Free Unionist Officers'** movement seized power on 1 September 1969, the **Revolutionary Command Council** (RCC) **nationalized** foreign-owned banks, converting them into Libyan joint-stock companies as part of a broader policy aimed at eliminating all vestiges of colonialism. One British, one **Egyptian**, and two **Italian** banks were affected. The first of those, Barclays, had established itself in Libya during the British occupation in the 1940s and successfully withstood pressure for Libyanization during the regime of King **Idris** I; rather than offer majority control to the revolutionary government, it chose to pull out of Libya altogether. Under the bank nationalization law approved by the RCC, the Libyan government became the majority shareholder in all banks.

In 2002, the banking sector became the first sector targeted for privatization in which foreign investors could participate. However, foreign interest in the banks mooted for privatization proved very limited, in large part because the banks concerned had high levels of nonperforming loans and operated within a bureaucratic and regulatory system in need of modernization. It quickly became obvious that an overhaul of the entire financial system was required before foreign investors would show much interest.

In part to address these concerns, the **General People's Congress** (GPC) in January 2005 passed **Law** No. 2 to combat money laundering. Drafted with international assistance and designed to begin the process of bringing the banking sector in line with international standards regarding banking oversight, the law requires the Central Bank of Libya to create a Financial Information Unit to monitor banking and financial-sector activities. Additional legislation designed to shore up banking, credit, and currency supervision is also pending before the GPC.

As part of its efforts to increase foreign investment through the liberalization and privatization of the **economy**, in March 2005 the GPC also approved legislation that permits foreign banks to open branches in Libya for the first time since the 1970s. According to the new law, foreign banks opening operations must satisfy a minimum capital requirement of $50 million. In July 2005, BAWAG P.S.K., an Austrian bank, became the first Western bank to open a branch in Libya. In addition to overhauling the banking sector and inviting in foreign banks, Libya is also moving to privatize a number of state-owned banks.

BARBARY STATES. As long as the American colonies remained a part of the British imperial system, American ships engaged in the Mediterranean **trade** enjoyed such immunities from Barbary corsairs as the British government bought by payments of tribute to the rulers of Algiers, **Morocco**, **Tripoli**, and Tunis. Once the colonies declared independence, however, this protection was immediately withdrawn, and the pirates proved useful to **Great Britain** in throttling the commerce of its rebellious possessions. After independence was won, the **United States** continued to be faced with the uncertainties of Mediterranean privateering.

As early as 1776, the Continental Congress approached **France** with a proposed treaty, one article of which sought explicit protection from the Barbary States. When the treaty was finally concluded in 1778, France agreed to employ its good offices and interposition in cases of depredation by Barbary corsairs. The following year, Congress appointed a committee of three to prepare for direct negotiations with the Barbary States, and in 1783, it resolved to send ministers plenipotentiary to the region to conclude treaties of amity and commerce and to procure safe conduct passes.

Following the seizure by Algiers in 1785 of two American schooners, the *Maria* and the *Dauphin*, the United States evoked its 1778 treaty with France; however, the good offices of the latter failed to materialize. With direct negotiations the next obvious resort, the U.S. government dispatched ministers plenipotentiary to Morocco and Algiers. The mission to Morocco met with early success, and a treaty of peace and friendship was soon concluded. Backed by Britain, the regency of Algiers proved more intransigent, though, and a treaty of peace and amity was not concluded until September 1795. Through the terms of the agreement, the United States paid a substantial ransom for the release of American captives and agreed to deliver annual presents to Algiers in the form of naval and military stores. Washington also agreed to give Algiers a 36-gun frigate, appropriately named the *Crescent*, which it delivered in 1798.

A Treaty of Peace and Friendship between Tripoli and the United States, guaranteed by the dey and regency of Algiers, was signed on 4 November 1796. It promised protection and free passage for the naval vessels of both states and instituted a system of passports to ensure their protection. The treaty recognized money and presents paid to the bey of Tripoli but clearly stated that no periodic tributes or further payments would be made by either party.

In 1801, the pasha of Tripoli demanded better terms than he had received in 1796. Bolstered by growing American nationalism, the United States responded with a more aggressive approach. Tripoli had the reputation of being a nest of corsairs; however, it was never a major corsairing **port**. Contemporary studies rightly confine Tripoli to a relatively minor role. This relative weakness vis-à-vis other corsairing ports helps explain why Washington chose to make it an example of its new policy against corsairing.

In a dramatic expansion of its naval presence in the region, the U.S. government dispatched a naval squadron to the Mediterranean with orders to blockade and bombard Tripoli. At the same time, President Thomas Jefferson in May 1804 appointed William Eaton, a former U.S. consul in Tunis, to be the navy agent for the Several Barbary Regencies. It also agreed to support an overland expedition by Eaton to overthrow the Tripoli government. Commanding a small military force, Eaton left **Egypt** in the spring of 1805, seizing the port of Derna, several hundred miles east of Tripoli, in late April.

As Eaton slowly proceeded in a westerly direction toward Tripoli, the pasha made overtures for peace, which the United States soon accepted. In addition to the withdrawal of American forces from

Derna, the terms of the settlement provided for the release of all prisoners on both sides, with the United States giving the regency of Tripoli an ex gratia payment of $60,000 because the latter held considerably more prisoners than did the United States.

BARUNI, SULEIMAN (SULAYMAN AL-BARUNI). A **Berber** of the Ibadi sect from Fesatu in **Jabal Nefusah**, Suleiman Baruni was a prominent man of letters, known as a historian of North Africa and **Islam**. Following a traditional Muslim upbringing, he developed into an outspoken politician who was elected to represent **Tripolitania** in the newly reopened **Ottoman** parliament after 1908. Suspected of harboring ambitions for an autonomous Ibadi province in the western mountains, Baruni was imprisoned for subversive activity during the reign of Abdul Hamid II.

When war broke out between **Italy** and the Ottoman Empire, Baruni quickly supported the latter. In 1916, Baruni returned to Tripolitania as the Ottoman-appointed governor of Tripolitania, **Tunisia**, and Algeria. A member of the ruling Council of Four of the 1918 **Tripoli Republic**, he later rallied to the Italian cause after the promulgation of the **Legge Fondamentale** and visited Rome to join in the celebrations that surrounded its announcement. The Italian authorities, in the belief that Baruni still harbored ambitions for an autonomous Ibadi province, considered his adherence to the Tripoli Republic to be merely tactical.

The Italians had long entertained hopes of dividing the Berbers of the Jabal from their **Arab** counterparts, and their arbitrary and divisive administration of Berber areas soon resulted in a full-scale civil war in the early months of 1921. By the summer of that year, most of the Berber population had taken refuge in coastal areas under the Italian flag. Blamed by fellow Berbers for the disorders, Baruni ended his career in Libya despised by the other republican leaders who held him responsible for Italian gains. In November 1921, Suleiman Baruni left Libya for the last time. He traveled to **France**, **Egypt**, Turkey, and Mecca before finally settling in Oman, where he was appointed finance minister. *See also* YOUNG TURK REVOLUTION.

BASIC PEOPLE'S CONGRESS (BPC). When the **Revolutionary Command Council** (RCC) overthrew the monarchy in the **One Sep-**

tember Revolution in 1969, the three levels of subnational government were the zone, the municipality or branch municipality, and the **trade unions** or professional associations. At the lowest level, zone residents elected a **people's committee** to administer the affairs of the zone, which did not include a congress or legislative body. The next echelon of government was the municipality. In the case of larger urban areas, municipalities were divided into branch municipalities; for example, the city of **Tripoli** was divided into five branches. All zones were components of either a municipality or a branch municipality. Each municipality or branch municipality elected a legislative assembly known as the Basic People's Congress. Meeting quarterly, the BPC made recommendations or decisions on administrative matters within its jurisdiction, such as **roads**, sewage, **water resources**, and public clinics. The BPC also debated the agenda of the **General People's Congress** (GPC) in advance of the latter's annual meeting. The BPC selected its own chairman, as well as a five-member people's committee that had day-to-day administrative responsibility. All voting in the BPC was public—either by a show of hands or by a division into yes-no camps.

In those instances where a municipality was divided into more than one branch, a municipal People's Leadership Committee was established to coordinate the activities of the branch municipalities. The municipal People's Leadership Committee was made up of the chairmen and deputy chairmen of the branch people's committees. Committee members selected one of their number to be chairman, who would then become the equivalent of the mayor of a municipality in the United States. In those municipalities not large enough to be divided into branches, the chairman of the single municipal people's committee served as the head of the municipality.

In 1978, the General People's Committee at the national level was decentralized to include a similar structure at the municipal level. Municipal general people's committees were elected by the BPC for a term of three years. They were responsible for the coordination of activities between the GPC and the BPC.

In addition to the zone and municipal committees and congresses, Libyan workers were organized into trade unions and professional associations. Each union or professional association elected its own people's committee to administer its affairs. In turn, these committees participated in a federation of unions at the national level. The national federation of unions and professional associations sent representatives to the GPC to address issues of special relevance to them, but these individuals were not allowed to vote on major policy issues. While the unions and professional associations brought necessary expertise to selected issues, the Leader of the Revolution, **Muammar al-Qaddafi**, insisted that their views as citizens be represented through the people's committees and BPCs.

Libyan universities were also managed to a large degree by student unions; therefore, each college or faculty in Libya's three universities (Tripoli, Benghazi, and Beida) elected a chairman and a committee to administer the college. Representatives of these committees formed the university student union, which, along with the president of the university, was responsible for running the institution. The president of the university served at the pleasure of the members of the student union. Like trade unions and professional associations, university student unions attended the GPC in a nonvoting capacity.

In 1984, a new **law**, which attempted to clarify the power of the BPCs, stipulated that the local congresses were the real expression of popular authority in Libya. They were entitled to promulgate legislation and in theory even to determine the **foreign policy** of the country. The new law also made the BPCs responsible for developing Libya's **economic** plans and approving the **budget**. In addition, they were to control the executive branch and oversee the popular committees. Since that time, experience has shown that the actual roles and responsibilities of the BPCs are somewhat less than the ideal pattern outlined in the 1984 law.

Qaddafi again modified the operative political structure in 1991–1992, dividing the country into 1,500 **communes**, each with its own budget together with executive and legislative powers formerly vested in the BPCs. That said, delegates to the GPC continue to be chosen by the BPCs and the latter continue to meet regularly to discuss the latest political actions and observations of the Leader of the Revolution as well as to consider general economic and social issues facing Libya on the domestic and international levels. On the other hand, local congresses do not have any legislative power or responsibility, despite what *The Green Book* says. Instead, laws are created by the Secretariat of Justice in cooperation with the general secretary of the GPC. In this role of approving the ideas defined and clarified by Qaddafi and the GPC structure, the BPCs have become, in effect, the consulting instruments of the revolution. *See also* DE-CLARATION OF THE ESTABLISHMENT OF THE PEOPLE'S AUTHORITY.

BENGHAZI (BANGHAZI). Capital of **Cyrenaica** and second largest city in Libya. With a population of approximately 950,000 people, Benghazi is situated on the eastern side of the Gulf of **Sidra**, with a **port** built around a large double harbor. It is the major commercial center for eastern Libya. Mostly a postwar development, contemporary Benghazi displays little of its ancient heritage.

Originally known as **Euesperides**, Benghazi was founded by **Greek** settlers moving westward. The city later became a part of the **Roman** Empire, but very little is known of its early history. Like many North African cities, Benghazi suffered considerable damage at the hands of the **Vandals**, and after a brief period of repair under the Byzantines, it fell into obscurity. It was not until the 15th century that Benghazi was rediscovered by **Tripolitanian** merchants who took the city into a new and prosperous phase. Under first the Turks and later the **Karamanlis**, Benghazi again fell into disrepair. It was only during the second **Ottoman** occupation that the city once more recovered its fortunes.

In the 19th century, the only other significant settlement along coastal Cyrenaica was Darnah, which lay six or seven days' journey east of Benghazi. Most of the inhabitants of both Benghazi and Darnah originated in trading families from **Tunisia** and Tripolitania, especially the city of **Misurata**. Indeed, the political divisions of the people of Benghazi mirrored those of Misurata. The two opposing factions included the Kawabi, the **tribe** of the Muntasir family, and the *khouloughlis*, which included the Kikhiyah family, a branch of the Adghams. Historically, the urban population of Benghazi has had much more contact with the urban centers of Tripolitania than it had with the rural bedouin of the region.

A walk around the older sections of contemporary Benghazi is especially rewarding. While there are no outstanding historical monuments in the city, the covered souks or markets are open daily. Souq al-Jreed, the main covered market, is located off Sharia Umar al-Mukhtar. The tomb of **Sidi Umar-al Mukhtar**, the most famous freedom fighter of the resistance, is located nearby. Gar Younis University is also worth a visit.

BENGHAZI DECLARATION. In the **Benghazi** Declaration, dated 2 August 1972, Libyan leader **Muammar al-Qaddafi** and Egyptian president Anwar al-Sadat announced plans to merge their respective governments on or before 1 September 1973. The agreement established a unified political command with seven joint committees to lay the foundations for **unity** in such areas as **constitutional** matters, political organization, legislation and the judiciary, finance and administration, and **education**, science, culture, and public information. In a subsequent meeting, the defense and national security committee was subdivided into defense, security, and foreign affairs committees, increasing the total number to nine. The city of Cairo was declared the capital of the new state, and its form of government was described as a consultative, democratic, and republican system.

By early 1973, it was increasingly obvious that the two states were drifting apart. For one thing, the joint committees formed to advance the union were bureaucratic in operation, and the capabilities of many of their members were limited. Second, many aspects of the two societies were fundamentally different, and each was often critical of the other. Major **foreign policy** differences also separated the two states. **Egypt** pursued a broad policy of **Arab** solidarity and reconciliation, while Libya was more selective in its friends and openly hostile to many governments in and out of the Arab world. Finally, the personalities of the two leaders proved incompatible, with Qaddafi concluding that Sadat was not a true revolutionary and was not sincerely concerned with the liberation of Palestine from **Israel**.

In June 1973, Qaddafi arrived in Cairo for an unscheduled visit in which he was highly critical of many aspects of Egyptian society. His erratic, uncompromising behavior confirmed the doubts of many Egyptians who already had severe misgivings about the proposed union. Qaddafi's next step was to organize a motorcade of some 20,000 vehicles, which attempted to drive east from the Libyan-**Tunisian** border to Cairo in support of immediate union with Egypt, but Egyptian authorities stopped the motorcade. This so-called **Green March** was the last official Libyan attempt to export the cultural revolution to Egypt.

The Egyptians shelved the merger plans but at the same time sought to enable Qaddafi to preserve appearances. On 29 August 1973, the unified political command created to effect union announced a series of largely symbolic measures scheduled to become effective on 1 September 1973. The announcement created a joint constitutional assembly and a free economic zone on the Egyptian-Libyan border. On 10 September, a supreme planning council was formed, with ministers replacing the ambassadors of the two states in Cairo and **Tripoli**. Designed to preserve the principle of Arab unity, the plan for union by stages, together with Qaddafi's behavior during the October 1973 Arab-Israeli War, isolated Libya from the Arab world in general and Egypt in particular. *See also* FEDERATION OF ARAB REPUBLICS; TRIPOLI CHARTER.

BERBERS. Once dominant throughout North Africa, the Berbers of Libya today are a marginal, conservative people generally living in mountain refuge areas or in **desert** localities, driven there over the centuries by successive waves of invaders. Cultural and linguistic distinctions mostly differentiate the Berber from the **Arab**. Distantly related to Arabic, the Berber language has no written form; consequently, little literary culture has developed. Unlike the Arabs, who tend to see themselves as part of a larger Arab nation, the Berbers find identity in smaller groupings, like the clan or a section of a **tribe** that lives together. While a few can be found in **Cyrenaica**, most of the Berbers in Libya reside in **Tripolitania**. *See also* ZIRID DYNASTY.

BEY AL-KABIR, WADI. A large drainage basin in northeast **Tripolitania**, which has several tributaries originating in the southeastern part of the **Hamadah al-Hamra**. North of Ngem, these tributaries join forming the Wadi Bey al-Kabir, which trends northeast until it reaches the Mediterranean Sea east of Buerat.

BIN HALIM, MUSTAFA (1921–). Prime minister of the **United Kingdom of Libya** from April 1954 to May 1957. Born in **Egypt** where his family was in exile, Bin Halim studied at a French school in Alexandria before graduating in engineering from the Egyptian (now Cairo) University. While at university, Bin Halim met **Sayyid**

Muhammad Idris al-Madhi al-Sanusi, who was then in exile in Egypt, and developed a friendship with Idris's personal secretary, Ibrahim al-Shalhi. Before independence, Bin Halim returned to Libya and proved himself an active and effective public administrator, serving the **Cyrenaican** government as minister of public works and communications. In this time frame, Bin Halim cemented his relationship with Shalhi and his close associate, Sayyid Abd-Allah Abid, a member of the Sanusi family. Known as "the triumvirate," the three men collaborated to attain great success in business and government.

Mustafa Bin Halim reluctantly joined the **Muhammad al-Saqizli** government as minister of communications with the tacit understanding it would lead to higher political posts. However, no one, including Bin Halim, expected that he would be the king's choice as successor to the short-lived Saqizli government. The new government was a strong one, receiving the support of **opposition** elements, and it enjoyed an enviable tenure of three years despite five cabinet reshuffles. The conclusion in 1954 of the **American-Libyan Agreement** with the **United States**, the opening in 1955 of diplomatic relations with the **Soviet Union**, and acceptance of the Eisenhower Doctrine were among the more controversial **foreign policies** of the Bin Halim government. Regional conflicts, together with power struggles within the royal household, eventually led to the fall of the government in mid-1957. Bin Halim later served King Idris as a special adviser and then as ambassador to **France**. Retiring from public service, he then returned to private business.

BIN UTHMAN, MUHAMMAD (1920–). Prime minister of the **United Kingdom of Libya** from October 1960 to March 1963. Born in **Fezzan** and educated in local religious schools, Muhammad Bin Uthman studied history and **law**. A self-made man, he distinguished himself in the local politics of the Fezzan, where he was an early supporter of a Sanusi monarchy. Before becoming prime minister, he served in various cabinets as minister of **health**, national **economy**, and finance. His administration was plagued by ongoing conflict between federal and provincial authorities as well as a monarchy growing increasingly remote from its people. During Bin Uthman's tenure, the king moved his administrative capital to the remote location of

Beida, which added to the general confusion and lack of cohesion in the administration of the country.

BLACK AFRICANS. Descendants of sub-Saharan **Africans**, mostly from the **Sudan** or West Africa, live in both the **desert** and coastal communities of Libya. Many of them are descended from former slaves, while others came to **Tripoli** during World War II.

BORDERS. *See* FRONTIERS.

BREGA PETROLEUM MARKETING COMPANY. In July 1970, Libya announced the establishment of the Brega Petroleum Marketing Company, a subsidiary of the **National Oil Company** (NOC), to market Libyan **petroleum** products abroad. At the time, the single source of crude oil for Brega came from the Libyan government exercising its option, detailed in concession contracts, to take all or part of its royalty in kind rather than in cash. After 1973, Brega received crude oil from its production share in the participation agreements negotiated by the revolutionary government with the foreign oil companies.

The exodus of **United States** oil companies from Libya in 1986 hastened Brega's emergence as an international presence on world crude oil markets. At the time, several distinct characteristics typified its policies and practices. The main market for Libyan crude oil continued to be Western Europe, especially **Italy** and West **Germany**, and Brega preferred to sell its crude oil to state oil companies. Beginning in the early 1970s, Brega linked sales contracts to exploration commitments whenever possible, and it continued this practice throughout the following decade. Barter trade, debt repayment agreements, and the avoidance of spot market sales were other practices that characterized Brega's marketing policies in the 1980s.

In October 1990, Libya dissolved the Brega Petroleum Marketing Company and transferred its activities to a department within NOC. It is believed that this move was taken to enable NOC to better control export destinations and sales arrangements in the face of the growing threat of **economic** sanctions by the **United Nations**. In 1992, the new marketing organization tightened its control over sales by issuing regulations covering restricted destinations in sales contracts. At the end of 1994, Libya again altered its price formula for term contracts, and it continued thereafter to adjust its policies periodically to the rules and regulations of the petroleum industry.

While Libya has pursued relatively cautious and conservative marketing and pricing policies over the last three decades, it can be expected to be more aggressive in the future. To meet its stated objective of increasing oil production to 3 million barrels a day by 2015, Libya will need to secure a greater share of the overall **Organization of Petroleum Exporting Countries** (OPEC) quota. In 2004–2005, Libya produced almost to capacity and maintained its output at a little more than 1.6 million barrels a day or approximately 110 percent of its present quota of 1.5 million barrels a day. With NOC probably unable to increase its capacity above 2 million barrels a day for another year, recent calls for quota increases have been muted. However, to return to a production level of 3 million barrels a day, Libya can at some point be expected to become much more forceful in its demand for a higher OPEC quota.

BU MARYAM. The Agreement of Bu Maryam, concluded between the **Sanusi Order** and **Italian** forces in 1921, proved to be the last attempt to negotiate control of **Cyrenaica**. Under the terms of the arrangement, mixed camps of Sanusi and Italian soldiers were organized and made jointly responsible for the security of the countryside. Given the deep-seated animosity between the two sides, the agreement was short-lived.

BUDGETS. Budget methodology and fiscal policy after 1959 tended to follow the recommendations of the World Bank mission that visited Libya that year. The change in government from a federal to a unitary form in 1963 facilitated the integration of provincial fiscal administrations with the central government. Thereafter, the promise of large **petroleum** revenues enabled the government to introduce an extensive **development plan**, which included the provision that not less than 70 percent of future oil revenues should be allocated to development financing. In 1966, Libya experienced its first budget surplus, as oil revenues began to increase spectacularly.

Under the monarchy, the national budget was prepared by the Ministry of Finance, approved by the parliament, and signed into law by the king. It consisted of a current expenses budget and, after 1962, a development budget. In the aftermath of the 1967 Arab-**Israeli** war, a supplemental budget was added to cover increased defense outlays and annual subsidies to **Egypt**, Jordan, and Syria.

After the monarchy was overthrown, the annual budget was presented in the form of separate budgets for administrative expenses, development expenditures, and special expenditures. Before 1974, the fiscal year began in April; but since January 1974, the fiscal year has been concurrent with the calendar year. After the **Declaration of the Establishment of the People's Authority** in 1977, the final step in the formal budgeting process for both the administrative budget and the development budget has been their review and approval by the **General People's Congress** (GPC). Special expenditures not included in the formal budget are approved by the GPC in the course of the year. Special expenditures include grants, loans, subsidies, and the purchase of military equipment. The total amount budgeted for special expenditures is never made public because of defense-related items; however, incomplete data on individual accounts are sometimes released.

As much as 80 percent of the administrative budget is spent by the federal government, with the remainder transferred to municipalities and public entities. After 1969, development expenditures were generally higher than administrative expenditures as the revolutionary government carried out its pledge to use oil revenues to build for the future. The development budget covers **economic** and social projects but also includes working capital for public corporations and some lending and operating expenditures. All budgets are amended and revised in the course of the year to reflect increases for specific projects or programs as well as the increased costs of imported items for development projects.

As might be expected, the bulk of the government's revenues are drawn from the hydrocarbon (**petroleum** and **natural gas**) sector in the form of taxes, royalties, profits, and fees. More than 85 percent of revenues came from hydrocarbons in 2003–2004, and this trend is expected to continue in the foreseeable future. Revenue sources outside the hydrocarbon sector include profits from other government enterprises, import duties, income taxes, and miscellaneous taxes and fees.

Budget transparency is slowly improving but remains a major obstacle to a detailed analysis of the government budget. As the International Monetary Fund emphasized in its March 2005 report, Libya's statistical base suffers from shortcomings in the "quality, coverage, timeliness, and consistency of data." The secretary of finance discloses minimal information about the budget, accounting and auditing practices are weak, and no effective requirements to ensure public accountability are in place. Officially, there are two separate budgets, one for recurrent government expenditures and the other for development expenditure; however, major spending decisions are the prerogative of Libyan leader **Muammar al-Qaddafi** and his inner circle, which has contributed in the past to unpredictable budgetary decisions.

BULGARIA. Under the terms of the third **Exploration and Production-Sharing Agreement**, which awarded the Bulgarian oil company Geocom an exploration block in 1988, Bulgaria attempted to participate in the **petroleum** industry in Libya for many years, but eventually abandoned the block in 2005.

Diplomatic relations, on the other hand, have focused almost exclusively in recent years on a controversial case involving the imprisonment since 1999 of five Bulgarian nurses and a Palestinian doctor charged with deliberately infecting 426 children in a **Benghazi** hospital with HIV. Initially, they were also charged with working for the Mossad, the **Israeli** intelligence service, but this charge was later dropped. The six defendants, who were sentenced to death by firing squad in May 2004, claim they are innocent. They assert they were tortured to obtain their confessions, but nine Libyan policemen and a physician were cleared in June 2005 of allegations of torturing the five nurses to force them to confess. Numerous HIV experts, including Dr. Luc Montagnier, discover of the AIDS virus, have testified that the children were infected as the result of poor hygiene at the hospital and that the epidemic was under way before the nurses ever arrived. These experts believe Libya has made the defendants scapegoats rather that admitting the HIV infections were the product of poor hospital hygiene, an argument rejected by Libyan authorities.

The case has damaged Libyan ties with the **European Union** and the **United States**, both of which reject the evidence against the nurses, demanding they be freed. In an effort to resolve the issue, Libya urged Bulgaria in the fall of 2005 to offer the families of the infected children financial compensation for their pain, comparable to Libya's payments for the **Lockerbie incident**; however, Bulgaria has rejected this approach on the grounds the nurses are innocent and should be freed. Most recently, Bulgaria asked the World **Health** Organization to intervene in the case.

– C –

CENTRAL AMERICA. In the first decade of the Libyan revolution, efforts by the government of **Muammar al-Qaddafi** to destabilize pro-Western governments were most pronounced in **Africa**; however, it soon expanded such efforts to include Latin America, especially Central America and the Caribbean Basin. Libyan **foreign policy** in this regard was motivated by three interrelated objectives. First, Libyan representatives sought to promote Qaddafi as a legitimate Third World leader with an attractive and workable sociopolitical philosophy, the **Third Universal Theory**. Second, the Libyans hoped to undermine the interests of the **United States** in a region that had traditionally been under its influence. Finally, Libya hoped to be of assistance in enabling liberation groups in these and other areas to free themselves from the domination of foreign interests.

As early as 1977, Qaddafi recognized Cuban efforts to fight American imperialism and invited Fidel Castro to visit Libya. Following the visit, Libya established diplomatic relations with Cuba and began an era of close cooperation. Embassies were opened in Havana and Tripoli, and cooperative agreements were concluded addressing **trade**, technology, and **economic** issues as well as scientific and cultural exchanges. After 1977, the two states supported each other on a variety of regional and international issues, including Zionism as racism, Third World politics, the Palestinian right to self-determination, Nicaragua, and El Salvador.

The Qaddafi government also established close bilateral relations with the Sandinista government in Nicaragua. At the outset, it would appear that the **Palestine Liberation Organization** (PLO), together with the Cuban government, assisted Libya in establishing ties with the Sandinistas; but after 1979, there was no longer need for inter-mediaries. During the final stages of the guerrilla war against the So-moza regime, the Sandinistas combined Libyan money and PLO technical assistance to obtain arms from both North Korea and Viet-nam. After the Sandinista victory, Libyan-Nicaraguan relations con-solidated and expanded, including a $100 million Libyan loan in 1981. Libya also financed agricultural projects in Nicaragua, and in January 1985 Nicaragua announced a $15 million trade agreement in-volving Libyan **petroleum**. In addition to economic assistance, the Qaddafi government also provided the Sandinista government with military assistance, ranging from small arms and ammunition to an-tiaircraft guns and surface-to-air missiles.

In the Caribbean, the Libyan government established especially good relations with the New Jewel Movement of Grenada during the 1979–1983 reign of Maurice Bishop. In addition, Qaddafi invited leftist leaders and associated revolutionaries from Antigua and Bar-buda, Barbados, Dominica, the Dominican Republic, St. Vincent and the Grenadines, St. Lucia, and elsewhere to come to Libya for semi-nars and paramilitary training. Libya also established a **People's Bu-reau** in Grenada to serve as a center for the distribution of economic and other support to leftist groups on the islands of the Caribbean.

Despite such efforts, Libya never became a major diplomatic force in Central America or the Caribbean. The Third Universal Theory was un-appealing to most Latin Americans, as it was to the majority of Africans, and generated little interest or support. The Qaddafi regime did channel some economic and military aid to revolutionary groups and radical governments in the area, but in the end, this support had minimal long-term impact on the economics or politics of the region. By the mid-1980s, the small amount of political capital that Libyan diplomacy had built up in Central America and the Caribbean Basin had been largely expended, and Libyan foreign policy again turned its attention to Africa and the Middle East. In September 2001, Libya did pledge $2 billion in development assistance to several Caribbean states, raising concern in Washington about renewed Libyan influence in the region; however, lit-tle came of this reported Libyan initiative.

CHAD. The Republic of Chad, a landlocked state in the center of the northern **Africa** subregion, is the fifth largest political entity on the

African continent. It is bounded on the north by Libya, on the west by Niger and Nigeria, on the south by Cameroon and the Central African Republic, and on the east by **Sudan**. Chad remained under French occupation until 1960 when it finally gained independence. The first president of the new state was François Tombalbaye, who adopted a pro-French policy and maintained good ties with **Israel**. In the beginning, he did not give any political posts to representatives of the Muslim majority occupying the northern section of Chad, although he later modified this policy.

Once Libya achieved independence in 1951, its African policy focused on Chad. Diplomatic relations with the remainder of the states in sub-Saharan Africa were of little consequence and were generally conducted within the framework of the **Organization of African Unity** (OAU). In 1955, Libyan motorized units penetrated the disputed Aouzou Strip in northern Chad, considered by the **Ottomans** to be an integral part of their North African province; however, the Libyans were soon driven out by French troops. With the outbreak of the Chadian rebellion in 1965, the Libyan monarchy opposed the government, initially providing support to the Front for the National Liberation of Chad (Frolinat), the major rebel organization. Diplomatic relations between the two governments later improved, however, and just a few months before the **One September Revolution** in 1969, the governments of Libya and Chad signed agreements designed to improve mutual communications, the upkeep of **Islamic** institutions in Chad, and the status of Chadian workers in Libya.

After two years of often stormy relations, the **Revolutionary Command Council** finally reestablished diplomatic ties with Chad in April 1972. In return for Libyan friendship, a withdrawal of official support for Frolinat, and a promise of aid from Libya and other **Arab** states, the Chadian government broke diplomatic relations with Israel in November 1972. At the time, this was considered a major diplomatic victory for Libyan policy in sub-Saharan Africa, which had focused since 1969 on undermining Israeli influence on the continent. This growing reconciliation between Chad and Libya was crowned by a treaty of friendship signed in December 1972.

For the remainder of the decade, the Libyan government was deeply involved in the internal affairs of Chad. In fact, it was largely due to Libya's diplomatic and military intervention that the Chadian civil war became irrevocably internationalized as early as 1978. In 1980, the two governments concluded a new treaty of friendship that provided Libyan support for Chadian independence and territorial integrity, laying the groundwork for increased Libyan involvement in the second half of the year. It was also the forerunner of a Libyan communiqué issued in January 1981 that stated that Libya and Chad had agreed to work together toward the realization of total **unity**. International reaction to the proposed merger was immediate and largely critical. The chairman of the OAU called for a withdrawal of Libyan forces from Chad, and an emergency OAU meeting convened later in the month condemned the suggested union. An African peace-keeping force was later sent to Chad, but it failed to prevent the collapse of the Chadian government in June 1982.

In 1983, the Libyan government threw its weight behind a rebel faction and against a Chadian government that enjoyed official recognition by the vast majority of the OAU membership. As Libya reinforced its military presence and imposed civilian administration in northern Chad, Colonel **Muammar al-Qaddafi** aggressively defended Libya's right to intervene in African affairs, describing Chad as a mere extension of the **Socialist People's Libyan Arab Jamahiriya**. In November 1984, Libya and France announced the completion of a mutual phased withdrawal of armed forces in Chad; however, within a week, the French government was forced to admit that a sizable Libyan force remained in the country.

The stalemate in Chad continued until 1987, when the Libyan intervention in northern Chad, not seriously challenged since the early 1970s, suddenly crumbled. After a series of lightning victories by lightly armed but highly mobile Chadian troops, Libya was forced to withdraw into the Aouzou Strip. The Libyan withdrawal from northern Chad was a humiliating military defeat as well as a major setback for Qaddafi's vague plans to create an Islamic federation from Mauritania to Sudan. While the Libyan government soon rejected a Chadian proposal to bring the issue of the Aouzou Strip before the **International Court of Justice** (ICJ), it later accepted this prospect as part of a wider settlement concluded the day before the 20th anniversary of the One September Revolution.

Dated 31 August 1989, the Libya-Chad peace accord called for an end to the fighting over the disputed Aouzou Strip. All hostilities were to cease, and the signatories were to conclude a treaty of friendship. In addition, all Chadian and Libyan forces were to withdraw from the disputed territory, where they would be replaced by African observers who would remain until a settlement was reached. Finally, the treaty gave the signatories one year to resolve their dispute through a political settlement. If that proved impossible, they were to take the question of the sovereignty of the Aouzou Strip to the ICJ for resolution.

Despite a number of unsuccessful meetings in 1989–1990, the disputants were unable to negotiate a settlement, and the dispute over the sovereignty of the Aouzou Strip was eventually placed before the ICJ. Committing itself to a lengthy legal battle, Libya was determined to challenge the OAU principle that African **frontiers** should remain as they were fixed by the colonial powers. In the interim, its political prospects improved in late 1990 with the swift and unexpected fall of the Chadian government of the pro-Western president, Hissené Habré. Many African governments again expressed concern that Libya appeared poised to use Chad as a springboard to extend its influence throughout the region.

In early 1994, the ICJ delivered its judgment in the territorial dispute between Chad and Libya, ruling that the boundary between the two neighbors was fixed in a 1955 treaty concluded by France and the **United Kingdom of Libya**. The line referred to in the 1955 treaty had been featured on most maps and atlases as the boundary between the two states since 1919. The decision of the court constituted a resounding defeat for Libyan claims in the area. On 7 January 2002, following three days of Qaddafi-led negotiations in Tripoli, a representative of the Chadian government and the leader of the rebels concluded a peace agreement, ending the civil war in Chad. *See also* FOREIGN POLICY; THIRD UNIVERSAL THEORY.

CHALGAM, MOHAMMED ABDERRAHMAN. Secretary of foreign affairs and international cooperation in the General People's Committee (2000–). *See also* FOREIGN POLICY; GENERAL PEOPLE'S CONGRESS.

CHEMICAL WEAPONS. The sensitivity of the **United States** government to the proliferation of chemical weapons erupted on

24 December 1987 in a front-page article in the *New York Times* in which the administration of President Ronald Reagan charged Libya was building a factory near Rabta that U.S. officials strongly suspected would be used to produce chemical weapons. In addition to the charges related to the production facility, the article also mentioned reports that Libya had used poison gas in its war with **Chad** and that Iran and Libya enjoyed a trade relationship in chemical arms. The article marked the outset of a prolonged, serious international crisis based on Washington's charge that Libya was constructing a chemical weapons production facility, a development it was determined to prevent.

Libya responded quickly to the charge, denying that the plant under construction at Rabta was intended for this purpose. At the same time, Libyan officials condemned the embargo implemented earlier by the U.S. government, especially what they described as the Reagan administration's ban on the sale of medical supplies and medicines to Libya. A distortion of U.S. policy, the Libyan charge set the stage for the subsequent Libyan rationale that the U.S. embargo gave it no choice but to construct a factory to produce pharmaceuticals.

Expanding its initial charges against Libya, the Reagan administration in September 1988 announced that Libya appeared to be nearing full-scale production of chemical weapons. The following month, the director of the Central Intelligence Agency (CIA) said that Libya was building the largest chemical weapons facility in the world. By the end of 1988, U.S. officials were reported to have ascertained that Libya was creating a staggering manufacturing complex to produce chemical weapons at Rabta. Speculation emerged that Libya had received assistance from nearly a dozen firms in Eastern and Western Europe as well as Japan. Increasing the pressure, Reagan stated in a television interview that the United States was considering some type of military attack on the alleged chemical weapons factory. Given the 1986 air attack on Libya, such statements by the American president were credible and taken seriously in Tripoli.

Libya reacted vociferously to U.S. pressure in a wide variety of international forums, including bilateral diplomatic contacts, **international organizations**, and a steady flow of press releases. Throughout the period, Libya claimed the technical complex under construction at Rabta was nothing more than a pharmaceutical facility designed to produce medicines for the alleviation of sickness and disease. Never wavering from this position, Libya argued that its interest in chemical industries was legitimate and challenged the U.S. government, instead of making false charges against Libya, to destroy its own **weapons of mass destruction**.

While Washington continued its public accusations that Libya was building a chemical weapons facility, it also exerted quiet diplomatic pressure on the governments of the international companies thought to be involved in the construction of the Rabta complex. Possible links to **German** firms, in particular, had surfaced over a period of several years; nevertheless, the government of West Germany steadfastly maintained that it had no knowledge of prosecutable offenses—until early 1989, when it finally issued a report that acknowledged the involvement of a number of German firms, especially Imhausen-Chemie, in the construction of the Rabta complex. Subsequent decisions by Bonn to tighten export regulations and to increase penalties for violations were welcomed in Washington.

The chemical weapons issue lay dormant for almost a year until reports of new activities at Rabta surfaced in early 1990. Again working through the *New York Times*, the George H. W. Bush administration released information indicating that Libya had begun production of small quantities of mustard gas under a limited production posture but was striving to reach full-scale production capacity. Reports suggested small quantities of the nerve gas Sarin were also being produced. The U.S. government estimated that 30 tons of mustard gas had been manufactured in 1989 and that a building had been completed at Rabta in which to load the gas into plastic containers. Like Reagan, President Bush refused to rule out a military attack on the Rabta facility.

In March 1990, the United States revealed that the chemical complex at Rabta appeared to be on fire. The Libyan press agency soon confirmed this report, blaming the United States, **Israel**, and Germany for the incendiary act. Other Libyans attributed the fire to **terrorist** organizations, and at least one Libyan dissident group claimed responsibility. Regarding the damage caused by the fire, assessments varied from modest to very serious damage. U.S. officials initially stated that the plant was inoperable, but the Bush administration later announced that the fire could have been a hoax and that the plant might not be seriously damaged after all.

The alleged fire at the Rabta technical complex temporarily defused the chemical weapons issue. However, the U.S. government again charged in late 1991 that Libya was producing poison gas at Rabta as well as building another factory nearby for the manufacture of chemical weapons. Washington also charged that Libya was expanding its chemical weapons program and dispersing chemical stockpiles to avoid detection. In early 1993, Libya denied the U.S. allegations that it was constructing a chemical weapons plant near Tripoli and invited any neutral international group to inspect the construction site in question. Later in the year, the United States warned Thailand that Thai contractors appeared to be the principal companies involved in the construction of chemical weapons plants in Libya.

In February 1996, the U.S. government once again renewed charges that Libya was actively involved in the proliferation of chemical weapons. U.S. intelligence sources identified a factory located in Tarhuna, scheduled for completion in 1997, as the world's largest chemical weapons plant. Libya again denied it was involved in the manufacture of chemical weapons and described the factory under construction as simply part of an irrigation project.

It was not until early 2004, after Libya had unilaterally renounced weapons of mass destruction, that the full extent of its chemical weapons program became known. According to the Organization for the Prohibition of Chemical Weapons, which oversaw the destruction of Libya's stockpile of chemical weapons, Libya had manufactured a large quantity of mustard gas and possessed precursor chemicals for the production of nerve gas. It also had more than 3,000 empty bomb casings designed to carry chemical weapons, although it lacked the long-range missiles or other systems necessary to deliver chemical weapons beyond its own borders. *See also* FOREIGN POLICY.

CLEANSING COMMITTEE. Cleansing committees, also referred to as purification committees, were established in Libya on 1 September 1994. Their stated aim was to identify and eliminate counterrevolutionaries as well as to prevent **people's committee** members from accumulating too much wealth and power. Libyans were required to give a cleansing committee situated in their area of residence a periodic accounting of their material wealth and means of acquiring it.

Cleansing committee members were also called upon to reflect accurately the personality and politics of Libyan leader **Muammar al-Qaddafi**. The cleansing committee effort was reinvigorated in the spring of 1996 in an effort to root out corruption and speculation.

CLIMATE. With the Mediterranean Sea and the **Sahara Desert** being the dominant influences, up to five separate climatic zones have been recognized in Libya. Throughout the coastal lowlands, the climate tends to be Mediterranean with hot summers and mild winters. Rainfall is scarce, and the dry climate results in good year-round visibility. In the highlands, the weather is cooler, and frosts occur at maximum altitudes. The **desert** interior experiences very hot summers and extreme diurnal temperature ranges.

Less than 2 percent of Libya receives enough rainfall for settled **agriculture**. The heaviest precipitation occurs in the **Jabal al-Akhdar**. Elsewhere, rainfall is erratic, and sustained showers are often followed by prolonged, severe periods of drought. The limited, irregular pattern of rainfall is reflected in the absence of permanent rivers or streams; moreover, the approximately 20 perennial lakes in Libya are all brackish or salty. As might be expected, the existing patterns of rainfall have severely limited the country's level of agricultural development.

The prevailing winds along the coast of Libya are from the northeast, with occasional north winds. In the summer, hot winds sometimes blow northward from the desert. Known as the *ghibli*, this weather condition often raises the ambient temperature substantially above normal and fills the air with sand and dust. In the south, the prevailing winds are from either the northeast or the southwest and shift from one area to another. The winds blowing north from the Sahara Desert are intensely hot in the summer and often very cold in the winter. *See also* WATER RESOURCES.

COMMON MARKET FOR EASTERN AND SOUTHERN AFRICA (COMESA). COMESA is a free trade area with 21 member states stretching across **Africa** from **Egypt** to Namibia. Formed in December 1994, COMESA replaced a Preferential Trade Area, which had existed since 1981. Libya became a full member at the 10th COMESA Summit in June 2005. *See also* AFRICAN UNION; COMMUNITY OF SAHEL-SAHARAN STATES; UNITY.

COMMUNES. Muammar al-Qaddafi proposed in 1991–1992 that Libya be divided into some 1,500 communes, each of which would become a self-governing replica of the larger state, with its own **budget** and legislative and executive powers. Each commune was to create its own 13-man cabinet, two members of which would form part of a larger national cabinet, whose exact functions were not detailed; moreover, it remained unclear exactly how this new cabinet, composed of 3,000 members, would operate. With each commune responsible for its own defense, Qaddafi's proposal has been interpreted by some observers as another attempt to fragment the **armed forces**. While the commune concept might be reinvigorated at a later date, it is more likely yet another example of the ephemeral nature of Libyan political institutions under Qaddafi. *See also* BASIC PEOPLE'S CONGRESS; GENERAL PEOPLE'S CONGRESS.

COMMUNITY OF SAHEL-SAHARAN STATES (COMESSA; CEN-SAD). COMESSA was established in February 1994, following a conference of **African** leaders in **Tripoli**. In addition to Libya, the founding members were Burkina Faso, **Chad**, Mali, Niger, and **Sudan**. The Central African Republic and Eritrea joined the organization in April 1999, and Djibouti, Gambia, and Senegal in February 2000. Other African states have joined since then and more are in the process.

A Libyan **foreign policy** initiative, the COMESSA project included creation of the Eastern and Southern African Trade and Development Bank with 75 percent Libyan capital, together with regional initiatives such as upgrading the Trans-Saharan Highway. COMESSA is headquartered in Tripoli. *See also* AFRICAN UNION; COMMON MARKET FOR EASTERN AND SOUTHERN AFRICA; UNITY.

CONSTITUTION OF LIBYA. The constitution promulgated in **Benghazi** on 7 October 1951 provided for a **United Kingdom of Libya** consisting of the provinces of **Cyrenaica**, **Tripolitania**, and the **Fezzan**. Under a hereditary monarchy, the system of government was representative, with **Islam** designated the official state **religion**. The 1951 constitution provided for executive, legislative, and **judicial** branches of government.

Section 36 of the constitution defined 39 powers given to the federal government. Among the more important were foreign affairs, war and peace, treaties, nationality, defense, atomic energy, taxation, **education**, the minting of coins, and the issuance of money. Section 38 of the constitution enumerated 27 powers to be shared concurrently by federal and provincial authorities, including shipping and navigation, insurance, public meetings, labor and social security, and public **health**. All residual powers, those not specifically defined in the constitution, were vested in the provincial governments.

The 1951 constitution recognized **Muhammad Idris al-Mahdi al-Sanusi** and his male successors as the monarchy of Libya. Since the king had no immediate successor, it was determined that the order of succession would be resolved in a royal decree within one year of the date of the constitution's promulgation. Provisions for a regency were also detailed in the document.

A bicameral parliamentary system was established in Libya consisting of a Senate and a House of Representatives. The Senate was composed of 24 members, eight from each of the three provinces; half of each province's members were to be appointed by the king, the other half elected by provincial legislative councils. Unlike the Senate, the House of Representatives was meant to represent Libya at large, with one deputy elected for every 20,000 inhabitants. Under this formula, Tripolitania received 35 seats, Cyrenaica 15, and the Fezzan 5.

The federal system established by the 1951 constitution was the subject of much criticism. Opponents argued that federation in an underpopulated country like Libya weakened central authority and made the state more vulnerable to outside influence. It was also difficult to maintain three provincial governments and a central government without imposing a crushing tax burden on the populace. Finally, critics emphasized that the Libyan population was both numerically small and generally homogeneous, two criteria often considered supportive of a unitary system.

Faced with constant criticism, King Idris on 27 April 1963 approved an amendment to the constitution that abolished the federal system and replaced it with a unitary one. The amendment brought the provinces of Tripolitania, Cyrenaica, and the Fezzan together in a united kingdom with a parliamentary legislature. In the process, the three provinces were divided into 10 administrative units or **governorates**, and all provincial executive and legislative councils were abolished. The amended 1951 constitution remained the basis for Libyan government until the **Revolutionary Command Council** replaced it in 1969 with the **Constitutional Proclamation**.

CONSTITUTIONAL PROCLAMATION. On 11 December 1969, the **Revolutionary Command Council** (RCC) replaced the 1951 **Constitution of Libya** with a constitutional proclamation whose preamble emphasized the revolutionary government's intention to fight reactionary forces and colonialism and to eliminate obstacles to Arab **unity**. It summarized the revolution's goals as **freedom, socialism**, and unity. The first article of the proclamation held that Libya constituted part of the **Arab** nation and reiterated the commitment to comprehensive Arab unity. It also described Libya as part of **Africa**, a concept that took on fresh meaning in the 1970s as **Muammar al-Qaddafi**'s efforts at Arab unity faltered and he looked to pan-African or pan-**Islamic** unity as an option. The second article described Islam as the state **religion**, but gave no clear indication as to the strong emphasis on Islam that would characterize the Libyan revolution and thus differentiate it from those in neighboring Arab states.

Eight of the remaining 15 articles in the first chapter dealt with some aspect of Libyan socialism. Founded on the principle of social justice, Article 6 gave socialism a practical application in the form of self-sufficiency in production and equity in distribution. Articles 7 and 8 promised an increase in public ownership, while guaranteeing nonexploitative private ownership a place in the new **economic** system. Articles 14 and 15 addressed the social welfare aspects of socialism, establishing **education** and **health** care as rights for all Libyan citizens.

The second half of the proclamation outlined the operative governmental structure. The RCC was described as the highest authority in the Libyan Arab Republic and was given both executive and legislative functions. Over the next six years, the RCC, under Qaddafi's leadership, ruled Libya through the issuance of resolutions, decrees, and **laws**.

The 1969 constitutional proclamation was to remain in force until the completion of the so-called nationalist democratic revolution, when it would be replaced by a permanent constitution. This has never occurred, and with the political system undergoing continuous change after 1969, the system functioning today bears little resemblance to the one detailed in the proclamation. It is now doubtful the constitutional proclamation will ever be replaced by a constitution. *The Green Book* describes man-made law, including constitutions, as illogical and invalid, concluding that the genuine law of society is tradition or religion. *See also* GENERAL PEOPLE'S CONGRESS; THIRD UNIVERSAL THEORY.

CORSAIRS. *See* BARBARY STATES.

COUNCIL OF MINISTERS. On 7 September 1969, the **Revolutionary Command Council** announced it had appointed a Council of Ministers to conduct the government of the new republic. **Mahmud Suleiman al-Maghrabi**, an American-educated technician imprisoned since 1967 for political activities, was named prime minister. He presided over an eight-member council consisting of six civilians and two military officers. The Council of Ministers was replaced after the **Declaration of the Establishment of the People's Authority** in 1977 by the General People's Committee.

CUF, WADI AL-. A drainage system on the **Jabal al-Akhdar** in **Cyrenaica**. The Wadi al-Cuf and the Wadi **Derna** run parallel to the edge of the escarpment in opposite directions away from the high part of the terrace south of Ras el-Hilal. They both turn at right angles and descend to the sea transversely to the escarpments and terraces.

CYRENAICA. The largest of Libya's three historic regions, occupying the eastern half of the country. Constituting an area of approximately 790,000 square kilometers (305,000 square miles), Cyrenaica's boundaries stretch eastward from the Gulf of **Sidra** to the **Egyptian** border and southward from the Mediterranean Sea to **Chad** and **Sudan**. Cyrenaica is generally subdivided into three geographical regions: the coastal plain; the **Jabal al-Akhdar** area, including eastern Cyrenaica; and the **Sahara Desert**.

    Benghazi, the second largest city in Libya and the commercial center for the eastern half of the country, is located on the eastern side of the Gulf of Sidra. Cyrenaica is also the location of several spectacular **Greek** cities of antiquity, notably **Cyrene** and **Apollonia**. The landscape of the region is very attractive, especially along the coastline.

Over the centuries, Cyrenaica has maintained especially close ties to Egypt. Cyrenaican bedouins, defeated in **tribal** wars, migrated to Egypt, eventually settling there as peasants. Other tribal members retained their nomadic way of life but also relocated to Egypt. During the period of **Italian** occupation, Cyrenaicans received arms and supplies from Egypt in support of their struggle against the invaders. Eventually, Italian authorities were forced to erect a barbed wire fence along the length of the Egyptian-Libyan border to stop the passage of military supplies to the insurgents. In 1922, **Sayyid Muhammad Idris al-Mahdi al-Sanusi**, head of the **Sanusi Order** and the first leader of independent Libya, sought refuge in Egypt, where he remained for almost 30 years. Other émigrés from Libya also sought refuge in Egypt, and many were offered Egyptian citizenship. In a word, the ties between Cyrenaica and Egypt are old and strong and bear the stamp of both tradition and legitimacy.

With a population of about 1,000,000 people, approximately 20 percent of Libya's total, Cyrenaica today is an extremely important **economic** center. The Jabal al-Akhdar, together with Al-Kufrah and other irrigated areas in the south, remain important centers of **agriculture**. However, it is the **petroleum** sector that now drives both regional and national economies. Petroleum deposits in the south account for almost all of Libya's exports and an estimated 33 percent of gross domestic product. The development of the petroleum **industry** over the last three decades has resulted in modernization of the **port** at Benghazi as well as the construction of several oil-exporting facilities along the coast of Cyrenaica.

CYRENAICAN DEFENSE FORCES. The Cyrenaican Defense Forces were largely composed of remnants of the Sanusi Liberation Forces that assisted the Allies in the North African theater during World War II. They were formally established in August 1949 as the defense forces of the newly independent **Cyrenaica**. Trained and equipped by the British, the defense forces emerged at independence in 1951 as the army of King **Idris** I. Members of the Cyrenaican Defense Forces were chosen from the major **tribes** of the **Jabal al-Akhdar** on the basis of loyalty to the monarchy. *See also* ARMED FORCES.

CYRENE. After **Leptis Magna**, Cyrene is generally considered the second most important archeological site in Libya. It is the most splendidly preserved of the five **Greek** cities of **Cyrenaica** known as the Pentapolis. Its buildings were originally modeled after those at Delphi. Apart from the ruins themselves, their location is also noteworthy, as they sit on a bluff overlooking the sea. This ancient city covers a huge area and is still not completely excavated.

Thought to have been founded around 631 B.C., the early history of Cyrene is shrouded in legend. With Barka, Berenice, Tocra, and **Apollonia**, Cyrene was a member of the Pentapolis, a federation of five cities that traded together and shared a common coinage. It eventually became a part of the **Roman** Empire and later suffered serious damage during a **Jewish** revolt in Cyrenaica in A.D. 115. By the fourth century, Cyrene and the other cities of the Pentapolis lay virtually deserted.

– D –

DEBRI, YOUSSEF. The head of the Libyan intelligence services until 1996 when he was replaced by **Musa Kusa**. A colonel in the Libyan **armed forces**, Debri later became head of the Libyan-**Egyptian** production company Al-Shoaa.

DECLARATION OF THE ESTABLISHMENT OF THE PEOPLE'S AUTHORITY. Issued on 2 March 1977, the Declaration of the Establishment of the People's Authority stated that direct popular authority would thereafter be the basis for the Libyan political system. This declaration was not a **constitution**, as some observers suggested, but its central principle relating to people's authority, coupled with other resolutions adopted at the same time, fundamentally revised the governmental organization described in the 1969 **constitutional proclamation**. The March 1977 declaration also changed the official name of the country from Libya to the **Socialist People's**

Libyan Arab Jamahiriya. *Jamahiriya* was a newly coined Arabic word with no official definition, albeit translated unofficially as "people's power" or "state of the masses."

Under the new political system, the people would exercise their authority through **people's committees**, people's congresses, **trade unions** and professional associations, and the **General People's Congress** (GPC). Elections would be direct, with all voting consisting of a show of hands or a division into yes-no camps. Suffrage and committee/congress membership were open to all Libyan citizens 18 years of age or older in good legal and political standing.

Muammar al-Qaddafi was designated general secretary of the GPC, and the remaining members of the now defunct **Revolutionary Command Council** composed the General Secretariat. A General People's Committee was also named to replace the **Council of Ministers**. Its 26 members were designated secretaries instead of ministers.

In theory, the residents of each zone would elect their own people's committee. Similarly, the residents of each branch municipality or municipality would elect their own **Basic People's Congress** (BPC). The members of a BPC would then elect a chairman and a five-member branch or municipal people's committee. The General People's Congress was to consist of the chairmen of the BPCs, the branch and municipal people's committees, and representatives of the people's committees for unions, professional associations, and student unions. *See also* REVOLUTIONARY COMMITTEES.

DERNA, WADI. A drainage system on the **Jabal al-Akhdar** in **Cyrenaica**. The Wadi Derna and the Wadi **al-Cuf** run parallel to the edge of the escarpment in opposite directions away from the high part of the terrace south of Ras el-Hilal. They both turn at right angles and descend to the sea transversely to the escarpments and terraces.

DESERT. While Libya constitutes a part of the **Sahara Desert**, less than 20 percent of the country is covered by sand dunes, notably the Awbari and Murzuk Sand Seas in the **Fezzan** and the Kalanshiyu and Rabyanah Sand Seas in **Cyrenaica**. A much greater part of the country is covered by *hamadah*, an Arabic term designating a flat rocky plain, or *sarir*, flat gravel plain.

In the deserts of Libya, the surfaces of rocks are subject to great extremes of temperature. The processes of heating, cooling, and slow chemical alteration combine to produce granular disintegration and exfoliated peeling, which results in the characteristic aspect of desert weathering. The absence of plant cover in the Libyan Desert both contributes to and accelerates the process of granular disintegration, producing fine sand, which accumulates around detached boulders and at the base of hills.

Winds of high velocity are a common **climatic** phenomenon in the deserts of Libya. Sandstorms lift up and carry sand and dust in sufficient quantities to blacken the sky. Locally, these winds are termed *ghibli*.

DEVELOPMENT PLANS. From the outset, planning was an important ingredient in the Libyan revolutionary government's approach to **economic** development. A three-year plan was announced in 1973, and it was followed by five-year plans beginning in 1976. When compared to the monarchy, the revolutionary government committed to a faster rate of development through higher levels of expenditure. Funding for this accelerated development was insured by the **petroleum** policies of controlled production and increased price followed after 1969.

The development plans of the revolutionary government placed special emphasis on the creation of viable productive sectors in **agriculture** and **industry**. For example, the first five-year plan envisioned an annual increase of 10 percent in gross national output, 25 percent in industrial output, and near self-sufficiency in food production by 1980. More than 15 percent of the **budget** was allocated to agriculture, with industry receiving the second-highest allocation. In the second five-year plan, the allocation for industry was greater than that for agriculture, and self-sufficiency in industrial production also became a key regime goal. Unfortunately, development planning often confused expenditure with implementation, and both the agricultural and industrial sectors experienced difficulty absorbing the target levels of investment. As a result, the quest for self-sufficiency, despite regime propaganda to the contrary, was never fully rewarded with viable accomplishment.

Financial pressures during the decade of the 1980s led Libya to make significant modifications to its earlier development strategy.

The 1981–1985 development plan set the tone for the decade with its wariness toward total dependency upon oil revenues. Emphasizing economic diversity, the plan allocated 17 percent of investment to agriculture and 22 percent to industry. Unfortunately, the decision to move away from a reliance on petroleum came too late to save the 1981–1985 plan, which had to be abandoned in the face of declining oil revenues. As early as 1982, Libya experienced cash flow problems due to oil price reductions and began to scale back development projects. Eventually, the plan was largely suspended, and restrictions were placed on imports. The sharp collapse of oil prices in 1985 exacerbated Libya's economic woes, highlighting the need for a long-term structural adjustment program.

During the 1990s, the economic sanctions imposed by the **United Nations** further disrupted development plans in Libya. Year after year of economic sanctions took a toll on the Libyan economy, increasing unemployment levels and the rate of inflation. While politics played a role, steadily deteriorating economic conditions eventually led Libya to expel hundreds of thousands of expatriate workers. That said, according to an official report issued by the government in mid-2005, Libya had spent around DN51 billion on development projects from 1970 to the end of 2003.

With the lifting of international sanctions in 2003, Libya's approach to development planning changed dramatically. A program of economic liberalization and privatization introduced in 2002 gained momentum in 2003–2005. Central to an understanding of this plan is the goal to increase oil production to 3 million barrels a day by 2015, an objective achievable only if Libya can generate upwards of $30 million in foreign investment by 2010. Libya looks set to achieve its development plans in the hydrocarbons sector; however, the reform process in other areas of the economy is expected to be slower.

DINAR (DN). The unit of currency in Libya since 1 September 1971, when it replaced the Libyan pound. The dinar is divided into 1,000 dirhams.

DJERBA DECLARATION. *See* ARAB ISLAMIC REPUBLIC.

DUWUD. A small, distinctive group of negroid people of unknown origin. Living near the salt lakes of the western **Fezzan**, they subsist mainly on a type of red crayfish.

– E –

ECONOMY. Following the discovery of major **petroleum** and **natural gas** deposits in 1959, the Libyan economy followed an autarkic pattern in which many sectors demonstrated only a limited response to market forces. The economy was further distorted by the economic sanctions progressively imposed first by the **United States** beginning in the mid-1970s and later by the **United Nations** beginning in the early 1990s. At the same time, available data on the economy have long been incomplete and unreliable, further hampering detailed economic analysis. The substantial economic rent derived from hydrocarbon-related production, in particular, limited and distorted the published information.

The Libyan economy since the early 1960s has depended primarily on oil revenues, which contributed practically all export earnings and around one-quarter of the gross domestic product (GDP). Nominal GDP in current dollars was estimated to be $29 billion in 2004; GDP per capita was around $7,000, among the highest in **Africa**. Economic growth strengthened after 2003 with the lifting of UN sanctions and Libya's renunciation of **weapons of mass destruction**. The real growth rate in 2005 was estimated to be 4.3 percent.

Given Libya's heavy dependence on hydrocarbon-related industries, Libyan officials have been especially interested in attracting foreign participation in other economic sectors as part of a broader emphasis on liberalization and privatization. Freed from economic sanctions, foreign direct investment in Libya in 2004 totaled some $4 billion, 20 percent of all investment in Africa and well ahead of fellow oil producers Angola and Nigeria. Libyan oil reserves are currently estimated to exceed 36 billion barrels, with natural gas reserves estimated at 1.31 trillion cubic meters. *See also* AGRICULTURE; BUDGETS; DEVELOPMENT PLANS; EMPLOYMENT; FISHING; INDUSTRY; MINING; SOCIALISM.

EDUCATION. At the outset of the independence era, the **United Kingdom of Libya** offered its citizens limited educational opportunities. Primary schools were few in number, and there were only two secondary schools. A teachers' training school for **women** in **Tripoli** provided the only effective school **health** service in the entire country. At the same time, there were several dozen **Italian** schools and a single **Jewish** school, but for a variety of reasons, these were largely unavailable to Libyan students. The curriculum in Libyan primary schools was based on the **Egyptian** syllabus and included such subjects as Arabic, English, science, geography, history, **religious** studies, and mathematics.

The 1951 **Constitution of Libya** stressed the right of every citizen to education, made elementary education compulsory for children of both sexes, and declared elementary and primary education in public schools to be free. These provisions were the foundation of the modern educational system in Libya, and in moving to enact them, the monarchy made tremendous strides in building schools, training teachers, and teaching students. The first university opened on 15 December 1955 with the founding of the Arts and Education Department at the University of Libya in Benghazi.

School enrollment increased from 34,000 on the eve of independence to around 360,000 at the time of the **One September Revolution** in 1969. Moreover, a growing number of females were attending school by 1969, and the number of available schools had markedly increased. School enrollment had increased to 1.3 million by 1988, and while comparable numbers are not available for 2005, the combination of population growth and rural–urban dislocation has continued to increase school enrollment. A literacy rate estimated to be above 82 percent in 2003 is one indication of progress made since 1951.

Expanding and redirecting the educational policies of the monarchy, the revolutionary government has achieved advances both in the size of the student population and in the number of educational facilities. Education is free at all levels, and university students receive substantial maintenance grants. Moreover, the length of compulsory education has increased to nine years and is now between the ages of 6 and 15 or until completion of the preparatory cycle of secondary school. The geographical distribution of schools has also expanded to bring education within reach of more rural people. Adult education has also been stressed, as has vocational and technical training to develop needed skills in such fields as **agriculture, industry**, and business. Finally, the revolutionary government has largely merged secular and religious education.

Although advances in the provision of education are undeniable, the impact of the revolution on the quality of education is much more difficult to assess. Under the revolutionary government, education in Libya was not a goal in itself but rather a means to create a new kind of citizen. While the speed and direction of such attempts remain unclear, the government's efforts to transform educational institutions and regulate curriculum had far-reaching sociopolitical implications. On university campuses, for example, **revolutionary committees** created in the second half of the 1970s assumed tight control over activities and regularly subjected students returning from study abroad to hostile questioning. Too often, the net result was a poorly motivated student body taught by an uncommitted faculty that was generally anxious and insecure.

In the late 1970s and early 1980s, Libyan students living outside the country organized demonstrations and invasions of Libyan **people's bureaus** abroad. This led the **Muammar al-Qaddafi** regime to recall up to 5,000 students attending Western universities. In 1985, the government also canceled the study grants and travel permits of most students studying outside Libya. At home, students in 1984–1985 participated in demonstrations organized by the **Muslim Brotherhood**, activities that resulted in the arrest and the subsequent execution by hanging of two students. In spring 1986, students at Al-Fateh University organized protests in response to Qaddafi's ongoing campaign to reduce Western influence and increase Arabization, leading to attempts to close the facilities.

In July 1992, the government announced a new round of reforms to its educational system, measures which constituted a redefinition of the role of education in Libya. The 1992 **law** represented a renewed effort by Qaddafi to instill a heightened sense of revolutionary spirit in Libyan students. For example, the law defined the role of Libyan universities as developing citizens with both specialized scientific training and the ideological convictions necessary to perform their obligations to the **Arab** nation and the **jamahiriya**. University students were described as being the vanguard in the awakening of Arab and **Islamic** civilization.

The new law contained no new initiatives in the administration of universities, which have continued to be administered, at least in theory, by popular committees supervised by revolutionary committees. In spite of the financial difficulties experienced by Libya in recent years, education has remained free for all students of Arab nationality. Below the university level, the 1992 law included few reforms, principally in the duration of school cycles, which did little to change the prevailing system. At the lower levels of the educational system, the primary intent of the new law also appeared to be development of a more activist, revolutionary student.

In recent years, there have been indications the politicization of higher education in Libya has resulted in widespread political alienation among university students and other **youth**. Like most revolutionary governments, the Qaddafi regime seeks to nurture and sustain its **economic** and political initiatives. In this regard, grievances in Libya appear to derive primarily from the regime's political and ideological rigidity and only secondarily from general economic uncertainty. At the same time, the student body on most Libyan campuses is divided, consisting of both supporters and **opposition** to the government. In the existing sociopolitical milieu, it is difficult to address fundamental questions relating to the quality or diversity of education or the capability of the system to prepare Libyans to become self-sufficient in the posthydrocarbon era. Consequently, it is hard to assess the actual levels of education or evaluate whether Libyans are being trained in a manner relevant to the country's needs.

EGYPT. In the run-up to Libyan independence, Egypt felt it should have a say in the final disposition of the former **Italian** colony. In a September 1946 memo to the Big Four Powers (**France, Great Britain**, the **Soviet Union**, and the **United States**), Egypt asked to be consulted on the fate of Libya. At the same time, it suggested a plebiscite be conducted to determine whether Libyans preferred independence or union with Egypt. A year later, it submitted a second memorandum to the Big Four Powers asking for a modification of the Egypt-Libya border to return to Egypt border areas it claimed had been usurped during the Italian occupation of Libya.

Following independence, the **Idris** regime followed a pro-Western policy, concluding a variety of air base and other agreements with the major Western powers. At the same time, Egyptian president Gamal Abdul Nasser was following **nationalist**, **Arab unity** policies diametrically opposed to the regional interests of the Western powers. Nasser sought to prevent the Libyan monarchy from granting military facilities to the Western governments, and when it failed to do so, Egypt orchestrated a press campaign against the policies of the Idris government.

In his youth, **Muammar al-Qaddafi** had been strongly influenced by Nasser and the 1952 Egyptian revolution. As a result, the three goals proclaimed by the Qaddafi-led **Revolutionary Command Council** when it seized power from the monarchy on the **One September Revolution** in 1969 were **freedom, socialism**, and unity— the same three goals Nasser had proclaimed at the outset of the Egyptian revolution. Like Nasser, Qaddafi based his variant of Arab **nationalism** on a glorification of Arab history and culture that viewed the Arabic-speaking world as the Arab nation.

At his first press conference in February 1970, Qaddafi produced a formula for Arab union; thereafter, he proclaimed the unification of Arab governments into a single state as an absolute necessity. Initially, his approach to Arab unity focused eastward on the pan-Arab core. Apart from his admiration for Nasser, Qaddafi saw Egypt as the essential nucleus for an Arab union.

At the conclusion of an Arab summit meeting in Morocco in December 1969, the heads of state of Egypt, Libya, and **Sudan** moved their discussions to **Tripoli**. Further talks resulted in a tripartite agreement known as the **Tripoli Charter**, which established a supreme planning committee and a common security system. Less than a year later, in November 1970, the heads of state—with Egypt now represented by Anwar al-Sadat six weeks after President Nasser had died of a heart attack—met again in Cairo, where they formed a tripartite federal union. Syria later joined the federal plan, and in April 1971 the governments of Egypt, Libya, and Syria announced the formation of a tripartite federation known as the **Federation of Arab Republics** (FAR). In contrast to the Tripoli Charter, the FAR established a political union at the outset. The constitution of the new federation stated that the union of the three Arab republics would have one flag, one capital, and one socialist, democratic political system.

In a confidential memo to President Sadat, Qaddafi in February 1972 proposed an immediate and total union between their two countries. When the latter failed to respond, Qaddafi repeated his proposal in a public statement six months later. Sadat traveled to Libya, and on 2 August 1972, in the so-called **Benghazi Declaration**, Egypt and Libya announced plans to merge their respective states before 1 September 1973.

On the surface, union offered both Egypt and Libya tangible **economic** and political benefits. Nevertheless, the two states gradually moved apart after the August 1972 agreement. Union discussions proceeded at a slow pace and were eventually overtaken by political events. In February 1973, a Libyan plane violated Sinai airspace and was downed by **Israeli** fighter planes, resulting in more than 100 deaths. Qaddafi blamed Sadat for not intervening and orchestrated anti-Egyptian demonstrations in Libya. The Egyptian consulate in **Benghazi** was attacked, and Egyptian citizens working in Libya were branded a fifth column. In June, Qaddafi arrived in Cairo for an unscheduled visit, during which he was sharply critical of Egyptian society. He next organized a 20,000-vehicle motorcade to drive from the Libya-**Tunisia** border to Cairo in support of immediate union with Egypt. This so-called **Green March**, the first public manifestation in Libya of the new governing concept of the masses, proved to be the last official attempt to export the revolution to Egypt. Egyptian authorities stopped the motorcade at the border and shelved plans for a merger.

Sadat's assassination later offered the potential for improved relations with Egypt, but Qaddafi's radical foreign policies soon torpedoed this prospect, and his relations with President Hosni Mubarak were no better. In March 1983, Libya called for Egypt's suspension from the **nonaligned movement**; and in January 1984, Libya openly resisted the readmission of Egypt to the Organization of the Islamic Conference. In the coming months, Libya was implicated in a plot to deploy mines in the Red Sea, a Libyan pilot claimed his government had plans to bomb the Aswan Dam, and Egypt foiled a Libyan plot to assassinate a former Libyan prime minister. In autumn 1985, Libya suddenly expelled tens of thousands of Egyptian workers, an act that Mubarak labeled inhumane.

Libyan-Egyptian relations later improved in the early 1990s after President Mubarak attended a ceremony in Libya marking the conclusion of the first phase of the **Great Manmade River** project. A few weeks earlier, Mubarak had decreed that all obstacles to free movement between the countries should be removed. Almost immediately, daily cross-border traffic surged to a level of some 10,000 people.

The thaw in bilateral relations was accelerated by Libya's balanced response to the Iraqi invasion of Kuwait, which was viewed in Tripoli more as a crime against the Arabs than a Western plot to punish Iraq. Egypt seized the opportunity to convince its Western allies that increased ties with Libya would moderate Qaddafi's behavior. Egyptian officials also hoped their influence on Libya might help rehabilitate the Qaddafi regime in the eyes of the West, where Qaddafi remained an anathema.

In January 1994, Egypt warned Libya against infringing on Egyptian sovereignty following the disappearance in Cairo of the Libyan dissident, **Mansour Kikhia**. And in 1996 and after, efforts by the United States and the **United Nations** to tighten sanctions against Libya led to uncertain but periodic restrictions on cross-border trade. With the lifting of UN sanctions in 2003, Egyptian-Libyan cooperation steadily increased, and bilateral talks between Qaddafi and Mubarak became commonplace. Among other topics, the two neighbors focused on finding a regional solution to the crisis in Sudan's Darfur province. *See also* FOREIGN POLICY.

ELECTRICITY. Libya lacks coal, wood, and hydroelectric resources but has sizable hydrocarbon reserves. Therefore, most of its electrical energy is produced by thermally generated plants fired by **natural gas** or **petroleum**. Small diesel plants often provide electricity in isolated areas, but they are relatively uneconomical and have been replaced where practical by larger gas-fueled plants.

Despite its abundant hydrocarbon reserves, the revolutionary government also pursued the acquisition of nuclear power generating plants. In 1975, the **Soviet Union** agreed to provide Libya with its first nuclear reactor, a 10-megawatt research facility. Three years later, Moscow also agreed to build a combined nuclear power plant and research center with a capacity of 300 megawatts. The two governments later discussed expanding their nuclear cooperation to include a power station with two 400-megawatt units. In 1985, the Soviets agreed to help Libya build a nuclear reactor with the understanding it would not be convertible to military uses. Two decades later, the French government in June 2005 announced it was prepared to respond favorably to Libyan requests for nuclear technology transfers. At the same time, French officials hastened to add that a nuclear program with Libya would be open to inspection by the International Atomic Energy Agency. *See also* DEVELOPMENT PLANS.

EMPLOYMENT. The heavy flow of urban migration after independence, combined with the **petroleum** wealth that rapidly transformed Libya from a country having one of the lowest per-capita incomes to one of the richest nations in the world, drastically changed traditional Libyan employment patterns. By the mid-1970s, almost half the economically active population was employed in either public administration or the construction **industry**. In turn, the **agricultural** sector, which had occupied more than half of the country's workers before independence, dropped to less than a 20 percent share. Of the urban workers not employed in public administration or construction, a large majority were working in service sector occupations, many of which were connected to the petroleum sector.

As a result, unemployment in Libya virtually ceased to exist. Any able-bodied male could find a job, and many applicants became increasingly selective about the type of work they were willing to accept, especially if they possessed specialized skills or training. Agricultural labor, in particular, was hard to find, and wage rates became so high that few farmers could afford to hire help.

As the Libyan labor market tightened, expatriate workers, many of them from nearby **Arab** countries, flowed into Libya in search of jobs. Where there had been only 17,000 such workers in 1964, the total rose to 223,000 by 1975 and continued to grow into the next decade. Most foreign workers entered Libya under contract for specific periods of time, and they were not permitted to change jobs without first returning home to sign a new agreement. To attract skilled labor, the revolutionary government offered liberal allowances and customs exemptions in addition to travel costs and social benefits similar to those available to Libyan citizens. Employment preference was given to people from neighboring Arab states, followed by the citizens of other Muslim nations.

The social impact of the presence of a large alien population was minimal. Expatriate workers generally adjusted well to the rather austere living conditions of revolutionary Libya, while the Libyan people mostly remained aloof from them. Their political significance, on the other hand, was less predictable, as the government occasionally used workers from neighboring states as political pawns in support of its **foreign policy** objectives.

In late 1995, for example, Libya asked the **United Nations** for permission to repatriate more than 1,000,000 **African** workers. Libya cited the poor state of the Libyan **economy** in support of its request, but some observers viewed the policy as a means to protest against the economic sanctions imposed by the United Nations. At the same time, the economic slowdowns that periodically plagued Libya have been a legitimate cause for occasional reductions in the foreign workforce.

With the lifting of UN sanctions in 2003 and the moves toward liberalization and privatization after 2003, Libya has grappled with a growing unemployment problem. Official estimates in 2005 indicate that 13 percent of Libyans are unemployed, but unofficial estimates put the number of unemployed and underemployed at a much higher level. In addressing this problem, the assistant secretary for services in the General People's Committee, **Maatuq Mohammed Maatuq**, in March 2005 cautioned foreign companies that Libyan **law** requires all jobs not demanding special skills—such as drivers, guards, and maintenance workers—should go to Libyan citizens. In addition, he reminded them that Libyan nationals should have the same treatment as foreign workers with regard to wages, **health** insurance, and other benefits.

ENEMIES OF GOD GROUP. One of many small domestic groups that periodically surface in **opposition** to the **Qaddafi** regime.

ENI. ENI SpA is one of **Italy**'s largest companies, operating in the **petroleum** and **natural gas**, petrochemicals, and oil field services industries. Its wholly owned subsidiary **Agip** has long been a major oil producer in Libya.

ETHIOPIA. Ethiopia is located in eastern central **Africa** just above the equator. It is bounded on the north and west by **Sudan**, on the east by the Red Sea and Djibouti, on the southeast by Somalia, and on the south by Kenya.

The modern history of Ethiopia can be loosely divided into three distinct periods. During the first period (1941–1974), the country was ruled by Emperor Haile Selassie I, who controlled a patrimonial, feudal system. Dependent on the British government, which had returned him to power in 1941 after the defeat of the **Italians**, the Haile Selassie regime pursued largely pro-Western policies. As British power in the region declined, Haile Selassie turned increasingly to the **United States** for aid and support. After concluding a military agreement granting land facilities in return for military hardware and training, the United States became the main supplier of arms and economic assistance to Ethiopia.

During this first period, the Ethiopian government was generally viewed by Libya as an anti-**Arab** and anti-Muslim state serving as a Western base on the African continent. Consequently, Libya extended its full support to the Eritrean Liberation Front (ELF) in its struggle against the Haile Selassie regime. In addition to opening an ELF office in **Tripoli**, Libya extended economic and military aid and also solicited support for the ELF from other Arab and Muslim countries. Furthermore, Libya expressed its displeasure with the regime by backing Somalia in its dispute with Ethiopia over the Ogaden region. In early 1973, Libya even called for the **Organization of African Unity** to move its headquarters from the Ethiopian capital to Cairo because of Ethiopia's diplomatic ties with **Israel**; however, Libya withdrew this request later in the year after Ethiopia broke diplomatic relations with the **Jewish** state.

Failing to deal with Eritrean and Somali secessionist movements and the country's chronic underdevelopment, Emperor Haile Selassie was deposed in 1974, and Ethiopia entered a second period of political change. From September 1974 to February 1977, a military council known as the Dergue ruled the country. The Dergue was initially headed by General Aman, a moderate officer and politician who was widely considered a friend of the United States. Although Aman was later assassinated after resigning from office, his successors maintained generally good relations with the United States, in large part because of their dependence on U.S. military supplies. At the same time, the military council demonstrated a desire to improve diplomatic relations with the Arab countries and to support their cause against Israel. As a consequence, Libya approached the new regime with a more positive attitude, although it did not give up its support for the Eritrean people. Libya was especially critical of Ethiopian arms deals with the United States, accusing the military council of preparing to launch attacks on both Eritrea and Sudan.

The third period in contemporary Ethiopian political history opened in February 1977 when Lt. Col. Mengistu Haile Mariam came to power. His regime took more of an anti-Western approach than had its predecessors, denouncing the United States and making it clear that Ethiopia was no longer an American ally in the region. Mengistu allied Ethiopia with the **Soviet Union** and increasingly pursued Marxist-Leninist policies at home. At the same time, the Ethiopian government continued to struggle with the problems of uniting the country, as well as with a variety of regional issues, including the rebellion in Sudan.

Libya sent an official delegation to Ethiopia in June 1977, and several cooperative agreements were signed by the two countries. Thereafter, Libyan policy toward Ethiopia was generally characterized by a high level of support and collaboration. Cooperation between the two states reached a peak in 1981 when Libya and Ethiopia joined South Yemen in concluding a treaty of friendship and cooperation. At the time, the signatories stated in a joint communiqué that they intended to be a material force against any form of conspiracy or imperialist aggression that might threaten the peoples of their three states. *See also* FOREIGN POLICY.

EUESPERIDES. An ancient **Greek** city located on the outskirts of modern-day **Benghazi**, Euesperides did not figure large in history. It was first mentioned in 515 B.C. in connection with the revolt of Barca from the Persians, when a punitive expedition was sent by the satrap in **Egypt** and marched as far west as Euesperides. The settlement was subjected to sporadic attacks from Libyan **tribes** in the Syrtic region over the next two to three centuries, and around 405 B.C., more settlers came from Naupactus, in part to complement and supplement a population devastated by ongoing conflict. The earliest site of the city seems to have been in the north, in the slightly higher ground, but the earliest levels probably do not predate the mid-sixth century B.C. The lower city and the walls were laid out between 375 and 350 B.C., and there was more building in the area between 350 and 325 B.C. Occupation of the city apparently dropped after approximately 275 B.C. In the latter fourth century, Euesperides backed the losing side in the revolt led by Thibron, a Spartan adventurer who was defeated by **Cyrene** in alliance with Libyan tribes. Extensive archaeological excavations have been conducted at Euesperides, especially by the Ashmolean Museum at Oxford University.

EUROPEAN UNION (EU). In the early 1990s, the member states of the European Union reassessed their approach to the Mediterranean region, electing to expand and reform their relations with the Mediterranean countries. In November 1995, the 15 EU governments joined 12 North **African** and Middle Eastern governments to sign the Barcelona Declaration of the Euro-Mediterranean Partnership. The declaration, which aimed to establish a Mediterranean Free Trade Area (MEFTA) by 2010, invited cooperation in a broad range of political, social, and **economic** areas. Because Libya was under **United Nations** sanctions at the time, however, it was not invited to join in the Barcelona process.

Once the **Lockerbie incident** suspects were remanded into custody and the UN suspended its sanctions in April 1999, Libya moved quickly to strengthen diplomatic and commercial ties with key European states. The EU encouraged the Libyan initiatives, announcing in spring 1999 its intention to reassess Libyan participation in the regional Barcelona process; Libya was granted observer status for the first time at the April 1999 Euro-Mediterranean conference, returning again in 2001. In September 1999, the EU lifted most of its remaining sanctions on Libya, retaining only an arms embargo.

Libya later embraced the principles of the Barcelona Declaration —including commitments to democracy, regional stability, market economies, and free **trade**—without formally committing to the declaration itself. In so doing, Libya announced it believed **Israel** and the Palestinian Authority should be excluded from the 27-nation partnership until they reached a final peace agreement. EU officials responded in January 2000 that it was unacceptable for Libya to make its agreement to the Barcelona process contingent on a resolution of the Israeli-Palestinian dispute. Libyan authorities later confirmed **Tripoli**'s ongoing interest in participating in the Barcelona process, but stated Libya was unable at the time to make a formal commitment to the Barcelona Declaration. Libyan leader **Muammar al-Qaddafi**'s reluctance to become an active member in a Euro-Mediterranean partnership, when combined with his mentoring efforts in **Africa**, evidenced a Libyan desire to play the role of intermediary between Africa and Europe, a new objective for Libyan **foreign policy**.

Commercially, the EU in the 1990s attracted 85 percent of all Libyan exports, with **Germany**, **Italy**, and Spain collectively absorbing 80 percent of this total. The EU also provided 75 percent of Libyan imports, with Germany and Italy being the major players and **Great Britain** also a significant exporter. In non**petroleum** sectors, European companies also enjoyed the bulk of contracts, although Turkish companies dominated in construction and South Korean firms in **water resource** management. In October 2004, the EU finally ended 12 years of sanctions against Libya and also eased the arms embargo.

Libya's future with the European Union remains uncertain. It is the only country in the southern Mediterranean not to have signed the Association Agreement, and most EU member states would welcome its active participation. One obstacle is Israel, which is a founding member of the Barcelona process. If Libya were to join, it would have to recognize to some degree the existence of the state of Israel and sit on the same committees and working groups with Israelis. With this and other issues to resolve, Libya looks content for the time being to remain a passive observer in the Barcelona process, limiting its participation to attending foreign affairs ministerial meetings, high-level political dialogue gatherings, and the Euro-Mediterranean committee.

EVACUATION DAY. National holiday celebrating the evacuation of British forces from Libyan soil on 28 March 1970. *See also* ADEM BASE, AL-.

EXPLORATION AND PRODUCTION-SHARING AGREEMENT (EPSA). After the **Revolutionary Command Council** (RCC)

nationalized the **petroleum industry** in 1973, it converted the existing concessionary agreements into exploration and production-sharing agreements. Under the terms of EPSA-1, introduced in 1974, the oil companies were given five years for exploration, after which the award expired if no oil was found; if the companies located oil, they were given rights for 30 years of production. Onshore production was shared, with the government taking 85 percent and the oil company 15 percent. The split for offshore production was 81–19 in the government's favor.

The terms for EPSA-2, introduced in 1980, were similar to EPSA-1, with the important difference that the sharing pattern now varied according to the prospects of the acreage. The **National Oil Company** (NOC) retained the 85–15 split for top-category concessions, but dropped it to 81–19 for medium-category concessions and 75–25 for less promising areas.

After the **United States** ordered all American oil companies and personnel out of Libya in 1986, Libya relaxed the terms of its exploration and production-sharing agreements in an effort to attract oil companies not then working in the country. Introduced in 1988, the terms of EPSA-3 again varied with the prospects of the acreage, ranging from 70–30 in NOC's favor for acreage in the first-class category to 65–35 for second-class acreage. The Libyan government was successful in this phase in assigning exploration blocks to oil companies new to Libya, such as the Romanian State Oil Company, Rompetrol, and **Bulgaria**'s Geocom; nevertheless, almost no new crude oil deposits were discovered over the next 16 years.

Once the **United Nations** had lifted its economic **sanctions** and the **Muammar al-Qaddafi** regime had renounced **weapons of mass destruction**, Libya announced a new round of exploration and production-sharing agreements in support of its long-term objective to increase oil production to 3 million barrels a day by 2015. Launched in August 2004, the first round of EPSA-4 offered 58 blocks in nine onshore and six offshore exploration areas for open, competitive bidding. With only small amounts of oil discovered in Libya in the 1974–2004 period, international interest in the new blocks was high; 122 companies registered to bid, and 63 were eventually approved to bid. When the results were announced on 29 January 2005, U.S. oil companies were the big winners, with Occidental Petroleum involved in 9 of the 15 exploration areas and Chevron Texaco and Amerada Hess each picking up one area. The other four went to Algeria's Sonatrach, Petrobras of Brazil, Verenex Energy of Canada, and Oil India.

The first round of EPSA-4 was followed by a second round in fall 2005, in which the number of exploration areas increased from 15 to 26. When the results were announced in October 2005, ExxonMobil was the only American firm to win acreage. **Italy**'s **ENI** took four areas, Japan's Mitsubishi Oil took four, and **Great Britain**'s BG Group took three alone or in association with others. The remaining eight areas were awarded to a variety of Asian and European firms. *See also* SEVENTH NOVEMBER ZONE.

– F –

FAREGH (AL-FARIGH), WADI AL-. The principal drainage system in the Sirte area of **Cyrenaica** on the western border with **Tripolitania**. Flowing westward, the Wadi al-Faregh discharges into the great depression of Sabkhat Kurkurah south of Marsa al-Brega and southeast of Al-Agheila. With the exception of the Wadi al-Faregh and a few other limited exposures in the small depression, there are no rock outcrops in this region.

FATEH REVOLUTION, AL-. *See* ONE SEPTEMBER REVOLUTION.

FEDERAL PROCESSION. *See* FEDERATION OF ARAB REPUBLICS.

FEDERATION OF ARAB REPUBLICS (FAR). Less than a year after the conclusion of the **Tripoli Charter**, the heads of state of Libya, **Egypt**, and **Sudan** met in Cairo on 8 November 1970 to form a tripartite federal union. At its own initiative, Syria joined the federal plan on 27 November, and on 17 April 1971, Egypt, Libya, and Syria announced the formation of a tripartite federation; pleading internal political problems, the Sudanese government did not immediately accede, but the way was left open for its later membership.

FAR statutes placed it somewhere between a federal and confederal system. The new structure was directed to lay the groundwork for a common **foreign policy** and a combined military command, but the member states retained their own diplomatic relations with outside states and their own **armed forces**. A council of the three state presidents, each of whom would serve a two-year term as federation president, was to be the supreme authority. At the outset, this supreme body of three was designed to function on the basis of a majority vote; however, Egyptian concern that this would lead to its domination by the more radical policies of Libya and Syria led to this being changed to the principle of unanimous vote. The statutes also created a federal parliament composed of an equal number of representatives from each member state and entrusted with federal legislative functions. Until such time as a single political structure was established, each state remained responsible for organizing its own political activity; nevertheless, political groups in one state were prohibited from operating in another state except through the officially recognized political front command.

Over the next two years, Libya unsuccessfully pressured Sudan to join the new organization. In the interim, the momentum for Arab **unity** stalled as the organizational shortcomings of the federation and the policy conflicts of its constituent parts became increasingly evident. The heads of state of the member governments signed the draft constitution of the federation in August 1971, and the document received the customary near-unanimous approval of the electorates of the individual states on 1 September. Egyptian president Anwar al-Sadat was named the first president of the presidential council in October, and after a federal cabinet was formed, the new federative entity was declared officially in existence on 1 January 1972. Thereafter, the newly created federal structures worked closely with the constituent governments to initiate a series of gradual measures that would slowly amend existing rules and regulations to promote Arab unity through increased individual interchange.

Muammar al-Qaddafi soon became frustrated with the slow progress being made toward Arab unity, however, and in February 1972, he proposed to Sadat immediate, total unity. When the Egyptian president failed to respond, the Libyan leader continued to repeat his proposal. At the beginning of August, Sadat traveled to **Benghazi**

where he found Qaddafi ready for immediate union. While Sadat preferred a more gradual approach, on 2 August 1972 he signed the **Benghazi Declaration**, by which Egypt and Libya agreed to merge on or before 1 September 1973.

FEKINI, MUHIADDIN (1923–). Prime minister of the **United Kingdom of Libya** from March 1963 to January 1964. Muhiaddin Fekini, who earned a doctor of jurisprudence degree from the University of Paris, possessed an unusually wide range of domestic and **foreign policy** experience. He was president of the **Tripolitanian** Executive Council and later minister of justice for a brief period in 1956, ambassador to **Egypt** in the 1950s, and ambassador to the **United States** and to the **United Nations** concurrently in 1960–1963. A Westernized, intellectual politician, Americans often compared Fekini with Adlai Stevenson. During his tenure, the Libyan government changed from a federal to a unitary system. His administration also gave **women** the right to vote. On 22 January 1964 demonstrations in support of the Palestinian cause broke out in a number of Libyan cities; the demonstrations left several Libyan students injured and eventually led to Fekini's resignation. *See also* IDRIS AL-MAHDI AL-SANUSI, SAYYID MUHAMMAD.

FEZZAN (FAZZAN). One of Libya's three historic regions. Covering an area of approximately 475,000 square kilometers (184,000 square miles), it is located in the southwestern part of the country. Geographically, it is a great topographic basin in the northern **Sahara Desert** that is largely covered by the Awbari Sand Sea in the north and the Murzuk Sand Sea in the south. The average elevation of Fezzan is less than 460 meters (1,500 feet) above sea level compared to the average elevation of the surrounding **desert**, which is about 1,000 meters (3,300 feet).

Since ancient times, Fezzan has been tied commercially, **religiously**, and politically to what the **Arabs** used to call Bilad al-Sudan, an area stretching from West **Africa** to the Nilotic **Sudan**. Many of the great **trade** routes from central Africa to the Mediterranean coast passed through Fezzan. Murzuk, a walled oasis town and capital of the region, became one of the major trading posts of the Saharan trade with the Mediterranean. The

Bornu–Kawar–Fezzan–**Tripoli** and the Kano–Air–Ghat–**Ghadames** –Tripoli trade routes, both of which operated until the mid-19th century, crossed Fezzan. A third trade route, Wadai to Al-Kufrah to **Benghazi**, functioned into the early 20th century, largely because it was used by members of the **Sanusi Order** to propagate their faith. The wealth of Fezzan lay in its oasis entrepôts for the caravan trade.

The historic ties of Fezzan, and to some extent **Cyrenaica** as well, with the territories now constituting the Republic of **Chad** strengthened in the late 19th century. **Sayyid Muhammad bin Ali al-Sanusi** established the Sanusi Order in Cyrenaica in 1842 and later spread his revivalist movement south to Chad, where he built a strong and enthusiastic following. In Wadai, Sultan Muhammad Sharif and his successors, Ali and Yusuf, became followers of the Sanusi Order. By 1899, the Sanusi had established a headquarters in Gouro, Chad, where there were 10 lodges, compared to 15 in the Fezzan.

Fezzan, as well as Cyrenaica, also has strong historic ties to what is today the Democratic Republic of Sudan. A 17th-century manuscript on Fezzan traces those relations back to the end of the 16th century, when **tribes** from Fezzan sought refuge in Sudan to escape **Ottoman** persecution. It would appear that Sudanese tribesmen later joined these refugees from Fezzan in raiding Ottoman forces in Fezzan. As a result, the ties of Fezzan to Chad and Sudan, together with the northern parts of Mali and Niger, are at least as old as those of Cyrenaica to **Egypt** and **Tripolitania** to **Tunisia**.

Contemporary Fezzan remains a vast but largely uninhabited area of varied desert terrain. A population of less than 500,000 people is largely concentrated along the various wadi systems. While most parts of Fezzan are covered by large areas of sand seas, many of the wadi areas include small **agricultural** projects fed by underground **water resources**. Lovers of the desert will find the Fezzan area offers some of the best scenery and experiences found anywhere in the Sahara. There are picturesque landscapes in abundance, with unique rock formations and some of the best prehistoric art to be found in Africa. The **tourism** potential of this part of Libya is fantastic, and the infrastructure necessary for tourism is being developed.

FISHING. Libyan coastal waters in the Mediterranean Sea and Gulf of **Sidra** contain relatively large sponge beds as well as fishing grounds that include tuna, sardines, and red mullet. With some 1,600 kilometers (1,000 miles) of coastline and access to the **Libya-Tunisia continental shelf**—second-largest in the Mediterranean—Libya would thus appear to have every opportunity for a productive fishing industry. Nevertheless, there was relatively little indigenous fishing along the coast until very recently. A variety of factors, including coastal waters noted for frequent storms, a lack of natural harbors, the absence of a seafaring tradition, indifference to fish consumption, and a small and scattered population, contributed to this situation.

During the period of **Italian** occupation, substantial efforts were made to exploit the resources of Libyan waters. As early as 1912, boats from Naples undertook fishing trials off **Tripoli** and Italian interests conducted an inconclusive survey of Libyan fishing prospects. Additional survey work was conducted in 1923 and 1927. Throughout the period, the Italian government attempted to regulate and control the exploitation of offshore resources. After 1921, an attempt was made to cultivate pearls in Libyan coastal waters; however, it never progressed beyond the experimental stage. On the other hand, both tuna fishing and sponge fishing reached their peak production in the interwar era.

Under the monarchy, the fishing **industry** received little emphasis; fishing methods remained primitive, with processing plants generally poorly equipped and confined to the **Tripolitanian** coast. This situation changed after 1969 as the revolutionary government viewed an expanded fishing industry as an integral part of its **economic** diversification policies. Determined to elevate the industry to an optimum level, the government improved **port** facilities at Homs, **Tripoli**, and Zanzur and constructed refrigeration facilities at Sirte, Tobruk, Derna, Marsa Susa, Ayn al-Ghazalah, and Marsa Sabratah. Later, a modern fisheries complex was constructed at Zuwarah. Finally, joint venture companies with foreign partners—from Benin, Guinea, **Malta**, Mauritania, South Yemen, Spain, and elsewhere—were founded to encourage more efficient fishing in deeper waters. The Libyan government remains committed to a policy of fisheries expansion; however, the fishing industry has suffered, like most sectors of the economy, from the occasional decline in **petroleum** revenues.

FOREIGN POLICY. After World War II, two rival systems, the Middle Eastern and the **Arab**, struggled for dominance in the Middle

East and North Africa. The **United States**, backed by NATO, was the architect of the Middle Eastern system. Preoccupied with the Soviet threat, this group largely viewed the region in geographic terms and expected the Arab states to join a security alliance. In contrast, the Arab system viewed the area not as a geographic expanse between Europe and Asia, but as one nation with common interests and security priorities distinct from those of the West; in place of the **Soviet Union**, the Arab view saw **Israel** as the central threat.

The **United Kingdom of Libya**, under the leadership of King **Idris** I, cooperated with the Middle Eastern system and limited its participation in the Arab system. Supporting selected Arab causes such as the Algerian independence movement, the monarchy took little active part in the Arab-Israeli dispute or in the tumultuous inter-Arab politics of the 1950s and 1960s. As a result, Libya came under growing criticism from key members of the Arab system, especially the government of **Egyptian** president Gamal Abdul Nasser.

In this context, 1967 proved a pivotal year for the monarchy, as the nature and extent of the Six-Day War was the catalyst for the September 1969 coup d'état. Popular reaction in Libya to the June 1967 conflict was widespread and violent, and the prime minister was forced to resign on the grounds that Libya had not done enough to assist its Arab brethren in the Arab-Israeli conflict. In response, the Idris regime made some token gestures toward the Arab system but sought to retain its **nonaligned** orientation.

On 1 September 1969, the **Libyan Free Unionist Officers**, under the leadership of **Muammar al-Qaddafi**, overthrew the monarchy and established a revolutionary government. Where the monarchy had carefully limited its participation in the pan-Arab movement while accommodating to and cooperating with the NATO allies, Qaddafi quickly moved Libya into a close association with the Arab system. For him, the concept of the Arab nation was an ideological bond joining a people with a common cultural history and a faith in their destiny as equal to any other race on Earth.

From the outset of the **One September Revolution**, Qaddafi was a strong advocate of Arab **unity**. At his first press conference in February 1970, he produced a formula for a united Arab politics; thereafter, he considered the unification of Arab governments into a single state an absolute necessity. Over the next two decades, he persisted in pursuing practical attempts at Arab unity even after the idea was widely discredited elsewhere in the Arab world. In 1969–1974, for example, he engaged in union discussions with Egypt (twice), Syria, **Sudan**, and **Tunisia** (twice).

After 1974, Qaddafi continued to discuss Arab unity but more as a long-term goal than an immediately achievable objective. By this time, Qaddafi appeared to recognize more clearly the rivalries and divisions in the path of Arab unity, even though he did not forgo his dream of union. In 1980, Libya and Syria proclaimed a merger, declaring their intent to form a unified government, and in 1984 Libya and **Morocco** announced a federation, known as the **Arab-African Union**. Five years later, Libya joined Algeria, Mauritania, Morocco, and Tunisia in the **Arab Maghrib Union**.

Thereafter, Qaddafi gradually shifted the focus of Libyan foreign policy from the Arab world to **Africa**. In the 1970s, sub-Saharan Africa had been the scene of intense Libyan diplomatic activity aimed at supplanting Israeli influence; however, by the early 1980s, Libya's involvement in **Chad** had raised concerns that success there would lead to Libyan intervention elsewhere in Africa. Qaddafi maintained his ties to Africa during the period of the **United Nations** embargo, and in 1999, when sanctions were suspended, he launched a series of initiatives. Focused on Africa to the virtual exclusion of the Middle East, he proposed a United States of Africa in 1999 and was accorded a prominent speaking role at the opening ceremonies of the **African Union** in 2002.

A third dimension to Libyan foreign policy under Qaddafi, in addition to its emphasis on the Middle East and Africa, involved the Libyan leader's support for **jihad**, which became the action element of his variant of Arab **nationalism**. Broadening and distorting the traditional concept of jihad, Qaddafi saw it as the means to achieve social justice around the world. Jihad found its most practical expression in support for the Palestinian cause; however, Qaddafi's approach led him to support a wide variety of other "liberation movements," including the Irish Republican Army and **Moro National Liberation Front**.

Diplomatic relations with the United States quickly deteriorated after the 1969 revolution and were seriously strained after 1979 when Libya failed to protect the U.S. embassy in Tripoli as it was stormed by Libyan students. During the 1980s, the Ronald Reagan administration increased diplomatic, economic, and military pressure on Libya, unfairly depicting Qaddafi as a Soviet puppet and branding him an international menace. Throughout the 1990s, the Qaddafi regime attempted to reestablish relations with the United States, but it was unable to do so until the **Lockerbie incident** was settled and Libya renounced **weapons of mass destruction**.

Libya enjoys a wide range of commercial and diplomatic ties with key European states, including **France**, **Germany**, **Great Britain**, **Italy**, and **Russia**. In recent years, members of the **European Union** have purchased around 85 percent of Libyan exports and supplied some 75 percent of Libyan imports. The EU has invited Libya to join the Euro-Mediterranean partnership, but to date Libya has elected to remain an observer to the Barcelona process.

Libya in 1951 was the first state to be created by the UN General Assembly, but it was not until the early 1990s that the United Nations again played a central role in Libyan diplomacy. In January 1992, UN Security Council Resolution 731 condemned the destruction of Pan Am flight 103 and UTA flight 772 and called on Libya to remand the suspects in the Lockerbie bombing, disclose all it knew about the bombings, cease its support for **terrorism**, and pay appropriate compensation. When Libya did not respond, the United Nations imposed mandatory sanctions. The UN sanctions were suspended in 1999 after the Qaddafi regime remanded the two Libyan suspects into custody and were finally lifted in 2003 after Libya compensated the families of the victims of the attacks. In February 2000, Libya contributed officers to a UN peacekeeping mission for the first time in a decade. In January 2003, it was elected chairman of the UN Commission on **Human Rights**.

In addition to the United Nations and the international bodies already cited, contemporary Libyan foreign policy includes active cooperation with a number of other **international organizations**, from the International Atomic Energy Agency to the International Monetary Fund to the **Organization of Petroleum Exporting Countries**.

FRANCE. During the late **Ottoman Empire** period, several major European powers—France in particular—expressed interest in Libya both as a **frontier** district and transit region. At the time, the paramount interest of France was in the protection of the **African** colonies it governed. In May 1910, a Franco-Turkish agreement concerning the Libya-**Tunisia** border was concluded, but demarcation operations were soon interrupted, first by the start of the **Italian** occupation and later by World War I. Following the Italian invasion, French forces in November 1911 occupied the oasis of Janet, located in southwestern Libya. While French aims were not clear, it would appear France planned to encroach progressively upon Libya's borders to the point that much, if not all, of Libya would be annexed.

The southern border of Libya, because of the diverse interests concerned, was the most hotly disputed region. Local chiefs and Sanusi **religious** leaders joined French and Ottoman forces in a fierce struggle for commercial and political influence and control. The **Sanusi Order** had begun to penetrate into central Africa in the second half of the 19th century, and as the number of its followers expanded, their political influence in the region increased dramatically. At the same time, France was increasingly aggressive in its penetration of Equatorial Africa. French efforts in this regard received an additional stimulus at the end of the century when France and **Great Britain** concluded a treaty in March 1899 that in effect divided the region between them, leaving France free to proceed north of Lake **Chad**. In the early 20th century, the Ottoman administration attempted to establish itself on the ground in southern Libya, but the available resources proved inadequate to protect Ottoman interests for an extended period of time.

France and the **United Kingdom of Libya** negotiated a friendship treaty not long after Libya's independence, resulting in the **Franco-Libyan Agreement** of 10 August 1955. With the conclusion of the Algerian War in 1962, the French government achieved a remarkable postcolonial recovery in most of Africa and the Middle East. By February 1970, for example, Egyptian president Gamal Abdul Nasser could comment that France was the only Western power with a Middle Eastern policy free of imperialist ambitions and thus acceptable to **Arab** states. An early turning point in Franco-Libyan relations came in January 1970 when Paris agreed to sell the revolutionary government 110 Mirage fighter aircraft. Both signatories viewed the agreement, the largest French armaments sale in history to that date, as a major **economic** and diplomatic coup.

Over the next few years, France continued to make diplomatic and commercial gains in Libya. In 1974, for example, the two states concluded an agreement in which Libya exchanged **petroleum** supply guarantees for technical assistance and financial cooperation. Thereafter, diplomatic relations between Libya and France began to deteriorate. **Muammar al-Qaddafi** increasingly criticized French willingness to sell arms to both sides in the Middle East conflict; and as Libyan relations with **Egypt** soured, he also criticized the sale of French weapons to the government in Cairo. A more fundamental and serious source of disagreement was Libya's increasingly aggressive policies in sub-Saharan Africa, a traditional sphere of French influence.

Diplomatic relations between Libya and France later improved for a time in the early 1990s. France credited Qaddafi with assisting in the April 1990 release of three European hostages taken prisoner more than two years earlier by a Libyan-backed **terrorist** group. Orchestrated by Qaddafi, ostensibly as a humanitarian gesture, their freedom coincided with the delivery to Libya of three Mirage fighters impounded by France since 1986.

The French government later supported **United Nations** sanctions for Libya and continued its investigation into the destruction of UTA flight 772 over Niger in September 1989. In mid-1997, French investigators asked a Paris court to try Qaddafi's brother-in-law and five other Libyan operatives in absentia on charges of blowing up the French airliner and killing 171 people. French officials believed the Libyan government ordered the strike in retaliation for France's deployment of troops to resist the Libyan invasion of Chad in the second half of the 1980s. Evidence in support of the French charges included confidential documents dating to one year before the bombing that instructed Libyan agents to plan a strike against France. In addition, a Congolese witness testified that Libyan operatives had paid a friend to check onto UTA flight 772 from Brazzaville to Paris with a Samsonite suitcase containing a bomb.

In March 1999, the French court condemned six Libyans to life imprisonment, in absentia, for the UTA bombing. The court ruling stressed the involvement of the Libyan secret services in the attack but did not raise the issue of Qaddafi's personal responsibility. In response, SOS-Attentats, a French advocacy group, filed a lawsuit in

June 1999 for complicity in murder on behalf of the victims of the UTA attack, naming Qaddafi, the Libyan head of state, as a codefendant. In July 1999, Libya paid 200 million francs ($33 million) in compensation to the relatives of the victims of the bomb attack.

Hamstrung by legal proceedings, French diplomatic and commercial interests struggled to exploit the international rehabilitation of Libya. France in November 1999 invited the Libyan foreign minister to take part in a preparatory meeting for the Franco-African Summit in Paris, although Qaddafi was not invited to attend the summit. In April 2000, the French stand at the Tripoli International Fair was second in size only to that of **Italy**, and the French secretary of state for industry—the first French minister to visit Libya since the imposition of UN sanctions in 1992—completed numerous official visits during the fair.

While some progress was made, the legal wrangling in Paris repeatedly slowed or blocked French initiatives in Libya, where officials suggested the proceedings against Qaddafi were driven in part by **Israeli** interests. A French court ruling in October 2000 upheld a magistrate's finding that heads of state could be prosecuted for complicity in terrorist attacks. By December, relations had deteriorated to the point there was concern in Paris that Qaddafi supporters in protest against the French judiciary might attack the French embassy. This threat was taken seriously, since Qaddafi in February 1980 had allowed irate mobs to sack the French embassy in **Tripoli** and the French consulate in **Benghazi**.

Following a period of uneasy relations, France in early 2001 began to promote more aggressively French commercial interests in Libya and later to press for Qaddafi's active support in the war on terrorism. In response, Qaddafi declared that he was prepared to fight terrorism, but he rejected the **United States**' simplistic view that anyone not "with us" should be considered as aiding the terrorists. After Libyan foreign minister **Mohammed Abderrahman Chalgam** visited France in November 2001 to attend a meeting of **European Union** and Mediterranean region foreign ministers, French foreign minister Hubert Védrine visited Libya in February 2002.

The normalization of Franco-Libyan relations continued at various levels throughout the year. A joint committee met to discuss a variety of subjects, from stronger cooperation in the cultural, scientific, technical, and economic fields to Libyan relations with the EU. Air **transportation** links between Paris and Tripoli were resumed in February 2002 after a 10-year halt. That September, the French company Bouygues Offshore announced a 33-million-euro contract with Libya as part of the **Western Libya Gas Project**. And in October, France's Schneider Electric announced it would provide the power management system, medium voltage switchgear, and transformers for two major oil and **natural gas** sites in Libya.

Franco-Libyan ties received a boost in January 2004 when Libya agreed to increase its compensation to the families of the victims of the UTA bombing. French president Jacques Chirac met with Libyan prime minister **Shokri Ghanem** in Paris in April 2004, a month after British prime minister Tony Blair had met with Qaddafi in Libya; Chirac then visited Tripoli in November, the first French leader to travel to Libya in more than two decades. In June 2005, the French government announced it was prepared to respond favorably to Libyan requests for nuclear technology transfers for **electricity** production, adding that any nuclear program with Libya would be open to inspection by the International Atomic Energy Agency.

FRANCO-LIBYAN AGREEMENT. Dated 10 August 1955, this treaty provided that perpetual peace and friendship should govern future relations between Libya and **France**. In the central agreement, the French government promised to withdraw its forces from the **Fezzan** within 12 months of the enforcement of the treaty and to cede its **airports** in the area to Libyan control. In turn, the Libyan government agreed to future consultations on issues of mutual interest. In the financial agreement, the French government agreed to contribute the sum of 130 million French francs in 1955 and another 350 million in 1956 for the economic development of Libya. Both states promised to observe the most-favored-nation clause in foreign **trade** and to promote **economic** and commercial cooperation. They also agreed to promote the exchange of cultural facilities and publications, and Libya promised to introduce French language instruction into its institutions of higher learning.

FREEDOM. One of the three goals of the 1969 Libyan revolution. The other two are **socialism** and **unity**. These goals are the same ones proclaimed by Gamal Abdul Nasser at the outset of the 1952 **Egyptian** revolution. The similarities in the ideology of the two revolutions are significant because **Muammar al-Qaddafi** was speaking almost two decades after Nasser and well after certain policies associated with the revolutionary trinity had been generally discredited elsewhere in the **Arab** world.

Qaddafi conceived of freedom as three interrelated concepts: liberation of the individual from poverty, ignorance, and injustice: liberation of the homeland (Libya) from imperialist and reactionary elements; and the economic, political, and social emancipation of the entire Arab world. The ideological values that governed policies in these areas were closely integrated. Consequently, internal and external developments were closely tied, and actions that might conventionally be seen in terms of **foreign policy** became equally pertinent to domestic affairs and vice versa.

Initially, Qaddafi concentrated on highly symbolic acts of national independence, which were widely popular and thus increased the legitimacy of the revolutionary government. For example, on 19 September 1969, the **Revolutionary Command Council** (RCC) issued an order that all signs, cards, and tickets in Libya should be written in the Arabic language only. Later, the RCC addressed larger issues, such as the renewal of the base agreements negotiated by the American and British governments in 1954 and 1953, respectively, and due to expire in the early 1970s. Qaddafi pressured both governments for early termination of those agreements. Once that was achieved, the dates of the American and British withdrawals became official national holidays that typically included a strongly nationalistic address by Qaddafi.

FRONTIERS. Regional conflicts in the second half of the 20th century, which were mostly quiescent by the 21st century, traced their origins to the process of frontier creation during the colonial period. This was true of the Libyan occupation of the Aouzou Strip in **Chad**, tensions with **Tunisia** over the **Jifarah Plain** and **Ghadames** tripoint, the dispute with Niger over the Toummo Oasis, and the crisis with Algeria in the Ghat border region. In addition to bilateral conflicts, multilateral relations in North **Africa** also suffered from problems associated with ill-defined borders. Attempts to promote

Maghrib **unity**—for example, the **Arab-African Union** and the **Arab Maghrib Union**—were undermined to a greater or lesser extent by unresolved territorial conflicts.

In the Libyan case, its contemporary borders originated from three related but distinct categories of negotiations. The boundaries between Tunisia and **Tripolitania** and between **Egypt/Sudan** and **Cyrenaica** exemplify the first class, which focused on the location of existing precolonial boundaries. The second category of negotiations, exemplified by the Ghat region, concerned the interpretation of treaties drawn up between colonial powers or different administrations within a colony. The third class dealt with border negotiations, which were largely a response to domestic or European issues. The Chad-Libya border proposed in 1935 is often cited as an example of this category of negotiation.

In the east, the borders of Libya are the product of agreements between Egypt and **Italy** in 1925–1926—which superceded an 1841 treaty between the **Ottoman Empire** and Egypt—together with 1934 agreements between **Great Britain** and Egypt on the one side and Italy on the other. The latter settlement transferred to Libya the Sarra Triangle, territory lying to the south of 22 degrees north latitude and allocated earlier to Sudan under an 1899 convention.

In the west, Libya's frontiers with Algeria and Tunisia are the result of early negotiations between French authorities in Algeria and Tunisia and Ottoman authorities in **Tripoli**. After 1902, parallel discussions between representatives from **France** and Italy took place, ongoing talks eventually codified through negotiations in 1919. The settlement in the west was finalized through agreements in 1955 and 1956 between Libya and France. As a result, the border between Libya and Tunisia has been demarcated and is no longer in dispute.

Talks between France and Italy in 1914 delimited the Libya-Algeria border from Ghadames to Ghat. Consequently, this section of the frontier is no longer disputed, either; however, the border to the south of Ghat remains controversial. A September 1919 exchange of notes between France and Italy is the only documentation laying down principles of delimitation for the section of the border from Ghat to the tripoint between Algeria, Libya, and Niger. The same exchange of notes also defines the overall delimitation down to the Toummo Oasis. Unfortunately, the wording of this document is ambiguous, in that it simply states the border should follow the line of mountain peaks, leaving Italy direct communication links between Ghat and Toummo.

Algeria later held that the frontier line passed through the Anai Pass, even though other interpretations excluded this possibility, providing Libya with a large increase in territory toward In Ezzane. This confusion stemmed in part from the fact that Italy did not begin to occupy the territory until the late 1920s and in part from subsequent internal French decisions that impacted on a detailed definition of the border region. Meetings were held in 1909 and 1932 to clarify the outstanding border issues, and the 1955–1956 agreements confirmed existing arrangements for delimiting the border. Nevertheless, no attempt was made either to delimit or to demarcate the region. Consequently, there is ongoing danger of conflict because Algerian military forces have encroached on territory claimed by Libya. While Libya to date has not employed military force to assert its claim, this option remains open, despite the fact that the Arab Maghrib Union agreement, concluded in 1989, guarantees the territorial inviolability of member states and encourages them to settle disputes by negotiation, not war.

The southern border of Libya is the product of turn-of-the-century negotiations between France and Great Britain, talks that aimed to delimit their respective zones of influence in Africa. According to the Anglo-French declaration of 1899, the British and French zones of influence would in the future be divided by a line running southeast from the intersection of 16 degrees east longitude and the Tropic of Cancer until it intersected the 24th meridian. Unfortunately, the arrangement did not include a map—or in any case, a map has never been found, although one is mentioned in a 1902 exchange of notes. The failure to include a map as part of the agreement later took on some significance because a controversy developed over the exact location of the line referred to in the 1899 declaration.

Toward the end of the Italo-**Sanusi** wars in Libya, Italian officials began to claim territories far to the south of the 1899 line on the grounds these areas had been controlled by the Ottoman administration and thus Italy, as the successor state to the Ottoman Empire, could claim the same territorial extent as its predecessor. Concerned with Italian claims, the French government sought to resolve the issue in the 1935 Laval-Mussolini treaty, which ceded to Libya a large stretch of Chad, the so-called Aouzou Strip, parallel to the existing frontier. This treaty was approved by the parliaments of both countries but did not come into force because ratifications were not exchanged.

In August 1955, France and Libya concluded an agreement that dealt with a range of issues, including the question of frontiers. In article 3 of the treaty, the signatories recognized the frontiers arising from international instruments in force at the time of Libyan independence. An appendix to the agreement listed those instruments, including the 1899 Anglo-French declaration, the 1902 Anglo-French exchange of notes, and the 1919 Anglo-French convention. However, there was no reference in the agreement to the 1935 Laval-Mussolini treaty. France thus retained control of the Aouzou Strip, which was to remain an integral part of Chad.

While the 1955 agreement might suggest that Libya had abandoned its claims to the Aouzou Strip, the Libyan monarchy and later the **Muammar al-Qaddafi** regime sustained claims to the disputed territory. Following the overthrow of the monarchy, Qaddafi established diplomatic ties with Chad in 1972, and his government thereafter remained deeply involved in the internal affairs of Chad for much of the next two decades. It was only in August 1989 that Libya and Chad concluded a peace accord calling for an end to the fighting over the disputed Aouzou Strip. The agreement gave the signatories one year to negotiate a political settlement. If that proved impossible, they were to take the question of the sovereignty of the Aouzou Strip to the **International Court of Justice**. The court eventually heard the case and ruled in favor of Chad, concluding the 1955 treaty determined the boundary between Chad and Libya. *See also* LIBYA-TUNISIA CONTINENTAL SHELF.

– G –

GARAMANTES. A **tribal** confederation first mentioned by Herodotus in the fifth century B.C. The political power of the Garamantes was limited to a chain of oases some 400 kilometers (250 miles) long in the Wadi **Ajal**. However, because they occupied the oases on the most direct route from the Mediterranean Sea to central Africa—the so-called Garamantean Road—they controlled trans-**Saharan** trade from **Ghadames** south to the Niger River, east to **Egypt**, and west to Mauritania.

GENERAL PEOPLE'S CONGRESS (GPC). The General People's Congress in 1976 became the national-level representative body in Libya. Delegates to the GPC are usually the chairmen of the **basic people's congresses** and the branch or municipal people's congresses, as well as representatives from the university student unions and professional associations. The number varies from session to session but normally approximates 1,000 delegates. The general secretary of the GPC is its chief executive, and the General Secretariat of the GPC is the chief executive's staff and advisory body. The General People's Committee, which consists of a general secretary and a number of secretaries, serves as a cabinet, replacing the former **Council of Ministers**.

Muammar al-Qaddafi was the general secretary of the GPC from 1977 until 1979, when he relinquished the post to concentrate on what he described as "revolutionary activities with the masses." During Qaddafi's tenure as GPC general secretary, the remaining members of the **Revolutionary Command Council** (RCC) constituted its General Secretariat; they too resigned their posts in 1979 to focus on revolutionary activities. Regardless of position or title, Qaddafi and a close band of associates, including the remaining members of the RCC, control and direct the Libyan government. Members of the General People's Committee and the secretariat of the GPC are selected by them and serve at their convenience.

Scheduled to meet annually, normally for two weeks in January or February, the GPC became the major forum in which the government plans, programs, and policies were discussed and ratified. Formal ratification carried with it the responsibility for implementation by the people's congresses and **trade unions** and associations. At its first session in 1976, the General Secretariat of the GPC began submitting major government policies and plans to the congress for review and authorization. For example, both the general administrative **budget** and the 1976–1980 **development plan** were submitted, as were major domestic and **foreign policy** items. On the other hand, there have always been undefined limits to the subjects allowed on the GPC agenda. Libya's intervention in **Chad**, for example, was not discussed at its sixth session in January 1981.

With the abolition of both the RCC and the Council of Ministers, all executive and legislative powers in theory became vested in the GPC. In reality, the GPC delegated many of its duties to the General Secretariat and the General People's Committee. In December 1978, for example, the GPC authorized the General People's Committee to appoint ambassadors and the secretary of foreign affairs to receive the credentials of foreign diplomats.

The fourth session of the GPC illustrated some of the limits to its power and authority. In the first two days of the December 1978 congress, several representatives called for an increase in salaries, despite the fact the recently published part 2 of *The Green Book* called for their abolition. Other representatives demanded an end to the military draft after the General Secretariat had announced universal conscription for all young people. As a result of these and similar actions, the meeting was adjourned on the third day, officially out of respect for the death of the president of Algeria. Unofficially, delegate independence convinced the General Secretariat of the need to reassert control over the organization.

In early March 1988, the GPC met in Ras Lanuf, where Qaddafi took the lead in promoting **economic** liberalization. He called for the creation of more cooperatives, for **women** to take their place alongside men in the workforce, and for the development of programs to halt the migration from the countryside to the cities. Later, he personally mounted a bulldozer to knock down the walls of a major prison in **Tripoli**, announcing that all prisoners—with the exception, as it turned out, of 100 political prisoners—were being released. In June 1988, the GPC reconvened to adopt a manifesto entitled the **Great Green Charter on Human Rights in the Era of the Masses**, which restricted the scope of the death penalty and expressed its total abolition as the eventual aim. It also outlawed degrading punishment and the ill-treatment of prisoners and proclaimed everyone's right to a free trial.

In March 1989, the GPC met in **Benghazi**, where it approved a series of measures aimed at achieving greater economic efficiency as well as aligning the national economy with Libya's partners in the newly created **Arab Maghrib Union**. Many of these issues reflected themes and priorities long advocated by Qaddafi. Earlier, he had called for an end to government control over **trade**, greater tolerance of private business, and improved efficiency in state enterprise. Economic as opposed to ideological issues dominated the GPC meeting the following year. When the General Secretariat demanded budget cuts, the delegates responded with calls for more subsidies, more free services, and no new duties or taxes. Nevertheless, the congress found time to elevate Qaddafi to the status of supreme leader, a position that appeared to give him the authority to overrule any policy decision with which he disagreed.

The GPC continued to function with little change in authority, structure, or operation throughout the 1990s. At the turn of the century, Qaddafi abolished most central government functions, devolving responsibilities to the 26 municipal councils making up the GPC. At the same time, central control was retained in the areas of defense and security, energy, **foreign policy**, infrastructure, social security, and trade, all of which report to the General People's Committee. **Zenati Mohammed al-Zenati** has been the general secretary of the General People's Congress for a number of years, a notable tenure in a political system known for reorganization and change. **Shokri Ghanem** was named general secretary of the General People's Committee, in effect prime minister, in June 2003.

While the general secretary and the General Secretariat closely supervise the activities of the GPC, the congress has served over the years as a clearinghouse and sounding board for the views of the Libyan people as transmitted by their representatives on the lower congresses, committees, and functional organizations. Moreover, for the first time in the nation's history, subnational government requires popular participation in the selection of local leadership and allows popular involvement in the local policy-making process. It also provides an effective organization for the national leadership to communicate its ideas and objectives to the people. In this regard, while Qaddafi and his close associates remain the primary decision makers in Libya, the political system created by him has produced a level of representation and participation hitherto unknown in Libya. *See also* DECLARATION OF THE ESTABLISHMENT OF THE PEOPLE'S AUTHORITY; REVOLUTIONARY COMMITTEE.

GERMANY. Libyan relations with Germany, like those with **France**, have suffered from long-standing legal proceedings. When the **United States** bombed Libya in 1986, U.S. secretary of state George Shultz claimed that radio intercepts related to the bombing of the La Belle discothèque in West Berlin—which killed three people and injured 229 others—were the "smoking gun" that proved Libyan complicity in **terrorism**. Eleven years later, a trial opened in Germany in an effort to bring to justice individuals accused of bombing the disco at the behest of Libya. As the La Belle proceedings played out, Libya appeared satisfied with a German relationship grounded on mutual commercial interest but characterized by a certain distance best described as normalcy at a low level. German chancellor Gerhard Schroeder met briefly in Cairo with Libyan leader **Muammar al-Qaddafi** in the spring of 2000, and one of Qaddafi's sons visited Expo 2000 in Hanover that September. In addition, the chief of the Federal German Intelligence Service met on several occasions with his Libyan counterpart in 1999–2000 to discuss terrorism issues. Berlin also approached **Tripoli** from time to time in search of a moderating influence with the **Organization of Petroleum Exporting Companies** (OPEC) on **petroleum** price policy, as well as a mediating role in conflicts with radical Muslims.

Libyan relations with Germany in 2001–2002 were constrained by ongoing legal proceedings concerning the 1986 La Belle attack. Finally, after a four-year trial, a German regional court in mid-November 2001 found four people guilty of involvement in planting the bomb at the disco. The judge in the case indicated the court was convinced that the Libyan state was at least to a large extent responsible for the attack. Suggesting it was planned by members of the Libyan secret service in senior positions in the Libyan embassy in East Berlin, he added that the four people found guilty had been manipulated by the Libyans into planting the bomb. The judge complained about the limited willingness of the U.S. and German governments to share intelligence information, stating that the personal responsibility of Qaddafi had not been proven. Libyan foreign minister **Mohammed Abderrahman Chalgam**, in a November 2001 interview, immediately denied that Libyan officials had been involved in the La Belle bombing; nevertheless, the court ruling, and subsequent attempts to obtain financial compensation for the victims, cast a long shadow over commercial and diplomatic relations with Germany.

In early September 2004, Libya finally signed an agreement to pay $35 million in compensation to the more than 160 non-U.S. victims of the 1986 bombing. With the conclusion of the agreement, German exports to Libya, which had reached 314 million euro in the first six months of 2004, were expected to increase. Germany was already Libya's second largest trading partner behind **Italy**.

Chancellor Schroeder traveled to Libya in October 2004 and met with Qaddafi. This was the first time a German chancellor had visited Libya. Schroeder visited a site in Libya operated by Wintershall, the oil arm of chemicals giant BASF, which had been active in Libya since 1958. With five oil fields and an offshore drilling site, Wintershall accounts for some 10 percent of Libyan oil production, making it the country's third largest oil producer. Less than a week later, the German industrial conglomerate Siemens announced it had secured a $224 million order to modernize Libya's **electricity** network. In May 2005, Schroeder repeated an earlier invitation to Qaddafi to pay an official visit to Germany. *See also* FOREIGN POLICY.

GHADAMES. The Ghadames oasis is located in the Libyan **Sahara Desert** and forms part of the subregion of Gharyan in the **Ghadames Basin**. It lies some 630 kilometers (390 miles) southwest of **Tripoli**, close to the junction of the borders of Algeria, Libya, and **Tunisia**. The oasis is situated on an ancient and important **trade** route connecting central Africa and the Mediterranean coast. Collectively, these factors made historic Ghadames one of the more important of Libyan cities. Known as the "Pearl of the Desert," Ghadames is famed for its traditional **desert** architecture. The old town is a classic example of how traditional settlement can respond successfully to local geographical, environmental, and social conditions. With thick mud-brick walls, the old town is a quiet and cool retreat from the desert sun. It is also a labyrinth where dark streets are illuminated only by the occasional overhead skylight or open square. UNESCO inscribed Ghadames on the World Heritage List in 1987.

GHADAMES BASIN. The Ghadames Basin is separated from its southern extension, the **Murzuk Basin**, by the Al-Qarqaf Platform.

Some consider the Ghadames and Murzuk basins to be a single sedimentary basin because they have similar geological features. There was limited foreign **petroleum** exploration activity in the Ghadames Basin during the reign of the monarchy. Oil companies sunk wells and discovered oil deposits, but no one considered the finds profitable enough to develop. More recently, the **National Oil Company** of Libya has discovered several small oil fields and proceeded with their development. *See also* KUFRAH BASIN; SIRTE BASIN.

GHANEM, SHOKRI (SHUKRI) MUHAMMAD. Elected secretary general (prime minister) of the General People's Committee in June 2003, Dr. Ghanem is an experienced **petroleum** economist. He earned his B.A. in economics from the University of Libya, **Benghazi**, followed by M.A. degrees in both economics and law and diplomacy from the Fletcher School of Law and Diplomacy at Tufts University in Boston, and a Ph.D. in international economics, also from the Fletcher School.

In addition to teaching assignments at Al-Fateh University, **Tripoli**, and elsewhere, Ghanem has held a number of senior government positions, including director of foreign **trade** at the Ministry of the **Economy**, undersecretary and chief adviser at the Ministry of Petroleum, and chief economist and director of energy studies at the Arab Development Institute. He has also served as the director of the research division of the **Organization of Petroleum Exporting Countries** (OPEC). Ghanem has authored several books, including *The Pricing of Libyan Crude Oil*, and numerous articles.

GIARABUB (JAGHBUB). A remote oasis in northeastern Libya about 250 kilometers (150 miles) south of Tobruk. **Sayyid Muhammad bin Ali al-Sanusi** moved his headquarters from its original location in the **Jabal al-Akhdar** to Giarabub in 1856. Although the site had few resources and little water, it stood on important **trade** and pilgrimage routes. As such, it was probably the ideal location at the time to be in touch with **Sanusi Order** lodges in **Cyrenaica**, **Tripolitania**, the Western Desert of **Egypt**, and **Sudan**. Moreover, its remote location helped the Grand Sanusi turn it into a virtually impregnable fortress. Giarabub became the intellectual center of the Sanusi Order and remained so even after the transfer of its headquarters to Al-Kufrah in 1896.

The university founded in Giarabub became second in importance in Africa only to Al-Azhar in Cairo. At Giarabub, the *Ikhwan*—the brothers of the order—trained in missionary work on behalf of this revivalist movement, which sought to gain a following among the receptive peoples of central Africa.

GOVERNORATES. The three traditional regions of Libya were divided into 10 governorates in 1963. Seven years later, the revolutionary government adjusted the names and boundaries of many governorates, which resulted in one each for **Benghazi**, Derna, Gharian, **Jabal al-Akhdar**, Khalig, Homs, **Misurata**, **Sebha**, **Tripoli**, and Zawiya. This division of government was abolished in 1975 as part of the move toward a new political system based on direct popular authority.

GRAND SANUSI. *See* SAYYID MUHAMMAD BIN ALI AL-SANUSI.

GRAZIANI, RODOLFO (1882–1955). The **Italian** general responsible for pacifying the **Fezzan** in the late 1920s. Thereafter, he was appointed vice governor of **Cyrenaica** and given a similar mission. Marshal Graziani's notoriously harsh—albeit successful—methods included **terrorism**, public executions, and concentration camps.

GREAT BRITAIN. From the beginning, the revolutionary government in Libya was highly critical of British policy in the Middle East dating as far back as the 1917 Balfour Declaration. In addition, it strongly condemned Great Britain's close economic, political, and military ties with the **Idris** regime. While the British government agreed to an expeditious withdrawal from the Libyan base facilities covered by the 1953 **Anglo-Libyan Agreement**, a variety of other issues combined to strain bilateral relations throughout the early years of the revolution. After Britain suspended armament agreements negotiated with the monarchy and refused to consider subsequent Libyan contracts, the **Revolutionary Command Council** nationalized British Petroleum's oil interests. The official justification for **nationalization** was retaliation for alleged British complicity in the Iranian occupation of three disputed islands in the Persian Gulf, but the British government recognized that the decision was also influenced by broader policy disagreements, including Libyan intervention in British negotiations with **Malta** over base leases on the island as well as alleged Libyan support for elements of the Irish Republican Army.

Once its own North Sea oil fields began producing high-quality crude, the British government became something of an exception in Western Europe as the only government not dependent to some degree on Libyan oil imports. In part for this reason, diplomatic relations with Libya remained circumspect even after commercial relations began to expand. For example, when Libyan exiles in Europe were repeatedly attacked in the spring of 1980, the British government took a firm stand against what it viewed as a mounting Libyan campaign of political **terrorism**. In April 1984, Great Britain broke off diplomatic relations with Libya and ordered the closure of the Libyan embassy after political demonstrations in front of the embassy led to the death of a London policewoman; the shots that killed the policewoman were believed to have been fired from inside the embassy.

Representatives of the British and Libyan governments did hold talks in Rome in March 1985 in an effort to improve relations; however, little progress was made after **Muammar al-Qaddafi** repeated threats to retaliate against any European state harboring Libyan dissidents. As a result, no meaningful improvement in Libyan relations with Great Britain occurred in the 12-month period prior to the April 1986 American air attack on Libyan targets from British bases. Great Britain later banned Libyan Arab Airways flights after evidence in a London trial implicated the national carrier in terrorist activities in Britain. The Libyan government responded to this decision, and a related British one to break off diplomatic relations with Syria, by closing its airspace to British aircraft—a move that had little practical effect, as British carriers had not flown to Libya since the summer of 1986.

Over the next decade, British relations with Libya continued to be strained. In mid-1995, the British defense secretary expressed fears Libya possessed or was developing the capacity to hit British military facilities on Cyprus and Gibraltar with ballistic missiles. He added that an increasingly large area of Europe, over the next 5 to 10 years, would be threatened by missile attacks from adjacent states, although he did not identify Libya as the only potential source of missile attacks.

Six months later, the British government expelled a senior Libyan diplomat, charging him with spying and the intimidation of Libyan opponents to the Qaddafi regime. Khalifa Ahmed Bazelya, head of the Libyan interest section at the Saudi Arabian embassy in London, was asked to leave Great Britain by Christmas Day 1995 after being officially charged with activities incompatible with his diplomatic status. The Foreign Office in London insisted that the expulsion of the Libyan diplomat was unconnected with the death the previous month of Ali Mohamed Abouzid, an outspoken critic of the Qaddafi government who was found stabbed to death in his London grocery store. On the other hand, Libyan experts suggested that Bazelya, who headed the official Libyan news agency in London, was in charge of monitoring the acts of Libyan dissidents. In theory, this would have made him responsible for any actions taken against the dissidents by Libyan authorities.

After Libya surrendered the two suspects in the **Lockerbie incident**, Britain in July 1999 agreed to restore diplomatic relations if Libya would acknowledge its involvement in the 1984 murder of the policewoman, Yvonne Fletcher. Libya later signed a statement accepting general responsibility for the actions of those in the Libyan **People's Bureau** at the time of the shooting. In addition, it expressed deep regret to Fletcher's family for what had occurred, offered to pay compensation, and agreed to help investigate the murder. This cleared the way for the October 1999 visit to Libya of a large British trade delegation, including more than 50 delegates from **petroleum**, **natural gas**, construction, and engineering companies, in search of business contracts. In November, British foreign secretary Robin Cook announced that Libya had completed the requisite compensation payment, removing the final obstacle to the restoration of full diplomatic relations. Richard Dalton, the new British ambassador to Libya, took up his post in December, describing his appointment as a fresh start for Anglo-Libyan relations.

In January 2000, Britain announced the discovery at Gatwick Airport outside London of Scud missile components in transit to Libya disguised as automobile parts. The British lodged an official protest, accusing Libya of a clear breach of the **European Union** arms embargo. The incident proved an embarrassment to both states, as it later turned out that the British had been aware of the pending shipment as early as April 1999. Nevertheless, British officials opened a commercial fair in Tripoli in May 2000 that involved 60 British firms and was the largest of its kind since the suspension of sanctions.

In March 2003, Libyan officials approached the British government, initiating talks with Great Britain and the **United States** aimed at dismantling Libya's unconventional weapons program. Those negotiations proved successful; and in December 2003, Libya announced that it had decided of its own free will to be entirely free of internationally banned weapons. Even as the British hailed the decision, the Libyan government credited Great Britain and Prime Minister Tony Blair for doing the most to bring Libya out of isolation.

GREAT GREEN CHARTER ON HUMAN RIGHTS IN THE ERA OF THE MASSES. Intended to open the way for increased **economic** and political liberalization, the Great Green Charter was a manifesto adopted by the **General People's Congress** (GPC) in June 1988. Its 27 articles addressed a variety of personal guarantees and rights. The document guaranteed **freedom** of movement and respect for personal liberty. It restricted the scope of the death penalty, while expressing the abolition of capital punishment as the ultimate aim of the government. The charter also outlawed degrading punishment and the ill-treatment of prisoners and proclaimed the right of everyone to a fair trial. The document invited opponents of the Qaddafi regime to return to Libya without fear of reprisals, although few dared take advantage of the offer.

The Great Green Charter was issued at a time when **Muammar al-Qaddafi** was openly questioning the role of the Libyan security services and **revolutionary committees**. In spring 1988, the Libyan leader was highly critical of the failings of the rule of **law** in Libya and acknowledged that abuses had taken place in the past. In a remarkable volte-face, he suddenly became the foremost Libyan advocate of legality, freedom, and **human rights**. In an effort at consistency, Qaddafi proposed the codification of such principles by the GPC in what eventually became this charter.

While the Great Green Charter was viewed by many observers as a positive step, critics pointed out that the document lacked many provisions necessary to give Libyans the civil and political rights traditionally assumed under domestic law. Article 11 characterized private property as sacred and protected, but added it could be circumscribed by the public interest—without defining what the "public interest" might entail. Article 25 called on each member of the *jamahiriya* to defend his or her country to the death. The following article, which outlawed all acts contrary to the principles and rights of the charter, created gray areas that could be considered treasonous by the government if it so desired. Article 27 endorsed **The Green Book** as the guide for the liberation of the world.

While many aspects of the Great Green Charter were thus legitimate objects for concern, the Qaddafi regime did attempt to implement some of the charter's provisions in the spring and summer of 1989. That March, the GPC adopted a law calling for an independent **judiciary**, and it later extended this call to include strengthening the people's courts and expanding legal accountability. In May, Libya signed the **United Nations** Convention against Torture and Other Cruel, Inhuman, or Degrading Treatment or Punishment.

In the end, the Great Green Charter on Human Rights can best be described as an attempt to codify many of the principles long advocated by Qaddafi. The essence of the charter had been foreshadowed in the three parts of *The Green Book* published after 1975 although a few of the stipulations represented a retreat from earlier pronouncements. However, basic rights continued to be denied to the citizens of Libya. There remained no room for a free press, on the understanding that the Libyan people were free to express themselves at the people's congresses. There was no right to strike, because Libyans were in theory the owners of the factories in which they worked. Rights for **opposition** groups were not specified, again because, in theory, they were free to express their opposition within the congress and committee system.

GREAT MANMADE RIVER (GMR). In 1983, Libya embarked on a new phase of development, involving the **transportation** of underground water via pipeline hundreds of kilometers from its origins in the southern **desert** to planned **agricultural** projects along the

Mediterranean coast. When finally completed, the GMR will consist of more than 4,000 kilometers (2,500 miles) of pipeline intended to transport 5.6 million cubic meters of fresh water a day from underground desert aquifers to the coastal plain.

The first phase of the project called for laying 1,800 kilometers (1,140 miles) of 3.7-meter (12-foot) concrete pressure pipes. These connected 108 wells in the Tazerbo region and 126 wells in Sarir to the coastal towns of Sirte and **Benghazi**. This first phase of the GMR used gravity flow to move the water through the system. Once the project was extended and the flow increased, pumping stations were required. Phase one of the GMR was declared complete in 1991.

The second phase of construction was awarded to Dong Ah, the same South Korean contractor responsible for phase one. The second-phase requirements were similar to those of the first, the most important exception being an attempt to accelerate the rate at which the project would be completed. The demand for water in **Tripoli** and elsewhere along the coastal plain has grown considerably since the conception of the GMR project; consequently, it was decided in 1990 to bring two million cubic meters on board in one stage instead of two as originally planned. That said, pumping fresh water from desert aquifers has proven more complicated than drilling for **petroleum**, and the project has not moved forward according to schedule. On the contrary, a five-year project is now in its 22nd year.

In theory, up to 80 percent of the water provided by the GMR will be devoted to agriculture in an effort to make Libya self-sufficient. According to the original plan, final completion of the project will provide irrigation to an additional 450,000 acres of land in winter and 250,000 acres in summer for grain cultivation. This elevation in grain production, coupled with an increase in the number of sheep to three million, could be expected to transform the country from a net importer of foodstuffs to a net exporter. In reality, though, coastal demand for water for domestic and industrial use has increased faster than forecast. Years of overpumping of the coastal aquifers around Tripoli have allowed seawater to seep into freshwater reservoirs, contaminating the capital's drinking supplies. Economics also play a part, as urban and industrial uses cover the mounting costs of the GMR system to a much greater extent than agriculture.

The GMR project is not without its critics. Detractors say the project is too costly and encourages agricultural development that will always require government subsidies. Once the GMR is completed, recent studies project an average cost of $0.65 per cubic meter of water. If accurate, this would make the GMR cost-effective for municipal purposes but not for agricultural use, where few crops can produce a compensating return. On the other hand, it makes the project an attractive alternative to desalination, which experts suggest would cost between $1.00 and $1.50 per cubic meter of water. Some have charged the scheme may damage the North African aquifer system, but others claim the water supplied by the GMR will be sufficient to supply Libya's water needs for 800 years.

In June 1995, Dong Ah announced that it had been awarded a $5.7 billion contract to build the third phase of the GMR. Six years later, Libya concluded a new agreement with Dong Ah, in which the South Korean firm agreed to repair leakage from pipelines constructed in the first phase and to complete the estimated 5 percent of work outstanding on the second phase. The deal averted a $1.3 billion lawsuit threatened by Libya if Dong Ah stopped work on the project, but it did not mean the GMR was nearing completion.

Libya awarded a total of almost $2 billion in contracts for the third phase of the GMR in August 2005. The largest contract, totaling some $1.1 billion, went to SNC Lavalin, a Canadian company, and covered a four-year extension to its operation of a pipe manufacturing plant at Sarir. Another contract covering engineering, procurement, and construction went to Tekfen of Turkey and covered work over the next five years. Libya also awarded two contracts related to the intended end-use of the water supplied by the GMR, namely agriculture. Brown and Root North Africa was awarded a one-year contract to complete the **Umar al-Mukhtar** Reservoir, which will supply water for agriculture around Benghazi, and two Indonesian firms were contracted to build large water storage tanks south of Tripoli for use in coastal agriculture projects.

The final cost of the Great Manmade River has yet to be determined, but current estimates, including related infrastructure, generally exceed $25 billion. The completion date also remains uncertain, but the most recent contract awards suggest it will take 5–10 more years, or up to 30 years in total to finish the project. *See also* WATER RESOURCES.

GREAT SEPTEMBER REVOLUTION. *See* ONE SEPTEMBER REVOLUTION.

GREAT SOCIALIST PEOPLE'S LIBYAN ARAB JAMAHIRIYA. *See* SOCIALIST PEOPLE'S LIBYAN ARAB JAMAHIRIYA.

GREEK INFLUENCE. The region of **Cyrenaica**, which occupies the eastern half of Libya, derives its name from **Cyrene**, founded in 631 B.C. as the first Greek city in North Africa. Within two centuries, four more cities had been founded on the North African shore, thereby bringing all of Cyrenaica under Greek influence. The other four cities were Barce (Al Marj), Hesperides (later Berenice, present-day **Benghazi**), Teuchira (later Arisione, present-day Tukrah), and **Apollonia** (Susah, the port of Cyrene). Collectively, these five cities, all of which became republics and experimented with a variety of democratic institutions, came to be known as Pentapolis (five cities).

Tradition has it that the citizens of Cyrene and Carthage agreed to set the border between their competing spheres of influence at the point where runners starting from either city should meet. When the brothers Philaeni, representing Carthage, met the runners from Cyrene on the southern shore of the Gulf of **Sidra**, the Greeks refused to believe that the runners from Carthage had run a fair race. To demonstrate to Cyrene the good faith of Carthage, the two Philaeni brothers agreed to be buried alive on the spot. Consequently, the Altars of Philaeni, which the Greeks built over the graves of the two brothers, mark the traditional boundary between Cyrenaica and **Tripolitania**.

The inhabitants of Pentapolis aggressively resisted invaders from east and west; however, due to intense intercity rivalries, they were seldom able to mount a common front against their foes. This weakness led to their eventual conquest by the army of Cambyses II, fresh from the conquest of **Egypt**, in 525 B.C. Pentapolis existed as the westernmost province of the Persian Empire for the next two centuries, but it returned in 331 B.C. to Greek rule under Alexander the Great of Macedonia. Eight years later, upon the death of Alexander,

the region was incorporated with Egypt and given to Ptolemy. Cyrenaica remained under Greek rule, its kings drawn from the Ptolemaic
royal house, until 74 B.C. when it was joined to Crete as a **Roman**
province.

The economic and political life of Pentapolis was not unduly affected by the political turmoil that periodically plagued Cyrenaica.
The region grew rich from the production of grain, wine, wool, and
stockbreeding as well as from silphium, an herb that grew only in
Cyrenaica and was widely regarded as an aphrodisiac. The city of
Cyrene became one of the great intellectual and cultural centers of
the Greek world, rightly famous for its medical school, learned acad-
emies, and architecture. The city was also home to a school of
thinkers, the Cyrenaics, who expounded a doctrine of moral cheer-
fulness that defined happiness as the sum of human pleasures.

GREEN BOOK, THE. **Muammar al-Qaddafi** outlined the major
tenets of the **Third Universal Theory** in three parts of *The Green
Book* published beginning in 1975. Part 1, entitled "The Solution of
the Problem of Democracy: The Authority of the People," developed
the political base for the system of congresses and committees implemented throughout Libya in the first decade of the revolution. In
the second part, entitled "The Solution of the Economic Problem: Socialism," Qaddafi explored the economic dimensions of the Third
Universal Theory. Finally, in the third part, entitled "The Social Basis of the Third Universal Theory," he developed the social aspects of
his concept. In many respects, the third part proved the most controversial, as Qaddafi's views on **women**; minorities; melodies and arts;
and sport, horsemen, and shows remain an endless source of debate.
See also DECLARATION OF THE ESTABLISHMENT OF THE
PEOPLE'S AUTHORITY; GENERAL PEOPLE'S CONGRESS;
SOCIALISM.

GREEN MARCH. Frustrated with the failure of early attempts to unite
with **Egypt**, **Muammar al-Qaddafi** arrived in Cairo in June 1973 for
an unscheduled visit in which he was highly critical of Egyptian society. Returning to **Tripoli**, the Libyan leader organized a motorcade
of some 20,000 vehicles to drive from the Libyan-**Tunisian** border to
Cairo in support of an immediate union with Egypt. Termed the

Green March by Libyan officials, this motorcade proved to be the first public demonstration of the new governing concept of the masses. It was also the last official effort to export the Libyan revolution to Egypt. Egyptian authorities stopped the motorcade at the border. *See also* BENGHAZI DECLARATION; UNITY.

GREENSTREAM PIPELINE. *See* WESTERN LIBYA GAS PROJECT.

GULF CRISIS. The Iraqi invasion of Kuwait in early August 1990 put Libya in a difficult international position. On the one hand, the **Muammar al-Qaddafi** regime had long been the **Arab** world's strongest advocate of enhanced Arab **unity**. On the other, it found the **United States**–dominated buildup in the Gulf to be totally unacceptable. Qaddafi later explained that his rejection of the U.S. presence in the region was the major reason why Libya voted against early **Arab League** resolutions on the crisis.

The first official response of the Qaddafi government was to announce in early September 1990 a seven-point peace plan. Supposedly drawn up after consultations with the governments of Iraq, Jordan, and **Sudan**, the plan envisaged Iraq keeping Kuwait's Bubiyan Island at the head of the Gulf and the Kuwaiti half of the Rumeila oil field in return for withdrawing from the remainder of Kuwait. While the official Libyan news agency reported that the Saudi government welcomed the plan, its central provisions were clearly unacceptable to Kuwait as well as most other Arab and Western governments. As outlined by Qaddafi, the plan did not clearly endorse the two key factors shared in all **United Nations** and Arab League resolutions on the crisis—the unconditional withdrawal of Iraqi troops from Kuwait and the restoration of the Kuwaiti amirate.

Throughout the remainder of the dispute, Qaddafi searched unsuccessfully for a policy that would allow him to play, or at least appear to play, a significant role in resolving the crisis. Public statements supportive of Iraq, coupled with Western press allegations of sanctions-busting, were combined with overt acts in support of the allied cause. At the end of October 1990, for example, Qaddafi expelled a Palestinian group, the Palestine Liberation Front, after it threatened to attack U.S. interests in response to the Gulf Crisis. The leader of the group, Abu Abbas, was banned from entering Libya, and the front's training camps in Libya were closed.

In early January 1991, Qaddafi made a final attempt to find what he termed a peaceful Arab solution to the crisis in Kuwait. Meeting in the Libyan seaside town of **Misurata**, the heads of state of **Egypt**, Sudan, and Syria joined Qaddafi for discussions that were ultimately unsuccessful in contributing to a resolution of the problem. Thereafter, the Libyan government was no more than an observer to the subsequent diplomatic and military events that climaxed in the forcible expulsion of Iraq from Kuwait.

In retrospect, Qaddafi's marginal involvement in the Gulf Crisis produced both gains and losses for Libyan **foreign policy**. The most tangible gain was an immediate, albeit temporary, improvement in diplomatic relations with Egypt. Qaddafi and Egyptian president Hosni Mubarak met regularly in a show of solidarity, and in December 1990 the two heads of state signed several accords pledging further economic cooperation between their respective countries. However, the improved relations with Egypt came at the expense of deeper relations with fellow members of the **Arab Maghrib Union** (AMU), who tended to be wary of Qaddafi's overtures to Egypt. Libya's AMU partners also viewed the economic arrangements between Libya and Egypt as coming at their own expense.

The Gulf Crisis also produced a short-term increase in **petroleum** prices, which boosted Libya's oil export revenues. The rise in oil prices also exposed the limitations of Libya's oil production capacity, which had become severely limited due to the economic sanctions imposed by the United States and the United Nations. Oil prices later dropped steadily until they eventually reached levels below those of August 1990.

– H –

HAMADAH AL-HAMRA (HAMMADAH AL-HAMRA). Known as the Red Rocky Desert, this region of some 80,000–90,000 square kilometers (30,000–35,000 square miles) includes the western part of **Tripolitania** south of the **Jifarah Plain** and a lesser area of northern **Fezzan**. The well-known oasis of **Ghadames** lies in the southwest part of the Hamadah al-Hamra near the Algerian-**Tunisian** border. The eastern part is a dissected plateau. The Hamadah al-Hamra is cut by numerous wadis, some of which form wide depressions or floodplains. Such features are most frequent in the northern part of the **desert**, where a cover of sand is commonly present. In the south, the Hamadah al-Hamra falls gradually into a monotonous gravel plain. The southern boundary of the Hamadah al-Hamra is marked by a line of precipitous cliffs, beyond which lies a vast lowland covered by the sand dunes of the Ubari Sand Sea.

HAMZA, AWAD ALI (1943–). An original member of the **Revolutionary Command Council** (RCC). Like eight other RCC members, Hamza was a member of the political study cell that **Muammar al-Qaddafi** formed at the military college in **Benghazi** in the early 1960s. He also shared a poor, bedouin background with most of his revolutionary colleagues. Hamza was accused in 1975 of plotting against Qaddafi and was imprisoned along with **Bashir Saghir al-Hawaadi** and 20 senior military officers.

HASSI MESSOUD, TREATY OF. A mutual defense pact concluded by Algeria and Libya in 1975. While the signatories pledged to come to each other's aid if attacked, the Algerian government did not provide military assistance to Libya in its 1977 border war with **Egypt**. On the other hand, Algerian diplomacy did help end the fighting.

HAWAADI, BASHIR SAGHIR AL- (BESHIR SAGHIR HAWADY; BASHIR SAGHIR HAWWADI) (1941–). An original member of the **Revolutionary Command Council** (RCC). Like **Awad Ali Hamza**, Hawaadi was a member of the political study cell that **Muammar al-Qaddafi** organized at the military school they attended in **Benghazi**. In addition to RCC membership, Hawaadi served as chairman of the **Arab Socialist Union**, which Qaddafi formed in June 1971. He was accused in 1975 of plotting against Qaddafi and imprisoned. The abortive revolt by Hawaadi, following on the heels of a failed coup by fellow RCC member **Omar Mehishi**, effectively spelled the end of the RCC. By 1976, the RCC was reduced from its original 12 members to the five that constituted the elite leadership of the revolution for much of the next 20 years.

HAWARIA, BATTLE OF. One of the final engagements in the **Italian** conquest of Libya. The battle of Hawaria took place in Western **Cyrenaica** outside the oasis of Al-Kufrah in 1932.

HAWWAZ, ADAM SAID. One of only two senior military officers not purged at the outset of the **One September Revolution**, the other being **Musa Ahmad**. Hawwaz initially served as minister of defense in the eight-member **Council of Ministers** appointed in early September 1969. Two months later, he was arrested in connection with an abortive plot against the revolutionary government. Hawwaz, together with alleged co-conspirator Ahmad, was sentenced to a long prison term, which was later increased.

HEALTH. At the outset of the revolution in 1969, the major health hazards endemic in Libya included typhoid and paratyphoid, infectious hepatitis, leishmaniasis, rabies, meningitis, schistosomiasis, and venereal diseases. Childhood diseases such as whooping cough, mumps, measles, and chicken pox were common, and epidemics of cholera occasionally broke out. Malaria was officially thought to have been eliminated in the previous decade; nevertheless, malaria suppressants were recommended for travelers to **desert** oasis areas.

Faced with this situation, the revolutionary government made rapid strides in improving overall health conditions. Welfare became much more a public than a private function, and free medical care of increasingly better quality was made available to all citizens. The number of physicians and surgeons practicing in Libya increased fivefold between 1965 and 1974, and there were corresponding increases in the number of dentists and other medical and paramedical personnel. Medical personnel were most numerous in **Tripoli** and **Benghazi**, but new clinics with resident staffs of physicians and medical support personnel were also increasingly common in the oasis communities.

Schools of nursing have existed in Libya since the early 1960s, and the faculties of medicine at the universities of Tripoli and Benghazi include specialized courses for nurses and technicians. On the other hand, the first school of medicine was not established until 1970, and there was no school of dentistry until 1974. By 1978, almost 500 students were enrolled in Libyan medical schools, and the dental school in Benghazi had graduated its first class of 23 students. In addition, a number of Libyan students were pursuing graduate medical studies abroad.

The number of hospitals also increased substantially during the first years of the revolution, as did various kinds of clinics and health centers. The government purchased a mobile dental unit for use in servicing desert oasis communities and experimented with the construction of hospital ships to serve coastal communities. While the bulk of hospital beds continued to be found in the urban areas, smaller hospitals of standard design were constructed in more and more areas of the country.

This improved provision for health care, coupled with heightened attention to preventive medicine and general sanitation, led to substantially improved living standards. While a high rate of trachoma formerly left 10 percent or more of the population with impaired vision or blindness, new glaucoma centers and an intensive antiglaucoma program appear to have brought the disease largely under control. With the construction of several tuberculosis care centers, the incidence of that disease has also been drastically reduced. Finally, the number of active leprosy cases has dropped to the point that health authorities have shifted their attention from caring for the disease to studying its social repercussions.

The most visible health issue in recent years centered on a Palestinian doctor and five **Bulgarian** nurses found guilty by a Libyan court of knowingly infecting 426 Libyan children with the AIDS virus. Arrested in 1999, the six were sentenced to death by firing squad in May 2004. The Supreme Court was scheduled to rule on their appeal in May 2005, but at the last moment, delayed its decision until November 2005. Outside medical experts have testified that the AIDS epidemic broke out before the arrival of the doctor and nurses at the hospital and was due to poor hygiene at the Benghazi hospital where the incident took place. The **European Union**, **United States**, and **United Nations**, among other bodies, have condemned the verdict; nevertheless, the Libyan government has so far refused to release the prisoners. *See also* SCREWWORM FLY.

HEMEIDI, KWEILDI AL- (KUWAYLDI AL-HUMAYDI; KHEWEILDY HAMIDY; KHUWAILDI HAMIDI) (1943–). An original member of the **Revolutionary Command Council** (RCC).

Hemeidi was one of the eight RCC members who were also members of the first political study cell organized by **Muammar al-Qaddafi** when all were students at the military school in **Benghazi**. He served the revolution as both minister of the interior and commander of the militia. In the aftermath of an abortive coup in August 1975, Hemeidi joined **Abdel Salaam Jalloud**, **Mustafa al-Kharuubi**, **Abu Bakr Yunnis Jaabir**, and Qaddafi as the five remaining original RCC members. This group of men constituted the elite of the Libyan leadership for much of the next two decades. Hemeidi later served on the **General People's Committee** as secretary for internal affairs.

HIGHER COUNCIL FOR NATIONAL GUIDANCE. An organization created by the **Revolutionary Command Council** (RCC) on 10 September 1972 to increase unity of thought among Libyan citizens in the existing phase of revolutionary transformation, as well as to lay the cultural basis for future ideological **education**. The council membership consisted of the RCC chairman; the **Arab Socialist Union** (ASU) general secretary; the ministers of education, information and culture, **youth** and social affairs, and planning; the presidents of the universities of **Tripoli** and **Benghazi**; the administrative chairmen of religious endowments; the chairman of the **Islamic Call Society**; and the ASU secretary of thought and culture. Its teachings centered on **Islam**, Arabism, and the relationship between Libya and the international community.

HIZB AL-TAHRIR AL-ISLAMI. *See* ISLAMIC LIBERATION PARTY.

HIZBULLAH. *See* PARTY OF GOD GROUP.

HOUNI, ABDEL MENIN AL- (ABDUL MONIEM TABER AL-HUNY; ABDUL MUNIM AL-TAH AL-HUNI) (1941–). An original member of the **Revolutionary Command Council** (RCC). Houni was a member of the first political study cell organized by **Muammar al-Qaddafi** at the military school in **Benghazi**. Unlike many of his RCC colleagues, he came from an urban, middle-class background. Houni served as minister of foreign affairs. Implicated in a failed coup attempt in 1975, he was exiled to **Egypt**.

HOUSING. After independence, urban migration led to an acute housing shortage. The **Idris** Housing Project of the 1960s proved an expensive fiasco, and on the eve of the revolution, the lack of adequate housing remained a critical social problem. While a government report in the mid-1970s showed 150,000 families still in need of homes, housing construction under the **Revolutionary Command Council** was already a conspicuous achievement. By the early 1980s, most hovels and tenements had given way to modern apartment blocks with electric lights and running water.

In March 1978, the **General People's Congress** issued **Resolution Four**, which detailed new guidelines for home ownership. The resolution stated that Libyan families, with the exception of widows dependent on rental income or families with at least one son over the age of 18, had the right to own just one house. Non-Libyans and Libyans with a need for short-term accommodations were guaranteed access to rental housing. By September 1978, most tenants of housing previously owned by government agencies or private companies had become the owners of their residences. Thereafter, the government concentrated its efforts on the confiscation and redistribution of properties owned by individuals.

HUMAN RIGHTS. Unable to tolerate dissent, the **Muammar al-Qaddafi** regime was rightly criticized from the outset of the **One September Revolution** for a deplorable human rights record. The 1970s and early 1980s were marked by a policy of savage repression of anyone who opposed regime policies. Participants in failed attempts to overthrow the revolutionary government, and later **Islamist** militants, were executed publicly. In 1980, the government initiated a policy of extrajudicial executions of political opponents, termed "stray dogs," with **revolutionary committees** empowered to implement this policy at home and abroad. The brutal legacy of the first three decades of the revolution included arbitrary arrest, detention without trial, torture, disappearances, unfair trials, and the death penalty. However, this history did not prevent Libya's election to chair the **United Nations** Commission on Human Rights in 2003.

With the resolution of the **Lockerbie incident** and the renunciation of **weapons of mass destruction**, the Qaddafi regime acknowledged deficiencies in the area of human rights, as well as the need to institutionalize international human rights standards. Beginning in 2004, Libya took notable steps to improve its human rights practices, including the reopening of its borders to international human rights monitors. In February 2004, Amnesty International, a London-based nongovernmental organization (NGO), made its first visit to Libya in 15 years; its visit was followed by a similar mission in May 2005 by Human Rights Watch, a New York–based NGO.

In April 2004, Amnesty International issued a scathing report, "Time to Make Human Rights a Reality," calling on the Qaddafi regime to address the grave human rights concerns detailed therein. Among other detainees, Amnesty International highlighted the case of Fathi al-Jahmi, a member of the **Basic People's Congress** who had been arrested and sentenced to a year in jail for demanding democratic reforms. Released in March 2004, he was again detained and beaten after he gave interviews to Arabic satellite channels.

In January 2005, Libya closed the People's Court, a tribunal convened periodically to try crimes against the state, transferring the cases it was then reviewing to regular criminal courts. In addition, Libyan officials were reportedly preparing new penal and criminal procedure codes, which they said would reduce the number of crimes punishable by death. In October 2005, the Supreme Court announced that 86 members of the **Muslim Brotherhood**, arrested in 1998 and sentenced by the People's Court in 2002 to prison terms ranging from 10 years to life imprisonment, would be retried by the criminal courts.

The **United States** government in its most recent annual report on human rights practices, dated 28 February 2005, described the Qaddafi regime as an authoritarian government with a poor human rights record, emphasizing that the Libyan government continues to commit serious abuses. The White House later suggested in August 2005 that Libya must clean up its human rights record before it would receive additional concessions from Washington.

Following its May 2005 visit to the country, Human Rights Watch stated that Libya had taken important first steps to improve its human rights record but suggested serious problems remained. These problems include violence against detainees, restricting freedom of association and expression, the incarceration of political prisoners, and problems in the administration of justice. As an example, journalist and writer Daif al-Ghazal was abducted and murdered in June 2005 by armed men who said they were national security officials. While the authorities denied involvement, Ghazal had been increasingly strident in his criticism of the Qaddafi regime in general and government corruption in particular. Human rights groups believe he was murdered by revolutionary committee members.

Libya also remains under fire for human rights abuses in the case of five **Bulgarian** nurses and a Palestinian doctor detained in 1999 for allegedly infecting 426 Libyan children with HIV. Sentenced to death in 2004, the detainees since their arrest have repeatedly accused Libyan security officials of using rape and torture to extract confessions. When a **Tripoli** court in June 2005 acquitted nine policemen and a doctor accused of mistreating the six detainees, the verdict contributed to a deterioration in Libya's relations with the **European Union** and United States.

Given the questionable state of human rights in Qaddafi's Libya, organizations such as Libya Watch for Human Rights and other civil rights campaigners expressed understandable concern when the British government in October 2005 signed a deportation agreement with Libya on the understanding that Libyan nationals returned to Libya would not be mistreated. As a signatory to the European Convention on Human Rights, **Great Britain** is not permitted to deport people to countries where they may face mistreatment or torture. The fate of five Libyan nationals currently under detention in England was the immediate cause of concern.

– I –

IBN TASHFIN, YUSUF. Ibn Tashfin, an early **Almoravid** leader, founded Marrakesh in 1062, which became the Almoravid capital. Ibn Tashfin invaded Spain in 1086 and eventually controlled territory as far north as Toledo. In the Maghrib, he moved eastward from **Morocco** into Algeria, capturing Tlemcen, Oran, and Algiers. Ibn Tashfin is also credited with the construction of some notable mosques in North Africa, including those in Tlemcen and Algiers.

IBN TUMART (1080–1130). Founder and spiritual leader of the **Almohad dynasty**. The details of Ibn Tumart's life are not established enough to satisfy the rigor of modern historians; however, traditional accounts concur in the essential details. Born by some accounts as late as 1091, the young Ibn Tumart was obsessed with learning and reportedly spent almost his entire youth in study. At the age of 18, he left North Africa to travel to Spain and later to the Orient, which at the time was a center of **Islamic** learning and culture. During these travels, tradition has it that he studied with the most eminent and learned scholars; however, it has never been possible to detail exactly his intellectual genealogy.

Ibn Tumart returned to the Maghrib around 1116. This was a period in North African history in which the Fatimids sent the Bani Hilal west to punish the **Zirids**. In the process, the so-called Hilalian invasions unsettled the traditional order in North Africa. Moving east to west along the Mediterranean Sea, Ibn Tumart passed through lands controlled by the Zirids and the Hammad before arriving in the western Maghrib controlled by the **Almoravids**. Traveling widely in **Morocco**, he soon found substantial reason for criticizing the manner in which the Almoravids were governing the country. Eventually banished from Marrakesh, Ibn Tumart returned to his native village. Attracting a host of students from many places, he was later proclaimed mahdi of the Almohads. *See also* ABD AL-MUMIN.

IBRAHIM, AHMED MOHAMMED. Assistant secretary of the **General People's Congress** since 2005. Ibrahim was formerly secretary of higher **education** in the General People's Committee. He has been a vocal opponent of the privatization initiatives championed by **Shokri Ghanem**, secretary general of the General People's Committee, charging that they are sabotaging the people's socialist system in Libya.

IDRIS I, KING. *See* IDRIS AL-MAHDI AL-SANUSI, SAYYID MUHAMMAD.

IDRIS AL-MAHDI AL-SANUSI, SAYYID MUHAMMAD (1890–1983). Descendant of a distinguished **Arab** family long resident in North Africa that traces its ancestry from the Prophet Muhammad through the Prophet's daughter Fatima and her husband Ali. A grandson of **Sayyid Muhammad bin Ali al-Sanusi**, founder of the **Sanusi Order**, Sayyid Muhammad Idris al-Mahdi al-Sanusi was schooled in traditional **Islamic** studies at Al-Kufrah. The outbreak of World War I found Sayyid Idris in Medina in the midst of a religious pilgrimage. Returning to **Cyrenaica**, he assumed leadership of the Sanusi Order and concluded peace agreements in 1917 with **Great Britain** and **Italy**. The negotiation of these arrangements brought diplomatic and political status to the Sanusi Order, but it did not bring peace to Cyrenaica.

In October 1920, the Italian government recognized Idris as the hereditary amir of Cyrenaica in return for the implementation of new political accords concluded in 1919. The 1920 agreement was short-lived, however, and by the end of 1921, diplomatic relations between the Sanusi Order and Italy were again strained. The crisis came to a head at the end of 1922 when Idris realized the peace he had negotiated was breaking down and that Italy and the Sanusi Order could not share Cyrenaica between them. Accordingly, Idris left for exile in **Egypt**, leaving more-martial members of the order to wage what ultimately proved to be a fruitless war against Italy.

With the outbreak of World War II, Idris began pressing the question of independence with British authorities in Cairo. However, Libyans in general and Cyrenaicans in particular accepted deferment of international decisions on their future as long as the war lasted. The conclusion of World War II found Cyrenaica stronger than **Tripolitania**. Idris was a convincing leader, widely accepted in Cyrenaica, and recognized and respected by the British authorities. Faced with the real possibility of renewed Italian administration, Libyans in both Cyrenaica and Tripolitania increasingly accepted Idris as the one leader who could unite Libya.

After considerable debate and political infighting, Libya finally achieved independence in December 1951 as the **United Kingdom of Libya**. The **Constitution of Libya** established a hereditary monarchy with a federal state divided into the three provinces of Cyrenaica, **Fezzan**, and Tripolitania. A conservative, traditionalist monarchy, the Idris regime emphasized Libyan-Arab brotherhood and solidarity, but its policies seldom went beyond lip service unless under extreme pressure. For example, King Idris I blocked Libyan membership in the **Arab League** until 1953, and his government always fell short of offering tangible support for the Arab cause in the Middle East. When Libya concluded a treaty with **Tunisia** in 1957, hailing it as a model of bilateral collaboration, Arab **nationalist** critics denounced the agreement as little more than an instrument for harmonizing the policies of the signatories with those of the West.

Both the appearance and the reality of the monarchy's dependence on the West rested on the financial and political assistance generated by British and American military bases in Libya. The close association of the monarchy's apparent Western orientation to its need for military base revenues became apparent once **petroleum** exports reduced its dependence on those revenues. As early as 1964, the Libyan government asked Great Britain and the **United States** to reconsider their future status at those bases. The United States responded by accepting in principle a withdrawal from the **Wheelus Air Base**, while Britain actually began evacuating troops from **Tripoli** in 1965.

In reality, King Idris I was never as pro-Western as many observers in and out of the Arab world believed. While the monarchy maintained a cordial relationship with the Western powers, its approach was based not on a widespread commitment to Western ideals and traditions but on the monarchy's belief that the Western powers remained in the best position to guarantee Libya's security. In fact, the monarchy worked to minimize the impact of Western sociopolitical values and structures on Libya.

While enriching the government, oil revenues in the 1960s also awakened the Libyan populace, and in the process, drew additional attention to the conservative nature of the king. The socioeconomic change that accompanied the oil revolution precipitated a demand for political change that the monarchy was unwilling or unable to accommodate. By the end of the decade, increasing numbers of the Libyan populace, in particular its younger, more articulate segments, had concluded that the domestic and foreign policies of King Idris were parochial, if not corrupt, and must be changed. In short, the monarchy failed to overcome the negative impact of **tribal**, provincial, and **religious** loyalties and the positive appeal of a vibrant pan-Arabism.

The Idris regime was eventually overthrown by the **Libyan Free Unionist Officers** movement in 1969 in the **One September Revolution**. Abroad at the time, King Idris never returned to Libya. He settled in Egypt and lived in exile in Cairo until his death on 25 May 1983 at the age of 94.

INDUSTRY. Italy promoted industrial development in Libya during the Italian occupation from 1911 to 1943. By 1938, almost 800 firms were operating in the country, most of them devoted to the manufacture of basic goods for domestic consumption. The more important articles produced included building materials, metal products, **agricultural** foodstuffs, and tobacco. Most of these factories were small in size and located in **Tripoli, Benghazi, Misurata**, or Derna. Four out of five were operated by Italians. While many were damaged in World War II, similar industries emerged in the 1950s with increased local ownership. Industrial training centers were also established in Tripoli and Benghazi.

In 1961, Libya established its first Ministry of Industry. Manufacturing was officially recognized in the first five-year **development plan** (1963–1968), where it was accorded 3 percent of planned expenditure. However, the disbursement of development funds remained low throughout the decade. As late as 1969, the ratio of actual to planned investment in industry was estimated to be less than 10 percent. Moreover, the monarchy limited direct investment in the industrial sector to fewer than 10 companies.

After the 1969 revolution, government policy changed dramatically, and more attention was paid to the development of public-sector projects. In 1970, the government created the National Public Organization for Industrialization (NPOI) as the body responsible for implementing the public sector's development plan. Within a decade, the NPOI had funded 91 projects with an estimated capital investment of DN500 million. As public-sector investment increased, private-sector investment declined because of actual or anticipated government policies.

In spite of government plans, the development of heavy industry proceeded slowly. At the beginning of the 1980s, the only major **petroleum** refinery was at Zawiya, while **natural gas** exports were possible only because Esso and Occidental had completed facilities in 1968–1972. A methanol plant was commissioned in 1977 and an ammonia plant began production in 1980. A West **German**–built chemical complex was also operating near the **Tunisian** border. Plants producing ammonia, methanol, monoethylene glycol, polypropylene, fertilizers, iron and steel, and aluminum later entered into production. After two decades of limited investment in heavy industry, the privatization policies pursued by Libya after 2003 are resulting in a large number of new projects.

The development of light industry was less challenging for Libyan officials. The emphasis remained on the processing of local materials for domestic consumption as well as on import substitution. The government also attempted to consolidate light industry into larger, more efficient units. Committed to the integration of heavy and light industry, the development of a sophisticated intermediate industry has proved to be a challenging process.

INTERNATIONAL COURT OF JUSTICE (ICJ). The history of the **Socialist People's Libyan Arab Jamahiriya** is remarkable in that Libya has been involved over the last two decades in no less than three separate cases before the International Court of Justice. These cases dealt with the **Libya-Tunisia continental shelf**, the Libya-Malta continental shelf, and the Libya-Chad land **frontier**. Libya viewed the resolution of continental shelf issues with **Malta** and **Tunisia** as largely technical adjustments leading to the final resolution of boundaries in undermarcated areas. Both judgments were largely, if not wholly, favorable to Libya. On the other hand, the situation was different in the case of the land boundary dispute with **Chad**. In the area of the Aouzou Strip, the international boundary line rejected by Libya had achieved widespread international recognition based on traditional practice, and the issue was finally resolved in favor of Chad.

The dispute involving delimitation of the Libya-Tunisia continental shelf was brought before the ICJ in 1978. The disputants asked the court to determine the principles and rules of international law that might be applied to delimit the area of the continental shelf appertaining to the two parties. In so doing, the ICJ was asked to take into account both equitable principles and the relevant circumstances that characterize the area. It was also asked to consider recent legal trends regarding the Third Conference on the Law of the Sea.

Before the ICJ, Libya and Tunisia adopted similar positions on the applicable law. Both parties relied on natural prolongation and eschewed equidistance. On the other hand, they disagreed about both the facts of the dispute and the application of the law to these facts. Libya's principal argument was that the continental shelf was a prolongation to the north of the continental landmass and that a boundary due north from Ras Ajdir would reflect this prolongation. In a countermemorial, Libya later softened this position when it recognized the equity of an adjustment of the line to the northeast opposite the point of significant change in the general direction of the Tunisian coast.

Relying principally on geomorphology and historic fisheries, Tunisia argued that the natural prolongation of the continent in the area was much farther east and that the continental shelf at issue was, in effect, a submerged portion of Tunisia.

Rejecting the proposals of both parties, the ICJ treated the boundary areas as two sectors, proposing a line of delimitation in two segments. The first segment began at the outer limits of the territorial sea and ran at a bearing of 26 degrees east of north from Ras Ajdir to a point on the parallel of latitude drawn from the most westerly point of the Tunisian coastline between Ras Kaboudia and Ras Ajdir. The second segment, more seaward off the coast, veered to the east at a bearing of 52 degrees east of north to reflect the radical change in the direction of the Tunisian coast. At the same time, the court concluded that the Kerkennah Islands should not be given full effect in determining the direction of the coast. Therefore, this segment of the boundary was drawn parallel to a line extending from the westernmost point of the Gulf of Gabes and bisecting the angle formed by a line from that point to Ras Kaboudia and a line drawn from that same point along the seaward coast of the Kerkennah Islands.

Pursuant to a special agreement, Libya and Malta had earlier, on 23 May 1976, submitted a dispute to the ICJ concerning the delimitation of the continental shelf underlying the Mediterranean Sea between the two countries. Under the terms of this special agreement, the court was asked to decide which principles of law were applicable to the dispute and how such principles would be applied. However, the task of drawing the actual boundary line was to be left to the two parties in subsequent negotiations.

On 3 June 1985, the ICJ delivered a judgment that was limited both by the terms of the special agreement and by the competing claims of the **Italian** government, which was not a party to the dispute. The court found that the law governing the case was customary international law, which required the delimitation be effected in accordance with equitable principles taking into consideration all relevant circumstances. In applying such principles, the ICJ rejected Libya's contention that the natural prolongation of the land under the sea was the primary basis of title to the continental shelf. Instead, it accepted Malta's argument that the concept of the exclusive economic zone, as embodied in customary international law, required that natural prolongation be defined in part by the distance from the shore, irrespective of the physical nature of the intervening seabed.

Accordingly, the ICJ began the process of delimitation by drawing an imaginary line between Libya and Italy as if Malta did not exist. Next, it adjusted this line, out of equitable considerations, by eliminating from the baseline formed by the Maltese coast that portion of the line extending to the islet of Filfla. Finally, the court adjusted the line northward toward Malta, taking into account the disparity between the respective lengths of the Libyan and Maltese coasts as well as the fact that Malta is a relatively minor feature of the central Mediterranean.

After years of conflict, Libya and Chad concluded a peace agreement in August 1989, calling for an end to fighting over the Aouzou Strip. Both states were to withdraw from the disputed territory, where they would be replaced by a group of **African** observers who would remain until a settlement was reached. The agreement also called on the signatories to resolve their differences through a political settlement. However, if that proved impossible, they were to take the question to the ICJ for resolution.

Unable to resolve their differences, the disputants submitted the dispute to the ICJ in August 1990. Libya argued before the court that there was no existing boundary with Chad and asked the court to determine one. In support of its position, Libya presented an ingenious case based on a wide array of arguments that sought to demonstrate geographic, historic, and administrative links between Libya and northern Chad. According to the Libyan brief, the **Ottoman Empire** had extended its administration south from Libya into Chad by delegation of authority to the indigenous inhabitants. At the same time, the **Sanusi Order**, based in Libya, had also extended Libyan influence over northern Chad. Finally, Libya argued before the ICJ that control of the Tibesti Mountains by Libya was necessary to prevent hostile incursions from the south.

In contrast, Chad took the position that a recognized frontier between itself and Libya had existed without dispute until the 1970s. Arguing that the object of the case was to arrive at a firm definition of that frontier, it simply asked the court to determine the course of the frontier in accordance with the principles and rules of international law applicable in the matter between the parties.

The ICJ delivered its judgment on 3 February 1994, ruling that the boundary between Libya and Chad was defined by the Treaty of

Friendship and Good Neighborliness concluded by **France** and the **United Kingdom of Libya** on 10 August 1955. Specifically, it found the course of the boundary to run from the point of intersection of the 24th meridian east and the parallel 19 degrees 30 seconds of north latitude, in a straight line, to the point of intersection of the Tropic of Cancer with the 16th meridian east; and from that point, in a straight line to the point of intersection of the 15th meridian east and the parallel 23 degrees of north latitude. The line referred to in the 1955 treaty had commonly featured on maps and atlases as the Chad-Libya boundary since 1919. Since the ICJ did not recognize any Libyan claims to the south of that line, Chad emerged as the clear winner in this case. *See also* SIDRA, GULF OF; PETROLEUM.

INTERNATIONAL ORGANIZATIONS. Libya is a member of the African Development Bank (ADB), **African Union** (AU), Arab Bank for Economic Development in Africa (ABEDA), Arab Fund for Economic and Social Development (AFESD), **Arab League** (AL), Arab Monetary Fund (AMF), **Arab Maghrib Union** (AMU), **Common Market for Eastern and Southern Africa** (COMESA), Council of Arab Economic Unity (CAEU), Customs Cooperation Council (CCC), Economic Commission for Africa (ECA), Food and Agriculture Organization (FAO), Group of 77 (G-77), International Atomic Energy Agency (IAEA), International Bank for Reconstruction and Development (IBRD), International Civil Aviation Organization (ICAO), International Criminal Police Organization (Interpol), International Development Association (IDA), International Federation of Red Cross and Red Crescent Societies (IFRCS), International Finance Corporation (IFC), International Fund for Agricultural Development (IFAD), International Labor Organization (ILO), International Maritime Organization (IMO), International Monetary Fund (IMF), International Olympic Committee (IOC), International Organization for Migration (IOM), International Organization for Standardization (ISO), International Telecommunications Satellite Organization (INTELSAT), International Telecommunications Union (ITU), Islamic Development Bank (IDB), Multilateral Investment Guarantee Agency (MIGA), **Nonaligned Movement** (NAM), Organization for the Prohibition of Chemical Weapons (OPCW), **Organization of Arab Petroleum Exporting Countries** (OAPEC), **Organization of Petroleum Exporting Coun-**

tries (OPEC), Organization of the Islamic Conference (OIC), Permanent Court of Arbitration (PCA), **United Nations** (UN), United Nations Conference on Trade and Development (UNCTAD), United Nations Educational, Scientific, and Cultural Organization (UNESCO), United Nations Industrial Development Organization (UNIDO), United Nations Institute for Training and Research (UNITAR), Universal Postal Union (UPU), World Customs Organization (WCO), World Federation of Trade Unions (WFTU), World Health Organization (WHO), World Intellectual Property Organization (WIPO), World Meteorological Organization (WMO), World Tourism Organization (WTO), and World Trade Organization (WTO; observer status).

ISLAM. With the **Arab** conquest after the seventh century, Islam began to penetrate North **Africa**. Over the next 12 centuries, the North African shore, especially Libya, assumed a distinct Arab-Islamic character. In the early 19th century, **Sayyid Muhammad bin Ali al-Sanusi** founded the **Sanusi Order**, an Islamic revival movement. Centered in **Cyrenaica**, Sanusism later spread to the **Fezzan**, although it never achieved the widespread following in **Tripolitania** that it enjoyed in eastern and southern Libya. More a **religious** than a political movement, it aimed at purifying Islam and educating the Libyan people in Islamic principles. At the same time, Sanusism was like other **Sufi** movements in that its proselytizing activities often had strong political overtones.

When the **Italians** invaded Libya in 1911, the Libyans generally viewed their colonial policies as an attack against Islam and responded by declaring **jihad**. In this sense, it was more religious zeal than **nationalism** in the European sense that provided the motivation to resist Italian occupation. Four decades later, Islam as epitomized by the Sanusi movement gave continuity and legitimacy to the monarchy established in 1951. The role of religion as a legitimizing force declined in the ensuing two decades for a variety of reasons, including increased **education** and urbanization. Nevertheless, Islam continued to exert a major influence on Libyan society. Conservative attitudes dominated and people's values and behavior remained a function of their religious background and attachment.

Today, the vast majority of Libyans belong to the Sunni branch of Islam and adhere to the Malikite school of Islamic **law**. One of four orthodox Sunni schools, the Malikite rite holds that the Koran and the *hadith* are the principal sources of truth. In line with their orthodox Islamic beliefs, Libyan Muslims also practice the Five Pillars of Islam: the profession of faith, alms giving, prayer five times daily, fasting during the holy month of Ramadan, and pilgrimage to Mecca.

When the **Revolutionary Command Council** (RCC) overthrew the monarchy and seized power on 1 September 1969, the religious complexion of the revolution, like many of its essential aspects, remained obscure. The **constitutional proclamation** issued in December 1969 simply stated that Islam was the official religion of the state, and Arabic, the language of the Koran, was its official language. At the same time, the RCC moved quickly to establish its Islamic credentials. Alcohol and gambling were banned immediately and the *sharia* was later established as the official source of law. The revolutionary government also clamped down on the activities of religious groups such as the **Muslim Brotherhood**, the **Islamic Liberation Party**, and the **Islamic Jihad Organization**.

Muammar al-Qaddafi later moved to reinstate sharia law in Libya and to abrogate the European laws imposed by the monarchy because he felt the latter violated Islamic principles. In the process, he exploited opportunities that enabled him to pose as the defender of sharia law and successfully associated his new regime with the defense of Islamic values. Such actions created the false impression that Libya had reimposed Islamic law under Qaddafi's leadership when in fact the real accomplishments of his regime were somewhat more modest.

In conjunction with domestic reform, Qaddafi also attempted to influence the international Islamic movement. His government hosted a variety of Islamic conferences in Libya and abroad in states such as Barbados, Cyprus, and Togo. In addition, Qaddafi established the **Islamic Call Society** to actively promote Islamic religion and culture abroad, especially in Africa. Closely associated with the domestic Institute of Islamic Studies, the activities of the Islamic Call Society linked the internal and external political and religious concerns of the Libyan government. Unfortunately, the society's occasional association with political and subversive acts sometimes undermined its influence as a religious body.

In Libya itself, **opposition** to the Qaddafi government based on Islamic precept has been noteworthy, and the regime has long considered it a serious threat. At the same time, Islamic opposition in Libya is neither cohesive nor necessarily part of a wider movement with origins based outside the country. Consequently, the Qaddafi government has generally tried to steer a middle path between hard-line religious opponents of his regime and the population as a whole, which appears mostly opposed to militant Islam. *See also* THIRD UNIVERSAL THEORY.

ISLAMIC CALL SOCIETY (JAMIYAT AD-DAWA AL-ISLAMIYA). An organization created by the revolutionary government in 1972 ostensibly to act as a missionary body for **Islam**. Its representatives occasionally were reported to be also engaging in political or subversive roles in their host countries. The society has periodically convened conferences in Libya to educate and motivate its members.

ISLAMIC JIHAD ORGANIZATION (MUNAZZAMAT AL-JIHAD AL-ISLAMI). A fundamentalist movement opposed to the **Muammar al-Qaddafi** regime. Thought to have been eliminated in 1973, evidence surfaced in the mid-1980s that the organization was still active. In September 1986, Libyan security forces arrested 26 men accused of being members of the Islamic Jihad Organization. Charged with two assassinations and various acts of sabotage, nine of the men were hanged in televised executions in February 1987. *See also* OPPOSITION.

ISLAMIC LEGION. In May 1979 at an **Islamic** conference in **Morocco**, the Libyan foreign minister called for the creation of a pan-Islamic military force. At the end of the decade, the Islamic Legion, partially composed of mercenaries from the Sahel and the **Sahara**, appeared in public for the first time. Its official aim was to buttress the Palestinian struggle, as well as to support Islamic movements struggling against oppression. In March 1985, Libyan leader **Muammar al-Qaddafi** announced the formation of a national Command of the Revolutionary Forces of the Arab World or Pan-Arab Command, a shadowy group of which little more was heard.

ISLAMIC LIBERATION FRONT. A small, fundamentalist **opposition** group in Libya.

ISLAMIC LIBERATION PARTY (HIZB AL-TAHRIR AL-ISLAMI). Founded in Jordan in the 1950s, the Islamic Liberation Party has focused on the purification of **Islamic** society and the restoration of the original integrity of the Muslim world. In repeated attempts to infiltrate the Libyan **armed forces**, the Islamic Liberation Party has long posed a threat to the **Muammar al-Qaddafi** regime. A remarkably persistent organization, its activities inside and outside Libya have adversely affected Libyan relations with neighboring states. The Islamic Liberation Party in Libya is believed to have links with similar organizations in other parts of North **Africa, Egypt**, and Jordan. In addition to the military, it appears to have made inroads among university students in **Benghazi** and **Tripoli**. *See also* OPPOSITION.

ISLAMIC MILITANT GROUP (IMG). A small, fundamentalist **opposition** group in Libya about which little is known. The Islamic Militant Group reportedly attempted to assassinate **Muammar al-Qaddafi** in March 1996. Government forces clashed with IMG units in eastern Libya one month later.

ISLAMIC REVOLUTION. In July 1978, the **Muammar al-Qaddafi** regime declared an "**Islamic** revolution" in an effort to bring **religious** authorities in Libya into conformity with the **Jamahiriya**.

ISLAMIC VANGUARD. A small, fundamentalist **opposition** group in Libya.

ISLAMISM. The term *Islamism* generally refers to the revival in **religious** awareness, confidence, and identity that has occurred throughout the Islamic world in recent decades. Libyan leader **Muammar al-Qaddafi**'s unorthodox interpretation of **Islam**, coupled with his attempts to use Islam in support of the revolution, put him on a collision course with Libya's traditional religious leadership. Rebuffed by the **ulama**, Qaddafi launched a direct assault on their authority and privilege, stoking Islamist opposition from clergy and layman alike.

Largely homegrown groups such as the **Islamic Liberation Party**, **Islamic Militant Group**, **Islamic Jihad Organization**, and **Libyan Islamic Fighting Group** exemplify the militant side of Islamist opposition in Libya. The **Muslim Brotherhood**, by comparison, is a more moderate group with links to one of the better-known organizations in the region.

In the first two decades of the revolution, the Qaddafi regime pursued relentless repressive measures against Libya's religious leadership, and when those policies provoked a violent reaction from Islamist groups, his security forces crushed the **opposition** in the early to mid-1990s. A nuisance to the Qaddafi regime, Islamist groups have never presented a real threat to its survival. In the wake of the 11 September 2001 **terrorist** attacks on the **United States**, Qaddafi was an early recruit to the war on terrorism because Libyan authorities viewed al-Qaeda and related Islamist groups as a common threat.

ISRAEL. The proclamation of the state of Israel in 1948 provoked ugly demonstrations in Libya as it did elsewhere in the **Arab** world. Unable to express their growing anger over events in Palestine directly against Zionists in that distant region, Libyan Arabs joined their neighbors in venting it locally upon **Jews** who in most cases had little or no connection with Zionism. The **United Kingdom of Libya** under King **Idris** I sympathized with the Palestinians, but took no active role in supporting them. For example, the monarchy acted firmly in quelling serious domestic disturbances precipitated by the 1967 Arab-Israeli War. In part for this reason, the monarchy came under increasing pressure in the 1960s from Arab **nationalist** governments such as **Egypt**, which demanded Libya use its burgeoning **petroleum** revenues to support a more aggressive policy against Israel.

Following the overthrow of the Idris regime, the **Revolutionary Command Council** (RCC) moved Libyan **foreign policy** from sympathy for the Palestinians to active support for their struggle against Israel. The Palestinian cause was placed at the forefront of all Arab causes as **Muammar al-Qaddafi** and his fellow RCC members described the road to Palestine as the path to the liberation of Arabs everywhere. Palestine was considered an integral part of the Arab nation, which could never be truly free and united until Palestine was liberated. In this light, Qaddafi dismissed the Zionist presence in Palestine as nothing more than the latest bridgehead or military base to protect imperialist and neocolonialist interests in the Middle East.

The revolutionary government pledged all material and moral capabilities to the Palestinian cause and declared that Libyan diplomatic relations with other states would be largely dictated by their stand on the Palestinian issue. The Qaddafi government soon made good on this threat, especially in **Africa** south of the **Sahara Desert**, where Libyan **economic** and diplomatic assistance was largely determined by a state's termination of diplomatic relations with Israel.

Libyan foreign policy in Africa met with early success in **Chad** and Uganda, and by mid-1973, the governments of Burundi, Congo, Mali, and Niger had also severed diplomatic relations with Israel. By the end of 1973, another 20 African states had ended diplomatic ties with Israel, and many of them had established relations with Libya for the first time.

Qaddafi maintained the anti-Israeli emphasis of Libyan foreign policy in Africa after 1973 but gave additional attention to the related goals of attacking colonialism and neocolonialism. In the process, Libya failed to consolidate its early diplomatic gains; by the end of the decade, its influence in Africa was on the wane. Throughout the 1980s, African states, one by one, resumed diplomatic relations with Israel.

Qaddafi also expressed his rejectionist posture toward Israel through diplomatic and financial support for the **Palestine Liberation Organization** (PLO) and other more radical Palestinian and non-Palestinian factions. His support for the latter, in what Western governments often considered **terrorist** activities, led frequently to conflicts with the more moderate stance of the PLO. In the aftermath of the Israel-PLO peace agreement in 1995, for example, Qaddafi first attempted to expel several thousand Palestinians living in Libya and later declared that all Palestinians would eventually have to leave Libya.

Qaddafi's opposition to Israel remained total, but the strategies he followed in his first two decades of power left him isolated and ineffective. As events unfolded in the Middle East, his hard line on Israel appeared less and less tenable. At the same time, **United Nations** sanctions, coupled with increasingly effective Western security measures, made rejectionist terrorism a difficult policy to sustain.

Once the UN sanctions were lifted, the Qaddafi regime opened a cautious dialogue with Israel. While the details of contacts between Libyan and Israeli officials remained closely guarded, **media** reports of official and unofficial contacts regularly surfaced. A central issue in bilateral negotiations was believed to be the question of compensation for property left behind by Libyan Jews, many of whom now live in Israel, together with the preservation of Jewish communal sites in Libya. **Saif al-**

Islam al-Qaddafi stated publicly in May 2005 that Libya had no qualms about dealing with Israel; nevertheless, other Libyan officials have sought to tie the issue of compensation for Libyan Jews to the question of Israeli compensation for Palestinian refugees. *See also* POGROM.

ITALO-SANUSI WARS. *See* ITALY.

ITALY. Italy was one of the last European powers to engage in imperial expansion. The Italian city-states were not united until the second half of the 19th century, and consequently Italy was unable to exploit effectively the early colonial opportunities that **Africa** offered neighboring European states. At the turn of the 20th century, Libya was one of the last African territories not occupied by Europeans; and its proximity to Italy made it a primary objective of Italian colonial policy. Italy saw itself carrying on the traditions of the **Roman** Empire, even though Italian unification had occurred only a few decades earlier and Italy was not a leading power at the time.

Visionaries in Rome hoped to return Italy to its former greatness by creating a modern empire. In this regard, many Italians believed it was a historic right, as well as an obligation, to apply Italian sovereignty to those regions once ruled by the Roman Empire. Italy began to penetrate **Ethiopia** in 1879, but its expansion there suffered a severe blow with the defeat of Italian forces at Adowa in 1896. Partially in search of revenge for this humiliating defeat, Italy next turned its attention to Libya.

In addition to issues of historical right and national pride, many Italians viewed overseas expansion as the solution to a number of vexing internal problems. At the dawn of the 20th century, a newly unified Italy still suffered from mutual suspicion and internal conflict among its regions. Many Italian leaders saw a foreign war as a means to divert attention away from internal divisions, unite the population, and increase pride in the homeland. At the same time, overseas expansion offered a means to test the skills and weapons of the highly rated Italian armed forces.

Many Italians also believed the colonization of Libya offered an ideal settlement region for countrymen wishing to emigrate. Italian emigration to the United States exceeded 650,000 people in 1910, while emigration to other areas like Argentina was becoming more difficult because of the distance and expense involved. In contrast, Libya was situated close to Italy, enjoyed a pleasant **climate** with favorable coastal terrain, and was only sparsely populated. Remote myths regarding the fertility of certain areas of Libya only added to the enchantment of this promised land.

Finally, Italy was in need of cheap raw materials and markets for the development of its own economy. Based on the limited information available, many Italians also assumed the colonization of Libya would address this problem in a positive fashion. Little did they know that Libya's **agriculture** was poor, its **industry** limited, and much of its territory empty. Ironically, the **Ottoman** authorities contributed to this lack of information and thus inadvertently encouraged one of the principal arguments for the subsequent Italian invasion. Afraid that foreign explorers and **tourists** would be a first step toward occupation, Ottoman administrators in Libya actively discouraged Westerners, especially Italians, from surveying or otherwise touring the country. In consequence, there was very little reliable, up-to-date information available on Libya, with the notable exception of the report of the Jewish Territorial Organization that toured northern **Cyrenaica** in 1908 and concluded that the area was unfit for large-scale European settlement.

The Italian government declared war on the Ottoman Empire in September 1911, seizing **Tripoli** in October. In November, Italy announced its annexation of the North African province, and the war for control of Libya was joined. Embarrassed with the sorry state of provincial defenses, Ottoman authorities soon began sending military officers to Libya to organize resistance to the Italian invasion. By the end of 1911, an important group of Ottoman officers had arrived from Istanbul. Known as the Special Organization, this group functioned as a pan-**Islamic** secret intelligence unit. Their primary objective was to meet and defeat what the Ottomans considered to be the principal dangers to the empire—local separatist movements and European occupation. These officers took command of the military resistance to the Italians, and in the process, their enthusiasm for the defense of the province bolstered Libyan loyalty to pan-Islamic and Ottomanist ideologies. Consequently, early Turkish resistance received growing Libyan support, and despite an October 1912 treaty in which the Turks abandoned Libya to Italian administration, Libyan forces continued to oppose Italian rule in a struggle that assumed aspects of a holy war. By early August 1915, the

Italians controlled little more than the Libyan coastal cities of Tripoli, **Benghazi**, Derna, and Tobrak.

From 1917 to 1923, known as the period of accords, the Italian government negotiated with a variety of Libyan factions, such as the **Tripoli Republic**, in an effort to consolidate its occupation of the country peacefully. These efforts were largely unsuccessful, as neither side would abandon its claims to control of Libya. After the Fascist takeover of Italy in October 1922, the Mussolini government implemented a more rigid colonial policy. In early 1923, the Italian armed forces embarked on a brutal reconquest of Libya, known as the *Riconquista*. Enjoying an overwhelming superiority in men and equipment, the Italian army had some 20,000 men in the field by 1926, while Libyan guerrilla forces seldom numbered more than 1,000.

Tripolitania and the **Fezzan** were soon pacified, and the struggle then centered on Cyrenaica, where Sanusi **tribesmen** effectively employed guerrilla warfare characterized by raids, ambushes, and sabotage. In an effort to deny resistance fighters access to their people, the Italian authorities in turn increasingly emphasized repression and **terrorism**—men, women, and children were detained in concentration camps, wells were blocked, and **livestock** slaughtered. Active resistance in Cyrenaica finally ended in September 1931 when **Sidi Umar al-Mukhtar**, the most effective Cyrenaican resistance leader, was captured and hanged. On 24 January 1932, the Italian authorities declared an official end to the war begun in 1911.

After 1934, the Libyan territories of Tripolitania and Cyrenaica, together with a military administration in the Fezzan, which was referred to as South Tripolitania, were administered by a governor-general, who in 1937 was redesignated the first consul. He was supported by a general consultative council and a council of government made up exclusively of Italians. On 9 January 1939, the colony of Libya was incorporated into metropolitan Italy and thereafter considered an integral part of the Italian state.

During World War II, **Great Britain** occupied Tripolitania and Cyrenaica, and **France** gained control over the Fezzan. While the division of Libya between two new colonial masters appeared to augur ill for the future, it eventually led to a declaration of independence in December 1951.

After the **One September Revolution** in 1969, the early diplomatic relations between the **Revolutionary Command Council** (RCC) and

Italy were strongly influenced by the bitter heritage of the colonial period. When the revolutionary government seized power, a large and economically important Italian community resided in Libya, although it tended to live apart, with its own schools, churches, and customs. After **Muammar al-Qaddafi** announced in June 1970 that the time had come to avenge the Italian occupation, the RCC in October confiscated Italian-owned property and expelled 20,000 Italian residents. Diplomatic relations between the two states did not improve until after 1975, when a tentative agreement was reached regarding compensation for the property confiscated in 1970.

In October 1978, Qaddafi remarked that modern Italy was not the imperialist power of the past, and over the next decade, Italy became Libya's main commercial partner as well as one of Europe's strongest advocates of an ongoing dialogue with the Libyan government. As the decade of the 1990s opened, Italians dominated the expatriate business community in Libya, with an estimated 57 Italian firms operating there. Still, the improvement in diplomatic relations between Rome and Tripoli did not stop Qaddafi in October 1989 from demanding Italian compensation for the thousands of Libyans killed, injured, or deported during the 1911–1943 period of Italian occupation.

In April 1992, Italy joined other European nations in honoring the mandatory **United Nations** Security Council sanctions imposed on Libya. Libyan diplomats were asked to return home and flights were canceled in compliance with the sanctions, which blocked arms sales and air travel to Libya and called for the expulsion of most Libyan diplomats. At the same time, Italy was less than enthusiastic about subsequent **United States** attempts to expand the sanctions to include a full **petroleum** embargo, and Italian companies maintained the oil and **natural gas** exploration and drilling contracts they had with Libya.

Italy was an early champion of Libyan rehabilitation. Italian foreign minister Lamberto Dini visited Libya to meet with Qaddafi just one day after the two **Lockerbie incident** suspects were flown to the Netherlands for trial. Italian companies also rushed to expand commercial ties in Libya with **ENI**, the oil and gas group, landing a $5.5 billion natural gas project in July 1999. That December, Italian prime minister Massimo D'Alema flew to Tripoli for a two-day visit, the first by a Western leader in eight years. D'Alema's visit reinvigorated extensive bilateral **economic** ties, which had slowed but never stopped during the embargo years. In a joint statement during the visit, D'Alema and Qaddafi agreed to work together to fight **terrorism**. Over the next year, dialogue between the two governments emphasized infrastructure and development projects, where other European states focused almost exclusively on the petroleum sector.

During the Italian foreign minister's August 2000 visit to Tripoli, both countries agreed they had a role to play in strengthening relations between **Africa** and Europe, stressing the need to relaunch the **Arab Maghrib Union** (AMU) as well as to utilize fully other Mediterranean forums. In committing to build a rehabilitation center for the handicapped and a production unit for artificial limbs, both of which were aimed primarily at victims of World War II, Italy also acknowledged a need to address its colonial legacy. Italy later wrote off $260 million in Libyan debts as part of a deal to compensate Libya for damages and suffering during colonial rule.

Libyan relations with Italy in the 2001–2002 period remained a mix of old and new. Speaking in September 2001 on the 70th anniversary of the hanging of Libyan resistance leader **Sidi** Umar al-Mukhtar, Qaddafi encouraged all African states to press for damages from the European countries that had colonized their territories and enslaved their people. Members of Italy's right-wing National Alliance party later voiced satisfaction in December 2001 when they succeeded in inserting into the 2002 budget a government pledge to consider additional compensation for the 20,000 Italians expelled from Libya in 1970. At the same time, Italian officials joined the Qaddafi regime in touting Libya as a natural bridge between Europe and Africa, emphasizing Qaddafi's leadership role in Africa.

In June 2002, ANSA, Italy's national press agency, and JANA, Libya's official news agency, concluded a long-term collaboration accord, the first joint initiative between their respective press organs, aimed at boosting information exchanges between the two states. Libya later closed its **airports** and **ports** and severed telecommunications with the outside world in October 2002 in what it called a Day of Mourning for the victims of the Italian occupation. Shortly thereafter, Italian prime minister Silvio Berlusconi began an official visit to Libya with a round of talks with Qaddafi focused on improved commercial relations.

Libya provides about 25 percent of Italy's total energy imports, and with the activation of a new underwater gas pipeline, its share will increase to 30 percent. This Greenstream pipeline, part of an $8.6 billion gas project by Italy's ENI and Libya's **National Oil Company** (NOC), came on line in early October 2004. Central to the **Western Libya Gas Project**, the 520-kilometer (830-mile) pipeline connects Mellitah in Libya to Gala in Sicily. Libya continues to invest in Italy, and commercial ties are expected to increase further when the two sides resolve their dispute over the colonial past. In a disagreement linked in part to Libyan claims for reparations, 120 Italian firms are still waiting for repayment of credits extended to Libyan bodies, mostly state-owned firms, for work completed in the 1970s and 1980s. The disputed amount totals some 877 million euro; however, Italian firms maintain the total would climb to 1.75 billion euro if interest were taken into consideration.

Prime Minister Berlusconi again met with Qaddafi in late August 2004. With Libya second only to **Morocco** as a transit point for immigration to Europe, talks centered on stopping the tide of illegal immigrants flooding Italy from Libya. Italian and Libyan officials announced in February 2005 the creation of joint teams of specialists to share information and lead targeted inquiries against people traffickers. In addition, Libya continued to press Italy for compensation for damages suffered during the Italian occupation, asking Italy to finance a coastal highway from **Tunisia** to **Egypt** to close accounts with its colonial past. Italy agreed to fund the feasibility study for the project, but not the entire project. While Berlusconi thought he had reached an agreement with Qaddafi in 2004 to end Libya's annual anti-Italian celebrations, Libya again celebrated in October 2005 its Day of Revenge, marking the Italian invasion of Libya in 1911 and the confiscation of Italian properties in 1970. *See also* EUROPEAN UNION; FOREIGN POLICY; YOUNG TURK REVOLUTION.

– J –

JAABIR, ABU BAKR YUNNIS. *See* YUNNIS JAABIR, ABU BAKR.

JABAL AL-AKHDAR. A high plateau in **Cyrenaica** known as the Green Mountain because the relatively greater rainfall in the region supports a thin forest. With maximum altitudes of around 900 meters (3,000 feet), this limestone plateau descends gradually southward into a rocky, semidesert area.

The northern face of the Jabal al-Akhdar is cut by several wadis flowing northward toward the **Marj Plain**; however, most of them terminate at the foot of the Jabal escarpment. In the Jabal area, the wadis radiate from the high watershed and follow the general slope of the land. The most important drainage systems are the Wadi **Derna** and the Wadi **al-Cuf**.

The higher precipitation and humidity of the Jabal area result in forested areas on the slopes of the northern face of the escarpment and perennial vegetation on the upper plateau. Rainfall increases as the elevation increases from the coast to the upper Jabal, but then decreases toward the interior and is rare in the **desert**. The main crops grown in the Jabal al-Akhdar area include wheat and barley, olives, dates, citrus fruits, grapes, and vegetables. Grazing has long been an important source of **agricultural** income.

JABAL NAFUSAH. A rock plateau in **Tripolitania** with a steep north face and a gentle south slope interrupted by some north-facing escarpments. Located in northwestern Libya, it has elevations up to 1,000 meters (3,300 feet). Because of its elevation, the Jabal Nafusah region receives more rain than most parts of Libya and thus is well populated and partly cultivated.

JALLOUD, ABDEL SALAAM (ABDUL SALAAM JALLOUD; ABDEL SALEM JALLOUD) (1941–). Boyhood friend of **Muammar al-Qaddafi** and member of the first political study cell organized by Qaddafi among students at the secondary school in **Sebha**. Under Qaddafi's direction, this early study cell discussed **Egyptian** president Gamal Abdul Nasser's speeches and plotted means of implementing the Egyptian revolution in Libya. At this early stage, it was already clear to the nascent revolutionaries that a military coup was the only means likely to alter the organization and substance of Libyan politics. Consequently, Qaddafi urged members of this first study cell to enter military college instead of pursuing alternate careers. Jalloud was perhaps Qaddafi's closest confidant at the time, and although he had planned to enter medical school, he altered his plans and entered the military college at Qaddafi's urging.

Jalloud was an original member of the **Revolutionary Command Council** (RCC). He served first as prime minister and later as executive secretary of the **General People's Congress** (GPC) when that body was created in 1976. While his political fortunes have risen and fallen, Jalloud remained Qaddafi's chief deputy for much of the first two decades of the revolution. In the early 1980s, Jalloud ran afoul of the **revolutionary committees**. While heading the committees, he attempted to curb their excesses, including the public hangings, but proved no match for them. Not only were his orders ignored, but in a show of force, revolutionary committee members arrested members of Jalloud's family and eliminated his supporters from their ranks. Since that time, his role in the government has been marginalized by Qaddafi, who turned increasingly to his own relatives for support.

JAMAHIRIYA (JAMAHIRIYYA). Newly coined Arabic word that has no official translation but unofficially is understood to mean "state of the masses," "people's authority," or "people's power." The Libyan revolutionary government uses the term to convey the idea that the Libyan people rule themselves without interference from a state administration. **Muammar al-Qaddafi** has also described the jamahiriya as a state run by the people without a government. The **Declaration of the Establishment of the People's Authority**, issued on 2 March 1977, officially designated Libya as the **Socialist People's Libyan Arab Jamahiriya**. After 1986, many Libyans began to refer to their country as the Great Socialist People's Libyan Arab Jamahiriya. Because these official titles are so cumbersome, most observers continue to refer to the country as Libya.

JAMIYAT AD-DAWA AL-ISLAMIYA. *See* ISLAMIC CALL SOCIETY.

JERBA (DJERBA) DECLARATION. *See* ARAB ISLAMIC REPUBLIC.

JEWS. During the **Karamanli dynasty**, Libyan Jews held the official status of *dhimmi* under **Islamic law**, a category or definition that allowed them to run their internal affairs and also permitted them wide-ranging participation in the **economic** and social life of the country. In this period of Libyan history, state-supported piracy was undermined by the Great Powers of Europe, as well as the **United States**, a process that affected all of **Tripolitanian** society, including the Jewish minority. The ongoing success of the world powers in reducing the activities of pirates operating out of **Tripoli** and other **Barbary State** ports meant a significant decrease in state revenues. To cover expenses, the Karamanli administration was forced to levy heavier taxes, including special taxes on Jews, increasing discontent in both urban and rural areas of Libya.

In 1835, the **Ottoman Empire** established direct rule over Libya, ending the reign of the Karamanli dynasty. Throughout the remainder of the century, the Ottoman administration took steps to introduce reforms in Libya parallel to its modernizing efforts elsewhere in the empire. Among other things, these reforms involved a change in the civil status of Jews, in effect elevating them to the status of subjects of the empire equal to all other subjects. In addition, many of the more progressive Ottoman governors took active steps to encourage the small group of wealthy Jewish merchants to become more involved in the development of the region's economy. At the same time, any assessment of the steps taken to increase the status and role of Jews must take into account the reluctance of the Muslim population at large to change their perception of the dhimmi. In the traditional discourse of Muslim life in North Africa in general and Libya in particular, it remained common to refer to Jews in terms that took for granted their lowly position in society as a whole.

The relatively brief period of **Italian** occupation (1911–1943) was characterized by dramatic if contradictory shifts in the position of Libyan Jews. Toward the end of Turkish rule, a small group of the Jewish elite had begun to express pro-Italian sentiments; and after Italian forces occupied the country, they often turned to the Libyan Jews, who spoke Italian as well as Arabic, to serve as middlemen in their relationships with the Muslim population. The subsequent rise of Fascism later resulted in an official policy of coolness toward the Jewish minority, but this did not prevent Jews from continuing to link themselves with the growing European population of Tripoli. And for various reasons, including the importance of Jews to the local economy, **Italo Balbo**, the Italian governor of Libya, worked to delay the implementation in Libya of the racial laws enacted in 1938 in Italy. While the last years of Italian administration brought hardships to Jews in the form of forced labor and deportation to concentration camps in Tripolitania, the Italians are generally remembered as having treated Jews relatively well and as having taken steps to improve their position in Libya.

The period immediately following the end of World War II was characterized by a state of euphoria in which Jewish-Muslim relations, especially in smaller towns and rural areas, seemed to settle down as both groups evidenced a sincere desire to work together. Jews joined the city of Tripoli police force, something that had not occurred under Italian rule, and patrolled together with Muslims. Anticipating better relations, many Jews moved into apartments in the new city, which they rented from Italians who had returned to the mainland. While the period of immediate euphoria declined as postwar economic dislocations set in, a deceptive sense of normalcy prevailed at the everyday level.

At the same time, the establishment of British administration increased expectations and support for complete freedom from colonial rule. In the charged and uncertain political atmosphere that developed, anti-Jewish riots broke out in late 1945 in which more than 130 Jews, and one Muslim, were killed in several days of rioting in Tripoli and nearby rural communities. The definitive history of the 1945 **pogrom** has yet to be written; however, many observers believe the riots can be seen, at least in part, as a symbolic statement claiming restoration of the proper order of Muslim sovereignty. Whatever the complete cause for the riots, their effect on the Jewish population of Libya was soon clear. Libyan Jews after 1948 began to emigrate in increasing numbers to **Israel**.

Anti-Jewish violence again erupted in Tripoli in 1967, and in 1970 the revolutionary government confiscated most remaining Jewish property, compensating its owners with government bonds. By the early 1970s, a Jewish population that had numbered around 35,000 in 1948 had been reduced to no more than 100, with virtually all Jews eventually leaving Libya. The full extent to which Libyan persecution of its Jewish population was tied to the establishment of the state of Israel, as opposed to intrinsic anti-Semitism, was made clear in 1976 at the International Conference on Zionism and Racism in Tripoli. At that time, Libyan leader **Muammar al-Qaddafi** offered Libyan passports to members of the Neturei Karta, an ultra-orthodox Jewish sect opposed to the existence of Israel. Almost three decades later, Qaddafi in 2004 offered to compensate Jews returning to Libya for lost properties if Israel agreed to compensate Palestinians for similar losses.

JIFARAH (GEFARA) PLAIN. The Jifarah Plain, a triangular area of approximately 15,000 square kilometers (6,000 square miles) lying in the northwestern corner of Libya, is bounded on the north by the Mediterranean Sea and on the south by the **Jabal Nafusah** and Jabal Gharian. Its southern edge is a high escarpment that extends from the **Tunisian** border near Nalut eastward to the vicinity of Homs on the coast. The elevation of the Jifarah Plain ranges from 10–20 meters (30–60 feet) above sea level near the coast to around 200 meters (700 feet) at the foot of the Jabal escarpment. Along the Mediterranean coast, the Jifarah Plain is heavily populated with urban areas, including the city of **Tripoli**.

JIHAD. The struggle to spread the triumph of **Islam** is seen as a permanent duty by Muslims. It is often interpreted narrowly to mean holy war, in accordance with the *sharia*, against non-Muslims. In the context of **Muammar al-Qaddafi**'s ideology, jihad is the action element of his variant of **Arab nationalism**. In the broadest sense, he sees jihad as a means to achieve greater social justice inside and outside of Libya. From this angle, revolutionary ideology in Libya initially considered communism and imperialism as equal threats to Islam. However, as the 1970s progressed, it was imperialism that was increasingly identified as jihad's prime target.

The concept of jihad found its most practical expression in Qaddafi's fervent support for the Palestinian movement. In the early 1970s, Qaddafi advocated direct military action against **Israel**. He continued this policy after the October 1973 war strengthened the **Palestine Liberation Organization** (PLO), and the oil weapon proved to be a more effective instrument in support of Arab goals.

Toward the end of the 1990s, when the creation of ad hoc, surrogate groups made it possible for many leaders of governments or movements to pursue the armed struggle while disassociating themselves from such activities, Qaddafi continued his public support. In the end, his advocacy of the use of force in support of the Palestinian cause contributed to a public feud with PLO Chairman Yasser Arafat in late 1979. It also impacted adversely on his aspirations to regional and international leadership. More recently, Qaddafi has devoted much time and attention to differentiating between revolutionary violence, which he continues to support in theory if not in practice, and **terrorism**, which he opposes.

Qaddafi's approach to jihad has also led him to support, at one time or another, a diverse collection of "liberation movements" around the world, including the Somali National Salvation Front, the Irish Republican Army, and Muslim separatist elements in the Philippines. With the exception of Islamic minority groups, Qaddafi's support for liberation movements has seldom been a question of doctrine or vital national interest. Instead, he has seen such support as simply another means to strike at imperialism. At the same time, he has tried to use these activities to increase his own legitimacy by enhancing his domestic and international reputation. *See also* JIHAD FUND.

JIHAD FUND. In January 1970, the **Revolutionary Command Council** (RCC) gave practical expression to **Muammar al-Qaddafi**'s emphasis on **jihad** with the creation of the Jihad Fund. Its objectives included the support of armed struggle for the liberation of usurped **Arab** territories from Zionist control. Funded initially from public and private contributions, the RCC soon established a jihad tax to increase the financial strength of the fund.

The Jihad Fund exemplified Qaddafi's view that the Palestinian issue was the major threat to the integrity of **Islam** and the Arab world. He saw Palestine as an integral part of the Arab nation and believed the latter could never be truly free and united until the former was completely liberated. The enemy was Zionism, seen as a European political movement—not the Jewish people as such—together with the imperialist and colonialist powers responsible for imposing this indignity on the Arab nation. In this sense, Qaddafi's hostility toward the state of **Israel**, expressed in his support for jihad, encompassed the entire ideological system of Arab **nationalism**.

JIHAD GROUP. A small, fundamentalist **opposition** organization with few contacts outside Libya.

JUDICIAL SYSTEM. From the outset, the **Revolutionary Command Council** (RCC) indicated that it planned to place the Libyan judicial system in an **Islamic** context. On 28 October 1971, the RCC established a legislative review and amendment committee, composed of leading Libyan legal experts, to ensure that existing **laws** conformed with the basic tenets of the *sharia*. Two years later, the RCC promulgated a law that merged the existing civil and sharia courts into a single judicial system. The revised court system consisted of four levels, with the Partial Court, existing in most villages and towns, being the primary level. The Court of First Instance served as a court of appeal for the Partial Court; in addition, it was the court of original jurisdiction for all cases involving damages of more than DN100.

Appeals Courts, the third level, sat in **Tripoli**, **Benghazi**, and **Sebha**. As their name suggested, they heard cases referred from a Court of First Instance. The Appeals Courts had no original jurisdiction except for cases involving felonies or high crimes. The Supreme Court, the highest level, sat in Tripoli and was composed of five chambers specializing in civil and commercial, criminal, administrative, **constitutional**, and personal cases. Each chamber consisted of a five-judge panel, with the majority establishing a decision. Before its formal abolition in 1977, the RCC appointed all judges. Thereafter, they were appointed by the **General People's Congress**, with the General Secretariat and the secretary of justice making the actual decision. Except in political cases, both judicial independence and due process have been generally respected in the revised court system.

In addition to the regular court system, a variety of other organizations are involved in the administration or enforcement of Libyan justice. The Supreme Court for Judicial Authorities plays an administrative role, supervising and coordinating the various courts. The prime responsibility of the Council of State is to deliver advisory legal opinions for government bodies on draft legislation or other actions or regulations being considered. Conspiracies against the state have been referred to special ad hoc military courts.

In 2004, Libyan leader **Muammar al-Qaddafi** called for the abolition of the People's Court, which convened periodically to try crimes against the state; however, it continued to try cases into 2005. Qaddafi also stated opposition to the death penalty in 2004; nevertheless, executions have continued to occur. Two Turkish citizens sentenced to death for murder in 1995 and four Egyptian nationals convicted of murder in 2004 were executed in 2005. A Palestinian doctor and five Bulgarian nurses, detained since 1999, were on death row in 2005 for allegedly infecting hundreds of Libyan children with HIV.

– K –

KA'ABAR, ABDUL MAJID ('ABD AL-MAJID KU'BAR; ABDUL AL-MAJID KUBAR) (1909–). Prime minister of the **United Kingdom of Libya** from May 1957 to October 1960 with five cabinet reshuffles. Serving as King **Idris**'s fourth prime minister, Abdul Majid Ka'abar was a **Tripolitanian**, while his two immediate predecessors were from **Cyrenaica**. A member of a family that had distinguished itself in **nationalist** activities, Ka'abar worked his way up in local Tripolitanian politics until he was appointed a member of the National Constituent Assembly in 1950. In the first general election, held in 1952, he entered parliament, where he served as speaker of the house almost uninterruptedly until he formed his government in 1957.

As prime minister, Ka'abar's chief preoccupation was to ensure the continuation of the foreign aid necessary to balance the federal **budget**. Domestically, his administration introduced a new and fairer election **law** in 1959 and conducted a relatively quiet general election in January 1960. Ka'abar initiated monthly press conferences in which he discussed the policies of his administration and answered questions; this practice evidenced a new willingness on the part of the government to improve its communications with the Libyan people. A growing financial scandal centered on the cost of a **road** being built in the **Fezzan** to **Sebha** led to the fall of his government. Originally scheduled to be built in three years at a cost of $5.3 million, cost overruns for the highway led to later estimates of three times that amount. Fearing a vote of no confidence, Ka'abar resigned rather than defend himself before parliament.

KARAMANLI, AHMED (AHMED QARAMANLI) (?–1745). After seizing **Tripoli** in 1711, Ahmed Karamanli purchased his confirmation as pasha-regent from the **Ottoman Empire** with goods stolen from Turkish officials murdered during the coup. While Karamanli continued to recognize nominal Ottoman suzerainty, he created the **Karamanli dynasty**, an independent hereditary monarchy with a government largely **Arab** in composition. Reigning from 1711 to 1745, Ahmed Karamanli pursued an active **foreign policy** with the European powers while extending his political authority into **Cyrenaica**.

KARAMANLI (QARAMANLI) DYNASTY. Under the rule of **Ahmed Karamanli** and his successors, Libya enjoyed a largely independent status, which was recognized by the **Ottoman Empire** from 1711 until 1835. However, the Karamanli regime declined after the death of Ahmed in 1745. Ahmed was succeeded by his son, Muhammad, who ruled until his death in 1754. The reign of Ali I, which stretched from 1754 to 1795, was corrupt and inefficient and led to a confused civil war at the end of the century. Finally, Yusuf Karamanli, one of three sons of Ali I, returned to **Tripoli** and installed himself as pasha. In a throwback to the reign of Ahmed, Yusuf tamed the **tribes** of the interior while defying both Ottoman and British naval power by supporting Napoleon Bonaparte during his 1799 **Egyptian** campaign.

At the end of the century, the **United States** came into conflict with the Karamanli regime. Representatives of President John Adams in 1799 agreed to pay Tripoli $18,000 annually in return for a promise that Tripoli-based corsairs would not molest American shipping. This agreement was similar to others concluded with the rulers of **Morocco**, Algiers, and Tunis. Two years later, however, Yusuf Karamanli demanded a new agreement with a $250,000 annual stipend, and when the U.S. government refused, the American consulate in Tripoli was attacked and the U.S. consul was expelled. Taking these actions as a declaration of war, the U.S. government dispatched a flotilla to the Mediterranean, attacked Tripoli-based vessels, and initiated a partial blockade of the coast. After considerable fighting, Karamanli was finally compelled to conclude peace with the United States in 1805.

The final years of the Karamanli dynasty were characterized by a severe economic crisis compounded by growing social problems and deepening political malaise. In the aftermath of the Napoleonic Wars, the European powers ended the piracy of the **Barbary states**. The end of the corsair system dealt a devastating blow to the economy of the Karamanlis. Deprived of tribute payments, Tripoli found itself unable to pay for basic imports or to service its foreign debt. The subsequent increase in customs duties, together with the imposition of extraordinary taxes on luxury commodities and consumer goods, provoked considerable domestic opposition that degenerated into civil war.

The first serious revolt against the tax policy of the government was initiated in the summer of 1831 by a seminomadic tribe dwelling in the south of Libya in the **Fezzan** and Surt areas. Unrest quickly spread to southern and eastern **Tripolitania** and soon posed a serious threat to the Karamanli regime. At the same time, the government's accumulated external debt, estimated at 750,000 francs or $500,000, passed overdue with the pasha unable to satisfy his creditors in **France** and **Great Britain**. Receiving no satisfaction, these overseas creditors pressed their consuls in Tripoli for assistance in receiving their money. Having exhausted all other means to generate the revenues necessary to meet his financial burdens, Karamanli attempted to impose an emergency tax on his auxiliary force, the *khouloughlis*. Viewing the imposition of taxes as an end to their privileged status, this traditionally tax-exempt military contingent soon initiated the most serious revolt in the history of the Karamanli dynasty.

When the khouloughlis mounted an attack on Tripoli, Yusuf Karamanli realized his hopeless position and abdicated in favor of his son, Ali II, who ruled from 1832 to 1835. At this point, the Ottoman government responded to Ali's calls for assistance by sending troops to Libya to put down the rebellion and restore public order. In the process, Ali II was bundled aboard a warship and carried into exile; thereafter, Turkish troops restored Ottoman rule in Tripoli.

KAWZ, BATTLE OF. One of the final engagements in the **Italian** conquest of Libya. The battle of Kawz took place in western **Cyrenaica** approximately halfway between **Benghazi** and Al-Kufrah in 1931.

KHARUUBI, MUSTAFA AL- (MUSTAPHA KARAUBY; MUATAPHA KHARUBY; MUSTAPHA KHARRUBI; MUSTAPHA AL-KHAROUBI) (1941–). Boyhood friend of **Muammar al-Qaddafi** and original member of the **Revolutionary Command Council** (RCC). Mustafa al-Kharuubi was one of eight RCC members who joined the revolution as members of the political study cell organized by Qaddafi at the military school in **Benghazi**. After the RCC seized power in 1969, he became director of military intelligence. An abortive coup attempt led by fellow RCC member **Omar Mehishi** in August 1975 left only Kharuubi and four other original RCC members in power. These five men, led by Qaddafi, served as the elite of the Libyan leadership for the next two decades. Kharuubi served the revolutionary government in a variety of positions, including commander of the army's Inspector General Corps and secretary of state security on the General People's Committee. In June 1995, the **opposition** group Libyan Patriotic and Democratic Forces reported that Kharuubi had resigned as inspector general.

KIKHIA, MANSOUR (MANSUR R. KIKHIYA). Born into an aristocratic clan in **Benghazi**, Mansour Kikhia studied in Cairo and then at the Sorbonne in Paris, where he earned a **law** degree in the 1960s. He entered the Libyan foreign service under the reign of King **Idris**, but when the **Revolutionary Command Council** seized power in 1969, he embraced the revolution, which he viewed as a redress of the servile, pro-Western policies of the monarchy.

One of the few highly educated members of the revolutionary government, Kikhia rose quickly to become foreign minister, a post from which he resigned in 1973 after a falling out with **Muammar al-Qaddafi** over Libyan ties to **terrorist** movements in Western Europe and the Middle East. After reconciling with the Libyan leader, Kikhia returned to government in 1975 as the Libyan ambassador to the **United Nations**. In 1980, he again broke with Qaddafi and defected, eventually settling in the **United States** and emerging in the mid-1980s as a leading **opposition** figure abroad.

In December 1993, while attending a conference of the Arab Organization of Human Rights, a group that he founded and on which he served as a board member, Kikhia disappeared from a hotel room in Cairo. His disappearance coincided with calls from **revolutionary committees** in Libya to crush traitors and spies. In a speech the preceding month, Qaddafi had declared that opponents of his regime who had escaped to America deserved to be slaughtered. The disappearance of Kikhia focused renewed attention on violence and **human rights** violations by the Qaddafi regime and also damaged its diplomatic relations with **Egypt**. Many people, inside and outside Libya, believe Kikhia was abducted in Cairo by Libyan intelligence agents, who then drove him to Libya in a car with Libyan diplomatic plates.

KUFRAH (KUFRA) BASIN. The Kufrah Basin is one of four sedimentary basins in Libya holding promise of **petroleum** deposits. Located in **Cyrenaica** in the southeast part of the country, the Kufrah Basin has structural elements of varying ages and trends. It contains Paleozoic strata that are partly marine but appears to lack suitable hydrocarbon source rocks. There have been no significant oil discoveries to date there.

KUSA, ISSA. A shadowy figure about whom very little is known. He is widely believed to be a member of the "gang of five" that has run Libya since the mid-1990s. The other four members are **Muammar al-Qaddafi**, **Mohammed Saud**, **Ammar al-Taief**, and **Musa Kusa**.

KUSA, MUSA. The head of Libyan intelligence services since 1996. Musa Kusa was the deputy head of intelligence in 1988 when he was alleged to have been involved in the bombing of Pan Am flight 103 over **Lockerbie**, Scotland. Prominent in efforts to co-opt members of the **opposition**, he played a lead role in the negotiations with **Great Britain** and the **United States** that eventually led to Libya's renunciation of **weapons of mass destruction** in December 2003. Kusa is widely believed to be a member of the "gang of five" that has run Libya since the mid-1990s. The other four members are **Muammar al-Qaddafi**, **Mohammed Saud**, **Ammar al-Taief**, and **Issa Kusa**.

– L –

LABOR. *See* EMPLOYMENT.

LAW. Under the monarchy, Libya imported codified laws from **Egypt**, which were in turn based on **French** Napoleonic law. These laws were applied within a dual **judicial system** of courts, in which the *sharia* courts retained special jurisdiction over those cases arising under **Islamic** law. The sharia law of the Maliki school was applied by these courts in matters of personal status.

After the overthrow of the monarchy, **Muammar al-Qaddafi** moved to reinstate sharia law and to abrogate the European laws he felt violated Islamic principles. In the process, he exploited opportunities that enabled him to pose as the defender of sharia law and thus successfully associated his new regime with the defense of Islamic values. Such actions created the false impression that Libya had reimposed Islamic law under Qaddafi's leadership, when the real accomplishments of his regime were more modest.

In October 1971, a new law established a committee entrusted with the Islamization of Libyan law. Specifically, the committee was empowered to ascertain where in Libyan law there existed conflicts with the fundamental principles of the sharia and then to prepare new legislation to eliminate those conflicts. The most notable achievement of this committee was the drafting of new criminal laws based on the laws set forth in the Koran. In this regard, it should be recognized that sources of Islamic law generally provide little guidance in the criminal area; however, the serious *hadd* crimes set forth in the Koran do provide scriptural authority for principles regarding substantive offenses, rules of proof, and applicable penalties.

The first of the new hadd laws, which revived the crimes of *theft* and *brigandage*, was enacted in October 1972. The law of theft, in particular, was very narrowly defined under the new Libyan law. In order to constitute an act of theft—for which amputation could be imposed—both sharia and Libyan law required that the item must be licit, have a certain minimum value, and be an item to which the thief had no valid claim. Otherwise, the Libyan law provided that only penalties applicable under secular law could be imposed.

Laws reviving the hadd crimes of *fornication* and *false accusation of unchastity* were enacted in October 1973 and September 1974, respectively. In the case of the law relating to *slanderous accusation*, the Libyan law followed the pertinent sharia provisions much more closely than did the other laws. The penalty was set at 80 lashes and subsequent unacceptability of court testimony by any individual convicted under the provisions of the law. The rules of proof also mirrored sharia standards, requiring a confession from the accused or the testimony of two male Muslim witnesses with the appropriate technical legal requirements of rectitude.

A law prohibiting the *consumption of alcohol* was enacted in November 1974. Whereas the traditional sharia law concerned only the drinking of alcohol, the new Libyan law was much broader in application as it addressed acquisition, possession, manufacture, and trading in alcohol as well as offering or giving it to another person. In this case, the new Libyan law was clearly an outgrowth and extension of the prohibition on alcohol use imposed by the **Revolutionary Command Council** in 1969. The law set the penalty for the consumption of alcohol at 40 lashes for a Muslim.

From the examples cited above, it is clear that the revolutionary government in Libya focused on the reinstatement of hadd offenses, while avoiding sharia rules in areas that would threaten orderly **economic** development or the modernization of institutions, such as contract, commerce, and property law. The gap that appeared between the heralded, official policy of Islamization and the modest practical achievements of the program was a natural result of the inherent conflict in Qaddafi's intent to use Islamization as a legitimizing device while at the same time pursuing a revolutionary, **socialist** society.

In June 1988, the **General People's Congress** adopted the **Great Green Charter on Human Rights in the Era of the Masses**, a manifesto that addressed a variety of personal rights and guarantees in an apparent attempt to open the way for increased economic and political liberalization. The document guaranteed **freedom** of movement and respect for personal liberty, and it restricted the scope of the death penalty, indicating that its abolition was the ultimate goal of the government. The charter also outlawed degrading punishment, together with the ill-treatment of prisoners, and proclaimed the right of everyone to a fair trial.

Viewed by many analysts as a concrete, positive step, critics pointed out that the provisions of the Great Green Charter failed to give Libyan citizens the civil and political rights traditionally assumed under domestic law. For example, one article in the charter called on each member of the **jamahiriya** to defend the country to the death, while another outlawed all acts contrary to the principles of the charter. The document also endorsed *The Green Book* as the guide for the liberation of the world. While many of the provisions of the Great Green Charter addressed subjects of concern in Libya, the document proved to be little more than an attempt to codify principles long advocated by Qaddafi.

Externally, Qaddafi's interest in international law grew as he attempted to resolve **frontier** disputes with his neighbors—several of which were brought before the **International Court of Justice**—as well as conflicts with the Western powers. Nevertheless, his efforts to wield it effectively in support of Libyan **foreign policy** objectives were generally unimpressive.

LEADER OF THE REVOLUTION. *See* QADDAFI, MUAMMAR AL-.

LEGGE FONDAMENTALE. An agreement between the **Tripoli Republic** and the **Italian** government in June 1919, the Legge Fondamentale (Fundamental Law)—or as it is sometimes called, the Statuto—was extended to cover **Cyrenaica** in October of that year. Both versions of the **law** provided for a special form of Italian-Libyan citizenship and granted all such citizens the right to vote in **local government** elections. These new citizens were exempted from military conscription, and their taxing power rested with the locally elected parliament. The laws also provided for local administrative positions to be appointed by the Italian governor based on nominations from a 10-man council, eight of whose members would be Libyans selected by the parliament. *See also* RAJMA, ACCORD OF AL-.

LEPTIS MAGNA (LEPCIS MAGNA). One of the finest examples of an African city during the **Roman** period. The importance of Leptis Magna lies in its location in relationship to the Mediterranean Sea and the relatively well-watered hinterland of **Tripolitania**. The key factor in the development of the city was its geographical position, sheltered by a promontory at the mouth of the Wadi Lebda. Leptis Magna displayed the process of growth that other Roman town-plans have made familiar —a nuclear core with divergent, though mostly rectilinear, enlargements. Leptis eventually became more important than the sister ports of Oea (**Tripoli**) and **Sabratah**.

Wealthy private citizens contributed to the early development of Leptis Magna in the first century A.D. In the second century, the Roman emperor Septimus Severus and his two sons contributed in significant ways to the cultural and architectural development of the city. With the decline of seaborne trade that followed serious economic crises at the end of the third century, raids by Libyan tribes on Leptis Magna became bolder and more ruthless. Following an invasion of the city by the **Vandals**, commerce came to a halt, the harbor silted up, and the Leptis Magna was abandoned.

Widely regarded as the best Roman site in the Mediterranean, Leptis Magna is clearly the most impressive archeological site in Libya. The Severan Arch, thought to have been erected in honor of a visit from Emperor Septimius Severus in A.D. 203, is a grand affair. Decorative carvings adorn the upper levels, although most of the carved marble friezes that formerly decorated the top of the arch have been moved to the museum. The Hadrianic baths complex, the largest outside Rome, is thought to have been dedicated around A.D. 126 and later extended. In the center of the building, a *frigidarium* or cold room paneled with marble has a roof supported by eight massive columns. Other buildings on the site that should not be missed include the colonnaded street, Severan Forum, circus, and amphitheater.

LIBIA. Ancient term applied to the area previously occupied by classical civilizations and known today as the **Socialist People's Libyan Arab Jamahiriya**. The **Italian** government and its administrators in Libya consciously used the name Libia to stress the region's **Roman** antecedents, buttressing their colonization efforts.

LIBYA HUMAN AND POLITICAL DEVELOPMENT FORUM. A London-based **opposition** group committed to regime change in Libya. Describing itself as an "independent forum for research and study," the Libya Human and Political Development Forum is a generally reasoned and reliable source for articles and information on contemporary events in Libya.

LIBYAN. Name derived from the ancient Egyptian Lebu or Rebu and applied in the second millennium B.C. to a **tribe** or groups of tribes in **Cyrenaica**. The **Greeks** later used the term to describe the Hamitic peoples of northwest Africa.

LIBYAN DESERT. *See* SAHARA DESERT.

LIBYAN FREE UNIONIST OFFICERS. The secret army organization that claimed credit for organizing and executing the **One September Revolution** that ousted the **Idris** regime on 1 September 1969. It was headed by a 12-member directorate that immediately designated itself the **Revolutionary Command Council**.

LIBYAN GENERAL PETROLEUM COMPANY (LIPETCO). *See* NATIONAL OIL COMPANY.

LIBYAN ISLAMIC FIGHTING GROUP. An **opposition** force thought to be made up largely of Libyans who fought against **Soviet** forces in Afghanistan. The Libyan Islamic Fighting Group, also known as the Libyan Militant Islamic Group, first surfaced in 1995; however, some sources claim it was established as early as 1991. Declaring the **Muammar al-Qaddafi** regime un-**Islamic**, the group pledged to overthrow it, claiming responsibility for failed assassination attempts against the Libyan leader in 1996 and 1997. The head of Libyan intelligence, **Musa Kusa**, reportedly met with representatives of the group in August 1999 to discuss a return to Libya in exchange for a cessation of their activities; however, the group later denied the talks had occurred. The **United States** government, in its *Patterns of Global Terrorism 2003* report, designated the Libyan Islamic Fighting Group a foreign **terrorist** organization on the grounds that it opposed the United States as well as the Qaddafi regime. In early October 2005, the British Home Office also added the Libyan Islamic Fighting Group, which has members in **Great Britain**, to its list of banned terrorist organizations.

LIBYAN MARTYRS MOVEMENT. A militant **opposition** movement active in Libya for more than a decade. The Libyan Martyrs Movement claimed responsibility in 1996 for several armed attacks against government installations in and around **Benghazi**. The head of Libyan intelligence, **Musa Kusa**, reportedly met in August 1999 with representatives of the group to discuss a return to Libya in exchange for a cessation of their activities; the Libyan Martyrs Movement made no public comment on the meeting, but it has been largely quiescent since that time.

LIBYAN MILITANT ISLAMIC GROUP. *See* LIBYAN ISLAMIC FIGHTING GROUP.

LIBYAN NATIONAL ARMY. The Libyan National Army largely consists of Libyan military officers and men captured in the mid-1980s during the fighting in **Chad**. In the aftermath of the war, they decided in June 1988 to form an army and join the **opposition** to the **Muammar al-Qaddafi** regime as the military arm of the **National Front for the Salvation of Libya** (NFSL). The decision to join the NFSL was driven by Col. Khalifa Haftar, a member of the Farjani **tribe** and the commander of what became the Libyan National Army in the spring of 1988. In December 1990, political events in Chad caused the Libyan National Army to move out of Chad to other **African** countries and the **United States**. Washington has long supported the NFSL.

LIBYAN NATIONAL PARTY. An **opposition** group seeking to overthrow the **Muammar al-Qaddafi** regime.

LIBYAN PETROLEUM LAW. The Libyan Petroleum Law was enacted on 21 April 1955, with the final text published in the *Official Gazette* on 19 June 1955. The new **law** contained several innovative features that combined to foster the development of a competitive and prosperous **petroleum industry** throughout the 1960s. At a time when there was no shortage of production elsewhere in the world, the success of the 1955 **Petroleum** Law in getting foreign oil companies to begin exploration in Libya came about largely through its attractive financial terms. Any company fortunate enough to discover oil could anticipate good profits due to the favorable tax structure contained in the law. In addition, the 1955 Petroleum Law provided foreign oil companies with strong assurances, lowering their perception of risk.

In August 1960, the **Idris** government announced it intended to amend some of the provisions of the 1955 Petroleum Law. In so doing, it noted that it was following the example of several other oil-producing states, namely, Iran, Kuwait, Saudi Arabia, and Qatar. At the same time, the government stated that it would not make any new concessions until it had completed the anticipated changes in the existing law. The most significant amendments made to the 1955 law concerned the basis on which royalties were calculated and allowable cost deductions. In an effort to increase government income from oil production, the amendments stipulated that future royalties would be calculated on the posted price rather than the market price of oil. For the same reason, the Libyan government curtailed the costs allowed as deductions to the foreign oil companies by abolishing the depletion allowance.

The 1955 Petroleum Law succeeded in attracting many different oil companies to Libya to prospect for oil. Once these companies had begun to make important discoveries in which they had vested interests, Libya took a tougher stand in terms of its share of the earnings, working within the existing legal framework by interpreting the existing law to its benefit and then amending certain provisions of the law. The monarchy never demanded more than 51 percent participation and never sought **nationalization**. The most important and lasting success of the 1955 Petroleum Law was its ability to attract foreign oil companies other than the majors. Decades later, this enabled the Libyan oil industry to continue production almost without a hitch when the **United States** ordered American oil companies to leave Libya in the mid-1980s.

LIBYAN PRODUCERS AGREEMENT. In the wake of the **One September Agreement**, which led to an increase in the posted price of Libyan **petroleum**, the foreign oil companies working in Libya agreed on 15 January 1971 to act in concert vis-à-vis the Libyan government to prevent the latter from forcing further concessions from individual companies. In the pact, the signatories agreed not to make an agreement or an offer of an agreement with the Libyan government, as it applied to the government take of crude oil, without the concurrence of all producers. If the Libyan government cut the production of one of the signatories, the others also agreed to make good the loss of oil at cost from their Libyan production or from other production if Libyan oil was not available. The amount of oil to be supplied in this manner would be 100 percent of cutbacks in 1971, 80 percent in 1972, and 60 percent in 1973. The existence of the agreement was known to the Libyan government, but its details were kept secret for some time. The full text was not made public until 1974 when the H. R. Hunt oil company filed a claim for damages against Mobil for allegedly violating the agreement.

On 20 January 1972, the Gulf states and the oil companies who were party to the **Teheran Agreement** concluded a new accord, termed the First Geneva Agreement, which raised posted oil prices by a fixed percentage and also provided for quarterly adjustments as the value of the dollar moved up or down. The Libyan government remained aloof from these general negotiations but later achieved a better result on its own. The increasingly aggressive Libyan policy on dollar fluctuations caused the signatories to the Libyan Producers Agreement to broaden their understanding to cover enforced adjustment for currency fluctuations. Nevertheless, the revolutionary government negotiated final agreements with each oil company in May 1972 that contained the same features as the First Geneva Agreement and were effective retroactively from 20 January 1972.

On 1 June 1973, the parties to the First Geneva Agreement signed a subsequent accord to reflect the February 1973 devaluation of the dollar. On this occasion, the Libyan government signed separate but identical agreements with the oil companies on the same day. As a result, all of the **Organization of Petroleum Exporting Countries** nations, including Libya, had incorporated by mid-1973 both inflation and dollar escalation factors into their posted prices until the end of 1975. *See also* NATIONALIZATION; TRIPOLI AGREEMENT.

LIBYAN STUDIES CENTER. The Libyan Studies Center, formally known as Markaz Dirasat Jihad al-Libiyyin Dhud al-Ghazw al-Italyani (Center for the Study of the **Jihad** of the Libyans against the **Italian** Occupation), is one of several research units founded by the **Muammar al-Qaddafi** government in the late 1970s to support the rewriting of Libyan history to include not only the **Sanusi Order** and **Cyrenaica** but also other populations and regions. Opening its doors in 1978, the Libyan Studies Center, as well as the other newly created research bodies, contributed to the research, writing, and dissemination of a new interpretation of Libyan history.

While scholarship on the prehistoric and classical periods was not abandoned, the Qaddafi regime encouraged study of the **Ottoman Empire** and Italian occupation. The Sanusi were given their due, especially the role of the sheiks in the resistance to the Italians; however, information on the dark side of the family that led the Sanusi Order also became more readily available. Equally important, research was encouraged on the role of Ottoman officers from elsewhere in the **Arab** and **Islamic** world in aiding the Libyan resistance against the Italians. For example, both Mustafa Kemal, better known later as the leader of republican Turkey, and Abd al-Rahman Azzam, the first head of the **Arab League**, fought side by side with the Libyans against the Italian invaders. The new scholarship also emphasized the role of the **Tripoli Republic** in upholding the interests of **Tripolitanians** after World War I.

Taking the work of the Libyan Studies Center as an example of this new brand of Libyan history, early publications included translations of the memoirs of figures as disparate as Italian prime minister Giovanni Giolitti and Ottoman minister Enver Pasha, both of whom played important roles in the Italo-Turkish war (1911–1912). The center also published biographies of important figures in the resistance, such as **Umar al-Mukhtar**, and accounts of significant military battles. At the same time, the center interpreted its mandate broadly to include general regional and local histories, for example, scholarly studies of the **Fezzan** and the oasis city of **Ghadames**.

Finally, the Libyan Studies Center published the semiannual *Majallat al-Buhuth al-Tarikhiya* (Historical Studies Review), which included articles on such subjects as the role of **tribal** structure in the organization of resistance in Cyrenaica. Collectively, the work published by the Libyan Studies Center and similar research bodies contributed to an interpretation of Libyan society as cohesive, **nationalist**, anti-imperialist, and loyal to its Arab and Muslim culture.

By the mid-1980s, the close nexus between the interests of the regime and its finance of historical research raised the issue of politically subservient history. In a fluid political climate such as that which existed in Libya, the context of historical interpretation could and did change suddenly and dramatically. Consequently, studies greeted with enthusiasm in the late 1970s sometimes found themselves confined to the restricted access rooms of Libyan libraries less than a decade later. In 1984, Habib al-Hisnawi, a U.S.-trained Libyan historian, in a discussion of the Libyan Studies Center warned an audience in Tunis of the dangers of official history that wholly or mostly supported ideological or political ends. By that time, the ideological framework of the Qaddafi regime was firmly in place, and independent, professional historians in Libya had outlived their usefulness.

LIBYA-SYRIA UNION. Toward the end of 1980, Libyan leader **Muammar al-Qaddafi** initiated a new phase in his search for greater **Arab unity**. In a speech marking the 11th anniversary of the **One September Revolution**, he proposed that his government merge with Syria's. In a characteristic pose, he then threatened to resign from office and enlist as a freedom fighter in Palestine if his proposal was not adopted. The Syrian government accepted almost immediately, and the following day, both governments declared their intention to work toward a unified government. On 10 September 1980, a 13-point statement was issued that indicated Libya and Syria intended to form a unitary state. While the form of the future government was not specified, the declaration stated that it would have popular democratic institutions that would enable the masses to exercise a full role in building their society and future. Opposed to Zionism, imperialism, and reaction, the new state was described as both a base for the Arab revolutionary movement and a nucleus for widespread Arab unity. The statement also indicated that other Arab states wishing to join the Libya-Syria union would be welcome.

After this promising start, the Libya-Syria union lapsed because the two states could not agree on the operative governmental institutions for a unified state. The Syrian government preferred a loose federation, while Libya pressed for the adoption of its own political system. In August 1981, Qaddafi journeyed to Syria in an effort to add substance to the union; his visit led to a joint statement that Libya and Syria had agreed to resume talks aimed at merger. One week later, Qaddafi again voiced disappointment that a union had not been consummated, blaming the failure on unspecified regional and separatist factors as well as the bureaucrats left to implement the union. A more balanced appraisal would have included the difficulties involved in uniting disparate cultures and **economies** with single-minded political leaders separated physically by hundreds of kilometers. Union talks between Libya and Syria continued for several more years, but nothing substantive was achieved. *See also* BENGHAZI DECLARATION; FEDERATION OF ARAB REPUBLICS.

LIBYA-TUNISIA CONTINENTAL SHELF. Libya and **Tunisia** share a land frontier extending 460 kilometers (285 miles) from Bur al Hattabah to Ras Ajdir on the Mediterranean coast. The most striking feature of this boundary is a radical change in the direction of the Tunisian coast approximately 156 kilometers (97 miles) northwest of the terminus of the international boundary line. The second significant geographical feature in the area is a group of Tunisian islands, the Kerkennah group, which are located 18 kilometers (11 miles) off the Tunisian coast south of Ras Kaboudia.

The first offshore **petroleum** concession in the area was granted in 1964, and thereafter a significant amount of hydrocarbon exploration and drilling occurred. The Tunisian concession line of 21 October 1966 was bounded on the east by a stepped line running at a bearing of approximately 26 degrees, roughly perpendicular to the general direction of the coast in the vicinity of Ras Ajdir. Two years later, Libya granted a concession to the Tunisian line and subsequent Libyan concessions followed the same 26-degree line. In 1974, Tunisia granted additional concessions that extended east to an equidistant line. At the same time, both parties claimed larger geographical areas.

The dispute was eventually submitted to the **International Court of Justice** (ICJ) by a special agreement pursuant to Article 40 of the statute of the ICJ on 1 December 1978. Rejecting the boundary proposals of both parties, the ICJ elected to treat the boundary areas as two sectors, proposing a line of delimitation in two segments. The first such segment began at the outer limits of the territorial sea and ran at a bearing of 26 degrees east of north from Ras Ajdir to a point on the parallel of latitude drawn from the westernmost point of the Tunisian coastline between Ras Kaboudia and Ras Ajdir. The second segment of the boundary, more seaward off the coast, veered to the east at a bearing of 52 degrees east of north to reflect the radical change in the direction of the Tunisian coast. At the same time, the ICJ concluded that the Kerkennah Islands should not be given full effect in determining the direction of the coast. Therefore, this segment of the boundary was drawn parallel to a line extending from the most westerly point of the Gulf of Gabes and bisecting the angle formed by a line from that point to Ras Kaboudia and a line drawn from that same point along the seaward coast of the Kerkennah Islands.

In March 1988, the disputants signed an agreement implementing the judgment of the ICJ. In a second agreement signed the same day, representatives of Libya and Tunisia also established a joint exploration zone. *See also* FRONTIERS; MALTA.

LIBYA-TUNISIA UNION. Diplomatic relations between Libya and **Tunisia** improved in the summer of 1970 when **Muammar al-Qaddafi** was received on a visit to Tunisia with great honor and respect. At the same time, the new friendship was slow to expand, as the Tunisian government maintained its moderate stance on the Arab-**Israeli** issue and continued its close ties with the West. Qaddafi returned to Tunisia on an official visit in December 1972. Frustrated with the slow progress in union talks with **Egypt**, he unexpectedly proposed to the Tunisian government an immediate, total union.

While the sudden offer caught the Tunisians off guard, they eventually rejected the proposition. Explaining that his government had no disagreement with a distant target of Arab **unity**, the Tunisian president explained that he preferred to move toward it gradually through increased political and **economic** cooperation. On 17 December 1972, Libya and Tunisia took a step in this direction as they signed a joint communiqué that focused on specific projects such as joint exploitation of the **Libya-Tunisia continental shelf**; increased cooperation in the areas of education, information, and defense; and the expansion of agreements through which Tunisians could freely enter Libya to work. The two governments also agreed to meet quarterly at the prime ministerial level to advance coordination and cooperation. The first such meeting was held in Tripoli in January 1973. Overall, the Libyan and Tunisian governments signed some 15 accords in 1972–1974, but most of them were never implemented.

Two years later, Qaddafi made a second proposal to Tunisian president Habib Bourguiba. In January 1974, Qaddafi visited the Tunisian island of Djerba, where he and Bourguiba negotiated in a single session the creation of an Arab Islamic Republic. The new organization was to have a single constitution, a single president, a single army, and the same legislative, executive, and judicial powers. The new proposal evidenced even less planning than the earlier one, and senior members of the Tunisian government were stunned when their ailing president accepted it. Once the Tunisian prime minister had returned from abroad and the Tunisian foreign minister was dismissed, the Tunisian government allowed the unity pact to lapse, and it soon became a dead letter. In November 1974, a Libyan delegation visited Tunisia in an unsuccessful attempt to breathe new life into the Arab Islamic Republic, to no avail.

LION OF THE DESERT. Funded by the Libyan government and widely distributed, this film starred Anthony Quinn in the role of **Umar al-Mukhtar**. Released in the **United States** in 1979, *Lion of the Desert* was generally faithful to the historical record of the Sanusi sheik, an active and effective guerrilla leader against the **Italians** in 1911–1917 and again in 1923–1931. The film is also an excellent example of the **Muammar al-Qaddafi** government's attempt, particularly in the late 1970s and early 1980s, to rewrite Libyan history to include not only the **Sanusi Order** and **Cyrenaica** but other populations and regions as well.

LITORANEA. As recently as the early 1930s, the easiest way to travel between **Tripolitania** and **Cyrenaica** remained, as it always had been, by sea. By 1935, **roads** had been built from Zuara to **Misurata** in Tripolitania and from Derna to **Ajdabiyah** in Cyrenaica; nevertheless, some 500 kilometers (300 miles) of highway was still needed to join the two provinces of northern Libya. This work was begun by the **Italians** in late 1935 and completed about 18 months later. The new highway, known as the Litoranea, was one of the more impressive works of Fascism, skirting the coast from **Tunisia** to **Egypt** and passing through most of the towns and population centers.

The Italian government contended that the road was built for **tourism**, but its military potential was quickly recognized. The Litoranea made policing the colony by motorized troops easier and less expensive because the number of garrison posts could be reduced. In addition, the new highway vastly improved the capacity of Italian military planners to move forces east or west to meet possible future interventions by British troops from Egypt or French forces from Tunisia. During World War II, the road became a two-way invasion route that carried Italian and German armies into western Egypt in 1940, 1941, and 1942 and British forces into Libya in 1940–1941, 1941–1942, and 1942–1943. Ironically, the final installment of the building cost of the road appeared in the 1943–1944 Italian budget, a year after the highway carried conquering British forces across Libya from Egypt.

LIVESTOCK. The revolutionary government initiated a variety of measures designed to make the country self-sufficient in meat, poultry, and dairy products. Herds of sheep, cattle, and poultry were slowly increased, while the number of goats and camels decreased. Sheep and goats are used for meat, milk, and wool and are found throughout the country with the largest flocks at the Al-Kufrah settlement project. Along the coast, thousands of acres of pastureland were fenced, and both cattle breeding stations and livestock fattening pens were established. To increase meat and milk production, particular emphasis was placed on dairy cattle. Dairy farms were built, breeding cattle imported, and special fodder plants constructed. Everywhere, the government encouraged the use of modern range management practices to prevent overgrazing and to optimize the use of available pasture. *See also* AGRICULTURE.

LOCAL GOVERNMENT. After the **Revolutionary Command Council** (RCC) seized control of Libya, it moved to consolidate its power base by reducing **tribal** and regional power, increasing political participation, and implanting local leadership supportive of revolutionary goals. To promote these ends, the RCC in 1970–1971 promulgated **laws** establishing a Ministry of Local Government. At the same time, it increased the power of local authorities to implement the policies of the national government and redesignated some of the names and boundaries of the existing 10 **governorates**. In this last move, former tribal areas were divided into administrative zones based on population density and geographical divisions. The new zones crossed old tribal boundaries and combined different tribes into a single zone. Rezoning reduced regional identity and accompanying social and political power and relocated traditional administrative centers. It was especially effective when buttressed by supportive actions such as changing the title of the local leadership from sheik to zone administrator and replacing traditional leaders with new ones who qualified for leadership on the basis of standardized civil service examinations. The RCC began to replace traditional leaders with modernizing leaders as early as October 1969.

The RCC scrapped this policy of building a core of revolutionary administrators less than two years after its initiation. The fatal weakness of the newly appointed leaders was their lack of the background and attitudes toward change necessary to generate popular representation and participation. As a result, subnational government continued to function largely as a hierarchical system, rather than the popular system the RCC desired. In this sense, the performance of the revolutionary administrators mirrored a failure of the RCC both in underestimating the power base of the traditional leadership and in overestimating the appeal of its own reforms.

The year 1972 also marked the passage of Law No. 130, new legislation that attempted to rationalize subnational government. The former district and subdistrict divisions were abolished, reducing subnational administration to the governorate and municipality. At both levels, the principal organ of local government became the council, which had both executive and legislative powers. At the governorate level, executive power was exercised by the governor, while the mayor wielded similar power at the municipal level. The RCC appointed both governors and mayors.

A council was created in each of the 10 governorates and 46 municipalities. The membership on these councils comprised both appointed and elected seats, with many members also belonging to the **Arab Socialist Union**. Governorate and municipal councils were given the responsibility for implementing the policies of the central government as well as local planning for areas such as **health**, **education**, social assistance, **agriculture**, local **industry**, and **transportation** services. All council decisions were subject to review by the prime minister, who had the power to reject them; he was also empowered to dissolve councils. Eventually, the Ministry of Local Government was abolished, and its functions were taken over by the Ministry of the Interior.

On 15 April 1973, Libyan leader **Muammar al-Qaddafi** proclaimed a popular revolution and called on the Libyan people to elect **people's committees** at the zone, municipal, and governorate levels. Shortly thereafter, the RCC promulgated Law No. 78, which clarified the administrative responsibilities of the people's committees, transferring to them the authority and functions of the governorate and municipal councils established in 1972. In February 1975, the RCC abolished the governorates, establishing the municipality as the only geographical and administrative subdivision in Libya. Qaddafi again modified the local political landscape in 1992, dividing Libya into 1,500 **communes**, each with its own **budget** as well as executive and legislative functions. In 2000, the Libyan leader abolished most central government executive functions, devolving responsibility to the 26 municipal councils making up the **General People's Congress**. *See also* BASIC PEOPLE'S CONGRESS; DECLARATION OF THE ESTABLISHMENT OF THE PEOPLE'S AUTHORITY; REVOLUTIONARY COMMITTEE.

LOCKERBIE INCIDENT. On 21 December 1988, Pan Am flight 103, on a flight from London to New York, exploded over Lockerbie, Scotland, killing all 259 passengers, as well as 11 persons on the ground. In the wake of the Lockerbie incident, **United States** policy toward Libya progressively hardened. Following the indictment of two Libyan citizens, Abdel Basset Ali al-Megrahi and Al-Amin Khalifa Fhimah, as perpetrators of the attack, Washington aggressively pushed for **United Nations** Security Council Resolution (UNSCR) 731, eventually passed in January 1992, which called for Libyan cooperation in the investigations into the destruction of the Pan Am flight and the later bombing of UTA flight 772 over Niger in 1989. UNSCR 731 specifically called upon Libya to remand the two suspects in the Lockerbie bombing for trial in **Great Britain** or the United States, disclose all it knew about the bombings, take concrete steps to cease its support for **terrorism**, and pay appropriate compensation. When Libya failed to cooperate, the United Nations adopted wide-ranging sanctions against Libya, including an embargo on arms sales and air travel.

In November 1993, the United Nations tightened its sanctions after concluding that the **Muammar al-Qaddafi** regime had defied its order to surrender the two suspects. Eleven of the 15 members of the Security Council voted for a new resolution that froze Libyan assets overseas, banned some sales of **petroleum** equipment, and tightened the earlier decision to end commercial air links with Libya; China and the three Islamic members—Djibouti, **Morocco**, and Pakistan—abstained.

In addition to supporting the UN sanctions, the United States extended its bilateral sanctions regime. In early 1993, it banned American law firms or their foreign branches from offering legal services to the Libyan government or its agencies; in 1996, the Iran-Libya Sanctions Act imposed sanctions on foreign individuals or companies investing $40 million or more a year in **natural gas** or oil projects in Libya or Iran. Washington also called repeatedly for a global embargo on Libyan oil sales; however, it was unable to win the support of key European governments, especially **Germany** and **Italy**, which were heavily dependent on Libyan oil supplies. In April 1996, the relatives of the victims of Pan Am flight 103 filed a $10 billion lawsuit against Libya.

The Libyan government in August 1998 finally accepted a compromise proposal to try the two Lockerbie suspects in the Netherlands, remanding the two suspects into custody in April 1999. In response, the UN Security Council adopted UNSCR 1192, which called for sanctions to be suspended as soon as the suspects were handed over. With the suspension of UN sanctions, Qaddafi moved aggressively to end Libya's diplomatic isolation, focusing first on the **African** continent. He also moved to strengthen long-term commercial and diplomatic ties with key European states.

For the first time in 18 years, representatives of the U.S. government in May 1999 met with Libyan officials to discuss the steps Libya needed to take before sanctions would be lifted permanently. While the handover of the two suspects in the Lockerbie bombing marked a positive first step, American officials emphasized that any further improvement in bilateral relations would depend on Libyan compliance with the requirements set forth in all applicable Security Council resolutions.

In March 2000, the State Department dispatched four consular officials to Libya to assess travel safety for U.S. citizens. The decision to investigate travel safety to Libya generated considerable criticism in the U.S. Congress and elsewhere, especially among the relatives of the victims of the Pan Am bombing. Therefore, it came as no surprise that months passed with no decision announced. In the interim, the U.S. Senate in late April 2000 passed a nonbinding resolution requesting the White House not to lift the travel ban before the end of the Lockerbie trial.

On 31 January 2001, following a 12-year investigation and an 84-day trial that cost an estimated $106 million, three Scottish judges sitting in a special court in the Netherlands found only one of the two defendants guilty in the Lockerbie trial. Abdel Basset Ali al-Megrahi, a former Libyan intelligence agent, was convicted and sentenced to a long prison term; an appellate court ruling in March 2002 upheld the guilty verdict.

With the conclusion of the Lockerbie trial, U.S. and British officials opened talks with Libya's UN envoy to detail the steps Libya must take to permanently end the UN sanctions regime. The White House and 10 Downing Street later issued a joint statement in February 2001 in which President George W. Bush and Prime Minister Tony Blair called on Libya to comply with all relevant Security Council resolutions, especially UNSCR 731.

In a carefully worded statement, Libya in August 2003 finally accepted responsibility for the bombing of Pan Am flight 103 and transferred $2.7 billion to the Bank for International Settlements in Switzerland to compensate the families of the victims. Libya also announced a final compensation deal with the relatives of those killed in the 1989 UTA bombing. On 12 September 2003, the UN Security Council permanently lifted its 11-year-old sanctions regime on Libya, bringing some closure to the Lockerbie incident.

– M –

MAATUQ, MAATUQ MOHAMMED. The assistant secretary for services in the General People's Committee (2004–). Maatuq has also served as the secretary for **education** and vocational training in the General People's Committee. *See also* GENERAL PEOPLE'S CONGRESS.

MAGHRABI, MAHMUD SULEIMAN AL-. On 7 September 1969, the **Revolutionary Command Council** (RCC) announced it had appointed a **Council of Ministers** to conduct the government of the new republic. Mahmud Suleiman al-Maghrabi, a U.S.-educated technician imprisoned in 1967 for political activities, was designated the prime minister. He presided over an eight-member council consisting of six civilians and two military officers. The Maghrabi cabinet fell in December 1969 after the two military officers, neither of whom were members of the RCC, were linked to a plot to overthrow the government. Maghrabi sought exile in **Great Britain** in 1977, where he remained active in the **opposition** to the **Muammar al-Qaddafi** regime.

MAHDI AL-SANUSI, SAYYID MUHAMMAD AL- (1844–1902). Eldest son and successor to **Sayyid Muhammad bin Ali al-Sanusi**. During the four decades of his leadership of the **Sanusi Order**, the number of *Zawaayaa* or **religious** lodges is estimated to have increased fourfold. Marked by a strong personality and considerable organizational talents, Mahdi brought the Sanusi Order to the peak of its influence. By the time of his death, he had established 146 lodges in **Africa**. Equally important, if not more so, he had brought almost all of the bedouins in **Cyrenaica** under the Order's influence. Mahdi moved the Order's headquarters 650 kilometers (400 miles) south from **Giarabub** to the oasis at Al-Kufrah, which was closer to **Sudan** and the Sahel. From that location, he could better supervise Sanusi missionary activities, which were under threat from the **French**, who saw the Order as a rival to their colonial expansion into Saharan and sub-Saharan Africa. After his death, the fortunes of the Sanusi Order declined, chiefly because the European colonial powers had begun to challenge its influence in north-central Africa. *See also* IDRIS AL-MAHDI AL-SANUSI, SAYYID MUHAMMAD; SHARIF, SAYYID AHMAD AL-.

MAHMUDI, ALI BAGHDADI AL-. The current deputy secretary (deputy prime minister) of the General People's Committee. *See also* GENERAL PEOPLE'S CONGRESS.

MAJANIN, WADI AL-. Located in **Tripolitania**, the Wadi al-Majanin is the largest north–south drainage system of the **Jifarah Plain**. It has a watershed area of approximately 650 square kilometers (250 square miles). Located in an area of relatively high rainfall, damaging floods occasionally occur at **Tripoli** and elsewhere along its course.

MALTA. In 1523, the Knights of the Order of St. John of Jerusalem were forced out of their base on Rhodes by a lengthy **Ottoman** siege. In 1530, the Order of St. John, eventually known as the Order of Malta, moved to the island of Malta where it was again the target of Ottoman forces. In 1565, the Ottoman fleet invaded Malta but failed to destroy the Order. Thereafter, its presence on the island remained an irritant for the Muslim world for the next two centuries. During this period, Malta maintained regular contact with the **Barbary states** and later the **Karamanli dynasty** in Libya.

An early **foreign policy** objective of the **Revolutionary Command Council** (RCC) was to reduce the presence of NATO forces in the Mediterranean Sea. In support of this goal, it intervened in 1971 in Maltese negotiations on the future status of British and NATO facilities on the island. The RCC reportedly promised Malta a sizable amount of **economic** aid if the latter would reduce or eliminate existing NATO facilities. Libyan overtures did not prevent Malta from concluding a new, seven-year treaty covering both British and NATO forces; however, the terms of the agreement represented something of a Libyan victory. The negotiations were prolonged and allowed Malta to obtain increased revenues for the base facilities as well as to voice stronger claims to national independence and neutrality. Moreover, the final settlement included a clause that precluded the use of Maltese facilities for attacks against Arab states.

Diplomatic relations between Libya and Malta were generally cordial over the next few years. In 1976, the two governments agreed to refer an offshore oil dispute to the **International Court of Justice** (ICJ). This issue was especially sensitive for Libya as it involved potential new **petroleum** discoveries that would likely become operational in the 1990s when Libya's onshore production was expected to decline. An opportunity for even closer economic and military relations appeared to present itself in 1979 as **Great Britain** prepared to evacuate its forces from Malta; however, diplomatic relations actually deteriorated. At issue was the failure of Libya to compensate Malta for the financial losses resulting from the British withdrawal. An ongoing strain in Maltese relations with Libya were occasional claims from the former that the latter failed to deliver promised economic assistance or **trade** opportunities.

In 1979–1980, Libya closed broadcasting and educational facilities on Malta; and in August 1980, Malta looked to **Italy** instead of Libya to guarantee its neutrality. Diplomatic relations improved later in the decade, and Malta and Libya in 1984 signed a Friendship Treaty with cultural, economic, social, and security clauses. In June 1985, the ICJ finally ruled on the offshore oil dispute. The ICJ accepted Malta's argument that the concept of the exclusive economic zone required that natural prolongation be defined in part by the distance from the shore, irrespective of the physical nature of the intervening seabed. At the end of 1985, Libya and Malta concluded a demarcation agreement implementing the ICJ decision.

In the military clauses of the 1984 treaty, Libya and Malta agreed to exchange information on security matters, and Libya agreed to provide the Maltese armed forces with weapons and training. Libya subsequently considered the exchange of military information to be a vital part of its defense policy, especially after the 1986 **United States** attack on **Benghazi** and **Tripoli**. Libyan leader **Muammar al-Qaddafi** credited the advance information of the attack received from Malta with saving his life.

Consequently, it is not surprising that Libya resisted Maltese attempts in late 1989 to abrogate the military clauses in the 1984 treaty. In the face of a pending Mediterranean superpower summit, Malta approached Libya with a view to renewing only the economic, social, and cultural aspects of the agreement. Qaddafi refused this request on the grounds that the military clauses were an integral part of the total pact. Reluctant to antagonize its most important trading partner, the Maltese prime minister eventually returned to Valletta empty-handed. Libya and Malta did not agree on terms for extending the Friendship Treaty until February 1990. *See also* ROGER II.

MAQARYIF, IMHAMMAD ABU BAKR AL- (ABU BAKR MGARIEF; MUHAMMAD ABU BAKR AL-MUQARYAF) (1940–1972). An original member of the **Revolutionary Command Council** (RCC) and one of eight RCC members who were a part of the political study cell formed by **Muammar al-Qaddafi** at the **Benghazi** military college. Maqaryif served the revolution both as military commander of Benghazi and as minister of **housing**. He died in an automobile accident in 1972.

MARJ PLAIN. The coastal lowland area of **Cyrenaica**, corresponding to the **Jifarah Plain** of **Tripolitania**, is known as the Marj Plain. Forming a crescent approximately 200 kilometers (125 miles) long between **Benghazi** and Derna, it extends inland less than 50 kilometers (30 miles). To the north, it quickly narrows to a point where it is less than a kilometer (half a mile) wide at Tulmaythah (Tolemaide). The Marj Plain is extensive northeast of Benghazi, where it is called the Benghazi Plain. Behind the Marj Plain, the terrain rises abruptly to form the **Jabal al-Akhdar**.

MARRIAGE CUSTOMS. Marriage in Libya is more a family than a personal affair and more a social contract than a sacrament. Because of the limited social contact among the sexes, younger men and **women** enjoy few acquaintances with members of the opposite sex. Many marriages are still arranged by the parents either through friends or a professional matchmaker. There is a preference for marriages between the children of brothers; otherwise, unions most often occur between people of similar social standing. A 1972 **law** states a girl cannot be married against her will or before the age of 16. If a father forbids a girl who is a minor to marry the man of her choice, she may petition the court for permission to proceed with the marriage. However, traditional family relations in Libya would make this a very difficult thing for any girl to do.

The law provides that couples must consent to a union, but in practice, they often play little part in the arrangements. While young men may express a preference as to a future partner, the contract will establish the terms of the marriage as well as the recourse if they are violated. On the other hand, the revolutionary government did enact several laws that improved the position of women with respect to marriage. Men are now prohibited from marrying an alien woman, even an **Arab** from another country, and men in the employ of the state cannot marry non-Arab women. Finally, legislation passed by the revolutionary government gives women divorce rights nearly equal to those of men. On the other hand, children born of Libyan men are eligible for Libyan citizenship while the reverse is not automatically true.

Overall, the legal status of women with regard to marriage and divorce has definitely improved in recent years, but questions remain as to how deeply it has taken root in traditional Libya. Many sectors of society continue to be reluctant to acknowledge changed circumstance, and Libyan women remain hesitant to claim new privileges.

MAZIQ, HUSSEIN (HUSAIN MAZIGH; HUSAIN MAZIQ) (1916–?). Prime minister of the **United Kingdom of Libya** from March 1965 to June 1967. A long-time **Cyrenaican** politician, Hussein Maziq acquired most of his political ability from practical experience. His formal education was limited to primary school followed by night school. His extensive government service began when he was named secretary of the interior in 1943 under the British administration. He became *wali* of Cyrenaica in 1953 and minister of foreign affairs in the **Mahmud al-Muntasir** government. Maziq came to office at a time when student and worker opposition to the monarchy was on the rise. Although his main concern was internal order and balance, he was eventually dismissed by King **Idris** after his administration proved unable to cope with public disorders in the aftermath of the June 1967 **Arab-Israeli** War.

MEDIA. Newspapers and periodicals in Libya are published by the Jamahiriya News Agency, the Press Service, and trade unions. The main newspapers are *Arraid* and *El Balag*. The Socialist People's Libyan Arab Jamahiriya Broadcasting Corporation broadcasts in both Arabic and English from **Tripoli** and **Benghazi**.

MEHISHI, OMAR (OMAR ABDULLAH MEHEISHY; OMAR ABDULLAH MUAHISHI) (1941–1983?). Member of the political study cell organized in **Misurata** by **Muammar al-Qaddafi** when the latter moved there from **Sebha** to continue his secondary studies. At the urging of Qaddafi, Mehishi entered military college rather than pursuing a civilian career. He was an original member of the **Revolutionary Command Council** (RCC), where he served as the minister of planning. In his early 20s at the time, he was the youngest minister in the **Arab** world. Members of the RCC engaged in an intense internal power struggle in 1974–1975. In the end, Mehishi led an unsuccessful coup attempt in August 1975 and subsequently fled to **Tunisia**. According to Mehishi, his showdown with Qaddafi involved the misallocation of funds. As planning minister, Mehishi resisted a Qaddafi attempt to reallocate to foreign adventures funds meant for local development.

The events of August 1975 spelled the end of the RCC. With no institutionalized **opposition** left, Qaddafi moved to consolidate his position throughout the remainder of the year. Mehishi left Tunisia and took asylum in **Egypt**, where he reportedly founded a short-lived opposition group known as the Libyan National Grouping. He suffered a nervous breakdown in 1981 and, after receiving treatment in Kuwait, moved to **Morocco**. As the Libya-Morocco rapprochement developed, eventually culminating in the Treaty of Oujda, Qaddafi reportedly demanded Mehishi's return as part of the deal. In November 1983, Moroccan authorities returned him to Libya where he was arrested and presumably executed.

MINING. Apart from hydrocarbons, commercially viable mineral resources in Libya are limited to the iron ore deposits in the Wadi ash-Shati Valley near **Sebha** and scattered deposits of gypsum, limestone, cement rock, salt, and building stone. Small deposits of phosphate rock, manganese, barite-celestite, sodium carbonate, sulfur, and alum also exist but not in commercial quantities.

The Wadi ash-Shati iron ore deposit is located west of Brak in the Sebha region. One of the largest such deposits in the world, it outcrops or underlies an enormous area in the Shati Valley. While little of the deposit is believed to be of the highest grade, the iron ore content ranges between 25 percent and 50 percent and is estimated to total between 1.8 and 3.3 billion tons. Unfortunately, the distances and technical problems involved in mining the deposit have hampered profitable exploitation. Iron ore deposits are also known to exist southwest of **Tripoli** at Dor al Goussa and Jabal al Haruj al Aswad as well as at Al-Kufrah, but they are not commercially viable under existing conditions.

Salt flats are widely scattered throughout the northern part of Libya. Formed by evaporation at lagoonal deposits along the coast and in closed depressions in the **desert** interior, they cover large areas, especially along the Gulf of **Sidra**. Although production is relatively small-scale, an output of some 30,000 tons per annum makes them one of the largest nonhydrocarbon extraction **industries** in Libya. The most important salt works are located around **Benghazi** and at Mallahat east of Tripoli.

Gypsum is the only other mineral found on any large scale in Libya. Significant deposits are located in **Tripolitania** at Bir al-Ghanam, Yifran, Nalut, and Mizdah. Output from the various gypsum workings in Libya was recently estimated to be some 4,000 tons a year.

Sulfur traces have been reported at scattered points in the salt flats of the Sirtica Basin and in parts of the **Fezzan**. Sodium carbonate is also formed as a crust at the edges and bottoms of a number of dry lakes in the Fezzan. Marketed in Sebha, it is used in **petroleum** refining as well as in soap making and water refining. Small deposits of manganese can also be found in a few areas, although none are being exploited. Such deposits exist at Awbari, Al-Kufrah, Nalut, and Wadi ash-Shati.

MISURATA (MISRATAH; MISRATA). Main city on the coast of **Tripolitania** east of **Tripoli**. Since the days of the **Ottoman Empire**, when it was the second city of the Regency, Misurata has been an important administrative center on the eastern edge of the province. It also served for centuries as an important staging area for **African trade** caravans. Misurata was a major caravan entrepôt, and its merchants supported the local carpet industry for which it is still known. The location of Misurata also made it an important station for communication with both **Cyrenaica** and the **Fezzan**.

Much of the history of Misurata is the product of the Muntasir and Adgham clans, two families that long dominated the town. The Muntasirs often led the local **Arab** population in disputes with the Adgham-led *khouloughlis*. The city is surrounded by a relatively large area of cultivable land and is also noted as a handicrafts center. Its recent prosperity is due in part to a relatively new steel mill, which created something of an economic boom in the town.

MORO NATIONAL LIBERATION FRONT (MNLF). The Moro National Liberation Front is a Muslim separatist movement in the Philippines to which the **Muammar al-Qaddafi** government has periodically provided aid. MNLF leader Nur Misuari long pushed for implementation of the Tripoli Accord, signed in Libya by the government of former Philippine president Ferdinand Marcos in 1976 under the auspices of the Organization of the Islamic Conference (OIC). The agreement stipulated that a provisional government under MNLF control and overseeing 13 out of 25 Mindanao provinces would be established immediately without referendum.

In mid-1996, Misuari flew to Tripoli to seek Qaddafi's support before agreeing to head a Manila-proposed Southern Philippines Council on Peace and Development. Misuari needed Qaddafi's assistance to convince his more militant colleagues to accept the government proposal. Under the terms of the new deal, Misuari became chairman of the autonomous council for three years, after which a plebiscite was to be held to determine which provinces would be included in a permanent autonomous structure. The arrangement was immediately challenged by the Moro Islamic Liberation Front (MILF), a more radical insurgent group, which continued skirmishing with the Philippine army.

Thereafter, Libyan involvement in the Philippines decreased but did not end. In August 2000, Libya, under the guise of the **Qaddafi International Foundation for Charity Associations**, an organization headed by **Saif al-Islam al-Qaddafi**, agreed to pay $1 million for each of 12 foreign hostages held by Muslim rebels in the southern Philippines. Four years later, in November 2004, Libya sent four peacekeepers to the Philippines to oversee implementation of the cease-fire negotiated by the Philippine government and the MILF.

MOROCCO. Occasionally, it has been suggested that the **Revolutionary Command Council** (RCC) had no policy toward Morocco—or the Maghrib in general—during the early years of its rule. On the contrary, less than three months after the overthrow of the monarchy, **Muammar al-Qaddafi** removed Libya from the Permanent Consultative Committee for the Maghrib, an organization King **Idris** I had earlier joined. This move reflected concern on the part of the RCC that membership in a traditional, regional bloc of North **African** states might detract from plans for greater **Arab unity**. Diplomatic relations with Morocco were especially tense in the early years of the revolution, when both states engaged in hostile propaganda. The government of King Hassan II resented Libyan support for Moroccan dissident groups, while the RCC viewed King Hassan's regime as corrupt, feudal, and reactionary. Given the monarchy's ties to the West and its lack of commitment to Palestine, Morocco was a natural target for the RCC because its policies in these areas were very similar to those of King Idris.

Relations between Libya and Morocco improved after a tactical rapprochement in mid-1981. At the time, Libya hoped to restore full diplomatic relations; but it was unwilling to meet a Moroccan precondition that called for an end to Libyan support for the Polisario Front. In any case, Libya did moderate its support for the Polisario at **Organization of African Unity** meetings that summer, while Morocco refused to condemn heightened Libyan involvement in **Chad**. Such mutual restraint suggested that a temporary compromise had been reached and led to Qaddafi's first visit to the Moroccan capital since 1969. At the time, Libya agreed to suspend aid to the Polisario in return for a Moroccan pledge not to condemn Libyan involvement in Chad. Morocco also promised to help improve Libya's strained relations with **Egypt** and Saudi Arabia. A new element in the 1983 rapprochement was Morocco's willingness to turn over Libyan dissidents—for example, **Omar Mehishi**—to the Qaddafi government.

Once diplomatic relations were resumed, a joint Libyan-Moroccan commission met in January 1984. It agreed to a variety of projects, including increased **trade** relations and cooperation in the **industrial** sphere, a joint **bank**, and the exploration of opportunities for Moroccan construction companies in Libya. Eight months later, the two governments concluded a union agreement, known as the Treaty of Oujda, calling for the creation of a federation in which each state would retain its sovereignty. While the union promised some benefit to both countries, its long-term prospects were never good, as the political outlooks of the signatories were often diametrically opposed to each other. In the end, Morocco declared the agreement null and void on 29 August 1986.

Less than three years later, in February 1989, Libya and Morocco joined Algeria, Mauritania, and **Tunisia** in a regional body intended to improve **economic** cooperation. Inspired by the European Community, the **Arab Maghrib Union** (AMU) was considered by its member states to be essential in the face of the upcoming single European market. Libya's relations with Morocco, like its ties with the AMU, traveled a winding road in later years. Throughout most of the 1990s, Morocco and Libya remained at opposite ends of the spectrum on important ideological and political issues, and the development of meaningful economic ties through the AMU was also hampered by contentious regional issues.

At the turn of the century, conditions seemed right for an improvement in multilateral relations through the AMU as well as Libya's bilateral relations with Morocco. In 2000–2001, the **Lockerbie incident** was in the process of resolution, the violence in Algeria was moderating, and a solution to the Western Sahara issue appeared possible. When King Mohammed visited Qaddafi in January 2001, his first visit to Libya since his enthronement in mid-1999, talks focused on improved bilateral relations and increased trade. Five months later, Libyan foreign minister **Mohammed Abderrahman Chalgam** turned to the **Sahara Desert** issue, labeling the Algeria-Morocco dispute the main obstacle to joint Maghrib action and calling for his neighbors to abolish barriers, **frontiers**, and passports. Thereafter, stronger bilateral ties with Morocco, as well as the other Maghrib states, were held hostage to the policy disputes dividing the AMU. The AMU summit, originally scheduled for 1999, was repeatedly postponed, and in May 2005, Morocco again rejected Algerian attempts to include the Western Sahara issue on the AMU agenda. *See also* FOREIGN POLICY.

MUGHARIAFF, MUHAMAD AL- (MUHAMMAD YUSUF AL-MAQARYAF). An economist, ex-state controller, and former Libyan ambassador to India, Muhamad al-Mughariaff founded the **National Front for the Salvation of Libya** (NFSL) in 1980. Since that time, he has remained head of the NFSL, making it one of the most active and effective Libyan **opposition** movements in exile.

MUHAAFAZAAT. The **governorates** into which Libya's three traditional regions were divided in 1963. They were abolished in 1975.

MUKHTAR, SIDI UMAR AL- (c. 1862–1931). Born of the Minifa **tribe** and educated first at the **Sanusi Order** school at Janzur and afterward at **Giarabub**, Umar al-Mukhtar took a prominent part in the first phase of the **Italian** conquest (1911–1917) and in blocking Italian penetration during and after World War I. An active and highly effective guerrilla leader after 1923, he became a hero of the **Cyrenaican** resistance movement. Captured and then hanged on 16 September 1931, effective resistance to the Italian occupation ended with his death. On 24 January 1932, Italian authorities declared an end to the war begun in 1911. The name of Sidi Umar al-Mukhtar is often employed by the **Muammar al-Qaddafi** regime to emphasize the need to continue the struggle for national liberation.

MUNAZZAMAT AL-JIHAD AL-ISLAMI. *See* ISLAMIC JIHAD ORGANIZATION.

MUNTASIR, MAHMUD AL- (1903–?). First prime minister of the **United Kingdom of Libya**, from December 1951 to February 1954. Muntasir was born into a distinguished **Tripolitanian** family and educated at the University of Rome. He was not involved in early Libyan **nationalist** movements, concentrating instead on family business affairs. As befitting a traditional leader in an **Islamic** society, Muntasir achieved some **religious** authority and prestige. In the mid-1930s, he served as director of religious endowments and chairman of the Muslim high school council.

In 1950, Muntasir was named vice president of the Tripolitanian Administrative Council, and the following year, he served in the national assembly. Appointed Libya's first provisional prime minister in March 1951, Muntasir later formed the first national government under the 1951 **Constitution of Libya**, with a cabinet reshuffle in September 1953. The conflict between national and provincial authorities was the major challenge faced by his government and the eventual reason for its downfall. After his resignation, he was appointed Libyan ambassador to London.

Muntasir returned as prime minister from January 1964 to March 1965. Faced with a growing wave of **Arab** nationalism, one of his first acts was to recommend the nonrenewal of the base agreements negotiated by Libya in the early 1950s with **Great Britain** and the **United States**. A general election was held in October 1964, but King **Idris** later dissolved the new parliament because of mounting public unrest over the validity of the general election. Weary of politics, Muntasir resigned on 21 March 1965, citing reasons of poor health.

MUNTASSER, OMAR AL- (OMAR MONTASSER; OMAR MUSTAFA MONTASSER) (1939–). Omar al-Muntasser was educated in **Egypt** and at the American University in Beirut. He joined the Libyan operation of Mobil Oil Corporation in 1960 and was chairman of the **National Oil Company** (NOC) in 1975–1979. He later served as the secretary of heavy **industry** on the General People's Committee of the **General People's Congress** (GPC) until that post was abolished in 1986. In February 1987, the GPC elected Muntasser secretary general of the General People's Committee.

MURZUK BASIN. One of four sedimentary basins in Libya holding promise of **petroleum** deposits, the Murzuk Basin is situated in the **Fezzan** and is separated from its northern extension, the **Ghadames Basin**, by the Al-Qarqaf platform. Some consider the Murzuk and Ghadames basins to be the same sedimentary basin and thus argue that Libya has only three sedimentary basins with oil deposits. Located far from the seacoast and in inhospitable terrain—sand dunes in the region sometimes exceed 300 meters (1,000 feet) in height—the remoteness of the Murzuk Basin discouraged oil exploration in the early days. However, in the 1980s, Eastern European oil companies discovered significant deposits of petroleum reserves in the Murzuk Basin, including a large field containing some two billion barrels.

MUSLIM BROTHERHOOD. Founded in **Egypt** in the 1920s, this movement has long played an active role in Libyan politics. After independence, it criticized the **Idris** regime because of both its pro-Western policies and the particular practices of the **Sanusi Order**. When **Muammar al-Qaddafi** came to power, he rightly viewed the Muslim Brotherhood as a serious threat to his regime, as the two movements differed on every issue from **Arab nationalism** to direct popular democracy to the status of **women** in **Islamic** society. These policy differences were perceived by the revolutionary government to be so profound and so serious that it moved to eliminate the influence of the brotherhood completely. Successful in its efforts, the regime had largely eradicated the Muslim Brotherhood in Libya by 1984. Thereafter, if its members played a political role, it was largely through the medium of other **opposition** movements such as the **National Front for the Salvation of Libya**.

– N –

NAJM, MUHAMMED (MOHAMAD NAJIM; MOHAMAD NEJM; MUHAMMAD NAJM) (1942–). An original member of the **Revolutionary Command Council** (RCC), Muhammed Najm was one of eight RCC members who was also a member of the political study cell formed by **Muammar al-Qaddafi** at the military college in **Benghazi**. He served the revolutionary government as minister of municipality and later as minister of **education** and **housing**. Najm withdrew from the RCC in 1975 as the result of intense policy conflicts that split the organization into pro-Qaddafi and anti-Qaddafi factions.

NATIONAL CONFERENCE OF THE LIBYAN OPPOSITION. A coalition of Libyan **opposition** groups that met in London in June 2005 to develop a strategy to topple the **Muammar al-Qaddafi** regime. Agreeing on the need for regime change, the final conference declaration explicitly rejected foreign military support, holding the **United Nations** responsible for restoring the 1951 **Constitution of Libya**.

NATIONAL DEMOCRATIC GROUPING. An **opposition** group seeking to overthrow the **Muammar al-Qaddafi** regime.

NATIONAL FRONT. When the news reached **Sayyid Muhammad Idris al-Mahdi al-Sanusi** that the Council of Foreign Ministers, meeting in Paris in the spring of 1946, was considering the fate of the **Italian** colonies, he returned to Cairo to confer with British authorities in order to keep himself informed as to the outcome of the Paris meetings. His sudden departure, which was misunderstood by Libyan leaders in **Cyrenaica** to imply a protest against British reluctance to transfer authority to him, prompted **tribal** chiefs to address a manifesto to British authorities expressing regrets at the departure of Sayyid Idris and demanding the fulfillment of the country's national aspirations. Specifically, the manifesto demanded acknowledgment of independence and the formation of a constitutional government, recognition of the Sanusi Amirate under Sayyid Idris, and immediate transfer of the administration to the Cyrenaicans.

Upon his return to Cyrenaica in July 1946, Sayyid Idris gave approval for the creation of a National Front (al-Jabha al-Wataniya) to present the Cyrenaican case to the international commission of inquiry that was sent to Libya to ascertain the wishes of the people as to their political future. The organization also sought to coordinate the activities of older, established political leaders with the rising influence of younger **nationalists**. Membership in the National Front, intended to represent both desert tribes and urban dwellers, soon increased to 75, including a working committee of 19.

The National Front made its first official declaration on 30 November 1946. Addressed to the British authorities, the manifesto demanded recognition of the Sanusi Amirate under Sayyid Idris and permission to form a national government to administer the country in preparation for complete independence. Moderate and reasonable in tone, the wording of this initial declaration reflected the concern of Cyrenaican leaders that Italy's interests in **Tripolitania** were still strong and might yet succeed in getting the upper hand and thwarting independence. If Cyrenaica was to unite eventually with Tripolitania, as many international councils suggested, Cyrenaican leaders felt it vital first to ensure their own independence.

When the British authorities showed some willingness to transfer powers from the British military to Cyrenaican hands, the broader question of Libyan **unity** became a subject of controversy in Cyrenaica. Politicians of all ages tended to agree on the Sanusi Amirate; however, they split over the issue of union with Tripolitania. The younger politicians tended to insist on unity with Tripolitania under Sanusi leadership, which weakened and compromised the position of elder politicians more focused on Cyrenaica.

NATIONAL FRONT FOR THE SALVATION OF LIBYA (NFSL; AL-JABHA AL-WATANIYYA LI-INKADH LIBYA). The most active of the **opposition** groups in exile is the National Front for the Salvation of Libya. It was founded on 7 October 1981, the 30th anniversary of the promulgation of the **Constitution of Libya** under the monarchy by Dr. **Muhamad al-Mughariaff**. The founding date highlights the constitutional nature of the political system the NFSL wants to establish after the overthrow of the **Muammar al-Qaddafi** regime. In the immediate post-Qaddafi era, the NFSL plans to establish a constitutional government and a supreme council to rule for a maximum of one year, while general elections are held and a new constitution adopted.

The NFSL is not the only opposition movement to Qaddafi, but it is the most important. In this role, it has tried to provide a neutral umbrella under which all shades of opposition could gather—unlike many other opposition groups, most of which have tended to be identified with explicit currents of **Arab** or Libyan political thought. It is also noteworthy that the NFSL espouses a liberal democratic political and economic ideology and that its ranks include a multitude of political factions and ideologies from liberal democrats to traditional supporters of the Sanusi to former sympathizers of the **Muslim Brotherhood**. Nevertheless, the vision of the NFSL remains a synthesis of the **religious** and cultural legacy of the Libyan people prior to the **One September Revolution**. As such, it seeks a new Libya that would include the basic freedoms, constitutional democratic rule, and sanctity of private property absent in the Qaddafi era.

In June 2005, the NFSL helped organize a two-day congress of Libyan opposition groups in London. Reflecting its long-term program, the final declaration of the conference explicitly rejected foreign military support to topple the Qaddafi regime, calling for **United Nations** assistance in restoring the 1951 constitution. The NFSL is a member of the **National Conference of the Libyan Opposition**.

NATIONAL OIL COMPANY (NOC). With a view to increasing its control over the **petroleum** industry, Libya in April 1968 announced the establishment of the Libyan General Petroleum Company, known as LIPETCO, noting that its charter was to enter into new partnerships with international oil companies on terms more beneficial to Libya. The **Council of Ministers** had the final authority over both the acreage allocated to LIPETCO and any participation agreements negotiated by the new company. In turn, LIPETCO assumed the government's share in any joint oil exploration and development ventures as well as the government's right to participate in existing and future concessions. LIPETCO was the forerunner of the National Oil Company, also known as the National Oil Corporation, established by Law No. 24 dated 5 March 1970.

Operating under the supervision of the minister of petroleum, the mission of NOC from the outset was to achieve Libya's **development plans** in the hydrocarbon sector. The new **law** limited future joint ventures to those in which the foreign partner assumed all the risk in the exploration period and insisted that NOC's share be fixed at a given percentage from the start of operations. It also authorized NOC to enter into contractual agreements, which bore fruit in the **exploration and production-sharing agreements** (EPSAs) embarked upon after 1974. On 4 July 1970, Law No. 69 transferred all marketing of oil products in Libya to NOC. The following year, the **Brega Petroleum Marketing Company** was established as an NOC subsidiary to carry out these activities.

Since 1970, the National Oil Company and its 33 subsidiaries have controlled the Libyan petroleum and **natural gas** industry, upstream and downstream. NOC and its subsidiaries in 2005 accounted for around 63 percent of Libyan oil production. The main subsidiary production companies are the Waha Oil Company (WOC) and the Arabian Gulf Oil Company (AGOCO). When U.S. oil companies withdrew from Libya in 1986, WOC was created to assume operation from Oasis Oil Co., a joint venture of NOC (59.16 percent), Conoco (16.33), Marathon (16.33), and Amerada Hess (8.16). WOC production dropped during the years of **United States** and **United Nations** economic sanctions because its oil fields were equipped with American equipment for which it could not acquire spare parts. AGOCO is the second largest NOC subsidiary, with production coming mainly from the Sarir, Nafoora/Aguila, and Messla fields. With the award of new EPSAs in 2005, NOC's share of production will drop in the future.

NATIONAL PUBLIC ORGANIZATION FOR INDUSTRIALIZATION (NPOI). An organization created by the **Revolutionary Command Council** in 1970 to implement its public-sector **development plan**. *See also* INDUSTRY.

NATIONALISM. From the beginning, **Arab** nationalism was the central element of **Muammar al-Qaddafi**'s ideology and probably his primordial value. Like **Egyptian** president Gamal Abdul Nasser, Qaddafi based his variant of Arab nationalism on a glorification of Arab history and culture that views the Arabic-speaking world as the Arab nation. Libya is the heart, the vanguard, and the hope of the Arab nation and thus the custodian of Arab nationalism. Acknowledging the "backwardness" of the Arab nation, Qaddafi lays the blame for the existing situation on four centuries of stagnation under **Ottoman** rule, the subjugation and exploitation of first colonialism and then imperialism, and finally the repression and corruption of reactionary, monarchical rule. At the very core of his approach to Arab nationalism is the belief that the Arab people are equal if not superior to the other peoples of the world and have the right and the duty to manage their own resources and shape their own destiny.

A survey of 500 male and female students at Garyounis University, released in 2001, suggests the Qaddafi regime has been largely successful in creating a national identity based on Arab nationalism, as opposed to the regional or local identities previously dominant in Libya. The majority of the students surveyed did not distinguish **Islam** from Arabism as a source of personal identity, instead stating the two elements were equally important to them. *See also* THIRD UNIVERSAL THEORY.

NATIONALIZATION. On 7 December 1971, the **Revolutionary Command Council** (RCC) nationalized the British Petroleum Company's share of the British Petroleum–N. B. Hunt Sarir field. British Petroleum was replaced by the Arabian Gulf Exploration company, and the **petroleum** production of the other companies operating in Libya was frozen to prevent them from supplying British Petroleum. On 16 December 1971, the oil companies responded by amending the **Libyan Producers Agreement** to cover total or partial nationalization of the properties of any party by the Libyan government. The RCC depicted the nationalization of British Petroleum as a protest against **Great Britain**'s failure to intervene to prevent the shah of Iran from occupying the Greater and Lesser Tunb Islands off the coast of the United Arab Emirates. In this sense, the political rationale behind the nationalization of British Petroleum put its case in a different category from later actions. At the same time, decisive action on the part of the RCC set the stage for Libya's growing emphasis in 1972–1973 on participation in the petroleum sector.

Less than a year later, the revolutionary government accepted a proposal by the Italian oil producer **ENI** and its subsidiary **Agip** for 50 percent state participation in their concession. Libya then focused its attention on N. B. Hunt, where it argued that 50 percent state participation was not negotiable and was only a first step toward even greater state participation. After N. B. Hunt rejected Libya's participation terms and also refused to market what had once been British Petroleum's share of Sarir crude oil, Libya nationalized N. B. Hunt on 11 June 1973. In justifying this action, **Muammar al-Qaddafi** argued the right to nationalize was a basic right of any state with oil deposits.

In August 1973, **Abdel Salaam Jalloud** intervened in ongoing talks regarding state participation in the oil industry. He made it clear that the revolutionary government was now demanding 51 percent of net book value of all the oil companies. Agreements incorporating those terms were signed the same month with Occidental and Oasis, the largest independent and major group producers, respectively. On 1 September 1973, the fourth anniversary of the revolution, Libya announced a general nationalization decree that covered 51 percent of the assets and business of all the oil-producing majors and their partners operating in Libya. The major oil producers, under the terms of the Libyan Producers Agreement, tried to stand behind N. B. Hunt, but they were unable to provide effective support. With worldwide demand exceeding supply, there were simply too many willing buyers to make a boycott of Libyan crude effective.

The terms of the September 1973 nationalization decree included similar provisions for each producer. Libya took 51 percent of the assets and business of the companies concerned, with the exception of Esso's gas liquefaction plant. Compensation was decided by three-man committees consisting of representatives from the Appeals Court, the Libyan **National Oil Company**, and the Ministry of the Treasury. While the oil companies all protested the actions of the Libyan government, they eventually agreed over the next four years to individual settlements. The year 1973 thus marked the high point of the Libyan emphasis on participation, although selected refinements to the general nationalization decree occurred thereafter. By 1976, the state's share of total Libyan oil production, excluding royalty oil, had reached 64 percent. *See also* ONE SEPTEMBER AGREEMENT; TEHERAN AGREEMENT; TRIPOLI AGREEMENT.

NATURAL GAS. Despite extensive plans for gas-based industrialization, Libya was slow to develop a clearly defined policy on natural gas. On the one hand, enhanced utilization of associated gas was generally encouraged by **petroleum** regulations governing conservation, which imposed penalties for the excessive flaring of natural gas. On the other hand, with the exception of a couple of fields formerly owned by Esso, natural gas fields in Libya were mostly abandoned with their wells plugged. The revolutionary government in the early years was also largely unsuccessful in taking its hard negotiating position on oil prices to the issue of liquefied natural gas (LNG) exports.

That said, Esso Sirte did construct a liquefied natural gas plant at Marsa al-Brega in 1968. Its main pipeline was a 170-kilometer (105-mile), 90-centimeter (36-inch) unit from the Zelten field, originally designed to carry seawater as part of an oil-field reinjection program. The

Raguba field provided a secondary supply via a 97-kilometer (60-mile), 56-centimeter (22-inch) spur, with additional sources of natural gas available from fields owned by Oasis and Amoseas. Libya later refused to include this LNG plant in its **nationalization** agreement with Esso.

By the 1980s, Libya had begun to reevaluate its long-term policies regarding the exploitation of natural gas reserves. In line with other members of the **Organization of Arab Petroleum Exporting Companies**, Libya reduced the flaring of associated natural gases. It also awarded a growing number of gas-related contracts to European firms and expanded its coastal gas pipeline.

Recent estimates by the **National Oil Company** (NOC) put Libya's proven natural gas reserves at 1.49 trillion cubic meters, the third highest in **Africa** behind Algeria and Nigeria. Annual production approximates 10 billion cubic meters a year, and production is expected to increase rapidly with the development of the **Western Libya Gas Project** (WLGP), which comprises gas extraction from various fields in Wafa in the **Ghadames Basin** together with the NC-41 field off the coast of Libya.

Two factors help explain Libya's present emphasis on expanding natural gas production. First, the government hopes to use more gas and less oil for domestic power generation, freeing up oil production for export. Second, Libya's natural gas reserves are largely unexplored, as well as unexploited, and are anticipated to be much larger than current estimates. Large new discoveries have been made in recent years in the Ghadames and el-Bouri fields as well as in the **Sirte Basin**, and the latest round of exploration and production awards are expected to produce large new finds in the relatively near future.

The potential thus exists for a large increase in Libyan gas exports to Europe. The WLGP alone calls for Libya to export 8 billion cubic meters of natural gas annually to **France** and **Italy** over a 24-year period beginning in 2006. Not surprising, international interest in Libyan natural gas production has rapidly increased. For example, energy giant Royal Dutch Shell announced a long-term deal with NOC in May 2005. The agreement covers the rejuvenation of the existing LNG plant at Marsa al-Brega, together with the exploration and development of five major blocks, covering 20,000 square kilometers (7,700 square miles), in the Sirte Basin. Subject to gas availability, Shell also agreed to undertake jointly with NOC the development of a new LNG facility.

NONALIGNED MOVEMENT (NAM). The **Muammar al-Qaddafi** regime has been an active, often enthusiastic, but highly unpredictable participant in the Nonaligned Movement (NAM). In September 1973, Qaddafi attended a NAM conference in Algeria where he posed as the champion of the Palestinians, quarreled with Fidel Castro about the **Soviet Union**, and generally isolated himself from mainstream NAM members. In September 1986, less than six months after the **United States** had bombed **Benghazi** and **Tripoli**, the Libyan leader attended the eighth NAM meeting in Zimbabwe, where he was widely expected to seek sympathy and support against additional outside aggression. Despite a conference resolution condemning the raid, Qaddafi instead lectured the group, accusing NAM of not being nonaligned at all but instead of being allied with the former colonial powers in the West. *See also* POSITIVE NEUTRALITY; THIRD UNIVERSAL THEORY.

– O –

OIL. *See* PETROLEUM.

OIL INVESTMENTS INTERNATIONAL COMPANY (OIIC). Formerly known as the Foreign Petroleum Investments Corporation, Oil Investments International Company, a state holding company registered in Curaçao in the Netherlands Antilles, was established in April 1988 to oversee Libyan investments overseas in the **petroleum**, **natural gas**, petrochemical, and energy sectors. Over the next few years, OIIC acquired a majority share in several European refineries, distribution networks for refined products, and retail service centers. By the early 1990s, OIIC controlled an estimated 250,000 barrels a day of refining capacity and some 3,000 service stations in several European countries.

ONE SEPTEMBER AGREEMENT. Occidental was the first foreign **petroleum** company to reach a pricing agreement with the **Revolutionary Command Council** (RCC). It made an offer in early September 1970, which was accepted by the Libyan government and then backdated to 1 September to coincide with the first anniversary of the revolution. Over the next few weeks, similar agreements were reached with the other oil companies operating in Libya. The highlights of these agreements included increasing the posted price of a barrel of oil by 30 cents, with an additional two-cent increase on 1 January of each of the five succeeding years. This marked the first significant increase in the posted price of oil since the formation of the **Organization of Petroleum Exporting Countries** (OPEC) in 1960.

The new posted price was also subject to a new escalation based on the specific gravity of the petroleum extracted—two cents a barrel for each API (American Petroleum Institute) degree above 40 and minus 1.5 cents a barrel for each API degree below 40. This proviso, which eventually altered the oil industry's entire gravity differential structure, favored Libya's lighter crudes. In terms of oil revenues, the impact of the revised gravity escalation formula was to augment the agreed-upon increase in the posted price of oil. The oil companies further agreed to make retroactive payments for underpricing Libyan oil after 1965 or the start of production, whichever came first. The agreements also ended the old 50–50 profit sharing pattern based on posted price, and the income tax rate increased as high as 58 percent, with a new average of around 54 percent. Finally, the RCC imposed harbor dues on all oil tankers, and the total salaries of all foreign workers were now to be paid in foreign currency.

The worldwide impact of the One September Agreement and its successors was enormous. Since its creation, OPEC had been largely successful in blocking the downward movement of oil prices, but the oil companies had been equally successful in blocking upward movement. The RCC changed this situation overnight. At the same time, it ended the myth that the oil companies were the sole determinants of the posted price of crude oil. In the process, Libyan policy drove up the market price of oil to a level that enabled the oil companies to make a nice profit in 1970 even after they paid the higher posted price.

As the negotiations leading to the One September Agreement progressed, most OPEC states remained aloof; only Iraq and Algeria actively supported Libyan policy. However, once the agreements were concluded, the Libyan government emerged temporarily as a leader of the oil-producing states as the latter hastened to negotiate similar agreements. Libyan influence was clearly visible at the 21st OPEC conference, held in Caracas in December 1970. A resolution adopted by the meeting mirrored the Libyan settlement in that it called for negotiations with the oil companies aimed at raising the posted price, increasing taxes, and adopting a new gravity differential scheme. In support of these objectives, the conference formed a committee to negotiate on behalf of the six Gulf states. *See also* LIBYAN PRODUCERS AGREEMENT; NATIONALIZATION; TEHERAN AGREEMENT; TRIPOLI AGREEMENT.

ONE SEPTEMBER REVOLUTION. The revolution planned and executed by the **Libyan Free Unionist Officers** movement that overthrew the monarchy of the **United Kingdom of Libya** on 1 September 1969. The Libyan Free Unionist Officers movement was led by a Central Committee of 12 officers who soon designated themselves the **Revolutionary Command Council** (RCC). Initially, the composition of the RCC remained anonymous; however, within a week, it issued a terse press release announcing the promotion of **Muammar al-Qaddafi** to commander in chief of the Libyan **armed forces**. Thereafter, the RCC continued to be a relatively closed organization, but it was soon apparent that its chairman and the de facto head of state was Qaddafi.

Once it seized power, the immediate objectives of the RCC were twofold: consolidation of its power and the socioeconomic and political development of Libya. To achieve these objectives, it sought to increase the mobilization and participation of the populace and to improve the technical capacities and responsiveness of governmental institutions. Like many developing states, its basic problem was the creation of an institutional framework that generated the levels of mobilization and participation necessary to achieve its objectives but did so within the centralized, authoritarian political system insisted upon by the RCC.

OPPOSITION. Throughout the 1970s, the **Muammar al-Qaddafi** regime followed an increasingly radical socioeconomic policy that included **housing** redistribution and currency exchange and led, by the end of 1981, to the state takeover of all import, export, and distribution functions. The resultant widespread redistribution of wealth and power directly affected the economic well-being of different sectors of the population, activating dormant political opposition. Members of the nascent middle class, who had prospered after 1969 as the revolutionary government's emphasis on the service and housing sectors created lucrative opportunities in **trade**, real estate, and small consumer manufacture, were especially affected. Opposition was not limited to a single socioeconomic group, however; it included many farmers, educated elites, and government officials. Outside the country, organized opposition existed among student groups and self-imposed exiles, with a number of such groups operating in Western Europe and the Middle East.

Opposition to the government based on **Islamic** precept is especially noteworthy, as it has existed for some time and is considered by the regime to present a serious threat. Widespread throughout Libyan society, Islamic opposition is neither cohesive nor necessarily part of the broader movement with origins based outside Libya itself. The **Islamic Liberation Party**, **Islamic Militant Group**, **Islamic Jihad Organization**, and **Libyan Islamic Fighting Group** represent the violent side of Islamic opposition. On the other hand, the **Muslim Brotherhood** has clear links with one of the better-known Islamic organizations in North **Africa** and the Middle East.

In the 1990s, Qaddafi, like many rulers in the Muslim world, became increasingly concerned about the threat of Islamic fundamentalism. While often referring to such militants as "mad dogs" and "**terrorists**," he called for a stricter application of *sharia*, advocating amputation for robbery and public flogging for adultery in an apparent attempt to increase his popularity and political legitimacy. In February 1994, the **General People's Congress** (GPC) extended the application of Islamic **law** and granted new powers to Libya's **religious** leaders, including the right to issue religious decrees. In short, Qaddafi tried to steer a middle path between hard-line religious opponents of his government and the wider population opposed to militant Islam.

Exiled Libyan opposition groups are numerous but generally lack cohesion and integration. The more visible of these organizations include the Libyan Constitutional Union, Libyan National Movement, Libyan National Party, Movement of the Popular Struggle for Libya, Libyan Liberation Organization, Army Organization for the National Salvation of Libya, Libyan National Grouping, and **National Front for the Salvation of Libya**. A Libyan campaign against exiled dissidents, promoted by the newly formed **revolutionary committees**, generated global notoriety in the early 1980s when more than a dozen dissidents were assassinated.

In a populist gesture, Qaddafi summoned the diplomatic corps in March 1988 to Furnaj Prison, where he mounted a bulldozer and breached the walls of the facility. Several hundred prisoners were then released from Furnaj as well as several thousand from prisons else-where in Libya. At the time, Qaddafi claimed to be tormented by the idea of people behind bars, realizing the futility of imprisonment as a punishment. A few days later, he reportedly went to the emigration of-fice and personally destroyed lists of Libyans forbidden to leave the country, mostly for political reasons. He also repeated a suggestion that the country should be defended by a **people's militia**. Qaddafi's **human rights** initiatives in this period culminated in the adoption in 1988 of the **Great Green Charter on Human Rights**, which promised basic guar-antees to Libyan citizens, but its adoption did little to change the over-all context of the policies pursued by Qaddafi since the early 1970s.

In March 1990, economics as opposed to ideology dominated the proceedings of the GPC. Delegates rejected government efforts to re-duce expenditures; instead, they called for lower taxes, free **health** care, cheaper housing loans, and increased government spending on state-owned **industries**. Qaddafi responded to these criticisms by attacking corruption in government. Later in the session, the GPC elevated Qaddafi to the status of supreme leader, a position that appeared to give him the authority to overrule any policy decision with which he dis-agreed. Later in the year, major changes were made in the composition of the General People's Committee of the GPC. The appointment of a new secretary general and replacement of several key secretaries on the General People's Committee were steps widely interpreted at the time as a victory for hard-liners.

Another failed coup attempt occurred in October 1993, and large numbers of arrests followed the rebellion of an army unit near **Mis-urata**. Growing dissatisfaction with selected regime policies was com-pounded by worsening economic conditions in the wake of the imposi-tion of **United Nations** sanctions over the **Lockerbie incident**. Reported dissatisfaction among key Libyan **tribal** groups at this time posed yet another threat to Qaddafi's carefully balanced hold on power. In the second half of the 1990s, opposition groups continued to report regular acts of sabotage and clashes with the Qaddafi regime.

After more than three decades in power, some opposition to the Qaddafi regime still exists, but it is badly fragmented and must deal with sustained regime support, especially among younger, less well-to-do elements of society. This support has been generated both by Qaddafi's charismatic leadership and by the regime's distributive economic policies. Qaddafi has also balanced skillfully the three insti-tutions—the Libyan **armed forces**, GPC, and revolutionary committees —that form the basis of his support. The careful juxtaposition of these three separate but related institutions, intertwined as they are with tribal alliances, has allowed him to dominate the overall political system.

Moreover, Qaddafi has taken extraordinary and often violent mea-sures to limit collaboration between domestic and foreign opponents. In addition to operational difficulties, the various opposition groups face extensive internal repression as well as state terrorism abroad. Under these circumstances, meaningful institutional or political change toward any form of democracy seems highly unlikely. As a result, a legacy of the post-Qaddafi era could be a new ideological and political system completely unlike the **jamahiriya** system imposed upon Libya today.

In July 1999, the Libyan ambassador to the United Nations met in New York with a small group of Libyan dissidents, unsuccessfully seek-ing support for the Qaddafi regime. In August 1999, two **Islamist** movements, the **Libyan Martyrs Movement** and the Libyan Militant Islamic Group, better known as the Libyan Islamic Fighting Group, re-portedly met with Libya's chief of intelligence to discuss allowing them to return to Libya in exchange for a cessation of their activities. The Libyan Islamic Fighting Group later denied the talks had occurred, and the Libyan Martyrs Movement made no public comment on the re-ported meeting. Two factors—the success of government efforts against regime opponents and a shortage of funds previously provided by Saudi dissident Osama bin Laden—may have encouraged opposition groups to seek accommodation with Qaddafi. The Libyan UN ambassador again met with opposition figures later in the year in another unsuc-cessful attempt to co-opt them.

In April 2000, the Islamic Observation Centre, a London-based group, reported that Libya had executed three of eight Islamic militants recently extradited from Jordan. **Benghazi** was a center of anti-Qaddafi activity in the mid-1990s, and antiregime activities, including the as-sassination of two senior security officers, were again reported in mid-August 2000. Six opposition organizations, the Libyan Change and Re-form Movement, Libyan Constitutional Grouping, Libyan Islamic Group, Libyan National Organization, Libyan National Democratic Rally, and the National Front for the Salvation of Libya, met in August 2000 to discuss a joint strategy. However, ideological differences and factional disputes continued to bedevil efforts to present a united front. This was evident in the vagueness of the joint statement issued at the end of their meeting, which emphasized agreement only on ending the regime and establishing an alternative one.

Consequently, there appeared to be little immediate prospect of a coordinated campaign against the Qaddafi regime. On the other hand, opposition groups clearly saw the need to command some international attention in a period in which the Libyan government was enjoying considerable success, beginning with the suspension of the UN sanctions regime. With a plethora of opposition groups already in existence, a new Libyan opposition organization, the National Reform Congress, announced its formation in mid-August 2000, calling for a just and civilized multiparty system in Libya.

In a controversial move, Libya in late October 2000 officially asked Interpol for assistance in arresting 17 Libyans living abroad, including a number of prominent Libyan dissidents. International human rights groups continue to document hundreds of political prisoners in Libya, some held without charge or trial, and many for over a decade. For example, Amnesty International reported two prisoners of conscience, Abdullah Ahmed Izzedin and Salem Abu Hanak, were sentenced to death in February 2002, while scores of others in the same trial received sentences ranging from 10 years to life in prison. The defendants were among 152 professionals and students arrested in 1998 on suspicion of supporting either the Libyan Islamic Group or the Muslim Brotherhood. Many of these detainees were scheduled for release in late May 2005, but their liberation was postponed at the last moment.

Following the release of dozens of political prisoners and prisoners of conscience on 1 September 2002, Qaddafi falsely claimed that Libyan jails were now empty with the exception of a few "heretics" linked to the Taliban or al-Qaeda. He indicated these prisoners would be treated the same way the **United States** was treating prisoners at Guantánamo Bay, with no right to defend themselves, no access to lawyers, and no respect for their human rights. Later in the month, the Libyan Islamic Fighting Group challenged claims of the **Qaddafi International Foundation for Charity Associations**, an organization run by the Libyan leader's son, **Saif al-Islam al-Qaddafi**, that Libyan jails no longer held prisoners of conscience. In the context of so-called attempts "to appease America and the West," the group accused the regime of deliberately underestimating the number of political prisoners in jail, especially Islamic fundamentalists.

Major divisions over vision and tactics continue to split Libyan opposition groups in exile, limiting their activities to remote and ineffective criticism of the regime. The fragmented nature of the opposition was amply demonstrated in late June 2005 when approximately 300 opposition members, representing many but not all Libyan opposition groups, convened a two-day congress in London. In a statement before the conference opened, the organizers stressed that political change in Libya should be undertaken without foreign interference, criticizing the United States for normalizing ties with the Qaddafi regime and practicing a double standard when it came to human rights violations in Libya. But, while agreeing on the need for regime change in Libya, Qaddafi's opponents could not come to a consensus on the best strategy to achieve that result. Calling for the formation of a transitional government in Libya, the final declaration of the **National Conference of the Libyan Opposition** held the United Nations responsible for restoring the 1951 **Constitution of Libya**. At the same time, a number of participating organizations emphatically rejected foreign military support to topple Qaddafi, specifically the use of U.S. tanks.

ORGANIZATION OF AFRICAN UNITY (OAU). Created in Addis Ababa, Ethiopia, on 25 May 1963, the Organization of African Unity was once the world's largest regional organization. A compromise between statists and unionists, the policy of the organization was driven by several acknowledged norms of action. These included a recognition of the sovereign state as the basic legitimizing unit of **African** politics, a preference for intrasystem solutions to African problems rather than external ones, and a rejection of wars of conquest as acceptable policy alternatives. **Muammar al-Qaddafi**'s ideology, which centers on pan-**Arabism**, anti-Zionism, and **Islam**, repeatedly clashed with the norms and values of the OAU and thus often led to conflict and controversy within the organization.

Initially, the OAU adopted a cautious but positive attitude toward the fledgling **Revolutionary Command Council** (RCC). The latter quickly allied itself with the **Egyptian** government, which enjoyed enormous prestige and support in the region, and this close association with Egypt encouraged other OAU states to welcome the new Libyan regime. The early domestic policies of the revolutionary government, which stressed sovereignty and independence from the West, were also welcomed by OAU members who pursued similar policies in their own countries.

This period of relative harmony in Libyan relations with the OAU lasted until 1972. Following Nasser's death in 1970, the Egyptian government increasingly emerged as a stumbling block on the road to Arab **unity**. In turn, the Libyan government turned to pan-**Islamism** as an alternative and took to criticizing African governments that it considered unfaithful or pro-Zionist. **Tripoli** aligned itself with some of the more notorious dictatorships in the region, such as the Ugandan government of Idi Amin Dada, and was charged with economic or political intervention in the internal affairs of a growing number of African states.

After 1978, Libyan relations with the OAU entered a new phase in which isolation turned to ostracism. The principal issue was Libya's growing involvement in **Chad** and the repercussions that diplomatic relationship, together with related talk of a pan-Islamic African federation, had for the remainder of Sub-Saharan Africa. In 1980, Libya and Chad negotiated a treaty of friendship that provided Libyan support for Chadian independence and territorial integrity and thus laid the groundwork for increased Libyan involvement in Chadian domestic affairs. It was also the forerunner of a January 1981 Libyan communiqué which stated that Chad and Libya had agreed to work together toward the realization of complete unity. In response to the proposed merger, the chairman of the OAU called for a withdrawal of Libyan forces from Chad, and an emergency OAU meeting that convened later also condemned the suggested union. Libyan policy toward Chad eventually led to canceling Tripoli's designation as the site for the 1982 OAU summit. In the process, Qaddafi was denied the presidency of the organization, an embarrassing and disappointing turn of events for the Libyan leader.

Following the suspension of UN sanctions in April 1999, Qaddafi attended the 35th OAU summit in Algiers in July, where he was feted as a long-lost brother by fellow heads of state. Resurrecting his vision for African unity, he called for creation of a Pan-African Congress to boost unity, together with an Integration Bank to accelerate implementation of a treaty for the Economic Community of Africa. At the same time, he invited African leaders to attend an extraordinary OAU summit in Tripoli, timed to coincide with the 30th anniversary of the **One September Revolution**, to discuss a restructuring of the OAU charter to strengthen relations among member states. The Algiers summit, in a closing statement, called for the complete and immediate lifting of all sanctions against Libya.

While many African leaders took a cautious approach to Qaddafi's invitation, most agreed to participate in the extraordinary summit in Tripoli out of respect for a veteran revolutionary whose steadfast support for liberation movements had helped end colonialism on the continent. Nevertheless, few expected concrete results from the meeting. In advance of the summit, Qaddafi called for the creation of a United States of Africa, pressing the issue in a meeting of African foreign ministers convened prior to the summit. In the end, African leaders refused to endorse his call for a United States of Africa but did issue a declaration at the end of the summit calling for the strengthening of the OAU and the rapid creation of a pan-African parliament, African Monetary Union, and African Court of Justice. Qaddafi reiterated his call for African unity in April 2000 at the **European Union**–Africa summit in Cairo and in July 2000 at the OAU summit in Togo.

The **African Union**, a regional organization modeled after the EU and intended to rejuvenate an impoverished continent, replaced the 35-year-old OAU in July 2002.

ORGANIZATION OF ARAB PETROLEUM EXPORTING COUNTRIES (OAPEC). OAPEC was established in January 1968 to coordinate member economic activity in the **petroleum** industry. Its member states include Algeria, Bahrain, **Egypt**, Iraq, Kuwait, Libya, Qatar, Saudi Arabia, Syria, and the United Arab Emirates.

ORGANIZATION OF PETROLEUM EXPORTING COUNTRIES (OPEC). Established in 1960, OPEC coordinates the **petroleum** policies of the major oil-producing states. Its member states have included Algeria, Ecuador, Gabon, Indonesia, Iran, Iraq, Kuwait, Libya, Nigeria, Qatar, Saudi Arabia, the United Arab Emirates, and Venezuela. Libya joined OPEC in 1962 to prevent the major oil companies from reducing their posted price for oil, the basis of taxable income for governments of producing countries. The Libyan monarchy shared OPEC's stand on the need to maintain government income from the taxation of oil production. At the same time, it was reluctant to provoke foreign oil companies over the issue of the posted price of oil at a time when confrontation with the oil companies might slow development of the Libyan oil industry. Consequently, the Libyan government under King **Idris** I was pleased to profit from OPEC gains in negotiations with the oil companies but unwilling to endorse OPEC policies that might threaten its relationship with the companies that had started production in Libya.

The revolutionary government that seized power from the monarchy in the **One September Revolution** in 1969 immediately reversed the oil policies of the monarchy. For a short time, it was the aggressive oil policies of the **Revolutionary Command Council** that led the industry, while other OPEC members looked on from the sidelines, mostly implementing the initiatives as they succeeded in Libya. First, the revolutionary government increased the posted price of oil, which led to a sharp decline in oil output but a jump in oil revenues. Later, it seized control of oil production in Libya by **nationalizing** the oil companies.

In recent times, Libyan oil production has been restrained by OPEC production quotas. As an OPEC member, Libya is required, at least in theory, to restrict its crude oil output to the levels set by OPEC to stabilize prices. In the early 1980s, Libya refused to adhere to its allocation and continued to produce more than its due until OPEC revised member quotas in 1983. OPEC again revised the quotas in 1984, 1986, 1988, and 1997, and Libya appeared to produce within these limits although it protested occasionally that its allocation had been set too low. In any case, a number of factors, including the sanctions imposed by the **United States** and the **United Nations**, combined throughout most of the 1990s to make it unclear as to whether Libya could substantially exceed its OPEC allowance even if it so desired. In the early 21st century, Libya has pressed periodically for increased production quotas, and having announced plans to return its oil production to three million barrels a day by 2015, it will surely continue to press for larger quotas in the future.

OTTOMAN EMPIRE. Contemporary Libya was Ottoman territory for most of the period from 1551 to 1911. The Ottomans governed Libya through a pasha appointed by the sultan. In turn, the pasha was dependent upon the *janissaries*, an elite military caste stationed in Libya to support Turkish rule. In matters of taxation and **foreign policy**, the sultan allowed the local *divan* or council considerable autonomy.

After 1661, Turkish power declined and the janissaries, together with local corsairs, often manipulated the divan. In the end, the janissaries began designating among their own number a *dey* or local chief. Between 1672 and 1711, some 24 deys attempted to control the increasingly chaotic political situation in Libya. In 1711, **Ahmed Karamanli**, an officer in the Turkish army, led a popular revolt against the ruling dey, founding the **Karamanli dynasty**, which governed Libya for next 124 years.

In 1835, the Ottomans overthrew the Karamanli dynasty and reestablished direct control over **Cyrenaica** and **Tripolitania**. Ottoman reoccupation marked a turning point in the history of Libya. The restoration of Ottoman rule signaled the end of the long period of decentralized political rule that had prevailed under the Karamanlis. Under the new regime, Libya became more directly responsible to and hence more closely linked to the Sublime Porte—the government of the Ottoman Empire. In support of a new policy of consolidating central power over distant provinces, the Ottoman authorities in Libya were expected to use every political and economic resource—**trade**, taxes, or otherwise—in support of centralization.

The new political establishment had a major impact on the traditional patterns of life of many segments of Libyan society. With the consolidation of Ottoman rule, the power of influential groups was destroyed, and new patterns of relationships developed between the local population and their rulers. For example, the process of implementing direct government control over the interior of Libya alienated **tribal** leaders, who had enjoyed autonomous status and socioeconomic privileges under the Karamanlis. These tribal forces now found themselves under a more centralized political system that expected them to perform regular fiscal obligations. The new demands of the Ottoman administration created strong opposition, leading eventually to a series of local uprisings between 1835 and 1858.

The decade of the 1850s marked the end of the transitional stage of Ottoman rule in Libya. In the early 1860s, Ottoman administrators began to implement a variety of political and administrative changes in the province. As a result, Ottoman rule became more centralized and Libya became more highly integrated with the central authority of the Sublime Porte. New institutional developments included the establishment, for the first time, of administrative and village councils, together with municipalities and a court system. New methods of tax assessment and collection were introduced, along with postal and telegraph services, **educational** reforms, and **health** services. While major institutional and administrative reforms followed the end of the transitional period, Turkish rule over the years became increasingly remote, with Turkish control over Libya reaching a low ebb at the outset of the 20th century.

Italy encountered only minimal resistance when it moved to occupy Libya after declaring war on the Ottoman Empire on 29 September 1911. By the middle of 1912, the Ottoman government in Istanbul had weakened further in its determination to support resistance in Libya. Concerned with events in the Balkans, the Sublime Porte opened negotiations with Italy, and a treaty of peace was concluded shortly after the Balkan Wars broke out in October 1912. The Ottomans did not cede sovereignty over their North African province, but the sultan did issue a declaration to his Libyan subjects granting them full and complete autonomy. At the same time, he reserved the right to appoint an agent charged with protecting Ottoman interests in Libya and agreed to withdraw Ottoman officers, troops, and civil officials. The Italians, in turn, reaffirmed their annexation of the province, an act not recognized by international law until after the 1924 Allied peace settlement with Turkey.

The outbreak of World War I saw the reappearance of Ottoman influence in Libya. While the Ottoman government had formally withdrawn from the province, authorities in Istanbul continued to encourage local Libyan forces in their resistance to the Italians. When Italy entered the war on the side of the Entente powers, the Ottoman Empire and its German allies hoped to use the few remaining troops in Libya to spark a revolt against the British, French, and Italian presence in North Africa. The eventual failure of Ottoman efforts to dislodge the European powers occupying Libya—efforts that revealed the continuing importance of pan-**Islamic** loyalties in Libya—left the province with leaders more interested in solidifying local authority than in developing wider loyalties. By the end of World War I, these local Libyan leaders had largely given up hope for reincorporation into a larger Ottoman or Islamic political union. *See also* OTTOMAN REFORMS; YOUNG TURK REVOLUTION.

OTTOMAN REFORMS. When the **Ottomans** reoccupied the former autonomous province of Libya in 1835, they found a war-torn country, undermined by years of strife and neglect. It took the new governors almost 20 years to reestablish order. But by the mid-1850s, Libya had become fertile ground for the reforms that flowered during the Ottoman *tanzinlat*, or reform, period. For the next 25 years, the Ottomans proceeded with administrative, **economic**, and **educational** reforms, as **agriculture** slowly supplanted the commerce of the dying caravan **trade**. Land reform and agricultural development, by encouraging settlement and loosening kinship ties, undermined the **tribal** organization of nomadic pastoralism. The activities of the **Sanusi Order**, whose commercial and political organizations also encouraged educational development and more sedentary living, provoked similar changes.

The consolidation of Ottoman control in the province of **Tripoli** set the stage for subsequent developments elsewhere in Libya. Ottoman administrators attacked the entrenched power of Libyan tribes in the belief that the traditional decentralization of the Ottoman Empire, largely dependent on local notables for the administration of the provinces, was dangerously outmoded. In its place, the reformers hoped to create a more efficient administrative system capable of reviving Ottoman power in the face of European expansion.

Two major reforms implemented in the 1860s, land reform and administrative reorganization, reflected the conviction of Ottoman policy makers that fixed settlement was a key to achieving the social and economic development necessary to rejuvenate the empire. They established criminal and civil courts that for the first time separated the duties of administrators and judges. The postal system was reorganized, and in 1861 the administration opened a telegraph line between Tripoli and **Malta**. To encourage commerce between city and countryside, a new gate was opened in the city wall of Tripoli in 1865. Additional adjustments to the administrative system were made throughout the century as the trend toward settlement and urbanization made municipal government increasingly possible.

Following the promulgation of the Ottoman code of land law, private ownership and registration were introduced to the settled areas of **Tripolitania** and the urban areas of **Cyrenaica**. Tribal lands were divided, and ownership of the land was assigned to individuals who paid a small fee for registration. Land reform in Libya was relatively successful, in that most of the redistributed land remained in the hands of farmers. In part because agriculture in Libya was a risky business, tribal sheiks did not amass large concentrations of property as happened else-where in the empire.

Eight decades of Ottoman administration in Tripoli clearly produced a social and economic transformation of the province. A series of Ot-toman governors combined to establish order, reorganize administra-tion, encourage settlement, and increase education. Agriculture and pas-toralism, slowly replacing long-distance trade as primary sources of revenue, moved from subsistence to revenue-generating activities. The political consequences of this economic and social transformation were later manifested in Ottoman policies that successfully mobilized popu-lar feeling in defense of the province against European encroachment. *See also* YOUNG TURK REVOLUTION.

OUJDA, TREATY OF. *See* ARAB-AFRICAN UNION.

– P –

PALESTINE LIBERATION ORGANIZATION (PLO). Libyan for-eign policy after 1969 included a rejectionist stance on the **Arab-Israeli** conflict that increasingly clashed with the more moderate stance of the Palestine Liberation Organization. For example, the **Muammar al-Qaddafi** regime in mid-1995 began expelling thousands of Palestinian residents as punishment for the PLO's peace agreement with Israel. Ap-proximately 30,000 Palestinians resided in Libya at the time, and many of them had been there for decades. At the same time, Qaddafi urged other Arab countries to throw out their Palestinian refugees. The depor-tations followed reports of clashes between Libyan security forces and Muslim fundamentalists in the eastern **port** of **Benghazi**. Qaddafi later halted the exodus of Palestinians to give the Arab world time to develop plans to deal with the expulsions, but he insisted that all Palestinians would eventually have to be removed from Libya. Long estranged from Yasser Arafat, Qaddafi called in October 2005 for an international in-vestigation into what he termed the murder of the late Palestinian leader. *See also* THIRD UNIVERSAL THEORY.

PARTY OF GOD GROUP (HIZBULLAH). The Party of God Group is a relatively small, **Islamic** fundamentalist **opposition** movement in

Libya. Alleged conspirators from the group were executed by the Libyan government in 1986 and 1987.

PEOPLE'S BUREAU. The current name used by Libya for its embassies around the world. In response to a call from **Muammar al-Qaddafi**, Libyan students abroad gradually assumed control of most embassies. After electing a **people's committee**, they renamed the embassies "people's bureaus" and reconstituted their leadership. This process generated considerable confusion and consternation in the foreign ministries and embassies of the world.

PEOPLE'S COMMITTEE. On 15 April 1973, **Muammar al-Qaddafi** proclaimed a **popular revolution** and called for the Libyan people to elect people's committees. Like the **Arab Socialist Union**, the people's committee structure was given both a geographical and a functional basis. Geographically, committees were formed at the zone, municipal, and **governorate** levels. At the zone level, direct popular elections were used to fill seats on the people's committee. Zone people's committees then elected representatives to constitute the municipal people's committee, and the municipal committees selected representatives to form the governorate committee.

Later in the year, the **Revolutionary Command Council** (RCC) promulgated **Law** No. 78 to clarify the administrative responsibilities of the people's committees. The law transferred the functions and authority of governorate and municipal councils established in 1972 to the people's committees at the same levels. The chairmen of the governorate people's committees, in effect, became governors, while the chairmen of the municipal people's committees became mayors. The RCC also authorized the election of people's committees in public corporations, institutions, companies, and universities as well as in other sectors, such as hospitals, convalescent homes, and government printing plants.

The terms of the people's committee members were set at three years, but the members could be removed earlier by a two-thirds vote of the membership. In addition, the RCC reserved for itself the right to dissolve a people's committee at any time or to expel one or more of its members. This actually happened several times during the summer and fall of 1973. In some cases, as many as three or four elections were held before a suitably revolutionary group of lower-level employees emerged as members of the people's committee. The government security services also used the elections to expose and denounce individuals opposed to or simply ambivalent about the objectives of the revolutionary government. Finally, the law empowered the RCC to create new people's committees whenever and wherever needed.

The creation of the people's committee system marked a significant stage in the political evolution of Libya. For the first time in Libyan history, the subnational political system actively encouraged popular participation in the selection of local leadership and allowed substantial local involvement in the local policy-making process. With the formation of people's committees, the RCC increased the political involvement and experience of the Libyan people and focused their attention on the issues of most importance to the local community.

Still not satisfied with the existing level of popular participation, Qaddafi at the 1974 National Congress called for a further refinement of subnational administrative machinery. Stressing the primacy of the people's committees in administrative affairs, the congress responded by recommending the elimination of the governorates. In February 1975, the RCC issued a law abolishing the governorates and reestablishing a ministry of municipalities. Two months later, another RCC law formally established the municipality as the single geographical and administrative subdivision in Libya.

The 52 municipal branch people's committees in Libya are augmented by some 375 people's committees, responsible for specific state sectors. For example, the people's administration is responsible for the functional equivalents of the ministries of reform, planning, social security, light **industry**, public services, **housing**, justice, sports, and the **economy**. The secretaries of the basic people's committees and the municipal branch people's committees are represented on the general people's specialized committees, each of which appoints a secretary and which collectively form the General People's Committee. The composition of the General People's Committee must be approved by the **General People's Congress**. *See also* BASIC PEOPLE'S CONGRESS.

PEOPLE'S MILITIA. In 1989, **Muammar al-Qaddafi** issued a decree that announced the dissolution of the Libyan **armed forces** and their replacement by what he termed the "armed people." At the same time, key personnel and commands were retained albeit under different titles. Consequently, the move appeared to be largely a symbolic gesture in the direction of Qaddafi's long-standing goal of replacing institutions with popular organizations. *See also* DECLARATION OF THE ESTABLISHMENT OF THE PEOPLE'S AUTHORITY.

PEOPLE'S SOCIAL GUIDE. A new class of political activist and policy maker reportedly created by **Muammar al-Qaddafi** in 1996 as a rival to nominees to the **General People's Congress**. The Libyan leader supposedly divided Libya into 48 zones and nominated a coordinator for each zone termed a "people's social guide." The exact role of these guides in the overall Libyan political system remains unclear.

PETROLEUM. Oil deposits in commercial quantities were first discovered in Libya in 1959 when American prospectors—working under the favorable terms of the 1955 **Libyan Petroleum Law**—confirmed their location at Zelten in **Cyrenaica**. The substantial oil reserves identified were quickly developed, and Libya began exporting crude oil in 1961. Libya joined the **Organization of Petroleum Exporting Countries** (OPEC) in 1962 and immediately came under heavy pressure to adopt the organization's pricing policies. Libya's first decade as a petroleum producer witnessed dramatic increases in oil production and oil revenues, but not in the posted price of oil. The Libyan monarchy agreed with its critics that the posted price was undervalued and unjust; nevertheless, it chose to pursue a volume-oriented, as opposed to a price-oriented, oil policy. This was especially true after the June 1967 **Arab-Israeli** War closed the Suez Canal, increasing the demand for Libyan oil. The foreign oil companies working in Libya rapidly expanded their production in order to take advantage of the transportation savings derived from not having to ship Persian Gulf oil to Europe via the Cape of Good Hope. By the time the monarchy was overthrown in September 1969, Libya's daily oil production was on a par with that of Saudi Arabia.

The revolutionary government immediately reversed the oil policies of its predecessor, moving quickly to increase the posted price of oil. The result was a sharp decline in oil output, coupled with a jump in oil revenues. In terms of daily output, oil production in 1974 was less than half what it was in 1969. While production later increased to some two million barrels a day in the second half of the 1970s, it was again reduced to approximately one million per day after 1981. The price per barrel rose from $2 a barrel in 1969 to as high as $41 a barrel in 1981. In the meantime, the revolutionary government seized control of oil production, **nationalizing** the oil companies. The combined result of the oil policies initiated by the revolutionary government was to extend greatly the life of Libyan oil reserves while swelling oil revenues to more than $22 billion in 1980, after which they dropped off sharply for the remainder of the decade.

The **United States** government imposed restrictions on trade with Libya as early as 1974; and in 1986, it ordered all American companies and U.S. citizens to leave the country. The companies affected by this decision included Conoco, Marathon, and Amerada Hess. In the short term, the U.S. government's recall of all American oil companies affected exploration more than production. Many Libyans had gained considerable production experience with U.S. companies in the decades after oil was first discovered in 1959, and they put that knowledge to good use after 1986.

In late 1988, the petroleum sector received welcome news in that the $2 billion Bourri offshore field, reported to have reserves of up to two billion barrels, was set to start producing. Located approximately 115 kilometers (70 miles) northwest of **Tripoli**, this field was developed by the **Italian** firm **Agip**. Its wells were viewed as an important lifeline by a Libyan government haunted by the prospect of its onshore fields drying up.

During the 1990s, the production of Libyan oil flagged for a variety of reasons, including the imposition of **economic** sanctions by the United States and **United Nations**, falling demand, OPEC quotas, and aging fields. Very few new oil fields were put into production after the mid-1970s, and Libya did not issue detailed field reserve and production figures for them. A series of **exploration and production-sharing agreements** (EPSAs) were awarded in the three decades after 1974, but they resulted in only small discoveries of new crude oil deposits. At the same time, the **Muammar al-Qaddafi** regime found it difficult to increase production from existing fields while also replacing production losses with new reserves.

In a major policy shift, Qaddafi in June 2003 called for the privatization of the Libyan oil industry, together with other sectors of the Libyan economy. This announcement led Libya to launch a new round of EPSAs in August 2004. Known as EPSA-4, 15 exploration blocks were awarded to international bidders in the spring of 2005; a new round of awards, EPSA-5, was awarded later in the year. In the interim, oil prices increased to around $60 a barrel, generating a substantial increase in petroleum revenues.

Libya's crude oil production peaked at 3.3 million barrels a day in 1970, dropping to less than a million in the mid-1980s. Production later increased to 1.4 million barrels a day, and Libya hopes to return to three million barrels a day by 2015. In support of these ambitious production targets, Libya has substantial crude oil reserves and expects more to be discovered. According to the **National Oil Company**, proven oil reserves rose from 36 billion barrels in 2003 to more than 39 billion barrels in 2004, making Libya's proven oil reserves the largest in **Africa**. *See also* DEVELOPMENT PLANS; LIBYAN PRODUCERS AGREEMENT; NATURAL GAS; ONE SEPTEMBER AGREEMENT; ORGANIZATION OF ARAB PETROLEUM EXPORTING COUNTRIES; SEVENTH NOVEMBER ZONE; TRIPOLI AGREEMENT.

PHOENICIANS. An Eastern Mediterranean people whose homeland included the coastal regions of contemporary Syria, Lebanon, and northern **Israel**, the Phoenicians were extremely skillful navigators and accomplished merchants. They founded colonies throughout the Mediterranean Basin, among the most successful of which was Carthage, located along the coast of modern-day **Tunisia**. Based on Phoenician practice, the social, religious, and governmental concepts of Carthage had a strong influence on surrounding **Berber** populations.

POGROM. The period immediately following the end of World War II was characterized in Libya by a state of euphoria in which **Jewish**-Muslim relations, especially in smaller towns and rural areas, seemed to settle down and both groups evidenced a sincere desire to work peacefully together. In the prevailing milieu, the anti-Jewish riots that broke out in **Tripoli** on Sunday, 4 November 1945, were almost totally unexpected. The immediate cause of the riots remains unclear; official British inquiries mentioned a fight that had taken place between a Jew and a Muslim, as well as brawling between the youth of the two communities that had become a common Sunday evening event in new city life. A Jewish community report stressed that the initial rioting had occurred simultaneously in several different places, which suggested some planning and coordination had been involved.

The anti-Jewish rioting, which involved shop looting, arson, and physical attacks, quickly grew in intensity. In Tripoli, Jews living outside the Jewish quarter suffered the most, while those residing inside were able to isolate themselves in the old Jewish section. The next day, the only official response to the riots was a curfew announcement and the appearance of a few troops in the streets, who failed to react against the mobs. In fact, firm and effective government action to stop the rioting did not occur until the evening of 6 November and the morning of 7 November. During this period, 38 Jews and one Muslim were killed in the city of Tripoli alone.

The riots spread from Tripoli to other towns, with attacks on Jewish populations in outlying areas sometimes beginning several days after the outbreak of violence in Tripoli. In the villages, the death toll totaled almost a hundred people—all Jews—more than double that in Tripoli. In at least one instance, a forced conversion to **Islam** occurred, and throughout **Tripolitania**, nine synagogues were burned and 35 Torah scrolls ruined. In addition to the loss of life, there was heavy damage to property from burning and looting, estimated at the time at 268 million military authority lire.

The anti-Jewish riots of 1945 were a turning-point in Jewish-Muslim relations in Libya, as well as in the relationship of Jews to Libya itself. Dealing a severe blow to any Jewish sense of security, the pogrom challenged, if not destroyed, any illusions Libyan Jews held about taking initiatives in Libya. While almost three years of political upheaval were yet to pass before the state of **Israel** emerged as a reality in May 1948, the 1945 riots were clearly a central factor in bringing about mass emigration from Libya to Israel after 1948. Many Jews would probably have emigrated eventually anyway from an independent Libya, as they did from other North African states under different circumstances; however, the emigration would almost surely have been much more gradual if the riots had not occurred. While the 1945 pogrom remains a controversial event, it is increasingly clear today that the episode must be placed in the perspective of traditional Libyan Muslim notions concerning Jews and the threat to these notions posed by the **Italian** occupation.

POLITICAL PARTIES. Numerous political groups emerged in Libya in the aftermath of World War II. Oppressed during the long years of **Italian** occupation and denied the right to organize political associations, Libyan leaders, especially in **Tripolitania**, took full advantage of their new freedom to organized political parties at the conclusion of the war. The Nationalist party, organized by a few **nationalists** under the leadership of Ahmad al-Faqih Hasan in 1944, presented itself as the political party representing the aspirations of the country at large. Its platform stood for the ascendancy of Tripolitania within a united and independent Libya; if that proved impossible, the Nationalists called for a trusteeship of a united Libya under the administration of the **Arab League**.

In turn, the United National Front, formed in May 1946, attempted to enlist the support of **Sayyid Muhammad Idris al-Mahdi al-Sanusi** to include Tripolitania as well as **Cyrenaica** under his amirate by advocating a united, independent Libya under Sanusi leadership. A third political party, the Free National Bloc, was composed of dissident elements from the United National Front opposed to the extension of Sanusi influence in Tripolitania; formed in May 1946, it advocated the creation of a constitutional assembly to plan the future form of government for Libya. Other political parties active in Libya in the late 1940s included the Egyptian-Tripolitanian Union party, which called for a union of Tripolitania (and Cyrenaica) with **Egypt**, the Labor party, and the Liberal party.

All the political parties formed in Libya at the end of World War II favored a free, united Libya with membership in the Arab League. The main point of contention centered on the leadership of the new state, with some parties favoring Sayyid Idris and some not. For the future of Libya, it proved fortunate that the traditional elites in Cyrenaica and Tripolitania, as well as in the **Fezzan**, eventually agreed in 1950 to form a united, federal Libya under the leadership of Idris as king.

It is interesting to note that all of the political parties that emerged after the war, which were in large part responsible for shaping the national political system, later dissolved or, failing to formulate new principles attractive to the body politic, faded into obscurity. Lacking real ideological differences or broad policy concerns and programs, the early political parties achieved the goal of independence but then lost their raison d'être. King Idris I outlawed political parties after the November 1952 national elections, reducing the role of the Libyan parliament to little more than a rubber stamp for decisions made by the king and his *diwan*.

The **Revolutionary Command Council** maintained the monarchy's ban on the organization and operation of political parties. The December 1969 Decision on the Protection of the Revolution, the Penal Code, and Law No. 71 of 1972 collectively rendered political party activity of any sort a crime and constituted a strict injunction against unauthorized political activity.

Like many contemporary Islamic thinkers, **Muammar al-Qaddafi** rejects the political party system, not because it is incompatible with the Koran or *sharia* but because he is unfavorably impressed with party organization and competition. In *The Green Book*, he describes the political party as the modern dictatorial instrument of governing and the party system as an overt form of dictatorship.

Qaddafi's condemnation of the political party system is multifaceted. He argues that political parties, because they are generally made up of people of similar beliefs, represent and promote the interests of only one or more segments of society. Such segments form parties to attain their ends and impose their doctrines on society as a whole. In such a system, competition between parties frequently escalates, often resulting in the dominant party or parties ignoring the rights and interests of minority party members. Qaddafi also argues that political parties, in their struggle to gain power, often destroy the accomplishments of their predecessors, even if those accomplishments are for the general good. His solution to these dilemmas is the system of congresses and committees that he established in Libya. *See also* BASIC PEOPLE'S CONGRESS; GENERAL PEOPLE'S CONGRESS; PEOPLE'S COMMITTEE.

POPULAR COMMITTEE. *See* PEOPLE'S COMMITTEE.

POPULAR CONGRESS. *See* BASIC PEOPLE'S CONGRESS.

POPULAR REVOLUTION. On 15 April 1973, the 1,402nd anniversary of the Prophet Muhammad's birth, **Muammar al-Qaddafi** announced a popular revolution based on a five-point program.

1. All existing **laws** must be repealed and replaced by revolutionary enactments designed to produce the necessary revolutionary change.
2. All feeble minds must be weeded out of society by taking appropriate measures toward perverts and deviationists.
3. An administrative revolution must be staged to eliminate all forms of bourgeoisie and bureaucracy.
4. Arms must be distributed to the people who will point them at the chest of anyone who challenges the revolution.
5. A cultural revolution must be initiated to get rid of all imported poisonous ideas and to fuse the people's genuine moral and material potentialities.

To consummate the revolution, Qaddafi declared the Libyan people must seize power through **people's committees**, which were to be elected throughout the country in villages, schools, **airports**, popular organizations, and even private foreign companies, including the oil companies.

Initially, there was little in the way of guidelines or procedures set for the election of these committees, and this led to considerable uncertainty in the early stages of the revolution. Direct popular election was largely restricted to organizations within zones, with the more general levels of representation being achieved by the election of representatives of zone committees to municipal and provincial committees. Direct elections were also held in public corporations and selected government bureaucracies. On the other hand, the **Revolutionary Command Council** (RCC) evidenced concern that anarchy could develop, because it did not allow the popular revolution to take over the revolutionary administration. People's committees were not permitted in government ministries. *See also* BASIC PEOPLE'S CONGRESS; GENERAL PEOPLE'S CONGRESS; PEOPLE'S COMMITTEE.

POPULATION MOVEMENTS. Petroleum wealth has transformed Libya, a sparsely populated country, bringing dramatic demographic changes. Spatial duality has intensified sharply due to strong rural-to-urban migration as well as an increase in interregional migration. The main cause for the differing levels of development among regions is the concentration of development programs in certain urban areas. As a result, the regions containing the most important urban centers have increased in prosperity while the others have become less developed or even depressed. Predictably, the inhabitants of the less developed regions have continued to move in increasing numbers to the more developed areas. The large majority of these migrants are rural people who have changed their occupations and place of residence. They have left work in the rural sector and sought **employment** in the cities in the **industrial** and service sectors. The agrarian sector now employs less than 25 percent of the workforce, while the percentage of nomads and semi-nomads has declined to less than 10 percent of the population.

One of the consequences of the enormous **economic** and social development programs financed by growing oil revenues was a substantial increase in the demand for labor, an increase that the Libyan workforce was unable to satisfy. Participation rates for Libyan **women** in the workforce have remained among the lowest in the world. In turn, the level of male participation declined over the years due to the expansion of **educational** opportunities at the secondary and higher levels as well as the introduction of compulsory military service.

The Libyan government sought to satisfy the growing demand for labor by importing large numbers of foreign workers. By the mid-1970s, foreign workers were estimated to represent approximately a third of the entire workforce, and by the early 1980s, almost half. At the same time, it should be emphasized that the percentage of foreign nationals was still much lower than in the Gulf states, where foreign nationals often outnumbered nationals.

The drop in oil prices in the late 1980s and early 1990s, coupled with the corresponding sharp decline in government revenues, combined to bring about a marked reduction in the number of foreign workers. In 1985, for example, Libya expelled tens of thousands of foreign workers, including a large number of **Egyptians** and **Tunisians**. At the same time, the government pursued more energetically a policy of Libyanization of the labor force. A decade later, Libya requested permission from the **United Nations** to repatriate more than one million **African** workers due to the poor state of the sanctions-hit Libyan economy.

Urbanization has also played a key role in population redistribution in recent decades. Following independence, Libya began to experience a marked shift in the level of urbanization, with the major towns beginning to dominate the economic and political life of the country. **Tripoli** and **Benghazi**, the major administrative, commercial, educational, and industrial centers of Libya, have become increasingly predominant. Reliable figures on the level of urbanization are not available, but it is estimated that at least 85–90 percent of the 2005 population lives in urban areas.

PORTS. Libya has long been hampered by a lack of good seaports. For decades, **Tripoli** and Tobruk had the only deepwater harbors. In the early days of the revolution, port congestion was so bad that cargoes were often diverted to **Tunisian** ports, unloaded, and shipped overland to Libya. By the mid-1970s, port congestion was costing the country an estimated $175 million a year in extra handling costs.

The revolutionary government addressed the seaport problem by upgrading the existing ports at Tripoli, **Benghazi**, and Tobruk. The modernization programs included automated cargo-handling equipment, new navigational equipment, refrigerated warehouses, and additional docking space. Moreover, a new port was constructed at Qasr Ahmad near **Misurata**, with smaller ports opened at Derna and Zuwarah. Specialized oil-exporting seaports connected to the various oil fields by pipelines were also located at Marsa al-Brega, As-Sidr, Ras Lanuf, Marsa al-Hariqah, and Qaryat az-Zuwaytinah. *See also* TRANSPORTATION.

POSITIVE NEUTRALITY. A major element in the **Arab** definition of neutralism is the primacy of national independence, self-determination, and nonintervention. Largely a response to the bipolarization of international power, *positive neutrality* in the Arab world has generally meant the pursuit of an independent policy in accord with Arab national interests, frequently defined in terms of the revolutionary trinity: **freedom**, **socialism**, and **unity**.

The brand of positive neutrality frequently espoused by Arab revolutionary governments is an integral part of **Muammar al-Qaddafi**'s ideology. He professes a belief in the unity of Third World causes and has proclaimed a policy of absolute neutrality between East and West. Qaddafi has rejected foreign controls of any kind and promised vigorous ideological and operational hostility to any form of imperialism, anywhere. *See also* SOVIET UNION; THIRD UNIVERSAL THEORY; UNITED STATES.

PUNIC INFLUENCE. The region of **Tripolitania** was settled by the **Phoenicians** in 900 B.C. in order to extend the influence of Carthage over the west coast of North Africa. The Punics established permanent settlements, building three large coastal cities—Oea (**Tripoli**), Labdah (later **Leptis Magna**), and **Sabratah**—known collectively as Tripolis (three cities). By the fifth century, Carthage, the greatest of the overseas Punic colonies, had extended its hegemony across much of North Africa. Unlike the Greeks in **Cyrenaica**, the Punics in Tripolitania established and cultivated excellent relations with the **Berber** populations, trading with their southern neighbors as well as teaching and learning from them. In consequence, the Berbers in short order were largely Punicized in language and custom. Carthage, together with Tripolis, was later able to draw support from these Berber tribes during the Punic Wars of 264–241 and 218–201 B.C.

The Punic Wars doomed Carthage, ending its former glory. The **Romans** sacked the city in 146 B.C. to forestall any future Carthaginian revival. Nevertheless, the influence of Punic civilization on the North African region continued to be strong. Displaying a remarkable gift for cultural assimilation, the Berbers readily synthesized Punic cults into their folk religion. In the late Roman period, the Punic language was still spoken in the towns of Tripolitania as well as by the Berber farmers in the coastal countryside.

– Q –

QADDAFI, AISHA AL- (1978–). Muammar al-Qaddafi's single surviving daughter after an adopted daughter, Hannah, was killed in the April 1986 bombing raid by the **United States** on his **Bab al-Aziziya** residence in Tripoli. Named after Qaddafi's mother, Aisha graduated with a **law** degree from Al-Fateh University.

QADDAFI, MUAMMAR AL- (MU'AMMAR QADHDHAFI; MU'AMMAR AL-QUADDAFI) (1942–). Born in a bedouin tent in the desert near Sirte, Muammar al-Qaddafi is part of a family descended from a small **tribe** of **Arabized Berbers**, the Qadadfa, who are stockherders with holdings in the Hun Oasis some 250 kilometers (150 miles) south of Sirte. As a child, he herded the family flocks, spending long hours alone. His first formal **education** took place in a Muslim elementary school, which was followed by secondary school in **Sebha** and later in **Misurata**. Looked down upon by his classmates due to his impoverished background, the young Qaddafi is said to have slept in a mosque at night and returned to the family encampment on weekends.

During his formative years, decisive political events in the Middle East, including the 1948 Arab defeat by **Israel** in Palestine and the 1952 **Egyptian** revolution, deeply influenced his world outlook. Qaddafi later claimed that he began to plan the overthrow of King **Idris** I while still in school. Accounts differ as to when he became an activist; however, his boyhood friends included several men who participated in the overthrow of King Idris and then served the government. Examples are **Abdel Salaam Jalloud**, regarded for many years as the number two man in the Qaddafi regime; **Mustafa al-Kharuubi**, a commander of the Army Inspector General Corps; and **Abu Bakr Yunnis Jaabir**, onetime army chief of staff.

Actively involved in student protests during the 1956 Suez Crisis, Qaddafi was accused of fomenting a student strike and expelled from secondary school. He completed his secondary education under the direction of a private tutor in Misurata, where he showed special interest in the study of history. Over the next two years, Qaddafi studied history at the University of **Tripoli**, but he was not an academic success and ended his university studies.

At the time, a career in the **armed forces** offered exciting opportunities for higher education and upward socioeconomic mobility, especially for young men from the lower economic levels of Libyan society. For many, the armed forces also represented the most obvious avenue for political action and rapid change. Like his mentor, Egyptian president Gamal Abdul Nasser, Qaddafi saw an army career not in pure military terms but as a means for enhanced political participation. Hence, his army career from the beginning was as much a revolutionary as it was a military vocation.

In 1963, Qaddafi entered the Libyan Royal Military Academy in **Benghazi**, graduating in 1965; his classmates included many future members of the **Revolutionary Command Council** (RCC). Before graduation, Qaddafi received training at a military school in Turkey. Commissioned a communications officer, he later attended a British army advanced signals course in the United Kingdom. One of the most poignant early photographs of the future Leader of the Revolution shows him strolling the streets of London dressed in traditional Libyan robes during his brief time abroad. Qaddafi's association with the **Libyan Free Unionist Officers** movement began during his cadet days and intensified after the Arab defeat in the 1967 war with Israel. Convinced the monarchy had to be replaced, the Libyan Free Unionist Officers were only one of several groups plotting against the Idris regime when they successfully overthrew the king on 1 September 1969 in the **One September Revolution**.

After seizing power, the central committee of the Libyan Free Unionist Officers movement designated itself the ruling RCC, with Qaddafi as commander in chief of the armed forces and de facto head of state. In theory, the RCC functioned as a collegial body in which the membership discussed issues and policies until a consensus emerged. In practice, Qaddafi was increasingly able to impose his will through a combination of personality and argument to the extent that all major policy statements bore the imprint of his thinking. In September 1976, he announced a plan to create a new, national-level representative body called the **General People's Congress** (GPC) to replace the RCC as the supreme instrument of government. He served as general secretary of the GPC in 1977–1979, but then resigned to concentrate on what he termed "revolutionary activities with the masses." Retaining his position as de facto commander in chief, he adopted the title Leader of the Revolution.

Domestically, Qaddafi trumpeted **socialism** as the solution to humanity's **economic** problems, but his variant of Arab socialism was doctrinal rather than pragmatic. It was also highly **nationalistic** in an area of the world where socialism and nationalism have often been found together. Early statements underscored the indigenous nature of Libyan socialism, describing it as an integral part of Libyan political culture as well as a necessary corrective action. Qaddafi argued that socialism stemmed from the heritage of the Libyan people and the heart of the Libyan nation. His approach thus resembled what had happened elsewhere in the Middle East, where the origins and character of socialism have invariably been discussed in the context of local history and customs.

Overseas, Qaddafi pursued an aggressive **foreign policy** based on his interpretation of Arab nationalism, neutrality, and Arab **unity**. Upon seizing power, the RCC immediately opened negotiations with the **United States** and **Great Britain** aimed at an early termination of the standing agreements providing for foreign military bases in Libya. **Italian**-owned assets were soon confiscated, and the Italians living in Libya were expelled in mid-1970. At the same time, the RCC pursued other policies designed to emphasize its opposition to colonialism and imperialism. The Qaddafi regime consistently advocated **jihad**, broadly defined to include economic and political as well as military actions, as the solution to the Arab-**Israeli** dispute. Its stance on the Palestinian issue also influenced its policy toward an overall Middle East settlement in addition to many other areas of foreign policy, especially its posture toward **terrorism**.

Qaddafi was a particularly strong and vocal advocate of Arab unity. Where the Libyan monarchy had limited its participation in the pan-Arab movement, cooperating with the NATO allies, Qaddafi quickly moved Libya into a close association with the Arab system. Focused on the Arab world, he often referred to the "Arab nation" not in geographical terms but as an expression of conviction and guidance. To Qaddafi, the concept of the Arab nation was an ideological bond joining a people with a common cultural history and a faith in their destiny.

As the revolution unfolded, Qaddafi developed a theoretical underpinning, known as the **Third Universal Theory**, for his domestic and foreign policies. The theory, expounded in *The Green Book*, was an attempt to develop an alternative to capitalism and communism, both of which he declared unsuitable for Libya. Qaddafi based the Third Universal Theory on nationalism and **religion**, two forces he described as the paramount drivers of history and humankind. Nationalism was seen to be the natural result of the world's racial and cultural diversity and thus both a necessary and a productive force. Arab nationalism was considered to have especially deep and glorious roots in the ancient past. Because the Arab nation was the product of an age-old civilization based on the heavenly and universal message of **Islam**, Qaddafi argued that it had the right as well as the duty to be the bearer of the Third Universal Theory to the world.

QADDAFI, AL-MUATASSIM BILLAH AL- (1974–). Muammar al-Qaddafi's fourth son. Following graduation from Al-Fateh University, he served as an officer in the Libyan **armed forces**. In May 2005,

a French court found Muatassim, known as Hannibal, guilty of striking his pregnant companion in a Paris hotel, handing him a four-month suspended sentence.

QADDAFI, MUHAMMED AL- (1971–). Muammar al-Qaddafi's eldest son and only child by his first wife. Head of the Libyan Olympic Committee, as well as a local soccer club, he shares a passion for soccer with his half-brother, Saadi.

QADDAFI, AL-SAADI AL- (1973–). Muammar al-Qaddafi's third son. Saadi is a graduate of the Military Engineering Academy, an army officer, and the president of the Libyan Football Federation. A soccer enthusiast, he joined the board of directors of Juventus, an **Italian** football club, in 2002 after the Libyan Arab Foreign Investment Company acquired a 7.5 percent stake in the club. His subsequent attempts to play professional football in Italy were unsuccessful.

QADDAFI, SAIF AL-ISLAM AL- (1972–). Muammar al-Qaddafi's eldest son by his second wife. He graduated from Al-Fateh University in 1994 with a B.S. degree from the Architectural Engineering and Planning Department. After working at the Industrial Research Center and the National Consultancy Office, he earned an M.B.A. from IMADEC University, an American-run institution in Vienna, graduating in 2000. Saif is president of the **Qaddafi International Foundation for Charity Associations**, a supposedly nongovernmental organization he founded in 1997, officially to serve as an umbrella body for Libyan charitable activities. The foundation has been involved in a number of high-profile domestic and **foreign policy** issues in recent years in what some observers see as a deliberate attempt to elevate the role of Saif in the social and political life of Libya. Widely rumored to be a potential successor to his father, Saif has repeatedly denied any interest in politics, stating he has no plan to succeed his father as head of state.

QADDAFI, WANIS AL- (WANIS AL-GADDAFI; WANIS AL-QATHAFI) (c. 1922–). Last prime minister of the **United Kingdom of Libya**, from September 1968 to September 1969. Wanis al-Qaddafi was a former head of the **Cyrenaican** executive council and an experienced cabinet member, having served previously as minister of foreign affairs, the interior, labor and social affairs, and planning and development. Somewhat conservative, Wanis al-Qaddafi represented the pragmatic, technical approach to government. He was the last prime minister to serve under King **Idris** I. His government was overthrown by the **Libyan Free Unionist Officers** on 1 September 1969.

QADDAFI HUMAN RIGHTS CHARITABLE FOUNDATION. Long associated with the **Qaddafi International Foundation for Charity Associations**, the Qaddafi Human Rights Charitable Foundation focuses on **human rights** issues. In September 2005, the foundation launched a hotline on the website of the Qaddafi International Foundation for Charity Associations, complete with telephone numbers, regular mail, and e-mail addresses, through which people can report human rights violations.

QADDAFI INTERNATIONAL FOUNDATION FOR CHARITY ASSOCIATIONS. Saif al-Islam al-Qaddafi was the founder of the Qaddafi International Foundation for Charity Associations and has remained its president from the beginning. The foundation in recent years has been involved in a wide range of domestic and **foreign policy** issues, from paying ransoms for hostages held by **Islamist** extremists in the Philippines in 2000 to sending medical aid to Iraq in 2003 to promoting **human rights** in Libya in 2005. Allegedly a nongovernmental, nonprofit organization, the foundation provides Saif al-Qaddafi with the structure and organization necessary to impact on public policy decisions inside and outside Libya.

QADDAFI INTERNATIONAL PRIZE FOR HUMAN RIGHTS. An award established by the Libyan government to recognize annually a Third World figure in the forefront of "liberation struggles." Founded in Switzerland under a $10 million trust, the first winner of the $250,000 award, jailed black South African activist Nelson Mandela, was named in 1989. Subsequent winners have included Native Americans and the children of the Palestinian uprising against the **Israeli** occupation. In 1996, Libya awarded the prize to Louis Farrakhan, leader of the Nation of **Islam**, a Chicago-based organization founded in 1930. After a prolonged controversy, Farrakhan eventually traveled to Libya to accept the award, although he declined the $250,000 honorarium that normally accompanies the award until such time as he obtains permission from a **United States** court to accept it. The U.S. Treasury Department had earlier rejected Farrakhan's request for an exemption from U.S. sanctions, which barred virtually all economic ties with Libya. The U.S. government also refused to allow the Nation of Islam to accept a $1 billion donation from Libya.

QALAT AL-ZAYTUNA, AGREEMENT OF. An April 1919 agreement between the **Tripoli Republic** and **Italy** that laid the groundwork for the **Legge Fondamentale**.

QARAMANLI. *See* KARAMANLI, AHMED; KARAMANLI DYNASTY.

QARAWI, MUKHTAR ABDULLAH AL- (MUKHTAR ABDULLAH GERWY; MUKHTAR ABDULLAH AL-KIRWI) (1943–). An original member of the **Revolutionary Command Council** (RCC). Mukhtar Abdullah al-Qarawi was also a member of the political study cell established by **Muammar al-Qaddafi** at the **Benghazi** military college. He withdrew from the RCC in 1975 after intense policy conflicts between Qaddafi and a coalition of RCC members divided the organization.

QASR BU HADI, BATTLE OF. In April 1915, a major battle in Sirte turned into a rout of the **Italians** after Libyans whom the Italians thought to be friendly unexpectedly joined the forces attacking them. As a result, the Italians lost more than 500 dead, several thousand rifles, and several million rounds of ammunition. Also known as Gardabiyya, the battle of Qasr Bu Hadi temporarily ended any semblance of Italian control in the hinterlands of Libya. Thereafter, the Italians were forced to withdraw from the interior to the coast. For the duration of World War I, which Italy entered in May 1915, the Italian occupation was limited to **Tripoli**, **Benghazi**, and a few other coastal areas.

QATTAR, WADI AL-. The most important drainage system of the **Cyrenaican** coastal plain. It starts at the southwestern flank of the **Jabal al-Akhdar** and flows toward the **Marj Plain**. Even though it is an important drainage system, its water is above ground only during heavy floods.

– R –

RAJMA, ACCORD OF AL-. On 25 October 1920, **Italy** reached an agreement with **Sayyid Muhammad Idris al-Mahdi al-Sanusi**, granting him what the Italians considered a purely ceremonial title of amir of **Cyrenaica**. He was also given permission to organize the autonomous administration of Ajadabiyyah, Aujila, **Giarabub**, Jalu, and Al-Kufrah oases, with the last becoming his seat of government. In return, Idris agreed to cooperate in applying the **Legge Fondamentale** of Cyrenaica, to dismantle Cyrenaican military units, and not to tax the local population beyond the religious tithe; however, the most important concession—the breakup of military units—was never accomplished.

As part of the accord, Idris was granted a personal stipend of 63,000 lire a month, with additional payments of 93,000 lire monthly being paid to other members of the Sanusi family. In addition, the Italians agreed to cover the costs of administering and policing the areas under Sanusi control, payments that included 2.6 million lire for general expenses. Stipends were also paid to **tribal** sheiks and administrators of the Sanusi *zawiya*. In effect, the Italian government attempted to bribe the elite of the entire country to accept its rule.

RELIGION. Long a dominant influence on Libyan society, religion played a central role in Libyan politics after independence in 1951; and its role increased after the revolutionary government seized power in 1969. The 1951 **Constitution of Libya** declared **Islam** to be the religion of the state. When the monarchy was ousted in 1969, the revolutionary government issued a **constitutional proclamation** reaffirming Islam as the religion of the state and also making Arabic, the language of the Koran, the state's official language. The 1977 **Declaration of the Establishment of the People's Authority**, which amended the constitutional proclamation, made the Koran the **law** of society in Libya.

In the **Third Universal Theory**, Libyan leader **Muammar al-Qaddafi** argued that **nationalism** and religion were the paramount drivers of history and mankind. His subsequent attempts to manipulate Islam in support of the revolution generated considerable internal **opposition**. In particular, the revolutionary government's unorthodox interpretation of Islam, coupled with its efforts to use Islam to support the revolution, put it in direct conflict with the country's traditional religious leadership. Rebuffed by the **ulama**, Qaddafi undertook a determined assault on the religious establishment of Libya, and **Islamist** opposition to the Qaddafi regime fragmented under constant pressure from government security forces. There have been influential ulama in Libya, such as Sheik al-Bishti, the former imam of Tripoli, but there are no contemporary theologians or authors with influence remotely similar to that of **Sayyid Muhammad Idris al-Mahdi al-Sanusi**.

Most Libyans today belong to the Sunni branch of Islam and adhere to the Malikite school of Islamic law, a rite that holds the Koran and the *hadith* to be the principal sources of truth. Unlike the **Arabs** of Libya, the minority **Berber** community belongs to the Kharijite sect of Islam, which emphasizes the equality of believers to a greater extent than does the Malikite school. A small group of **Tuareg** nomads, scattered in the southwestern **desert**, adhere to a form of Islam that incorporates nonorthodox magical elements. A few hundred **Tebu** also live in small isolated groups in southern Libya. Converted to Islam by the **Sanusi Order**, they retain earlier beliefs and practices.

Beginning in the 1940s, Libya's small **Jewish** population suffered increasingly harsh treatment, and today no more than a handful of Jews remain in Libya. The resident Christian community, numbering some 50,000, are mainly expatriates working in the **petroleum** industry. A variety of Christian denominations are found in Libya, Roman Catholicism, reflecting the large expatriate **Italian** community, being the most common. *See also* ISLAMIC CALL SOCIETY.

RESOLUTION FOUR. A **General People's Congress** resolution issued in March 1978 that established new guidelines for home ownership. *See also* SOCIALISM.

REVOLUTION. *See* POPULAR REVOLUTION.

REVOLUTIONARY COMMAND COUNCIL (RCC). The **Socialist People's Libyan Arab Jamahiriya** is a unitary state governed by a unique organization of congresses and committees. This system of government evolved slowly after the **Libyan Free Unionist Officers** movement, led by a central committee of 12 officers, executed a well-planned coup d'état on 1 September 1969 and overthrew the monarchy that had ruled the **United Kingdom of Libya** since independence in 1951.

The central committee immediately renamed itself the Revolutionary Command Council. The RCC was designated the highest authority in the Libyan Arab Republic and exercised both executive and legislative functions. As such, it was empowered to take whatever measures it deemed necessary to protect the regime or the revolution. Such measures could take the form of proclamations, **laws**, orders, or resolutions. The 1969 **constitutional proclamation** specifically gave the RCC the power to declare war, conclude and ratify treaties, appoint diplomatic envoys and receive diplomatic missions, proclaim martial law, and control the **armed forces**. The RCC was further empowered to appoint a **Council of Ministers**, consisting of a prime minister and ministers; the council's function was to implement the state's general policy as defined by the RCC. The RCC could also dismiss the prime minister or his ministers. The resignation of the prime minister automatically resulted in the resignation of the entire Council of Ministers.

The **One September Revolution** was completed without the participation of any organized civilian groups, and initially the RCC maintained its military character. Later, the RCC appointed civilians to the Council of Ministers to help operate the government, but even then, it reserved supreme authority in all fields for itself.

The members of the RCC shared similar backgrounds, motivations, and worldviews. Most were from lower-middle-class families and minor **tribes** and attended the Libyan military academy at a time when a military career offered opportunities for higher **education** and upward socioeconomic mobility. The language of the RCC was the language of **Arab nationalism**, guided by the precepts of the Koran and the *sharia* and strengthened by a conviction that only the RCC understood and spoke for the masses.

RCC chairman **Muammar al-Qaddafi** quickly became the dominant figure in the revolutionary government. While never given formal authority over his RCC colleagues, Qaddafi was able to impose his will through a combination of personality and argument. In theory, the RCC functioned as a collegial body, with the members discussing issues and policies until enough of a consensus evolved to establish a unified position. In practice, as the revolution unfolded, Qaddafi increasingly exercised the final choice in major decisions, and the Libyan people increasingly looked to his public statements to guide their own behavior. By 1975, he had become the only member of the RCC to initiate major political programs or policies. In this manner, Qaddafi attempted to generate support for the revolution and to legitimize its new political institutions through increasingly charismatic leadership.

The executive-legislative system composed of the RCC and the Council of Ministers operated into 1977, but on 1 September 1976, the seventh anniversary of the revolution, Colonel Qaddafi introduced a plan to reorganize the government. The key feature of this proposal was the creation of a new, national-level representative body called the **General People's Congress** to replace the RCC as the supreme instrument of government.

REVOLUTIONARY COMMITTEES. A completely new echelon of subnational government created in 1976–1977, although they were not mentioned in *The Green Book* and their existence was not widely known outside Libya until 1979 when the **General People's Congress** (GPC) first described their official functions. The first revolutionary committee was created in **Tripoli**, followed by the creation of similar committees in Tarhuna, **Benghazi**, Tukra, and Bani Walid. Revolutionary committees were organized in virtually all government departments and agencies as well as within the **Basic People's Congresses** (BPCs), the **people's committees** of **trade unions** and professional associations, the university student unions, and the **armed forces**.

The revolutionary committee system was established to raise the political consciousness of the people, especially in those areas influenced by traditional or petit bourgeois ideas or individuals. It was also expected to counter the growing tendency of the BPCs to advocate parochial interests and concerns instead of taking a broader view of the nation's needs. Examples of this former tendency were the excessive budgetary demands made by the committees at the Fourth GPC and the reluctance of people's committees west of Tripoli to support the reallocation of coastal farming land.

Revolutionary committees reported directly to **Muammar al-Qaddafi**, and he convened them periodically both individually and en masse. Since all members were self-proclaimed zealots, the revolutionary committees became the true cadres of the revolution. In explaining their role, Qaddafi repeatedly emphasized that the people's committees exercised *administrative* responsibilities while the revolutionary committees exercised *revolutionary* control.

In fact, the revolutionary committees increasingly set and enforced the agendas at local congress meetings, often through intimidation. They quickly became the only official organization in Libya allowed to engage in revolutionary activities. Revolutionary committee members also became part of what came to be known as revolutionary courts. With lawyers now unable to maintain a private practice, the revolutionary courts usurped the power of the existing **judicial system** in Libya. Their creation marked the beginning of a seven-year period notable for an arbitrary and repressive system of revolutionary justice that contributed to growing tension and discontent within Libya.

Early in the second half of the 1980s, Qaddafi began to indicate in some of his speeches that he was aware of the negative impact the revolutionary committees were having on many aspects of life in Libya. His attempts to restore some element of order and stability proved highly selective but nonetheless significant. In 1987–1988, Qaddafi increasingly described the revolutionary committees as overzealous and power-hungry. Eventually, they lost a substantial number of their responsibilities, especially in the police, security, and intelligence arenas. In 1988, for example, the newly created Secretariat for Mass Mobilization and Revolutionary Leadership assumed many of the functions previously accomplished by the revolutionary committees.

Qaddafi again modified the Libyan political structure in 1992, dividing the country into 1,500 **communes**, each with its own executive and legislative functions, responsibilities formerly vested in the BPCs. Both the communes and the BPCs are supervised by revolutionary committees directed by secretaries appointed by Qaddafi.

RICONQUISTA (1923–1932). In spring 1923, **Italy** abrogated all accords with the various factions in Libya and began its reconquest. The military operations undertaken by Italian authorities to pacify Libya were long, difficult, and costly, but they were eventually successful. Northern **Tripolitania** was subdued by the end of 1924, and by the beginning of 1928, the acting head of the **Sanusi Order** had submitted to the Italian commander in **Cyrenaica**. With the northern **Fezzan** already in Italian control, the Italian authorities united Tripolitania and Cyrenaica in January 1929 under the rule of Marshal **Pietro Badoglio**. In Cyrenaica, a brief truce was declared in the spring of 1929; however, during the summer, resistance again flared under the leadership of **Sidi**

Umar al-Mukhtar. In the face of extreme Italian brutality, Libyan resistance continued until fall 1931 when Mukhtar was finally captured and hanged. On 24 January 1932, Marshal Badoglio declared the rebellion in Cyrenaica broken.

ROADS. Libya has a surfaced road system totaling some 48,000 kilometers (30,000 miles). Most major towns and villages, including **desert** oases, are accessible by car or truck. In the larger cities, traffic levels are high and increasing. Major highways include the 1,600-kilometer (1,000-mile) coastal highway from the **Tunisian** border to **Egypt** as well as roads from **Tripoli** to **Sebha**, Sebha to Ghat, Sebha to **Chad** and Niger, and **Ajdabiyah** to Al-Kufrah. *See also* LITORANEA; TRANSPORTATION.

ROGER II (1095–1154). The Norman king of Sicily from 1130 to 1154. After occupying **Malta**, he invaded **Tripolitania** with the intent of building an African empire. Initially successful, he was later forced out by the **Almohads**.

ROME. In the third century B.C., Rome and Carthage began a competition for control of the central Mediterranean that ended with Rome's destruction of its rival after the Third **Punic** War in 146 B.C. At the time, the Roman provinces of Africa corresponded roughly to the territory previously controlled by Carthage. Early Roman efforts at colonization in North Africa were haphazard and largely consisted of a few large **agricultural** estates. The systematic colonization of the Maghrib did not begin until around a century later.

In 46 B.C., Julius Caesar awarded land grants in North Africa to the soldiers who had defeated Juba, the Numidian king who had allied with Pompey in the civil wars. By 27 B.C., Roman rule had expanded to encompass virtually all of modern **Tunisia** north of the **desert**. These early settlers fully exploited the agricultural possibilities of the land, and as a result, the Maghrib became a granary for Rome. The Romans also used their legions to complete public works such as building **roads**, **ports**, aqueducts, and baths.

The heavy imperial tax burden sparked a revolt in the major cities of North Africa in A.D. 238. While order was eventually restored, the bloody suppression of the revolt devastated many of the important towns of the Maghrib. Consequently, the **economic** center of gravity of the region tended to shift to the smaller towns of the interior, which had been spared the worst effects of the revolt. The resulting projection of the heavy hand of imperial rule into the interior further antagonized relations between the Romans and native **Berbers**.

The rapid spread of Christianity into the interior of Africa in the first and second centuries added new complications to an already explosive situation. Christianity came to be viewed as a means of dissent, and many Berbers converted to the faith, not out of conviction but because they regarded Christian beliefs as a challenge to Roman rule. Early in the fourth century, the Donatist schism with the mainstream Church hierarchy split the Christians in the province. For more than a century thereafter, revolts flared in Berber areas under the banner of Donatism. This ongoing religious conflict further weakened Rome's political authority in North Africa, thus expediting the **Vandal** takeover in the early fifth century.

RUSSIA. Libyan ties with Russia are both complex and paradoxical. While Russia stopped importing Libyan **petroleum** with the collapse of the **Soviet Union** in 1990, Libya still owes Russia an estimated $4 billion, mostly for previous arms sales. Throughout the 1990s, Libya was in no hurry to pay the outstanding balance because the debt helped shield it from tighter **United Nations** sanctions. In 1994, a cash-strapped Russia, fearing Libya would be unable to repay its debts, threatened to veto a Security Council resolution restricting the export of Libyan oil. In the end, Russian opposition resulted in a watered-down resolution that included a prohibition on the export of oil-related equipment to Libya but no restrictions on the sale of oil.

From the Libyan perspective, the area of greatest need for Russian assistance continues to be in the military field. The huge Soviet-made Libyan arsenal is in desperate need of maintenance, much of which only Russia can provide. An unknown but presumably large segment of Libya's military hardware is currently inoperable due to poor servicing and a lack of spare parts. Under the terms of the UN embargo, Russia was unable to sell military hardware to Libya or to service the equipment already owned by the Libyan military.

With the suspension of UN sanctions, the Russian government, a major arms supplier to **Tripoli** during the first two decades of the revolution, immediately assumed an aggressive commercial stance in Libya.

The chairman of the international affairs committee of the Russian State Duma in April 1999 hailed the suspension of sanctions as a long-awaited event. A Russian **trade** ministry press release in October 1999 argued that Russia was now free to resume arms sales to Libya even as a Russian trade delegation visited Tripoli to negotiate a resumption of military-technical cooperation. In June 2000, the Russian firm Promeksport announced it was resuming deliveries of ammunition to Libya and undertaking repair of armored equipment and air defense systems. Russian foreign minister Igor Ivanov in May 2001 called for a complete lifting of international sanctions against Libya.

In November 1999, a Russian company had concluded a contract with the **National Oil Company** to build a branch of the Khums-Tripoli gas pipeline, estimated to cost more than $150 million. A joint Libyan-Russian commission for **trade**, economic, scientific, and technical cooperation, initially focused on Russian investment in oil and **natural gas** projects, began to meet regularly and expanded its scope by November 2000 to include **agriculture**, **banking**, nuclear power, and **transportation** projects. Discussions also continued on the issue of Libyan debts outstanding from the Cold War era. *See also* FOREIGN POLICY; POSITIVE NEUTRALITY.

– S –

SABHA. *See* SEBHA.

SABKHAT TAWURGHA. An immense coastal marsh that extends along the Libyan coast from **Misurata** to Buerat. It is separated from the Mediterranean Sea by a belt of partly cemented coastal dunes. The water of the Sabkhat is largely floodwater from the **Wadi Soffegin** and the **Wadi Zamzam**, supplemented by spring discharge at Tauorga, and infiltration from the sea through the coastal dunes.

SABRATAH (SABRATHA). Sabratah is a well-preserved **Roman** city located approximately 70 kilometers (45 miles) from **Tripoli**. The ruins themselves are less attractive than those found at **Leptis Magna**, but the site enjoys a spectacular view of the sea. The modern town of Sabratah grew around the ruins.

The ancient city dates from the Roman occupation of **Tripolitania** and was built during the first and second centuries A.D. Destroyed by the **Vandals**, it was rebuilt during the **Arab** occupation and then neglected by the Turks. Sabratah was evacuated and partially restored during the **Italian** occupation. The earliest parts of the city are in the western area, which corresponds roughly to the original **Punic** city.

Monuments that should be visited include the great forum, which dates from a fourth-century restoration; its location away from the center of the city suggests the builders expected Sabratah to expand. The Basilica of Apuleius, which originally served as a law court, dates from around A.D. 440 in its final form as a church. The theater is the most outstanding monument at Sabratah. Built in the late second century, it has been beautifully restored with an unusual backdrop consisting of 108 Corinthian columns. The design, reputed to be a replica of the palace built by Septimius Severus in Rome, bears a passing resemblance to Petra in Jordan.

SADAWI, BASHIR AL-. *See* TRIPOLITANIAN-CYRENAICAN DEFENSE COMMITTEE.

SADR, MUSA AL-. The spiritual leader of the Muslim Shiite sect in Lebanon, Musa al-Sadr disappeared in August 1978 while on a visit to Libya to secure economic and material assistance for his movement, Amal. While **Muammar al-Qaddafi** later described Sadr as an agent of the shah of Iran, Libya repeatedly denied any knowledge of his fate. His whereabouts remain a mystery that continues to trouble Libyan diplomatic relations with Lebanon and Iran as well as with Shiite communities everywhere.

SAHARA DESERT. A barren wasteland of rocky **desert** plateaus and sand dunes that supports minimal human habitation, the Sahara Desert covers most of the interior of North **Africa** and, along with the Mediterranean coast, is Libya's most prominent natural feature. In the Sahara, **agriculture** is possible only in a few scattered oases. Due to the scarcity of arable land, there is severe overpopulation at many of these oases. Land-use patterns vary from nomadic grazing to intensive irrigation farming. The most significant physical characteristic of the Sahara Desert is the lack of rainfall, which is generally less than 10 centimeters

(4 inches) per year with relative humidity in the range of 5 percent. Due to the scarcity of water, the occasional desert rainfall is of great geomorphic importance. Desert rains often occur as torrential downpours over restricted areas, while no rain may fall in adjacent areas for years.

The northeastern portion of the Sahara is also known as the Libyan Desert or Cyrenaican Desert. It is centered in **Cyrenaica** and is among the largest deserts in the world, extending from the slopes of the **Jabal al-Akhdar** at about 31 degrees north latitude to the southern border of Libya. Contrary to popular belief, less than 20 percent of Libya is covered by sand dunes, notably the Awbari and Murzuk sand seas in the **Fezzan** and the Kalanshiyu and Rabyanah sand seas in central **Cyrenaica**. A much greater part of the Libyan Desert is covered by rocky or gravelly plains.

A limestone plateau is located along the slopes of the Jabal al-Akhdar in the northern part of the Libyan Desert. An undulating plain that slopes gently southward to almost sea level, this plateau contains several closed basins and depressions that collect the floodwaters of the Jabal. It also includes a line of oases, including Marada, Augila (Awjilah), Gialo, and **Giarabub** (Al-Jaghbub), which constitute the lowest part of the Libyan Desert. From this line, the ground gradually rises to the south reaching an elevation of 350 meters (1,150 feet) above sea level at Al-Kufrah and about 600 meters (2,000 feet) at the foot of the Jabal Arkenu and Jabal Awenat. In the southwestern part of the desert, the Jabal Eghei rises to heights of 750–1,000 meters (2,500–3,300 feet).

South of the Cyrenaican platform, the Sarir Calanscio occupies an area of 120,000 square kilometers (47,000 square miles), while the Great Kalanshiyu Sand Sea and the Rabyanah Sand Sea cover 100,000 square kilometers (39,000 square miles) and 70,000 square kilometers (27,000 square miles), respectively. South of these great sand dune areas and gravel plains, the Libyan Desert consists of rocky plains and hills separated by gravel plains and minor sand areas. The isolated oases of Bzema, Al-Kufrah, Rabiana, and Tazerbo are among the few populated areas in this vast desert.

High-velocity winds are also a common phenomenon in the deserts of Libya. These winds often act effectively as a transporting medium in that they lift sand and dust into the air in sufficient volume to blacken the sky. Locally, these winds are termed *ghibli*, and humans and animals caught in them can be in danger of suffocation. Eroded rocks in the desert often assume fantastic and unusual forms as a result of wind erosion and the abrasive action of sand-filled winds. The Ghost Mountains of the Tibesti range are a good example of such wind-carved rock forms.

SAKISLI, MOHAMMED AL-. *See* SAQIZLI, MUHAMMAD AL-.

SANCTIONS, ECONOMIC. *See* UNITED NATIONS; UNITED STATES.

SANUSI, ABDULA AL- (ABDULLAH SANUSI). Abdula al-Sanusi, the brother-in-law of **Muammar al-Qaddafi**, is married to the sister of Qaddafi's wife; they have five children. Like **Abdel Salaam Jalloud**, Sanusi is a member of the Magharha **tribe**, and his marriage into Qaddafi's family enabled Qaddafi to replace Jalloud with Sanusi without offending the Magharha. Abdula al-Sanusi is the de facto internal and external security chief and appears to have become the second-in-command in Libya. Some observers believe he was the mastermind behind the **Lockerbie incident** as well as the kidnapping of the dissident **Mansour Kikhia**, but these charges remain unproven.

SANUSI, SAYYID MUHAMMAD BIN ALI AL- (c. 1787–1859). Algerian scholar who established the **Sanusi Order** in **Cyrenaica** in 1842. Born to a distinguished family of sharifs in a village near Mustaghanim in Algeria about 1787, the Grand Sanusi was educated at Mustaghanim, then at Mazun, and later at the famous mosque school at Fez, **Morocco**. Studying the usual subjects of the time, which included theology, jurisprudence, and the exegesis of the Koran, he developed an interest in mysticism, coming under the influence of the Moroccan Order of the Tijaniya Darwishes. He left Morocco in his 30s and traveled extensively in North Africa and the Middle East before arriving in Cyrenaica in the early 1840s. After founding the mother lodge of the Sanusi Order at Beida in the **Jabal al-Akhdar**, he later moved its center to **Giarabub**.

The teachings of Sayyid Muhammad bin Ali al-Sanusi advocated a combination of **Sufism** and orthodoxy that proved well suited to the bedouins of Cyrenaica. He forbade fanaticism and the use of stimulants and stressed hard work in earning a livelihood. To spread the influence of the Sanusi doctrine, the Grand Sanusi instructed his followers to build rest houses for travelers along the **trade** and pilgrimage routes passing through Libya. Eventually, these structures became more than rest stops as they functioned as **religious** centers, schools, and social and commercial centers. The Grand Sanusi died at Giarabub on 7 September 1859 and was buried there. *See also* IDRIS AL-MAHDI AL-SANUSI, SAYYID MUHAMMAD; AL-SHARIF, SAYYID AHMAD.

SANUSI, HRH MUHAMMAD HASAN-ELRIDA AL-. A grandnephew of King **Idris I** and the crown prince of Libya if the monarchy were to be restored. Long content to remain in the shadows, Muhammad al-Sanusi was increasingly visible in 2004–2005 as the **opposition** to the **Muammar al-Qaddafi** regime sought to organize. *See also* IDRIS AL-MAHDI AL-SANUSI, SAYYID MUHAMMAD; SANUSI ORDER.

SANUSI, SAYYID MUHAMMAD IDRIS AL-MAHDI AL-. *See* IDRIS AL-MAHDI AL-SANUSI, SAYYID MUHAMMAD.

SANUSI ORDER. **Sayyid Muhammad bin Ali al-Sanusi** established the Sanusi Order in **Cyrenaica** between **Benghazi** and Derna in 1842. A strictly orthodox order of **Sufis**, the Sanusi were a revivalist rather than a reformist movement, dedicated to spreading **religious** enlightenment into areas where **Islam** was at best only lightly observed. They concentrated their influence away from the main political centers of the Mediterranean Sea and North Africa and among the more inaccessible peoples of the **Sahara Desert** and **Sudan**. The brothers of the order, known as *Ikhwan*, carried their message to large parts of Islamic and pagan **Africa**, eventually establishing at least 146 *zawaya* or lodges in the region. In most areas, the Sanusi brought law and order, curbed raiding, encouraged peaceful **trade**, and promoted **agriculture** in a remarkable civilizing mission amid highly unpromising surroundings. With the **Italian** occupation of Cyrenaica in 1932, the Sanusi Order largely ceased to exist as a religious, political, or social organization in either French or Italian colonial territory.

SAQIZLI, MUHAMMAD AL- (MUHAMMAD AL-SAKIZLY; MOHAMMED AL-SAKISLI). Prime minister of the **United Kingdom of Libya** from February to April 1954. A self-made statesman of great personal integrity, Saqizli was closely associated with the elder politicians and thus experienced difficulty in commanding the respect of the younger generation. King **Idris I** invited Saqizli, the chief of the Royal Diwan, to form a new government, in which Saqizli also served as foreign minister. Given the complex domestic and foreign problems facing Libya at independence, there was some question from the start as to why a more flexible and dynamic person than Saqizli, who was meticulous and legal oriented, was not chosen to replace **Mahmud al-Muntasir**. Apparently, the king selected Saqizli because he believed him the best candidate to address the difficult **constitutional** issues facing Libya. From the start, the tenure of the Saqizli government was not expected to be long, and this proved to be the case. Involved in a power struggle between the royal household and the cabinet, Saqizli resigned after his attempt to dissolve the **Tripolitanian** legislative assembly was declared unconstitutional.

SAUD, MOHAMMED. Coordinator of the **revolutionary committees**, Saud is widely believed to be a member of the "gang of five" that has run Libya since the mid-1990s. The other four members are **Muammar al-Qaddafi**, **Ammar al-Taief**, **Issa Kusa**, and **Musa Kusa**.

SCREWWORM FLY. In its first known appearance outside the Western Hemisphere, the screwworm fly, a blue-green insect about three times larger than a housefly, was first spotted in North **Africa** in July 1988. It spread rapidly across some 18,000 square kilometers (7,000 square miles) surrounding the Libyan capital of **Tripoli**. The cross-Atlantic journey of the fly, which had already proven destructive of **livestock** in the Americas, alarmed health and **agricultural** officials worldwide.

Known in its larval stage as the New World screwworm, it is a fast-breeding, flesh-eating pest that poses a serious threat to African livestock and wildlife. The female fly settles in wounds—a tick bite is sufficient—and within a few days can kill its animal host by eating away at tissues and spawning meat-eating larvae that cause a painful death. The fly also attacks human beings.

In mid-1990, the International Fund for Agricultural Development (IFAD) announced a one-year pilot project south of Tripoli aimed at eradicating the screwworm parasite. The project called for airlifting up to 100 million sterilized screwworms a week to Tripoli from a sterilizing unit in Texas in an attempt to disrupt the reproductive cycle of the fly. The scheme included setting up 30 quarantine centers and bringing in agricultural specialists to coordinate the program. Later in the year, IFAD accelerated the program, calling for further aid to finance the scheme in 1991.

The appearance of the screwworm fly led to limited cooperation between Libya and the **United States**. Modifying its ban on American travel to Libya, Washington allowed U.S. technicians employed with **international organizations** to travel to Libya on international passports. American expertise was considered essential to any successful eradication campaign.

SEBHA. Sebha is the capital of the **Fezzan** and the major **transportation** center for southwestern Libya. Contemporary Sebha is largely modern with rather commonplace architecture. The town's main claim to fame is as the place where **Muammar al-Qaddafi** was educated and began his political activities. The school where Qaddafi studied has been renamed the Point of Light School, and his old classroom has been decorated with oil paintings that depict scenes from his life.

SEPTEMBER 1 REVOLUTION. *See* ONE SEPTEMBER REVOLUTION.

SEVENTH NOVEMBER ZONE. Libya made a surprise award in September 1988 when it awarded the 3,000-square-kilometer (1,160-square-mile) **petroleum** block known as Seventh November to the joint Libyan-Tunisian Exploration and Exploitation Company. The award was preceded by a multiyear dispute between Libya and **Tunisia** concerning their offshore **frontier** and the oil and **natural gas** fields located on the disputed **Libya-Tunisia continental shelf**. At one point, tensions reached the stage that gunboats were dispatched to prevent exploration. Eventually, the two neighbors submitted their dispute to the **International Court of Justice** (ICJ), which delivered its judgment in February 1982. When Tunisia refused to accept the ruling of the court, additional hearings were required before a boundary acceptable to both sides was agreed upon in 1985.

Under the terms of the final ICJ adjudication, Libya and Tunisia agreed to undertake joint exploration of the continental shelf traversing the offshore boundary. The Seventh November zone covers 1,600 square kilometers (600 square miles) on the Libyan side and 1,400 square kilometers (550 square miles) on the Tunisian side. It is believed to contain three oil- and gas-bearing structures, a major one on the Libyan side and two smaller ones on the Tunisian side.

SHAKSHUKI, FAWZI (FAWZI AL-SHAKSHUKI). A cabinet minister throughout most of the 1980s, Fawzi Shakshuki served first as minister of planning and later as secretary of **petroleum** on the General People's Committee to the **General People's Congress**. In a surprise move, Shakshuki was replaced as secretary of petroleum in October 1990 by **Abdullah Salem al-Badri**, former chairman of the **National Oil Company**.

SHARIF, SAYYID AHMAD AL- (?–1933). Son of Sayyid Muhammad al-Sharif, the younger brother of **Sayyid Muhammad al-Mahdi al-Sanusi**. Sayyid Ahmad al-Sharif assumed the leadership of the **Sanusi Order** after the death of his uncle in 1902. Sharif lacked the organizational and tactical skills of Sayyid Muhammad, however, and consequently the war with **France**'s colonial forces was not a success. His leadership of the order fell into three periods: 1902–1912, when he opposed French expansion in the **Sahara Desert**; 1912–1918, when he directed the bedouins of **Cyrenaica** against the **Italians** and British; and after 1918, when he went into exile. He died in 1933 in Saudi Arabia. *See also* IDRIS AL-MAHDI AL-SANUSI, SAYYID MUHAMMAD.

SIDRA (SIRTE), GULF OF. The large gulf in the Mediterranean Sea off the central Libyan coast. Its northern limit is the parallel of latitude at 32 degrees 30 minutes north. This line links the outermost points of the cities of **Benghazi** and **Misurata** and measures 296 nautical miles long; the longest perpendicular distance from the line to the Libyan coast is 96 nautical miles. The Gulf of Sidra thus encloses 70,560 square kilometers (27,520 square miles) or approximately 2.8 percent of the Mediterranean Sea. The line marking the extent of the gulf, a boundary proclaimed unilaterally by the Libyan government, defines an area Libya considers to be internal waters, although this claim has been strongly contested by a number of other states.

The Libyan government first declared its sovereignty over the waters of the Gulf of Sidra in a 9 October 1973 proclamation, the contents of which were communicated to the **United Nations** in a *note verbale* 10 days later. In this note, the Libyan government argued that the Gulf of Sidra, surrounded by land boundaries on three sides, was located within the territory of the Libyan Arab Republic, constituted an integral part of Libya, and was under its complete sovereignty. The note then described the waters of the gulf as internal waters, beyond which commenced Libya's territorial waters. In support of its position, the Libyan government claimed an extended, de facto occupation and control of the gulf, an exercise of sovereignty that it said had gone unchallenged for an extended period of time. It also emphasized the sensitive nature of the gulf's waters to the security and safety of the Libyan state. The October 1973 communication defiantly concluded that public and private ships would no longer be allowed to enter the Gulf of Sidra without the prior permission of the Libyan Arab Republic.

A number of states, including the **United States**, immediately challenged the new claims of the Libyan government. Most of these protests were based on the argument that the Libyan action converted international waters into internal waters in an unlawful abuse of the high seas. In its February 1974 reply to the October 1973 declaration, the United States described the Libyan action as an unacceptable violation of international law. Citing the 1958 Convention on the Territorial Sea and Contiguous Zone, Washington argued that the body of water enclosed by the Gulf of Sidra could not be regarded as the juridical internal or territorial waters of the Libyan Arab Republic. In this regard, it emphasized that the Gulf of Sidra did not meet the international standards of past and effective exercise of authority, continuous exercise of authority, and acquiescence of foreign nations required in order to be regarded historically as Libyan internal or territorial waters. The United States concluded that Libya's declaration was really an attempt to expropriate a large area of the high seas by unilateral action for exclusive use, thereby encroaching upon the long established principle of freedom of the seas. The U.S. government in its February 1974 reply emphasized to Libya that Washington reserved its rights and the rights of its nationals in the Gulf of Sidra.

After 1974, the U.S. government repeatedly challenged Libyan claims in the Gulf of Sidra both by action and in formal protests. The Libyan government, in turn, protested what it saw as a repeated violation of its sovereign territory by U.S. forces, claiming a legitimate right to defend its territory. In 1975, for example, Libya protested the over-flight of gulf waters by U.S. aircraft. Libya lodged a similar protest in 1977 following additional overflights by the United States.

In August 1981, U.S. fighter planes operating from the aircraft carrier *Nimitz* intercepted and shot down two aircraft of the Libyan Air Force over the gulf. The American aircraft were taking part in naval exercises being conducted by the U.S. Sixth Fleet within the Gulf of Sidra. The United States had conducted 10 previous exercises in the vicinity of the gulf in 1977–1980, but this was the first time it had directly challenged Libya's claim to internal waters by conducting maneuvers within the Libyan-defined gulf closing line. The incident took place 60 miles off the Libyan coast, clearly within range of the Libyan claim.

A second incident occurred in March 1986 in the course of the fourth major naval exercise conducted by the U.S. Navy off the Libyan coast within a period of only three months. In this instance, U.S. aircraft were fired upon by surface-to-air missiles from an antiaircraft battery near Sirte. Over a two-day period, the United States responded by attacking the Sirte missile battery on two separate occasions as well as sinking four Libyan patrol craft. In both 1981 and 1986, the U.S. government justified its actions as necessary to maintain freedom of navigation in international waters.

In addition to the United States, the governments of **France**, **Great Britain**, Greece, **Italy**, **Malta**, Turkey, and the **Soviet Union** have all protested the attempted enclosure of the Gulf of Sidra by Libya. The Italian government expressed strong reservations immediately, which it repeated in its intervention before proceedings at the **International Court of Justice** involving the Libya-Malta continental shelf case. Similarly, the Maltese government in 1974 rejected the argument that the Gulf of Sidra was a part of Libyan territory or fell within Libyan sovereignty. Malta repeated these reservations in the course of the March 1986 UN Security Council debate occasioned by the Libya-U.S. military confrontation.

The **Arab League** has also been reluctant to uphold Libya's claims. While it condemned the use of force by the United States in 1981 and 1986, the Arab League did not support the legitimacy of the Libyan claim. The permanent observer of the League of Arab States, on the contrary, accepted the right of the United States to challenge the claim, although strongly disapproving of the violent means employed. Only

Burkina Faso and Syria accepted to some degree Libya's claim to ownership of the Gulf of Sidra. *See also* FRONTIERS.

SIRTE BASIN. A desolate region, extending some 500 kilometers (300 miles) along the Libyan coast on the Gulf of **Sidra**, also known as the Gulf of Sirte, where the **desert** extends northward to the Mediterranean. This area is of great historical significance as it has traditionally marked the division of the Maghrib and the Mashriq. To the west, **Tripolitania** has characteristics and a background similar to **Tunisia**, Algeria, and **Morocco**. To the east, **Cyrenaica** has been more closely associated with **Egypt** and the **Arab** states of the Middle East. Because of this traditional bifurcation, observers have long debated whether contemporary Libya should be considered part of the Maghrib or the Mashriq. Libya's location as a crossroads between east and west was often cited by Libyan leader **Muammar al-Qaddafi** in his attempts in the early years of the revolution to promote greater Arab **unity**.

Many of the crude oil fields discovered in Libya to date are located in the Sirte Basin, or Sirtica as it is often called. In 1995, there were 16 giant Sirte fields under production, each with original reserves of more than 500 million barrels of **petroleum**. The bulk of the early Sirte discoveries were at depths between 915 and 1,740 meters (3,000 and 5,700 feet), and the yields per well generally varied from good to exceptional. The oil found in the Sirte Basin is very light, with low sulfur although in some cases a high wax content.

In addition to the 16 Sirte fields, other producing oil fields in the basin have listed reserves of between 100 and 300 million barrels. Few smaller fields have been discovered, which is unusual for a sedimentary basin of this size. However, this may simply reflect a lack of incentive to find and develop smaller fields; in the 1950s and 1960s, the foreign oil companies had their hands full developing the larger fields they had discovered.

Apart from the Sirte Basin, there are three other sedimentary basins in Libya of Paleozoic origins. The **Murzuk Basin** and **Ghadames Basin** lie to the south and southwest, while the **Kufrah Basin** lies to the southeast. In the early days of exploration and development, none of these basins received more than cursory exploration by the foreign oil companies, who concentrated on the more promising Sirte Basin. Later, the Murzuk and Ghadames basins, in particular, were more important in terms of exploration and development.

SOCIALISM. One of the three goals of the 1969 Libyan revolution; the other two are **freedom** and **unity**. These are the same three goals proclaimed by **Egyptian** president Gamal Abdul Nasser at the outset of the 1952 Egyptian revolution. From the beginning, the revolutionary government in Libya trumpeted socialism as the solution to humanity's **economic** problems. Early **Revolutionary Command Council** statements emphasized the indigenous nature of Libyan socialism, describing it as an integral part of Libyan political culture as well as a necessary corrective action. **Muammar al-Qaddafi** argued repeatedly that socialism stemmed from the heritage of the Libyan people and the heart of the Libyan nation. In this regard, his approach to socialism resembled what had happened elsewhere in the Middle East, where the origins and character of socialism have invariably been discussed in the context of local history and customs.

Qaddafi also gave his socialism a strong **Islamic** base by arguing that Libyan socialism was the socialism of Islam. In general terms, he saw the egalitarian precepts of Islam as sustaining the working system of Libyan socialism. More specifically, he argued that the Muslim obligation for alms giving was the basis for the socialist spirit in Islam. Qaddafi also professed to see support in Muslim tradition for his policies on private property and **nationalization**.

Implicit after 1969, socialism did not assume a practical form in Libya until after 1975. This delay in implementation was due to the domestic **opposition** it was expected to engender. Instead, during the early years of the revolution, economic policy emphasized social welfare programs that enjoyed widespread popular support. Regime support for increased **housing** and improved **health** care was especially strong, while enthusiasm for **education** was comparatively less and somewhat selective. Moreover, Qaddafi later became increasingly preoccupied with giving education a military dimension as well as insuring that the curriculum reflected his own ideology. After an initial surge of investment in education, health care, and housing, allocation and spending declined either because of the limited absorptive capacity of the economy, a decision to shift resources from development into reserves, or the cash flow problems caused by arms expenditures.

In 1978, the Libyan approach to socialism began to clarify with the publication of part 2 of *The Green Book*, entitled "The Solution of the Economic Problem: Socialism." Here, Qaddafi defined people's basic needs as a house, an income, and a vehicle. He also described the renting out of houses and vehicles as forms of domination over the needs of others. Ownership of land was specifically prohibited because land was the property of society and not the individual. Qaddafi defined the accumulation of savings beyond a level necessary to satisfy individual needs as exploitative on the grounds that all societies suffer from a scarcity of economic goods and thus the accumulation of wealth beyond one's immediate needs was done only at the expense of others.

In part 2 of *The Green Book*, Qaddafi attempted to develop a theory of natural socialism based on equality among what he considered to be the three economic factors of production: raw materials, an instrument of production, and a producer. In Qaddafi's view, each of these factors was equally important to the process of production and thus each was entitled to an equal share in what was produced. The problem with earlier approaches to socialism, according to the Leader of the Revolution, was that they focused on ownership, wages, or only one of the factors of production. Consequently, they failed to address the real economic problem, which was production itself. Qaddafi advocated the abolition of both the wage system and the profit motive, suggesting these would lead to the disappearance of money. Depicting salaried employees as slaves, he urged them to rise up and become partners in production. Finally, almost as an afterthought, domestic servants were described in *The Green Book* as the slaves of the modern age and were told to find new jobs outside the home where they could also become partners in production.

The socialist theories outlined in *The Green Book* were gradually translated into **laws** that extended and tightened controls over private enterprise. Begun in 1975, this process accelerated after March 1978 when the general secretariat of the **General People's Congress** issued Resolution Four, which established new guidelines for home ownership. All Libyans were given the right to own their own home—but, with few exceptions, no one could own more than one. Six months later, after Qaddafi had urged greater self-management of public and private enterprise, workers rushed to take over some 200 companies. A widespread reorganization and redistribution of farms and land on the **Jifarah Plain** was discussed in 1978–1979, and the government actually closed some wells. In May 1980, all currency in denominations larger than one Libyan dinar was declared void, and citizens were given one week to exchange the money in their possession. With the maximum exchange set at 1,000 dinars, all deposits in excess of that amount were frozen, the depositors turned away with cash receipts. In early 1981, the general secretariat announced the state takeover of all import, export, and distribution functions by year end. A series of state-run central and satellite supermarkets were constructed to replace the private sector.

Clearly, a socialist revolution occurred in Libya after 1969. For more than a decade, the management of the economy was increasingly socialist in intent and effect. Wealth, whether held as housing, capital, or land, was either significantly redistributed or in the process of being redistributed. In turn, private enterprise was virtually eliminated and replaced by a centrally controlled economy. This process continued until the second half of the 1980s, when the revolutionary government signaled an interest in returning to a more open, free-enterprise system in a package of measures, often referred to as "green *perestroika*."

In March 1987, Qaddafi announced the first of a series of economic and political reforms that would modify many of the socialist policies followed earlier by his regime. In additional speeches, on 23 May and 1 September, the Leader of the Revolution called for a new role for the private sector, as well as for increased political liberalization. As part of a package of reforms, he also adopted a form of self-management that permitted the creation of cooperatives to which some partners could contribute labor while others contributed capital. In less than a year, approximately 140 companies had been turned over to self-management committees; in theory, these companies no longer received automatic subsidies from the government.

At the 1 September 1988 anniversary celebration, Qaddafi announced that the state import and export monopoly had been abolished. At the same time, many of the injunctions against the retail trade were lifted, and markets in the cities began to reopen. While the **petroleum** sector and heavy **industry** were exempt from the new privatization measures, most light and medium industries were turned over to self-management committees. In addition, physicians were allowed to reopen private clinics, although their fee schedules were still determined by the General People's Committee.

A complex web of economic and political factors combined to reverse the socialist policies followed by the Qaddafi regime for almost two decades. The state supermarket system faltered under the weight of corruption and a disorganized distribution system. The unofficially tolerated black market provided little relief to the average Libyan citizen. And the expulsion of large numbers of expatriate workers in 1985 and later brought much of the service and **agricultural** sectors to a standstill. Moreover, the combined impact of these economic issues was then intensified by the diplomatic isolation Libya experienced in the second half of the 1980s and most of the 1990s. Recognizing that domestic political discontent was approaching an explosive level, Qaddafi responded with a number of corrective measures that, in effect, reversed many of the socialist policies he had advocated since the early 1970s.

Stating that the nation's public sector had failed and should be abolished, Qaddafi called in 2003 for the privatization of the Libyan oil industry, together with other sectors of the Libyan economy. In response, Libya in October 2003 published a list of 361 firms in a variety of economic sectors targeted for privatization. In a further move to liberalize the economy, Libya decided in July 2005 to lift customs tariffs on 3,500 imported commodities.

SOCIALIST PEOPLE'S LIBYAN ARAB JAMAHIRIYA. On 2 March 1977, the **Declaration of the Establishment of the People's Authority** decreed that the official name of Libya had become the Socialist People's Libyan Arab Jamahiriya. Later, Libya was often also referred to as the Great Socialist People's Libyan Arab Jamahiriya, and in the aftermath of the 1986 bombing raids by the **United States**, it was also referred to as the Great Jamahiriya. For the sake of convenience, the continued use of "Libya" has remained widespread.

SOFFEGIN, WADI. The Wadi Soffegin is the most important drainage system in **Tripolitania**. Originating in the numerous headwater tributaries between Giado and Yafran, it rises in the folds of the Jabal south of Yafran, and flows southeastward past Mizda. Then, in a succession of great arcs, it continues eastward for about 250 kilometers (155 miles), entering the **Sabkhat Tawurgha** at the Gulf of **Sidra**.

SOVIET UNION. Russian interest in the Mediterranean Sea antedates the October 1917 Bolshevik Revolution. A traditional aim of tsarist diplomacy was control of the waterway connecting the Black Sea and the Aegean Sea. After World War II, the Soviet Union attempted to control

Libya as part of a broader policy of increasing its military presence in the Mediterranean and its political influence in the Middle East.

At the July 1945 Potsdam Conference, the USSR proposed the establishment of a Soviet trusteeship over **Tripolitania**. Two months later, it repeated this proposal at a meeting of the Council of Foreign Ministers in London, stating that 10 years should be adequate to prepare the area for independence. In recognition of the strategic location of Libya, as well as its value as a base for long-range bombers, the Soviet foreign minister argued that his country needed an outlet on the Mediterranean Sea and demanded that Libya be the site of such a base.

Both **France** and **Great Britain** opposed the Soviet proposal, and when the Council of Foreign Ministers reconvened in April 1946, the British government proposed immediate independence for Libya. Since this solution would frustrate Soviet designs in the region, the Soviet Union countered with a proposal for a collective trusteeship. When this alternative was rejected, the Soviets, alert to a possible Communist victory in the upcoming **Italian** general elections, supported the return of Libya to Italy.

In February 1947, the Big Four Powers (France, Great Britain, the Soviet Union, and the **United States**) signed a treaty of peace with Italy that left to the Big Four the final disposition of Italy's former colonies. While the Big Four were inclined to place Libya under some form of trusteeship, they could not agree on which powers should be involved. Deadlocked, they referred the question to the General Assembly of the **United Nations**, which proclaimed Libya independent on 24 December 1951. In this sense, the conflicting ambitions of the Big Four Powers, especially the policies of the Soviet Union, proved to be one of the principal assets enjoyed by Libya in its struggle for immediate independence.

The Soviet Union did not establish diplomatic relations with the **United Kingdom of Libya** until 1955, and for the remainder of the decade, diplomatic and commercial exchanges between the two states were minimal. Throughout the first decade of independence, the monarchy maintained a largely Western orientation because of its heavy dependence on the income and financial assistance generated by the British and U.S. military bases in Libya. At the same time, the discovery of **petroleum** in commercially exportable quantities in 1959 did prompt the monarchy to make minor modifications in the direction and emphasis of its **foreign policy**. As part of this redirection, commercial and diplomatic links with the Soviet Union were expanded modestly. Moscow participated in the annual Tripoli Trade Fair and a Soviet-Libyan **trade** agreement was concluded in 1963. Libyan parliamentary delegations visited the USSR in 1961 and 1968, and a Supreme Soviet delegation visited Libya in 1966.

On 1 September 1969, the **Libyan Free Unionist Officers** movement executed a successful coup d'état and initiated a radical reorientation of Libyan foreign and domestic policy. Three days later, the Soviet Union announced its official recognition of the Libyan Arab Republic, indicating a willingness to provide any assistance required. Thereafter, Soviet interests and activities in Libya gradually broadened. Initially, the revolutionary government carefully limited its expanded relationship with the Soviet Union to the commercial sphere, particularly the purchase of arms. The first consignment of Soviet military equipment arrived in July 1970 and was displayed at the parade on the first anniversary of the **One September Revolution**. Libya continued to purchase Soviet weaponry throughout the decade, including a $1 billion package in 1974–1975 that was its single largest arms agreement. By 1976, Libya was widely thought to have one of the highest per capita ratios of military equipment in the world. Soviet weapons were accompanied by Soviet military advisers and technicians; however, Libya attempted to minimize their numbers by utilizing advisers from other states like Cuba, Pakistan, and even the United States.

From the beginning, it was the seemingly insatiable Libyan appetite for modern armaments, combined with a foreign policy that increasingly isolated it from the West, that were the primary reasons for growing Soviet-Libyan ties. Ideological affinity played little role in their deepening commercial relationship. On the contrary, this early period was characterized by a degree of ideological antipathy. The revolutionary government's populist, **Islamic**, and **Arab nationalist** views had nothing in common with Soviet ideology. Still, increased involvement in Libya helped the Soviet Union pursue strategic and economic goals in the region, including diminishing Western influence, increasing its own voice in Middle Eastern and **African** affairs, and easing the logistical problems of maintaining a naval force in the Mediterranean Sea. The sale of arms also generated much-needed hard currency, and Libya was a potential source of oil when Soviet supplies ran short.

In the second half of the 1970s, the Soviet Union worked to expand technical interchange with Libya. In 1975, Moscow announced that it would provide Libya with its first nuclear reactor, a 10-megawatt research facility. Three years later, the Soviet Union also agreed to build a combined nuclear power plant and research center with a capacity of 300 megawatts. The two governments later discussed expanding their nuclear cooperation to include a power station with two 400-megawatt units.

Libyan leader **Muammar al-Qaddafi** never accomplished a threat made in October 1978 to join the **Warsaw Pact**, a defensive alliance of European Communist states; however, he continued to buy sophisticated Soviet arms, and the number of Soviet advisers in Libya increased over the years. Arms aid thus proved an effective instrument of Soviet policy in Libya as well as elsewhere in the Middle East. Moscow became **Tripoli**'s dominant military supplier, increasing its presence and influence in the country and the region. In the process, the Libyan **armed forces** acquired large quantities of modern, sophisticated weapons far in excess of their capacity to absorb and operate them. By the early 1980s, Libya had spent an estimated $12 billion on armaments, and its 55,000-strong armed forces were reported to have the highest ratio of military hardware to manpower in the Third World. The Libyans were also successful in upgrading the quality of their weapons, acquiring some of the most advanced systems in the Soviet inventory.

After 1984, Soviet concern with the direction and emphasis of Libyan policy increased, strengthening a growing reluctance to move too close to the Qaddafi regime. The reported Libyan bombing of Omdurman, a suburb of the **Sudanese** capital of Khartoum, in March 1984 and the suspected Libyan involvement in the mining of the Red Sea and Gulf of Suez in mid-1984 were both contrary to Soviet objectives. The Soviets also viewed Qaddafi's association with state-sponsored **terrorism** as counterproductive. Finally, as Libyan oil revenues dropped, the economic rewards of the Libyan connection diminished. Libya had reportedly purchased $15 to $20 billion worth of Soviet weapons by the end of 1986, but it was also estimated to owe the Soviets $5 to $7 billion in back payments.

After visiting Moscow in 1977 and 1981, Colonel Qaddafi paid his third official visit to the Soviet Union in October 1985. The objectives of his trip included Soviet assistance for the construction of a nuclear reactor convertible to military uses, additional military supplies, increased Soviet purchases of Libyan crude oil, and the conclusion of a treaty of friendship and cooperation. The official Soviet news agency described the discussions in Moscow as having occurred in an atmosphere of friendship and mutual understanding; however, Qaddafi left the Soviet capital with considerably less than his total package. The Soviets agreed to help with a nuclear reactor, but not one convertible to military uses. They referred the new Libyan arms requests to a commission and pressed for monies due for earlier purchases. A deal was struck for the purchase of additional Libyan oil for export to Yugoslavia, but it was not the doubling in the daily Soviet purchase sought by Libya. Finally, an agreement covering **economic**, trade, scientific, and technical cooperation through 2000 was negotiated, but there was no mention in the final communiqué of the friendship and cooperation treaty agreed to in principle two years earlier. Five months later, after Qaddafi ruled out any possibility of Soviet bases in Libya, the Soviets shelved plans to sign a friendship treaty.

The April 1986 **United States** bombing attack on targets around Tripoli and **Benghazi** strained already tense Soviet-Libyan relations. When Qaddafi again threatened to join the Warsaw Pact in the aftermath of the attack, he received no encouragement from Moscow. While the Soviet Union denounced the raids, it appeared content to promise Tripoli only that it would help Libya to rebuild its defensive capability. When **Abdel Salaam Jalloud** returned to Moscow in 1986, the Soviet government was reluctant to extend additional arms credits, rejected a proposed mutual defense treaty, and stressed the confusion that existed worldwide in differentiating between Libyan support for revolution and terrorism. The Soviet Union remained an ally of Libya, but it was an aloof, reluctant, and suspicious ally.

In the second half of the 1980s, the USSR further distanced itself from Libya, and the bilateral cultural, economic, and political agreements in place were increasingly subordinated to more simple arms-for-cash ties. In the process, the Soviet-Libyan relationship was strongly influenced by the economic and political reforms initiated by Soviet president Mikhail Gorbachev—reforms that eventually precipitated the collapse of the Soviet Union. Through a series of arms control agreements and summit meetings with U.S. presidents Ronald Reagan and George H. W. Bush, Gorbachev succeeded in developing a basis for diplomatic and economic cooperation with the United States. However, in the process, his promises of domestic political liberalization unleashed sociopolitical forces beyond his control.

In a brief period from 1989 to 1991, the Baltic republics asserted their national independence and the East European satellite states overthrew their Communist regimes and embraced a period of widespread reform. In response to these developments, opponents of Gorbachev's reform programs staged an abortive coup in 1991. Libya was among the first governments to recognize the Communist hard-liners in their failed attempt to displace Gorbachev and halt his reforms. While Gorbachev later resigned and was replaced by Boris Yeltsin, Qaddafi's quick decision to recognize the coup leaders contributed to a cooling of the relationship that continued in the aftermath of the implosion of the Soviet Union. *See also* POSITIVE NEUTRALITY.

STEADFASTNESS AND CONFRONTATION FRONT. Organized in December 1977, the Steadfastness and Confrontation Front expressed support for a variety of revolutionary movements in the **Arab** world. However, its main objective was to coordinate Arab opposition to Egyptian president Anwar al-Sadat's November 1977 peace initiative with **Israel**. Its founding members included Algeria, Libya, the **Palestine Liberation Organization**, South Yemen, and Syria. The Iraqi government also participated in the conference, but after a disagreement with Syria, it refused to sign the agreement. The Libyan government played an instrumental role in the formation of the organization. Its creation fulfilled a long-standing Libyan objective to organize an anti-Egyptian front.

SUDAN. A military coup d'état in May 1969 brought to power in Sudan a Revolutionary Command Council led by Jaffar al-Numayri. Under his leadership, the Sudanese government proclaimed a **socialist** revolution with **nationalist** goals and adopted pro-**Arab**, anti-imperialist policies. The pan-Arab approach of the Numayri regime endeared it to radical secular regimes in **Egypt** and Libya, but distanced it from the conservative monarchies of **Ethiopia** and the Arabian Peninsula.

Four months after the revolution in Libya and seven months after the revolution in Sudan, the two governments joined Egypt in December 1969 in signing a tripartite agreement known as the **Tripoli Charter**.

The agreement joined the three revolutionary governments in a so-called Arab Revolutionary Front, with a supreme planning committee and a common security system. The remainder of the pact was more circumspect as it established joint ministerial commissions to pursue coordinated policies but did not mention political union as a longer-term objective.

Soon after the conclusion of the Tripoli Charter, **Muammar al-Qaddafi** pushed both Egypt and Sudan for full constitutional union. Both governments rejected this approach, and subsequent talks at the ministerial level were limited to such issues as relaxation of customs duties and a freer flow of labor between the neighboring states. President Numayri later muted his socialist policies and backed away from **unity** proposals with Egypt and Libya.

A major difference in the **foreign policies** of Libya and Sudan soon surfaced when the latter forced five Libyan planes carrying military hardware to Uganda to land in Sudan and then refused to allow them to continue their journey. Libya viewed the Idi Amin regime in Uganda as an **Islamic**, anti-imperialist force in **Africa**, while Sudan saw it in a less favorable light. This diplomatic crisis, together with the rejection of the unity proposals in the Tripoli Charter, marked the beginning of Qaddafi's distrust of Numayri.

Sudan's relations with the **United States** began to improve in late 1974 when a pro-**Soviet** military regime overthrew the Ethiopian regime of Emperor Haile Selassie I, thereby ending a prolonged U.S. civilian and military presence in that country. Sudan became a preferred forward base for Washington, given the country's favorable location adjoining Ethiopia and the Red Sea and near the Arabian oil fields, and its opposition to the increasingly antagonistic regime in Libya. Khartoum welcomed the increased attention from Washington, together with the mounting levels of economic and military aid that came with it. Sudan also served as a strategic rear for Egypt, in part because the Numayri regime supported the Egyptian settlement with **Israel** and cooperated against Libya.

Diplomatic relations between Libya and Sudan improved after 1977 when Numayri entrusted Sadiq al-Mahdi, long-exiled leader of Sudan and a personal friend of Qaddafi, with the task of improving bilateral ties. Libya saw the Sadiq al-Mahdi mission as an opportunity to draw Sudan away from its close relationship with Egypt. While Libyan-Sudanese relations improved in the late 1970s as Sudan distanced itself from Egypt, they worsened again toward the end of 1980 when Libya dispatched troops to Chad.

Sensitive to the growing military forces on its borders, Sudan sought protection in the form of closer diplomatic relations with both Egypt and the United States. In early 1981, Numayri invited the Egyptian head of state to attend celebrations marking the 12th anniversary of his regime, an action that caused Libya as well as Syria to call upon the **Arab League** to take punitive actions against Sudan. Sudan also expressed interest in U.S. aid to improve Sudanese air and naval facilities, hinting that the United States and other friendly powers might utilize such facilities in time of crisis.

In 1981, the tripartite agreement between Libya, Ethiopia, and South Yemen exposed the vulnerability of the Numayri government, as the alliance appeared to encircle Sudan. In addition, the Libyan invasion of Chad put direct pressure on the western Sudanese province of Darfur. Libyan troops strayed across the border, Chadian forces crisscrossed the frontier, and Libyan bombers strafed Sudanese villages. The Numayri government was clearly unable to police and protect its own borders; instead, it had to rely on U.S. AWACS aircraft and Egyptian air defenses for surveillance.

Under increasing popular pressure, Numayri reversed course in 1983, aligning himself with the Islamic movement and adopting Islamic rules to govern the country. Nevertheless, Libya remained openly hostile to the Numayri administration; and when the latter was finally overthrown in 1985, Libya was the first to recognize the transitional government of Gen. Abd al-Rahman Siwar al-Dhabab. In April 1985, the self-styled Transitional Military Committee canceled a 1983 agreement calling for political and economic integration with Egypt; and days later, the Khartoum regime announced that Libya had initiated a political union with Sudan.

The initial policy line of the transitional government was that better diplomatic relations with Libya, Ethiopia, and the **Soviet Union** would not be at the expense of the United States and Egypt but instead would redress the balance and restore normal relations with all states. Not surprisingly, the Transitional Military Committee found its self-proclaimed good neighbor policy difficult to follow, with the result that Sudanese relations with Libya and its allies improved while those with Egypt and the United States deteriorated. Libyan military aid to Sudan increased, and the Khartoum government found itself increasingly embroiled in the mounting crisis between Libya and the United States.

When Sadiq al-Mahdi, leader of the Umma party, became prime minister in May 1986, he reinforced and consolidated the good neighbor policy begun by the transitional government. He cast his net wide, visiting Moscow, Washington, Tripoli, Riyadh, and Teheran, but he soon discovered the same contradictions that had complicated Sudanese diplomacy during the transitional period. Qaddafi's uninvited visit to Khartoum in September 1986, coupled with his renewed calls for unity and for subversion against Americans in the Middle East, were especially embarrassing. At the same time, complex domestic problems, particularly the ongoing conflict in the south, forced Sadiq al-Mahdi to continue to rely on Libyan military support. Mahdi was eventually overthrown in a coup d'état in June 1989.

The coup, engineered by Brigadier Omar Hassan Ahmad al-Bashir, was greeted initially with both enthusiasm and relief by a Sudanese people exasperated by the vacillating, incompetent government of Mahdi. However, these early attitudes began to change within days as the new government adopted a tough stance toward civil strife, imposed a state of emergency, suspended the constitution, and closed the parliament. This crackdown alienated supporters inside and outside the country. Qaddafi called for the release of Sadiq al-Mahdi and criticized the Islamic-oriented government in Khartoum for mixing religion and politics and for alienating non-Muslim communities. Libya continued to provide **petroleum** and military supplies to the Sudan, but it expected political dividends for its support.

In March 1990, Libya and Sudan concluded a Charter of Integration providing for coordination between their security and military forces as well as for joint efforts for the dissemination of Arabic culture and language. While Qaddafi criticized the politicization of Islam in Sudan, he embraced the Arabization of non-Arab peoples in the country. Libya also increased its military presence in Darfur, a battleground between Chadian forces and dissidents at the expense of local villagers. Darfur provided a vital sanctuary in Qaddafi's prolonged, eventually unsuccessful attempt to influence events in Chad. With the collapse of Libyan **foreign policy** toward Chad, Qaddafi's interest in and support for the Khartoum government also faded. Bilateral relations in the early 1990s were strained by Sudanese support for militant Islamic reformers, and Libya played a reduced role in Sudanese politics in the second half of the decade.

With the suspension of **United Nations** sanctions, Qaddafi reinvigorated Libya's African policy. As part of this effort, he mediated a dispute between Sudan and Uganda in May 2001 and played an active role in 2004–2005 in mediating an African solution to the conflict in Sudan's Darfur region. Providing leadership to a six-nation African mediation effort—its membership representing Libya, Chad, Egypt, Eritrea, Gabon, and Nigeria—Qaddafi worked tirelessly to persuade the conflicting parties to reach a settlement. The Libyan government also played an active role in supporting humanitarian efforts in Sudan, especially the transport of emergency supplies across Libya to war-torn Darfur.

SUFI. A mystical movement in **Islam**. Based on a renunciation of the world, the doctrine originated in the Middle East as a reaction to established Islam. It spread to North Africa in the 11th and 12th centuries, where it became particularly influential among the **Berbers**. Local Sufi saints, known as *marabouts* and thought to be blessed with *baraka*, established **religious** orders or schools, known as *zawiya*. Because the message of such movements addressed all aspects of society, their activities often had strong political overtones. The **Sanusi Order** in **Cyrenaica** had the strongest grip of any Libyan *tariqa* in modern times.

SUWAYHLI, RAMADAN AL- (RAMADAN AL-SHITAYWI AL-SUWAYHLI). A prominent **Tripolitanian nationalist** leader at the outset of the **Italian** occupation in 1911, Ramadan al-Suwayhli took the field against the Italians during the **Ottoman**-Italian war. After the conclusion of the 1912 peace treaty, he briefly cooperated with the Italians before leading the revolt against the Italian column at Sirte. With the outbreak of World War I, the Italians withdrew from **Misurata**, leaving Suwayhli, then in his early 30s and well known for his exploits at the battle of **Qasr Bu Hadi**, among the most prominent figures in town.

Like many Libyan notables at the time, Suwayhli was probably as interested in extending his own political influence as he was in serving the Ottoman cause. For several years, he succeeded in strengthening Misurata as a safe haven for Ottoman forces and an autonomous political district. In 1916, Suwayhli's forces clashed with Sanusi troops sent to Sirte to collect taxes from the local population. With the people of Sirte also being asked to pay taxes to his government in Misurata, the scarcity of resources had an adverse effect on the erstwhile united front against the Italians. In mid-1916, the leadership of the **Sanusi Order** opened negotiations with the British and Italians, leaving the Ottomans to pin their hopes on the forces of Suwyahli and **Suleiman Baruni**.

– T –

TAIEF, AMMAR AL-. A shadowy figure about whom very little is known. Taief is widely believed to be a member of the "gang of five" that has run Libya since the mid-1990s. The other four members are **Muammar al-Qaddafi**, **Issa Kusa**, **Musa Kusa**, and **Mohammed Saud**.

TEBU. An ancient, dark-skinned Saharan race of unknown origin. Converted to **Islam** by **Sanusi Order** missionaries in the 19th century, they retained many of their earlier **religious** beliefs and practices. Their language is related to a Nigerian tongue. Centered in the Tibesti Mountains and other parts of southern Libya and northern **Chad**, early Tebu **economic** organization was based on pastoral nomadism. Living in a naturally harsh environment, the Tebu traditionally widened their margin of survival by caravaning, slaving, and raiding. Beginning in the latter half of the 19th century, Tebu mobility was gradually curbed by the conquest and policing of the **Sahara Desert**, first by the colonial powers and later by the independent successor states of Libya and Chad. In the second half of the 20th century, the Tebu found themselves administered from centers such as **Benghazi** and Baida in Libya and N'Djamena in Chad. The presence of a Tebu minority in the **Fezzan** and **Cyrenaica** contributed to Libyan interest in the Chadian rebellion that was initiated in the 1960s.

TEHERAN AGREEMENT. A settlement concluded on 15 February 1971 between **petroleum** companies and the oil-producing states in the Gulf area, the Teheran Agreement stemmed from Libya's **One September Agreement** and incorporated many of the gains won by the Libyan government in 1970. The oil companies accepted an immediate posted oil price increase of 35 cents a barrel, to be followed by annual increases over the next five years, and the treatment of specific gravity levels was modified in favor of the oil-producing countries. In return, the Gulf states accepted the principle of no leapfrogging, agreeing not to negotiate individually for better terms, and also agreed not to limit production in order to achieve better financial terms.

The **Revolutionary Command Council** (RCC) adamantly opposed the terms of the Teheran Agreement. Where Libya rejected the principle of collective bargaining, the Gulf settlement spoke of a general increase in the posted price as if it applied to all **Organization of Petroleum Exporting Countries** (OPEC) members, including Libya. Tripoli also protested the level of price increases agreed upon and the value of the short-haul freight premiums specified for Libya. Finally, Libya rightly viewed the clauses in the Teheran Agreement that prohibited leapfrogging and production restrictions as designed to frustrate its efforts to seek better terms from its own oil producers. With the conclusion of this agreement, the limited OPEC leadership role that Libya had briefly enjoyed faded as the RCC soon opened new negotiations with Libyan oil producers aimed at more favorable terms. *See also* LIBYAN PRODUCERS AGREEMENT; NATIONALIZATION; TRIPOLI AGREEMENT.

TERRORISM. The concept of **jihad**, the action element of **Muammar al-Qaddafi**'s variant of **Arab nationalism**, found its most practical expression in his fervent support for the Palestinian movement. In the early 1970s, he advocated direct military action against **Israel**, and he continued this policy after the October 1973 war strengthened the **Palestine Liberation Organization** (PLO) and **petroleum** proved a more effective weapon in support of Arab goals.

Qaddafi's approach to jihad also led him to support, at one time or another, a variety of so-called liberation movements, including the Somali National Salvation Front, the Irish Republican Army, Muslim separatist elements in the Philippines such as the **Moro National Liberation Front**, and black militant movements in the **United States**. Qaddafi devoted considerable time in the 1970s and 1980s to differentiating between revolutionary violence, which he continued to advocate and support, and terrorism, which he claimed to oppose; however, many governments, especially that of the United States, failed to see the difference.

In the wake of the 11 September 2001 terrorist attacks on the United States, Qaddafi was an immediate convert to the George W. Bush administration's war on terrorism. Condemning the attacks, he expressed sympathy and support for the victims. While acknowledging political differences with the United States, he emphasized that they should not become a psychological barrier against offering humanitarian aid to U.S. citizens and all people in America who suffered from the attacks. At the same time, he expressed concern with President Bush's tendency to divide the world neatly into states "with the United States" or "with the terrorists." Qaddafi later argued that the United States had the right to take revenge for the attacks, calling them the worst form of terrorism. In the ensuing months, American and British officials held information-sharing sessions with their Libyan counterparts.

Long a target of **Islamist** fundamentalist groups, Qaddafi also rushed to share intelligence with Washington on alleged allies of Osama bin Laden such as the **Libyan Islamic Fighting Group**. In a move interpreted by some as an attempt to gain support from the West, Libya in January 2002 launched an Internet website offering a $1 million reward for information on terrorists—mostly regime opponents affiliated with Islamist movements—wanted by Libyan authorities. Al-Qaeda operatives in May 2005, in a move that highlighted the radical shift in Libyan policy with regard to terrorism in recent years, threatened to launch terrorist attacks against Libya if the Qaddafi regime did not release imprisoned followers. The move also suggested Libya's cooperation in the war on terrorism was having an effect on al-Qaeda operations.

THIRD CIRCLE. *See* AFRICA.

THIRD INTERNATIONAL THEORY. *See* THIRD UNIVERSAL THEORY.

THIRD UNIVERSAL THEORY. By late 1972, **Muammar al-Qaddafi** had begun to give the tenets of his strain of **Arab nationalism** a theoretical underpinning with the articulation of what came to be known as the Third Universal Theory. The theory sought to develop an alternative to capitalism and communism, both of which Qaddafi found unsuitable to the Libyan environment. It condemned both communism and capitalism as monopolistic—the former as a state monopoly of ownership and the latter as a monopoly of ownership by capitalists and companies. Initially, both the **United States** and the **Soviet Union** were grouped together as imperialist countries intent on obtaining spheres of influence in the Middle East. Qaddafi also denounced the atheistic nature of the Soviet regime.

Qaddafi based the Third Universal Theory on nationalism and **religion**, two forces he described as the paramount drives moving history and humankind. Nationalism was considered to be the natural result of the world's racial and cultural diversity and thus both a necessary and a productive force. Arab nationalism was considered to have especially deep and glorious roots in the ancient past. Because the Arab nation was the product of an age-old civilization based on the heavenly and universal message of **Islam**, Qaddafi argued it had the right and duty to be the bearer of the Third Universal Theory to the world.

Qaddafi never produced a coherent, comprehensive discussion of religion, but his thoughts in various seminars and statements focused on the centrality of Islam to religion and the Koran to Islam. Considering Islam to be God's final utterance to humanity, he argued there was nothing in life for which the principles were not found in Islam. For Qaddafi, the essence of religion was the unity of God; consequently, he made no distinction between what he called the followers of Muhammad, Jesus, and Moses. Since there was only one religion—Islam—he considered all monotheists to be Muslims. Qaddafi firmly believed that Islam was addressed not only to the followers of the Prophet Muhammad but that Islam meant a belief in God as embodied in all religions. He referred to his contention that anyone who believed in God and his apostles was a Muslim as the "divine concept of Islam."

Basing his call for Islamic revival on the Koran, Qaddafi argued that Muslims had moved away from God and the Koran and needed to return. In the process, he attempted to correct contemporary Islamic practices that in his mind were contrary to the faith. For example, he rejected formal interpretation of the Koran as blasphemy and sin, contending that the Koran was written in Arabic so that every Arab could read it and apply it without the help of others. Similarly, he criticized the *hadith* on the grounds the Koran was the only real source of God's word. Qaddafi was also critical of the various schools of Islamic jurisprudence on the grounds they were largely the product of a struggle for political power and thus unconnected to either Islam or the Koran.

While the similarities can clearly be overstated, there were some important continuities between the doctrines of the **Sanusi Order** and the fundamentalist elements of Qaddafi's reformist approach to Islam. To promote Islamic unity, the puritanical Sanusi Order accepted only the Koran and the Sunna as the basis for Muslim life, downplaying the role of the schools of Islamic **law**. Qaddafi emphasized these fundamentalist elements in the early years of the revolution due to their legitimizing effect. Later, however, his approach became increasingly reformist, if not secular.

In the process, the Islamic character of Qaddafi's brand of Arab nationalism and the supposed universal elements of the Third Universal Theory became increasingly paradoxical. In response, Qaddafi continued to emphasize the centrality of Islam to Arab nationalism while deemphasizing Islam's role in the Third Universal Theory. Although Qaddafi's thoughts on this complex relationship remained unclear, his argument that the Third Universal Theory was the basis for a new universal civilization centered on the Arab nation logically resulted in Islam continuing to have a central role. Consequently, any deemphasis of Islam was probably only a short-term tactic designed to give the Third Universal Theory wider appeal.

TOURISM. With the lifting of **United Nations** sanctions in 2003, the tourism industry expanded rapidly. Still a work in progress, the potential for tourism is enormous. The unspoiled coastline, **desert** expanses, natural scenery, and **Greek** and **Roman** ruins offer plenty for the tourist to see. To the west, the Roman ruins of **Leptis Magna** and **Sabratah** provide šome of the best-preserved Roman sites outside Italy. To the east, there are extensive Greek ruins at **Apollonia** and **Cyrene**. In the south, the **Sahara Desert** offers a striking landscape, prehistoric rock paintings, intriguing **Tuareg** culture, and a number of ancient towns, including the legendary caravan city of **Ghadames**, a UNESCO world heritage site.

Libya's tourist infrastructure, from domestic air **transportation** to hotels to restaurants, is not extensive but is developing rapidly. The number of tour operators offering visits to Libya, including cruise ship visits to coastal Greek and Roman sites, is also increasing. Europeans have been the most common visitors to Libya in recent years, but more and more American tourists can be seen as bilateral relations between Libya and the **United States** improve.

TRADE. Libya's primary exports are crude **petroleum** and associated refined products. According to the International Monetary Fund (IMF), approximately 90 percent of those exports go to Western Europe, mostly to **Italy**, Spain, and **Germany**. Imports are more diverse and include food products, machinery, manufactured goods, and **transportation** equipment. Approximately 70 percent of Libyan imports come from Western Europe, with Italy being the major source. The remainder is sourced from around the world; since 2003, U.S. suppliers have played a growing role. Libya's current account balance was $7.429 billion in 2004, according to IMF projections.

TRADE UNIONS. Since 1969, the revolutionary government has encouraged workers to organize into unions or professional associations. Each trade union or professional association elects a **people's committee** to administer its affairs. In turn, these committees participate in a federation of unions at the national level. The national federation of unions and professional associations sends representatives to the **General People's Congress** to address issues of special relevance to them; however, they are not allowed to vote on major policy issues. While the representatives of the trade unions and professional associations bring expertise on selected issues, their views as individuals can be expressed only through people's committees and their **Basic People's Congress**.

TRANSPORTATION. Before **petroleum** was discovered in commercially exploitable quantities, Libya was one of the poorest countries in the world. Consequently, the early years of independence were a time in which allocations to the transportation sector were modest. This situation quickly changed as oil revenues increased rapidly in the early 1960s. The first Five-Year **Development Plan** (1963–1968) allocated substantial funds to the production and services sectors. As a result, more than 800 kilometers (500 miles) of **road** had been constructed by 1968 with another 3,200 kilometers (2,000 miles) under construction, including a coastal highway.

In addition, other transportation facilities, such as the handling capacities of the **ports** of **Tripoli** and **Benghazi**, were also improved. The government constructed new storage areas and quays, as well as installing modern equipment for handling cargo. Air transport facilities were also improved with the construction of new runways and the purchase of new aircraft. On the other hand, the monarchy often experienced a shortfall between allocations to transportation and actual expenditures. A major reason for this problem was the difficulty experienced in mobilizing investment before appropriate studies had been conducted.

The revolutionary government brought new ideas and a new sense of urgency to development problems in general and the transportation sector in particular. Consequently, there was a substantial increase in government allocations to transport. A comparison of expenditure on transport in the periods 1963–1968 and 1971–1973 indicates actual spending by the revolutionary government ran at a rate of four times that achieved by the monarchy in the earlier period, adjusted for inflation. Clearly, **Muammar al-Qaddafi**'s government recognized early on the need to develop an appropriate infrastructure if it hoped to achieve related expansion objectives in the **agricultural** and **industrial** sectors.

The first Three-Year Development Plan (1973–1975) initiated major developments in the Libyan transportation system. Transport allocations were more than sevenfold greater than—and more than double the total allocations of—those of the 1963–1968 plan. In terms of expenditure, emphasis was placed on the nation's ports, as it was clear by the early 1970s that existing harbors could not cope with the growing demand for imports. Emphasis was also placed on the road network, which was generally inadequate to handle the growing traffic in passenger and commercial vehicles. Not surprisingly, this focus on transportation continued in subsequent development plans.

Whereas there were only about 6,000 kilometers (3,700 miles) of roads in Libya before the revolution, there are today more than 80,000 kilometers (50,000 miles), including some 48,000 kilometers (30,000 miles) of paved roads. Under successive development plans, roads have been improved and the system greatly expanded, including roads from **Fezzan** south into **Chad** and Niger and southwest into Algeria.

No railways have been in operation since 1965, and all of the previous rail systems have been dismantled. However, there are plans to construct a line from the **Tunisian** frontier to Tripoli and **Misurata** and then inland to **Sebha**. Other plans include a rail line from the **Egyptian** frontier to Tobruk. Seven rail lines totaling 2,757 kilometers (more than 1,700 miles) were under construction in 2004. The government hopes the planned railways will eventually form part of a network linking Libya with Egypt, Tunisia, and sub-Saharan **Africa**.

In addition to the steady improvement in the road network, there have also been ongoing improvements in air and sea transport. Tripoli inaugurated a new **airport** in 1978, and an international airport opened in Sebha in 1979. Overseas civilian air links, which were suspended in 1992–1999 due to **United Nations** sanctions, have been resumed by many carriers, including most major European and Middle Eastern airlines. The national carrier, Jamahiriya Libyan Arab Airlines, has also resumed international flights and is undergoing a substantial fleet modernization program. Major expansions have taken place over the years at Benghazi and Tripoli to relieve the acute congestion that occasionally prevailed at both ports. Specialized oil-exporting seaports were also constructed at several locations on the Mediterranean. Current plans include new projects to improve and expand the country's ports, together with plans to buy a number of new ships, including gas and oil tankers. *See also* LITORANEA.

TRIBES. Arab tribes have occupied Libya for at least nine centuries, to say nothing of the Arabs that arrived before the Hilalian invasion in the 11th century. **Tripolitania** has three tribes that trace their origins to the Bani Hilal and five tribes that go back to the Bani Sulaim. **Cyrenaica** was occupied mainly by the Bani Sulaim family of tribes. In Cyrenaica, these tribal families are divided into two main branches, the Jibarna and the Harabi. The Jibarna tribes are the Abid, Arafa, Awaqir, and Magharba. The Harabi tribes are the Abaidat, Ailat Fayid, Baraasa, Darsa, and Hasa.

In addition to the Saadi or dominant tribes, Tripolitania has two tribes and Cyrenaica six tribes, known as the Marabtin, that are of mixed origin. These tribes are believed to represent a mixture of the Arabs of the conquest period and the **Berbers**. The Marabtin tribes use earth and water through the grace of the Saadi tribes, of whom they are more or less clients. There are two categories of Marabtin. The first consists of those tribes, such as the Fawakhir, Minifa, Qatan, and Zuwaya, that live with the Saadi on what could be described as a fraternal or friendly basis. The second, including the Aulad Nuh and Aulad al Shaikh, lives more independently and sometimes acts as an arbitrator between the Saadi when conflicts or disputes arise.

Tribal life has long been the predominant pattern of existence in Libya. Each tribe has its own homeland, soil, pasture, and wells. These areas have no **frontiers** or definite boundaries and the main concern of all tribes is the source of water. As tribes divide into two or more primary divisions and then into subdivisions, the essential characteristics of each division or subdivision remain its lineage and geographical area. Divisions and subdivisions of tribes will defend their homeland from encroachment by another division or subdivision just like a tribe will defend itself against encroachment from another tribe.

The monarchy banned political parties soon after independence, and politics then became largely a contest of family, tribal, and parochial interests as networks of kinship and clan provided the organizational structure for political competition. Rather than rely on ideological loyalty or administrative competence, the monarchy delegated authority to locally powerful families, which consolidated their economic and political positions through intermarriage. In consequence, the tribal element constituted a core aspect of political leadership in the **United Kingdom of Libya** from 1952 to 1969, and many Libyans believed, with good reason, that only a few families controlled the country and determined its destiny.

Opposed in theory to family rule and family influence in Libyan politics, members of the **Revolutionary Command Council** that overthrew the monarchy in September 1969 attempted to weaken existing tribal loyalties and destroy tribal organization. These early efforts to eradicate political reliance on tribal affiliation and replace it with ideological loyalty were partially successful. Nevertheless, tribal relationships in Libya have retained much of their importance. Faced with growing political opposition, **Muammar al-Qaddafi** has relied increasingly in recent years on his family and fellow Qadadfa tribesmen for political support. He has repeatedly placed blood relatives in key intelligence and security positions as well as entrusting them with sensitive foreign assignments.

Not surprisingly, some members of the Qadadfa tribe have taken advantage of their privileged position to enrich themselves. In an ironic echo of the earlier complaints concerning nepotism that engulfed the **Idris** regime, Qaddafi published a letter in fall 1985 in which he publicly rebuked his relatives for disloyal behavior. Nonetheless, he continued thereafter to recruit heavily from the Qadadfa tribe and its allies to fill sensitive government posts.

TRIPOLI. Located in northeastern **Tripolitania**, Tripoli is the de facto capital of Libya, although the **Muammar al-Qaddafi** regime has made periodic attempts to decentralize the government by moving some departments to other areas of the country. In one such attempt, Qaddafi on 1 January 1987 declared Al-Jufra the new capital of Libya. Nevertheless, Tripoli remains the main business and cultural center, as well as the principal **port**, with a population in 2005 of approximately two million people. The city has lost most of its pristine allure but retains a good deal of character. There are many colonial buildings, historical mosques, and a lively medina. The architecture of the city is a jumble of Turkish and **Italian** colonial styles combined with the usual hallmarks of a thriving commercial center dating from the revolutionary era.

Known as Oea in antiquity, Tripoli was founded by the **Phoenicians** around 500 B.C. Tripoli is the only ancient city in Libya to have been continuously occupied; unfortunately, few relics of the early settlements remain. Following the fall of Carthage, Tripoli fell briefly under the jurisdiction of the Nubian kingdom before becoming a **Roman** protectorate. Under the Romans, the city grew prosperous, and together with **Sabratah** and **Leptis Magna**, supplied the Roman Empire with grain and slaves. Following a golden age in the second century A.D., Tripoli fell into decline. When the **Vandals** overran much of North Africa in the fifth century, the damage to the city was considerable, and it could well have been abandoned. But after the first **Arab** invasion, in the seventh century, a new town was built among the ruins of the old. Following the second Arab invasion in 1046, the old city walls were rebuilt using the Roman ruins as foundations.

The walled city of Tripoli has survived into modern times as one of the best-preserved **Islamic** towns in the Maghrib, retaining defensive walls together with many old houses and mosques. As a center of commerce, Tripoli shares many features with other Islamic towns on the Mediterranean coast from **Tunisia** to **Egypt** to Spain. The old walled city contains virtually all of Tripoli's historic buildings.

The most lasting architectural monuments in the old city were built by the Turks, who constructed mosques and souks that are still standing today. One of the more prominent mosques in the old city is the Darghut mosque, which takes its name from a Turkish governor who resided in Tripoli from 1556 to 1564. The building, which contains a number of Roman columns, was extensively restored after being severely damaged during World War II. The minaret of the Darghut mosque, in the **Ottoman** style like many others throughout the city, reflects the vigor of Turkish influence in Tripoli in the 16th century.

Another impressive mosque was founded by **Ahmed Karamanli** in 1736–1737. The Karamanli mosque is decorated with polychrome tiles known as qallaline that were manufactured in the 17th century in a suburb of Tunis by the same name. Qallaline and related tiles are common in Algeria and Tunisia but can also be found in Egypt. Their presence in Tripoli is significant as an indication of the extent to which the city shared in the fashions of Islamic art current in the major towns along the North African coast in the 18th and 19th centuries. The wall ceramics at the Karamanli mosque have formal repeated floral patterns and cover the outer wall of the prayer hall.

Tripoli Castle evolved over the centuries into a vast citadel consisting of a labyrinth of courtyards, alleyways, and houses. While the site itself dates from Roman times, most of the citadel's existing interior was constructed in the 17th and 18th centuries. Plans from the 17th century indicate that the castle at that time was totally surrounded by water.

TRIPOLI AGREEMENT. Backdated to 20 March 1971, the Tripoli Agreement was actually a series of separate pacts between Libya and the **petroleum** companies. While the structure of the settlements was similar to that of the **Teheran Agreement**, the Libyan government was successful in extracting improved terms from the oil companies. Libya achieved a new posted oil price of $3.32 a barrel, which was raised to $3.447 by immediately effective increases of 2.5 percent plus $0.05 a barrel. The new price included a premium to Libya to reflect, in a period of high oil tanker freight rates, the temporary advantage the closure of the Suez Canal and the rupture of the Tapline, an oil pipeline in Syria, had brought to Libya's short-haul crude. Finally, the new price was subject to the same gravity escalation agreed to in the **One September**

Agreement of 1970, and there was also a provision for annual price increases over the next five years.

The Tripoli Agreement established a minimum tax rate of 55 percent, with Occidental Petroleum paying 60 percent because of an earlier commitment to spend 5 percent of pretax profit on the development of an **agricultural** project at the Al-Kufrah Oasis. As compensation for underpricing during the 1960s, the oil companies also agreed to make a supplemental payment on every barrel of oil exported for the duration of their concessions. In addition, they accepted that in each year of the agreement they would collectively average at least one exploration rig in operation on concessions held individually or jointly. Libya was firm on this point, because it was concerned about a sudden fall in petroleum exploration and development as well as the natural reluctance of the oil companies to commit capital to a country, regardless of its oil prospects, that did not give full assurance as to the future security of their investments. While the additional financial commitment to satisfy the exploration requirement was relatively small—eight rigs at an average cost each of around $3.5 million annually—the oil companies gave way reluctantly on this point. Exact figures were never made public, but the price increases and retroactive payments in the Tripoli Agreement brought Libya an estimated $1 billion in additional revenues in the first year alone. *See also* LIBYAN PRODUCERS AGREEMENT; NATIONALIZATION.

TRIPOLI CHARTER. Muammar al-Qaddafi, the **Arab nationalist** par excellence, was also the consummate Arab unionist. He approached both ideals with a purist fanaticism that ignored the real obstacles in their path. At his first press conference, held in February 1970, he produced a formula for a united politics of the Arab world. His theme was the past failure of attempts at Arab **unity**, which he blamed on "Byzantine philosophies and sterile ideological disputes." His solution was a unified formula that grouped all Arabs into one Arab movement.

Qaddafi's early emphasis on Arab unity was soon rewarded with practical results. At the conclusion of an Arab summit meeting in **Morocco** in December 1969, the heads of state of **Egypt**, Libya, and **Sudan** returned to **Tripoli**, where they continued their discussions. Additional talks resulted in a tripartite agreement, dated 27 December 1969, and known as the Tripoli Charter. The agreement consolidated the three progressive revolutions into a so-called Arab Revolutionary Front, with a supreme planning committee and a common security system. The remainder of the charter was circumspect, establishing joint ministerial commissions to pursue coordinated policies but making no mention of an eventual political union. While the heads of state of the three governments agreed to meet at regular intervals, Egypt insisted that any attempts at economic integration be limited to concrete initiatives.

Shortly after the conclusion of the Tripoli Charter, Colonel Qaddafi pressed for a full constitutional union of the signatories. Both Sudan and especially Egypt rejected this proposal. The ensuing year was punctuated by a series of ministerial-level talks, which led to new agreements for increased technical cooperation, the relaxation of customs duties, and a freer flow of labor among the three states. *See also* BENGHAZI DECLARATION; FEDERATION OF ARAB REPUBLICS.

TRIPOLI REPUBLIC. Organized in the fall of 1918, this was the first formally republican government created in the **Arab** world. Its formation was strongly influenced both by an April 1917 modus vivendi, in which **Italy** granted the Sanusi local autonomy, and by President Woodrow Wilson's January 1918 declaration in support of national self-determination. When it became clear to **Tripolitanians** in late 1918 that they would no longer receive **Ottoman** support, the region's notables met to announce the creation of the Tripoli Republic.

The name of the new organization was chosen before the form of government was agreed upon and reflected republican sentiment as well as the inability of the founders to agree upon a single individual to act as head of state. For that reason, a Council of Four supported by a 24-member advisory group was eventually established to act as a ruling board. The Council of Four consisted of **Ramadan al-Suwayhli**, **Suleiman Baruni**, Ahmad al-Murayyid of Tarhuna, and Abd al-Nabi Bilkhayr of Warfalla. Members of both the council and the advisory group were carefully selected to represent the interests and regions of the province. Azizia was chosen as the headquarters of the republic.

The announcement of the formation of the Tripoli Republic, the proclamation of independence for Tripolitania, and the subsequent efforts of its leadership to plead their case for independence at the Paris Peace Conference generated little support among the major European powers. On the other hand, Italy agreed to meet with representatives of the republic in the hopes of negotiating an agreement similar to the 1917 accord with **Sayyid Muhammad Idris al-Mahdi al-Sanusi** in **Cyrenaica**. Negotiations opened in April 1919 and from the outset were characterized by misunderstanding and misapprehension on both sides. The Tripolitanians saw themselves as negotiating equals to the Italians in the sense that two independent governments might discuss a territorial dispute. In contrast, Italy saw its talks with republican leaders as the prelude to a new system of government in which it would rule through local chiefs.

While this basic misunderstanding was never resolved, the ensuing negotiations laid the groundwork for the promulgation of a **Legge Fondamentale** in June 1919 and its October 1919 extension in a comparable statute for Cyrenaica. The new **laws** provided for a special form of Italian-Libyan citizenship and accorded all such citizens the right to vote in elections for local parliaments. The parliament for Cyrenaica met five times before it was eventually dissolved in 1923; however, elections were never held in Tripolitania. In Cyrenaica, British intervention forced the Italians to work with the **Sanusi Order**, while in Tripolitania the Italians were under no such pressures and pursued a delaying tactic.

In the end, Italian authorities in Tripolitania never recognized the Tripoli Republic. While the membership of the council responsible for overseeing administrative appointments under the Legge Fondamentale was nearly identical with that of the founders of the Tripoli Republic, the Italians steadfastly refused to recognize the republic or acknowledge its authority to administer the hinterlands. Consequently, there was more competition than cooperation among the policy makers of the republic. In late 1919, for example, a quarrel broke out between Suwayhli and Abd al-Nabi Bilkhayr when the former refused to confirm several of the latter's family members in administrative positions in Warfalla. Bilkhayr also disapproved of Suwayhli's animosity toward the Sanusi Order, and both sides traded accusations over accounting for large sums of money sent from Istanbul during World War I. By mid-1920, Suwayhli felt sufficiently threatened to launch a campaign against his opponents in which his forces were defeated, and he was killed.

In fall 1920, the republican leadership called a general meeting in Gharyan shortly after the announcement of the Accord of **Al-Rajma**.

Recognizing that internal dissension was destroying the united front of the republic, the participants at Gharyan resolved that a single Muslim leader should be designated to govern the country. The conference also established a 14-member Council of the Association for National Reform and arranged to send an official delegation to Rome to inform the Italian government of its new organization. Among its stated aims, the association hoped to safeguard Arab rights as expressed in the fundamental law for Tripolitania, to increase understanding between Arabs and Italians based on complete equality and unity of interests, and to spread knowledge by all means available in order to bring Western civilization to a country that had preserved the glorious traditions of **Islam**. The elections called for by the Legge Fondamentale were never held, and the stated aims of the association proved far too ambitious.

Bereft of international support, the increasingly aggressive policies of the Italian government divided the republic and reduced its leadership. By 1923, when the Fascists were consolidating their power at home and beginning the military reconquest of Libya, the Tripoli Republic had ceased to exist. Italian policy during and after the *Riconquista* wreaked havoc with the nation's educated elite in Tripolitania as well as Cyrenaica, and in hindsight, it made the pretensions of the republic appear overly ambitious to say the least. Nevertheless, the creation of the Tripoli Republic marked an important early step in the political development of the region as a whole.

TRIPOLITANIA. The most populous of Libya's three historic regions, Tripolitania has approximately 80 percent of the country's total population, some 4 million people. Forming the northwestern part of the country, it covers an area of approximately 365,000 square kilometers (140,000 square miles) and extends southward from the Mediterranean Sea to an indefinite southern boundary at about latitude 29 degrees north.

The early history of Tripolitania was dominated by the influence of its major city, **Tripoli,** which for centuries was a terminus for caravans plying the **trade** routes of the **Sahara Desert** as well as a **port** sheltering pirates and slave traders. The cultural ties of Tripolitania are with the Maghrib, of which it is a part geographically and culturally and with which it shares a common history. Since ancient times, **Cyrenaica** has been drawn east toward **Egypt**, the **Fezzan** south toward **Chad** and the **Sudan**, and Tripolitania west toward **Tunisia**.

Studies completed in the 1950s and 1960s of the rural and urban populations of Tunisia note the extensive Libyan migration to the area. While this Tripolitanian migration to Tunisia has occurred for centuries, it was especially heavy during the **Italian** occupation of Libya, when thousands of Tripolitanians fled to escape the Italian invaders. In consequence, a great many Tunisians today are of Libyan descent, and the same families are often found on opposite sides of the Libya-Tunisia **frontier**; for example, Habib Bourguiba, a major figure in modern Tunisian history, is of Libyan descent.

Residents of Tripolitania developed their political consciousness in reaction to foreign domination, and it was from Tripolitania that the strongest impulses came for the unification of Libya. The **Tripoli Republic**, organized in 1918, was the first republican government created in the **Arab** world. Unfortunately, the creation of the Tripoli Republic, together with a declaration of independence for Tripolitania and later efforts to plead a case for independence at the Paris Peace Conference, generated little enthusiasm or support among the major world powers.

In the aftermath of World War II, numerous political groups and associations emerged in Libya, especially in Tripolitania. While all of the **political parties** formed in Libya favored a free, united Libya with membership in the **Arab League**, they differed in their choice of leadership for the new state. Eventually, the traditional elites in Tripolitania, Cyrenaica, and Fezzan agreed in 1950 to form a united, federal Libya under the leadership of King **Idris** I.

Today, the area surrounding Tripoli as far south as the **Jabal Nafusah** remains mostly **agricultural** land containing large groves of fruit and olive trees and date palms. The bulk of Libya's food comes from this region. Beyond Jabal Nafusah, the **desert** begins, with spectacular scenery most of the way south to Fezzan. Tripoli is the capital of Tripolitania, as well as the de facto capital of Libya.

TRIPOLITANIAN-CYRENAICAN DEFENSE COMMITTEE. A Libyan exile organization opposed to **Italian** rule, this committee was established in Damascus, Syria, in the interwar period. Under the leadership of Bashir al-Sadawi, a member of the 1922 **Tripolitanian** delegation to the Sanusi leader, **Sayyid Muhammad Idris al-Mahdi al-Sanusi**, it was only one of several émigré groups formed in **Egypt**, the Gulf, Saudi Arabia, and **Tunisia** in this time frame.

TUAREG (TOUAREG). A few thousand Tuareg nomads live in southwest Libya, wandering principally around the oasis towns of Ghat and **Ghadames**. They are a part of the larger Tuareg population living in neighboring Algeria and elsewhere in the **Saharan** region. Like other nomads of the **desert**, they have traditionally earned a livelihood by raiding sedentary settlements, acting as middlemen for the north–south caravan **trade** between the Mediterranean and sub-Saharan Africa, and extracting protection money from desert caravans and travelers. With the end of the caravan trade and the pacification of the desert, the Tuareg have been deprived of their traditional way of life, and many now live in a state of penury.

The Tuareg language derives from a **Berber** dialect. The Tuareg themselves adhere to a form of Sunni **Islam** with undertones of **Sudanese** and West African witchcraft, sorcery, and covert black magic. Tuareg men, but not **women**, wear veils. The blue dye used in the veils and in the clothing of noble men generally transfers to their skin earning them the name the "blue men." Marriage is monogamous, and women enjoy high status in Tuareg society.

TUNISIA. During the **Arab** conquest, contemporary Tunisia was known as Ifriqiya. The Arabs settled in Qayrawan and later expanded westward. Tunisia, along with the remainder of the Maghrib, came under **Almohad** control and was later ruled by the Hafsids. The Turks took over in 1574 and were later replaced by the **French**, who established a protectorate over Tunisia in 1881. The Young Tunisia political movement later became the Destour and finally the Neo-Destour Movement, headed by Habib Bourguiba. Bourguiba led the country to autonomy in 1954 and then to full independence in 1956.

During the **Idris** regime, Libyan **foreign policy** in the Maghrib centered on Tunisia. In January 1957, the two neighbors concluded a Treaty of Brotherhood and Good Neighborliness. A clause covering mutual defense established the principle that the two countries would consider themselves directly affected by any threat from a major foreign power against either of them. A second clause described one purpose of the agreement to be the harmonization of their foreign policies toward neighboring countries as well as toward both Eastern and Western states. The political implications of the treaty were not lost on the Mashriq, especially **Egypt**, as the agreement institutionalized Libya's position as part of the Maghrib. The Gamal Abdul Nasser government in Cairo viewed the treaty as an attempt by Libya to distance itself from Egyptian political influence and to strengthen its pro-Western position in the region through an alliance with another pro-Western state.

Muammar al-Qaddafi produced a formula for a united Arab politics at his first press conference when he described the unification of Arab governments into a single state as an absolute necessity. Given the relatively close relations between the Libyan monarchy and the Tunisian government, it was not surprising that diplomatic relations between the governments of Libya and Tunisia were cool in the immediate aftermath of the September 1969 coup d'état. However, by June 1970, relations had improved to the point that the two neighbors established a joint committee to settle outstanding issues and to exchange cultural programs.

Over the next five years, the Qaddafi regime engaged Tunisia in formal union discussions on two separate occasions. During an official visit to Tunisia in December 1972, Qaddafi unexpectedly proposed an immediate, total **Libya-Tunisia union**. Caught off guard, Tunisia first accepted and then rejected the offer. In January 1974, Libya and Tunisia announced the merger of their two states into the Arab Islamic Republic. This new proposal evidenced even less preparation than the earlier one, and Tunisia soon allowed the merger to lapse.

Unable to coerce Tunisia into union, the Qaddafi regime pressed the Tunisian government for a solution to their offshore dispute over the **Libya-Tunisia continental shelf**. Three years later, the issue was submitted to the **International Court of Justice** (ICJ). The disputants asked the ICJ to determine the rules of international law applicable to a determination of the area of the continental shelf appertaining to them. In so doing, the ICJ was asked to take into account both equitable principles and the relevant circumstances that characterize the area. In early 1982, the ICJ delivered a judgment that largely rejected the boundary proposals of both Libya and Tunisia. Instead, the ICJ laid down the general rule that delimitation would be effected in accordance with equitable principles and relevant circumstances. In March 1988, both parties to the dispute concluded an agreement implementing the judgment of the ICJ.

In the second half of the 1970s, diplomatic relations between Libya and Tunisia improved to the point that Qaddafi felt he could again propose to Bourguiba a federal union, this time also including Algeria. Tunisia expressed reluctance to enter into a federation with either regional power, although it left the door open for enhanced cooperation in the commercial sphere. Scorned and rejected, Qaddafi turned to subversion and sabotage.

In January 1980, Libyan-trained Tunisian commandos attacked the army barracks, national guard, and police station at Gafsa, a small town in southern Tunisia. Taking control of the town, the insurgents attempted unsuccessfully to foment an uprising against the Tunisian government. In the wake of the failed attack, diplomatic relations between Libya and Tunisia were tense for some time. While the details of the raid remain unclear, Libyan authorities appear to have masterminded the plot and armed and trained the commandos. The motive behind the Gafsa raid also remains unclear. The most plausible explanation is that Qaddafi supported the raid in retaliation for the rejection of his proposal for a federal union with Tunisia.

Nevertheless, the Qaddafi regime continued to explore unity, cooperation, and integration proposals with Tunisia for much of the following decade. Eventually, in the second half of the 1980s, relations between Libya and Tunisia improved, and in early 1989 Tunisia joined Libya, Algeria, Mauritania, and **Morocco** in creating the **Arab Maghrib Union** (AMU). Inspired by the European Community, the AMU is a regional organization intended to increase **economic** cooperation and efficiency; unfortunately, a number of contentious political issues to date have thwarted serious attempts at economic or political integration.

With the suspension of **United Nations** sanctions against Libya, Qaddafi moved to revitalize the AMU. In the process, bilateral relations with Tunisia expanded and improved. Following creation of a free **trade** zone, Libya and Tunisia resumed air connections disrupted since 1992. More recently, **Tripoli** has strengthened business links with Tunis, especially in the **tourism** sector, as Libya moved in 2005 to liberalize its **economy**.

– U –

UFFICIO FONDARIO. Land office established by the **Italian** government in Libya as part of a policy of providing land for Italian colonists. In the early 1920s, the Italian governor of **Tripolitania** passed a series of decrees which, among other things, provided that all uncultivated land would revert to the state after three years and that all land held by rebels or those who aided them would be confiscated. Such decrees led to a rapid increase in the amount of land made available to Italian colonists in both Tripolitania and **Cyrenaica**. Nevertheless, Italian capital did not move quickly to buy Libyan concessions, and Italian colonists were slow to immigrate to Libya. Laws promulgated in 1928 provided additional credits and subsidies to encourage colonists to settle in Libya, but immigration rates remained far below Italian expectations. *See also* BALBO, ITALO.

ULAMA. Men learned in **Islamic** traditions, especially its **laws**. Traditionally, Islamic scholars have played important sociopolitical roles as a buffer between the citizenry and government. The reformist elements of **Muammar al-Qaddafi**'s approach to Islam, such as the rejection of the *hadith*, the transcendence of God, and the purely human role of the Prophet, were a deliberate attempt to reduce the role of the ulama and to bring Islam under the control of the revolution. When Libya's **religious** leadership criticized these policies, Qaddafi purged them in mid-1978, emphasizing that mosques were meant to be places of worship and not arenas to discuss **economic**, social, or political questions. This denial of political influence to the ulama went beyond secularism, defined as the separation of church and state with the latter being supreme, as it was extended to every elite or popular body that might reduce regime power.

UMAYYAD DYNASTY (661–750). Members of the Umayyad family, among the most prominent merchants in pre-**Islamic** Mecca, held the office of caliph from 661 to 750. From their capital in Damascus, the Umayyads extended their power and influence westward into North **Africa**, Spain, and southern **France**. Strongly opposed by **Berber** and Byzantine forces, the **Arabs** were finally able to establish themselves along the North African littoral. Arab expansion was of considerable cultural significance to the Maghrib, as it brought with it the Islamic **religion** and the Arabic language. Unwilling to share power with non-Arabs, including those who had converted to Islam, the Umayyads were eventually overthrown by the **Abbasids**.

UNEMPLOYMENT. *See* EMPLOYMENT.

UNITED KINGDOM OF LIBYA. Granted independence in December 1951, Libya was the first **African** state to achieve independence from European rule and the first and only state to be created by the General Assembly of the **United Nations.** The 1951 **constitution of Libya** established a hereditary monarchy with a federal state divided into the three provinces of **Tripolitania, Cyrenaica,** and **Fezzan.** It also provided for executive, legislative, and **judicial** branches of government, including a parliament made up of a Senate and a House of Representatives.

The United Kingdom of Libya was a fragile product of bargains and compromises driven by both internal and external interests and pressures. It was thus a surprise to many observers that it lasted almost 18 years. During that time, it brought a certain precarious stability to the central Mediterranean. From 1951 to 1969, a total of 11 prime ministers and more than 40 different cabinets demonstrated an unexpected resilience in dealing with a succession of internal and external crises.

The 1951 constitution designated **Muhammad Idris al-Mahdi al-Sanusi,** together with his male successors, as the monarchy of Libya. Throughout most of the 1950s, the Libyan governments formed under the constitutional monarchy were too weak, poor, and inexperienced to have much choice in domestic or **foreign policy.** As a result, the Idris regime sought to balance the interests of the Western powers, upon whose support its economy depended, against the growing claims of Arab **nationalism.** The monarchy proved relatively successful in this regard, and annual foreign economic aid increased nearly fourfold in the 1950s.

At the outset of the 1960s, conditions in Libya were changing rapidly, and this led to new pressures on the policies of the kingdom. **Petroleum** revenues reached a level that assured future income for the state, while the combination of new, long-range aircraft and reduced international tensions meant that Libyan air bases were no longer central to Western defense strategies. As a result, the monarchy in 1964 asked **Great Britain** and the **United States** to reconsider the future status of their bases in Libya. The United States agreed in principle to withdraw, and Britain began evacuating troops in 1965.

At the same time, growing oil revenues, accompanied by improved economic conditions and greater social mobility, increased the demands, especially among younger Libyans, for a coherent ideology that would satisfy new, albeit vaguely understood, political and spiritual yearnings. The United Kingdom of Libya under the conservative, traditional monarchy of King Idris I attempted to respond to these needs but failed to understand and accommodate them just as it failed to satisfy the growing demands of Arab nationalists inside and outside Libya. By 1969, a growing number of Libyans, especially the younger segments of society, had come to view the policies of the monarchy as anachronistic. They welcomed the 1969 intervention of the **Libyan Free Unionist Officers** movement in the **One September Revolution** and the subsequent creation of the **Revolutionary Command Council**.

UNITED NATIONS (UN). At the end of World War II, the disposition of the **Italian** colonies was a question that needed to be considered prior to the conclusion of a treaty officially ending the state of war. In theory, Libya remained an Italian possession temporarily administered by **France** and **Great Britain**, but at the 1945 Potsdam Conference, Britain, the **Soviet Union**, and the **United States** had agreed that the Italian colonies seized during the war should not be returned to Italy. Thereafter, each of the Great Powers involved presented one or more proposals related to the future of Libya, but no compromise position proved possible. In February 1947, a peace treaty with Italy was finally concluded in which the latter renounced all rights to its **African** possessions; however, the language on the eventual status of the colonies was left vague. In the end, the Big Four Powers (France, Great Britain, the Soviet Union, and the United States) agreed to put the question before the UN General Assembly if they were unable to negotiate a compromise arrangement within a year of the date the peace treaty with Italy became effective.

In due course, the Libyan question was placed before the United Nations. In November 1949, the General Assembly adopted a compromise solution that called for the establishment by January 1952 of a sovereign state that would include the three historic regions of Libya. The General Assembly then established a UN commissioner and a Council of Ten—consisting of a representative from each of Libya's historic regions, one for Libyan minorities, and one each for **Egypt**, France, Great Britain, Italy, Pakistan, and the United States— to guide Libya through the transition period to independence. The

Council of Ten was also asked to assist a Libyan national assembly in drawing up a **constitution**.

The subsequent transition period was not without its problems, but a national constituent assembly was eventually created and met for the first time in November 1951. It authorized a federal system of government with a monarch as head of state and designated **Sayyid Muhammad Idris al-Mahdi al-Sanusi** as king. Committees of the assembly then drafted a constitution, which was officially adopted in October 1951. On 24 December 1951, King Idris I proclaimed the **United Kingdom of Libya** as a sovereign and independent state. Libya was the first African state to achieve independence from European rule and the first and only state created by the General Assembly of the United Nations.

Over the next four decades, Libya played an active role in the United Nations; however, it was not until the early 1990s that the United Nations again played a defining role in Libya. In January 1992, the United Nations through UN Security Council Resolution (UNSCR) 731 condemned the destruction of Pan Am flight 103 and UTA flight 772, which collectively resulted in the loss of several hundred lives. UNSCR 731, which continued by deploring the fact that the Libyan government had not responded effectively to requests to cooperate fully in establishing responsibility for these **terrorist** acts, urged Libya to provide a full and effective response so as to contribute to the elimination of international terrorism. Specifically, Libya was called upon to turn over two suspects in the **Lockerbie incident** for trial in Great Britain or the United States, disclose all it knew about the airplane bombings, take concrete steps to cease its support for terrorism, and pay appropriate compensation. When Libya failed to respond adequately to these requests, the United Nations imposed mandatory sanctions on 15 April 1992, including an embargo on arms sales and travel to Libya.

In Libya and elsewhere in the **Arab** world, the imposition of sanctions was greeted by a mixture of anger and resignation. Flags flew at half-mast in Libya, and the **Muammar al-Qaddafi** government declared 24 hours of national mourning. State-sponsored protests in **Tripoli** demonstrated against the unfairness of the sanctions imposed by the UN, and left-wing organizations throughout the Arab world dispatched delegates to Libya to express their solidarity. However, the UN sanctions also strained relations between Libya and its Arab neighbors, all of whom respected the embargo. The crisis had a particularly bad effect on the **Arab Maghrib Union**, which had been established to build a common market in North Africa.

After weeks of haggling and delay, the United Nations in November 1993 tightened the sanctions on Libya after concluding the Qaddafi regime had defied its order to surrender the two bombing suspects. Eleven of the 15 members of the Security Council voted for a new resolution that froze Libyan assets overseas, banned some sales of **petroleum** equipment, and tightened the earlier commercial air ban with Libya; China and the Security Council's three Islamic members— Djibouti, **Morocco**, and Pakistan—abstained.

The new round of sanctions, which cut Libya off from income it had been receiving from global investments, caused some inconvenience in **Tripoli**. On the other hand, Libya had had ample evidence the new restrictions were coming and was able to hide many of its offshore assets. Moreover, the new measures stopped well short of the total ban on oil exports the Security Council had imposed on Iraq for invading Kuwait. In addition, Belgian, French, Italian, and other oil companies were able to maintain the oil and **natural gas** exploration and drilling contracts they had with Libya. The U.S. government later emphasized it would continue to press for an oil embargo if the new sanctions did not cause Libya to hand over the suspects, but Western European countries and Russia continued to resist a total embargo because it would hurt their economic interests.

Qaddafi vowed to defy the UN ban on flights and also threatened to withdraw from the organization. To challenge the ban on flights, Libya flew pilgrims to Mecca in 1995 and Qaddafi flew to an Arab summit meeting in Cairo in mid-1996. In response to the earlier action, the Security Council in April 1995 eased the travel ban on Libyan flights to allow Libyan pilgrims to make the hajj to Mecca.

Eventually in August 1998, Qaddafi accepted a U.S.-British proposal to try the Lockerbie suspects in the Netherlands under Scottish law. In response, the UN Security Council unanimously adopted UNSCR 1192, calling for the sanctions to be suspended once Libya had remanded the two suspects. UN sanctions were suspended in April 1999, and with the conclusion of the trial and Libyan compliance with all applicable Security Council resolutions, the sanctions were lifted permanently in September 2003. In February 2000, Libya contributed officers to a UN peacekeeping mission for the first time in a decade. In January 2003, it was elected chairman of the UN Commission on **Human Rights**. In March 2005, amid talk of UN reform, Qaddafi called for the United Nations to scrap the Security Council and give its powers to the General Assembly if it hoped to become a democratic organization.

UNITED STATES. Libyan commercial and diplomatic relations with the United States date back to the second half of the 18th century. Increasingly plagued by privateers from the **Barbary States** of Algiers, **Morocco**, **Tripoli**, and Tunis, the U.S. government began concluding treaties of peace and amity in the 1790s, including one with Tripoli in 1796. Unfortunately, the peace was not long lived as the U.S. government took a more aggressive stance in 1801 after the bey of Tripoli demanded better terms than those negotiated only five years earlier. Washington dispatched a naval squadron to the Mediterranean, initiated a partial blockade of the Libyan coast, and eventually bombarded Tripoli. After considerable fighting, Yusuf **Karamanli** sued for peace with the United States in 1805.

American relations with the **United Kingdom of Libya** were mostly cordial, as the dependence of King **Idris** I on income from foreign military bases, including **Wheelus Air Base** near Tripoli, fostered a spirit of cooperation. In exchange for a 16-year lease on the air base, Washington granted Libya a wide-ranging program of economic, military, and technical assistance. The existence of large Western military bases in Libya, together with the dependence of the Libyan government on the income from these facilities, led many observers to describe the Idris regime as pro-Western. In many respects, this was a fallacy as it suggested a widespread commitment to Western traditions, ideals, and policies that simply did not exist, except perhaps in the minds of a few senior government officials.

While it agreed to Western military bases in return for much needed diplomatic and financial support, the monarchy tried to minimize the impact of the United States and other Western states on the sociopolitical values and structures of the country. It also emphasized its political nonalignment in international bodies such as the **United Nations** and **Organization of African Unity**. The close association between the monarchy's need for military base revenues and its Western orientation in general, and American orientation in particular, became clear once **petroleum** sales reduced its dependence on this income. As early as

1964, Libya asked the United States to reconsider the future status of Wheelus Air Base and accept in principle an early withdrawal.

Diplomatic relations between Washington and Tripoli were not good at any time after the **One September Revolution** in 1969, and they became especially strained after 1979 when Libya did little to protect the U.S. embassy from being stormed by students in the early days of the Iranian hostage crisis. Nevertheless, both governments tried to coexist with a mutually unsatisfactory diplomatic relationship that neither seemed willing to improve but both were unwilling to terminate. The election of Ronald Reagan worsened the prevailing state of affairs, as his administration increased diplomatic, military, and economic pressure on the **Muammar al-Qaddafi** regime. Unfairly and inaccurately described as a Soviet puppet, Qaddafi was labeled an international menace who should be restrained if not replaced. In less than a year, Reagan fundamentally altered U.S. policy toward Libya. In the process, Washington came to recognize Qaddafi not merely as an inconvenience but as an enemy.

The initial public step taken against Libya by the Reagan administration was the closure in May 1981 of the Libyan **People's Bureau** in Washington. The closure order cited a wide range of Libyan provocations, including alleged support for international **terrorism**. In a series of related steps, all Libyan visa applications were subjected to a mandatory security advisory opinion and American oil companies operating in Libya were advised to begin an orderly reduction of U.S. employees. To further isolate Qaddafi, Washington increased its support for countries opposed to Libya such as **Tunisia** and **Sudan**, attempted to coordinate its policies with those of Western European governments, and employed the calculated use of the threat of military intervention. In conjunction with this latter policy, the U.S. Navy shot down two Libyan aircraft over the Gulf of **Sidra** in August 1981.

In March 1982, the Reagan administration, charging that Libya was actively supporting terrorist and subversive activities, announced an embargo on Libyan oil and imposed an export license requirement for all U.S. goods destined for Libya, with the exception of food, medicine, and medical supplies. Washington also urged its allies in Europe to support the imposition of economic sanctions, but for various reasons, all of them declined. In early 1983, the United States dispatched AWACS aircraft to **Egypt** in response to an alleged Libyan threat to the Sudanese government. Although the crisis quickly subsided, the American response embarrassed the Egyptian government and thus underlined the difficulty of sanctioning Libya without incurring the wrath of other **Arab** and **African** states. Later in the year, President Reagan again urged Western European governments to curb exports to Libya.

In 1984, the United States restricted the movement of Libyan diplomats accredited to the United Nations, and in 1985, it banned the import of all Libyan petroleum products. Following terrorist attacks on the Rome and Vienna airports in December 1985, Washington once again urged the Europeans to join in imposing economic and political sanctions on Libya and again received a half-hearted response. For the third time since taking office, Reagan examined the option of a military strike but once more chose to limit his reaction to diplomatic and economic measures. Three months later, after new air and naval confrontations in the Gulf of Sidra and the bombing of a West Berlin discothèque, which radio intercepts attributed to Libya, the United States finally decided the military option was necessary, and American aircraft bombed what Washington described as centers of Libyan terrorist activity and training in **Tripoli** and **Benghazi**. One week later, the president publicly warned Libya to change its policies or face further military action.

Despite the American threat, the April raids had little sustained impact on Libyan **foreign policy**. Following a brief period of seclusion, Qaddafi returned to the world stage with the major tenets of his external policy intact. Washington responded with a heightened program of diplomatic, economic, and military pressure on the Libyan government but was unable to precipitate its downfall. While the policy of the Reagan administration was largely unsuccessful in redirecting Libyan foreign policy, it did focus attention on a major irony in the total U.S.-Libyan relationship. In part because of his esteem for American power and prestige, Qaddafi often betrayed a desire for U.S. recognition of his own power and importance. Consequently, the policies of the Reagan administration may have encouraged rather than discouraged the Libyan policies it appeared determined to check because the U.S. actions helped generate the international attention so desperately craved by the Leader of the Revolution.

Qaddafi greeted the advent of the George H. W. Bush presidency with cautious optimism, suggesting that a new administration in Washington offered an opportunity for improved bilateral relations. This did not prove to be the case. The Bush administration continued the policy of diplomatic isolation put in place by its predecessor. It also supported a covert policy to provide military aid and training to several hundred former Libyan soldiers. Set in motion during the final months of the Reagan administration, this covert operation hoped to use Libyan volunteers captured during the 1988 border fighting between Libya and **Chad** to destabilize the Qaddafi government.

In the aftermath of the December 1988 bombing of Pan Am flight 103 over Lockerbie, Scotland, the policy of the Bush administration toward Libya hardened. Following the indictment of two Libyan citizens as the perpetrators of the **Lockerbie incident**, Washington aggressively pushed for UN Security Council Resolution 731, passed in January 1992, which called for Libyan cooperation in the Lockerbie investigation. When Libya failed to cooperate, the United Nations adopted wide-ranging sanctions against Libya, including an embargo on arms sales and air travel. As it supported the UN sanctions, Washington extended the bilateral sanctions on Libya in place since 1986.

For much of the 1990s, U.S. policy toward Libya consisted largely of sanctions, sanctions, and more sanctions. In early 1993, Washington banned American law firms or their foreign branches from offering legal services to the Libyan government or its agencies. When the United Nations tightened its embargo against Libya later in the year, freezing Libyan assets overseas, banning selected sales of oil equipment, and further strengthening earlier flight bans, Washington enthusiastically supported the move.

After 1993, Washington called repeatedly for a worldwide embargo on Libyan oil sales; however, it was unable to win the support of key European governments, especially **Germany** and **Italy**, which were heavily dependent on Libyan oil supplies. In April 1996, the relatives of the victims of Pan Am flight 103 filed a $10 billion lawsuit against Libya. In the same month, in a move that mirrored American demands to turn over the two Libyans indicted in the Pan Am bombing, Qaddafi demanded that the United States surrender the pilots and planners involved in the 1986 air raids on Benghazi and Tripoli.

Later in the year, President Bill Clinton signed the controversial Iran-Libya Sanctions Act (ILSA) imposing sanctions on foreign individuals or companies that invested $40 million or more a year in **natural gas** or oil projects in either Libya or Iran. Libya was not the main target of these new sanctions; nevertheless, industry experts and analysts agreed the move would discourage international oil companies from making new investments in Libya. In part reflecting European dependence on Libyan oil, the **European Union** rejected the U.S. legislation and vowed to fight it.

The U.S. Treasury Department in July 1999 approved a controversial travel license, strongly criticized by some U.S. lawmakers, permitting Occidental Petroleum to visit Libya to inspect assets the company had abandoned in 1986. That August, three other U.S. oil companies — Conoco, Marathon Oil, and Amerada Hess — followed suit, applying for permission to visit Libya to assess assets they had left behind in the mid-1980s. Taking advantage of the eased sanctions introduced by the Clinton administration earlier in the year, Libya in November 1999 made its first purchase of U.S. wheat in 15 years.

In the final year of Clinton's second term, the future direction of U.S. policy toward Libya remained uncertain. In November 1999, less than three weeks after Washington approved the wheat sale to Libya, Secretary of State Madeleine Albright renewed a ban on use of U.S. passports for travel to Libya. While the annual renewal of the ban, required since 1981, had seldom attracted attention, the issue in 1999 was in doubt because some administration officials argued the ban should be allowed to lapse.

Qaddafi greeted the advent of the George W. Bush administration with optimism, and for once, he had not misread the American political scene. The early days of the new administration offered real promise for improved U.S.-Libyan relations. After one of the two defendants in the Lockerbie attack was found guilty in January 2001, talks opened with Libya's UN envoy to detail the steps Libya would have to undertake to terminate the UN sanctions regime. Bush and British prime minister Tony Blair issued a joint statement in February 2001 calling on Libya to comply with all relevant UN Security Council resolutions.

In May 2001, the White House unveiled an energy policy plan, recommending a review of existing unilateral sanctions and their impact on energy policy. A major issue in this regard was the 1996 Iran-Libya Sanctions Act, which was due for renewal in August 2001. The Bush administration pressed for a two-year extension, with the rationale that a short-term extension would give the United States more flexibility in dealing with both Tripoli and Teheran. However, Congress later approved a five-year extension, arguing that a shorter extension could send the wrong message, suggesting a lack of U.S. resolve to combat terrorism.

European allies of the United States, together with American oil companies, had long opposed ILSA, but the extension of sanctions was supported by influential interest groups in Washington, especially the relatives of the victims of Pan Am flight 103. Chris Patten, EU commissioner for external relations, decried the extension of ILSA on the grounds the European Union objected to unilateral sanctions laws with extraterritorial effects. A Libyan representative termed ILSA's renewal a cause for dismay, wrongly attributing it to illusions created by Zionist propaganda.

In September 2002 in his annual address commemorating the overthrow of the monarchy, Qaddafi emphasized that Libya was no longer a rogue state and would yield to international legitimacy. Adding that Libya had detained **Islamist** militants suspected of links with al-Qaeda, he reiterated a willingness to pay compensation to the families of the victims of the Lockerbie incident, a promise he kept 11 months later. He also warned against an attack on Saddam Hussein, saying it would turn Iraq into another Afghanistan. Urging Libyans to focus on Africa, he said Libya would turn its back on the Arabs and merge fully with the **African Union**. Qaddafi's speech was noteworthy in that it was directed not toward Libyans, as was normally the case, but to the West and especially the United States.

In March 2003, only weeks before the U.S. invasion of Iraq, Libyan officials approached the British government, initiating talks aimed at dismantling Libya's unconventional weapons program. After nine months of negotiations, Libya announced in December 2003 that it had decided of its own free will to be completely free of internationally banned weapons. The Bush administration welcomed the announcement, encouraging Libya to continue its support of the war on terrorism and initiating a series of steps to return Libya to the international community.

The U.S. government lifted the travel ban on Libya on 26 February 2004 and followed this on 23 April with an announcement of easing and lifting of sanctions. President Bush subsequently ended the national emergency with Libya, effectively lifting the remaining sanctions on 20 September. At the same time, the Bush administration asked Congress to lift the U.S. ban on Export-Import Bank loans to Libya, arguing that the action was necessary to help U.S. companies invest in Libya. In 2005, the United States approved a plan to reestablish military relations with Libya. In May 2006, the United States restored full diplomatic relations, removing Libya from the State Sponsors of Terrorism list.

UNITY. One of the three proclaimed goals of the **One September Revolution**. The other two were **freedom** and **socialism**. These were the same three goals proclaimed by Gamal Abdul Nasser at the outset of the 1952 **Egyptian** revolution. To understand the significance of **Muammar al-Qaddafi**'s emphasis on **Arab** unity, the movement must be put into historical perspective.

In the 1940s, the Syrian Baath party called for comprehensive Arab unity in the form of a single Arab state stretching from the Atlantic Ocean to the Persian Gulf. The exact means for achieving this end were left conveniently open. The pan-Arab ideal of the Baath party later became a goal of President Nasser and the United Arab Republic. Nasser argued that the Arab nations enjoyed a unity of language, **religion**, history, and culture, which they should take advantage of to create their own system of cooperation and defense. After the collapse of the United Arab Republic in 1961, Arab leaders continued to support the goal of Arab unity; but little substantive progress was made.

King **Idris** I carefully limited Libyan participation in the pan-Arab movement, while cooperating with the NATO allies. The revolutionary government, on the other hand, quickly moved Libya into a closer association with the Arab system. Qaddafi's interests focused on the Arab world, and like Nasser, he often referred to the "Arab nation," not in geographical terms but as an expression of conviction and guidance. The concept of the Arab nation was an ideological bond for Qaddafi that joined a people with a common cultural history and a faith in their destiny as equal to any race on Earth.

At the same time, Qaddafi believed the present weakness of the Arab people was the result of their disintegration into **tribal** states and regions, a process the colonial powers encouraged to help them dominate the Arab world. In this light, he viewed regionalism as an innovation of colonialism as well as the principal reason the Western powers were able to conquer the Middle East. He felt the Arab people must unite into a single Arab state if they were to regain their former glory and reach their full potential.

Qaddafi produced a formula for joint Arab politics at his first press conference in February 1970; thereafter, he described the unification of Arab governments into a single state as an absolute necessity. Over the next two decades, he persisted in pursuing practical attempts at Arab unity even after the idea was widely discredited elsewhere in the Arab world. Between 1969 and 1974, for example, he engaged in union discussions with Egypt (twice), Syria, **Sudan**, and **Tunisia** (twice).

While Qaddafi continued to discuss Arab unity after 1974, it was now more as a long-term goal than an immediately recognizable objective. The late 1970s were a period in which Qaddafi appeared to recognize more clearly the rivalries and divisions in the path of Arab unity, although he still refused to accept them. Consequently, it came as a surprise when Libya and Syria proclaimed a merger in September 1980 and declared their determination to form a unified government. Their subsequent difficulties in turning the proclamation into reality were not so surprising. Qaddafi, on the other hand, did not forgo his dream of Arab unity. In 1984, Libya and **Morocco** announced a federation, known as the **Arab-African Union**, in which the signatories retained their sovereignty. Five years later, Libya joined Algeria, Mauritania, **Morocco**, and Tunisia in the **Arab Maghrib Union**. Thereafter, Qaddafi focused increasingly on **African** unity, calling for a United States of Africa as early as 1999. Accorded a prominent speaking role at the opening ceremonies of the **African Union** (AU) in 2002, Qaddafi later hosted the 2005 AU summit in Sirte.

The future of the movement for Arab unity is more problematic today than it was when Qaddafi seized power in Libya more than three decades ago. In the wake of the **Gulf Crisis**, most analysts conceded the death of pan-Arabism as a practical proposition. Virtually all Arab regimes disapproved of Iraq's annexation of Kuwait, but only a slight majority of the **Arab League** was prepared to condemn the invasion outright. Other Arab states were more concerned with the rapid buildup of U.S. forces, charging that the dispatch of foreign forces preempted an Arab solution to the crisis. The subsequent invasion of Iraq in 2003 again highlighted the difficulties the Arab world has found in reaching common policy positions. In the wake of the American occupation of

Iraq, the Arab world appeared as divided as ever, with its member states having vastly different visions for the region's future.

URBANIZATION. *See* EMPLOYMENT; HOUSING; POPULATION MOVEMENTS.

– V –

VANDALS. Collective name for a group of Germanic tribesmen who entered North Africa from Spain early in the fifth century. By 430, Carthage, Hippo, and Cirta were the only three **Roman** cities in North Africa that had not fallen to the Teutonic onslaught. At the beginning of 435, the Vandal leader Gaiseric concluded a treaty with Emperor Valentinian III in which the emperor retained Carthage and its province but surrendered the other six Maghrib provinces to the Vandals. Nevertheless, four years later Gaiseric attacked Carthage and captured that city, too. In 455, the Vandals sailed to **Italy** and sacked Rome itself. The Vandals occupied North Africa for almost a century, settling along the coast and immediate hinterland.

VOLPI, COUNT GIUSEPPI. By profession, Count Giuseppi Volpi was a financier whose empire was based on electric power in his native Venetia. He was also the founder and director of several companies in the Balkans and carried out important diplomatic assignments for the **Italian** government. Volpi was one of the first of the major industrialists and bankers to join the Fascist party, and the Fascists celebrated him as one of their own. Appointed governor of **Tripolitania** in August 1921, his consistent, decisive policies contrasted sharply with those of earlier regimes. Volpi made two significant contributions to the **economic** and political development of Tripolitania. First, he resolved the stalemate in the political domain by directing the **Riconquista**, the reconquest of the area. He then successfully addressed the problem of creating a public domain for colonization purposes. Unlike many of his peers, Volpi felt strongly that policies in these two separate but related areas should naturally complement each other. With force alone insufficient to achieve development, the most effective strategy caused politics and economics to work hand-in-hand.

– W –

WARSAW PACT. A former defensive alliance of European Communist states before the implosion of the **Soviet Union**. While Libya continued to purchase Soviet arms, **Muammar al-Qaddafi** never followed up the threat he made in October 1978 to join the Warsaw Pact.

WATER RESOURCES. Rainfall in Libya is both scanty and erratic. Less than 2 percent of the country receives enough rainfall for settled **agriculture**; the heaviest precipitation occurs in the **Jabal al-Akhdar** region of **Cyrenaica**. The shortage of rainfall is reflected in the absence of permanent rivers or streams in Libya. Moreover, the 20 or so perennial lakes are all brackish or salty. Such circumstances have severely limited the revolutionary government's plans for agricultural development as the basis for a sound and varied **economy**.

Water resource management has been emphasized since the 1930s. The period of **Italian** occupation generated considerable scientific research and evaluation, which generally concluded that the available groundwater in the accessible coastal tracts was very limited and should be utilized with care. As a result, the **Jifarah Plain** in the northwest corner of Libya was largely managed throughout the 1930s as a dry farming region with supplementary irrigation. The subsequent period of British rule (1943–1951) produced little research and no change in water resource policy; however, following independence, a variety of governmental agencies worked to gain a better understanding of Libya's groundwater. Virtually all of these groups recommended extreme caution in the use of renewable resources. At the same time, many concluded that the water resources located in the extreme south should be developed to compensate for the emerging deficit on the coast.

Beginning in the late 1960s, responsibility for policy development on water resource management devolved to the government ministries responsible for land, water, and agricultural development. A wide variety of regional studies were concluded in this period. While the emphasis on the Jifarah Plain continued, all regions were covered to some degree by master planning studies that took into account numerous considerations, including water supply.

The most discussed water resources at the time were the great subterranean aquifers located in the southern **desert**. The best known of these was located at the Al-Kufrah oasis in southeastern Cyrenaica. When Occidental Petroleum Corporation applied for a **petroleum** concession in 1966, it agreed to commit 5 percent of its profits to the search for water and the development of agricultural projects. In March 1968, it discovered a huge underground water reservoir in the **Kufrah Basin**. Occidental planted the first crops there in fall 1968, but the government soon assumed control of the project and established the Al-Kufrah Agricultural Company.

The Al-Kufrah project was watered by central pivot irrigation, which provides water in a circular pattern. Most of the land was used to grow fodder for sheep raised in pens, but cereal crops were also grown. There is virtually no natural recharge of these underground reservoirs, so the water table will eventually drop; however, the reserves at Al-Kufrah are expected to last for 200 years.

Subterranean water was also located north of Al-Kufrah at Sarir and Jalu, as well as at **Sebha** in the southwestern desert. The major problem with these deposits was one of **transportation**, as they were separated from the populous coastal areas by vast stretches of empty desert. The cost of building **roads** to transport to coastal markets the produce grown at these remote sites restricted their development.

By the late 1970s, the level of understanding of government scientists and advisers had markedly increased. On the basis of studies already completed and the assumption that future government oil revenues would continue at least as high as those enjoyed at the time, Libya took a bold and controversial step. Almost as soon as agricultural production commenced at Al-Kufrah, the government decided to begin the massive civil engineering project known as the **Great Manmade River** (GMR). Initiated in 1983, this new phase of agricultural development involved transporting water via pipeline hundreds of kilometers from its origins in the southern desert to planned agricultural projects along the Mediterranean coast.

Originally conceived to be a five-year project, contracts for the third phase of the GMR were not awarded until 2005; and it now appears it will take up to 10 more years to complete the project. It also remains to be seen whether relocating water resources to the coast will contribute to agricultural output. Domestic and industrial use of water resources has grown much faster than anticipated in recent years, both increasing the salinity of coastal soils and diverting water resources from agriculture. Consequently, water resource management in Libya faces new challenges as the government seeks to balance earlier plans for agricultural expansion with new demands for a scarce resource.

WEAPONS OF MASS DESTRUCTION. The **Muammar al-Qaddafi** regime demonstrated interest in developing weapons of mass destruction from the outset of the **One September Revolution**. As early as 1975, the **Soviet Union** agreed to provide Libya with its first nuclear power plant; and in 1978, Moscow agreed to construct a nuclear power plant and research center with a capacity of 300 megawatts. By 1981, the two governments were discussing an expansion of their nuclear co-operation efforts to include a power plant with two 400-megawatt units.

Later in the decade, the emphasis shifted to the development of **chemical weapons**. The **United States** government in December 1987 charged that Libya was building a factory near Rabta that was suspected to be capable of producing chemical weapons. Two years later, the George H. W. Bush administration charged that up to 30 tons of mustard gas, together with small quantities of the nerve gas Sarin, had been produced at the Rabta facility. In early 1996, Washington renewed its charges that Libya was involved in the proliferation of chemical weapons, identifying a factory near Tarhuna, scheduled for completion in 1997, as the world's largest chemical weapons plant. The Qaddafi regime denied these charges, contending the Rabta facility was a pharmaceutical plant and the Tarhuna complex was part of an irrigation project.

The post-9/11 policy of the George W. Bush administration toward Libya highlighted the ambiguity of the war on **terrorism**. At a time when **Tripoli** appeared to be cooperating fully in the war on terrorism, Washington increased its rhetoric regarding Libyan development of weapons of mass destruction. In 2002–2003, John R. Bolton, undersecretary for arms control and international security, charged repeatedly that Libya was continuing its long-standing pursuit of nuclear weapons as well as moving to reestablish an offensive chemical weapons ability and continuing its alleged biological warfare program. In response to these charges, various Libyan officials—including **Saif al-Islam al-Qaddafi** in a Spring 2003 article in *Middle East Policy*—continued to deny the existence of unconventional weapons programs.

In December 2003, after nine months of difficult negotiations, the Qaddafi regime renounced unconventional weapons. It was only then that the full extent of its weapons of mass destruction programs became apparent. Over the years, Libya had manufactured a considerable amount of mustard gas and possessed the precursor chemicals necessary for the production of nerve gas. It also had more than 3,000 empty bomb casings designed to carry chemical weapons, although it lacked the long-range missile or other systems necessary to deliver chemical weapons beyond the nation's borders. Libyan officials acknowledged a past intent to develop biological weapons, but no active biological weapons program was discovered by international inspectors. Finally, Libya had an ambitious, albeit struggling, nuclear weapons program that had been successful in purchasing designs, components, and materials from a clandestine international supply network, although most experts agreed Libya was years, if not decades, away from actually developing a nuclear weapon.

While Libya renounced weapons of mass destruction in late 2003, the Qaddafi regime continues to pursue nuclear technology, allegedly for peaceful purposes. Talks on this subject were conducted in 2004 with **France** and **Russia**. In May 2005, France and Libya signed a letter of intent to cooperate in the development of a nuclear power project, involving the reactivation of a research reactor at Tajura for the production of radioisotopes for industrial and medical use. *See also* FOREIGN POLICY.

WESTERN LIBYA GAS PROJECT. The Western Libya Gas Project (WLGP) is designed to move **natural gas** and condensate from the onshore Wafa field, located near the Algerian border, and the offshore Bahr Essalam field, located 110 kilometers (68 miles) offshore in the Mediterranean, to a new processing plant on the Libyan coast at Mellitah.

The Greenstream pipeline, part of the $8.6 billion natural gas project by **Italy**'s **ENI** and Libya's **National Oil Company**, is central to the WLGP. The 520-kilometer (322-mile) pipeline connects Mellitah in Libya to Gela in Sicily. With the full activation of the pipeline, Libya will provide some 30 percent of Italy's energy imports.

The first awards for construction of the treatment centers, processing facilities, and pipeline for the WLGP were made in early 2002. The Greenstream pipeline came on line in October 2004 with the commencement of onshore production from the Wafa field. Trial production from the offshore Bahr Essalam field began in August 2005.

The WLGP is proving to be an excellent advertisement for Libya's natural gas sector, long subordinate to the **petroleum** sector. Libya's proven natural gas reserves total 1.49 trillion cubic meters, the third highest in **Africa** behind Algeria and Nigeria, and its unproven reserves are estimated to be as much as double this amount. The WLGP demonstrates there is market demand and the necessary production and distribution facilities available for Libyan natural gas.

WHEELUS AIR BASE. An American air base maintained near **Tripoli** during the **Idris** regime under the terms of the **American-Libyan Agreement**, Wheelus served as a training base for **United States** and NATO pilots as well as a strategic staging area for U.S. forces. The sparse population and year-round sunshine of Libya provided an attractive alternative to congested European airspace, yet was close enough to targets in Eastern Europe and the **Soviet Union** to be operationally useful. The air base had a profound impact on the domestic economy of Libya, especially in and around Tripoli. It also served as an effective propaganda machine through which American ideas, music, and newspapers were introduced. A prompt U.S. evacuation of Wheelus Air Base was one of the first demands of the **Revolutionary Command Council**, which overthrew the monarchy in September 1969. Once the U.S. forces had evacuated the base, the revolutionary government made 11 June, the date of the American evacuation, an official public holiday.

WOMEN. The longest section of part 3 of *The Green Book* is devoted to the rights and duties of women. **Muammar al-Qaddafi** urges them to take a more active role in society and says he intends to make them free, educated, armed, and capable of deciding their own destiny. Under the Qaddafi regime, women have been encouraged to participate actively in both the **people's committees** and the **Basic People's Congresses**, and the **revolutionary committees** were given the specific objective of increasing female political and administrative roles. As a result, the opportunities for Libyan women gradually increased after 1969. In the field of **education**, for example, one of the revolution's more impressive achievements has been the rate at which the quantity of education available to females has advanced.

On the other hand, many aspects of their role in Libyan society have not changed as fast as Qaddafi's rhetoric would suggest. The 1972 **law** on **marriage** and divorce was an anomaly, in that it was at the time both the most recent of such laws in the Muslim world and among the most conservative and backward-looking. Largely accepting the traditional *sharia* regime, it amounted to an affirmation of the status quo with an implicit confirmation of the superiority of the husband's legal position as presupposed in traditional law.

Libyan women have proved generally receptive to the idea of venturing into occupational spheres that were previously considered exclusively male. At the same time, they have not been eager to efface all of the social differences between the two sexes, because doing so would not only bring new rights but would also restrict existing privileges. Many Libyan males have also been reluctant to expand female job opportunities, because such action would both impact on the breadwinning role of the male and threaten his comprehensive domestic leadership. It would also amplify the status of women, endangering male paternalism. As a result, female participation in socioeconomic and political activities has increased, but the scope and level of such activities remains somewhat limited.

Neither the 1969 **Constitutional Proclamation** nor the 1977 **Declaration of the Establishment of the People's Authority** addressed women's rights; however, the **Great Green Charter on Human Rights** adopted in 1988 makes limited provision for the rights of women. Article 17 of the Charter bans discrimination based on color, culture, race, and religion, but it does not disallow gender-based discrimination. The content of the article is thus consistent with the teachings of *The Green Book*, in which Qaddafi argues that the physical makeup of women precludes gender equality.

Article 21 of the Great Green Charter, which discusses the personal status of women, is also consistent with *The Green Book*. This section describes marriage as a partnership of equals into which no woman should be forced. Concerning divorce, the Charter states that no married couple should be allowed to divorce without a fair trial or mutual agreement, and when divorce occurs, the Charter gives the wife both the house and custody of the children. These provisions of the Charter, which fly in the face of the Koran and sharia, are also consistent with the philosophy in *The Green Book*. While Libyan women, especially those with children, clearly face obstacles to becoming equal participants in society, the Charter demonstrates the extent to which Qaddafi is willing to disregard **Islamic** doctrines when they do not agree with his own precepts and principles.

In the second half of the 1990s, Qaddafi appeared for a time to modify his relatively liberal policy toward women in an effort to preempt **Islamist** criticism of his regime. Once that **opposition** had been contained, however, he called in 2003 for women to take up military training and to assume a larger role in the development of the country. In Libya today, the status of women remains unequal to that of men; however, the opportunity for them to make notable social progress has definitely increased in recent years. Female participation in the workforce, especially in the service sector, also continues to increase in spite of the persistence of traditional mores that often discourage female participation in public life.

WORLD COURT. *See* INTERNATIONAL COURT OF JUSTICE.

– Y –

YOUNG TURK REVOLUTION. In 1908, a group of young Turkish army officers, including Enver Bey, Jemal Pasha, and Mustafa Kemal, joined like-minded civilian revolutionaries in a revolt against the arbitrary rule of the sultan. The Young Turk movement largely consisted of political reformers, many of whom had traveled in Europe and been influenced by European ideas, who were critical of the **Ottoman** sultanate. The immediate interest of the Young Turks was a restoration of the constitutional rule abolished by Abdul Hamid II 40 years earlier. Many **Arabs** in Istanbul and in Arab provinces such as Libya welcomed the new era promised by the Young Turks. These Arabs hoped the declared spirit of equality would end Turkish domination and increase autonomy for Arab provinces.

Following the Young Turk Revolution, the Ottoman provinces that make up modern Libya entered more than a decade of political turbulence. The nature of the upheavals, together with their timing and participants, profoundly influenced subsequent Libyan conceptions of the country's place in modern **Islamic** and Arab identities. In the end, Libya remained generally loyal to the pan-Islamic aspirations associated with the empire and did not, for the most part, turn to Arab **nationalism** at this point in its history.

At the beginning of the 20th century, the issues that preoccupied Arabs elsewhere in the Ottoman Empire were also apparent in Libya. While not one of the most cosmopolitan provinces in the empire, Libya and its elite were more closely attuned to events in Istanbul than was immediately apparent. First of all, the final decades of the 19th century had been a time of relative prosperity in Libya. The province remained the last outpost of the trans-**Saharan** trade, and Libyan merchants retained widespread commercial ties with the remainder of the empire. Secondly, Abdul Hamid II often used the provinces of North Africa as a form of Saharan Siberia, where his more troublesome political opponents could be exiled to prisons or minor posts at the farthest reaches of the empire. One unexpected result of this practice was that the Libyan elite was exposed to much of the intellectual ferment of the time. Turkification policies, the neglect of Arabic in schools, and religious reform were issues of great importance to Libyans and to residents of the other provinces of the Ottoman Empire.

On the other hand, there was little evidence of separatist sentiment in Libya at this time. Some Europeans, quick to identify local sources of dissatisfaction with the Ottoman administration, thought they had found such a cleavage in Sanusi dissatisfaction with Ottoman policy over French incursions into **Chad**. Sanusi leaders advocated a policy of direct military confrontation with **France**, while the Ottoman administration preferred to temporize in the vain hope of winning French support against **Italy**'s designs on the province. A difference of opinion existed on this issue, but it was not the genesis of a separatist movement.

In a similar vein, **Suleiman Baruni**, leader of the Ibadi sect of **Berbers** in **Tripolitania** and also a deputy in the newly reopened Ottoman parliament after 1908, was suspected of harboring ambitions for an autonomous Ibadi province in the western mountains. Imprisoned for subversive activity during the reign of Abdul Hamid, Baruni appears to have envisioned an Ibadi province within the religious and political sovereignty of the Ottoman Empire rather than a fully independent entity.

If there was little evidence of separatist activity in Libya during this period, there was dissatisfaction with Ottoman policies. In spite of active Young Turk opposition to Italian penetration, local enthusiasm for the new regime in Istanbul was far from unanimous. Turkification language policies were not popular, while the new freedoms were welcomed by only a small fraction of the population. Opposition also grew out of more immediate interests, especially a campaign to rid the local administration of the reactionary supporters of Abdul Hamid.

The Italian invasion of Libya in 1911 followed on the heels of the Young Turk Revolution. The Young Turk movement saw the defense of this Ottoman province as a moral obligation as well as a political necessity and encouraged Ottoman officers throughout the empire to converge on Libya to repulse the European invaders. In consequence, by the time World War I began, Libya had already experienced several years of Ottoman-led resistance to Italian encroachment. World War I, in which the Ottoman Empire confronted major European powers, including Italy, cemented the loyalty of most of Libya's elite to the impotent empire and its pan-Islamic rationale. Islam later provided the most persuasive and effective ideological rationale to rally Libyan opposition to continued Italian occupation.

Following the defeat of the Ottoman Empire, an element of the Libyan elite attempted to establish an independent political administration on republican grounds, but the effort floundered on internecine disputes. Turning once more to **religiously** inspired leadership to oppose European rule, Islamic symbols and attachments, as opposed to Arab symbols and attachments, proved to be the most widely embraced political identity in Libya. Provincial patriotism, as well as a wider loyalty to the Ottoman Empire, were both expressed in the idiom of Islam.

YOUTH. A noteworthy characteristic of contemporary Libyan demography is an extremely youthful population. At the outset of the revolution in 1969, the Libyan population was one of the youngest in the world, with some two-thirds under the age of 25; a 2004 estimate suggests that more than a third of the population is now 14 or younger. Libya has one of the world's faster rates of population growth, so this age profile will continue in the foreseeable future.

The revolutionary government of **Muammar al-Qaddafi** has devoted considerable time and effort to mobilizing Libyan youth in support of the revolution; however, the limited empirical data available suggest such efforts have enjoyed only qualified success. A detailed analysis of Libyan political culture, published in 2001 and based on a survey of 500 students at Garyounis University in **Benghazi**, found the revolutionary government has enjoyed considerable success in reproducing its values among the younger generation. Its accomplishments were most notable in the area of gender issues, together with its policies on **Arab nationalism**, Arab **unity**, and the Palestinian issue. At the same time, the Qaddafi regime appeared to have failed in its efforts to create politically participant citizens and to develop acceptable alternatives to kinship ties. According to the survey, **tribes** continued to be a source of both individual identity and economic welfare, and they remained a source of political identity. Of most interest to the revolutionary government, the survey found that most Libyan youth did not accept their role in the system of **people's committees** and popular congresses created by Qaddafi and were not actively participating in that system.

YUNNIS JAABIR, ABU BAKR (ABU BAKR YUNIS JABER; ABU BAKR YOUNIS JABR; ABU BAKR YUNIS JABIR) (1940–). Boyhood friend of **Muammar al-Qaddafi** and an original member of the **Revolutionary Command Council** (RCC). Abu Bakr Yunnis Jaabir was one of eight RCC members who were also participants in the political study cell established by Qaddafi at the military college in **Benghazi**. Initially, he served the revolutionary government as chief of staff.

Following the abortive August 1975 coup led by fellow RCC member **Omar Mehishi**, Abu Bakr Yunnis Jaabir was one of the five remaining RCC members who constituted the top regime elite for much of the next two decades. He has served the Qaddafi regime in a variety of positions, most notably commander in chief of the Libyan Arab **armed forces**.

– Z –

ZAMZAM, WADI. A large drainage basin that originates on the eastern flank of the **Hamadah al-Hamra** and parallels the Wadi **Soffegin**. It eventually empties into the extreme southern part of the **Sabkhat Tawurgha**.

ZAWI, FARHAT AL-. Farhat al-Zawi spent his youth in **France** and **Tunisia**, spoke French, and upon his return to Libya, became a judge in his hometown of Zawiya. Twice dismissed for political intrigue before the **Young Turk Revolution**, he eventually joined **Suleiman Baruni** in supporting the Committee of Union and Progress. By the end of October 1911, both men were traveling their districts preaching resistance and calling for volunteers to oppose the **Italian** invasion. *See also* OTTOMAN EMPIRE.

ZENATI, ZENATI MOHAMMED AL-. Secretary general of the **General People's Congress** since 1999.

ZIONISM. *See* ISRAEL; JEWS; POGROM.

ZIRID DYNASTY (c. 970–c. 1150). **Berber** dynasty that ruled the northern parts of present-day Algeria, Libya, and **Tunisia** from the late 10th to the mid-12th centuries. In the aftermath of the Hilalian invasion, Zirid rule was confined to a small strip of territory along the Tunisian coast. When the Norman rulers of southern Italy arrived, the Zirids put up little resistance, accepting the dominance of **Roger II** by around 1150.

ZLEITNI, ABDEL-HAFEZ. Head of the higher planning council of the **General People's Congress** (2003–). Zleitni was chairman of the **National Oil Company** in 2001–2003.

Appendix A:
Libya Fact Sheet

GEOGRAPHY

Area: 1,759,540 sq km (686,221 sq mi)
Coastline: 1,770 km (1,097 mi)
Climate: Mediterranean along coast; dry, extreme desert interior
Terrain: Mostly barren, flat undulating plains, plateaus, depressions
Land Use

Arable land: 1.03%
Permanent crops: 0.19%
Other: 98.78%

PEOPLE

Population: 5,631,585 (2004 est.)
Age Structure

0–14: 34.2%
15–64: 61.7%
65 and older: 4.1%

Population Growth Rate: 2.37% (2004 est.)
Birthrate: 27.17 births/1,000 population (2004 est.)
Death Rate: 3.48 deaths/1,000 population (2004 est.)
Infant Mortality Rate: 25.7 deaths/1,000 live births (2004 est.)
Life Expectancy at Birth: 76.28 years
Ethnic Composition: Berber and Arab

Foreign Residents: 3% of population, including Americans, Egyptians, Indians, Italians, Greeks, Maltese, Pakistanis, Thai, Tunisians, and Turks

Religions: Sunni Muslims (97%)

Languages: Arabic; English and Italian also widely understood in urban areas

Literacy: 82.6% of population age 15 and over can read and write

GOVERNMENT

Head of State: Muammar al-Qaddafi

Capital: Tripoli

Constitution: 11 December 1969; amended 2 March 1977

Political System: Legislative authority vested in the General People's Congress, which exercises its authority through the General People's Committee

Legislative Branch: Unicameral

Judicial Branch: Supreme Court

Political Parties: None

Independence: 24 December 1951

National Day: Revolution Day, 1 September (1969)

Flag: Plain green, the traditional color of Islam, the state religion

ECONOMY

Overview: Socialist-oriented economy heavily dependent on oil revenues, which contribute practically all export earnings and about one-third of gross domestic product (GDP)

Labor Force: 1.51 million (2003 est.)

Agricultural Products: Wheat, barley, olives, dates, citrus, vegetables, peanuts, meat, eggs

Industries: Petroleum, food processing, textiles, cement, handicrafts

Currency: One Libyan dinar (LD) equals 1,000 dirhams

Fiscal Year: Calendar year

	1990	1995	2000	2004
Real GDP (annual % change)	8.2%	–0.3%	4.4%	2.8%
Consumer Prices (annual % change)	8.6%	8.3%	–2.9%	2.2%

TRANSPORTATION

Railways: No railways have been in operation since 1965; seven lines under construction, totaling 2,757 km (1,709 mi)
Highways

Total: 83,200 km (51,584 mi)
Paved: 47,590 km (29,506 mi)
Unpaved: 35,610 km (22,078 mi)

Waterways: None
Pipelines: Crude oil 7,252 km (4,496 mi); gas 3,611 km (2,239 mi)
Merchant Marine: 20 ships
Airports: 140 (2003 est.)

Sources: International Monetary Fund, *World Economic Outlook*, www.imf .org/external/pubs/ft/weo/2005/02/index.htm (September 2005); Central Intelligence Agency, *The World Factbook*, www.cia.gov/cia/publications/factbook/ geos/ly.html (September 2005).

Appendix B:
Karamanli Dynasty, 1711–1835

Ahmed Karamanli	1711–1745
Mohammed Karamanli	1745–1754
Ali (I) Karamanli	1754–1795
Yusuf Karamanli	1795–1832
Ali (II) Karamanli	1832–1835

Appendix C:
Turkish Governors of Libya, 1835–1911

Mustafa Nedjib Pasha	1835
Mohamed Raif Pasha	1835–1836
Taher Pasha	1836–1837
Hassan Pasha El Jashmalli	1837–1838
Askar Ali Pasha	1838–1842
Mohamed Ameen Pasha	1842–1847
Mohamed Ragheb Pasha	1847–1848
Hadj Ahmed Ezzat Pasha	1848–1852
Mustafa Noori Pasha	1852–1855
Othman Pasha	1855–1857
Ahmed Ezzat Pasha	1857–1860
Mahmood Nadim Pasha (Mahmud Nadim Pasha)	1860–1866
Ali Rida Pasha (Ali Ridha Pasha)	1866–1870
Mohamed Halat Pasha	1870–1871
Mohamed Resheed Pasha	1871–1872
Ali Rida Pasha (Ali Ridha Pasha) [second time]	1872–1874
Sami Pasha	1874–1875
Assem Pasha	1875–1876
Mustafa Pasha	1876–1878
Ali Kemali Pasha	1878
Mohamed Sabri Pasha	1878
Mohamed Djelal-ed-din Pasha	1878–1879
Ahmed Ezzat Pasha [second time]	1879–1880
Mohamed Nazef Pasha	1880–1882
Ahmed Rassem Pasha (Ahmad Rasim)	1882–1896
Namek Pasha (Namiq Pasha)	1896–1899
Hashem Pasha	1899–1900

Hafez Pasha	1900–1903
Hassan Hosni Pasha	1903–1906
Rajab Pasha (Rajib Pasha)	1906–1909
Ahmed Fawzi Pasha	1909
Ibrahim Pasha	1909–1911
Ahmed Rashim Pasha (secretary general)	1911

Appendix D:
Libyan Cabinets, 1952–1969

Mahmud al-Muntasir

24 December 1951–18 February
1954 (cabinet modified
14 May 1952, 26 April 1953,
18 September 1953)

Muhammad al-Saqizli
(Muhammad al-Sakizly,
Mohammed al-Sakisli)

18 February–11 April 1954

Mustafa Bin Halim

11 April 1954–26 May 1957
(cabinet modified 19
December 1954, 26 April
1955, 26 March 1956, 30
October 1956, 14 March 1957)

Abdul Majid Ka'abar
('Abd al-Majid Ku'bar,
Abdul al-Majid Kubar)

26 May 1957–16 October 1960
(cabinet modified 24 April
1958, 11 October 1958,
15 November 1958, 6 February
1960, 29 September 1960,
5 October 1960)

Muhammad Bin Uthman

16 October 1960–19 March 1963
(cabinet modified 3 May 1961,
15 October 1961, 27 January
1962, 3 February 1962, 11
October 1962, 1 March 1963)

Muhiaddin Fekini
(Mohyil Din Fkeni,
Muhi al-Din Fakini,
Muheddin Fkeni)

19 March 1963–22 January 1964
(cabinet modified 13
November 1963)

Mahmud al-Muntasir
[second time]

22 January 1964–20 March 1965
(cabinet modified 25 March
1964, 26 May 1964, 10
November 1964, 29 July 1964,
29 October 1964)

Hussein Maziq (Husain Mazigh,
Husain Maziq)

20 March 1965–1 July 1967
(cabinet modified 2 October
1965, 20 March 1966, 4 April
1964)

Abdel Qadir Badri
(Abdul Gader al-Badri,
Abdul Qader al-Badri)

1 July–24 October 1967 (cabinet
modified 7 July 1967)

Abdel Hamid Bakkush
(Abdul Hamid al-Bakkush)

24 October 1967–4 September
1968 (cabinet modified
4 January 1968)

Wanis al-Qaddafi
(Wanis al-Gaddafi,
Wanis al-Qathafi)

4 September 1968–1 September
1969 (cabinet modified 9 June
1969)

Appendix E:
Revolutionary Command Council, January 1970

Col. Muammar al-Qaddafi (Mu'ammar Qadhdhafi; Mu'ammar al-Quaddafi)

Maj. Adbel Salaam Jalloud (Abdul Salaam Jalloud; Abdel Salem Jalloud)

Maj. Bashir Saghir al-Hawaadi (Beshir Saghir Hawady; Bashir Saghir Hawwadi)

Capt. Mukhtar Abdullah al-Qarawi (Mukhtar Abdullah Gerwy; Mukhtar Abdullah al-Kirwi)

Capt. Abdel Menin al-Houni (Abdul Moniem Taber al-Huny; Abdul Munim al-Tah al-Huni)

Capt. Mustafa al-Kharuubi (Mustapha Karauby; Mustapha Kharuby; Mustapha Kharrubi; Mustapha al-Kharoubi)

Capt. Kweildi al-Hemeidi (Khuwayldi al-Humaydi; Kheweildy Hamidy; Khuwaildi Hamidi)

Capt. Muhammed Najm (Mohamad Najim; Mohamad Nejm; Muhammad Najm)

Capt. Awad Ali Hamza

Capt. Abu Bakr Yunnis Jaabir (Abu Bakr Yunis Jaber; Abu Bakr Younis Jabr; Abu Bakr Yunis Jabir)

Capt. Omar Mehishi (Omar Abdullah Meheishy; Omar Abdullah Muhaishi)

Lt. Imhammad Abu Bakr al-Maqaryif (Abu Bakr Mgarief; Muhammad Abu Bakr al-Muqaryaf)

Appendix F:
Libyan Government, October 2005

REVOLUTIONARY LEADER (HEAD OF STATE)

Muammar al-Qaddafi

GENERAL PEOPLE'S COMMITTEE

Secretary (Prime Minister)   Shokri Ghanem
Deputy Prime Minister   Ali Baghdadi al-Mahmudi
Assistant for Services   Maatuq Mohammed Maatuq

KEY MINISTERS

Economy and Foreign Trade   Abd al-Qadir Bilkhair
Energy   Fathi bin Shatwan
Finance   Mohammed Ali al-Huwaiz
Foreign Affairs and International   Mohammed Abderrahman
  Cooperation   Chalgam
Justice and Public Security   Mohammed Ali al-Misurati
Planning   Taher al-Hadi al-Jehaimi

GENERAL PEOPLE'S CONGRESS

Head of Higher Planning Council   Abdel-Hafez Zleitni
Secretary   Zenati Mohammed Zenati
Assistant Secretary   Ahmed Mohammed Ibrahim
Foreign Affairs   Suleiman Sasi al-Shahumi
Popular Committees   Ibrahim ali Ibrahim
Popular Congresses   Ibrahim abd al-Rahman Abjad
Social Affairs   Amal Nuri Abdullah Safar
Tourism   Umar al-Mabruk al-Tayyif
Trade Unions, Federations,   Mohammed Jibril al-Urfi
   and Vocational Associations

NATIONAL OIL COMPANY CHAIRMAN

Abdullah Salem al-Badri

CENTRAL BANK GOVERNOR

Ahmed Munaisi Abdel-Hamid

Appendix G:
Recoverable Oil Reserves, 1967–2004

Year	Reserves
1967	29.2
1970	29.2
1975	26.1
1980	23.0
1985	21.3
1990	22.8
1995	29.5
2000	36.0
2004	39.1

Sources: Organization of Petroleum Exporting Countries, *Annual Statistical Bulletin*, 2004, www.opec.org/library/Annual%20Statistical%20Bulletin/ asb2004.htm (2004); BP, *Statistical Review of World Energy*, www.bp .com/liveassets/bp_internet/globalbp/STAGING/global_assets/downloads/S/ statistical_review_of_world_energy_full_report_2004.pdf (June 2004).

Appendix H:
Selected Chronology of Sanctions against Libya

1978   May: U.S. government bans the export of military equipment to Libya, including aircraft and selected agricultural and electronic equipment.

1981   U.S. government asks all U.S. citizens to leave Libya.

1982   March: U.S. government bans all exports to Libya with the exception of food and medicine.

1983   U.S. government asks other nations to support curbs on exports to Libya.

1984   April: London police besiege Libyan embassy. Shots are fired and a policewoman is killed. Great Britain breaks diplomatic relations with Libya, closes Libyan embassy.

1986   January: U.S. government increases economic sanctions on Libya in the wake of late-1985 terrorist attacks on Rome and Vienna airports. **April:** U.S. conducts air strikes around Tripoli and Benghazi. European Community reduces Libyan diplomatic missions in Europe. **June:** U.S. government orders all American oil companies to leave Libya. **December:** U.S. ban on economic activities with Libya is extended for one year. Annual extensions continue thereafter.

1988   December: Pan Am flight 103 explodes over Lockerbie, Scotland.

1989   September: UTA flight 772 explodes over Niger.

1992   January: UN Security Council approves Resolution 731, asking Libya to cooperate with pending Pan Am and UTA bombing investigations. **March:** UN Security Council Resolution 748 adopts sanctions for three months if Libya fails to surrender Lockerbie suspects.

September: UN sanctions renewed for three months and later repeatedly renewed.

1993   February: United States bans U.S. law firms or their foreign branches from offering legal services to the Libyan government or its agencies. **November:** United Nations tightens its embargo against Libya, freezing Libyan assets overseas, banning selected sales of oil equipment and further strengthening earlier flight bans.

1995   March: United States presses the United Nations for tougher sanctions against Libya, up to and including a worldwide embargo on oil sales. **April:** UN Security Council eases travel ban on Libyan flights to allow pilgrims to visit Mecca. **October:** Libya announces it will no longer seek a seat on the UN Security Council, citing U.S. domination of organization.

1996   April: Relatives of Pan Am flight 103 bombing victims file a $10 billion lawsuit against Libya. **June:** Qaddafi flies to an Arab summit meeting in Cairo, ignoring a UN ban on flights from Libya. **August:** U.S. president Bill Clinton signs Iran-Libya Sanctions Act (ILSA), imposing sanctions on foreign individuals or companies investing $40 million or more a year in gas or oil projects in Libya or Iran.

1999   April: Libya remands two suspects in Lockerbie bombing. United Nations suspends sanctions in place since 1992.

2001   August: U.S. Congress renews ILSA, tightening Libyan provisions.

2003   August: Libya agrees to pay $2.7 billion to 270 families of Pan Am flight 103 victims. Libya later agrees to supplement prior payout to families of victims of UTA flight 772. **September:** United Nations permanently lifts sanctions. **December:** Libya renounces unconventional weapons.

2004   February: United States lifts travel ban on Libya. **April:** United States eases sanctions on Libya. **September:** United States effectively lifts remaining sanctions on Libya.

2006   May: United States restores full diplomatic relations, removing Libya from the U.S. State Department list of State Sponsors of Terrorism and omitting it from the annual certification of countries not fully cooperating with American antiterrorism efforts.

Glossary

Amir
Title of an independent chieftain; literally "commander."

Baraka
Quality of blessedness or grace, which is usually found in *marabouts* as well as other divinely favored persons; also refers to the charisma that endows the blessed with a special capacity to rule.

Barbary
Geographic term that stems from "Berber." The Barbary states extended from Libya to Morocco.

Defterdaz
Turkish term for office of the treasurer created by the Ottoman administration in Libya in the 1840s.

Dey
Originally, a junior officer commanding a company of *janissaries*; title after 1611 of the head of government of Tripolitania.

Dhimmi
Islamic legal concept dealing with protecting non-Muslims under Muslim rule; *dhimmi* carries the meaning of "contract," but not a contract between equals. The term took on a special meaning in Libya, where it referred largely to the Jewish community.

Dinar
Unit of currency in Libya.

Divan
Council of senior civilian officials and military officers during the Ottoman and Karamanli periods. The composition of the Divan varied over the centuries; often it consisted of the commander of the navy, the minister of finance, the sheiks in charge of the cities, and the commander of the *janissaries*.

Ghibli
Hot desert wind.

Guelta
Rocky hollow that collects rainwater; a type of natural cistern that is an important source of drinking water for nomads.

Hadith Traditions or collected sayings of the Prophet Muhammad; tradition relating to the life and actions of the Prophet. Each incident is carefully evaluated and positions are formed as to its likelihood of being a correct account. The orthodox collections of Hadith comprise the literary record of the Prophet's *Sunna* or customary practice.

Hajj (*Hadj*) Pilgrimage to Mecca, the fifth pillar of Islam. Also, one who has performed this act of faith.

Hegira The Prophet Muhammad's migration back to Mecca from Medina. The Islamic calendar starts from this event, traditionally dated to 16 July 622 on the Western calendar.

Ijma Use of consensus to establish agreed Islamic doctrine.

Ikhwan Brethren. Also, members of Sufi Order, and a specialized servant class in the Sanusi Order that held administrative and ritual posts and enjoyed considerable authority and influence.

Imam Religious leader or authority on Islamic theology and law in a mosque, community, or locale.

Jabal (*Djebel*) Mountain.

Janissaries Elite Turkish infantry; servants or slaves of the sultan.

Jihad Holy war.

Khouloughlis (*Kouloughlis*; *Kulughlis*; *Qulaughlis*) Distinct caste of mixed Turkish and Arabic parentage found in Tripolitania, the offspring of Turkish men and local women; literally "sons of servants" or "sons of slaves."

Koran Sacred book of Muslims containing the word of God as revealed to and recited by the Prophet Muhammad.

Maghrib The Western Islamic world, i.e., northwest Africa, traditionally comprising Algeria, Morocco, and Tunisia with Tripolitania sometimes added; literally "Place where sun sets."

Mahdi Envoy of God sent to complete the work of the Prophet Muhammad.

Marabout (*Marabut*) Saintly or venerated, often charismatic, Muslim leader; also, a descendant or leader of a Sufi

	order. Not usually a member of the *ulama*, a marabout is often called in to arbitrate tribal disputes.
Mashriq	The Eastern Islamic world, i.e., the Middle East. Cyrenaica before independence was sometimes considered part of the Mashriq.
Medina	The old native quarter of a North African city.
Moor	Urban Arab in Tripolitania during the dynastic and Ottoman periods.
Mufti	Islamic jurisconsultant; interpreter of the law.
Munas	Turkish garrisons.
Mutassarif	Turkish term for governor of a subprovince.
Nahiyah	(*Nahiye*) Ottoman administrative district.
Ottoman	Of the Islamic caliphate based in Turkey that controlled much of the central Middle East between 1300 and 1914.
Pasha	Turkish officer or official of high rank; governor of an Ottoman province or mayor or governor of a town.
Pashalik	Region under the control of a pasha.
Qaid	Official appointed to head the Jewish community; probably the most preeminent of individuals within the Jewish community to have access to the Ottoman court. This position enabled the government to place its tax-collecting burden on the shoulders of one man, who then had to concern himself with how this burden would be distributed within the community.
Qiyas	Practice of reasoning by analogy in order to amplify the Hadith and the Koran.
Sahel	Western stretch of the Sahara Desert bordering on the Atlantic Ocean; traditionally considered to consist of the band of African states (Mauritania, Mali, Niger) bordering the Sahara to the south and west.
Sayyid	Honorific title.
Sharia	Islamic law based on Muhammad's revelation; literally "the way."
Sharif	A descendant of Muhammad through his daughter Fatima.
Sheik	(*Shaykh*; *Cheikh*) A spiritual leader, elder, arbiter, or religious teacher; also, a descendant of an important Almohad family.

Shiite   Follower of a branch of Islam that developed from the conviction that the cousin and son-in-law of Muhammad, Ali ibn Abi Talib, was his rightful successor.

Shurfa   Descendants of the Prophet Muhammad considered to have special virtues and generally given special status in Islamic societies.

Sidi   Honorific title.

Souk   Traditional, covered market.

Sufi   Muslim mystic.

Sunna   Body of Islamic custom and practice based on the Prophet Muhammad's words and deeds, a source of authority in Islam second only to the Koran.

Sunni   Muslims who follow the customs (*sunna*) of the Prophet; specifically, the branch of Islam that accepts as legitimate the reigning caliphs who followed the Prophet Muhammad. Sunnis acknowledge the authority of the Koran and Sunna as interpreted by the *ulama*; the vast majority of Muslims are Sunnis, including most residents of Libya.

Tanzimat   Administrative reforms undertaken in the Ottoman Empire in the mid-19th century.

Tariqa   (*Tariqah*) A body of rituals practiced by Muslim brotherhoods; literally "way" or "path."

Ulama   Learned persons and religious leaders well versed in Koranic studies; the intellectual or religious elite whose opinions count in Islamic societies.

Umma   The community of Muslims worldwide.

Vilayet   (*Wilayah*) Administrative division of the Ottoman Empire comparable to a province and administered by a *wali*.

Wadi   River or dry riverbed. A wadi may become a swift, violent stream after heavy rains; many *wadis*, especially larger ones in areas of heavier rainfall, contain a subterranean flow a short distance below the surface.

Wali   (*Vali*) Chief administrator at the district level in Libya during the Ottoman era.

Zawiya   (*Zawiyah*; *Zawia*; plural *Zawaya*) Religious lodge or order founded by a person renowned for religious knowledge or holiness; also buildings for religious study or monasteries, often constructed at tribal centers, oases, and the junctions of trade and pilgrimage routes.

Bibliography

CONTENTS

I. INTRODUCTION

At the outset of the One September Revolution in 1969, only a handful of books on Libya were available to the general reader. Fortunately, this situation improved over the next decade, in large part due to widespread interest in the policies of the revolutionary government led by Muammar al-Qaddafi. The economic sanctions imposed by the United States in the 1980s and by the United Nations in the 1990s later stifled field research in Libya, creating a new gap in scholarship. With the lifting of those sanctions, scholarly output on Libya has again increased.

In addition to the extensive bibliography found in this fourth edition of the *Historical Dictionary of Libya*, a relatively comprehensive, albeit increasingly dated, bibliography is available in volume 79 of the World Bibliographical Series, entitled *Libya* and compiled by Richard I. Lawless. Also useful is the volume entitled *A Concise Bibliography of Northern Chad and Fezzan in Southern Libya* (1983), edited by Mohamed A. Alawar. Older but still helpful bibliographies include *Libya, 1969–1974: A Bibliography*, edited by Aghil M. Barbar; *A Bibliography of Libya*, edited by Roy W. Hill; *The Middle East: A Selected Bibliography of Recent Works, 1970–1972 Supplement*, edited by

H. Howard; and *Index Libycus: Bibliography of Libya, 1957–1969, with Supplementary Material, 1915–1956*, edited by Hans Schlüter.

The best general introductions to contemporary Libya are Dirk Vandewalle's *Libya since Independence: Oil and State-Building* (1998) and *Libya's Qaddafi: The Politics of Contradiction* (1997) by Mansour O. El-Kikhia. Vandewalle concentrates on the domestic policies of the Qaddafi regime, while El-Kikhia covers both its domestic and foreign policies. *Qadhafi's Libya, 1969 to 1994*, edited by Dirk Vandewalle and published in 1995, is a companion volume to his fuller study and El-Kikhia's, providing background and detail to the broader issues raised in the later works. For those familiar with the French language, Edmond Jouve, provides a contemporary portrait of Qaddafi in *Mouammar Kadhafi: Dans le concert des nations* (2004). Guy Arnold's *Maverick State: Gaddafi and the New World Order* also remains useful, especially on external relations. In contrast, *Libya: The Struggle for Survival*, 2nd ed., by Geoff Simons is a conventional summary of Libyan history that adds nothing to earlier work by John Wright and others.

In *Libya: Qadhafi's Revolution and the Modern State*, Lillian Craig Harris provides a readable survey of Libyan geography, society, history, economics, and politics with a focus on the Qaddafi regime to 1986. *Libya: A Country Study*, edited by Harold D. Nelson and a part of the Area Handbook Series, is useful but dated. Another rewarding survey is *The Making of a Pariah State: The Adventurist Politics of Muammar Qaddafi* (1987) by Martin Sicker. French-language studies include *La Libye contemporaine* by Juliette Bessis and *La Libye nouvelle: Rupture et continuité*, edited by G. Albergoni et al. François Burgat and André Laronde, in *La Libye*, provide an overview of Libya suitable for the traveler or general reader.

An introduction to the early history of the region can be found in *History of the Maghrib* by Jamil M. Abun-Nasr; *The History of the Maghrib: An Interpretive Essay* by Abdallah Laroui; and *The North African Provinces from Diocletian to the Vandal Conquest* by B. H. Warmington. More specialized volumes include *The Garamantes of Southern Libya* by C. Daniels; *Antiquities of Tripolitania* by D. E. L. Haynbes; and *The Coast of Barbary* by Jane Soames.

A variety of books exist on the period of Ottoman rule. The traditional studies include Ernest N. Bennett's *With the Turks in Tripoli*; Anthony Joseph Cachia's *Libya under the Second Ottoman Occupation, 1835–1911*; Godfrey Fisher's *Barbary Legend: War, Trade and Piracy in North Africa, 1415–1830*; and Ray W. Irwin's *Diplomatic Relations of the United States with the Barbary Powers, 1776–1816*. Richard B. Parker's *Uncle Sam in Barbary: A Diplomatic History* is a new addition to the literature. Parker relates historical events along the North Africa coast to contemporary issues in a well-researched and meticulously written book. Other recent studies on the same period include Franklin Lambert's *The Barbary Wars* and Richard Zacks's *The Pirate Coast*.

Ali Abdullatif Ahmida, in *The Making of Modern Libya: State Formation, Colonization, and Resistance, 1830–1932*, explores the nature of the state and political economy of Tripolitania, Cyrenaica, and the Fezzan. His analysis emphasizes the impact of Ottoman state centralization, the decline of the Saharan trade, and the penetration of European financial capital. Ahmida contributes to our understanding of Cyrenaican tribal structures as well as the Libyan reaction to Italian colonialism. He continues his work in *Forgotten Voices: Power and Agency in Colonial and Postcolonial Libya* (2005).

Much of the literature on the period of Italian occupation is available only in the Italian language. While some of it is listed in the bibliography, it will not be emphasized here. A welcome exception is *Modern and Contemporary Libya: Sources and Historiographies*, a collection of English- and French-language essays edited by Anna Baldinetti. The standard English-language source remains Claudio G. Segre's *Fourth Shore: The Italian Colonization of Libya* (1974). Others of note include William C. Askew's *Europe and Italy's Acquisition of Libya, 1911–1912*; Thomas Barclay's *Turco-Italian War and Its Problems*; and George H. Becker's *Disposition of the Italian Colonies*. On the transition period from Turkish to Italian rule, *Italo-Turkish Diplomacy and the War over Libya, 1911–1912* by Timothy W. Childs and Rachel Simon's *Libya between Ottomanism and Nationalism: The Ottoman Involvement in Libya during the War with Italy (1911–1919)* are recommended. On the transition from colonialism to independence, see Scott L. Bills's *Libyan Arena: The United States, Britain, and the Council of Foreign Ministers, 1945–1948*.

John Wright's *Libya: A Modern History* (1982) continues to be the best available general history of modern Libya. Expanding the story begun in his 1969 study, entitled *Libya*, Wright focuses on the post-1900 era. For political development in the 19th and 20th centuries, see Lisa Anderson's pioneering work, *The State and Social Transformation in Tunisia and Libya, 1830–1980*.

E. E. Evans-Pritchard's *Sanusi of Cyrenaica* and Nicola A. Ziadeh's *Sanusiyah: A Study of a Revivalist Movement in Islam* are invaluable for any examination of the Sanusi Order. A more recent study published in 1995 by Knut S. Vikor entitled *Sufi and Scholar on the Desert Edge: Muhammad b. Ali al-Sanusi and His Brotherhood* is highly recommended. The *Bedouin of Cyrenaica: Studies in Personal and Corporate Power* (1990) is a stimulating and controversial collection of essays published over the last several decades by the late Emrys L. Peters.

For the troubled history of Libyan Jews, see Renzo De Felice's *Jews in an Arab Land: Libya, 1835–1970*. A more recent study published by Harvey E. Goldberg in 1990, *Jewish Life in Muslim Libya: Rivals and Relatives*, is also recommended. Rachel Simon's *Change within Tradition among Jewish Women in Libya* (1992) remains a pioneering study of Jewish women in an Arab state. She examines the changing status of Jewish women in Libya from the second half of the 19th century until 1967, when most Jews left the country.

For an examination of contemporary sociopolitical events, the single most rewarding volume remains *Libyan Politics: Tribe and Revolution* by John Davis. Focusing on the Zuwaya tribe, the author provides a penetrating analysis of what it is like to be the subject of a revolutionary government, especially in a society in which any kind of government is a fairly recent phenomenon. At the same time, Amal Obeidi's *Political Culture in Libya* (2001) is a welcome addition to the literature. Based on a 1994 survey of 500 students at Garyounis University, this is one of the very few empirical studies of popular attitudes in Libya to be published since Qaddafi came to power in 1969. While her survey results and consequent observations must be tempered by the limited sample and the timeliness of the data, Obeidi's book offers fresh thinking supported by field research on issues at the heart of economic, political, and social change in Libya.

Libya: The Elusive Revolution by Ruth First remains extremely valuable on the early years of the One September Revolution. Those readers conversant in French will also find Guy Georgy's *Kadhafi: Le berger des Syrtes* of value. Other studies that should be consulted, in addition to those mentioned earlier, include *Libyan Sandstorm: The Complete Account of Qaddafi's Revolution* by John K. Cooley; *Qaddafi and the Libyan Revolution* by David Blundy and Andrew Lycett; *Qadhafi's Libya* by Jonathan Bearman; and *Gadafi: Voice from the Desert* by Mirella Bianco. *Libya since the Revolution: Aspects of Social and Political Development* by Marius K. Deeb and Mary Jane Deeb provides valuable information on the role of women, education, and Islam in revolutionary Libya. *Libya since Independence*, edited by J. A. Allen, includes chapters on economic, political, and social development.

To understand contemporary politics in Libya, the reader is well advised to begin with Majid Khadduri's *Modern Libya: A Study in Political Development*, which focuses on the independence era and the early years of the United Kingdom of Libya. *Libya: The Years of Hope*, the memoirs of Mustafa Ahmed Bin Halim, prime minister of Libya from April 1954 to May 1957, is also recommended. However, it should be read with care as Bin Halim was considered by some to be an unabashed self-promoter. In the absence of additional published works, a Ph.D. dissertation, completed in 1971 at Tufts University by Elizabeth R. Hayford, entitled "The Politics of the Kingdom of Libya in Historical Perspective" is essential to a study of the this period. Salaheddin Salem Hasan's Ph.D. dissertation, "The Genesis of the Political Leadership of Libya, 1952–1969: Historical Origins and Development of Its Component Elements," completed at George Washington University in 1973, is also valuable.

A survey of the early organization of the revolutionary government is found in *Politics and Government of Revolutionary Libya* (1975) by Henri Pierre Habib. More recent and more detailed analyses of political structures can be found in *Political Development and Bureaucracy in Libya* by Omar I. El

Fathaly, Monte Palmer, and Richard Chackerian, as well as in El Fathaly and Palmer's *Political Development and Social Change in Libya*. The most comprehensive English-language analysis of the Libyan system of government published to date remains the chapter by Ronald Bruce St John on the "Socialist People's Libyan Arab Jamahiriya" in volume 1 of the *World Encyclopedia of Political Systems and Parties* (1987). Hanspeter Mattes and Moncef Djaziri later explored selected aspects of the Libyan political system in separate essays published in *Qadhafi's Libya, 1969 to 1994*, edited by Dirk Vandewalle.

The ideology of the Libyan revolution is best introduced through a reading of the three slender volumes of *The Green Book*. Published independently after 1975, these books are collected in *Qaddafi's Green Book: An Unauthorized Edition*, edited by Henry M. Christman. Mohamed El-Khawas provides a more detailed analysis of the Third Universal Theory in *Qaddafi: His Ideology in Theory and Practice*. Mahmoud Mustafa Ayoub places the Third Universal Theory in a religious context in *Islam and the Third Universal Theory: The Religious Thought of Mu'ammar al-Qadhadhafi*.

The single most rewarding volume on the Libyan economy remains the study entitled *Libya: The Political Economy of Oil* (1996) by Judith Gurney. It builds on the earlier work of J. A. Allen in *Libya: The Experience of Oil*. On the oil industry, see *The Libyan Oil Industry* by Frank C. Waddams, *The Pricing of Libyan Crude Oil* by Shukri Mohammed Ghanem, and *Libya: Its Oil Industry and Economic System* by Abdul Amir Q. Kubbah. Aspects of development economics are discussed in *The Economic Development of Libya*, edited by Bichara Khader and Bashir El-Wifati. Various sectors of the Libyan economy are covered in *Social and Economic Development of Libya*, edited by E. G. H. Joffé and K. S. McLachlan, and *Planning and Development in Modern Libya*, edited by M. M. Buru, S. M. Ghanem, and K. S. McLachlan.

Ronald Bruce St John provides the most detailed examination to date of the prolonged, often tortured relationship between Libya and the United States in *Libya and the United States: Two Centuries of Strife* (2002). A broader survey of Libyan foreign policy, still valuable albeit dated, can be found in *Qaddafi's World Design: Libyan Foreign Policy, 1969–1987*, also by Ronald Bruce St John. Edward P. Haley focuses on contemporary Libyan foreign policy toward the United States in *Qaddafi and the United States since 1969*. Mahmoud G. El Warfally covers related ground from a totally different perspective in *Imagery and Ideology in U.S. Policy toward Libya, 1969–1982*. *Qaddafi, Terrorism, and the Origins of the U.S. Attack on Libya* by Brian L. Davis is also of interest. In *El Dorado Canyon: Reagan's Undeclared War with Qaddafi*, Joseph T. Stanik focuses on military operations between Libya and the United States in the 1980s.

Khalil I. Matar and Robert W. Thabit, in *Lockerbie and Libya*, provide a case study of the politics surrounding the 1988 bombing of Pan Am flight 103 over

Lockerbie, Scotland. In *Libya and the West: From Independence to Lockerbie*, Geoff Simons analyzes UN involvement in the domestic and international affairs of Libya. Finally, *Libya's Foreign Policy in North Africa* by Mary-Jane Deeb and *The Green and the Black: Qadhafi's Policies in Africa*, edited by René Lemarchand, explore often little-known but highly significant parameters of Libyan foreign policy in Africa. In contrast, Mohamed O'Bai Samura's *Libyan Revolution: Its Lessons for Africa* and Themba Sono's *Libya: The Vilified Revolution* are little more than apologies for the Qaddafi regime.

Current events in Libya are widely reported in the world press. In the United States, the *New York Times* and the *Washington Post* provide the most reliable, regular coverage, while in Great Britain the *Times* is recommended. The best Spanish newspapers to consult are *El País* and *Informaciones*, and there is no rival to *Le Monde* in the French press. A London-based weekly magazine, the *Middle East Economic Digest*, provides more in-depth analysis, as does the Paris-based weekly magazine *Jeune Afrique*. A variety of more scholarly journals can also be recommended, including *Libyan Studies*, published in London; the *Journal of Libyan Studies*, published in Oxford in 2000–2003; *Maghreb-Machrek*, published in Paris; and *The Middle East Journal* and *Middle East Policy*, published in Washington, D.C.

There are dozens of websites related to Libya available today, and the number grows each year. For current events, among the most reliable are www.libyadaily.com and www.allafrica.com. For official Libyan government positions and statements, see www.alfajraljadeedeng.com, www.algathafi.org, www.gaddaficharity.org, www.jamahiriyanews.com, www.jananews.com, and www.libya-un.org. For more general information, the following are recommended: www.libya-on-focus.com, www.libyaonline.com, www.libyanet.com, www.libyancentre.org, and www.mediterraneanco.com/libya.

The following bibliography has been broken down into subject categories to facilitate the location of desired materials. While many books contain information on more than one heading or subheading, they have usually been listed only once under the central subject they address. Edited volumes are typically listed only once, although occasionally chapters of special interest in an edited volume have been listed separately.

II. GENERAL

A. Bibliographies and Dictionaries

Alawar, Mohamed A., ed. *A Concise Bibliography of Northern Chad and Fezzan in Southern Libya*. Wisbech, U.K.: Arab Crescent, 1983.

Allan, J. A. *A Select Map and Air-Photo Bibliography of Libya with Special Reference to Coastal Libya*. London: Luzac, 1970.

Barbar, Aghil M. *Government and Politics in Libya, 1969–1978: A Bibliography*. Monticello, Ill.: Vance Bibliographies, 1979.

———. *Libya, 1969–1974: A Bibliography*. Washington, D.C.: Middle East Institute, 1974.

———. *The Population of Libya*. Monticello, Ill.: Vance Bibliographies, 1980.

———. *Public Administration in Libya: A Bibliography*. Monticello, Ill.: Vance Bibliographies, 1979.

———. *Urbanization in Libya*. Monticello, Ill.: Vance Bibliographies, 1977.

Beschorner, Natasha. *Bibliography of Libya, 1970–1990*. London: School of Oriental and African Studies, University of London and Society for Libyan Studies, 1990.

Ciarli, Stefano, and Keith McLachlan. "A Bibliographic Review: Studies of Libya's International Borders." *Libyan Studies* 27 (1996): 89–98.

Cricco, Massimiliano. "The Image of Colonel Qaddafi in American and British Documents (1969–1971)." *Journal of Libyan Studies* 3, no. 2 (Winter 2002): 32–40.

Harmon, R. B. *Administration and Government in Libya: A Selected Bibliography*. Monticello, Ill.: Vance Bibliographies, 1982.

Hill, Roy Wells. *A Bibliography of Libya*. Durham, U.K.: University of Durham, Department of Geography, 1959.

Howard, H. *The Middle East: A Selected Bibliography of Recent Works, 1970–1972 Supplement*. Washington, D.C.: Middle East Institute, 1972.

Landau, Jacob M. "Some Russian Publications on Libya." *Middle Eastern Studies* 15, no. 2 (May 1979): 280–82.

Lawless, Richard I., comp. *Libya*. World Bibliographical Series, vol. 79. Oxford: Clio, 1987.

Mattes, Hanspeter. "Revolutionary Libya in Western Research." *Journal of Libyan Studies* 3, no. 2 (Winter 2002): 70–78.

Megreisi, Youssef El-. "A Guide to a Selection of Manuscripts and Documents in the Public Record Office Relating to Libya." *Journal of Libyan Studies* 2, no. 2 (Winter 2001): 111–227.

St John, Ronald Bruce. *Historical Dictionary of Libya*. 3rd ed. Lanham, Md.: Scarecrow, 1998.

Santucci, J.-C., and M.-C. Gessay-Burgat. "The Economy of Libya: A Select Bibliography." In *The Economic Development of Libya*, ed. Bichara Khader and Bashir el-Wifati, 228–49. London: Croom Helm, 1987.

Schlüter, Hans. *Index Libycus: Bibliography of Libya, 1957–1969, with Supplementary Material, 1915–1956*. Boston: G. K. Hall, 1972.

Sjöström, Isabella W. "Note on the Contents and Accessibility of Some Italian Archives with Relevance to Libyan Studies." *Libyan Studies* 27 (1996): 85–87.

Vandewalle, Dirk. "Research Facilities and Document Collections in the Socialist People's Libyan Arab Jamahiriyah." *MESA Bulletin* 28, no. 1 (1994):
9–13.

Venuta, Pierluigi. "Libyan Studies on Italian Colonialism: Bibliographical and
Historiographical Considerations." *Journal of Libyan Studies* 2, no. 1 (Summer 2001): 48–60.

B. General Information and Interdisciplinary Studies

Audihert, Pierre. *Libye*. Paris: Éditions de Seuil, 1979.

Bailey, Donald M. "Photographs of Libya 2." *Libyan Studies* 27 (1996): 67–70.

Baldanetti, Anna, ed. *Modern and Contemporary Libya: Sources and Historiographies*. Rome: Istituto Italiano per L'Africa e L'Oriente, 2003.

Bates, Oric. *The Eastern Libyans: An Essay*. London: Frank Cass, 1970.

Bisson, Danielle, Jean Bisson, and Jacques Fontaine. *La Libye: A la découverte
d'un pays*. Paris: Éditions l'Harmattan, 1999.

Blunsun, Terence. *Libya: The Country and Its People*. London: Queen Anne,
1968.

Borglid, Kars-Ola. *Libyen*. Stockholm: Liberforlag, 1977.

Carpenter, John Allen, and James Hughes. *Libya*. Chicago: Children's Press,
1977.

Clarke, J. "Libya Takes Her Place in the World." *Geographical Magazine* 42
(November 1969): 87–91.

Copeland, Paul W. *The Land and People of Libya*. Philadelphia: J. B. Lippin-
cott, 1967.

Fergiani, Mohammad Bescir, comp. *The Libyan Jamahiriya*. London: Darf,
1983.

Gueneron, Hervé. *La Libye*. Paris: Presses Universitaires de France, 1976.

Habib, Henri. *Libya Past and Present*. 2nd ed. Valletta, Malta: Aedam Publishing, 1979.

Hajjaji, S A. *The New Libya: A Geographical, Social, Economic and Political
Study*. Tripoli: Government Printing Press, 1967.

Hardy, Paula, and Simon Clark. *Libya*. Richmond, U.K.: Zerzura Editions, supported by Condrill, 2002.

Kiker, Douglas. "Libya." *Atlantic Monthly* 225, no. 6 (June 1970): 30–38.

Libya. Ministry of Information and Culture. *This Is Libya*. Tripoli: n.p., 1968.

Mattes, Hanspeter. "Revolutionary Libya in Western Research." *Journal of
Libyan Studies* 3, no. 2 (Winter 2002): 70–78.

Murabet, Mohammed. *Facts about Libya*. Valletta, Malta: Progress Press, 1964.

Nafa, M. A. *Libya*. London: Arab Consultants, 1976.

Nelson, Harold D. *Libya: A Country Study*. 3rd ed. Washington, D.C.: GPO,
1979.

Owen, Roger. *Libya: A Brief Political and Economic Survey*. London: Oxford University Press, 1961.

Raoul-Duval, Claude. *Ciel de sable*. Paris: France-Empire, 1978.

Schliephake, Konrad. *Libyen: Wirtschaftliche und soziale Strukturen und Entwicklung*. Hamburg: Institut für Afrika-Kunde im Verbund der Stiftung Deutsches Übersee Institut, 1976.

Seale, Patrick. *The Hilton Assignment*. New York: Praeger, 1973.

Steer, George Lowther. *A Date in the Desert*. London: Hodder and Stoughton, 1939.

Vandewalle, Dirk, ed. *Qadhafi's Libya, 1969–1994*. New York: St. Martin's Press, 1995.

Vidergar, John J. *The Economic, Social and Political Development of Algeria and Libya*. Monticello, Ill.: Vance Bibliographies, 1977.

Wandell, Walt. *Rivers to the Sea: A Profile of Modern Libya*. Wiesbaden, West Germany: You and Europe Publications, 1966.

Wright, John L. *Libya: A Modern History*. Baltimore: Johns Hopkins University Press, 1982.

C. Guides and Yearbooks

Azema, James. *Libya Handbook*. Bath, U.K.: Footprint Handbooks, 2000.

Gandini, Jacques. *Libye du sud-est*. Calvisson: Éditions Jacques Gandini, 1992.

———. *Libye du sud-ouest: Le Fezzan*. Calvisson, France: Éditions Jacques Gandini, 1995.

Ham, Anthony. *Libya*. Melbourne: Lonely Planet, 2002.

Haynes, D. E. L. *An Archaeological and Historical Guide to the Pre-Islamic Antiquities of Tripolitania*. Tripoli: Antiquities Department of Tripolitania, 1959.

Joffé, E. G. H. [George]. "Libya." In *Tuttle Guide to the Middle East*, ed. Peter Sluggett and Marion Farouk-Sluggett, 161–81. Boston: Charles E. Tuttle, 1992.

Mazard, Béatrice. *La Libye*. Lyon: Éditions Xavier Lejeune, 1999.

McLachlan, Anne, and Keith McLachlan. *Egypt Handbook with Libya*. 2nd ed. Chicago: Passport Books, 1998.

Ward, Philip. *Sabratha: A Guide for Visitors*. Stoughton, Wis.: Oleander Press, 1970.

———. *Touring Libya: The Southern Provinces*. London: Faber and Faber, 1968.

———. *Tripoli: Portrait of a City*. Stoughton, Wis.: Oleander Press, 1969.

Wyman, P. *Leptis Magna, Sabratha, Oea*. London: Ginn, 1971.

D. Travel and Description

Alexander, F. G. *Wayfarers in the Libyan Desert*. New York: G. P. Putnam's Sons, 1912.

Amato, A. *Itinerari Fezzanesi*. Tripoli: n.p., 1932.

Bagnold, R. A. *Libyan Sands: Travels in a Dead World*. 1935. Reprint. London: Michael Haag, 1987.

Carl, L., and J. H. Petit. *Tefedest: A Journey to the Heart of Sahara*. London: Allen and Unwin, 1954.

Diole, P. *Dans le Fezzan inconnu*. Paris: A. Michel, 1956.

Eydoux, H. P. L. *L'Exploration du Sahara*. Paris: Éditions Gallimard, 1938.

Falls, J. C. Ewald. *Three Years in the Libyan Desert*. 1913. Reprint. London: DARF Publishers, 1985.

Holmboe, Knud. *Desert Encounter: An Adventurous Journey through Italian Africa*. London: George G. Harrap, 1936.

Jarvis, C. S. *Three Deserts*. London: J. Murray, 1936.

Kohl, Ines. "The Lure of the Sahara: Implications of Libya's Desert Tourism." *Journal of Libyan Studies* 3, no. 2 (Winter 2002): 56–69.

Marozzi, Justin. *South from Barbary: Along the Slave Routes of the Libyan Sahara*. London: Flamingo, 2002.

Missouri, Moftah. *La Libye des voyageurs (1812–1912)*. Lausanne: Favre, 2000.

Monod, Théodore, and Edmond Diemer. *Zerzura: L'oasis légendaire du desert Libyque*. Paris: Vents du Sable, 2000.

Pesco, A. *Colours of Libya: A Pictorial Book*. London: Oleander, 1972.

Pliez, Olivier. *Villes du Sahara: Urbanisation et urbanité dans la Fezzan libyen*. Paris: Éditions du Centre National de la Recherche Scientifique, 2003.

Preston, H. Lloyd, and D. Quincy Smith. *Tripolitania and Cirenaica: With Detailed Coast-wise Itineraries Auto-Circuits and Tourist Routes in the Interior*. Paris: Herbert Clark, 1930.

Sèbe, Alain, Berny Sèbe, and Daniel Richelet. *Redjem: Libye des grands espaces*. 2nd ed. Turin: Graf Art, 2000.

Thwaite, Anthony. *The Desert of Hesperides: An Experience of Libya*. London: Secker & Warburg, 1969.

Tondeur, Freddy. *Libye, royaume des sables*. Paris: Éditions Fernand Nathan, 1969.

Ward, Philip, and Angelo Pesce. *Motoring to Nalut*. Tripoli: Oasis Oil Company of Libya, 1970.

III. CULTURE

A. Archaeology and Prehistory

Adams, Neil. "Greek and Roman Inscriptions from Cyrene." *Libyan Studies* 34 (2003): 43–64.

———. "A Statue of Dionysos from the Sanctuary of Apollo at Cyrene." *Libyan Studies* 32 (2001): 87–91.

Applebaum, S. *Jews and Greeks in Ancient Cyrene.* Leiden: E. J. Brill, 1979.

Ashton, Sally-Ann. "A Preliminary Report on the Small Finds from Excavations at Lepcis Magna, 1994–1995." *Libyan Studies* 27 (1996): 11–15.

Ayoub, M. S. *Excavations at Germa, the Capital of the Garamantes.* Tripoli: Department of Antiquities, 1962.

———. *Excavations in Germa (Fezzan): Cemetery of Saniat Ben-Howidy.* Tripoli: Department of Antiquities, 1968.

———. *The Expedition of Cornelius Balbus, 19 B.C.* Tripoli: Department of Antiquities, 1968.

———. *Fezzan: A Short History.* Tripoli: Department of Antiquities, 1968.

———. *The Rise of Germa.* Tripoli: Department of Antiquities, 1968.

Bacchielli, Lidiano. "Pittura funeraria antica in Cirenaica." *Libyan Studies* 24 (1993): 77–116.

———. "Un santuario di frontiera, fra Polis e Chora." *Libyan Studies* 25 (1994): 45–59.

Bailey, Donald M. "Crowe's Tomb at Benghazi: A Postscript." *Libyan Studies* 19 (1988): 87–94.

———. "Photographs of Libya 1." *Libyan Studies* 26 (1995): 79–81.

———. "Some Beechey Plans of Buildings at Apollonia." *Libyan Studies* 12 (1981): 61–74.

Barich, Barbara E. "Rock Art and Archaeological Context: The Case of the Tadrart Acacus (Libya)." *Libyan Studies* 21 (1990): 1–8.

Barker, Graeme, ed. *Farming the Desert: The UNESCO Libyan Valleys Archaeological Survey.* Vol. 1: *Synthesis.* Paris: UNESCO Publishing; Tripoli: Department of Antiquities (S.P.L.A.J.); London: Society for Libyan Studies, 1996.

———. "From Classification to Interpretation: Libyan Prehistory, 1969–1989." *Libyan Studies* 20 (1989): 31–43.

———. "Prehistoric Rock Art in Tripolitania." *Libyan Studies* 17 (1986): 69–86.

Barnett, Tertia. "Rock-art, Landscape and Cultural Transition in the Wadi al-Ajal, Fazzan." *Libyan Studies* 33 (2002): 71–84.

Barton, Ian M. "Possible Sabrathan and Oean Amphora Stamps." *Libyan Studies* 27 (1996): 9–10.

Bentaher, Fuaad. "General Account of Recent Discoveries at Tocra." *Libyan Studies* 25 (1994): 231–43.

——. "Site d'un arc à Tokra et l'aménagement urbain de la ville." *Libyan Studies* 32 (2001): 95–106.

Berger, Friedrich. "More Tethering Stones." *Libyan Studies* 28 (1997): 27–28.

Boardman, John. "Reflections on the Greek Pottery Trade with Tocra." In *Libya in History*, ed. Fawzi F. Gadallah, 89–91. Benghazi: University of Libya, 1968.

"British Archaeology in Libya, 1943–1970." *Libyan Studies* 1 (1970): 6–11.

Brogan, Olwen. "First- and Second-Century Settlement in the Tripolitanian Pre-Desert." In *Libya in History*, ed. Fawzi F. Gadallah, 121–30. Benghazi: University of Libya, 1968.

Brogan, Olwen, and D. J. Smith. *Ghirza: A Libyan Settlement of the Roman Period*. Tripoli: Department of Antiquities of Tripolitania, 1984.

Burn, L. M. "Hellenistic Terracotta Figures of Cyrenaica: Greek Influences and Local Inspirations." *Libyan Studies* 25 (1994): 147–58.

Buttrey, Ted V. "Coins and Coinage at Euesperides." *Libyan Studies* 25 (1994): 137–45.

Buzaian, Ahmed. "Excavations at Tocra, 1985–1992." *Libyan Studies* 31 (2000): 59–102.

——. "Preliminary Report on Two Seasons of Excavations at Balagrae (al-Beida)." *Libyan Studies* 33 (2002): 125–31.

Buzaian, Ahmed, and John A. Lloyd. "Early Urbanism in Cyrenaica: New Evidence from Euesperides (Benghazi)." *Libyan Studies* 27 (1996): 129–52.

Caputo, Giacomo. *Le sculture del teatro di Leptis Magna*. Rome: L'Erma di Bretschneider, 1976.

Chamoux, François. "La Cyrénaïque, des origines a 321 A.C. d'après les fouilles et les travaux récents." *Libyan Studies* 20 (1989): 63–70.

——. "Sur quelques inscriptions grecques trovés à Apollonia de Cyrénaïque." In *Libya in History*, ed. Fawzi F. Gadallah, 45–51. Benghazi: University of Libya, 1968.

Chamoux, François, and Gilbert Hallier. "Un colombier en pierre de taille près d'Apollonia." *Libyan Studies* 25 (1994): 119–24.

Daniels, C. M. "Excavation and Fieldwork amongst the Garamantes." *Libyan Studies* 20 (1989): 45–61.

——. "The Garamantes." In *Geology, Archaeology and Prehistory of the Fezzan, Libya*, ed. W. Kanes, 31–52. Tripoli: Petroleum Exploration Society of Libya, 1969.

——. *The Garamantes of Southern Libya*. Stoughton, Wis.: Oleander Press, 1970.

——. "Garamantian Excavations (Germa), 1977." *Libyan Studies* 8 (1977): 5–7.

Dobias-Lalou, Catherine. "Langue et Politique: Á Quoi Sert le Dialecte dans la Cyrénaïque Romaine?" *Libyan Studies* 25 (1994): 245–50.

Dore, John N. "Is El Merj the Site of Ancient Barca? *Libyan Studies* 25 (1994): 265–74.

———. "ULVS [UNESCO Libyan Valleys Survey] XX: First Report on the Pottery." *Libyan Studies* 21 (1990): 9–17.

Dore, John N., and Nina Keay. *Excavations at Sabratha 1948–1951*. Vol. 11, *The Finds*. Part 1, *The Amphorae, Coarse Pottery and Building Materials*. Monograph No. 1. London: Society for Libyan Studies, 1989.

Dore, John N., and M. van der Veen. "ULVS [UNESCO Libyan Valleys Survey] XV: Radio-carbon Dates from the Libyan Valleys Survey." *Libyan Studies* 17 (1986): 65–68.

Edwards, David N. "The Archaeology of the Southern Fezzan and Prospects for Future Research." *Libyan Studies* 32 (2001): 49–66.

Fabbricotti, Emanuela. "Silphium in Ancient Art." *Libyan Studies* 24 (1993): 27–33.

———. "Statuette in calcare da Bu Senab." *Libyan Studies* 25 (1994): 219–30.

Fulford, M. G. "To East and West: The Mediterranean Trade of Cyrenaica and Tripolitania in Antiquity." *Libyan Studies* 20 (1989): 169–91.

Gilbertson, D. D., and N. W. T. Chisholm. "The UNESCO Libyan Valleys Survey XXVIII: Manipulating the Desert Environment: Ancient Walls, Floodwater Farming and Territoriality in the Tripolitanian Predesert of Libya." *Libyan Studies* 27 (1996): 17–52.

Gosline, Sheldon Lee. "Libyan Period Royal Burials in Context." *Libyan Studies* 26 (1995): 1–20.

Habicht, Ch. "Prosopograhica: Kyrene." *Libyan Studies* 27 (1996): 7–8.

Hayes, Peter P., and David J. Mattingly. "Preliminary Report on Fieldwork at Euesperides (Benghazi) in October 1994." *Libyan Studies* 26 (1995): 83–96.

Haynes, D. E. L. *The Antiquities of Tripolitania*. Tripoli: Department of Antiquuities, 1965.

Huskinson, Janet. *Roman Sculpture from Cyrenaica in the British Museum*. London: British Museum Publications, 1976.

Joly, F. *Lucerne del Museo di Sabratha*. Rome: L'Erma de Bretschneider, 1974.

Jones, G. D. B. "Town and City in Tripolitania: Studies in Origins and Development, 1969–1989." *Libyan Studies* 20 (1989): 91–106.

Kennet, D. "Pottery as Evidence for Trade in Medieval Cyrenaica." *Libyan Studies* 25 (1994): 275–85.

King, G. R. D. "Islamic Archaeology in Libya, 1969–1989." *Libyan Studies* 20 (1989): 193–207.

Laronde, Andre. "Le territoire de Taucheira." *Libyan Studies* 25 (1994): 23–29.

Lloyd, John A. "Urban Archaeology in Cyrenaica, 1969–1989: The Hellenistic, Roman and Byzantine Periods." *Libyan Studies* 20 (1989): 77–90.

Luni, M. "Il Forum—Caesareum di Cirene e la moderna riscoperta." *Libyan Studies* 25 (1994): 191–210.

Matthews, Kenneth D., Jr. *Cities in the Sand: Leptis Magna and Sabratha in Roman Africa.* Philadelphia: University of Pennsylvania Press, 1957.

Mattingly, David J. "Farmers and Frontiers: Exploiting and Defending the Countryside of Roman Tripolitania." *Libyan Studies* 20 (1989): 135–53.

——, ed. *Farming the Desert: The UNESCO Libyan Valleys Archaeological Survey.* Vol. 2, *Gazetteer and Pottery.* Paris: UNESCO Publishing; Tripoli: Department of Antiquities (S.P.L.A.J.); London: Society for Libyan Studies, 1996.

——. "Libyans and the Limes: Culture and Society in Roman Tripolitania." *Antiquité Africaines* 23 (1987): 71–94.

——. "Mapping Ancient Libya." *Libyan Studies* 25 (1994): 1–5.

Mattingly, David J., David Edwards, and John Dore. "Radiocarbon Dates from Fazzan, Southern Libya." *Libyan Studies* 33 (2002): 9–19.

McBurney, C. B. M. "Libyan Role in Prehistory." In *Libya in History*, ed. Fawzi F. Gadallah, 1–29. Benghazi: University of Libya, 1968.

Mohamed, Fadel Ali. "From the Memory of History: The Painted Room at Bardia." *Libyan Studies* 25 (1994): 287–91.

——. "The Horseman of Tobruk." *Libyan Studies* 28 (1997): 5–9.

Momono, S., et al. "Paleolithic Tools from Fezzan Province, Libya." *Kyoto University African Studies* 8 (1973): 167–82.

Mori, Fabrizio. "Prehistoric Saharan Art and Cultures in the Light of Discoveries in the Acacus Massif." In *Libya in History*, ed. Fawzi F. Gadallah, 31–39. Benghazi: University of Libya, 1968.

Mueller, Katja. "Dating the Ptolemaic City-Foundations in Cyrenaica: A Brief Note." *Libyan Studies* 35 (2004): 1–10.

Muzzolini, A. "Proposals for Updating the Rock-Drawing Sequence of the Acacus (Libya)." *Libyan Studies* 22 (1991): 7–30.

Paci, G. "Le iscrizioni in lingua latina della Cirenaica." *Libyan Studies* 25 (1994): 251–57.

Pesco, A., et al. *Pre-historic Rock Art of the Libyan Sahara.* Stoughton, Wis.: Oleander Press, 1974.

Presicce, Claudio Parisi. "La città dei re di Cirene." *Libyan Studies* 34 (2003): 9–24.

——. "La dea con il silfio e l'iconografia di Panakeia a Cirene." *Libyan Studies* 25 (1994): 85–100.

Rebuffat, R. "Notes sur le camp romain de Gholaia (Bu Njem)." *Libyan Studies* 20 (1989): 155–67.

Reynolds, Joyce M. "Inscriptions of Roman Cyrenaica." In *Libya in History*, ed. Fawzi F. Gadallah, 181–89. Benghazi: University of Libya, 1968.

——. "Twenty Years of Inscriptions." *Libyan Studies* 20 (1989): 117–26.

Sadawya, Awad M. "The Greek Settlement in Cyrenaica with Notes on Pottery Discovered There." In *Libya in History*, ed. Fawzi F. Gadallah, 93–98. Benghazi: University of Libya, 1968.

Shawesh, Abubaker Mohamed. "Traditional Settlement in the Oasis of Ghadames in the Libyan Arab Jamahiriya." *Libyan Studies* 26 (1995): 35–47.

Snape, Steven. "New Perspectives on Distant Horizons: Aspects of Egyptian Imperial Administration in Marmarica in the Late Bronze Age." *Libyan Studies* 34 (2003): 1–8.

Tagart, C. "A Glass Fish Beaker from Fezzan." *Libyan Studies* 13 (1982): 81–84.

Teichner, Felix. "Signa Venerandae Christianae Religionis: On the Conversion of Pagan Sanctuaries in the Dioceses of Africa and Ægyptus." *Libyan Studies* 27 (1996): 53–66.

Thorn, James Copland. "Reconstructing the Discoveries of Alan Rowe at Cyrene." *Libyan Studies* 25 (1994): 101–18.

———. "Warrington's 1827 Discoveries in the Apollo Sanctuary at Cyrene." *Libyan Studies* 24 (1993): 57–76.

Van der Veen, Marijke. "Garamantian Agriculture: The Plant Remains from Zinchecra, Fezzan." *Libyan Studies* 23 (1992): 7–39.

———. "The UNESCO Libyan Valleys Survey X: Botanical Evidence for Ancient Farming in the Pre-desert." *Libyan Studies* 16 (1985): 15–28.

Vickers, Michael, David Gill, and Maria Economou. "Euesperides: The Rescue of an Excavation." *Libyan Studies* 25 (1994): 125–36.

Vittozzi, Serena Ensoli. "L'iconografia e il culto di Aristeo a Cirene." *Libyan Studies* 25 (1994): 61–84.

Walda, Hafed M. "Lepcis Magna Excavations, Autumn 1995: Report on Surveying, Archaeology and Pottery." *Libyan Studies* 27 (1996): 125–27.

Walker, Susan. "Hadrian and the Renewal of Cyrene." *Libyan Studies* 33 (2002): 45–56.

———. "The Imperial Family as Seen in Cyrene." *Libyan Studies* 25 (1994): 167–84.

Wanis, Saleh. "A New Relief from Cyrene with a Libyan Scene." *Libyan Studies* 23 (1992): 41–43.

———. "A Scarab Seal from Cyrene." *Libyan Studies* 24 (1993): 35–36.

———. "Al-Waleed's Gold Dinar." *Libyan Studies* 22 (1991): 81–82.

Ward-Perkins, J. B. "Pre-Roman Elements in the Architecture of Roman Tripolitania." In *Libya in History*, ed. Fawzi F. Gadallah, 101–15. Benghazi: University of Libya, 1968.

Ward-Perkins, J. B., and R. G. Goodchild. "The Christian Antiquities of Tripolitania." *Archaeologia* 95 (1953): 1–84.

———. *Christian Monuments of Cyrenaica*. London: Society for Libyan Studies, 2003.

Welsby, Derek A. "The UNESCO Libyan Valleys Survey XXIV: A Late Roman and Byzantine Church at Souk el Awty in the Tripolitanian Pre-desert." *Libyan Studies* 22 (1991): 61–80.

White, Donald. "Before the Greeks Came: A Survey of the Current Archaeological Evidence for the Pre-Greek Libyans." *Libyan Studies* 25 (1994): 31–44.

Wilson, Andrew I., Paul Bennett, Ahmed Buzaian, Vanessa Fell, Ben Found, Kristian Göransson, Abbey Guinness, Jamal Hardy, Kerry Harris, Richard Helm, Alette Kattenberg, Estíbaliz Tébar Megías, Geoffrey Morley, Adrian Murphy, Keith Swift, Jessica Twyman, William Wootton, and Eleni Zimi. "Euesperides (Benghazi): Preliminary Report on the Spring 2004 Season." *Libyan Studies* 35 (2004): 149–90.

Wright, G. R. H. "A Funeral Offering near Euesperides." *Libyan Studies* 26 (1995): 21–26.

———. "The Martyrion by the City Wall at Apollonia: Its Structure and Form." *Libyan Studies* 24 (1993): 37–55.

———. "A Note on the Temple of Zeus at Cyrene and Its Re-erection." *Libyan Studies* 25 (1994): 185–90.

———. "Tombs at the Oasis of Jeghbub: An Exploration in 1955." *Libyan Studies* 28 (1997): 29–41.

B. Architecture

Aalund, F. *Ghadames: The Pearl of the Desert*. Tripoli: Architectural Conservation Planning in Libyan Arab Jamahiriya, 1987.

Abusbee, A. M. "The Churches of Cyrenaica: An Architectural and Art Historical Study." M.Litt. thesis, University of Newcastle, 1985.

Ahmed, S. "City of Ghadames." Ph.D. diss., University of Krakow, 1985.

Barbar, Ashil M. *Islamic Architecture in Libya*. Monticello, Ill.: Vance Bibliographies, 1979.

Cresti, Federico. "City and Territory in Libya during the Colonial Period: Sources and Research Documents." In *Modern and Contemporary Libya: Sources and Historiographies*, ed. Anna Baldinetti, 141–68. Rome: Istituto Italiano per L'Africa e L'Oriente, 2003.

Evans, J. Martin. "The Traditional House in the Oasis of Ghadames." *Libyan Studies* 7 (1976): 31–40.

Islamic Art and Architecture in Libya: Catalogue for the Exhibition. London: Libyan General Committee for Participation in the World of Islam Festival, 1975.

Kezeiri, S. K. "Here Today, Gone Tomorrow: The Problems of Deteriorating Historic Centres." *Libyan Studies* 16 (1985): 85–94.

Lafi, Nora, and Denis Bocquet. "Local Élites and Italian Town-Planning Procedures in Early Colonial Tripoli, 1911–1912." *Journal of Libyan Studies* 3, no. 1 (Summer 2002): 59–68.

Lars, E. *Ghadames: Structure foncière, organisation et structure social.* Lund, Sweden: Meddelard fran Lund Universitets Geografiska Institution, 1968.

Ramadan, A. M. *Reflections upon Islamic Architecture in Libya.* Tripoli: n.p., 1975.

Shawesh, A. M. "The Impact of Climate on Housing in the Libyan Desert: A Case Study of Ghadames City." M.I.H.Sc. thesis, University of Newcastle upon Tyne, 1992.

Walda, H. M., and S. Walker. "Ancient Art and Architecture in Tripolitania and Cyrenaica: New Publications, 1969–1989." *Libyan Studies* 20 (1989): 107–15.

——. "The Art and Architecture of Leptis Magna: Marble Origins by Isotopic Analysis." *Libyan Studies* 15 (1984): 81–92.

Ward-Perkins, J. B. "Pre-Roman Elements in the Architecture of Roman Tripolitania." In *Libya in History,* ed. Fawzi F. Gadallah, 101–16. Benghazi: University of Libya, 1968.

Welsby, Derek A. "ULVS [UNESCO Libyan Valleys Survey] XXV: The *Gsur* and Associated Settlements in the Wadi Umm el Kharab: An Architectural Survey." *Libyan Studies* 23 (1992): 73–99.

Wright, G. R. H. "Architectural Details from the Asklepeion at Balagrae (Beida)." *Libyan Studies* 23 (1992): 45–72.

C. Artisanry

Ciantar, Philip. "Continuity and Change in the Libyan Ma'luf Musical Tradition." *Libyan Studies* 34 (2003): 137–46.

El Mughrabi, Taher El Amin, Ali Mustafa Ramadan, and Ali Ammar El-Abani. *Shadows and Lights from Libyan Arab Republic.* Tripoli: Arabic House for Books, 1977.

Riley, J. A. "Islamic Wares from Ajdabiyah." *Libyan Studies* 13 (1982): 85–104.

——. "Pre-Islamic Pottery from Ajdabiyah." *Libyan Studies* 14 (1983): 138–42.

Ward, P. "Contemporary Art in Libya." *African Arts* (Summer 1971): 40–43.

D. Linguistics and Literature

Abdelkafi, Mohamed. *One Hundred Arabic Proverbs from Libya.* London: Vernon & Yates, 1968.

Aurayieth, Abdulhamid. "The Phonology of the Verb in Libyan Arabic." Ph.D. diss., University of Washington, 1982.

Elfitoury, Abubaker. "A Descriptive Grammar of Libyan Arabic." Ph.D. diss., Georgetown University, 1976.

Fagih, Ahmed. *Charles, Diana and Me, and Other Stories*. London: Kegan Paul International, 2000.

——. *Gardens of the Night: A Trilogy*. London: Quartet Books, 1995.

——. *Gazelles, and Other Plays*. London: Kegan Paul International, 2000.

——, ed. *Libyan Stories: Twelve Short Stories from Libya*. London: Kegan Paul International, 2000.

——. *Valley of Ashes*. London: Kegan Paul International, 2000.

——. *Who's Afraid of Agatha Christie? and Other Stories*. London: Kegan Paul International, 2000.

Garland, L. "L'Alphabet Libyque de Dougga." *Revue Occident Musulman Méditerranéen* 1–2 (1973): 361–68.

Jiyad, Mohammed Mossa. "A Linguistic Evaluative Study of the Textbooks Used to Teach English in Libya." Ph.D. diss., University of Texas, 1982.

Koni, Ibrahim Al-. *The Bleeding of the Stone*. New York: Interlink Books, 2002.

Owens, Jonathan. "The Syllable as Prosody: A Re-analysis of Syllabification in Eastern Libyan Arabic." *Bulletin of the School of Oriental and African Studies* 32, no. 2 (1980): 277–87.

Qaddafi, Muammar al-. *Escape to Hell, and Other Stories*. Montreal: Stanké, 1998.

Simon, Rachel. "Language Change and Sociopolitical Transformations: The Case of Nineteenth- and Twentieth-Century Libyan Jews." *Jewish History* 4, no. 1 (1989): 101–21.

——. "Literature as a Source for the History of Libyan Jewry during the Ottoman Period." In *New Horizons in Sephardic Studies*, ed. Yedida K. Stillman and George K. Zucker, 83–91. Albany: State University of New York Press, 1993.

Sraieb, Noureddine. "Introduction à la connaissance de la littérature libyenne contemporaine." In *La Libye nouvelle: Rupture el continuité*, ed. G. Alblergoni et al., 231–58. Paris: Éditions du Centre National de la Recherche Scientifique, 1975.

Ward, Philip. *Maps on the Ceiling: Libyan Poems*. Stoughton, Wis.: Oleander Press, 1972.

IV. ECONOMY

A. General

Agnaia, Almehdi A. "Assessment of Management Training Needs and Selection for Training: The Case of Libyan Companies." *International Journal of Manpower* 17, no. 3 (1996): 31–51.

Allan, J. A. "Changes in the Economic Use of Land in the Vicinity of Tripoli." Ph.D. diss., University of London, 1971.

——. "Libya Accommodates to Lower Oil Revenues: Economic and Political Adjustments." *International Journal of Middle East Studies* 15, no. 3 (August 1983): 377–85.

——. *Libya since Independence*. London: Croom Helm, 1982.

Allan, J. A., K. S. McLachlan, and M. M. Buru, eds. *Libya: State and Region, a Study of Regional Evolution*. London: SOAS Centre of Near and Middle Eastern Studies, 1989.

Almhdie, Abdoulhakem, and Stephen M. Nyambegera. "HRM in Libya." In *Managing Human Resources in Africa*, ed. Ken Kamoche, 169–82. New York: Routledge, 2004.

Altunisik, Meliha Benli. "External vs. Internal Debate Revisited: The Political Economy of Economic Reform Policies in Libya." Ph.D. diss., Boston University, 1995.

Amin, G. *The Modernization of Poverty*. Leiden: E. J. Brill, 1974.

Burgat, François. "The Libyan Economy in Crisis." In *The Economic Development of Libya*, ed. Bichara Khader and Bashir el-Wifati, 213–27. London: Croom Helm, 1987.

Buru, M. M., S. M. Ghanem, and K. S. McLachlan. *Planning and Development in Modern Libya*. London: Menas Press, 1982.

Dalton, W. "Economic Change and Political Continuity in a Saharan Oasis Community (Saw-Khah, al-Jufrah)." *Man* 8, no. 2 (June 1973): 266–84.

Fulford, M. G. "To East and West: The Mediterranean Trade of Cyrenaica and Tripolitania in Antiquity." *Libyan Studies* 20 (1989): 169–91.

Ghanem, Shukri M. "The Libyan Economy before Independence." In *Social and Economic Development of Libya*, ed. E. G. H. Joffé and K. S. McLachlan, 141–59. London: Menas Press, 1982.

Glavanis, Pandeli. "State and Labour in Libya." In *North Africa: Contemporary Politics and Economic Development*, ed. Richard Lawless and Allan Findlay, 120–49. London: Croom Helm and St. Martin's Press, 1984.

Joffé, E. G. H., and K. S. McLachlan, eds. *Social and Economic Development of Libya*. London: Menas Press, 1982.

Khader, Bichara, and Bashir el-Wifati, eds. *The Economic Development of Libya*. London: Croom Helm, 1987.

Mabro, Robert. "La Libye, un état rentier?" *Project* 39 (November 1969): 1090–1111. Reprinited in *Problèmes Economiques* (January 1, 1970): 2–27.

Mallakh, R. El. "The Economics of Rapid Growth: Libya." *Middle East Journal* 23, no. 3 (Summer 1969): 308–20.

Maouche, M. "Libye nouvelle aux portes de l'avenir." *Revolution Africaine* 358 (7 January 1971): i–xvi.

Payne, Rhys. "Economic Crisis and Policy Reform in the 1980s." In *Polity and Society in Contemporary North Africa*, ed. I. William Zartman and William Mark Habeeb, 139–67. Boulder, Colo.: Westview Press, 1993.

Souriau, Christiane. *Libye: L'économie des femmes*. Paris: Éditions L'Harmattan, 1986.

Terterov, Marat, and Jonathan Wallace, eds. *Doing Business with Libya*. 2nd ed. London: Kogan Page, 2004.

Vandewalle, Dirk. "Libya at Fifty: The (Mis) Fortunes of a Rentier State." *Journal of Libyan Studies* 2, no. 2 (Winter 2001): 65–76.

Wedley, W. "Libya: Super-Rich Labor-Poor." *Columbia Journal of World Business* 9, no. 2 (1974): 64–73.

Zayd, Mohammed. *Economic Transformation in the Jamahiriya*. Tripoli: n.p., 1982.

B. Agriculture and Pastoral Nomadism

"Agricultural Development in Libya after Oil." *African Affairs* 75 (July 1976): 331–48.

Allan, J. A. "Agricultural Development in Libya since Independence." In *Northern Africa: Islam and Modernization*, ed. Michael Brett. London: Frank Cass, 1973.

——. "Drought in Libya: Some Solutions Available to an Oil-Rich Government." *African Affairs* 73, no. 291 (April 1974): 152–58.

——. "Kufrah Agricultural Schemes." *Geographical Journal* 142 (March 1976): 39–56.

——. *Libya: Agriculture and Economic Development*. London: Frank Cass, 1973.

——. "Libyan Agriculture since Oil: Problems and Achievements." *Maghreb Review* 1, no. 1 (June–July 1976): 7–11.

——. "Management of Agricultural Resources in Coastal Libya." *Maghreb Review* 5, no. 5–6 (September–December 1980): 104–14.

——. "Managing Agricultural Resources in Libya: Recent Experience." *Libyan Studies* 10 (1979): 17–28.

——. "Should Libyan Agriculture Absorb Further Investment?" In *Planning and Development in Modern Libya*, ed. M. M. Buru, S. M. Ghanem, and K. S. McLachlan, 151–57. London: Menas Press, 1985.

——. "Some Recent Developments in Libyan Agriculture." *Middle East Economic Papers* (Beirut) (1969): 1–17.

——. "Water for Agriculture in the 1990s: Another Phase in Libya's Agricultural Development." In *The Economic Development of Libya*, ed. Bichara Khader and Bashire el-Wifati, 124–33. London: Croom Helm, 1987.

Allan, J. A., and K. S. McLachlan. "Libyan Agricultural Development since Independence." *African Affairs* 75, no. 300 (1976): 331–48.

Allan, J. A., K. S. McLachlan, and E. T. Penrose, eds. *Libya: Agriculture and Economic Development*. London: Frank Cass, 1973.

Atkinson, Ken. "Libya's Soil Resources and Their Potential for Sustained Agricultural Production." In *The Economic Development of Libya*, ed. Bichara Khader and Bashir el-Wifati, 134–56. London: Croom Helm, 1987.

Ballico, Petro. *L'opera di avvaloramento agricolo e zooternico della Tripolitania e della Cirenaica*. Rome: Abete, 1971.

Benkhail, A. S. "The Socio-Economic Impacts of Wadi Irrigation Projects: The Case of Wadi Darnah/Al Fatayah Scheme, Libya." Ph.D. diss., Clark University, 1985.

Benzabih, Hosney A. "Developing Trends of Farm/Rangeland Resources in the Eastern Zone of Libya." In *Planning and Development in Modern Libya*, ed. M. M. Buru, S. M. Ghanem, and K. S. McLachlan, 130–37. London: Menas Press, 1985.

Bukechiem, A. A. "The Management of Resources Use in Semi-Arid Lands: A Case Study of Agricultural Development in Jebel El Akhdar Region, North East Libya." Ph.D. diss., University of Newcastle upon Tyne, 1987.

——. "Utilisation of Groundwater in Jebel el Akhdar, North-East Libya, as a Basis of Agricultural Improvement with Special Emphasis on the El Marj Plain." *Libyan Studies* 24 (1993): 121–42.

Buroni, N. "Libya: Easy Oil, Difficult Agriculture." *Agricultural Forum* 12, no. 2 (February 1971): 63–67.

Buru, Mukhtar M. "The Tripoli Agglomeration: Land Use Changes and Land Use Options." In *Planning and Development in Modern Libya*, ed. M. M. Buru, S. M. Ghanem, and K. S. McLachlan, 110–29. London: Menas Press, 1985.

El Faedy, Mahjous Attia. "Agricultural Development in a Petroleum-based Economy: The Libyan Case." Ph.D. diss., University of Utah, 1982.

Hajjaji, Salem A. *The Agricultural Development Plans in the Socialist People's Libyan Arab Jamahiriya and the Five-Year Agricultural Transformation Plan (1976–1980)*. Tripoli: People's Establishment for Publishing, Distribution, Advertising and Printing, 1978.

Hill, R. W. "Some Problems of Economic Geography in Northern Tripolitania: A Study of Agriculture and Irrigation on the Jefara Plain." Ph.D. diss., University of Durham, 1960.

Lalevie, D., M. A. Schmeyla, and E. M. Lofevic. *Agriculture in Libya and a Plan for Its Development*. Tripoli: n.p., 1966.

——. *Importance and Feasibility of the Establishment of Large-Scale Modern Agro-Industrial Units in the Libyan Arab Republic*. Tripoli: n.p., 1974.

Laronde, A. "La vie agricole en Libye jusqu'à l'arrivée des Arabes." *Libyan Studies* 20 (1989): 127–34.

Libya. Ministry of Agriculture. *Report of Work of Agrarian Reform Development for the Year 1979*. Tripoli: Secretariat of Agriculture, 1979.

Marghani, Abdulkrim Mohamed Al-. "Libyan Settlements and Migration Adjustment." Ph.D. diss., Colorado State University, 1982.

Mattingly, D. J. "Farmers and Frontiers: Exploiting and Defending the Countryside of Roman Tripolitania." *Libyan Studies* 20 (1989): 135–53.

McLachlan, Keith. "The Role of Indigenous Farming in the Agrarian Structure of Tripolitania in the Nineteenth and Twentieth Centuries." In *Planning and Development in Modern Libya*, ed. M. M. Buru, S. M. Ghanem, and K. S. McLachlan, 33–45. London: Menas Press, 1985.

——. "Strategies for Agricultural Development in Libya." In *Libya since Independence*, ed. J. A. Allan, 9–24. London: Croom Helm, 1982.

Meheshi, Abdelkader Mostafa El. "The Transformation of Libyan Agriculture: The Impact of Oil Revenues on Agriculture of a Developing Country." Ph.D. diss., University of California, Riverside, 1980.

Najm, Mahmoud Abdalla. "Agricultural Land Use in the Benghazi Area, Libya: A Spatial Analysis of Cultural Factors Affecting Crop and Livestock Patterns." Ph.D. diss., Michigan State University, 1982.

Saber, Mabrouk Mohamed. "Land Settlement in the Libyan Sahara: The Kuira Settlement Project." Ph.D. diss., University of Kentucky, 1983.

Schliephake, Konrad. "Libyan Agriculture: Natural Constraints and Aspects of Development." *Maghreb Review* 5, nos. 2–4 (March–August 1980): 51–56.

Van der Veen, Marijke. "Garamantian Agriculture: The Plant Remains from Zinchecra, Fezzan." *Libyan Studies* 23 (1992): 7–39.

Wifati, Bashir M. el-. "Agricultural Development and Its Future in Libya." In *The Economic Development of Libya*, ed. Bichara Khader and Bashir el-Wifati, 157–82. London: Croom Helm, 1987.

——. "Some Socio-economic Considerations in the Bedouins' Agricultural Settlement (an Example from Libya)." Ph.D. diss., University of Missouri–Columbia, 1977.

Zagalla, Faisal Abdulazez. "Environmental Conduciveness for Building Rural Cooperative Institutions: The Case of KSP, Kufra, Libya." Ph.D. diss., Colorado State University, 1982.

C. Communications and Transport

Brandt, E. D. *Railways of North Africa: The Railway System of the Maghreb—Algeria, Tunisia, Morocco, and Libya.* Newton Abbot, U.K.: David & Charles, 1971.

Doxiadis Associates. *Transport in Libya: A General Survey and Study of Means of Communications.* Tripoli: Ministry of Planning and Development, 1965.

Elazzabi, Abulgasim M. "Transport and Investment in the Libyan Jamahiriya, 1963–1980." In *Libya since Independence*, ed. J. A. Allan, 92–100. London: Croom Helm, 1982.

———. "Transport Development in Libya." In *Libya: State and Region, a Study of Regional Evolution*, ed. J. A. Allan, K. S. McLachlan, and M. M. Buru, 173–78. London: SOAS Centre of Near and Middle Eastern Studies, 1989.

Harris, F. Martin, and Voorhees Associates. *Libyan Transportation Planning Study.* Tripoli: Secretariat of Communications and Marine Transport, 1985.

Marghani, Amin B. D. "Air Transport in Libya, 1951 to the Present Day." In *Planning and Development in Modern Libya*, ed. M. M. Buru, S. M. Ghanem, and K. S. McLachlan, 194–203. London: Menas Press, 1985.

———. "Politics and Aspects of the Development of Transport Systems in Libya: A Geographical Analysis." Ph.D. diss., University of London, 1987.

———. "Strategic Considerations and the Extent of the Domestic Air Network in Libya." In *Libya: State and Region, a Study of Regional Evolution*, ed. J. A. Allan, K. S. McLachlan, and M. M. Buru, 179–92. London: SOAS Centre of Near and Middle Eastern Studies, 1989.

D. Development

Abdussalam, Abderrahim Saleh. "External Forces, Economic Development and Regional Inequality in Libya." Ph.D. diss., University of Oklahoma, 1983.

Abohobiel, Abdulfattah Abdulsalam. "An Econometric Model for the Libyan Economy, 1962–1977." Ph.D. diss., Indiana University, 1983.

Abusneina, Mohamed Abduljalil. "Development Alternatives in a Surplus Economy with Skilled Labor Constraints: The Case of Libya." Ph.D. diss., Indiana University, 1981.

Alawar, Mohamed. "Fezzan: Population, Development and Economic Change." In *Planning and Development in Modern Libya*, ed. M. M. Buru, S. M. Ghanem, and K. S. McLachlan, 91–109. London: Menas Press, 1985.

Babour, El-. "Population Change and the Hierarchy of Central Places in North-Eastern Libya, 1954–1973." In *Libya: State and Region, a Study of Regional Evolution*, ed. J. A. Allan, K. S. McLachlan, and M. M. Buru, 137–49. London: SOAS Centre of Near and Middle Eastern Studies, 1989.

Bait-Elmal, Mohamed Abdalla. "The Role of Investment Tax Credit and Accelerated Depreciation in Stimulating More Investment: The USA Case and Its Implications to the Libyan Income Tax System." D.B.A. thesis, University of Kentucky, 1978.

Baryun, Nuri Abd. "Money and the Balance of Payments in an Oil-Producing Country: The Case of Libya." Ph.D. diss., Oklahoma State University, 1980.

Benkat, Omar Mukhtar. "Forecasting Models for Commercial Bank Asset Management: The Case of Libya." Ph.D. diss., University of Cincinnati, 1981.

Birks, Stace, and Clive Sinclair. "Libya: Problems of a Rentier State." In *North Africa: Contemporary Politics and Economic Development*, ed. Richard Lawless and Allan Findlay, 241–75. London: Croom Helm and St. Martin's Press, 1984.

Busniena, Saddeg M. "A Comparative Study of the Need for Achievement among Managers of Public vs. Private Organizations in the Libyan Arab Republic." Ph.D. diss., Louisiana State University, 1977.

Deeb, Mary-Jane. "Libya's Economic Development, 1961–1986: Social and Political Implications." *Maghreb Review* 12, no. 1–2 (January–April 1987).

Elhuni, Mustafa Salhen. "Economic Growth Constraints: The Cases of Libya and Other North African Countries." Ph.D. diss., Oklahoma State University, 1978.

Elmaihub, Saleh H. "Public Investment in a Capital Surplus Country: The Case of Libya." Ph.D. diss., Colorado State University, 1977.

Fakhery, Mahmoud Said El. "A Simulation Model of an Oil-based Economy: The Case of the Socialist People's Libyan Arab Jamahiriya." Ph.D. diss., University of Colorado, 1978.

Farley, Rawle. *Planning for Development in Libya: The Exceptional Economy in the Developing World*. New York: Praeger, 1971.

Fathaly, Omar I., and Fathi S. Abusedra. "The Impact of Socio-political Change on Economic Development in Libya." *Middle Eastern Studies* 16 (1980): 225–35.

Gazzo, Yves. *Pétrole et développement: Le cas libyen*. Paris: Económica, 1980.

Gehaw, Abdelsalam Ali El. "An Analysis of Effectiveness Auditing for Governmental Programs in the United States and Sweden with Application to Libya." Ph.D. diss., University of Missouri, 1980.

Ghanem, Shukri M. "Changing Planning Policies in Libya." In *Planning and Development in Modern Libya*, ed. M. M. Buru, S. M. Ghanem, and K. S. McLachlan, 220–29. London: Menas Press, 1985.

Higgins, Benjamin Howard. *The Economic and Social Development of Libya*. New York: n.p., 1953.

———. "Entrepreneurship in Libya." *Middle East Journal* 11, no. 3 (Autumn 1957): 319–23.

Kezeiri, Saad. "The Role of the State and the Development of Libya's Urban Centres." In *Libya: State and Region, a Study of Regional Evolution*, ed. J. A. Allan, K. S. McLachlan, and M. M. Buru, 151–71. London: SOAS Centre of Near and Middle Eastern Studies, 1989.

Kezeiri, Saad, and Richard Lawless. "Economic Development and Spatial Planning in Libya." In *The Economic Development of Libya*, ed. Bichara Khader and Bashir el-Wifati, 1–24. London: Croom Helm, 1987.

Libya. Ministry of Planning and Development. Census and Statistical Department. *Five-Year Economic and Social Development Plan, 1963–1968*. Tripoli: n.p., 1963.

Malhauf, Mohamed Farag. "The Jamahiriya Model in Planning, with Some Indication of Social and Economic Development and Change in Libyan Arab Society." In *The Economic Development of Libya*, ed. Bichara Khader and Bashir el-Wifati, 25–36. London: Croom Helm, 1987.

Mallakh, Ragei El. "The Economics of Rapid Growth: Libya." *Middle East Journal* 23, no. 3 (Summer 1969): 308–20.

McLachlan, Keith. "The Libyan South: Background to Current Developments and Future Outlook." In *The Economic Development of Libya*, ed. Bichara Khader and Bashir el-Wifati, 37–57. London: Croom Helm, 1987.

———. "Resources and Development in the al-Khalij Region of Libya." *Libyan Studies* 1 no. 1 (1980): 95–99.

Moustafa, Salem Mohamed. "An Economic Model of the Libyan Economy, 1962–1975." Ph.D. diss., Southern Methodist University, 1979.

Pinches, Christine Rider. "Economic Development: The Need for an Alternative Approach." *Economic Development and Cultural Change* 26 (October 1977): 136–46.

Pliez, Olivier. "Sebha, l'émergence d'une ville-carrefour dans le Sahara libyen." *Maghreb-Machrek* 170 (October–December 2000): 52–59.

Sankari, Farouk A. "Oil, Human Resources, and the Development Syndrome: The Libyan Case." *Studies in Comparative International Development* 16 (Spring 1981): 53–74.

Segal, M. "Libya's Economic Potential." *World Today* 28, no. 10 (October 1972): 445–51.

Sharif, Younis Hassan El. "An Empirical Investigation of Libyan Professional Accounting Services." Ph.D. diss., University of Missouri, 1978.

Watkins, W. S., and R. V. Price. "A Case Study of Regional Planning in Libya." In *Planning and Development in Modern Libya*, ed. M. M. Buru, S. M. Ghanem, and K. S. McLachlan, 204–19. London: Menas Press, 1985.

Zubi, Ramadam Yousif. "The Important Role of Manpower Planning, Education and Training in the Economic Development of Libya." *Libyan Studies* 23 (1992): 107–30.

E. Finance and Commerce

Abdussalam, Ali. "The Impact of Recent Economic Changes in Libya on Monetary Aggregates." In *Planning and Development in Modern Libya*, ed. M. M. Buru, S. M. Ghanem, and K. S. McLachlan, 77–90. London: Menas Press, 1985.

Adham, Mazen Abdussalam. "The Role of Money and Banking in the Libyan Development Process." Ph.D. diss., University of Colorado, 1979.

Baryun, Nuri A. "The Development of the Banking System in Libya." In *The Economic Development of Libya*, ed. by Bichara Khader and Bashir el-Wifati, 183–94. London: Croom Helm, 1987.

Boubakri, Hassen. "Exchanges transfrontaliers et commerce parallèle aux frontiers tuniso-libyennes." *Maghreb-Machrek* 170 (October–December 2000): 39–51.

Ghumati, Salem Meftah el Hula El. "Comparative Structural Analysis, Libyan Banking System vs. Banking System within the U.S." Ph.D. diss., Saint Louis University, 1979.

Green, Andrew Wilson, and Philip M. DeMoss. *The Money and Banking System of Libya*. Westchester, N.Y.: Green, 1977.

International Trade Center. *Libya: Market for Selected Manufactured Products for Developing Countries*. Geneva: n.p., 1969.

Joffé, E. G. H. [George]. "Trade and Migration between Malta and the Barbary States, 1835–1911." In *Planning and Development in Modern Libya*, ed. M. M. Buru, S. M. Ghanem, and K. S. McLachlan, 1–32. London: Menas Press, 1985.

Libya Commercial Law Service. *Libya*. Gainesville, Fla.: n.p., 1971.

Masri, Zienab Ismael El. "The Demand for Money in Developing Economies: The Case of Libya, Saudi Arabia and Iraq." Ph.D. diss., University of Missouri, 1962.

Oreibi, Misbah. "Foreign Trade and Development Policy in Libya." In *Planning and Development in Modern Libya*, ed. M. M. Buru, S. M. Ghanem, and K. S. McLachlan, 57–76. London: Menas Press, 1985.

Sharif, Ahmed Saaid El. "A Structural Model of the Monetary Sector of Libya." Ph.D. diss., Indiana University, 1979.

Wilson, Andrew. "Commerce and Industry in Roman Sabratha." *Libyan Studies* 30 (1999): 29–52.

F. Fisheries

Anderson, Ewan W., and Gerald H. Blake. "The Libyan Fishing Industry." In *Libya since Independence*, ed. J. A. Allan, 73–91. London: Croom Helm, 1982.

Blake, G. H. "The 1982 Convention on the Law of the Sea: Some Implications for Libya." *Libyan Studies* 15 (1984): 129–35.

———. "State and Region in Maritime Libya: A Framework for Planning and Management." In *Libya: State and Region, a Study of Regional Evolution*, ed. J. A. Allan, K. S. McLachlan, and M. M. Buru, 127–35. London: SOAS Centre of Near and Middle Eastern Studies, 1989.

G. Industry

Barker, Paul. "The Development of Libyan Industry." In *Libya since Independence*, ed. J. A. Allan, 55–71. London: Croom Helm, 1982.

Ewing, A. F., et al. "Industrial Co-ordination in Algeria, Libya, Morocco and Tunisia." In *Man, State and Society in the Contemporary Maghrib*, ed. I. William Zartman, 475–92. London: Pall Mall, 1973.

Jehaimi, Taher el-. "Industrial Development in Libya around the Year 2000." In *The Economic Development of Libya*, ed. Bichara Khader and Bashir el-Wifati, 73–80. London: Croom Helm, 1987.

Mehdawi, Mohamed M. El. "A Geographical Analysis of Industry in Libya with Special Reference to Industrial Location." Ph.D. diss., University of Durham, 1975.

Rifai, Mukhtar Mahmoud. "Interindustry and Programming Analysis: The Case of Libya." Ph.D. diss., University of Nebraska, 1981.

H. Labor

Abusneina, M. A. "Development Alternatives in a Surplus Economy with Skilled Labour Constraints: The Case of Libya." Ph.D. diss., Indiana University, 1981.

Belazi, O. M. "Human Resources Development: The Case of Libya." Ph.D. diss., Texas Tech University, 1973.

Bhairi, A. M. "Foreign Labour in Libya." Ph.D. diss., Oklahoma State University, 1981.

Birks, J. S., and C. A. Sinclair. "The Libyan Arab Jamahiriya: Labour Migration Sustains Dualistic Development." *Maghreb Review* 4, no. 3 (May–June 1979): 95–102.

Glavanis, Pandeli. "Nature of the State with Reference to Social Classes: Peripheral Capitalism and Labour in the Socialist People's Libyan Arab Jamahiriya." In *Social and Economic Development of Libya*, ed. E. G. H. Joffé and K. S. McLachlan, 281–93. London: Menas Press, 1982.

———. "State and Labour in Libya." In *North Africa: Contemporary Politics and Economic Development*, ed. Richard Lawless and Allan Findlay, 120–49. London: Croom Helm, 1984.

Gummed, Amer Ali. "High-Level Manpower Requirements for Economic Development in Libya." Ph.D. diss., Oklahoma State University, 1979.

Huni, A. M. El-. "Determinants of Female Labour Force Participation: The Case of Libya." Ph.D. diss., Oklahoma State University, 1978.

Mostafa, M. "Skilled Labor in Economic Development: The Libyan Case." M.A. thesis, University of California, 1972.

Norman, John. *Labor and Politics in Libya and Arab Africa*. New York: Bookman Associates, 1965.

Ramadan, A. K. "Migration, Labour Supply and Regional Development in Libya." Ph.D. diss., University of Oklahoma, 1979.

I. Mining and Minerals

Goudarzi, Gus Hossein. *Geology and Mineral Resources of Libya—A Reconnaissance*. Washington, D.C.: GPO, 1970.

Gurdon, Charles G. "A Preliminary Assessment of the Distribution of Non-hydrocarbon Minerals in Libya." In *Planning and Development in Modern Libya*, ed. M. M. Buru, S. M. Ghanem, and K. S. McLachlan, 178–93. London: Menas Press, 1985.

J. Petroleum

Adelman, M. "Politics, Economics and World Oil." *American Economic Review* 64, no. 2 (May 1974): 58–67.

Akins, J. "The Oil Crisis: This Time the Wolf Is Here." *Foreign Affairs* 51, no. 3 (April 1973): 162–90.

Allan, J. A. *Libya: The Experience of Oil*. London: Croom Helm, 1981.

———. "Libya Accommodates to Lower Oil Revenues: Economic and Political Adjustments." *International Journal of Middle East Studies* 15, no. 3 (August 1983): 377–85.

Amin, G. "New Trends in Oil Agreements and Their Impact on the Economics of Arab Oil." *Journal of the Middle East* 1 (January 1974): 75–91.

Barker, Paul, and Keith McLachlan. "Development of the Libyan Oil Industry." In *Libya since Independence*, ed. J. A. Allan, 37–54. London: Croom Helm, 1982.

Bernini, Simone. "Il petrolio nella storia del Regno di Libia." *Journal of Libyan Studies* 2, no. 2 (Winter 2001): 89–110.

Brown, R. W. "A Spatial View of Oil Developments in the Desert: Libya in the First Decade, 1955–1965." Ph.D. diss., Columbia University, 1969.

Couland, J., et al. "Pétrole et indépendance nationale." *Economie et Politique* 199 (February 1971): 25–44.

Ghanem, Shukri Mohammed. "The Libyan Role within OPEC." In *Planning and Development in Modern Libya*, ed. M. M. Buru, S. M. Ghanem, and K. S. McLachlan, 158–77. London: Menas Press, 1985.

——. "The Oil Industry and the Libyan Economy: The Past, the Present and the Likely Future." In *The Economic Development of Libya*, ed. Bichara Khader and Bashir el-Wifati, 58–72. London: Croom Helm, 1987.

——. *The Pricing of Libyan Crude Oil*. Valletta, Malta: Adams Publishing, 1975.

Gurney, Judith. *Libya: The Political Economy of Oil*. Oxford: Oxford University Press, 1996.

Khader, Bichara. "Libyan Oil and Money." In *The Economic Development of Libya*, ed. Bichara Khader and Bashir el-Wifati, 195–212. London: Croom Helm, 1987.

Kubbah, Abdul Amir Q. *Libya: Its Oil Industry and Economic System*. Beirut: Rihani Press, 1964.

Mahmud, Mustafa Bakar, and Alex Russell. "An Analysis of Libya's Revenue per Barrel from Crude Oil Upstream Activities, 1961–1993." *OPEC Review* 23, no. 3 (September 1999): 213–49.

McLachlan, K. "Libya's Oil Resources." *Libyan Studies* 20 (1989): 243–50.

Mehren, Robert B. von, and P. Nicholas Kourides. "International Arbitrations between States and Foreign Private Parties: The Libyan Nationalization Cases." *American Journal of International Law* 75, no. 3 (July 1981): 476–552.

Portman, H. "Oil and Oasis in Libya." *Swiss Review of World Affairs* 20, no. 4 (1970): 11–15.

Segal, Aaron. "Libya's Economic Potential." *World Today* 28, no. 10 (October 1972): 445–51.

Talha, Larbi. "Le pétrole et l'économie libyenne." *Annuaire de l'Afrique du Nord* 5 (1966): 153–234.

United States. Library of Congress. Foreign Affairs Division. *Chronology of the Libyan Oil Negotiations, 1970–1971*. Washington, D.C.: GPO, 1974.

Vigier, A. "Le pétrole: Après Teheran, Tripoli et Alger." *Economie et Politique* 202 (May 1971): 79–90.

Waddams, Frank C. *The Libyan Oil Industry*. London: Croom Helm, 1980.

Zaqaar, H. "The Libyan Oil Industry and Its Role in the National Economy." M.A. thesis, Howard University, 1970.

K. Trade

Boardman, John. "Reflections on the Greek Pottery Trade with Tocra." In *Libya in History*, ed. Fawzi F. Gadallah, 89–91. Benghazi: University of Libya, 1968.

Elfeituri, Attia E. "Import Demand and Economic Growth in Libya." Ph.D. diss., University of Pittsburgh, 1977.

Johnson, Marion. "Calico Caravans: The Tripoli-Kano Trade after 1880." *Journal of African History* 17, no. 1 (1976): 95–118.

Oreibi, Misbah I. "Foreign Trade and Development Policy in Libya." In *Planning and Development in Modern Libya*, ed. M. M. Buru, S. M. Ghanem, and K. S. McLachlan, 57–76. London: Menas Press, 1985.

Simon, Rachel. "The Trans-Saharan Trade and Its Impact on the Jewish Community of Libya in the Late Ottoman Period." In *Proceedings of the American Historical Association, 1987*. Ann Arbor, Mich.: University Microfilm International, 1988.

Srivastava, J. C. "Prospects of Trade with Oil-Rich Libya." *Africa Quarterly* 9, no. 2 (1969): 149–56.

Taleyarkhan, H. "Indo-Libyan Trade Possibilities." *Indo-African Trade Journal* 8, nos. 11–12 (1972): 40–44.

Wright, John. "Murzuk and the Saharan Slave Trade in the 19th Century." *Libyan Studies* 29 (1998): 89–96.

L. Water

Addison, H., and F. W. Shotton. "Water Supply in the Middle East Campaigns III: Collecting Galleries along the Mediterranean Coast of Egypt and Cyrenaica." *Water and Water Engineering* 49 (1986): 427–37.

Alghariani, Saad A. "Water Transfer versus Desalination in North Africa: Sustainability and Cost Comparison." *Libyan Studies* 34 (2003): 147–52.

Allan, J. A. "Capital Has Not Substituted for Water in Agriculture." In *Libya since Independence*, ed. J. A. Allan, 25–36. London: Croom Helm, 1982.

———. "Changes in the Economic Use of Land in the Vicinity of Tripoli." Ph.D. diss., University of London, 1971.

———. "Extremes of Resource Management: Libya's Water Strategy." Paper prepared for the Middle East Studies Association Conference held in San Francisco, November 1984.

———. "The Great Man-Made River." *Libyan Studies* 19 (1988): 141–46.

———. "Water for Agriculture in the 1990s: Another Phase in Libya's Agricultural Development." In *The Economic Development of Libya*, ed. Bichara Khader and Bashir el-Wifati, 124–33. London: Croom Helm, 1987.

———. "Water Resource Evaluation and Development in Libya, 1969–1989." *Libyan Studies* 20 (1989): 235–42.

Bukechiem, A. A. "The Management of Resources Use in Semi-arid Lands: A Case Study of Agricultural Development in Jebel El Akhdar, North-East Libya." Ph.D. diss., University of Newcastle upon Tyne, 1987.

——. "Utilisation of Groundwater in Jebel el Akhdar, North-East Libya, as a Basis of Agricultural Improvement with Special Emphasis on the El Marj Plain." *Libyan Studies* 24 (1993): 121–42.

Cremaschi, Mauro. "A History of Lakes and Watertables: The Paleoenvironmental Research in the Frame of the Fazz Project." *Libyan Studies* 35 (2004): 201–3.

Drake, Nick, Andrew Wilson, Ruth Pelling, Kevin White, David Mattingly, and Stuart Black. "Water Table Decline, Springline Desiccation and the Early Development of Irrigated Agriculture in the Wadi al-Ajal, Libyan Fezzan." *Libyan Studies* 35 (2004): 95–112.

Fontaine, Jacques. "La grand rivière artificielle libyenne." *Maghreb-Machrek* 170 (October–December 2000): 60–65.

Gilbertson, D. D., and N. W. T. Chisholm. "UNESCO Libyan Valleys Survey XXVIII: Manipulating the Desert Environment: Ancient Walls, Floodwater Farming and Territoriality in the Tripolitanian Predesert of Libya." *Libyan Studies* 27 (1996): 17–52.

Latham, John S. "A Rationale for a Green River to Supply the Jifarah Plain of North West Libya." In *Planning and Development in Modern Libya*, ed. M. M. Buru, S. M. Ghanem, and K. S. McLachlan, 138–50. London: Menas Press, 1985.

Simons, Geoff. "The Great Man-Made River Project: Technology, Evaluation, Politics." *Journal of Libyan Studies* 1, no. 2 (Winter 2000): 28–40.

Wright, E. P. "Groundwater Resources in Eastern Libya." *Libyan Studies* 8 (1977): 41–44.

V. HISTORY

A. General

Abun-Nasr, Jamil M. *History of the Maghrib*. 2nd ed. Cambridge: Cambridge University Press, 1975.

Anderson, Lisa. "Legitimacy, Identity, and the Writing of History in Libya." In *Statecraft in the Middle East: Oil, Historical Memory, and Popular Culture*, ed. Eric Davis and Nicolas Gavrielides, 71–91. Miami: Florida International University Press, 1991.

Baldinetti, Anna, ed. *Modern and Contemporary Libya: Sources and Historiographies*. Rome: Istituto Italiano per L'Africa e L'Oriente, 2003.

Bosworth, C. Edmund. "Libya in Islamic History." *Journal of Libyan Studies* 1, no. 2 (Winter 2000): 6–16.

Khalidi, Rashid, Lisa Anderson, Muhammad Muslih, and Reeva S. Simon, eds. *The Origins of Arab Nationalism*. New York: Columbia University Press, 1991.

Laroui, Abdallah. *The History of the Maghrib: An Interpretive Essay*. Princeton, N.J.: Princeton University Press, 1977.

Le Gall, Michel, and Kenneth Perkins. *The Maghrib in Question: Essays in History and Historiography*. Austin: University of Texas Press, 1997.

Patai, Raphael. *The Arab Mind*. Rev. ed. New York: Charles Scribner's Sons, 1983.

St John, Ronald Bruce. "Cyrenaica." In *Encyclopedia of the Modern Middle East and North Africa*, 2nd ed., ed. Philip Mattar, 1:655–56. New York: Thomson Gale, 2004.

———. "Libya." In *Encyclopedia of the Modern Middle East and North Africa*, 2nd ed., ed. Philip Mattar, 3:1410–15. New York: Thomson Gale, 2004.

———. "Tripolitania." In *Encyclopedia of the Modern Middle East and North Africa*, 2nd ed., ed. Philip Mattar, 4:2217–18. New York: Thomson Gale, 2004.

Soames, Jane. *The Coast of Barbary*. London: Jonathan Cape, 1938.

Wilson, Andrew. "Aerial Photographs of Sabratha and Garian." *Libyan Studies* 32 (2001): 107–13.

Wright, John. *Libya, Chad and the Central Sahara*. London: C. Hurst & Co., 1989.

B. Ancient

Adams, Neil. "Another Hellenistic Royal Portrait from the Temple of Apollo at Cyrene?" *Libyan Studies* 33 (2002): 29–44.

Baer, K. "The Libyan and Nubian Kings of Egypt: Notes on the Chronology of Dynasties XXII to XXVI." *Journal of Near Eastern Studies* 32 (January–October 1973): 4–25.

Bailey, Donald M. "Photographs of Libya 1." *Libyan Studies* 26 (1995): 79–81.

Baker, Graeme, John Lloyd, and Joyce Reynolds. *Cyrenaica in Antiquity*. British Archaeological Reports International Series No. 236. Occasional Papers No. 1. Oxford: Society for Libyan Studies, 1985.

Barker, G. W. W. "From Classification to Interpretation: Libyan Prehistory, 1969–1989." *Libyan Studies* 20 (1989): 31–43.

Barnett, Tertia. "Rock-art, Landscape and Cultural Transition in the Wadi al-Ajal, Fazzan." *Libyan Studies* 33 (2003): 71–84.

Benabou, Marcel. *La résistance africaine à la romanisation*. Paris: François Maspero, 1976.

Blake, H., A. Hutt, and D. Whitehouse. "Ajdabiyah and the Earliest Fatimid Architecture." *Libyan Studies* 2 (1971): 9–10.

Blas de Roblès, Jean-Marie. *Libye: Grecque, romaine et Byzantine*. Aix-en-Provence: Édisud, 1999.

Brett, M. "Ibn Khaldun and the Arabisation of North Africa." *Libyan Studies* 4 (January–February 1979): 9–16.

———. "Ifiqiya as a Market for Saharan Trade from the Tenth to the Twelfth Century A.D." *Journal of African History* 10 (1969): 347–64.

———. "The Journey of Al-Tijani to Tripoli at the Beginning of the Fourteenth Century A.D./Eighth Century A.H." *Libyan Studies* 7 (1976): 41–51.

———. "Libya: Some Aspects of the Mediaeval Period, First–Ninth Century H/Seventh–Fifteenth Century A.D." *Libyan Studies* 20 (1989): 209–14.

———. "Tripoli at the Beginning of the Fourteenth Century A.D./Eighth Century A.H." *Libyan Studies* 9 (1978): 55–59.

———. "The Zughba at Tripoli, 429H (1037–8 A.D.)." *Libyan Studies* 6 (1975): 41–47.

Brogan, Olwen. "First- and Second-Century Settlement in the Tripolitanian Pre-Desert." In *Libya in History*, ed. Fawzi F. Gadallah, 121–30. Benghazi: University of Libya, 1968.

———. "Hadd Hajar, a Clausura in the Tripolitanian Gebel Garian South of Asabaa." *Libyan Studies* 11 (1980): 45–52.

Charles-Picard, Gilbert. *La civilisation de l'Afrique romaine*. Paris: Librairie Plon, 1959.

Daniels, C. "The Garamantes of Fezzan." In *Libya in History*, ed. Fawzi F. Gadallah, 261–85. Benghazi: University of Libya, 1968.

———. "The Garamantes of Fezzan: Excavations on Zinchecra, 1965–1967." *Antiquaries Journal* 50, no. 1 (1970): 37–66.

———. *The Garamantes of Southern Libya*. Stoughton, Wis.: Oleander Press, 1970.

DiVita, Antonino, Ginette DiVita-Evrard, and Lidiano Bacchielli. *Libya: The Lost Cities of the Roman Empire*. Cologne: Könemann, 1999.

Edwards, David N., J. W. J. Hawthorne, John N. Dore, and David J. Mattingly. "The Garamantes of Fezzan Revisited: Publishing the C. M. Daniels Archive." *Libyan Studies* 30 (1999): 109–28.

Elmayer, A. F. "The Centenaria of Roman Tripolitania." *Libyan Studies* 16 (1985): 77–83.

Fabbricotti, Emanuela. "Thomas Ashby e la Libia." *Libyan Studies* 32 (2001): 115–31.

Filesi, T. "Un Ambasciatone Tripolino a Napoli e un Consule Napoletano a Tripoli nel 1742." *Africa* 26 (June 1971): 157–81.

Fontana, Sergio, and Fabrizio Felici. "Importazioni italiche in Tripolitania nella prima e media età imperiale." *Libyan Studies* 34 (2003): 65–84.

Fulford, M. G. "To East and West: The Mediterranean Trade of Cyrenaica and Tripolitania in Antiquity." *Libyan Studies* 20 (1989): 169–91.

Goodchild, R. G. "The Roman Roads of Libya and Their Milestones." In *Libya in History*, ed. Fawzi F. Gadallah, 155–71. Benghazi: University of Libya, 1968.

Hamdani, Abbas. "Some Aspects of the History of Libya during the Fatimid Period." In *Libya in History*, ed. Fawzi F. Gadallah, 321–46. Benghazi: University of Libya, 1968.

Haynes, D. E. L. *Antiquities of Tripolitania*. Tripoli: Antiquities Department of Tripolitania, 1955.

Jones, A. H. M. "Frontier Defence in Byzantine Libya." In *Libya in History*, ed. Fawzi F. Gadallah, 289–98. Benghazi: University of Libya, 1968.

Jones, G. D. B. "Town and City in Tripolitania: Studies in Origins and Development, 1969–1989." *Libyan Studies* 20 (1989): 91–106.

Kennet, Derek. "Pottery as Evidence for Trade in Medieval Cyrenaica." *Libyan Studies* 25 (1994): 275–85.

Keresztes, P. "The Constitutio Antoniniana and the Persecutions under Caracalia" *American Journal of Philology* 91, no. 4 (1970): 446–59.

———. "The Emperor Septimius Severus: Precursor of Decius." *Historia* 19 (1970): 565–78.

Kirwan, L. P. "Roman Expeditions to the Upper Nile and the Chad-Darfur Region." In *Libya in History*, ed. Fawzi F. Gadallah, 253–59. Benghazi: University of Libya, 1968.

Liebare, J. "Some Aspects of Social Change in North Africa in Punic and Roman Times." *Museum Africum* 2 (1973): 24–40.

Liverani, Mario. "The Garamantes: A Fresh Approach." *Libyan Studies* 31 (2000): 17–28.

———. "Rediscovering the Garamantes: Archaeology and History." *Libyan Studies* 35 (2004): 191–203.

Mackendrick, Paul. *The North African Stones Speak*. Chapel Hill: University of North Carolina Press, 1980.

Marquaille, Céline. "Ptolemaic Royal Cult in Cyrenaica." *Libyan Studies* 34 (2003): 25–42.

Martin, B. G. "Kanem, Bornu, and the Fezzan: Notes on the Political History of a Trade Route." *Journal of African History* 10, no. 1 (1969): 15–27.

Matthews, Kenneth D., Jr. *Cities in the Sand: Leptis Magna and Sabratha in Roman Africa*. Philadelphia: University of Pennsylvania Press, 1957.

Mattingly, David J. "Farmers and Frontiers: Exploiting and Defending the Countryside of Roman Tripolitania." *Libyan Studies* 20 (1989): 135–53.

———. "Mapping Ancient Libya." *Libyan Studies* 25 (1994): 1–5.

———. *Tripolitania*. Ann Arbor: University of Michigan Press, 1994.

McHugh, W. "Late Pre-Historic Cultural Adaptation in the Southeastern Libyan Desert." Ph.D. diss., University of Wisconsin–Madison, 1971.

Munzi, M., and M. Zennati. "Una postazione de miliari presso Abu Kammash (Tripolitania)." *Libyan Studies* 35 (2004): 123–30.

Norris, "The Libyan Fezzan: A Crossroads of Routes and a Thoroughfare of Arab and Berber Tribes Historically Connected with the Murabitun." *Libyan Studies* 34 (2003): 101–20.

Pennell, C. R. "Political Loyalty and the Central Government in Precolonial Libya." In *Social and Economic Development of Libya*, ed. E. G. H. Joffé and K. S. McLachlan, 1–18. London: Menas Press, 1982.

Pesco, A., et al. *Pre-historic Rock Art of the Libyan Sahara*. Stoughton, Wis.: Oleander Press, 1974.

Preece, Chris. "Marsa-el-Brega: A Fatal Port of Call." *Libyan Studies* 31 (2000): 29–58.

Presicce, Claudio Parisi. "La città dei re di Cirene." *Libyan Studies* 34 (2003): 9–24.

Ravin, Sue. *Rome in Africa*. 3rd ed. London: Routledge, 1993.

Rebuffat, R. "Routes d'Egypte de la Libye intérieure." *Studi Magrebini* 3 (1971): 1–20.

Reynolds, M. M. "Inscriptions of Roman Cyrenaica." In *Libya in History*, ed. Fawzi F. Gadallah, 181–89. Benghazi: University of Libya, 1968.

———. "Twenty Years of Inscriptions." *Libyan Studies* 20 (1989): 117–26.

Shawesh, Abubaker Mohamed. "Traditional Settlement in the Oasis of Ghadames in the Libyan Arab Jamahiriya." *Libyan Studies* 26 (1995): 35–47.

Smith, David, and James Crow. "The Hellenistic and Byzantine Defences of Tocra (Taucheira)." *Libyan Studies* 29 (1998): 35–82.

Smith, R. "The Army Reforms of Septimius Severus." *Historia* 21 (1972): 481–99.

Strzelecka, B. "Camps romains en Afrique du Nord." *Africana Bulletin* 14 (1971): 9–34.

Thompson, L. A. "Roman and Native in the Tripolitanian Cities in the Early Empire." In *Libya in History*, ed. Fawzi F. Gadallah, 235–50. Benghazi: University of Libya, 1968.

Uhlenbrock, Jaimee P. "The Cyrene Papers: The Second Report; The Oric Bates Expedition of 1909." *Libyan Studies* 30 (1999): 77–98.

UNESCO. *Libya antiqua*. Paris: UNESCO, 1986.

Walker, Susan. "Hadrian and the Renewal of Cyrene." *Libyan Studies* 33 (2002): 45–56.

Warmington, B. H. *The North African Provinces from Diocletian to the Vandal Conquest*. Cambridge: Cambridge University Press, 1954.

Wright, G. R. H. "Cyrene: Other Men's Memories." *Libyan Studies* 30 (1999): 99–108.

C. Early Colonial Occupation

Abou-El-Haj, Rifaat. "An Agenda for Research in History: The History of Libya between the Sixteenth and Nineteenth Centuries." *International Journal of Middle East Studies* 15, no. 3 (August 1983): 305–19.

Ahmida, Ali Abdullatif. *Forgotten Voices: Power and Agency in Colonial and Postcolonial Libya*. London: Routledge, 2005.

——. *The Making of Modern Libya: State Formation, Colonization, and Resistance, 1830–1932*. Albany: State University of New York Press, 1994.

Allison, Robert J. *The Crescent Obscured: The United States and the Muslim World, 1776–1815*. New York: Oxford University Press, 1995.

Anderson, Lisa S. "Legitimacy, Identity and the Writing of History in Libya." In *Statecraft in the Middle East: Oil, Historical Memory, and Popular Culture*, ed. by Eric Davis and Nicolas Gavrielides, 71–91. Miami: Florida International University Press, 1991.

——. "Nineteenth-Century Reform in Ottoman Libya." *International Journal of Middle East Studies* 16, no. 3 (August 1984): 325–48.

——. *The State and Social Transformation in Tunisia and Libya, 1830–1980*. Princeton, N.J.: Princeton University Press, 1986.

——. "Tribe and State: Libyan Anomalies." In *Tribes and State Formation in the Middle East*, ed. Philip S. Khoury and Joseph Kostiner, 288–302. Berkeley: University of California Press, 1991.

Ayoub, M. S. *A Short History of Fezzan*. Tripoli: n.p., 1967.

Baldinetti, Anna. "Italian Colonial Studies on the Sufi Brotherhoods in Libya." In *Modern and Contemporary Libya: Sources and Historiographies*, ed. Anna Baldinetti, 125–39. Rome: Istituto Italiano per L'Africa e L'Oriente, 2003.

Batis, O. *The Eastern Libyans: An Essay*. London: Frank Cass, 1970.

Bennett, Ernest N. *With the Turks in Tripoli*. London: Methuen, 1912.

Bixler, Raymond W. *The Open Door on the Old Barbary Coast*. New York: Pageant Press, 1959.

Boahen, A. Adu. *Britain, the Sahara and the Western Sudan, 1788–1861*. Oxford: Clarendon Press, 1964.

Bruce-Lockhart, Jamie. "Impressions of Fezzan in 1822: The Borno Mission Diaries of Lieutenant Hugh Clapperton, R.N." *Journal of Libyan Studies* 1, no. 1 (Summer 2000): 61–78.

Cachia, Anthony Joseph. *Libya under the Second Ottoman Occupation, 1835–1911*. Tripoli: Government Press, 1945.

Castor, H. *The Tripolitan War, 1801–1805*. New York: Watts, 1971.

Chicco, Gianni. "Crispi and the Question of the Tripolitanian Borders, 1887–1888." *East European Quarterly* 56, no. 2 (June 1982): 137–49.

Dearden, Seton. *A Nest of Corsairs: The Fighting Karamanlis of the Barbary Coast*. London: John Murray, 1976.

——, ed. *Tully's Ten Years' Residence at the Court of Tripoli*. London: Arthur Baker, 1957.

De Felice, Renzo. *Jews in an Arab Land: Libya, 1835–1970*. Trans. Judith Roumani. Austin: University of Texas Press, 1985.

Earle, Peter. *The Pirate Wars*. New York: Thomas Dunne, 2003.

Evans-Pritchard, E. E. *The Sanusi of Cyrenaica*. Oxford: Oxford University Press, 1949.

Field, Henry M. *The Barbary Coast*. 2nd ed. New York: Charles Scribner's Sons, 1894.

Field, James A., Jr. *America and the Mediterranean World, 1776–1882*. Princeton, N.J.: Princeton University Press, 1969.

Fisher, Godfrey. *Barbary Legend: War, Trade and Piracy in North Africa, 1415–1830*. London: Oxford University Press, 1957.

Folayan, Kola. "Tripoli and the War with the U.S., 1801–1805." *Journal of African History* 13, no. 2 (1972): 261–70.

———. *Tripoli during the Reign of Yusuf Pasha Qaramanli*. Ilé-Ifè, Nigeria: University of Ifè Press, 1979.

———. "Tripoli-Bornu Political Relations, 1817–1825." *Journal of the Historical Society of Nigeria* 5, no. 4 (June 1971): 463–76.

———. "The Tripolitan War: A Reconsideration of the Causes." *Africa* (Rome) 27, no. 1 (March 1972): 613–26.

Gall, Michel Le. "The Ottoman Government and the Sanusiyya: A Reappraisal." *International Journal of Middle East Studies* 21, no. 1 (February 1989): 91–106.

Horeir, Abdulmola S. El. "Social and Economic Transformations in the Libyan Hinterland during the Second Half of the Nineteenth Century: The Role of Sayyid Ahmad al-Sharif al-Sanussi." Ph.D. diss., University of California, Los Angeles, 1981.

Hume, L. J. "Preparations for Civil War in Tripoli in the 1820s: Ali Karamanli, Hassuna D'Ghies and Jeremy Bentham." *Journal of African History* 21, no. 3 (1980): 311–22.

Ibrahim, Abdallah Ali. "Evolution of Government and Society in Tripolitania and Cyrenaica (Libya), 1835–1911." Ph.D. diss., University of Utah, 1982.

Irwin, Ray W. *The Diplomatic Relations of the United States with the Barbary Powers, 1776–1816*. Chapel Hill: University of North Carolina Press, 1931.

Joffé, E. G. H. "British Malta and the Qaramanli Dynasty (1800–1835)." *Revue d'Histoire Maghrebine* (June 1981): 37–38.

———. "The French Occupation of the Western Jafara and the Village of Dahibat, 1890–1891." *Libyan Studies* 15 (1984): 113–28.

———. "Frontiers in North Africa." In *Boundaries and State Territory in the Middle East and North Africa*, ed. G. H. Blake and R. N. Schofield. London: Menas Press, 1987.

———. "Social and Political Structures in the Jafara Plain in the Late Nineteenth Century." In *Social and Economic Development of Libya*, ed. E. G. H. Joffé and K. S. McLachlan, 19–41. London: Menas Press, 1982.

———. "Trade and Migration between Malta and the Barbary States during the Second Ottoman Occupation of Libya (1835–1911)." In *Planning and De-*

velopment in Modern Libya, ed. M. M. Buru, S. M. Ghanem, and K. S. McLachlan, 1–32. London: Menas Press, 1985.

Lafi, Nora. *Une ville du Maghreb entre ancient régime et réformes ottomans: Genèse des institutions municipales à Tripoli de Barbarie (1795–1911)*. Paris: Éditions L'Harmattan, 2002.

Lambert, Franklin. *The Barbary Wars: American Independence in the Atlantic World*. New York: Hill and Wang, 2005.

Lane-Poole, Stanley. *The Barbary Corsairs*. New York: G. P. Putnam's Sons, 1890.

McLachlan, Keith. "The Role of Indigenous Farming in the Agrarian Structure of Tripolitania in the Nineteenth and Twentieth Centuries." In *Planning and Development in Libya*, ed. M. M. Buru, S. M. Ghanem, and K. S. McLachlan, 33–45. London: Menas Press, 1985.

———. "Tripoli and Tripolitania: Conflict and Cohesion during the Period of the Barbary Corsairs (1551–1850)." *Transactions of the Institute of British Geographers*, n.s. 3, no. 3 (1978): 285–94.

Parker, Richard B. *Uncle Sam in Barbary: A Diplomatic History*. Gainesville: University Press of Florida, 2004.

Pennell, C. R., ed. *Piracy and Diplomacy in Seventeenth-Century North Africa: The Journals of Thomas Baker, English Consul in Tripoli, 1677–1685*. Cranbury, N.J.: Associated University Presses, 1989.

———. "Political Loyalty and the Central Government in Precolonial Libya." In *Social and Economic Development of Libya*, ed. E. G. H. Joffé and K. S. McLachlan, 1–18. London: Menas Press, 1982.

———. "Tripoli in the Late Seventeenth Century: The Economics of Corsairing in a Sterile Country." *Libyan Studies* 16 (1985): 101–12.

———. "Work on the Early Ottoman Period and Qaramanlis." *Libyan Studies* 20 (1989): 215–19.

Pichon, Jean. *La question de Libye dans le règlement de la paix*. Paris: J. Peyronnet & Cie, 1945.

Rejob, Lotfi Ben. "To the Shores of Tripoli: The Impact of Barbary on Early American Nationalism." Ph.D. diss., Indiana University, 1982.

Roumani, M. "Zionism and Social Change in Libya at the Turn of the Century." *Studies in Zionism* 8, no. 1 (1987): 1–24.

St John, Ronald Bruce. *Libya and the United States: Two Centuries of Strife*. Philadelphia: University of Pennsylvania Press, 2002.

Simon, Rachel. *Libya between Ottomanism and Nationalism: The Ottoman Involvement in Libya during the War with Italy (1911–1919)*. Islamkundliche Untersuchungen, vol. 105. Berlin: Klaus Schwarz Verlag, 1987.

Triaud, Jean-Louis. *Tchad, 1900–1902: Une guerre franco-libyenne oubliée?* Paris: Éditions L'Harmattan, 1988.

Vella, A. P. "The Relations between the Order of Malta and Tripoli." In *Libya in History*, ed. Fawzi F. Gadallah, 349–79. Benghazi: University of Libya, 1968.

Wanis, Saleh, and Dorothy Thorn. "Mohammed el Adouli." *Libyan Studies* 26 (1995): 27–33.

Wheelan, Jeseph. *Jefferson's War: America's First War on Terror, 1801–1805.* New York: Carroll & Graf, 2003.

Wright, John. "Colonial and Early Post-Colonial Libya." *Libyan Studies* 20 (1989): 221–34.

——. "Consul Warrington's English Garden." *Libyan Studies* 35 (2004): 131–40.

——. "The Gateway to Africa: Consul Warrington and Tripoli." *Journal of Libyan Studies* 1, no. 2 (Winter 2000): 17–27.

——. "Nahum Slouschz and the Jews of Tripoli." *Journal of Libyan Studies* 3, no. 2 (Winter 2002): 41–55.

——. "Outside Perceptions of the Sanusi." *Maghreb Review* 13, nos. 1–2 (January–April 1988): 63–69.

——. "Sayyid Ahmad al-Sharif and the First World War." *Journal of Libyan Studies* 4, no. 1 (Summer 2003): 63–75.

Wright, Louis B. and Julia H. MacLeod. *The First Americans in North Africa: William Eaton's Struggle for a Vigorous Policy against the Barbary Pirates, 1799–1805.* Princeton, N.J.: Princeton University Press, 1945.

Zacks, Richard. *The Pirate Coast: Thomas Jefferson, the First Marines and the Secret Mission of 1805.* New York: Hyperion, 2005.

Ziadeh, Nicola A. *Sanusiyah: A Study of a Revivalist Movement in Islam.* Leiden: E. J. Brill, 1968.

D. Italian Occupation

Airò, Barbara. "Le discours colonial italien à travers les grammaires et les dictionnaires d'arabe parlé." In *Modern and Contemporary Libya: Sources and Historiographies*, ed. Anna Baldinetti, 113–23. Rome: Istituto Italiano per L'Africa e L'Oriente, 2003.

Allain, Jean-Claude. "Les débuts du conflict Italo-Turc: Octobre 1911–Janvier 1912 (d'après les archives françaises)." *Revue d'Histoire Moderne et Contemporaine* 18 (1971): 106–15.

Anderson, Lisa S. "The Development of Nationalist Sentiment in Libya, 1908–1922." In *The Origins of Arab Nationalism*, ed. Rashid Khalidi, Lisa Anderson, Muhammad Muslih, and Reeva S. Simon, 225–42. New York: Columbia University Press, 1991.

——. "Religion and Politics in Libya." *Journal of Arab Affairs* 1, no. 1 (October 1981): 53–77.

——. "States, Peasants and Tribes: Colonialism and Rural Politics in Tunisia and Libya." Ph.D. diss., Columbia University, 1981.

——. "The Tripoli Republic, 1918–1922." In *Social and Economic Development of Libya*, ed. E. G. H. Joffé and K. S. McLachlan, 43–65. London: Menas Press, 1982.

Appleton, Leonard. "The Question of Nationalism and Education in Libya under Italian Rule." *Libyan Studies* 10 (1979): 29–33.

Ashiurakis, Ahmed M. *A Concise History of the Libyan Struggle for Freedom*. Tripoli: General Publishing, Distributing, and Advertising Company, 1976.

Askew, William C. *Europe and Italy's Acquisition of Libya, 1911–1912*. Durham, N.C.: Duke University Press, 1942.

Atkinson, David. "The Politics of Geography and the Italian Occupation of Libya." *Libyan Studies* 27 (1996): 71–84.

Ausiello, Alessandro. *La politica italiana in Libia*. Rome: Scuola Tip., Don Luigi Guanella. 1939.

Baldinetti, Anna. "Italian Colonial Studies on the Sufi Brotherhoods in Libya." In *Modern and Contemporary Libya: Sources and Historiographies*, ed. Anna Baldinetti, 125–39. Rome: Istituto Italiano per L'Africa e L'Oriente, 2003.

——. "Libya's Refugees, Their Places of Exile, and the Shaping of Their National Idea." *Journal of North African Studies* 8, no. 1 (Spring 2003): 72–86.

——. "Note sul nazionalismo libico: L'attività dell'associazione 'Umar al-Mukhtar." *Journal of Libyan Studies* 2, no. 1 (Summer 2001): 61–68.

——. *Orientalismo e colonialismo: La ricerca di consenso in Egitto per l'impresa di Libia*. Rome: L'Istituto per l'"oriente "C. A. Nallino," 1997.

Barbar, Aghil Mohamed. "The Tarabulus (Libyan) Resistance to the Italian Invasion, 1911–1920." Ph.D. diss., University of Wisconsin–Madison, 1980.

Barclay, Thomas. *The Turco-Italian War and Its Problems*. London: Constable & Co., 1912.

Becker, George H. *The Disposition of the Italian Colonies, 1941*. Annemasse, France: n.p., 1952.

Beehler, W. H. *The History of the Italian-Turkish War (September 29, 1911, to October 18, 1912)*. Annapolis, Md.: Advertiser-Republican, 1913.

Belardinelli, A. *La Ghibla: Cenni sul territoria; Notizie storiche*. Tripoli: Governo della Tripolitania, 1935.

Bernini, Simone. "Ahmed al-Sharif e le missione de Khedive, 1912–1914." *Journal of Libyan Studies* 4, no. 1 (Summer 2003): 87–103.

——. "Correnti intellettuali, ideologie e proto-nazionalismo in Libia agli inizi del XX secolo." *Journal of Libyan Studies* 3, no. 2 (Winter 2002): 79–99.

——. "Nazionalismo e collaborazionismo in Libia: I colloqui di Tripolitania (novembre 1912)." *Journal of Libyan Studies* 1, no. 2 (Winter 2000): 54–67.

——. "Studi sulle origini del nazionalismo arabo in Libia." *Journal of Libyan Studies* 2, no. 1 (Summer 2001): 95–107.

Bono, Salvatore. *Le frontiere in Africa dalla spartizione coloniale alle vicende più recenti, 1884–1971.* Milan: Giuffrè, 1972.

———. "L'historiographie sur la résistance anticoloniale en Libye, 1911–1912." In *Modern and Contemporary Libya: Sources and Historiographies*, ed. Anna Baldinetti, 37–48. Rome: Istituto Italiano per L'Africa e L'Oriente, 2003.

———. "Una testimonianza di Alfredo Baccelli sulla Tripolitania (1914)." *Journal of Libyan Studies* 1, no. 2 (Winter 2000): 68–76.

Caimpenta, U. *Il Generale Graziani, L'Africano.* Milan: Edizioni Aurora, 1936.

Chicco, Gianni. "Crispi and the Question of the Tripolitanian Borders, 1887–1888." *East European Quarterly* 16 (June 1982): 137–49.

Childs, Timothy W. *Italo-Turkish Diplomacy and the War over Libya, 1911–1912.* Leiden: E. J. Brill, 1990.

———. "Mediterranean Imbroglio: The Diplomatic Origins of Modern Libya (The Diplomacy of the Belligerents during the Italo-Turkish War, 1911–1912)." Ph.D. diss., Georgetown University, 1982.

Cole, S. M. "Secret Diplomacy and the Cyrenaica Settlement of 1917." *Journal of Italian Studies* 2 (1979): 258–80.

Contini, Fluvio. *Storia delle istituzioni scolastiche della Libia.* Tripoli: Plinio Maggi, 1953.

Coro, Francesco. *Settantasei anni di dominazione turca in Libia (1835–1911).* Tripoli: Poligrafico Maggi, 1937.

Cresti, Federico. "City and Territory in Libya during the Colonial Period: Sources and Research Documents." In *Modern and Contemporary Libya: Sources and Historiographies*, ed. Anna Baldinetti, 141–68. Rome: Istituto Italiano per L'Africa e L'Oriente, 2003.

———. *Oasi di italianti: La Libia della colonizzazione agrarian tra fascismo, guerra e indipendenza (1935–1956).* Turin: Societ Editrice Internazionale, 1996.

———. "Progetto sociale e territoria nella colonizzazione demografica della Libia, 1938–1940." *Journal of Libyan Studies* 1, no. 1 (Summer 2000): 79–91.

Cumming, Duncan. "Libya in the First World War." In *Libya in History*, ed. Fawzi F. Gadallah, 383–92. Benghazi: University of Libya, 1968.

Degl'Innocenti, Maurizio. *Il socialismo italiano e la guerra di Libia.* Rome: Editori Riuniti, 1976.

Despois, Jean. *La colonisation italienne en Libya: Problèmes et mèthodes.* Paris: Larose, 1935.

Di Camerota, Paolo. *La colonizzazione africana nel sistema fascista: I problemi della colonizzazione nell'Africa italiana.* Milan: Fratelli Bocca, 1941.

Edeek, Mahmoud. "Les dimensions politiques, économiques et socials de la conquête italienne en Libye." In *Modern and Contemporary Libya: Sources and Historiographies*, ed. Anna Baldinetti, 91–97. Rome: Istituto Italiano per L'Africa e L'Oriente, 2003.

Epton, Nina. *Oasis Kingdom: The Libyan Story*. London: Jarrolds, 1952.

Fielding, Sean. *They Sought Out Rommel*. London: HMSO, 1942.

Folayan, Kola. "Italian Colonial Rule in Libya." *Tarikh* 4, no. 4 (1974): 1–10.

———. "The Resistance Movement in Libya." *Tarikh* 4, no. 3 (1973): 46–56.

Fowler, G. L. "The Role of Private Estates and Development Companies in the Italian Agricultural Colonization of Libya." In *Social and Economic Development of Libya*, ed. E. G. H. Joffé and K. S. McLachlan, 117–39. London: Menas Press, 1982.

Graziani, Rodolfo. *Cirenaica pacificata*. Milan: Mondadori, 1932.

———. *Die Eroberung Libyens*. Berlin: Vorhut-Verlag Otto Schlegel, n.d.

———. *Libia redenta*. Naples: Torella Editore, 1948.

———. *Verso il Fezzan*. Tripoli: F. Capocardo, 1930.

Great Britain. Foreign Office Historical Section. *Italian Libya*. Wilmington, Del.: Scholarly Resources, 1973.

Guardi, Jolanda. "Le discours colonial italien à travers le grammaires et les manuels d'arabe." In *Modern and Contemporary Libya: Sources and Historiographies*, ed. Anna Baldinetti, 99–112. Rome: Istituto Italiano per L'Africa e L'Oriente, 2003.

Hesnawi, Habib. "Italian Imperial Policy towards Libya, 1870–1911." In *Modern and Contemporary Libya: Sources and Historiographies*, ed. Anna Baldinetti, 49–62. Rome: Istituto Italiano per L'Africa e L'Oriente, 2003.

Italian Library of Information. *The Italian Empire: Libya*. New York: n.p., 1940.

Jerary, Mohammed Taher. "The Libyan Cultural Resistance to Italian Colonization." In *Modern and Contemporary Libya: Sources and Historiographies*, ed. Anna Baldinetti, 17–35. Rome: Istituto Italiano per L'Africa e L'Oriente, 2003.

La Libia in venti anni di occupazione italiana. Rome: Rassegna Italiana, 1933.

Labanca, Nicola. "Gli studi italiani sul colonialismo italiano in Libia." *Journal of Libyan Studies* 2, no. 1 (Summer 2001): 69–79.

Lischi, Dario. *Tripolitania felix*. Pisa: Nistri-Lischi, 1937.

Lombardi, P. "Italian Agrarian Colonization during the Fascist Period." In *Social and Economic Development of Libya*, ed. E. G. H. Joffé and K. S. McLachlan, 95–116. London: Menas Press, 1982.

Malgeri, F. *La guerra libica, 1911–1912*. Rome: Edizioni di Storia e Litteratura, 1970.

Maltese, Paolo. *La terra promessa: La guerra italo-turca e la conquista della Libia, 1911–1912*. Milan: Mondadori, 1976.

Mathuisieulx, H. M. de. *La Tripolitaine d'hier et de demain*. Paris: Libraire Hachette, 1912.

McClure, W. K. *Italy in North Africa: An Account of the Tripoli Enterprise*. London: Constable & Co., 1913.

McCullagh, Francis. *Italy's War for a Desert: Being Some Experiences of a War-Correspondent with the Italians in Tripoli.* London: Herbert and Daniel, 1912.

Minutilli, F. *La Tripolitania.* Turin: Fratelli Bocca, 1912.

Mozzati, Marco. "La vicenda degli operai libici militarizzati durante la Prima Guerra Mondiale: I potesi per una ricerca." *Journal of Libyan Studies* 2, no. 1 (Summer 2001): 80–94.

——. "Toward a Virtual Archive of Sources for the History of Libya in the Colonial Period." In *Modern and Contemporary Libya: Sources and Historiographies,* ed. Anna Baldinetti, 169–78. Rome: Istituto Italiano per L'Africa e L'Oriente, 2003.

Muller, Martine. "Frontiers—An Imported Concept: An Historical Review of the Creation and Consequences of Libya's Frontiers." In *Libya since Independence,* ed. J. A. Allan, 165–80. London: Croom Helm, 1982.

Ravagli, Federico. *Alba d'impero.* Bologna: Cappelli, 1938.

Romano, Sergio. *La quarta sponda: La guerra di Libia, 1911–1912.* Milan: Bompiani, 1977.

Ronnell, I. *British Military Administration of Occupied Territories, 1941–1947.* Westport, Conn.: Greenwood Press, 1970.

Rossi, Ettore. *Storia di Tripoli e della Tripolitania dalla conquista araba al 1911.* Rome: Istituto per L'Oriente, 1968.

Salerno, Eric. *Genocidio in Libia—Le atrocità nascoste dell'avventura coloniale, 1911–1931.* Milan: SugarCo Edizioni, 1979.

Segré, Claudio G. *Fourth Shore: The Italian Colonization of Libya.* Chicago: University of Chicago Press, 1974.

——. "Italian Development Policy in Libya: Colonialism as a National Luxury." In *Social and Economic Development of Libya,* ed. E. G. H. Joffé and K. S. McLachlan, 81–93. London: Menas Press, 1982.

——. "Italo-Balbo and the Colonization of Libya." *Journal of Contemporary History* 7, nos. 3–4 (July–October 1972): 141–56.

Serra, Fabrizio. *Italia e Senussia (Vent'anni di azione coloniale in Cirenaica).* Milan: Edizioni Fratelli Treves, 1933.

Simons, Geoff. "Towards Nationhood: European Invasion, Arab Resistance." *Journal of Libyan Studies* 2, no. 2 (Winter 2001): 46–64.

Sindacato Fascista Romano desli Autori e Scrittori. *Il libro coloniale del tempo fascista.* Rome: Il Sindacato, 1936.

Smith, Denis Mack. *Mussolini's Roman Empire.* London: Longman Group, 1976.

Traversi, Carlo. *Storia della cartografia coloniale italiana.* Rome: Istituto Poligrafico dello Stato, 1964.

Tumiati, Domenico. *Nell'Africa romana: Tripolitania.* Milan: Fratelli Treves, 1911.

Tuninetti, Dante Maria. *Il mistero di Cufra*. Benghazi: Nicola Calcagni, 1931.

Valabrega, G. "Quelques aspects de la politique italienne en Afrique du Nord." *Cahiers de la Tunisie* 29, nos. 117–18 (1981): 649–55.

Venuta, Pierluigi. "Libyan Studies on Italian Colonialism: Bibliographical and Historiographical Considerations." *Journal of Libyan Studies* 2, no. 1 (Summer 2001): 48–60.

Wright, John. "British and Italians in Libya in 1943." *Maghreb Review* 15, nos. 1–2 (1990): 31–36.

——. "Italian Fascism and Libyan Human Resources." In *Planning and Development in Modern Libya*, ed. M. M. Buru, S. M. Ghanem, and K. S. McLachlan, 46–56. London: Menas Press, 1985.

——. "Libya: Italy's Promised Land." In *Social and Economic Development of Libya*, ed. E. G. H. Joffé and K. S. McLachlan, 67–79. London: Menas Press, 1982.

——. "Mussolini, Libya and the Sword of Islam." *Maghreb Review* 12, nos. 1–2 (January–April 1987): 29–33.

——. "Poets, Pilots and Propaganda: Gabriele D'Annunzio and Italy's Libyan War, 1911–1912." *Journal of Libyan Studies* 2, no. 1 (Summer 2001): 5–23.

Zaccaria, Massimo. "The Other Shots: Photography and the Turco-Italian War, 1911–1912." In *Modern and Contemporary Libya: Sources and Historiographies*, ed. Anna Baldinetti, 63–89. Rome: Istituto Italiano per L'Africa e L'Oriente, 2003.

E. Independence Era

Anderson, Lisa. "'A Last Resort, an Expedient and an Experiment': Statehood and Sovereignty in Libya." *Journal of Libyan Studies* 2, no. 2 (Winter 2001): 14–25.

Annan, Muhammed abd Allah. *Libya of Idris el Sennousi*. Beirut: n.p., 1968.

"Annual Report of the French Government to the General Assembly Concerning the Administration of the Fezzan, 1950–1951." UN Document A/1390.

"Annual Report of the Government of the United Kingdom to the General Assembly Concerning the Administration of Cyrenaica and Tripolitania, 1950–1951." UN Document A/1390.

Annual Report of the UN Commissioner in Libya. Prepared in Consultation with Council for Libya. General Assembly. Official Records, 5th Session. Supplement #15. UN Document A/1340.

Baker, Coleman L. "The U.S. and Libya." *Military Review* 49, no. 4 (April 1969): 83–91.

Barbar, A. "Political Change in Libya: A Study in the Decline of the Libyan Traditional Elite." M.A. thesis, Georgetown University, 1974.

Bills, Scott L. *The Libyan Arena: The United States, Britain, and the Council of Foreign Foreign Ministers, 1945–1948*. Kent, Ohio: Kent State University Press, 1995.

Blackwell, Stephen. "Saving the King: Anglo-American Strategy and British Counter-subversion Operations in Libya, 1953–1959." *Middle Eastern Studies* 39, no. 1 (January 2003): 1–18.

Burr, J. Millard, and Robert O. Collins. *Africa's Thirty Years' War: Chad, Libya, and the Sudan, 1963–1993*. Boulder, Colo.: Westview Press, 1999.

Cecil, Charles O. "The Determinants of Libyan Foreign Policy." *Middle East Journal* 19, no. 1 (Winter 1965): 20–34.

Cricco, Massimiliano. *Il petrolio del Senussi: Stati Uniti e Gran Bretagna in Libia dall'indipendenza a Gheddafi (1949–1973)*. Florence: Edizioni Polistampa, 2002.

———. "La Libia nella politica delle grandi potenze (1951–1969)." Ph.D. diss., Università degli Studi di Firenze, 1999.

Haines, C. Grove. "The Problem of the Italian Colonies." *Middle East Journal* 1, no. 4 (October 1947): 417–31.

Hajjaji, Salem Ali. *The New Libya: A Geographical, Social, Economic and Political Study*. Tripoli: Government Printing Press, 1967.

Hassan, Salaheddin S. "The Genesis of the Political Leadership of Libya, 1952–1969: Historical Origins and Development of Its Component Elements." Ph.D. diss., George Washington University, 1970.

———. "A New System for a New State: The Libyan Experiment in Statehood, 1951–1969." In *Modern and Contemporary Libya: Sources and Historiographies*, ed. Anna Baldinetti, 179–94. Rome: Istituto Italiano per L'Africa e L'Oriente, 2003.

Hayford, Elizabeth R. "The Politics of the Kingdom of Libya in Historical Perspective." Ph.D. diss., Tufts University, 1970.

Khadduri, Majid. *Modern Libya: A Study in Political Development*. Baltimore: Johns Hopkins University Press, 1963.

Khalidi, Ismail Raghib. *Constitutional Development in Libya*. Beirut: Khayat's College Book Cooperative, 1956.

Le Gall, Michael. "The Historical Context." In *Polity and Society in Contemporary North Africa*, 3–18. Boulder, Colo.: Westview Press, 1993.

Lewis, William H. "Libya: The End of Monarchy." *Current History* 58 (January 1970): 34–38, 50.

Lewis, William H., and Robert Gordon. "Libya after Two Years of Independence." *Middle East Journal* 8, no. 1 (Winter 1954): 41–53.

Martel, André. "Histoire contemporaine de la Libye: Dimensions et recherches." *Annuaire de l'Afrique du Nord* (1966): 781–92.

Miles, Oliver. "Libya: Years of Change." *Libyan Studies* 35 (2004): 145–47.

Mogherbi, Mohammed Zahi El. "Arab Nationalism and Political Instability in Monarchical Libya: A Study in Political Ideology." M.A. thesis, Kansas State University, 1973.

Pelt, Adrian. *Libyan Independence and the United Nations*. New Haven, Conn.: Yale University Press, 1950.

———. "The United Kingdom of Libya from Colony to Independent State." UN Bulletin 2/15/52.

Rivlin, Benjamin. "Unity and Nationalism in Libya." *Middle East Journal* 13, no. 1 (January 1949): 31–44.

Sebki, H. *The United Nations and the Pacific Settlement of Disputes: Case of Libya*. Beirut: Dar el-Mashreq, 1970.

Second Annual Report of the UN Commissioner in Libya. Prepared in Consultation with Council for Libya. General Assembly. Official Records, 6th Session. Supplement #17. UN Document A/1949.

Sharabi, H. B. "Libya's Pattern of Growth." *Current History* 44 (January 1963): 41–45.

Simpson, Richard. "Military Artwork in Libya dating from the Second World War." *Libyan Studies* 35 (2004): 141–44.

St John, Ronald Bruce. "Muammar al-Qaddafi." In *Encyclopedia of the Modern Middle East and North Africa*, 2nd ed., ed. Philip Mattar, 3:1860–63. New York: Thomson Gale, 2004.

Stewart, Adrian. "Desert Battleground: The Libyan Campaigns in the Second World War." *Journal of Libyan Studies* 1, no. 1 (Summer 2000): 48–60.

———. "The Unintentional Tourists: British Servicemen in Libya, 1940–1943." *Journal of Libyan Studies* 3, no. 1 (Summer 2002): 42–58.

"Supplementary Report of United Kingdom of Great Britain and Northern Ireland to General Assembly Concerning the Administration of Cyrenaica and Tripolitania for 15 October–24 December 1951." UN Document A/2024.

Swetzer, R. L. *Wheelus Field: The Story of the U.S. Air Force in Libya; The Early Days, 1944–1952*. N.p.: Historical Division, Office of Information, U.S. Air Force in Europe, 1965.

United Nations. Department of Information. *Libya: The Road to Independence through UN*. New York: United Nations, 1952.

Villard, Henry S. *Libya: The New Arab Kingdom of North Africa*. Ithaca, N.Y.: Cornell University Press, 1956.

Wright, John. "Libya's Short Cut to Independence." *Journal of Libyan Studies* 2, no. 2 (Winter 2001): 77–88.

Ziadeh, Nicola A. *The Modern History of Libya*. London: Weidenfeld and Nicolson, 1967.

VI. JURIDICAL

A. Domestic

Ansell, Meredith O., et al. *The Libyan Civil Code: An English Translation and Comparison with the Egyptian Civil Code*. Stoughton, Wis.: Oleander Press, 1970.

Barger, John. "Gender Law in the Jamahiriyya: An Application to Libya of Mounira Charrad's Theory of State Development and Women's Rights." *Journal of Libyan Studies* 3, no. 1 (Summer 2002): 30–41.

Flanz, Gisbert H., and Ahmed Rhazaoui. "Libya." In *Constitutions of the Countries of the World*, ed. Albert P. Blaustein and Gisbert H. Flanz, 1–29. Dobbs Ferry, N.Y.: Oceana Publications, 1974.

Hinz, Almut. "The Development of Matrimonial Law in Libya." *Journal of Libyan Studies* 3, no. 1 (Summer 2002): 13–29.

Khalidi, Ismael Raghib. *Constitutional Development in Libya*. Beirut: Khayat's College Book Cooperative, 1956.

Layish, Aharon. *Shari'a and Custom in Libyan Tribal Society: An Annotated Translation of Decisions from the Shari'a Courts of Adjabiya and Kufra*. Leiden: Brill Academic Publishers, 2005.

Mayer, Ann Elizabeth. "Developments in the Law of Marriage and Divorce in Libya since the 1969 Revolution." *Journal of African Law* 22, no. 1 (Spring 1978): 30–49.

———. "In Search of Sacred Law: The Meandering Course of Qadhafi's Legal Policy." In *Qadhafi's Libya, 1969 to 1994*, ed. Dirk Vandewalle, 113–37. New York: St. Martin's Press, 1995.

———. "Libyan Legislation in Defense of Arabo-Islamic Sexual Mores." *American Journal of Comparative Law* 28 (1980): 287–313.

———. "The Regulation of Interest Charges and Risk Contracts: Some Problems of Recent Libyan Legislation." *International and Comparative Law Quarterly* 28 (1979): 541–59.

———. "Reinstating Islamic Criminal Law in Libya." In *Law and Islam in the Middle East*, ed. Daisy Hilse Dwyer, 99–114. New York: Bergin & Garvey, 1990.

Nafa, M. A. *Libya: Company and Business Law*. London: Arab Business Consultants, 1976.

B. International

Amos, J. V. "Libya–Chad: Borders and Territorial Disputes." *Conflict* 51 (1983): 1–18.

"The Aouzou Strip: Adjudication of Competing Territorial Claims in Africa by the International Court of Justice." *Case Western Reserve Journal of International Law* 23 (1991): 147–70.

Ben-Achour, Y. "L'affaire du Plateau Continental Tuniso-Libyen (analyse empirique)." *Journal du Droit International* (1993): 110.

Blake, G. H. "The 1982 United Nations Convention on the Law of the Sea: Some Implications for Libya." *Libyan Studies* 15 (1984): 129–35.

Blum, Y. Z. "The Gulf of Sidra Incident." *American Journal of International Law* 80 (July 1986): 668–77.

Brown, E. D. "The Tunisian-Libyan Continental Shelf Case: A Missed Opportunity." *Marine Policy* 7, no. 3 (1983): 142.

Christie, D. R. "From the Shoals of Ras Kaboudia to the Shores of Tripoli: The Tunisia-Libya Shelf Boundary Delimitation." *Georgia Journal of International and Comparative Law* 13 (Winter 1983): 1–30.

Degenhardt, H. W. *Chad–Libya: Borders and Territorial Disputes*. Harlow, U.K.: Longman, 1982.

"Diplomatic Missions: Appointment, Accreditation and Notification of People's Bureaus." *American Journal of International Law* 74 (October 1980): 921–28.

Feldman, M. B. "Tunisian-Libyan Continental Shelf Case: Geographic Justice or Judicial Compromise?" *American Journal of International Law* 77 (April 1983): 219–38.

Flores, Charles. *Shadows of Lockerbie: An Insight into the British-Libyan Relations*. Valletta, Malta: Edam Publishing, 1997.

Francioni, F. "The Status of the Gulf of Sirte and International Law." *Syracuse Journal of Law and Commerce* 11 (Autumn 1984): 311–26.

Gerson, Allan, and Jerry Adler. *The Price of Terror*. New York: HarperCollins, 2001.

Herman, L. L. "The Court Giveth and the Court Taketh Away: An Analysis of the Tunisia-Libya Continental Shelf Case." *International and Comparative Law Quarterly* 33 (October 1984): 825–58.

High Court of Justiciary at Camp Zeist [The Netherlands]. "Opinion of the Court Delivered by Lord Sutherland in Causa Her Majesty's Advocate *v.* Abdelbaset Ali Mohmed al Megrahi and Al Amin Khalifa Fhimah, Prisoners in the Prison of Zeist, Camp Zeist (Kamp van Zeist), The Netherlands." Case No: 1475/99. 31 January 2002.

Hodgson, D. C. "The Tuniso-Libyan Continental Shelf Case." *Case Western Reserve Journal of International Law* 16 (1984) 1–37.

International Court of Justice. *Application for Revision and Interpretation of the Judgment of 24 February 1982 in the Case Concerning the Continental Shelf (Tunisia v. Libyan Arab Jamahiriya). Pleadings, Oral Arguments, Documents*. 1982. B.ICJ/588.

——. "Application of the Government of Malta for Permission to Intervene in the Case Concerning the Continental Shelf (Tunisia/Libyan Arab Jamahiriya)." *International Legal Materials* 20 (March 1981): 329–31.

——. *Case Concerning Questions of Interpretation and Application of the 1971 Montreal Convention Arising from the Aerial Incident at Lockerbie (Libyan Arab Jamahiriya v. United Kingdom). Order of 14 April 1992. Reports of Judgments, Advisory Opinions and Orders.* 1992. B.ICJ/607.

——. *Case Concerning Questions of Interpretation and Application of the 1971 Montreal Convention Arising from the Aerial Incident at Lockerbie (Libyan Arab Jamahiriya v. United Kingdom). Order of 19 June 1992. Reports of Judgments, Advisory Opinions and Orders.* 1992. B.ICJ/613.

——. *Case Concerning Questions of Interpretation and Application of the 1971 Montreal Convention Arising from the Aerial Incident at Lockerbie (Libyan Arab Jamahiriya v. United States of America). Order of 19 June 1992. Reports of Judgments, Advisory Opinions and Orders.* 1992. B.ICJ/615.

——. *Case Concerning Questions of Interpretation and Application of the 1971 Montreal Convention Arising from the Aerial Incident at Lockerbie (Libyan Arab Jamahiriya v. United States of America). Reports of Judgments, Advisory Opinions and Orders.* 1992. B.ICJ/608.

——. *Case Concerning the Continental Shelf (Libyan Arab Jamahiriya v. Malta). Vol. I: Special Agreement: Memorials, Pleadings, Oral Arguments, Documents.* 1992. B.ICJ/580.

——. *Case Concerning the Continental Shelf (Libyan Arab Jamahiriya v. Malta). Vol. II: Pleadings, Oral Arguments, Documents.* 1992. B.ICJ/581.

——. *Case Concerning the Continental Shelf (Libyan Arab Jamahiriya v. Malta). Vol. III: Replies, Oral Arguments, Pleadings, Documents.* 1992. B.ICJ/618.

——. *Case Concerning the Continental Shelf (Libyan Arab Jamahiriya v. Malta). Vol. IV: Pleadings, Oral Arguments, Documents.* 1992. B.ICJ/619.

——. *Case Concerning the Continental Shelf (Libyan Arab Jamahiriya v. Malta). Vol. V: Maps, Charts, and Illustrations.* 1992. B.ICJ/620.

——. *Case Concerning the Territorial Dispute (Libyan Arab Jamahiriya v. Chad). Judgment of 3rd February 1994. Reports of Judgments, Advisory Opinions and Orders.* 1994. B.ICJ/648.

——. *Case Concerning the Territorial Dispute (Libyan Arab Jamahiriya v. Chad). Order of 14 April 1992. Reports of Judgments, Advisory Opinions and Orders.* 1992. B.ICJ/609.

——. *Case Concerning the Territorial Dispute (Libyan Arab Jamahiriya v. Chad). Reports of Judgments, Advisory Opinions and Orders.* 1994. B.ICJ/597.

——. "Judgment on the Application of Malta for Permission to Intervene in the Case Concerning the Continental Shelf (Tunisia/Libyan Arab Jamahiriya)." *International Legal Materials* 20 (May 1981): 569–88.

Leigh, Monroe. "Judicial Decisions: Case Concerning the Continental Shelf (Libyan Arab Jamahiriya/Malta)." *American Journal of International Law* 80, no. 3 (July 1986): 645–48.

——. "Judicial Decisions: Case Concerning the Contintental Shelf (Tunisia/Libyan Arab Jamahiriya)." *American Journal of International Law* 75, no. 4 (October 1981): 949–52.

Matar, Khalil I., and Robert W. Thabit. *Lockerbie and Libya.* Jefferson, N.C.: McFarland, 2004.

McDorman, C. "The Libya-Malta Continental Shelf (Libyan Arab Jamahiriya–Malta) International Court of Justice 1985 Case: Opposite States Confront the Court." *Canadian Yearbook of International Law* 24 (1986): 335–67.

McFinley, G. P. "Intervention in the International Court: The Libya/Malta Continental Shelf Case." *International and Comparative Law Quarterly* 34 (October 1985): 671–94.

Mehren, Robert B. von, and P. Nicholas Kourides. "International Arbitrations between States and Foreign Private Parties: The Libyan Nationalization Cases." *American Journal of International Law* 75, no. 3 (July 1981): 476–552.

Merrils, J. G. "Intervention in the International Court: Libya-Malta Continental Shelf." *Law Quarterly Review* 101 (1985): 11–15.

Monroe, L. "Judicial Decisions: Case Concerning the Continental Shelf (Libyan Arab Jamahiriya/Malta) International Court of Justice, June 3, 1985." *American Journal of International Law* 80 (1986): 645–48.

Ricciardi, M. M. "The Aouzou Strip: A Legal and Historical Analysis." *International Journal of International Law* 17 (1992): 301–488.

Simons, Geoff. "Lockerbie: Lessons for International Law." *Journal of Libyan Studies* 1, no. 1 (Summer 2000): 33–47.

Spinnato, J. M. "Historic and Vital Bays: An Analysis of Libya's Claim to the Gulf of Sidra." *U.S. Ocean Development and International Law* 3, no.1 (1983): 65–85.

Thomas, L. "Law of the Sea: Delimitation of the Libya-Malta Continental Shelf Case; International Court of Justice Judgment of 3 June 1985 (Libyan Arab Jamahiriya/Malta)." *Harvard International Law Journal* 27 (1986): 304–13.

United Nations. "Council Informed Agreement Reached on Chad-Libya Issue." *UN Monthly Chronicle* 25 (March 1978): 5–8.

Wlosowics, Z. "The Malta/Libya Case: Shelf Delimitation by the Distance Principle and How to Influence Decisions without Intervening." *Cambridge Law Journal* 44 (1985): 341–45.

Youssef, S. *L'affrontation arabe-américaine du Golfe de Sirt*. Nicosia, Cyprus: Foundation Al-Moukif, 1982.

VII. POLITICS

A. General

Abdrabboh, Bob, ed. *Libya in the 1980s: Challenges and Changes*. Washington, D.C.: International Economics and Research, 1985.

Ahmida, Ali Abdullatif. *The Making of Modern Libya: State Formation, Colonization, and Resistance, 1830–1932*. Albany: State University of New York Press, 1994.

Albergoni, G., et al. *La Libye nouvelle: Rupture et continuité*. Paris: Éditions du Centre National de la Recherche Scientifique, 1975.

Altunisik, Meliha Benli. "External vs. Internal Debate Revisited: The Political Economy of Economic Reform Policies in Libya." Ph.D. diss., Boston University, 1995.

Anderson, Frank. "Qadhafi's Libya: The Limits of Optimism." *Middle East Policy* 6, no. 4 (June 1999): 68–79.

Anderson, Lisa. "Qadhafi's Legacy: An Evaluation of a Political Experiment." In *Qadhafi's Libya: 1969 to 1994*, ed. Dirk Vandewalle, 223–37. New York: St. Martin's Press, 1995.

Arnold, Guy. *Maverick State: Gaddafi and the New World Order*. London: Cassell, 1996.

Barthel, Gunther, and Lothar Rathmann, eds. *Libya: History, Experiences and Perspectives of a Revolution*. Berlin: Akademie-Verlag, 1980.

Bearman, Jonathan. *Qadhafi's Libya*. London: Zed Books, 1986.

Ben-Halim, Mustafa Ahmed. *Libya: The Years of Hope*. London: AAS Media, 1998.

Bennett, Valeria Plave. "Libyan Socialism and Qaddafi's Policies." In *Socialism in the Third World*, ed. Helen Desfosses and Jacques Levesque, 99–100. New York: Praeger, 1975.

Bessis, Juliette. *La Libye contemporaine*. Paris: Éditions L'Harmattan, 1986.

Bezzina, Charles, ed. *The Green Book: Practice and Commentary*. Valletta, Malta: Edam Publishing, 1979.

Bianco, Mirella. *Gadafi: Voice from the Desert*. London: Longman Group, 1975.

Blake, G. H. "Political Geography in the Literature on Libya, 1969–1989." *Libyan Studies* 20 (1989): 259–62.

Blundy, David, and Andrew Lycett. *Qaddafi and the Libyan Revolution*. London: Weidenfeld and Nicolson, 1987.

Burgat, François. "Qadhafi's Ideological Framework." In *Qadhafi's Libya, 1969 to 1994*, ed. Dirk Vandewalle, 47–63. New York: St. Martin's Press, 1995.

Burgat, François, and André Laronde. *La Libye*. Paris: Presses Universitaires de France, 1966.

Burr, J. Millard, and Robert O. Collins. *Africa's Thirty Years' War: Chad, Libya, and the Sudan, 1963–1993*. Boulder, Colo.: Westview Press, 1999.

Cazalis, Anne-Marie. *Kadhafi: Le templier d'Allah*. Paris: Éditions Gallimard, 1974.

Christman, Henry M., ed. *Qaddafi's Green Book: An Unauthorized Edition*. Buffalo, N.Y.: Prometheus, 1988.

Cooley, John K. *Libyan Sandstorm: The Complete Account of Qaddafi's Revolution*. New York: Holt, Rinehart and Winston, 1982.

Cricco, Massimiliano. *Il petrolio del Senussi: Stati Uniti e Gran Bretagna in Libia dall'indipendenza a Gheddafi (1949–1973)*. Florence: Edizioni Polistampa, 2002.

Davis, John. *Libyan Politics: Tribe and Revolution*. London: I. B. Tauris, 1987.

Dawisha, Adeed. *Arab Nationalism in the Twentieth Century: From Triumph to Despair*. Princeton, N.J.: Princeton University Press, 2003.

Deeb, Marius K., and Mary-Jane Deeb. *Libya since the Revolution: Aspects of Social and Political Development*. New York: Praeger, 1982.

Deeb, Mary-Jane. "Political and Economic Developments in Libya in the 1990s." In *North Africa in Transition: State, Society, and Economic Transformation in the 1990s*, ed. Yahia H. Zoubir, 77–89. Gainesville: University Press of Florida, 1999.

Epton, Nina. *Oasis Kingdom: The Libyan Story*. London: Jarrolds, 1952.

Fallaci, Oriana. "Iranians Are Our Brothers: An Interview with Col. Muammar el-Qaddafi of Libya." *New York Times Magazine*, 16 December 1979, 40ff.

Frank, Sabine, and Martina Kamp, eds. *Libyen im 20. Jahrhundert: Zwischen Fremdherrschaft und nationaler Selbstbestimmung*. Hamburg: Deutsches Orient-Institut, 1995.

Georgy, Guy. *Kadhafi: Le berger des Syrtes; Pages d'éphéméride*. Paris: Flammarion, 1996.

Gerson, Allan, and Jerry Adler. *The Price of Terror*. New York: HarperCollins, 2001.

Golino, Frank Ralph. "Patterns of Libyan National Identity." *Middle East Journal* 24, no. 3 (Summer 1970): 338–52.

Gottfried, Ted. *Libya: Desert Land in Conflict*. Brookfield, Conn.: Millbrook, 1994.

Gregory, Harry. *Khadafy*. Toronto: PaperJacks, 1986.

Harris, Lillian Craig. *Libya: Qadhafi's Revolution and the Modern State*. Boulder, Colo.: Westview Press, 1986.

Hendiri, Said Abderrahmane al-. *Libyan-Chadian Relations, 1843–1975.* Tripoli: Markaz dirasat jihad Libiyyin didda ghazou al-Itali, 1984.

Ismael, Tareq Y. *The Middle East in World Politics: A Study in Contemporary International Relations.* Syracuse, N.Y.: Syracuse University Press, 1974.

Joffé, E. G. H. [George]. "Islamic Opposition in Libya." *Third World Quarterly* 10, no. 2 (April 1988): 615–31.

Jouve, Edmond. *Mouammar Kadhafi: Dans le concert des nations.* Paris: L'Archipel, 2004.

Khadduri, Majid. *Modern Libya: A Study in Political Development.* Baltimore: Johns Hopkins University Press, 1963.

Khalidi, Ismail Raghib. *Constitutional Development in Libya.* Beirut: Khayat Book and Publishing, 1956.

Khawas, Mohamed A. el-. *Qaddafi: His Ideology in Theory and Practice.* Brattleboro, Vt.: Amana Books, 1986.

Kikhia, Mansour O. el-. *Libya's Qaddafi: The Politics of Contradiction.* Gainesville: University Press of Florida, 1997.

Kyle, Benjamin. *Qaddafi.* New York: Chelsea House, 1987.

Lawson, Don. *Libya and Qaddafi.* New York: Franklin Watts, 1987.

"The Libyan Revolution in the Words of Its Leaders." *Middle East Journal* 24, no. 2 (Spring 1970): 203–19.

Matar, Khalil I., and Robert W. Thabit. *Lockerbie and Libya.* Jefferson, N.C.: McFarland, 2004

Mattes, Hanspeter. "Libya: The Desert Experience." *European Journal of International Affairs* 12, no. 2 (1991).

——. *Qaddafi und die islamistische Opposition in Libyen: Zum Verlauf eines Konflikts.* Hamburg: Deutsches Orient-Institut, 1995.

——. "Revolutionary Libya in Western Research." *Journal of Libyan Studies* 3, no. 2 (Winter 2002): 70–78.

Miles, Oliver. "Libya: Years of Change." *Libyan Studies* 35 (2004): 145–47.

Moll, Yasmin. "Repentant Rogue." *Egypt Today* 25, no. 6 (June 2004): 66–68.

Monti-Belkaoui, Janice, and Ahmed Riathi-Belkaoui. *Qaddafi: The Man and His Politics.* Aldershot, U.K.: Avebury, 1996.

Niblock, Tim. *"Pariah States" and Sanctions in the Middle East.* Boulder, Colo.: Lynne Rienner, 2001.

Obeidi, Amal. *Political Culture in Libya.* Richmond, U.K.: Curzon Press, 2001.

O'Sullivan, Meghan L. *Shrewd Sanctions: Statecraft and State Sponsors of Terrorism.* Washington, D.C.: Brookings Institution Press, 2003.

Piscatori, James P. *Islam in a World of Nation-States.* Cambridge: Cambridge University Press, 1986.

Qaddafi, Muammar al-. *Discourses.* Valletta, Malta: Adam Publishing, 1975.

——. "A Visit to Fezzan." In *Man, State, and Society in the Contermporary Maghrib,* ed. I. William Zartman, 131–36. New York: Praeger, 1973.

St John, Ronald Bruce. "Abu Bakr Yunis Jabir." In *Encyclopedia of the Modern Middle East and North Africa*, 2nd ed., ed. Philip Mattar, 4:2414. New York: Thomson Gale, 2004.

——. "The Ideology of Mu'ammar Al-Qadhdhafi: Theory and Practice." *International Journal of Middle East Studies* 15, no. 4 (November 1983): 471–90.

——. "Libya." In *Africa Contemporary Record*, ed. Colim Legum, 27:B621–B635. New York: Africana Publishing, 2004.

——. *Libya and the United States: Two Centuries of Strife*. Philadelphia: University of Pennsylvania Press, 2002.

——. "Libya Is Not Iraq: Preemptive Strikes, WMD, and Diplomacy." *Middle East Journal* 58, no. 3 (Summer 2004): 386–402.

——. "Libya's Foreign and Domestic Policies." *Current History* 80, no. 470 (December 1981): 426–29, 434–35.

——. "Muammar al-Qaddafi." In *Encyclopedia of the Modern Middle East and North Africa*, 2nd ed., ed. Philip Mattar, 3:1860–63. New York: Thomson Gale, 2004.

——. "Revolutionary Command Council." In *Encyclopedia of the Modern Middle East and North Africa*, 2nd ed., ed. Philip Mattar, 3:1921. New York: Thomson Gale, 2004.

——. "Socialist People's Libyan Arab Jamahiriya." In *World Encyclopedia of Political Systems and Parties*, 2nd ed., 1:685–93. New York: Facts on File Publications, 1987.

——. "The United States, the Cold War, and Libyan Independence." *Journal of Libyan Studies* 2, no. 2 (Winter 2001): 26–45.

Seale, Patrick, and Maureen McConville. *The Hilton Assignment*. London: Fontana/Collins, 1974.

Shahat, M. El. *Libya Begins the Era of the Jamahiriyat*. Rome: International Publication House, 1978.

Sicker, Martin. *The Making of a Pariah State: The Adventurist Politics of Muammar Qaddafi*. New York: Praeger, 1987.

Simon, Rachel. *Libya between Ottomanism and Nationalism: The Ottoman Involvement in Libya during the War with Italy (1911–1919)*. Islamkundliche Untersuchungen, vol. 105. Berlin: Klaus Schwarz Verlag, 1987.

Simons, Geoff. *Libya: The Struggle for Survival*. 2nd ed. New York: St. Martin's Press, 1996.

——. *Libya and the West: From Independence to Lockerbie*. Oxford: Centre for Libyan Studies, 2003.

——. "Libya Post-Saddam: Signposts to the Future." *Journal of Libyan Studies* 4, no. 1 (Summer 2003): 22–32.

Sono, Themba, ed. *Libya: The Vilified Revolution*. Langley Park, Md.: Progress Press, 1984.

Takeyh, Ray. "The Fate of the Permanent Revolution." *Journal of Libyan Studies* 3, no. 1 (Summer 2002): 6–12.

——. "Qadhafi and the Challenge of Militant Islam." *Washington Quarterly* 21, no. 3 (Summer 1998): 159–73.

Tremlett, George. *Gadaffi: The Desert Mystic*. New York: Carroll & Graf, 1993.

Vandewalle, Dirk. *Libya since Independence: Oil and State-Building*. Ithaca, N.Y.: Cornell University Press, 1998.

——. "The Libyan Jamahiriyya since 1969." In *Qadhafi's Libya, 1969 to 1994*, ed. Dirk Vandewalle, 3–46. New York: St. Martin's Press, 1995.

——. "Qadhafi's Failed Reforms: Markets, Institutions and Development in a Rentier State." In *North Africa: Development and Reform in a Changing Global Economy*, ed. Dirk Vandewalle. New York: St. Martin's Press, 1996.

Vikor, Knut S. "Al-Senusi and Qadhafi—Continuity of Thought?" *Maghreb Review* 12, nos. 1–2 (January–April 1987).

Villard, Henry Serrano. *Libya: The New Arab Kingdom of North Africa*. Ithaca, N.Y.: Cornell University Press, 1956.

Viorst, Milton. "The Colonel in His Labyrinth." *Foreign Affairs* 78, no. 2 (March–April 1999): 60–75.

Wright, John. *Libya, Chad and the Central Sahara*. London: C. Hurst & Co., 1989.

Yergin, Daniel. *The Prize: The Epic Quest for Oil, Money and Power*. New York: Free Press, 1992.

B. Domestic

Alexander, Nathan [Ronald Bruce St John]. "Libya: The Continuous Revolution." *Middle Eastern Studies* 17, no. 2 (April 1981): 210–27.

Allman, T. D. "Power and Paradox in Libya: Qadhafi's Restless Revolution." *Round Table* 259 (July 1975): 305–14.

Amnesty International. *Violations of Human Rights in the Libyan Arab Jamahiriya*. New York: Amnesty International Publications, various years.

Andel, H. "Libyen: Staatsstreich oder Revolution?" *Aussenpolitik* 21 (1970): 44–53.

Anderson, Lisa. "La Libye de Kadhafi." *Maghreb-Machrek* 170 (October–December 2000): 12–15.

——. "Libya's Qaddafi: Still in Command?" *Current History* 86, no. 517 (February 1987): 65–87.

——. "Muammar al-Qaddafi: The 'King' of Libya." *Journal of International Affairs* 54, no. 2 (Spring 2001): 515–17.

——. "Qadhdhafi and His Opposition." *Middle East Journal* 40, no. 2 (Spring 1986): 225–37.

Anderson, Scott. "Remember This Evildoer? Qaddafi's Campaign to Get off the Rogues' List." *New York Times Magazine*, 19 January 2003, 28–35, 44, 62–69.

Ansell, Meredith O., and Ibrahim Massaud al-Arif, eds. *The Libyan Revolution: A Sourcebook of Legal and Historical Documents*. Vol. 1, *1 September 1969–30 August 1970*. Stoughton, Wis.: Oleander Press, 1972.

Barbar, Ashil M. *Public Administration in Libya*. Monticello, Ill.: Vance Bibliographies, 1979.

Barger, John. "After Qadhafi: Prospects for Political Party Formation and Democratisation in Libya. *Journal of North African Studies* 4, no. 1 (Spring 1999): 62–77.

———. "From Qaddafi to Qadadfa: Kinship, Political Continuity, and the Libyan Succession." *Journal of Libyan Studies* 2, no. 1 (Summer 2001): 24–38.

Berween, Mohamed. "The Political Belief System of Qaddafi: Power Politics and Self-Fulfilling Prophecy." *Journal of Libyan Studies* 4, no. 1 (Summer 2003): 49–62.

Bleuchot, Hervè. "The Green Book: Its Context and Meaning." In *Libya since Independence*, ed. J. A. Allan, 137–64. London: Croom Helm, 1982.

———. "Les fondements de l'idéologie du Colonel Mouammar el-Kadhafi." *Maghreb* (March–April 1974): 21–27.

Borglid, Lars-Ola. *Revolution in Allah's Name*. Stockholm: Rahen & Sjogren, 1978.

Breton, H. "L'idéologie politique du régime républicaine en Libye." *Annuaire de l'Afrique du Nord* (1970): 231–41.

Cazalis, Anne-Marie. *Kadhafi: Le templier d'Allah*. Paris: Éditions Gallimard, 1974.

Cowles, Virginia Spencer. *The Phantom Major*. Washington, D.C.: Zender, 1979.

Davis, John. *Libyan Politics, Tribe and Revolution: An Account of the Zuwaya and Their Government*. London: I. B. Tauris, 1987.

———. "Politics in Libya: An Election to Popular Committees." *Maghreb Review* 5, nos. 5–6 (September–December 1980): 99–103.

———. "Qaddafi's Theory and Practice of Non-Representative Government." *Government and Opposition* 17, no. 1 (1982): 61–79.

De Candole, E. A. V. *The Life and Times of King Idris of Libya*. Manchester, U.K.: Jas. F. & C. Carter, 1990.

Dearden, Ann. "Independence for Libya: The Political Problems." *Middle East Journal* 4, no. 4 (October 1950): 395–409.

Decalo, Samuel. "Military Coups and Military Regimes in Africa." *Journal of Modern African Studies* 11, no. 1 (March 1973): 105–27.

Deeb, Marius K. "Militant Islam and Its Critics: The Case of Libya." In *Islamism and Secularism in North Africa*, ed. John Ruedy, 187–97. New York: St. Martin's Press, 1996.

——. "Radical Political Ideologies and Concepts of Property in Libya and South Yemen." *Middle East Journal* 40, no. 3 (Summer 1986): 445–61.

Deeb, Mary-Jane. "Militant Islam and the Politics of Redemption." *Annals* 524 (November 1992): 52–65.

——. "New Thinking in Libya." *Current History* 89, no. 546 (April 1990): 149–52, 177–78.

——. "Qadhafi's Changed Policy: Causes and Consequences." *Middle East Policy* 7, no. 2 (February 2000): 146–53.

Djaziri, Moncef. "Creating a New State: Libya's Political Institutions." In *Qadhafi's Libya, 1969 to 1994*, ed. Dirk Vandewalle, 177–200. New York: St. Martin's Press, 1995.

Dunne, Michele. "Libya: Security Is Not Enough." Policy Brief No. 32. Carnegie Endowment for International Peace, October 2004.

Evans, T. "The New Libya: Coming to Terms with Revolution in the Arab World." *Round Table* 239 (July 1970): 265–73.

Fathaly, Omar I. El. "Opposition to Change in Rural Libya." *International Journal of Middle East Studies* 11, no. 2 (April 1980): 247–61.

Fathaly, Omar I. El, and Monte Palmer. "Institutional Development in Qadhafi's Libya." In *Qadhafi's Libya, 1969 to 1994*, ed. Dirk Vandewalle, 157–76. New York: St. Martin's Press, 1995.

——. *Political Development and Social Change in Libya*. Lexington, Mass.: Lexington Books, 1980.

——. "The Transformation of the Elite Structure in Revolutionary Libya." In *Social and Economic Development of Libya*, ed. E. G. H. Joffé and K. S. McLachlan, 255–79. London: Menas Press, 1982.

Fathaly, Omar I. El, Monte Palmer, and Richard Chackerian. *Political Development and Bureaucracy in Libya*. Lexington, Mass.: Lexington Books, 1977.

First, Ruth. *Libya: The Elusive Revolution*. Harmondsworth, U.K.: Penguin, 1974.

Gaspard, J. "Making an Arab Revolution: Libya Finds Egypt's Pattern Inadequate." *New Middle East* 14 (November 1969): 15–20.

Golan, Galia. *Moscow and the Middle East: New Thinking on Regional Conflict*. New York: Council on Foreign Relations Press, 1992.

Habib, Henri Pierre. *Politics and Government of Revolutionary Libya*. Montreal: Cercle du Livre de France, 1975.

Habiby, Raymond N. "Mu'amar Qadhafi's New Islamic Scientific Socialist Society." *Middle East Review* 11, no. 4 (Summer 1979): 32–39.

——. "Qadhafi's Thoughts on True Democracy." *Middle East Review* 10, no. 4 (Summer 1978): 29–35.

Haddad, George M. *Revolutions and Military Rule in the Middle East: The Arab States*. Vol. 3, *Egypt, the Sudan, Yemen and Libya*. New York: Speller, 1973.

Hahn, Lorna. "Libya Waits in the Wings: The Qaddafi Question." *New Leader* 57, no. 12 (10 June 1974): 8–9.

Hajjar, Sami G. "The Jamahiriya Experiment in Libya: Qadhafi and Rousseau." *Journal of Modern African Studies* 1, no. 2 (June 1980): 181–200.

———. "The Marxist Origins of Qadhafi's Economic Thought." *Journal of Modern African Studies* 20 (1982): 361–75.

Hayford, Elizabeth R. "The Politics of the Kingdom of Libya in Historical Perspective." Ph.D. diss., Tufts University, 1971.

Hermassi, Elbaki, and Dirk Vandewalle. "The Second Stage of State Building." In *Polity and Society in Contemporary North Africa*, 19–41. Boulder, Colo.: Westview Press, 1993.

Hinnebusch, Raymond A. "Libya: Personalistic Leadership of a Populist Revolution." In *Political Elites in Arab North Africa: Morocco, Algeria, Tunisia, Libya, and Egypt*, ed. I. William Zartman, 177–222. New York: Longman, 1982.

Hinterhaff, E. "Implications of the Coup in Libya." *Contemporary Review* 216, no. 1248 (1970): 15–18.

Houderi, Ali El. "Interview." *Third World Forum* 7, no. 4 (August 1980): 1–3.

Hurni, Ferdinand. "Libya's Prosperous Revolution." *Swiss Review of World Affairs* (November 1976): 18–22.

Ibrahim, Ibrahim. "Forecast for the Future: State and Society in Egypt, Sudan, and Libya in 1995." In *The Next Arab Decade: Alternative Futures*, ed. Hisham Sharabi, 11–21. Boulder, Colo.: Westview Press, 1988.

Ibrahim, Muhammad. "The Sons Also Rise." *Foreign Policy* 139 (November–December 2003): 37–39.

Ismael, Tareq, and Jacqueline Ismael. "The Socialist People's Libyan Arab Great Jamahiriyah (SPLAJ)." In *Politics and Government in the Middle East and North Africa*, ed. Tareq Y. Ismael and Jacqueline S. Ismael, 487–512. Miami: Florida International University Press, 1991.

Joffé, E. G. H. "Islamic Opposition in Libya." *Third World Quarterly* 10, no. 2 (April 1988): 615–31.

Kuneralp, S. "Libya's Revolutionaries Are Fighting Back." *New Middle East* 23 (August 1970): 30–32.

Lewis, William. "Libya: Strategem and Deception." *Global Affairs* 5, no. 3 (Summer–Fall 1990): 132–45.

———. "Libya: The End of the Monarchy." *Current History* 58, no. 341 (1970): 34–48.

"Libya—A Revolution in Search of an Ideology." *Africa* 61 (September 1976): 58–65.

"Libyans Structure Their System." *Middle East* 77 (March 1981): 25–26.

Mack, David L. "Qadhafi Adjusts to Reality." *Middle East Institute Perspective*, 22 August 2003.

Martinez, Luis. "L'après-embargo en Libye." *Maghreb-Machrek* 170 (October–December 2000): 3–11.

Mason, John P. "Qadhdhafi's Revolution and Change in a Libyan Oasis Community." *Middle East Journal* 36, no. 3 (Summer 1982): 319–35.

Mattes, Hanspeter. *Qaddafi und die Islamistiche Opposition in Libyen: Zum Verlauf eines Konflikts.* Hamburg: Deutsches Orient-Institut, 1995.

———. "The Rise and Fall of the Revolutionary Committees." In *Qadhafi's Libya, 1969 to 1994,* ed. Dirk Vandewalle, 89–112. New York: St. Martin's Press, 1995.

McDermott, A. "Qaddafi and Libya." *World Today* 29 (1973): 391–408.

Muscat, Frederick. *My President, My Son.* Valletta, Malta: Edam Publishing, 1980.

National Front for the Salvation of Libya. *Libya: Daring to Hope Again.* Munich: National Front for the Salvation of Libya, 1984.

Naur, Maja. *Political Mobilization and Industrialization in Libya.* Copenhagen: Academisk Forlag, 1986.

Niblock, Timothy C. "Libya—The Emergence of a Revolutionary Vanguard." *New Statesman* 96 (22 September 1978): 356–57.

Okoro, J. "Libya Wobbles towards an Uncertain Future." *Africa Development* 11 (October 1970): 912.

Palmer, Monte, and Omar I. El Fathaly. "The Transformation of Mass Political Institutions in Revolutionary Libya: Structural Solutions to a Behavioral Problem." In *Social and Economic Development of Libya,* edited by E. G. H. Joffé and K. S. McLachlan, 233–53. London: Menas Press, 1982.

Possarnig, Renate. *Gaddafi: Enfant terrible der Weltpolitik.* Hamburg: Hoffman & Campe, 1983.

Reich, Bernard. "Socialist People's Libyan Arab Jamahiriya." In *The Government and Politics of the Middle East and North Africa,* ed. David E. Long and Bernard Reich, 359–79. Boulder, Colo.: Westview Press, 1980.

Rondot, Pierre. "Libye: Revolutionner l'arabisme." *Revue Française d'Études Politiques Africaines* 89 (May 1973): 13–18.

Ronen, Yehudit. "Qadhafi and Militant Islamism: Unprecendented Conflict." *Middle Eastern Studies* 38, no. 4 (October 2002): 1–16.

Roumani, Jacques. "From Republic to Jamahiriya: Libya's Search for Political Community." *Middle East Journal* 37, no. 2 (Spring 1983): 151–68.

———. "Libya and the Military Revolution." In *Man, State, and Society in the Contemporary Maghrib,* ed. I. William Zartman, 344–60. New York: Praeger, 1973.

St John, Ronald Bruce. "Libya's Revolution in a Vietnamese Mirror: Building a New Political Order." *Asian Affairs* [Dhaka] 7, no. 1 (January–March 1985): 11–42.

———. "Round Up the Usual Suspects: Prospects for Regime Change in Libya." *Journal of Libyan Studies* 4, no. 1 (Summer 2003): 5–21.

Salem, Hasan Salaheddin. "The Genesis of the Political Leadership of Libya, 1952–1969: Historical Origins and Development of Its Component Elements." Ph.D. diss., George Washington University, 1973.

Sanger, Richard H. "Libya: Conclusions on an Unfinished Revolution." *Middle East Journal* 29, no. 4 (Autumn 1975): 409–17.

———. "Libya's Multi-Step Revolution." Middle East Problem Paper No. 8. Washington, D.C.: Middle East Institute, 1974.

Schechterman, Bernard. "The Politics of Consensus: Qadhafi's Libyan Quest." *Journal of Political Science* 11, no. 1 (1983): 51–67.

Scott, A. M. *Procès à Khedafi*. Paris: Société Encyclopédique Française, 1973.

Shahat, M. El-. *Libya Begins the Era of the Jamahiriyat*. Tripoli: n.p., 1978.

Sheehan, E. "Colonel Qadhafi: Libya's Mystical Revolutionary." *New York Times Magazine*, 6 February 1972, 10–11, 56–59, 68–70.

Simons, Geoff. "Libya and Human Rights: The UDHR versus the International Green Charter." *Journal of Libyan Studies* 3, no. 2 (Winter 2002): 4–21.

Sury, Salaheddin Hasan. "The Political Development of Libya, 1952–1969: Institutions, Policies and Ideology." In *Libya since Independence*, ed. J. A. Allan, 121–36. London: Croom Helm, 1982.

Takeyh, Ray. "Qadhafi's Libya and the Prospect of Islamic Succession." *Middle East Policy* 7, no. 2 (February 2000): 154–64.

Vandewalle, Dirk Joseph. "The Failure of Liberalization in the Jamahiriyya." In *Qadhafi's Libya, 1969 to 1994*, ed. Dirk Vandewalle, 203–22. New York: St. Martin's Press, 1995.

———. "The Libyan Revolution after Twenty Years, Part I: Evaluating the Jamahiriyah." *Universities Field Staff International, Africa/Middle East*, no. 2 (1990–91).

———. "The Libyan Revolution after Twenty Years, Part II: A Libyan Perestroika?" *Universities Field Staff International, Africa/Middle East*, no. 8 (1990–91).

———. "The Political Economy of Maghribi Oil: Change and Development in Algeria and Libya." Ph.D. diss., Columbia University, 1988.

———, ed. *Qadhafi's Libya, 1969 to 1994*. New York: St. Martin's Press, 1995.

———. "Qadhafi's Perestroika: Economic and Political Liberalization in Libya." *Middle East Journal* 45, no. 2 (Spring 1991): 216–31.

Zartman, I. William. "State-Building and the Military in Arab Africa." In *The Many Faces of National Security in the Arab World*, ed. Bahgat Korany, Paul Noble, and Rex Brynen, 239–57. New York: St. Martin's Press, 1993.

C. International

Abdi, Nourredine. "Common Regional Policy for Algeria and Libya: From Maghribi Unity to Saharan Integration." In *Social and Economic Development of Libya*, ed. E. G. H. Joffé and K. S. McLachlan, 215–31. London: Menas Press, 1982.

Adam, R. "L'incidente del golfo della Sirte." *Revista di Diritto Internazionale* 64 (1981): 1025–28.

Alan, R. "African Horrorscope." *New Leader* 62 (15 January 1979): 9.

Albright, David E. "Soviet Policy." *Problems of Communism* 27 (January–February 1978): 20–39.

Alexander, Nathan [Ronald Bruce St John]. "The Foreign Policy of Libya: Inflexibility amid Change." *Orbis* 24, no. 4 (Winter 1981): 819–46.

Aliboni, R., et al. "The Political-Economic Relationship between Europe and the Maghreb." *Lo Spettatore Internazionale* 6, no. 4 (October–December 1971): 455–78.

Amoretti, Scarcia. "Libyan Loneliness in Facing the World: The Challenge of Islam?" In *Islam in Foreign Policy*, ed. Adeed Dawisha, 54–67. Cambridge: Cambridge University Press, 1983.

Amos, John W. "Libya in Chad: Soviet Surrogate or Nomadic Imperialist?" *Conflict* 5, no. 1 (1983): 1–18.

Anderson, Lisa. "Libya and American Foreign Policy." *Middle East Journal* 36, no. 4 (Autumn 1982): 516–34.

———. "Qadhdhafi and the Kremlin." *Problems of Communism* 34 (September–October 1985): 29–44.

Arab, Mohamed Khalifa. "The Effect of the Leader's Belief System on Foreign Policy: The Case of Libya." Ph.D. diss., Florida State University, 1988.

Auda, Abdel Malik. "An Evaluation of the Afro-Arab Cooperation Experiment." In *The Arabs and Africa*, ed. Khair El-Din Haseeb, 574–637. London: Croom Helm and Centre for Arab Unity Studies, 1985.

Azar, Edward E. "Soviet and Chinese Roles in the Middle East." *Problems of Communism* 28 (May–June 1979): 18–30.

Badday, M. "Libye: Les suites du coup de Tripoli." *Revue Française d'Etudes Politiques Africaines* (December 1969): 10–12.

Baker, Coleman L. "The United States and Libya." *Military Review* 49, no. 4 (April 1969): 83–91.

Bechtold, Peter K. "New Attempts at Arab Cooperation: The Federation of Arab Republics, 1971–?" *Middle East Journal* 27, no. 2 (Spring 1973): 152–72.

Beshir, Mohamed Omer. "The Role of the Arab Group in the Organisation of African Unity." In *The Arabs and Africa*, ed. Khair El-Din Haseeb, 223–56. London: Croom Helm and Centre for Arab Unity Studies, 1985.

Bibes, G. "Les Italiens de Libye et les relations italo-libyennes." *Maghreb* 42 (November–December 1970): 34–38.

Bills, Scott L. *The Libyan Arena: The United States, Britain, and the Council of Foreign Ministers, 1945–1948*. Kent, Ohio: Kent State University Press, 1995.

Binoche-Guedra, Jacques. "Quelques éléments pour situer le conflit tchado-libyen." *Maghreb-Machrek* 120 (April–June 1988): 96–102.

Blake, G. H. "The 1982 United Nations Convention on the Law of the Sea: Some Implications for Libya." *Libyan Studies* 15 (1984): 129–35.

Bleuchot, Hervé. "Les fondements de l'ideologie du Colonel Mouammar el-Kadhafi." *Maghreb* (March–April 1974): 21–27.

Bleuchot, Hervé, and Taoufik Monastiri. "La logique unitaire libyenne et les mobiles du Colonel Qadhafi." *Herodote* (March 1985): 81–89.

Blum, Y. Z. "The Gulf of Sidra Incident." *American Journal of International Law* 80 (July 1986): 668–77.

Boubakri, Hassen. "Exchanges transfrontalier et commerce parallèle aux frontiers tuniso-libyennes." *Maghreb-Machrek* 170 (October–December 2000): 39–51.

Boucek, Christopher. "The Abu Sayyaf Hostage Crisis and Libyan Foreign Policy in the Philippines." *Journal of Libyan Studies* 2, no. 1 (Summer 2001): 39–47.

———. "Libya's Curious Relationship with Mugabe's Zimbabwe." *Journal of Libyan Studies* 3, no. 2 (Winter 2002): 22–31.

Boureston, Jack, and Yana Feldman. "Verifying Libya's Nuclear Disarmament." In *Verification Yearbook 2004*, ed. Trevor Findlay, 87–105. London: VERTIC, 2003.

Brett, M. "The UN and Libya." *Journal of African History* 13, no. 1 (March 1972): 168–70.

Brewer, William D. "The Libyan-Sudanese Crisis of 1981: Danger for Darfur and Dilemma for the United States." *Middle East Journal* 36, no. 2 (Spring 1982): 205–16.

Brionne, B. "Libye-Soudan: Conflict inévitable?" *Défense National* 37, no. 12 (1981).

Calabrese, Jamie Ann. "Carrots or Sticks? Libya and the U.S. Efforts to Influence Rogue States." M.A. thesis, U.S. Naval Postgraduate School, Sepember 2004.

Campbell, John C. "Communist Strategies in the Mediterranean." *Problems of Communism* 28 (May–June 1979): 1–17.

Carveley, Andrew. "Libya: Act II." *Non-aligned Third World Annual* (1970): 111–36.

———. "Libya: International Relations and Political Purposes." *International Journal* 28, no. 4 (Autumn 1973): 707–28.

Cazadis, Anne-Marie. *Kadhafi: Le templier d'Allah*. Paris: Éditions Gallimard, 1974.

"Chad-Libya: Confrontation." *Africa* 21 (October 1971): 32–33.

Chandler, G. "Myth of Oil Power: International Groups and National Sovereignty." *International Affairs* 46, no. 4 (October 1970): 710–18.

Chaplin, Dennis. "Libya: Military Spearhead against Sadat?" *Military Review* 59, no. 11 (November 1979): 42–50.

Chasek, Pamela. "Revolution across the Sea: Libyan Foreign Policy in Central America." In *Central America and the Middle East: The Internationalization of the Crises*, ed. Dámian J. Fernández, 150–76. Miami: Florida International University Press, 1990.

Chidebe, Chris. "Nigeria and the Arab States." *American Journal of Islamic Social Sciences* 2, no. 1 (1985): 115–23.

Cleveland, Raymond H., et al. *A Global Perspective on Transnational Terrorism: A Case Study of Libya*. Research Report No. 25. U.S. Air Force Air War College. April 1977.

Collins, Stephen D. "Dissuading State Support of Terrorism: Strikes or Sanctions?" *Studies in Conflict and Terrorism* 27 (2004): 1–18.

Commaire, J. "Soudan-Libye: En marge de deux révolutions." *France Eurafrique* (October 1969): 36.

Cooley, John K. "The Libyan Menace." *Foreign Policy* 42 (Spring 1981): 74–93.
———. "The Shifting Sands of Arab Communism." *Problems of Communism* 24 (March–April 1975): 22–42.

Copson, Raymond W. "African Flashpoints: Prospects for Armed International Conflict." *Orbis* 25, no. 4 (Winter 1982): 903–23.

Cordell, Dennis D. "The Awlad Sulayman of Libya and Chad: Power and Adaptation in the Sahara and the Sahel." *Canadian Journal of African Studies* 19, no. 2 (1985): 319–44.

Cricco, Massimiliano. "The Image of Colonel Qaddafi in American and British Documents, 1969–1971." *Journal of Libyan Studies* 3, no. 2 (Winter 2002): 32–40.
———. "La vendita di armi sovietiche e italiana alla Libia nei documenti americani, 1970–1972." *Journal of Libyan Studies* 4, no. 1 (Summer 2003): 76–86.

Crocker, Chester A., chair. *U.S.-Libyan Relations: Toward Cautious Reengagement*. Atlantic Council Policy Paper, April 2003.

Crozier, Brian, ed. *Libya's Foreign Adventures*. Conflict Studies No. 41. London: Institute for the Study of Conflict, 1973.

Damis, John. "Morocco, Libya and the Treaty of Union." *American-Arab Affairs* 13 (Summer 1985): 44–55.
———. "The United States and North Africa." In *Polity and Society in Contemporary North Africa*, ed. I. William Zartman and William Mark Habeeb, 221–40. Boulder, Colo.: Westview Press, 1993.

Davis, Brian L. *Qaddafi, Terrorism, and the Origins of the U.S. Attack on Libya*. New York: Praeger, 1990.

Deeb, Marius, and Mary-Jane Deeb. "Libya: Internal Developments and Regional Politics." In *The Middle East Annual: Issues and Events*, ed. David H. Partington, 13–40. Boston: G. K. Hall, 1985.

Deeb, Mary-Jane. "The Arab Maghribi Union and the Prospects for North African Unity." In *Polity and Society in Contemporary North Africa*, ed. I. William Zartman and William Mark Habeeb, 189–203. Boulder, Colo.: Westview Press, 1993.

———. "The Arab Maghribi Union in the Context of Regional and International Politics." *Middle East Insight* 6, no. 5 (Spring 1989): 42–46.

———. "Qadhafi's Calculated Risks." *SAIS Review* 6, no. 2 (Summer–Fall 1986): 151–62.

———. *Libya's Foreign Policy in North Africa*. Boulder, Colo.: Westview Press, 1991.

———. "Libya's Foreign Policy in North Africa." Ph.D. diss., Johns Hopkins University, 1987.

"Diplomatic Missions: Appointment, Accreditation and Notification of People's Bureaus." *American Journal of International Law* 74, no. 4 (October 1980): 921–28.

Dunne, Michele. "Libya: Security Is Not Enough." Policy Brief No. 32, Carnegie Endowment for International Peace, October 2004.

Dyer, Gwynne. "Libya." In *World Armies*, 2nd ed., ed. John Keegan, 362–70. Detroit: Gale Research, 1983.

"Egypt-Libya, Mini-war." *Africa Institute Bulletin* 15, nos. 9–10 (1977): 272–76.

Evans, Trefor. "The New Libya: Coming to Terms with Revolution in the Arab World." *Round Table* (1970): 265–74.

Fallaci, Oriana. "Iranians Are Our Brothers: An Interview with Col. Muammar el-Qaddafi of Libya." *New York Times Magazine*, 16 December 1979, 40ff.

Fayeq, Omar. "Libya's Gains and Losses from the Gulf Crisis." *Middle East International* 402 (14 June 1991): 17–18.

Feldman, Mark B. "The Tunisia-Libya Continental Shelf Case: Geographic Justice or Judicial Compromise?" *American Journal of International Law* 77, no. 2 (April 1983): 219–38.

Francioni, F. "The Gulf of Sirte Incident (United States versus Libya)." *Italian Yearbook of International Law* 5 (1981): 85–109.

———. "The Status of the Gulf of Sirte in International Law." *Syracuse Journal of International Law* 1, no. 1 (Autumn 1984): 311–26.

Gaspard, J. "Making an Arab Revolution: Libya Finds Egypt's Pattern Inadequate." *New Middle East* 14 (November 1969): 15–20.

Ghanem, M. "International Relations with the Union of Arab Republics." *Journal of the Middle East* 1 (January 1974): 1–13.

Ghariani, Mustafa Sedd El. "Libya's Foreign Policy: The Role of the Country's Environmental and Leadership Factors, 1960–1973." M.A. thesis, Western Michigan University, 1979.

A Global Perspective on Transnational Terrorism: A Case Study of Libya. Maxwell Air Force Base, Ala.: Air War College, 1977.

"Gunboat Diplomacy, Lightning War and the Nixon Doctrine: U.S. Military Strategy in the Arabian Gulf." *Race and Class* 17 (Winter 1976): 303–18.

Gutteridge, William, ed. *Libya: Still a Threat to Western Interests?* Conflict Studies No. 160. London: Institute for the Study of Conflict, 1984.

Habeeb, William Mark. "The Maghribi States and the European Community." In *Polity and Society in Contemporary North Africa*, ed. I. William Zartman and William Mark Habeeb, 204–20. Boulder, Colo.: Westview Press, 1993.

Haddad, Saïd. "La politique africaine de la Libye: De la tentation impériale à la stratégie unitaire." *Maghreb-Machrek* 170 (October–December 2000): 29–38.

Haerr, R. C. "The Gulf of Sidra." *San Diego Law Review* 24 (1987): 751–67.

Haley, P. Edward. *Qaddafi and the United States since 1969*. New York: Praeger, 1984.

Harris, L. "North African Union: Fact or Fantasy?" *Arab Affairs* 12 (1990): 52–60.

Hartschorn, J. "From Tripoli to Tehran and Back: The Size and Meaning of the Oil Game." *World Today* 27, no. 7 (July 1971): 291–301.

Hasan, Yusuf Fadl. "The Historical Roots of Afro-Arab Relations." In *The Arabs and Africa*, ed. Khair El-Din Haseeb, 27–57. London: Croom Helm and Centre for Arab Unity Studies, 1985.

Haseeb, Khair El-Din. *The Arabs and Africa*. London: Croom Helm and Centre for Arab Unity Studies, 1985.

Haykal, M. "Egypt-Libya Union." *Africa* 23 (October 1973): 83–85.

Hodges, Tony. *Western Sahara: The Roots of a Desert War*. Westport, Conn.: Lawrence Hill, 1983.

Holley, Charles. "Libyan Foreign Policy: Consistent Objectives and Priorities But . . . ." *Middle East* 23 (September 1976): 25–29.

Hottinger, Arnold. "Colonel Ghadhafi's Pan-Arab Ambitions." *Swiss Review of World Affairs* 21, no. 3 (June 1971): 22–24.

———. "L'expansionnisme Libyen: Machrek, Maghreb et Afrique noire." *Politique Étrangère* 46, no. 1 (March 1981): 137–49.

Huliaras, Asteris. "Qadhafi's Comeback: Libya and Sub-Saharan Africa in the 1990s." *African Affairs* 100, no. 398 (2001): 5–25.

Inde, Gerd. *Zum Sowjetisch-Libyschen Verhältnis*. Cologne: Bundesinstitut fur Ostwissenschaftliche und Internationale Studien, 1975.

Jessup, Philip C. "Editorial Comment: Intervention in the International Court." *American Journal of International Law* 75, no. 4 (October 1981): 903–9.

Joffé, E. G. H. [George]. "Briefings: Libya and Chad," *Review of African Political Economy* 21 (May–September 1981): 84–102.

———. "La Libye et l'Europe." *Maghreb-Machrek* 170 (October–December 2000): 16–28.

———. "Libya: Who Blinked, and Why." *Current History* 103, no. 673 (May 2004): 221–25.

——. "Libya and Europe." *Journal of North African Studies* 6, no. 4 (Winter 2001): 75–92.

——. "Relations between Libya, Tunisia and Malta up to the British Occupation of Malta." *Libyan Studies* 21 (1990): 65–73.

Katzman, Kenneth. *U.S.-Libyan Relations: An Analytic Compendium of U.S. Policies, Laws & Regulations*. Atlantic Council Occasional Paper, August 2003.

Kearney, V. S. "Greening of Libya." *America* 142 (January 1980): 39–40.

Kerr, M. "The Convenient Marriage of Egypt and Libya." *New Middle East* 48 (1972): 4–6.

Khalid, Mansour. *Nimeiri and the Revolution of Dis-may*. London: KPI, 1985.

Khashan, H. "The Revival of Pan-Arabism" *Orbis* 35, no. 1 (1991): 107–16.

Khurana, T. "Indo-Libyan Trade Relations." *Indo-African Trade Journal* 7, no. 7 (1971): 30–33.

Korany, Bahgat, Paul Noble, and Rex Brynen, eds. *The Many Faces of National Security in the Arab World*. New York: St. Martin's Press, 1993.

Koury, E. *The Patterns of Mass Movements in Arab Revolutionary Progressive States*. New York: Humanities Press, 1971.

Lanne, Bernard. *Tchad-Libye: La querelle des frontières*. Paris: Éditions Karthala, 1982.

Layachi, Azzedine. "Images of Foreign Policy: The United States and North Africa." Ph.D. diss., New York University, 1988.

——. *The United States and North Africa: A Cognitive Approach to Foreign Policy*. New York: Praeger, 1990.

"Le Maghreb et la Libye devant la mort de Nasser." *Maghreb* 42 (November–December 1970): 13–16.

Leca, Jean. "La guerre franco-libyenne de 1900–1902." *Maghreb-Machrek* 120 (April–June 1988): 102–6.

Legum, Colin. "Libya's Intervention in Chad." In *Crisis and Conflicts in the Middle East*, ed. Colin Legum, 52–63. New York: Holmes and Meier, 1981.

Lemarchand, René. "Chad: The Road to Partition." *Current History* 83, no. 491 (March 1984): 113–16, 132.

——, ed. *The Green and the Black: Qadhafi's Policies in Africa*. Bloomington: Indiana University Press, 1988.

Lesch, Ann Mosely. "Sudan's Foreign Policy: In Search of Arms, Aid, and Allies." In *Sudan: State and Society in Crisis*, 43–70. Bloomington: Indiana University Press, 1991,

Lewis, William H. "North Africa: Struggle for Primacy." *Current History* 76, no. 445 (March 1979): 119–21, 131.

——. "U.S.-Libya Relations: A New Chapter?" *Atlantic Council Bulletin* 12, no. 4 (May 2001): 1–4.

——. "The War on Terrorism: The Libya Case." *Atlantic Council Bulletin* 13, no. 3 (April 2002); 1–4.

"Libya: Russian Rapprochement." *Africa Confidential* 15 (31 May 1974): 2–4.

Lycett, Andrew. "Libyans in Chad: Guests or Hosts?" *Middle East* 77 (March 1981): 26–28.

Majzoub, Mohamed Said. *La Libye et l'unité maghrebine*. Aix-en-Provence: Mémoire pour le Diplôme d'Études Supérieures, Faculté de Droit, 1970.

Mattes, Hanspeter. *Die innere und aussere islamische Mission Libyens*. Hamburg: Kaiser Grunewald, 1986.

——. "Libya's Economic Relations as an Instrument of Foreign Policy." In *The Economic Development of Libya*, ed. Bichara Khader and Bashir el-Wifati, 81–123. London: Croom Helm, 1987.

Mazrui, Ali. "Libya: A Superpower in Miniature?" *Africa Now* (May 1981): 51–52.

McConnell, James, and Bradford Dismukes. "Soviet Diplomacy of Force in the Third World." *Problems of Communism* 28 (January–February 1979): 14–27.

Mertz, Robert Anton, and Pamela MacDonald Mertz. *Arab Aid to Sub-Saharan Africa*. Munich: Chr. Kaiser Verlag, 1983.

Micallef, Joseph V. "Mediterranean Maverick: Malta's Uncertain Future." *Round Table* 275 (July 1979): 238–51.

Migliavacca, P. "Controversial Complementarity with Libya." *Politica Internazionale* 5, no. 2 (1986): 39–48.

Neuberger, Benyamin. *Involvement, Invasion and Withdrawal: Qadhdhafi's Libya and Chad, 1969–1981*. Occasional Papers No. 83. Shiloah Center for Middle Eastern and African Studies, Tel Aviv University, May 1982.

Neutze, Dennis R. "The Gulf of Sidra Incident: A Legal Perspective." *U.S. Naval Institute Proceedings* 108 (1982): 26–31.

N'Gangbet, Michel. *Peut-on encore sauver le Tchad?* Paris: Éditions L'Harmattan, 1984.

Ngansop, Guy Jeremie. *Tchad: Vingt ans de crise*. Paris: Éditions L'Harmattan, 1984.

Niblock, Tim. "The Foreign Policy of Libya." In *The Foreign Policies of Middle East States*, ed. Raymond Hinnebusch and Anoushiravan Ehteshami. Boulder, Colo.: Lynne Rienner, 2002.

Nizza, Ricardo. "Libya's Prussian Role in the Drive for Arab Unity." *New Middle East* 45 (June 1972): 4–7.

Ogunbadejo, Oye. "Qadhafi and Africa's International Relations." *Journal of Modern African Studies* 24, no. 1 (1986): 33–68.

——. "Qaddafi's North African Design." *International Security* 8, no. 1 (Summer 1983): 154–78.

Otayek, René. "La Libye révolutionnaire au sud du Sahara." *Maghreb-Machrek* 94 (October–December 1981): 5–35.

——. *La politique africaine de la Libye, 1969–1985*. Paris: Éditions Karthala, 1986.

Pajak, Roger F. "Arms and Oil: The Soviet-Libyan Arms Supply Relationship." *Middle East Review* 13, no. 2 (Winter 1980/81): 51–56.

———. "Soviet Arms Aid to Libya." *Military Review* (July 1976): 82–87.

Parker, Richard B. "Appointment in Oujda." *Foreign Affairs* 63, no. 5 (Summer 1985): 1095–1110.

———. *North Africa: Regional Tensions and Strategic Concerns.* New York: Praeger, 1984.

———. *Uncle Sam in Barbary: A Diplomatic History.* Gainesville: University Press of Florida, 2004.

Pernot, Maurice. "The Soviet Union and the Mediterranean." *Fortnightly Review* (December 1945): 363–68.

Pichon, Jean. *La question de Libye dans le règlement de la paix.* Paris: J. Peyronnet, 1945.

Pipes, Daniel. "No One Likes the Colonel." *American Spectator* 14, no. 3 (March 1981): 18–22.

Qadhafi, Saif Aleslam Al-. "Libyan-American Relations." *Middle East Policy* 10, no.1 (Spring 2003): 35–44.

Qora'i, Ahmed Yousef Al-. "The Scope of Actual Arab Political Interest in Africa." In *The Arabs and Africa*, ed. Khair El-Din Haseeb, 257–82. London: Croom Helm and Centre for Arab Unity Studies, 1985.

Rachid, C. "Projet de fusion Tunisie-Libye: Huit questions, huit responses." *African Affairs* 49 (4–17 February 1974): 10–13.

"Relations et échanges entre la Libye et des voisins maghrebins." *Maghreb* 35 (September–October 1969): 30–33.

Rodenbeck, Max. "Egypt and Libya: Towards Integration." *Middle East International* 407 (30 August 1991): 11.

Rondot, P. "L'union des républiques arabes." *Études* 336 (January 1972): 37–59.

———. "Vers une nouvelle république arabe unie." *Défense Nationale* 29 (March 1973): 73–82.

Ronen, Yehudit. "Libya's Intervention in Amin's Uganda: A Broken Spearhead." *Asian and African Studies* 26, no. 2 (1992): 173–83.

———. "Personalities and Politics: Qadhafi, Nasser, Sadat and Mubarak (1969–2000)." *Journal of North African Studies* 6, no. 3 (Autumn 2001): 1–10.

———. *Qadhafi's Christmas Gift: What's behind Libya's Decision to Renounce WMD?* Tel Aviv Notes. Moshe Dayan Center for Middle Eastern and African Studies, Tel Aviv University, 24 December 2003.

Rouleau, Eric. "Oil and Monarchies Don't Mix." *Africa Report* 14, no. 7 (November 1969): 24–27.

Rustow, Dankwart A. *Oil and Turmoil: America Faces OPEC and the Middle East.* New York: W. W. Norton, 1982.

St John, Ronald Bruce. "Apply 'Libya Model' to Iran and Syria." *Foreign Policy in Focus*, 21 October 2004, www.fpif.org/commentary/2004/0410libya.html.

———. "The Determinants of Libyan Foreign Policy, 1969–1983." *Maghreb Review* 8, nos. 3–4 (May–August 1983): 96–103.

———. "Libya and the United States: Elements of a Performance-based Roadmap." *Middle East Policy* 10, no. 3 (Fall 2003): 144–54. Reprinted in *Violence and Terrorism 05/06*, 8th ed., ed. Thomas J. Badey, 55–61. Dubuque, Iowa: McGraw-Hill/Dushkin, 2005.

———. "Libya in Africa, Looking Back, Moving Forward." *Journal of Libyan Studies* 1, no. 1 (Summer 2000): 18–32.

———. "Libya Is Not Iraq: Preemptive Strikes, WMD, and Diplomacy." *Middle East Journal* 58, no. 3 (Summer 2004): 386–402.

———. "Libya Is the Acid Test for Bolton Nomination." *Foreign Policy in Focus*, 16 May 2005, www.fpif.org/commentary/2005/0505libya.html.

———. "The Libyan Debacle in Sub-Saharan Africa, 1969–1987." In *The Green and the Black: Qadhafi's Policies in Africa*, ed. René Lemarchand, 125–38. Bloomington: Indiana University Press, 1988.

———. "Libyan Foreign Policy: Newfound Flexibility." *Orbis* 47, no. 3 (Summer 2003): 463–77.

———. "Libyan Terrorism: The Case against Gaddafi." *Contemporary Review* 1523, no. 261 (December 1992): 294–98.

———. "Libya's New Foreign Policy." *Contemporary Review* 243, no. 1410 (July 1983): 15–18.

———. "New Era in American-Libyan Relations." *Middle East Policy* 10, no. 3 (Summer 2002): 85–93.

———. *Qaddafi's World Design: Libyan Foreign Policy, 1969–1987*. London: Saqi Books, 1987.

———. "Qaddafi's World Design Revisited." *Global Affairs* 8, no. 1 (Winter 1993): 161–73.

———. "Separating Libyan Facts from Bush Fiction." *Foreign Policy in Focus*, 7 September 2004, www.fpif.org/commentary/2004/0409libyafacts.html.

———. "The Soviet Penetration of Libya." *World Today* 38, no. 4 (April 1982): 131–38.

———. "Terrorism and Libyan Foreign Policy, 1981–1986." *World Today* 42, no. 7 (July 1986): 111–15.

———. "The United States, the Cold War and Libyan Independence." *Journal of Libyan Studies* 2, no. 2 (Winter 2001): 26–45.

———. "Whatever's Happened to Qaddafi?" *World Today* 43, no. 4 (April 1987): 58–59.

Samura, Mohamed O'Bai. *The Libyan Revolution: Its Lessons for Africa*. Washington, D.C.: International Institute for Policy and Development Studies, 1985.

Sanders, S. W. "Why the U.S. Must Take a Stand on Qaddafi." *Business Week*, 3 March 1980, 41.

Sayigh, Yusif A. *Arab Oil Policies in the 1970s: Opportunity and Responsibility*. London: Croom Helm, 1983.

Schumacher, Edward. "The United States and Libya." *Foreign Affairs* 65, no. 2 (Winter 1986/87): 329–48.

Seale, Patrick, and Maureen McConville. *The Hilton Assignment*. New York: Praeger, 1973.

Segal, Aaron. "Spain and the Middle East: A Fifteen-Year Assessment." *Middle East Journal* 45, no. 2 (Spring 1991): 250–64.

Shaked, Haim, and Yehudit Ronen. "Shimmering Tension: Libyan-Egyptian Relations, 1954–1986." In *Conflict Management in the Middle East*, ed. Gabriel Ben-Dor and David B. Dewitt. Lexington, Mass.: Lexington Books, 1987.

Shams-Barragh, F. "Libya's Foreign Relations before and after the Discovery of Oil." M.A. thesis, Howard University, 1969.

Sharawi, Helmy. "Israeli Policy in Africa." In *The Arabs and Africa*, ed. Khair El-Din Haseeb, 285–343. London: Croom Helm and Centre for Arab Unity Studies, 1985.

Shembesh, Ali Muhammad. "The Analysis of Libya's Foreign Policy, 1962–1973: A Study of the Impact of Environmental and Leadership Factors." Ph.D. diss., Emory University, 1975.

Sicker, Martin. *The Making of a Pariah State: The Adventurist Policies of Muammar Qaddafi*. New York: Praeger, 1987.

Simons, Geoff. *Libya and the West: From Independence to Lockerbie*. Oxford: Centre for Libyan Studies, 2003.

Slonim, Shlomo. "Egypt, Algeria, and the Libyan Revolution." *World Today* 26, no. 3 (March 1970): 125–30.

Spinnato, J. W. "Historic and Vital Bays: An Analysis of Libya's Claim to the Gulf of Sidra." *Ocean Development and International Law* 13 (1983): 65–85.

Stanik, Joseph T. *El Dorado Canyon: Reagan's Undeclared War with Qaddafi*. Annapolis, Md.: Naval Institute Press, 2003.

Stevovic, Mihailo V. "Chad and Events Surrounding It." *Review of International Affairs* 32 (March 1981): 24–26.

Sultan, K. "Political Association and Maghreb Economic Development." *Journal of Modern African Studies* 10, no. 2 (1972): 191–202.

Takeyh, Ray. "The Evolving Course of Qaddafi's Foreign Policy." *Journal of Libyan Studies* 1, no. 2 (Winter 2000): 41–53.

——. "Libya: Opting for Europe and Africa, Not Ties with Washington." Policy Watch No. 486. Washington Institute for Near East Policy, 21 September 2000.

———. "Libya's Confident Defiance and ILSA." Policy Watch No. 553. Washington Institute for Near East Policy, 27 August 2001.

———. "Lockerbie Trial: At Last?" Policy Watch No. 460. Washington Institute for Near East Policy, 2 May 2000.

———. "A Lockerbie Trial Brief: The Tale of a Defector." Policy Watch No. 494. Washington Institute for Near East Policy, 13 October 2000.

———. "The Rogue Who Came In from the Cold." *Foreign Affairs* 80, no. 3 (May–June 2001): 62–72.

Terrill, A. "Libya and the Quest for Chemical Weapons." *Conflict Quarterly* 14, no. 1 (1994): 47–61.

Thompson, E. P., Mary Kaldor, et al. *Mad Dogs: The U.S. Raids on Libya*. London: Pluto Press, 1986.

Thompson, Virginia, and Richard Adloff. *Conflict in Chad*. London: C. Hurst & Co., 1981.

Thus Spoke Colonel Moammar Kaddafi. Beirut: Dar al-Awda, 1974.

Tripp, Charles. "Libye et l'Afrique." *Politique Étrangère* 49, no. 2 (1984): 317–29.

United States. *Termination of Certain Agreements with Libya*. Washington, D.C.: GPO, 1972.

United States. Library of Congress. Foreign Affairs Division. *Chronology of the Libyan Oil Negotiations, 1970–1971*. Washington, D.C.: GPO, 1974.

United States. Senate. *Inquiry into the Matter of Billy Carter and Libya*. 96th Cong., 2nd sess. Report no. 961015, October 2, 1980. Washington, D.C.: GPO, 1980.

Ware, Lewis B. *The Maltese-Libyan Entente in the Mediterranean Basin*. Maxwell Air Force Base, Ala.: Air War College, 1977.

Warfally, Mahmoud G. El. *Imagery and Ideology in U.S. Policy toward Libya, 1962–1982*. Pittsburgh: University of Pittsburgh Press, 1988.

Wheelan, Joseph. *Jefferson's War: America's First War on Terror, 1801–1805*. New York: Carroll & Graf, 2003.

Wiegele, Thomas C. *The Clandestine Building of Libya's Chemical Weapons Factory: A Study in International Collusion*. Carbondale: Southern Illinois University Press, 1992.

Wizarat al-I-lam wa-al-Thaqafah. *Gadafi's Day of Blood in the Sudan*. Khartoum: Ministry of Culture and Information, 1976.

Wright, Claudia. "Libya: Behind the Madman's Labels." *Macleans* 92 (16 July 1979): 26–27.

———. "Libya and the West: Headlong into Confrontation?" *International Affairs* 58, no. 1 (Winter 1981/82): 13–41.

Wright, John. "Chad and Libya: Some Historical Connections." *Maghreb Review* 8, nos. 3–4 (May–August 1983): 91–95.

———. *Libya, Chad and the Central Sahara*. London: C. Hurst & Co., 1989.

Wright, Louis B., and Julia MacLeod. *The First Americans in North Africa: William Eaton's Struggle for a Vigorous Policy against the Barbary Pirates, 1799–1805*. Princeton, N.J.: Princeton University Press, 1945.

Yodfat, Arieh. "The USSR and Libya." *New Outlook* 13, no. 6 (1970): 37–40.

Yousef, Ahmed. "The Impact of the Lockerbie Court Decision on Libyan-U.S. Relations." *Middle East Affairs Journal* 7, nos. 1–2 (Winter–Spring 2001): 31–48.

Zartman, I. William. "Explaining the Nearly Inexplicable: The Absence of Islam in Moroccan Foreign Policy." In *Islam in Foreign Policy*, ed. Adeed Dawisha, 97–111. Cambridge: Cambridge University Press, 1983.

———. "The Maghrib into the Future." In *Polity and Society in Contemporary North Africa*, ed. I. William Zartman and William Mark Habeeb, 241–49. Boulder, Colo.: Westview Press, 1993.

Zartman, I. William, and A. G. Kluge. "Heroic Politics: The Foreign Policy of Libya." In *The Foreign Policies of Arab States: The Challenge of Change*, ed. Bahgat Korany and Ali E. Hillal Dessouki, 236–59. Boulder, Colo.: Westview Press, 1991.

Zilian, F. "The US Raid on Libya—and NATO." *Orbis* 30, no. 3 (Fall 1986): 499–524.

Zoubir, Yahia H. "Libya in US Foreign Policy: From Rogue State to Good Fellow?" *Third World Quarterly* 23, no. 1 (2002): 31–53.

Zoubir, Yahia H., and Karima Benabdallah-Gambier. "Morocco, Western Sahara and the Future of the Maghrib." *Journal of African Studies* 9, no. 1 (Spring 2004): 49–77.

D. Official Libyan Publications

Al-Fateh Revolution in Ten Years. Printed in Italy and Switzerland, 1979. Distributed by the Libyan People's Bureau, Washington, D.C.

Libya. Department of Information and Cultural Affairs. *The Human March in the Libyan Arab Republic*. Tripoli: 1976.

Libya. General Administration for Information. *Popular Revolution and the People's Responsibilities*. Tripoli: 1973.

Libya. Ministry of Education and National Guidance. *On Evacuation of British Forces, Evacuation Day, March 31st, 1970*. N.p.: 1970.

Libya. Ministry of Foreign Affairs. Administration of Information and Cultural Affairs. *The Libyan Arab Republic: Facts and Figures*. Tripoli: 1975.

Libya. Ministry of Information. *Achievements of the First of September Revolution: Domestically, Nationally, Internationally*. Tripoli: 1971.

———. *First of September Revolution, Fifth Anniversary*. Tripoli: 1975.

Libya. Ministry of Information and Culture. General Administration for Information. *Aspects of First of September Revolution*. Tripoli: 1973.

———. *I. Broadlines of the Third Theory; II. The Aspects of the Third Theory; III. The Concept of Jihad; IV. The Divine Concept of Islam.* Tripoli: 1973.

———. *The Fundamentals of the Third International Theory.* Tripoli: 1974.

———. *The Libyan Arab Republic and the World.* Tripoli: 1974.

———. *The Revolution of 1st September the Fourth Anniversary.* Benghazi: 1973.

———. *The Revolutionary March.* Tripoli: 1973.

———. *The Third International Theory: The Divine Concept of Islam and the Popular Revolution in Libya.* Tripoli: 1973.

Qaddafi, Muammar al-. *Evacuation Day of American Troops, Uqba Ben Nafae Air Base.* Tripoli: Public Relations Department, Ministry of Education and National Guidance, 1971.

———. *The Green Book.* Part 1, *The Solution to the Problem of Democracy.* London: Martin Brian & O'Keefe, 1976. Part 2, *The Solution of the Economic Problem "Socialism."* London: Martin Brian & O'Keefe, 1978. Part 3, *The Social Basis of the Third Universal Theory.* Tripoli: Public Establishment for Publishing, Advertising and Distribution, n.d.

———. "Text of Address Delivered by RCC Chairman Col. Muammar Qadhdhafi in Opening Session of the EuroArab Youth Conference." Tripoli: General Administration for Information, Ministry of Information and Culture, 1973.

VIII. SCIENCE

A. General

Savitz, Gerald S. *Parmaceuticals in Libya.* Tripoli: Tarabulus, 1970.

B. Botany

Ali, S. I., and S. M. H. Jafri, eds. *Flora of Libya.* Tripoli: Al-Fateh University, 1976.

Durand, E., and G. Baratte. *Florae libycae prodromus: Catalogue raisonné des plantes de Tripolitaine.* Geneva: Romet, 1910.

Keith, H. G. *A Preliminary Check List of Libyan Flora.* Tripoli: Ministry of Agriculture and Agrarian Reform, 1965.

Kranz, Jurgen. *A List of Plant Pathogenic and Other Fungi of Cyrenaica (Libya).* Kew, U.K.: Commonwealth Mycological Institute, 1965.

Lairje, Abdulla Abdulla. "The Ecology and Macrofaunal Diversity of the Mediterranean Littoral Zone near Sussa, Libya, Africa." Ph.D. diss., Utah State University, 1979.

Pelling, Ruth, and Saleh al Hassy. "The Macroscopic Plant Remains from Euesperides (Benghazi): An Interim Report." *Libyan Studies* 28 (1997): 1–4.

Shawesh, Othman Mohamed. "Vegetarian Types of Semi-arid Rangelands in Northwestern Libya." Ph.D. diss., University of Wyoming, 1981.

Turner, D. "An Integrated Study of the Desert Grass, Panicum Turgidum Forsk., in a Fezzan Djebel System." *Libyan Studies* 14 (1983): 155–56.

Van der Veen, M. "The UNESCO Libyan Valleys Survey X: Botanical Evidence for Ancient Farming in the Pre-desert." *Libyan Studies* 16 (1985): 15–28.

White, Kevin, Nick Brooks, Nick Drake, Matthew Charlton, and Sue MacLaren. "Monitoring Vegetation Change in Desert Oases by Remote Sensing: A Case Study in the Libyan Fazzan." *Libyan Studies* 34 (2003): 153–66.

C. Geography and Geology

Ambraseys, N. N. "Material for the Investigation of the Seismicity of Libya." *Libyan Studies* 25 (1994): 7–22.

Ammar, A. Ammar. "An Analysis of Eocene Mass Movements in the Wadi Athrun, Cyrenaica." *Libyan Studies* 24 (1993): 19–26.

Anketell, J. M. "Quaternary Deposits on Northern Libya—Lithostratigraphy and Correlation." *Libyan Studies* 20 (1989): 1–29.

Anketell, J. M., and S. M. Ghellali. "The Karawah and Qarabulli Members of the Jifarah Formation—Late Pleistocene Aeolian and Lacustrine Deposits—Northwest Libya." *Libyan Studies* 23 (1992): 1–6.

——. "Quaternary Fluvio-aeolian Sand/Silt and Alluvial Gravel Deposits of Northern Libya—Event Stratigraphy and Correlation." *Journal of African Earth Sciences* 13 (1991): 457–69.

——. "Stratigraphic Aspects of the Gargaresh Formation, Tripolitania, Socialist People's Libyan Arab Jamahiriya." *Libyan Studies* 17 (1987): 123–31.

——. "Stratigraphic Aspects of the Qasr Al Haj Formation, Tripolitania, Socialist People's Libyan Arab Jamahiriya." *Libyan Studies* 18 (1988): 115–27.

——. "Stratigraphic Relationships of Basalt Lava Flows to the Pleistocene Sedimentary Sequence of the Mizdah Region, Tripolitania, Socialist People's Libyan Arab Jamahiriya." *Libyan Studies* 21 (1990): 61–63.

——. "Stratigraphic Studies on Quaternary Flood Plain Deposits on the Eastern Gefara Plain." *Libyan Studies* 14 (1983): 16–38.

Antonovic, A. "Geological Map of Libya, Mizdah (NI 33-1)." Tripoli: Industrial Research Centre, 1977.

Atkinson, David. "The Politics of Geography and the Italian Occupation of Libya." *Libyan Studies* 27 (1996): 71–84.

Atkinson, K., M. Bavis, and D. Johnson. "Man-made Oases of Libya." *Geographical Magazine* 45 (November 1972): 112–15.

Barker, G. W. W., D. D. Gilbertson, D. C. Griffin, P. P. Hayes, and D. A. Jones. "The UNESCO Libyan Valleys Survey V: Sedimentological Properties of Holocene Wadi Floor and Plateau Deposits in Tripolitania, Northwest Libya." *Libyan Studies* 14 (1983): 69–85.

Barker, G. W. W., and G. D. B. Jones. "The UNESCO Libyan Valleys Survey, 1979–1981: Palaeo-economy and Environmental Archaeology in the Pre-desert." *Libyan Studies* 13 (1982): 1–34.

——. "The UNESCO Libyan Valleys Survey, 1980." *Libyan Studies* 12 (1981): 9–48.

Bary, Erika de. *Im Bauch des Sandes*. Heusenstamm: Orion-Heimreiter, 1973.

Bary, Erwin von. *Sahara-Tagebuch*. Heusenstamm: Orion-Heimreiter, 1977.

Beadnell, H. J. L. "Libyan Sand Dunes." *Geographical Journal* 34 (October 1954): 337–40.

Blake, G. H. "Misurata: A Market Town in Tripolitania." Research Paper Series No. 9. Department of Geology, University of Durham, 1968.

——. "Political Geography in the Literature on Libya, 1969–1989." *Libyan Studies* 20 (1989): 259–62.

Brehony, J. A. N. "A Geographical Study of the Jebel Tarhun, Tripolitania." Ph.D. diss., University of Durham, 1960.

Buluga, Hadi M. R. "The Western Coastal Zone of Tripolitania: A Human Geography." M.Litt. thesis, University of Durham, 1960.

Buru, M. M. "El-Marj Plain: A Geographical Study." Ph.D. diss., University of Durham, 1965.

——. "A Geographical Study of the Eastern Jebel El Akhdar, Cyrenaica." M.Litt. thesis, University of Durham, 1960.

Coque, R. "Morphogenèse quaternaire du piémont mediterranéen du Djebel Akhdar (Cyrenaique)." *Annales de Géographie* 79 (1970): 375–85.

Danasouril, Gamal E. *Studies of the Geography of the Arab World in Africa*. Cairo: Anglo-Egyptian Bookshop, 1968.

Dardir, A. A. "Igneous Rocks and Mineral Deposits." *Geographical Journal* 146 (1980): 75–76.

Desio, Ardito. *Short History of the Geological, Mining and Oil Exploration in Libya*. Rome: Academia Nazionale dei Lincei, 1967.

Essed, A. S. "A Reconnaissance Bougher Gravity Anomaly Map of Libya." Ph.D. diss., Purdue University, 1978.

Fieller, N. R. J., E. C. Flenley, D. D. Gilbertson, and C. O. Hunt. "The Description and Classification of Grain Size Data from Ancient and Modern Shoreline Sands at Lepcis Magna using Log Skew Laplace Distributions." *Libyan Studies* 21 (1990): 49–59.

Flower, C. P. J. "Mapping the Libyan Valleys: An Application of GIS to the Libyan Valleys Survey." M.A. thesis, University of Leicester, 1993.

Flower, C. P. J., and D. J. Mattingly. "ULVS [UNESCO Libyan Valleys Survey] XXVII: Mapping and Spatial Analysis of the Libyan Valleys Data using GIS." *Libyan Studies* 26 (1995): 49–78.

Furon, R. *Le Sahara: Geologie, Resources, Minerales.* Paris: n.p., 1964.

Ghellali, S. M. "On the Geology of the Eastern Gefara Plain, North West Libya." Ph.D. diss., University of Manchester, 1977.

Ghellali, S. M., and J. M. Anketell. "The Suq al Jum'ah Palaeowadi, an Example of a Plio-Quaternary Palaeo-valley from the Jabal NaDusah, Northwest Libya." *Libyan Studies* 22 (1991): 1–6.

Ghuma, M. A. "The Geology and Geochemistry of the Ben Ghnema Backholikh, Tibesti Massif, Southern Libya." Ph.D. diss., Rice University, 1976.

Gilbertson, D. D., and C. O. Hunt. "The UNESCO Libyan Valleys Survey XXI: Geomorphological Studies of the Romano-Libyan Farm, Its Floodwater Control Structures and Weathered Building Stone at Site Lm 4, at the Confluence of Wasi el Amud and Wadi Umm el Bagul in the Libyan Pre-desert." *Libyan Studies* 21 (1990): 25–42.

Gilbertson, D. D., C. O. Hunt, and N. R. J. Fieller. "ULVS [UNESCO Libyan Valleys Survey] XXVI: Sedimentological and Palynological Studies of Holocene Environmental Changes from a Plateau Basin Infill Sequence at Grerat D'nar Salem, near Beni Ulid, in the Tripolitanian Pre-desert." *Libyan Studies* 24 (1993): 1–18.

Goudarzi, Gus Hossein. *A Geological Report on the Iron Deposits of Shatti Valley Area of Fezzan Province Libya.* U.S. Geological Survey Open File Report. Washington, D.C.: GPO, 1962.

——. *Geology and Mineral Resources of Libya—A Reconnaissance.* Washington, D.C.: GPO, 1970.

——. *A Summary of Geological History of Libya.* U.S. Geological Survey Open File Report. Washington, D.C.: GPO, 1959.

Gray, Carlyle, ed. *Symposium on the Geology of Libya, 1st.* Tripoli: University of Libya, Faculty of Science, 1969.

Groue, A. T. "Geomorphology of the Tibesti Region with Special Reference to Western Tibesti." *Geographical Journal* 126 (1960): 18–31.

Hajjaji, Salem Ali. *The New Libya: A Geographical, Social, Economic and Political Study.* Tripoli: Government Printing Press, 1967.

Hallett, Donald. *Petroleum Geology of Libya.* New York: Elsevier, 2002.

Hammuda, O. S., A. M. Sbeta, A. J. Mouzughi, and B. A. Eliagoubi. *Stratigraphic Nomenclature of the Northwestern Offshore of Libya.* Tripoli: Earth Sciences Society of Libya, 1985.

Haynes, V. "Quaternary Geology and Archaeological Observations." *Geographical Journal* 146, no. 1 (1980): 59–63.

Hey, R. W. "The Quaternary and Palaeolithic of Northern Libya." *Quaternaria* 6 (1962): 435–49.

Hinnawy, M. El, and G. Cheshitev. "Geological Map of Libya, Tarabulus (NI 33–13)." Tripoli: Industrial Research Centre, 1975.

Issawi, B. "Geology, Stratigraphy and Structure of Southwest Egypt." *Geographical Journal* 146, no. 1 (1980): 72–75.

Jacque, M. *Reconnaissance geologique, Fezzan oriental.* Paris: Compagnie Française del Petroles, 1962.

Johnson, Douglas I. *Jabal al-Akhdar, Cyrenaica: An Historical Geography of Settlement and Livelihood.* Chicago: University of Chicago, 1973.

Kanes, William H., ed. *Geology, Archeology and Prehistory of the Southwest Fezzan, Libya.* Castelfranco, Veneto, Italy: Grafiche Trevisan, 1970.

Karasek, Richard Mark. "Structural and Stratigraphic Analysis of the Paleozoic Murzuk and Ghadames Basins, Western Libya." Ph.D. diss., University of South Carolina, 1981.

Khoja, E. "Petrography and Diagenesis of Lower Paleocene Carbonate Reservoir Rock, Dahra Field, Libya." Ph.D. diss., Rice University, 1971.

Khuga, M. A. "The Jebel Garian in Tripolitania: A Regional Study." M.Litt. thesis, University of Durham, 1960.

Koehler, Robert Paul. "Sedimentary Environment and Petrology of the Ain Tobi Formation, Tripolitania, Libya." Ph.D. diss., Rice University, 1982.

McLachlan, K. S. "A Geographical Study of the Coastal Zone between Homs and Misurata, Tripolitania: A Geography of Economic Growth." Ph.D. diss., University of Durham, 1961.

Mijalkovic, N. "Geological Map of Libya, Al Qaddahiyah (NH 33–3)." Tripoli: Industrial Research Centre, 1977.

———. "Geological Map of Libya, Qasr Sirt (NH 33–4)." Tripoli: Industrial Research Centre, 1977.

Novovic, T. "Geological Map of Libya, Djeneien (NH 32–3)." Tripoli: Industrial Research Centre, 1977.

———. "Geological Map of Libya, Nalut (NI 32–4)." Tripoli: Industrial Research Centre, 1977.

Pesce, Angelo. *Gemini Space Photographs of Libya and Tibesti.* London: Academic Press, 1980.

Pyatt, F. B., D. D. Gilbertson, and C. O. Hunt. "ULVS [UNESCO Libyan Valleys Survey] XXII: Crustose Lichen Affecting the Geological Interpretation of Digital Landsat Imagery of the Tripolitanian Pre-desert." *Libyan Studies* 21 (1990): 43–47.

Salem, M. J., and M. T. Bubrewil, eds. *The Geology of Libya.* London: Academic Press, 1980.

Schurmann, H. M. E. *The Pre-Cambrian in North Africa.* Leiden: E. J. Brill, 1974.

Sheppard, T. "Desert Navigation." *Geographical Journal* 136 (1970): 235–39.

Soil Survey of Tauorsa, Tripolitania, Libya, 1961. Durham, U.K.: University of Durham, Department of Geography, 1961.

Thwaite, Anthony. *The Deserts of Hesperides*. London: Secker & Warburg, 1969.

Underwood, J., et al. "Patterned Ground in Southeast Libya." *Libyan Journal of Science* 1 (May 1971): 96–103.

United States. Defense Mapping Agency. Topographic Center. *Libya: Official Standard Names Approved by the United States Board on Geographic Names*. Washington, D.C.: GPO, 1973.

Wilson, Andrew, Paul Bennett, Ahmed Buzaian, and Alette Kattenberg. "The Effects of Recent Storms on the Exposed Coastline of Tocra." *Libyan Studies* 35 (2004): 113–22.

Witcomb, H. A. *Reconnaissance Report on the Geology and Hydrology of the Western Part of the Province of Fezzan*. Washington, D.C.: U.S. Department of the Interior, 1957.

Zivanovic, M. "Geological Map of Libya, Bani Walid (NH 33–2)." Tripoli: Industrial Research Centre, 1977.

D. Meteorology

Fantioli, Amilcare. *Contributo all climatologia della regioni interna della Libia*. Castelfranco, Veneto: Grafiche Trevisan, 1970.

E. Zoology

Anketell, J. M., and S. M. Ghellali. "Nests of a Tube-Dwelling Bee in Quaternary Sediments of the Jeffara Plain." *Libyan Studies* 15 (1984): 137–41.

Bundy, Graham. *The Birds of Libya*. London: British Ornithologists Union, 1976.

Cloudsley-Thompson, J. L. "Successful Desert Animals—Scorpions, Beetles and Lizards." *Libyan Studies* 24 (1993): 143–56.

Etchecopar, R. D., and Francois Hue. *The Birds of North Africa from the Canary Islands to the Red Sea*. Trans. P. A. D. Hollom. London: Oliver & Boyd, 1967.

Grover, J. "Notes about the Amphibians of Libya." *Libyan Journal of Science* [University of Libya, Tripoli] 1 (May 1971): 1–6.

Hamilton, William R. *The Lower Miocene Ruminants of Gebel Zelten, Libya*. London: British Museum, 1973.

Harris, John Michael. *Prodeinotherium from Gebel Zelten, Libya*. London: British Museum, 1973.

Hufnagle, Ernst. *Libyan Mammals*. Stoughton, Wis.: Oleander Press, 1972.

Ranck, Gary I. *The Rodents of Libya*. Washington, D.C.: Smithsonian Institution Press, 1968.

Sevase, Robert J. B. *Introduction to the Miocene Mammal Faunas of Gebel Zelter, Libya*. London: British Museum, 1973.

Toschi, Augusto. *Introduzione alla ornitologia della Libia*. Bologna: Laboratoria di Zoologia Applicata alla Caccia, 1969.

IX. SOCIETY

A. Anthropology

Albergoni, G., and J. Vignet-Zunz. "Aspects of Modernisation among the Bedouin of Barqah." In *Social and Economic Development of Libya*, ed. E. G. H. Joffé and K. S. McLachlan, 189–93. London: Menas Press, 1982.

Beneke, Roy H., Jr. *The Herders of Cyrenaica: Ecology, Economy, and Kinship among the Bedouin of Eastern Libya*. Illinois Studies in Anthropology No. 12. Urbana: University of Illinois Press, 1980.

Brett, Michael, and Elizabeth Fentress. *The Berbers*. Oxford: Blackwell, 1996.

Briggs, L. C. *Tribes of the Sahara*. Cambridge, Mass.: Harvard University Press, 1960.

De Felice, Renzo. *Jews in an Arab Land: Libya, 1835–1970*. Trans. Judith Roumani. Austin: University of Texas Press, 1985.

Dupree, Louis. "The Arabs of Modern Libya." *Muslim World* 64, no. 2 (1958): 113–24.

———. "The Non-Arab Ethnic Groups of Libya." *Middle East Journal* 12, no. 1 (Winter 1958): 33–44.

Goldberg, Harvey. *Cave Dwellers and Citrus Growers: A Jewish Community in Libya and Israel*. Cambridge: Cambridge University Press, 1972.

———. "Ecological and Demographic Aspects of Rural Tripolitanian Jews, 1853–1949." *International Journal of Middle East Studies* 2 (1971): 245–65.

———. "From Shaikh to Mazkin: Structural Continuity and Organizational Change in the Leadership of a Tripolitanian Jewish Community." *Folklore Research Center Studies* 1 (1970): 29–41.

———. "The Jewish Wedding in Tripolitania, a Study in Cultural Source." *Maghreb Review* 3, no. 9 (1978): 1–6.

———. "Rites and Riots: The Tripolitanian Pogrom of 1945." *Plural Societies* 8 (Spring 1977): 35–56.

Hunwick, John, and Eve Trout Powell. *The African Diaspora in the Mediterranean Lands of Islam*. Princeton, N.J.: Marcus Wienner, 2002.

Keenan, Jeremy. *The Tuareg People of Ahaggar*. London: Sickle Moon Books, 2002.

Mason, J. "The Social History and Anthropology of the Arabized Berbers of Augila Oasis in the Libyan Sahara Desert." Ph.D. diss., Boston University, 1971.

Milburn, M. "Socio-economic Change among the Fezzan Tuarez since 1800." In *Social and Economic Development of Libya*, ed. E. G. H. Joffé and K. S. McLachlan, 175–88. London: Menas Press, 1982.

Monod, Théodore, and Edmond Diemer. *Zerzura: L'oasis légendaire du desert Libyque*. Paris: Vents du Sable, 2000.

Najem, Faraj. "Libyan Tribes in Diaspora." *Libyan Studies* 34 (2003): 121–36.

Norris, H. T. "The Libyan Fazzan: A Crossroads of Routes and a Thoroughfare of Arab and Berber Tribes Historically Connected with Murabitun." *Libyan Studies* 34 (2003): 101–20.

Peters, Emrys L. "Aspects of the Family among the Bedouin of Cyrenaica." In *Comparative Family Systems*, ed. Meyer K. Nimkoff, 121–46. Boston: Houghton Mifflin, 1965.

———. "Cultural and Social Diversity in Libya." In *Libya since Independence*, ed. J. A. Allan, 103–20. London: Croom Helm, 1982.

Salheen El-Houni, Ahmad. "The Senusi Movement." *Libyan Review* 5, no. 1 (January 1969): 10–14.

B. Demography

Amara, Hamid Ait. "Demographic Pressures and Agrarian Dynamics." In *Polity and Society in Contemporary North Africa*, ed. I. William Zartman and William Mark Habeeb, 123–38. Boulder, Colo.: Westview Press, 1993.

Birks, J. S., and C. A. Sinclair. *International Migration Project: Libyan Arab Jamahiryah Case Study*. Durham, U.K.: University of Durham, 1978.

Elkahir, Yassin Ali. *Migrants in Tripoli*. Pittsburgh: University Center for International Studies, 1980.

Goldberg, Harvey E. "Ecologic and Demographic Aspects of Rural Tripolitanian Jewry, 1853–1949." *International Journal of Middle East Studies* 2, no. 3 (July 1971): 245–65.

Harley, R. "Distribution and Density of Population, 1954–1966." *Faculty of Arts Bulletin* [University of Libya, Benghazi] 3 (1969): 79–144.

Harrison, Robert S. "Migrants in the City of Tripoli, Libya." *Geographical Review* 57, no. 3 (July 1967): 397–423.

Lawless, R. I. "Population Geography and Settlement Studies." *Libyan Studies* 20 (1989): 251–58.

Lawless, R. I., and S. Keseiri. "Spatial Aspects of Population Change in Libya." *Mediterranée* 4 (1983): 81–86.

Libya. Ministry of Planning. Census and Statistical Department. *Demographic Parameters and Population Projections for the Libyan Population, 1975–2000*. Tripoli: Secretariat of Planning, 1979.

——. *Employment Census, 1980: Al Jufrah Baladiya*. Tripoli: Secretariat of Planning, 1980.

——. *Employment Census, 1980: Al Shati Baladiya*. Tripoli: Secretariat of Planning, 1980.

——. *Employment Census, 1980: Awbari Baladiya*. Tripoli: Secretariat of Planning, 1980.

——. *Employment Census, 1980: Ghat Baladiya*. Tripoli: Secretariat of Planning, 1980.

——. *Employment Census, 1980. Murzuk Baladiya*. Tripoli: Secretariat of Planning, 1980.

——. *Employment Census, 1980: Sabha Baladiya*. Tripoli: Secretariat of Planning, 1980.

——. *General Population Census of Libya, 1973: Preliminary Report*. Tripoli: Secretariat of Planning, 1973.

——. *Housing and Establishment Census*. Tripoli: Secretariat of Planning, 1973.

——. *Manpower and Human Resources Implications of the Long-Term Development Objectives, 1980–2000*. Tripoli: Secretariat of Planning, 1979.

——. *Population Census*. Tripoli: Secretariat of Planning, 1973.

——. *Report on the Second Phase of the Household Sample Survey (Benghazi Town)*. Tripoli: Secretariat of Planning, 1970.

Serge, C. "The Italian Demographic Colonization of Libya, 1922–1942." Ph.D. diss., University of California, Berkeley, 1970.

Soliman, N. "Analysis of Data on Fertility, Mortality and Economic Activity of Urban Population in Libya Based on a Household Sample Survey." *Memorandum of National Planning* [Cairo] (May 1971): 130.

Zuhri, Z. M. "Socio-economic Transformation and the Problem of Migration in Libya: A Case Study of Benghazi." Ph.D. diss., University of Hull, 1979.

C. Education

Abdulali, A. J. *Changing the Role of Inspector in the Libyan Educational System*. Pittsburgh: University of Pittsburgh, 1986.

Alarafi, Abdullah Belgassem. "Perceptions of Organizational Climate in Elementary and Intermediate Schools in Libya." Ph.D. diss., University of Oklahoma, 1980.

Appleton, L. "Italian Educational Policy towards Muslims in Libya, 1911–1928." M.Phil., University of London, 1980.

———. "The Question of Nationalism and Education in Libya under Italian Rule." *Libyan Studies* 10 (1979) 29–33.

Belazi, O. M. "Human Resources Development: The Case of Libya." Ph.D. diss., Texas Tech University, 1973.

Bony, Ahmed Mohammed. "An Evaluation of the Guidance and Counseling Service Needs in Libya as Perceived by Students, Teachers and Administrators." Ed.D. thesis, University of Northern Colorado, 1981.

Dughri, Abdurrazzagh Mahmud. "Human Resources Development and Educational Policy in Libya." Ph.D. diss., University of Pittsburgh, 1980.

Eldabri, Sadat Aburrazagh. "Education in Libya: An Historical Review and Report on the Status of Curriculum and Curriculum Planning." Ed.D. thesis, State University of New York (Buffalo), 1984.

Elkhanjari, Alkoni Ahmed. "Effects of Different Teaching Strategies and Preinstructional Backgrounds of the Learners upon the Instructional Effectiveness of Libyan High School Teachers." Ph.D. diss., University of Arizona, 1981.

Gallal, A. "Libraries in Libya." *UNESCO Bulletin for Libraries* 27, no. 5 (1973): 257–61.

Gummed, Amer Ali. "High-Level Manpower Requirements for Economic Development in Libya." Ph.D. diss., Oklahoma State University, 1979.

Heflins, Robert J. *Libya.* Washington, D.C.: American Association of Collegiate Registrars and Admissions Officers, 1972.

Kerdus, Salah. "The Literacy Programme in Libya." *Teachers of the World* 2 (1979): xi–xiii.

Libya. Ministry of Education. *The Development of Education in the Libyan Arab Republic.* Vol. 8. Tripoli: n.p., 1973.

Mogherbi, Mohamed Zahi El. "The Socialization of School Children in the Socialist People's Libyan Arab Jamahiriya." Ph.D. diss., University of Missouri, 1978.

Monastiri, Tawfiq. "The Organization of Primary Preparatory and Secondary Teaching in Libya from 1969 to 1979." In *Social and Economic Development of Libya*, ed. E. G. H. Joffé and K. S. McLachlan, 315–30. London: Menas Press, 1982.

———. "Teaching the Revolution: Libyan Education since 1969." In *Qadhafi's Libya, 1969 to 1994*, ed. Dirk Vandewalle, 67–88. New York: St. Martin's Press, 1995.

Nouri, Qais N. Al-. "Modern Professionalism in Libya: Attitudes of University Students." *International Social Science Journal* 27, no. 4 (1975): 691–702.

Pattison, J. G. "Socio-political and Cultural Factors Affecting Foreign Language Policy in Revolutionary Libya." M.Phil. thesis, London Institute of Education, 1984.

Preece, Chris. "Boreum, an Educational Resource." *Libyan Studies* 30 (1999): 53–68.

Savitz, Gerald S. *The Libyan Library Development Plan*. New York: n.p., 1970.

Steele-Creig, A. J. *A History of Education in Tripolitania from the Time of the Ottoman Occupation to the Fifth Year under British Military Occupation*. Tripoli: n.p., 1948.

Tessler, Mark. "Alienation of Urban Youth." In *Polity and Society in Contemporary North Africa*, ed. I. William Zartman and William Mark Habeeb, 71–101. Boulder, Colo.: Westview Press, 1993.

Vietmeyer, W. *Libya Primary Teacher Training, July 1965–November 1969*. Paris: UNESCO, 1970.

Young, T. *Libya: Education Statistics, January 1968–August 1969*. Paris: UNESCO, 1969.

D. Health

Abudejaja, A. H., M. A. Khan, R. Singh, A. Tower, M. Narayanappa, B. S. Gubta, and S. Umer. "Experience of a Family Clinic at Benghazi, Libya and Sociomedical Aspects of Its Catchment Population." *Family Practice* 4, no. 1 (1987): 19–26.

Barbar, Ashil M. *Health Care in Libya*. Monticello, Ill.: Vance Bibliographies, 1978.

Denti di Piraino, Alberto. *Un medico in Africa*. Milan: Lonsanesi, 1974.

Salem, Salem F. "The Health Care Delivery System in Libya with Special Emphasis on Public Health Care Services in Benghazi." *Libyan Studies* 27 (1996): 99–123.

United States. Interdepartmental Committee on Nutrition for National Development. *Libya*. Bethesda, Md.: Interdepartmental Committee on Nutrition for National Development, 1958.

E. Religion

Abdussaid, A. "Early Islamic Monuments at Ajdabiyah." *Libya Antiqua* 1 (1964): 115–19.

———. "An Early Mosque at Medina Sultan (Ancient Sort)." *Libya Antiqua* 3–4 (1967): 155–60.

Allan, J. W. "Some Mosques of the Jebel Nefusa." *Libya Antiqua* 9–10 (1973): 147–69.

Anderson, Lisa. "Religion and Politics in Libya." *Journal of Arab Affairs* 1 (1981): 53–77.

———. "Religion and State in Libya: The Politics of Qaddafi." *Annals of the American Academy of Political and Social Science* 483 (January 1986): 61–72.

Ayoub, Mahmoud Mustafa. *Islam and the Third Universal Theory: The Religious Thought of Mu'ammar al Qadhdhafi*. London: KPI, 1987.

Baldinetti, Anna. "Italian Colonial Studies on the Sufi Brotherhoods in Libya." In *Modern and Contemporary Libya: Sources and Historiographies*, ed. Anna Baldinetti, 125–39. Rome: Istituto Italiano per L'Africa e L'Oriente, 2003.

Bezirgan, Najm A. "Islam and Arab Nationalism." *Middle East Review* 11, no. 2 (Winter 1978/79): 38–44.

Bono, Salvatore. "Islam et politique coloniale en Libye." *Maghreb Review* 13, nos. 1–2 (January–April 1988): 70–76.

Deeb, Marius K. "Militant Islam and Its Critics: The Case of Libya." In *Islamism and Secularism in North Africa*, ed. John Ruedy, 187–97. New York: St. Martin's Press, 1986.

Dekmejian, Richard Hrair. "The Islamic Revival in the Middle East and North Africa." *Current History* 78, no. 456 (April 1980): 169–74, 179.

Evans-Pritchard. E. E. *The Sanusi of Cyrenaica*. Oxford: Oxford University Press, 1949.

Goldberg, Harvey E., ed. *The Book of Mordechai: A Study of the Jews of Libya*. Philadelphia: Institute for the Study of Human Issues, 1980.

———. *Cave Dwellers and Citrus Growers: A Jewish Community in Libya and Israel*. Cambridge: Cambridge University Press, 1972.

———. *From Shaikh to Mazkir: Structural Continuity and Organisational Change in the Leadership of a Tripolitanian Jewish Community*. Washington, D.C.: University Press of America, 1982.

———. *Jewish Life in Muslim Libya: Rivals and Relatives*. Chicago: University of Chicago Press, 1990.

———. "Jewish Life in Muslim Tripoli in the Late Qaramanli Period." *Urban Anthropology* 13, no. 1 (1984): 65–90.

———. "Language and Culture of the Jews of Tripolitania: A Preliminary View." *Mediterranean Language Review* 1 (1983): 85–102.

Habiby, Raymond N. "Mu'ammar Qadhafi's New Islamic Scientific Socialist Society." *Middle East Review* 11, no. 4 (Summer 1969): 32–39.

Halliday, Fred. *Islam and the Myth of Confrontation: Religion and Politics in the Middle East*. New York: I. B. Tauris, 1996.

Hutt, A. "Survey of Islamic Sites." *Libyan Studies* 3 (1972): 5–6.

Joffé, E. G. H. [George]. "Qadhafi's Islam in Historical Perspective. In *Qadhafi's Libya, 1969–1994*, ed. Dirk Vandewalle, 139–54. New York: St. Martin's Press, 1995.

Kepel, Gilles. *Jihad: The Trail of Political Islam*. Cambridge, Mass.: Belknap Press of Harvard University Press, 2002.

Limam, Haifa Malouf. "Tidjaniya, Sanusiya and Mahdiya as Studies in English Works." *Revue d'Histoire Mahgrebine* 4 (July 1975): 163–73.

Mason, John Paul. *Island of the Blest: Islam in a Libyan Oasis Community*. Papers in International Studies, African Series No. 31. Ohio University Center for International Studies, 1977.

———. "Oasis Saints of Eastern Libya in North African Context." *Middle Eastern Studies* 17 (July 1981): 357–74.

Mayer, Ann Elizabeth. "Islamic Resurgence or New Prophethood: The Role of Islam in Qadhdafi's Ideology." In *Islamic Resurgence in the Arab World*, ed. Ali E. Hillal Dessouki, 196–220. New York: Praeger, 1982.

Mitchell, E. "Islam in Colonel Qaddafi's Thought." *World Today* 38, no. 7–8 (July–August 1982): 319–26.

Muzikar, Josef. "Islam and the Ideology of Mu'ammar al-Qadhadhafi's Green Book: Part I, Part II." *Archív Orientální* 50 (1982): 1–21, 105–21.

Nomani, Farhad, and Ali Rahnema. "The Islamic Socialism of Qadhafi in Libya." In *Islamic Economic Systems*, 186–208. London: Zed Books, 1994.

Simon, Rachel. *Change within Tradition among Jewish Women in Libya*. Seattle: University of Washington Press, 1992.

———. "It Could Have Happened There: The Jews of Libya during the Second World War." *Africana Journal* 16 (1994): 391–422.

———. "The Sephardi Heritage in Libya." *Shofar* 10, no. 3 (1992): 90–112.

———. "Shlichim from Palestine in Libya." *Jewish Political Studies Review* 9, nos. 1–2 (1997): 33–57.

———. "The Social, Cultural and Political Impact of Zionism in Libya." *Jewish Poltical Studies Review* 6, nos. 3–4 (1994): 127–33.

Tozy, Mohammed. "Islam and the State." In *Polity and Society in Contemporary North Africa*, ed. I. William Zartman and William Mark Habeeb, 102–22. Boulder, Colo.: Westview Press, 1993.

Vatin, Jean-Claude. "Revival in the Maghreb: Islam as an Alternative Political Language." In *Islamic Resurgence in the Arab World*, ed. Ali E. Hillal Dessourki, 221–50. New York: Praeger, 1982.

Vikor, Knut S. "Opening the Maliki School: Mohammad b. 'Ali al-Sanusi's Views on the *Madhab*." *Journal of Libyan Studies* 1, no. 1 (Summer 2000): 5–17.

———. *Sufi and Scholar on the Desert Edge: Muhammad b. 'Ali al-Sanusi and His Brotherhood*. Evanston, Ill.: Northwestern University Press, 1995.

Wharton, Barrie. "'Between Arab Brothers and Islamist Foes': The Evolution of the Contemporary Islamist Movement in Libya." *Journal of Libyan Studies* 4, no. 1 (Summer 2003): 33–48.

Wright, John. "Nahum Slouschz and the Jews of Tripoli." *Journal of Libyan Studies* 3, no. 2 (Winter 2002): 41–55.

Ziadeh, Nicola A. *Sanusiyah: A Study of a Revivalist Movement in Islam*. Leiden: E. J. Brill, 1968.

F. Sociology

Ahmar, A. S. Al-. "The Changing Social Organisation of the Libyan Village." Ph.D. diss., University of Leeds, 1976.

Alawar, Mohamed. "Urbanization in Libya: Present State and Future Prospects." In *Social and Economic Development of Libya*, ed. E. G. H. Joffé and K. S. McLachlan, 331–53. London: Menas Press, 1982.

Allaghi, F. A. "Rural Women and Decision Making: A Case Study in the Kufra Settlement Project, Libya." Ph.D. diss., Colorado State University, 1981.

Anderson, Lisa. *The State and Social Transformation in Tunisia and Libya, 1830–1980*. Princeton, N.J.: Princeton University Press, 1986.

Ash, N. *Libya: Education, Health and Housing*. London: Hakima Press, 1980.

Atallah, B., et al. "Le phénomène urbain en Libye, problèmes juridiques et sociaux." *Annuaire de l'Afrique du Nord* 11 (1972): 79–103.

Baruni, M. Y. El-. *Personal Value Systems of Libyan Managers: An Exploratory Study*. St. Louis: St. Louis University, 1980.

Benzabih, H. A. "The Jabal Al-Akhdar: A Half-Century of Nomadic Livelihood." In *Social and Economic Development of Libya*, ed. E. G. H. Joffé and K. S. McLachlan, 195–206. London: Menas Press, 1982.

Birks, J. S., and C. A. Sinclair. *International Migration Project: Libyan Arab Jamahiryah Case Study*. Durham, U.K.: University of Durham, 1978.

——. "The Libyan Arab Jamahiriyya: Labour Migration Sustains Dualistic Development." *Maghreb Review* 4, no. 3 (May–June 1979): 95–102.

Blake, G. D. B. "Town and City in Tripolitania: Studies in Origins and Development, 1969–1989." *Libyan Studies* 20 (1989): 91–106.

Brandily, Monique. "Music and Social Change." In *Social and Economic Development of Libya*, ed. E. G. H. Joffé and K. S. McLachlan, 207–14. London: Menas Press, 1982.

Davis, John. *Libyan Politics, Tribe and Revolution: An Account of the Zuwaya and Their Government*. London: I. B. Tauris, 1887.

Fikry, Mona. "La femme et les conflits de valeurs en Libye." *Revue de l'Occident Musulman et de la Méditerranée* 18 (1974): 93–110.

Findlay, A. M. *Spatial Dimensions of Tunisian Emigration to Libya*. Durham, U.K.: University of Durham, 1978.

Foerster, Sharon Wilson. "The Effect of a U.S. Educational Experience on the Traditional Cultural Values of Libyan Students." Ph.D. diss., University of Texas, 1981.

Gannous, Subhi M. "Changing Social Relationships in a Libyan Semi-urban Situation." *International Social Science Journal* 31, no. 2 (1979): 250–62.

Goldberg, Harvey E. *Jewish Life in Muslim Libya: Rivals and Relatives*. Chicago: University of Chicago Press, 1990.

———. "Tailors in Tripoli in the Colonial Period." In *Social and Economic Development of Libya*, ed. E. G. H. Joffé and K. S. McLachlan, 161–73. London: Menas Press, 1982.

Habiby, Raymond N. "Mu'amar Qadhafi's New Islamic Scientific Socialist Society." In *Religion and Politics in the Middle East*, ed. Michael Curtis, 247–59. Boulder, Colo.: Westview Press, 1981.

Hajjar, S. G. "Qadhafi's Social Theory as the Basis of the Third Universal Theory." *Journal of Asian and African Studies* 17, nos. 3–4 (1982): 177–88.

Hajjar, S. G., and R. Kieron-Swaine. "Social Justice: The Philosophical Justifications of Qadhafi's Construction." *Africa Today* 31, no. 3 (1984): 17–44.

Hammali, Abdullah Amir El. "Aspects of Modernization in Libyan Communities." In *Social and Economic Development of Libya*, ed. E. G. H. Joffé and K. S. McLachlan, 295–313. London: Menas Press, 1982.

———. "Modernization Trends in Libya." Ph.D. diss., University of Pittsburgh, 1979.

Hopkins, Nicholas S. "Local Societies." In *Polity and Society in Contemporary North Africa*, ed. I. William Zartman and William Mark Habeeb, 168–85. Boulder, Colo.: Westview Press, 1993.

Kabir, Y. A. El. *Migrants in Tripoli: A Case Study of Assimilation*. Pittsburgh: University of Pittsburgh Center for International Studies, 1980.

Kezeiri, Saad Khalil. "Here Today, Gone Tomorrow: The Problems of Deteriorating Historic Centres." *Libyan Studies* 16 (1985): 85–94.

———. "The Problem of Defining a Small Urban Centre in Libya." *Libyan Studies* 15 (1984): 143–48.

———. "Re-structuring the Urban System in Libya." In *Social and Economic Development of Libya*, ed. E. G. H. Joffé and K. S. McLachlan, 355–59. London: Menas Press, 1982.

———. "Urban Planning in Libya." *Libyan Studies* 14 (1983): 9–15.

Khawas, M. El-. "The New Society in Qaddafi's Libya: Can It Endure?" *Africa Today* 31, no. 3 (1984): 17–44.

Kshedan, H. S. "The Spatial Structure of Tripoli, Libya: An Example of a Third World Socialist City." Ph.D. diss., University of Oklahoma, 1984.

Lafi, Nora. *Une ville du Maghreb entre ancient régime et réformes ottomans: Genèse des institutions municipales à Tripoli de Barbarie (1795–1911)*. Paris: Éditions L'Harmattan, 2002.

Lawless, R. I. "Population Geography and Settlement Studies." *Libyan Studies* 20 (1989): 251–58.

Layish, Aharon. *Divorce in the Libyan Family*. New York: New York University Press, 1991.

Mason, John P. *Island of the Blest: Islam in a Libyan Oasis Community*. Athens: Ohio University Center for International Studies, 1977.

——. "Petroleum Development and the Reactivation of Traditional Structure in a Libyan Oasis Community." *Economic Development and Cultural Change* 26 (July 1978): 763–76.

——. "Qadhdhafi's Revolution and Change in a Libyan Oasis Community." *Middle East Journal* 36, no. 3 (Summer 1982): 319–35.

Mayer, Elizabeth Ann. "Libyan Legislation in Defense of Arabo-Islamic Sexual Mores." *American Journal of Comparative Law* 28 (1980): 287–313.

Mead, Richard, and Alan George. "The Women of Libya." *Middle East International* 25 (July 1973): 18–20.

Misallati, A. S. O. "Tripoli, Libya: Structure and Functions as an Arab-Islamic City." Ph.D. diss., University of Kentucky, 1981.

Naur, Maja. "The Military and the Labour Force in Libya." *Current Research on Peace and Violence* 4, no. 1 (1981): 89–99.

——. *Social and Organizational Change in Libya.* Uppsala, Sweden: Scandinavian Institute of African Studies, 1982.

Nomani, Farhad, and Ali Rahnema. "The Islamic Socialism of Qadhafi in Libya." In *Islamic Economic Systems*, 186–208. London: Zed Books, 1994.

Nouri, Qais N. Al-. "Changing Marriage Patterns in Libya: Attitudes of University Students." *Journal of Comparative Family Studies* 11 (Spring 1980): 219–32.

Peters, Emrys L. *The Bedouin of Cyrenaica: Studies in Personal and Corporate Power.* Ed. Jack Goody and Emanuel Marx. Cambridge: Cambridge University Press, 1990.

——. "The Proliferation of Segments in the Lineage of the Bedouin of Cyrenaica (Libya)." In *Peoples and Cultures of the Middle East*, ed. Louise E. Sweet, 1:363–98. New York: Natural History Press, 1970.

Pliez, Olivier. *Villes du Sahara: Urbanisation et urbanité dans la Fezzan libyen.* Paris: Éditions du Centre National de la Recherche Scientifique, 2003.

Sharif, Ibrahim El Zaroug El. "Professional Occupational Adjustment of Libyans Educated in United States Universities." Ph.D. diss., University of Maryland, 1982.

Simon, Rachel. *Change within Tradition among Jewish Women in Libya.* Seattle: University of Washington Press, 1992.

Soliman, N. "Analysis of Data on Fertility, Mortality and Economic Activity of Urban Population in Libya Based on a Household Sample Survey." *Memorandum of National Planning* [Cairo] (May 1971): 130.

Souriau, C. "La société féminine en Libye." *Revue de l'Occident Musulman et la Mediterranée* 6 (1969): 127–55.

———. "Libye: Chronique sociale et culturelle." *Annuaire de l'Afrique du Nord* 8 (1969): 497–518.

Waheshy, A. B. El-. "Men's Attitudes towards Women's Role in Libya: An Indicator of Social Change." Ph.D. diss., University of Akron, 1981.

Zein, S. A. El-. "The Tuareg of South-western Libya." Ph.D. diss., University of Hull, 1979.

About the Author

Ronald Bruce St John received his B.A. from Knox College in Galesburg, Illinois, and his M.A. and Ph.D. from the Graduate School of International Studies, University of Denver, Colorado. He has visited Libya on numerous occasions and traveled over much of the country. His publications include *Libya and the United States: Two Centuries of Strife* (2002), *Qaddafi's World Design: Libyan Foreign Policy, 1969–1987* (1987), and the earlier editions of *Historical Dictionary of Libya* (1991, 1998). St John contributed a chapter to *The Green and the Black: Qadhafi's Policies in Africa* (1988), as well as the entries on Libya in *Governments of the World* (2005), *Worldmark Encyclopedia of Religious Practices* (2005), *Africa Contemporary Record* (2004, 2005), *Encyclopedia of the Modern Middle East and North Africa* (2004), and *World Encyclopedia of Political Systems and Parties* (1983, 1987). He has published more than 100 articles and reviews on Libya in a variety of professional journals, including *Global Affairs*, *International Journal of Middle East Studies*, *Maghreb Review*, *Middle East Journal*, *Middle East Policy*, *Middle East Studies Association Bulletin*, *Orbis*, and *World Today*. He has served on the International Advisory Board of the *Journal of Libyan Studies* and the Atlantic Council Working Group on Libya.